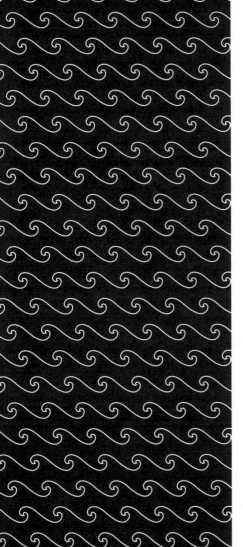

SECOND EDITION

AMERICAN FOREIGN POLICY AND PROCESS

To the Memory of My Father

SECOND EDITION

AMERICAN FOREIGN POLICY AND PROCESS

JAMES M. MCCORMICK
IOWA STATE UNIVERSITY

F.E. PEACOCK PUBLISHERS, INC.
ITASCA, ILLINOIS 60143

Copyright © 1992
F. E. Peacock Publishers, Inc.
All rights reserved
Library of Congress Catalog Card No. 91-67848
ISBN 0-87581-360-7
Printed in the United States of America
Printing: 10 9 8 7 6 5 4 3 2 1
Years: 96 95 94 93 92

CONTENTS

Chronologies, Documents and Document
Summaries, Figures, Tables, and Maps   x

Preface   XIII

PART I   VALUES AND POLICIES IN AMERICAN
FOREIGN AFFAIRS   1

CHAPTER 1   AMERICA'S TRADITIONS IN FOREIGN
POLICY   5

Values, Beliefs, and Foreign Policy   6

The United States: A New Democratic State   9

Isolationism in American Foreign Policy   11

Moralism in American Foreign Policy   25

Concluding Comments   32

Notes   33

CHAPTER 2   AMERICA'S GLOBAL INVOLVEMENT AND
THE EMERGENCE OF THE COLD WAR   39

The Postwar World and American Involvement   40

America's Globalism: The Truman Doctrine
and Beyond   49

Elements of Containment: Regional
Security Pacts   52

Elements of Containment: Economic and
Military Assistance   57

Elements of Containment: The Domestic
Cold War   61

The Korean War: The First Major Test of
Containment   66

Concluding Comments   70
Notes   71

CHAPTER 3   THE COLD WAR CONSENSUS AND
             CHALLENGES TO IT   77
             Key Components of the Cold War Consensus   78
             The Public and the Cold War Consensus   83
             Patterns of Interactions during the Cold War,
                1946–1972   86
             Challenges to the Cold War Consensus   92
             The Vietnam Debacle   103
             Concluding Comments   112
             Notes   112

CHAPTER 4   NIXON'S REALISM AND CARTER'S
             IDEALISM IN AMERICAN FOREIGN POLICY   117
             Realism and Idealism as Foreign Policy
                Concepts   118
             Realism and the Nixon Administration   119
             The Nixon-Kissinger Worldview in Operation   125
             Criticisms of the Nixon-Kissinger Approach   135
             Idealism and the Carter Administration   138
             The Carter Worldview in Operation   143
             Realism in the Last Year: A Response to Critics 160
             Concluding Comments   162
             Notes   163

CHAPTER 5   THE REAGAN ADMINISTRATION:
             A RENEWAL OF THE COLD WAR?   169
             The Values and Beliefs of the Reagan
                Administration   170
             The Policy Approach of the Reagan
                Administration   173
             The Reagan Worldview in Operation   179
             Challenges to the Reagan Approach   186

Policy Change: Accommodation with the
  Soviet Union   188
Policy Continuity: The Reagan Doctrine
  and the Third World   195
Concluding Comments   205
Notes   206

CHAPTER 6   THE BUSH ADMINISTRATION AND THE
            COLD WAR'S END   213
The Values and Beliefs of the Bush
  Administration   215
The Policy Approach of the Bush
  Administration   219
Political Change and Eastern Europe   225
Political Change and the Soviet Union:
  Before and After the August 1991 Coup   233
After the Cold War: Policy toward
  Central Europe   239
The Search for a New World Order   245
The Persian Gulf War: First Test of a New
  World Order?   247
Challenges to a New World Order   254
Concluding Comments   255
Notes   256

PART II   THE PROCESS OF POLICYMAKING   263

CHAPTER 7   THE PRESIDENT AND THE MAKING OF
            FOREIGN POLICY   265
Constitutional Powers in
  Foreign Policy   266
The Growth of Executive Dominance in
  Foreign Affairs   270
Concluding Comments   300
Notes   301

CHAPTER 8   CONGRESSIONAL PREROGATIVES AND
             THE MAKING OF FOREIGN POLICY   307
             Commitment Making   308
             War Powers   313
             Controlling the Purse Strings   325
             Congressional Oversight   331
             Congressional Change and Future Foreign
               Policymaking   339
             Concluding Comments   344
             Notes   344

CHAPTER 9   THE DIPLOMATIC AND ECONOMIC
             BUREAUCRACIES: DUPLICATION OR
             SPECIALIZATION?   353
             Bureaucratic Politics and Foreign Policymaking   354
             The Department of State   356
             The National Security Council   370
             Why Two Departments of State?   377
             Some Economic Bureaucracies and Foreign
               Policymaking   380
             Concluding Comments   386
             Notes   386

CHAPTER 10   THE MILITARY AND INTELLIGENCE
             BUREAUCRACIES: PERVASIVE OR
             ACCOUNTABLE?   393
             The Department of Defense   394
             The Intelligence Agencies   406
             CIA "Special Activities" and Policy Influence   413
             The Iran-Contra Affair: A Case of Failed
               Accountability   420
             Policy Coordination among Competing
               Bureaucracies   425
             Concluding Comments   430
             Notes   431

CHAPTER 11   POLITICAL PARTIES, BIPARTISANSHIP,
             AND INTEREST GROUPS   437
             Political Parties and the Bipartisan Tradition   438
             The Limits of Bipartisanship through the
               Vietnam Era   441
             Bipartisanship: Did It Ever Really Exist?   445
             Partisan Divisions Today: The Reagan
               and Bush Years   448
             Partisan Politics and the Future   451
             Interest Groups and the Foreign Policy Process   452
             The Impact of Interest Groups   460
             Concluding Comments   476
             Notes   476

CHAPTER 12   PUBLIC OPINION: MOODISH OR STABLE?   483
             Foreign Policy Opinion: Uninformed and
               Moodish   484
             Foreign Policy Opinion: Structured and Stable   494
             The Impact of Public Opinion on Foreign
               Policy   505
             Concluding Comments   510
             Notes   510

PART III   CONCLUSION   515

CHAPTER 13   AMERICAN FOREIGN POLICY IN THE
             POST–COLD WAR ERA   517
             A Nation Divided   518
             A New Foreign Policy Consensus   523
             Concluding Comments   533
             Notes   533

             A Selected Bibliography   537
             Index   553

CHRONOLOGIES, DOCUMENTS AND DOCUMENT SUMMARIES, FIGURES, TABLES, AND MAPS

CHRONOLOGIES

Chronology 3.1	Six Phases of the Cold War, 1945–1972	**88**
Chronology 3.2	The Growth of New Nations, 1945–1990	**99**
Chronology 6.1	The Democratization of Four Eastern European Nations, 1989–1990	**228**
Chronology 6.2	The Division and Reunification of Germany, 1945–1990	**232**
Chronology 6.3	Political Change within the Soviet Union, 1985–1991	**235**
Chronology 6.4	The Persian Gulf War, 1990–1991	**251**
Chronology 8.1	The War Powers Resolution and Presidential Reports to the Congress	**317**

DOCUMENTS AND DOCUMENT SUMMARIES

Document 1.1	Treaty of Peace and Friendship between the United States and Tripoli	**18**
Document 1.2	Wilson's Fourteen Points	**31**
Document 2.1	Excerpts from NSC-68, April 14, 1950	**62**
Summary 4.1	Major Agreements from the Moscow Summit, May 1972	**127**
Summary 4.2	Key Elements of the Shanghai Communique, February 27, 1972	**129**
Summary 4.3	A Description of the Three "Baskets" of the Helsinki Accords, August 1, 1975	**131**
Summary 4.4	The Panama Canal Treaties, September 1977	**155**
Summary 4.5	The Camp David Accords between Egypt and Israel, September 1978	**156**
Summary 6.1	Key Components of the Strategic Arms Reduction Treaty, July 1991	**243**
Summary 7.1	Presidential Foreign Policy Powers and the Courts: Some Recent Decisions	**283**

FIGURES

Figure 2.1	Patterns in Foreign Aid, 1945–1970	**60**
Figure 2.2	National Defense Expenditures and U.S. Armed Forces per 1000 Population, 1946–1968	**65**
Figure 3.1	The "Mistake" Question on Vietnam	**111**
Figure 4.1	The Principal Participants in the Balance-of-Power System Conceptualized by Nixon and Kissinger	**123**
Figure 9.1	The Structure of the Department of State	**357**
Figure 9.2	The Structure of a U.S. Mission Abroad—Venezuela	**360**
Figure 9.3	Career Foreign Service Officers and Political Friends as Ambassadors, Presidents Kennedy to Bush	**368**
Figure 9.4	The Structure of the National Security Council Staff under President Bush	**378**
Figure 10.1	The Structure of the Department of Defense	**395**
Figure 10.2	The Intelligence Community	**407**

Figure 10.3   National Security Council Policy Coordination
Committees in the Bush Administration   **429**
Figure 11.1   Bipartisan Foreign Policy Voting in the Congress,
1947–1988   **446**
Figure 11.2   Partisan Differences in Congressional Voting on
Foreign Policy Issues   **447**
Figure 11.3   Partisan Support in Congressional Voting on Four
Foreign Policy Issues, 1947–1988   **449**
Figure 12.1   Percent of the American Public Very Interested in
Various Types of News, 1974–1990   **486**
Figure 12.2   The Relative Importance to the American Public of
Foreign and Domestic Issues: 1982, 1986, and 1990   **489**
Figure 12.3   The Distribution of the Mass Public among the Four
Types of Foreign Policy Beliefs, 1974–1986   **497**

MAPS

Map 1.1   U.S. Involvements in Central America and the
Caribbean, 1898–1990   **23**
Map 2.1   Europe Divided between East and West after World
War II   **46**
Map 2.2   United States Collective Defense Arrangements   **54**
Map 2.3   The Korean War, 1950–1953   **67**
Map 3.1   Vietnam, 1954–1975   **106**
Map 4.1   Israel and Its Neighbors   **134**
Map 4.2   Southern Africa   **158**
Map 5.1   Central America   **182**
Map 6.1   The Persian Gulf and Southwest Asia   **248**

TABLES

Table   1.1   Content of International Agreements by the United
States   **15**
Table   3.1   The American Postwar Consensus in Foreign Policy   **79**
Table   3.2   Use of American Military Force during Four
Administrations, 1946–1968   **82**
Table   3.3   Attitudes toward Stopping the Spread of
Communism, 1950–1951   **84**
Table   3.4   Attitudes toward the Threat of Communism, 1948   **85**
Table   3.5   Attitudes toward the Use of Troops to Respond to
Communist Attacks, 1950   **86**
Table   3.6   Attitudes toward the Use of Troops in Central and
South America, 1947–1954   **87**
Table   3.7   The Domino Theory in Southeast Asia   **110**
Table   5.1   Major Weapons Systems Sought and Obtained by
the Reagan Administration, 1981–1988   **176**
Table   5.2   Key Components of the Intermediate Nuclear Forces
(INF) Treaty   **194**
Table   7.1   Some Foreign Policy Powers Shared between the
President and the Congress   **269**
Table   7.2   Treaties and Executive Agreements, 1789–1988   **276**
Table   7.3   Presidential Victories on Foreign Policy Votes in the
Congress: from Truman to Bush   **292**

Table 8.1   Late Reporting of International Agreements by the
Executive Branch to the Congress, 1981 and 1988   311
Table 8.2   Earmarked Foreign Assistance Funds in Fiscal Year
1990   329
Table 8.3   Committee and Subcommittee Hearings of the
House Foreign Affairs Committee, 80th–99th
Congresses   337
Table 9.1   Composition of the National Security Council   371
Table 11.1   Interest Group Activity over the Contra Aid Issue in
the 1980s   459
Table 11.2   Top 100 U.S. Defense Contractors and Their
Corporate Sales Ranks for FY 1988   467
Table 12.1   Level of Public Knowledge Regarding Which Side
the U.S. Government Supported in Nicaragua,
1983–1987   488
Table 13.1   Differences between the Leaders and the Public,
1990   522

PREFACE

American Foreign Policy and Process is a substantially revised, enlarged, and updated edition of what was originally published as *American Foreign Policy and American Values*. The book is intended to serve as a comprehensive text for the first course in U.S. foreign policy. In addition, it should be wholly suitable as a supplemental text in a global politics or comparative foreign policy course where American actions are analyzed. Further, it could also serve as a ready reference for the first graduate course in a study of American foreign policy or the foreign policy process.

Values and beliefs have been chosen as the basic organizing theme for the text because policy actions are always taken within a context of underlying values. Yet, this emphasis on values and beliefs does not promote a particular point of view. Indeed, the intent and the analyses presented here are the direct opposite of that approach: the presentation portrays how values and beliefs toward foreign affairs have changed over the course of the history of the Republic and how U.S. foreign policy has thus changed as well.

To accomplish this end, the text is divided into three parts. Part I, which consists of six chapters, focuses upon the values and beliefs that have shaped policy historically (Chapter 1), during the height of American globalism and the Cold War years (Chapters 2 and 3), during the immediate post-Vietnam years (Chapter 4), and during the separate administrations of Reagan (Chapter 5) and Bush (Chapter 6). In each of these chapters, of course, we discuss a wide variety of foreign policy actions that illustrate the various values and beliefs of the particular period or administration(s). Part II, which consists of six chapters as well, examines in some detail the policymaking process and how various institutions and groups—the president (Chapter 7), the Congress (Chapter 8), the key bureaucracies (Chapters 9 and 10), political parties and interest groups (Chapter 11), and public opinion (Chapter 12)—compete to promote their own values and beliefs in American policy abroad. At this juncture, too, we provide essential information on how foreign policy decisions are made and on the relative importance of the various institutions and groups involved in that process. Part III, which consists of a concluding chapter, discusses alternate views of what values and beliefs may shape American foreign policy as we approach the twenty-first century.

Those familiar with the first edition will recognize the second edition as a much more comprehensive volume. First, each chapter has been revised and fully updated to reflect important changes in both U.S. policy and the policymaking process. Second, the number of chapters and the treatment of various subjects have been expanded. The text now consists of thirteen, rather than ten, chapters. The new total was accomplished by adding some chapters, combining others, and dividing some previous ones into separate chapters. Chapter 6 on the Bush administration is entirely new, and Chapter 3 on the Cold War consensus has much that is new as well. Chapter 4 reflects a combining of the earlier separate chapters on Nixon and Carter. Chapters 9 and 10 reflect a decision to expand the discussion of the role of the bureaucracies from one to two chapters and to add a section on the foreign economic bureaucracies to the former. Chapters 11 and 12 contain separate treatments of political parties and interest groups in the first chapter and public opinion in the second. In the earlier edition, these topics were all combined into one chapter. Third, this revision incorporates a greater use of tables, figures, and maps to portray more fully the story of American foreign policy and the process of its formulation. Chronologies of major events (e.g., the changes in Eastern Europe and the course of the Persian Gulf War) and summaries of key documents (e.g., INF Treaty and the Panama Canal Treaties) have also been added to provide greater detail to the discussion and to enable students to gain a greater understanding of these important actions. Finally, and perhaps most importantly, the entire revision was undertaken with an eye toward including the latest scholarly research available on these various topics and providing the most up-to-date policy examples as well.

In the course of undertaking these substantial revisions, I have encountered a number of debts from many individuals and institutions. I am now happy to have the opportunity to acknowledge my thanks to them publicly. First of all, several colleagues at a variety of institutions—Michael Engelhardt of Luther College, Lloyd Jensen of Temple University, Joseph Lepgold of Georgetown University, Steven Koven of Iowa State University, John Outland of the University of Richmond, Steven Schwiezer of Benedictine College, and Donley Studlar of Oklahoma State University—took the time to review the first edition and made a number of specific suggestions for revisions. Second, several colleagues read the entire revised manuscript or portions of it and shared with me their comments and suggestions for further improvement: James Lindsay of the University of Iowa, Neil Mitchell of the University of New

Mexico, Eric Plutzer of Iowa State University, and Ann McLaurin of Louisiana State University—Shreveport. Moreover, I am particularly indebted to James Lindsay for his careful reading of the entire manuscript and for his very detailed suggestions for changing it. His efforts saved me from several inaccuracies and helped to improve the final product. In several instances, though, I was not always wise enough to follow his and others' suggestions. Perhaps by the time of another edition, I will have gained the wisdom that they had already displayed. Special thanks, too, go to my colleague and friendly competitor, Eugene R. Wittkopf of Louisiana State University, for his good advice and encouragement as I was completing this edition. He also generously facilitated my use of his recently published work on public opinion and bipartisanship in this volume, for which I am most grateful.

Third, colleagues and staff in the Department of Political Science at Iowa State University provided moral support, a congenial work environment, and, as necessary, gentle prodding in my efforts to complete the text. I particularly want to thank Don Hadwiger, Young Kihl, Richard Mansbach, Jorgen Rasmussen, and Jerry Shakeshaft for their help. Beverly Christensen, Ronna Eley, Pam Hinderaker, Elaine Hood, Kim Jensen, Lois Jacobson, Linda Powell, Darryl Samuels, Joyce Wray, and Renee Zirk generously afforded me various forms of clerical and research assistance during the course of doing these revisions, and I am now happy to thank them as well. Once again, too, I am grateful to the staff of the William Robert Parks and Ellen Sorge Parks Library at Iowa State University. They were superb in assisting me in obtaining various pieces of specific information on American foreign policy.

Fourth, my students in the U.S. foreign policy course at Iowa State University continue to serve as an inspiration for me. They have graciously endured many of the arguments (and their reformulations) discussed here over the past seventeen years. They continue to challenge and question my thinking on many of the questions and issues raised in the text. In doing so, they have assisted me in writing a better book, and I am now delighted to acknowledge their help.

Fifth, I would like to express my thanks to the American Political Science Association for affording me the opportunity to serve as a Congressional Fellow in 1986–1987 and to Roger Davidson who encouraged me in that direction. As a result of that experience, I had the good fortune to gain a greater understanding of congressional-executive relations in foreign policy by engaging in some "participant-observation" in the office of Congressman Lee Hamilton of Indiana. I am particularly grateful to Congressman Hamilton and his staff for allowing me to take an active part in the policy process and now to share some of that experience in this text.

Sixth, I had the good fortune of working with an excellent copy editor, Norman Mysliwiec, during the production stage of the book. He carefully perused the manuscript for potential inaccuracies and cheerfully brought to my attention several passages that needed clarification or correction. For that kind of attention to detail on my behalf, I am indeed grateful. Finally, I must acknowledge the assistance and encouragement provided by Leo A. W. Wiegman, college editor at F. E. Peacock Publishers, Inc. He also read the entire manuscript, offered numerous cogent comments, and, without exception, improved the quality of the book. More than that, however, Leo Wiegman has been a most gracious editor—wholly supportive and inevitably encouraging, even as my deadlines slipped away—with a keen sense of quality publishing. As always, too, the support of Ted Peacock is appreciated. From my first association with Peacock Publishers, I sensed the commitment by the organization to its authors and to quality publishing. Happily, I can report that those commitments were meaningful and remain wholly intact.

All of these individuals and institutions (and others whom I may have inadvertently omitted) deserve my heartfelt thanks. Nonetheless, final responsibility for this book rests with me. Any errors of fact and interpretation are mine alone.

James M. McCormick
Ames, Iowa

PART I VALUES AND POLICIES
IN AMERICAN FOREIGN AFFAIRS

In Part I of *American Foreign Policy and Process*, we survey the beliefs and values that have been the basis of America's foreign policy actions. While providing the reader with an overview of the beliefs that have shaped American foreign policy throughout its history, we place special emphasis on the post–World War II period—the era of greatest American global involvement. Values and beliefs have been chosen as the basic organizing scheme because policy actions are always taken within a value context. If the beginning analyst can appreciate how belief systems influence policy choices, he or she will be in a good position to understand the foreign policy actions of a nation.

But values and beliefs cannot be understood in isolation; their importance is useful only within the context of actual foreign policy behavior. Thus, as an aid in appreciating how beliefs and attitudes have shaped American policy, we provide a narrative of foreign policy actions that reflect the underlying belief systems during various periods of U.S. diplomatic history. It is our hope that by combining illustrations of beliefs and actions, the reader will come away better able to interpret the foreign policy of the United States.

Part I is divided into six chapters. In Chapter 1, we begin our analysis by surveying the impact of moralism and isolationism, the value orientations that have influenced American foreign policy historically. These fundamental beliefs are reviewed to illustrate how they affected American international behavior throughout the first 150 years of the nation and how they continue to influence American policy to the present day. In Chapter 2, we focus on the development of American globalism in the immediate post–World War II years and on how America's beliefs about the world changed sharply. We discuss in detail the emergence of the Cold War and the military, economic, and political dimensions of the new U.S. foreign policy doctrine—the global containment of communism. This doctrine represented a dramatic departure from America's isolationist past, since it called for universal action on the part of the United States, but it reflected substantial continuity as well, since it was highly moral in content. In Chapter 3, we continue this discussion of America's emerging globalism by describing the new set of values and beliefs—the Cold War consensus—that came to dominate America's thinking about its role in the world from the late 1940s to the mid-1960s. This consensus produced a discernible set of foreign policy responses by the United States, which are illustrated at this juncture. In Chapter 3, we also analyze how these Cold War beliefs came under attack from abroad (through the weakening of the Eastern and Western blocs, the emergence of the Sino-Soviet split, and the development of the nonaligned movement) and at home (principally over the Vietnam War) and how their cohesion within the American leadership and the public was lost.

With the breakdown of the Cold War consensus finalized by the Vietnam War, succeeding administrations attempted to bring forth new foreign policy perspectives to replace this shattered worldview. From the late 1960s to the present, the dominant foreign policy beliefs of U.S. policymakers have shown a considerable degree of fluctuation from one administration to the next. We have witnessed the movement from the realist approach adopted by the Nixon-Ford administrations, to the idealist approach of the Carter administration, and back to elements of the Cold War in the Reagan administration, especially in its first term. More recently, the Bush administration has again adopted a more realist approach as it seeks to deal with the apparent ending of the Cold War. Thus, the last half of Part I focuses on the differing value emphases within these administrations and the ways in which they produced differing U.S. foreign policy behaviors during the past two decades.

In Chapter 4, we compare the "realist" approach that President Richard Nixon and National Security Advisor Henry Kissinger brought to American foreign policy in the late 1960s and early 1970s with the "idealist" approach that President Jimmy Carter adopted in the late 1970s. Each administration adopted foreign policy perspectives that were at odds with the key values of the Cold War years: Nixon and Kissinger's approach through its policy of détente with the Soviet Union and China; Carter's approach with its emphasis on "global politics." These two administrations also differed from each other in their compatibility with America's historical foreign policy values. The Nixon-Kissinger approach challenged the past with its "power politics" emphasis in dealing with other states, while Carter's approach was more in tune with the past in that it sought to reintroduce a stronger moral content to U.S. actions abroad, especially with regard to global human rights. Neither approach, however, succeeded in maintaining the support of the American people for very long, and both came under attack from critics at home and abroad.

In Chapter 5, we survey the values and beliefs of the Reagan administration. While the Nixon and Carter administrations attempted to replace the values of the Cold War, the Reagan administration—in large measure—attempted to restore them. The Reagan administration turned away from the global approach that the Carter administration had initially adopted, embracing a bipolar view of the world—one closely reminiscent of the containment and Cold War policies of three decades earlier. While this approach enjoyed some initial success, it, too, encountered substantial resistance. By the beginning of Reagan's second term, a discernible change in course had taken place. His earlier approach was replaced by one that sought to be more accommodative in bilateral relations with the Soviet Union, even as it continued to challenge that nation for influence in other areas of the world.

The final chapter in Part I examines the values and beliefs of the Bush administration. While this administration has adopted many of the values and beliefs of the second term of the Reagan administration, it has also sought to put its own stamp on its foreign policy approach. Most notably, the Bush administration has tried to adopt foreign policy values that will allow it to address the changing global environment and the significant transformations that have taken place in the international communist movement. To date, this approach of accommodating the "end of the Cold War" and attempting to establish a "new world order" has reflected a combination of realist and idealist beliefs that may portend a new approach to the world by the United States in the years ahead.

CHAPTER 1 AMERICA'S TRADITIONS IN FOREIGN POLICY

"...peace, commerce, and honest friendship with all nations—entangling alliances with none...." PRESIDENT THOMAS JEFFERSON, FIRST INAUGURAL ADDRESS, MARCH 4, 1801

"I shall never, myself, consent to an entangling alliance. But I would gladly assent to a disentangling alliance—an alliance which would disentangle the people of the world from those combinations in which they seek their own separate and private interests and unite the people of the world to preserve the peace of the world upon a basis of common right and justice." PRESIDENT WOODROW WILSON, MAY 30, 1916

Politics, at its roots, deals with values and value differences among individuals, groups, and nations. Various definitions of the term *politics* attest to the central place that values play in political life. Political scientist Harold Lasswell has written, for example, that politics "is the study of influence and the influential. . . . The influentials are those who get the most of what there is to get."[1] What there is to get, Lasswell continued, is values such as "deference, income, and safety."[2] Drawing upon Aristotle and Max Weber, Robert Dahl notes that what seems to be common across different definitions of politics is that they deal with values such as power, rule, and authority.[3] David Easton's famous definition of politics is even more explicit in its assessment of the relationship between politics and values: "Politics is the authoritative allocation of values."[4] According to this definition, authority structures (e.g., governments) distribute something, and that something is values.

Values refer to "modes of conduct and end-states of existence" that guide people's lives. They are "abstract ideals" that serve as an imperative for action.[5] Further, values are viewed as "goods" (not in a material, but in an ethical sense) that ought to be obtained or maintained by a person or a society. In the Declaration of Independence, for instance, the values of life, liberty, and the pursuit of happiness were explicitly stated as reasons for creating the United States. These values, moreover, came to serve as guides to political action in the earliest days of the nation. Indeed, such values have remained important to this day. Liberty, or freedom, is emphasized again and again by American political leaders as one value that differentiates this nation from so many others.

VALUES, BELIEFS, AND FOREIGN POLICY

Because the essence of politics is so closely related to achieving and maintaining particular values, the analysis of values and beliefs was consciously chosen as the organizing theme for studying the foreign policy of the United States.[6] Further, since values and beliefs are the motivating forces for individual action—and because we shall make the assumption that foreign policy is ultimately the result of individual choice—their importance for foreign policy analysis becomes readily apparent. Thus, by identifying the values and beliefs that American society fosters, we ought to be in a good position to understand how they have shaped our actions toward the rest of the world.

Social psychologists have provided the best analysis of the relationships among values, beliefs, and the behavior of individuals.

Milton Rokeach defines beliefs as propositions "inferred from what a person says or does" and whose content "may *describe* an object or situation as true or false; *evaluate* it as good or bad; or *advocate* a certain course of action as desirable or undesirable." Individuals thus may have numerous beliefs, but some are more central than others in accounting for their behavior. These core beliefs are values. As Rokeach notes, "A value is a type of belief, centrally located within one's total belief system, about how one ought, or ought not, to behave, or about some end state of existence worth, or not worth, attaining." Although these values are likely to be few in number, they are crucial in understanding the attitudes and behaviors that an individual expresses.[7] By extension, then, nation-states would operate in the same way, since ultimately individuals comprise them.

Inevitably, of course, there will be some slippage in any direct analogy between individual and nation-state behavior, and we ought to discuss a few cautions in applying this approach to foreign policy analysis. First, such other factors as the personality traits of individual leaders, the effects of bureaucratic factors, and the restraints of the governmental process will intrude into any complete identification of the national values and beliefs.[8] While recognizing these factors, and the wealth of research that has gone into their analysis, the role of underlying values and beliefs remains critically important and should not be overlooked.

Even accepting this position, a second reason raises doubts about using this kind of values perspective: the very definition of national values is likely to be problematic. Whose values are we to identify? Should they be the values of political leaders or the public at large? While our analysis will focus primarily on the values held by the political elites, the values and beliefs of the public will also be examined.

A third caution in using the values approach to the study of American foreign policy is potentially more troubling. By focusing on values and beliefs, and by using them as the basis for explaining U.S. foreign policy, we are close to relying on the national character (or, more generally, the political culture) explanation of behavior.[9] As A. F. K. Organski has asserted, the national character approach makes several key assumptions:

> (1) that the individual citizens of a nation share a common psychological make-up or personality or value system that distinguishes them from the citizens of other nations, (2) that this national character persists without major changes over a relatively long period of time, and (3) that there is a traceable relationship between individual character and national goals.[10]

Such assumptions are very difficult to make. Thus, there are limitations to the national character approach as a meaningful explanation of foreign policy, and it cannot be relied on completely. Its use in a more limited sense to identify the "basic attitudes, beliefs, values, and value orientations" of a society as a beginning point for analysis is appropriate, however, since individuals (and, hence, nations) make decisions within the context of a particular array of values and beliefs.[11]

Although we recognize these limitations, we believe that this values approach is a sufficiently useful first step to warrant more coverage than it has received. Moreover, our analysis will not contend that values and beliefs are immutable. Rather, we shall emphasize the very opposite: the constancy of change, especially in the past several decades, as the United States has entered the global arena and has attempted to reshape it.

Beyond the utility of a values approach to analyzing the foreign policy of any nation, it is especially germane to the study of American foreign policy for at least three additional reasons. First, the nation was explicitly founded on particular sets of values, and these values made the United States view itself as different from the nations of the Old World from which it originated. In this view, politics was not to be conducted upon the principles of power politics, but rather on the basis of democratic principles. To many, then, America could act in the world only on the basis of moral principles or in defense of such principles. Domestic values, at all times, were to be the guide to political behavior. Whether the United States lived up to these standards is debatable, but the inevitable desire to justify actions within a value context emphasizes the role of such principles as guides to U.S. foreign policy.

Second, since American values toward international affairs have changed so rapidly in recent years, an understanding of these changes is especially important for U.S. foreign policy analysis. As we shall discuss, America moved from its isolationist past to an active globalism in the post–World War II years. Indeed, a particular set of values, often labeled the Cold War consensus, came to dominate the motivations of American policy actions from the late 1940s to at least the middle 1960s. In the post-Vietnam period (roughly 1973 and beyond), America's value orientation toward the world has changed a number of times—from the realism of the Kissinger-Nixon-Ford years, to the idealism of the Carter term, back to the Cold War values of the Reagan administration, and toward values emphasizing the "ending of the Cold War" during the Bush administration. With such discernible changes throughout the recent history of U.S. foreign policy, an understanding of these particular value orientations and their policy implications are an important step in understanding American behavior abroad in different periods.

Third, the lack of a foreign policy consensus at either the elite or mass levels in American society further invites the use of a values approach. According to several national surveys, none of the value perspectives of the post-Vietnam period has been fully embraced by the American public or its leaders. Both the public at large and the American leadership are deeply divided as to the appropriate set of values to guide American policy for the future. While we shall discuss these divisions fully in Chapters 12 and 13, suffice it to say that until these divisions are overcome, values and beliefs will remain a potent force for understanding American foreign policy.

In the remainder of this first chapter, then, we will sketch the historical values and beliefs of American society and then suggest how they have influenced our foreign policy toward the rest of the world, especially in the nation's first century and a half.

THE UNITED STATES: A NEW DEMOCRATIC STATE

Numerous scholars have noted that the United States was founded upon values that were different from those of the rest of the world.[12] It was to be a democratic nation in a world governed primarily by monarchies and other autocracies. Indeed, according to one historian, America's founders "didn't just want to believe that they were involved in a sordid little revolt on the fringes of the British Empire or of European civilization. They wanted to believe they were coming up with a better model, . . . a better way for human beings to form a government that would be responsive to them."[13] Thomas Jefferson stated this view best when he described the new American state as "the solitary republic of the world, the only monument of human rights. . . the sole depositary of the sacred fire of freedom and self-government, from hence it is to be lighted up in other regions of the earth, if other regions shall ever become susceptible to its benign influence."[14] Because of its democratic value emphasis, moreover, America developed with the belief that its society was unique and possessed a set of values worthy of emulation by others. In this sense, the country emerged as a deeply ideological society (although Americans do not readily admit it), and as one not always tolerant of those who hold contrary views.[15]

In 1776 the United States was explicitly conceived in liberty and equality, in contrast to other nations, where ascription and privilege were so important.[16] It emerged as an essentially free society in a world that stressed authority and order. This new American state, to a large measure, was dynamic, classless, and free, in contrast to Europe, which was largely classbound and restrictive.[17] (Revolutionary France does not fit this description, but "classbound and restrictive" certainly describe politics under the Concert of Europe.) Thus, the American Revolution was fought in defiance of the very principles by which Europe was governed. In this sense, there developed a natural aversion to European values—and foreign policies—which further reinforced America's beliefs in its own uniqueness.

The fundamental American beliefs that were perceived to be so different from European values of the time can be summarized in the notion of classical liberalism, especially as espoused by John Locke.[18] In this liberal tradition the individual is paramount, and the role of government is limited. Government's task is to do only what is necessary to protect the life and liberty of its citizens and to provide for their happiness. Citizens are generally left alone, free to pursue their own goals and to seek rewards based solely on their abilities.

From such a concern for the individual, personal freedom and personal achievement naturally emerged as cherished values in American society. Yet equality before the law was also necessary to ensure that all individuals could maximize their potential on the sole basis of their talents. In a society that placed so much emphasis on the freedom of the individual, however, equality was viewed in a particular way. What was guaranteed was *not* equality of outcomes (substantive equality) but equality of opportunity (procedural equality) for all.[19] Although all citizens were not guaranteed the same ultimate station in life, all citizens should (theoretically) be able to advance as far as their individual capabilities would take them. While equality of opportunity is thus important to American society, the freedom to determine one's own level of achievement remained the dominant characteristic of this new society.

The early leaders of the new American state differed from their European counterparts in a third important way: in the relationship between domestic values and foreign policy. Unlike the European states of the time, most of the new American leaders did not view foreign policy as having primacy over domestic policy in which the power and standing of the state must be preserved and enhanced at the expense of domestic well-being. Nor did these new leaders view foreign policy values and domestic policy values as distinct from one another, where one moral value system guided domestic action and another, by necessity, guided action between states. Instead, most early American leaders saw foreign policy as subservient to the interests of domestic policy and domestic values. One recent analysis of Thomas Jefferson's beliefs on the relationship between the domestic and foreign policy arenas best captures the predominant view at the outset of the American Republic: "the objective of foreign policy was but a means to the ends of posterity and promoting the goals of domestic society, that is, the individual's freedom and society's well-being."[20]

Such values and beliefs came to have important consequences for foreign policy actions by this new nation. Because the United States adopted a democratic political system, developed strong libertarian and egalitarian values domestically, and believed in the primacy of domestic over foreign policy, two important foreign policy traditions quickly emerged: isolationism and moralism.[21] Both traditions, moreover, were intended to assist in perpetuating unique American values: the former by reducing U.S. involvement in world affairs, and particularly those of Europe, the latter by justifying U.S. involvement abroad only for sufficient ethical reasons. At times, these two impulses pulled in different directions (one based on the urge to stay out of world affairs, the other based on the urge to reform world affairs through unilateral action), but both came to dominate the foreign policy action of the new state.

ISOLATIONISM IN AMERICAN FOREIGN POLICY

Since democratic values were so much at variance with those of the rest of the world, many early Americans came to view foreign nations, and especially European states, with suspicion.[22] They feared that the nation's values would be compromised by other states and that international ties would only entangle the United States in alien conflicts. From the beginning, therefore, there was a natural inclination in American society to move away from global involvement and toward isolationism. Throughout the greatest part of the history of this nation, in fact, isolationism best describes America's foreign policy approach.[23]

Although philosophical concepts influenced the isolationist orientation, it was also guided by some important practical considerations. First, the United States was separated geographically from Europe—the main arena of international politics in the eighteenth and nineteenth centuries—and from the rest of the world. Staying out of the affairs of other nations, therefore, seemed a practical course. Second, since the United States was a young, weak country with a small army and a relatively large land-mass, seeking adversaries and potential conflicts abroad would hardly be prudent. Third, domestic unity—a sense of nationalism—was still limited and merited more attention than foreign policy. Finally, the overriding task of settling and modernizing the American continent provided reason enough to adopt an isolationist posture.[24]

TWO STATEMENTS ON ISOLATIONISM

Early in the history of the country, two statements—Washington's Farewell Address and the Monroe Doctrine—effectively portrayed what isolationism meant and set limits to its application. The first president's Farewell Address of September 1796 was originally meant to thank the American people for their confidence in his leadership, but it also contained a series of warnings about problems that could arise and could threaten the continuance of the Republic. Washington admonished American citizens not to become involved in factional groups (i.e., political parties), sectional divisions (i.e., East versus West, North versus South), or international entanglements. His comments on international involvements are instructive in explaining what isolationism was to mean in determining American foreign policy for a century and a half.

America's attitude toward the world, Washington said, should be a simple one:

> Observe good faith and justice toward all nations. Cultivate peace and harmony with all. . . .
> In the execution of such a plan nothing is more essential than that permanent, inveterate antipathies against particular nations and passionate attachments for others should be excluded, and that in place of them just and amicable feeling toward all should be cultivated.[25]

He warned against the danger of forming close ties with other states:

> . . . a passionate attachment of one nation for another produces a variety of evils. Sympathy for the favorite nations, facilitating the illusion of an imaginary interest in cases where no real common interest exists, and infusing into one the enmities of the other, betrays the former into a participation in the quarrels and wars of the latter without adequate inducement or justification.[26]

And he provided a "rule of conduct" for the United States and admonished that any involvement in the Byzantine politics of Europe would not be in this country's best interest:

> The great rule of conduct for us in regard to foreign nations is, in extending our commercial relations to have with them as little *political* connection as possible. So far as we have already formed engagements let them be fulfilled with perfect good faith. Here let us stop.
>
> Europe has a set of primary interests which to us have none or a very remote relation. Hence she must be engaged in frequent controversies, the causes of which are essentially foreign to our concerns. Hence, therefore, it must be unwise in us to implicate ourselves by artificial ties in the ordinary vicissitudes of her politics or the ordinary combinations and collisions of her friendship or enmities.[27]

In sum, Washington suggested that while the foreign policy of the United States should not be totally isolationist (because economic ties with some states were good and useful, and amicable diplomatic ties with others were commendable), he strongly opposed the establishment of any permanent political bonds to other countries. Moreover, he directly warned against any involvement in the affairs of Europe.

While Washington's Farewell Address outlined a general isolationist orientation to the world, the Monroe Doctrine set forth specific guidelines for U.S. involvement or noninvolvement in international affairs. This doctrine—named after President James Monroe's seventh annual Message to the Congress, on December 2, 1823—was promulgated in part as a response to the possibility of increased activities by the European powers in the affairs of the American continents, especially when some Latin American states were moving toward independence or had just achieved it.[28] Monroe's message contained several distinct and identifiable themes: a call for future noncolonization in Latin America by the European powers and a "maintenance of the *status quo*" there, a declaration about the differences in the political systems of Europe and America, and a statement indicating that the United States would not interfere in the affairs of Europe.[29]

Monroe stated the first of these themes by declaring that the American continents "are henceforth not to be considered as subjects for future colonization by any European power." Such involvement in the affairs of the Americas would affect the "rights and interests" of the United States. Near the end of the message, he highlighted the differences in policies between the United States and Europe toward each other and toward Latin America:

> Of events in that quarter of the globe [Europe], with which we have so much intercourse and from which we derive our origin, we have always been anxious and interested *spectators*. . . . In the wars of the European powers in matters relating to themselves we have never taken any part, nor does it comport with our policy so to do. . . . With the movements in this hemisphere we are of necessity more immediately connected, and by causes which must be obvious to all enlightened and impartial observers. The political system of the allied powers is essentially different in this respect from that of America. These differences proceed from that which exists in their respective Governments. . . . We owe it, therefore, to candor and to the amicable relations existing between the United States and those powers to declare that we should consider any attempt on their part to extend their system to any portion of this hemisphere as dangerous to our peace and safety. With the existing colonies or dependencies of any European power we have not interfered and shall not interfere. But with the Governments who have declared their independence and maintained it, and whose independence we have, on great consideration and on just principles, acknowledged, we could not view any interposition. . . by any European powers in any other light than as the manifestation of an unfriendly disposition toward the United States.[30]

The Monroe Doctrine thus gave rise to the "two spheres" concept in American foreign policy by emphasizing the differences between the Western and Eastern hemispheres—the New World versus the Old World.[31] As Washington had done earlier, Monroe's statement called for political noninvolvement in the affairs of Europe. But Monroe's message did more than Washington's; it specified that the U.S. policy of political noninvolvement in European affairs did not apply equally to Latin American affairs. By asserting that the "rights and interests" of the United States would be affected by European involvements in the Western Hemisphere, it stipulated that the United States did, indeed, have political interests beyond its borders— particularly in Latin America. In this sense, U.S. political isolationism did not wholly apply to the Western Hemisphere. Instead, U.S. political interests in Latin America became widespread, and they had their origins in the Monroe Doctrine.

Taken as a whole, these two messages can be a valuable guide in understanding this country's isolationist orientation toward global affairs. The principles enunciated in them generally reflected the diplomatic practices of the United States throughout much of the nineteenth century and into the twentieth, and their words became the basis of the nation's continuing foreign policy.

TABLE 1.1 CONTENT OF INTERNATIONAL AGREEMENTS
BY THE UNITED STATES

Content	Years 1778–1899	Years 1947–1960
Alliance	1	1,024
Amity and Commerce	272	3,088
Boundary	32	4
Claims	167	105
Consular Activities	47	212
Extradition	47	12
Multilateral	37	469
Territorial Concessions	18	4
Total	621	4,918

Source: Calculated from Igor I. Kavass and Mark A. Michael, *United States Treaties and Other International Agreements, Cumulative Index 1776–1949,* Volume 2 (Buffalo, NY: Wm. S. Hein & Co., Inc., 1975), and from Igor I. Kavass and Adolf Sprudzs, *United States Treaties Cumulative Index 1950–1970,* Volume 2 (Buffalo, NY: Wm. S. Hein & Co., Inc., 1973). For a discussion of how the table was constructed, see the text and note 34.

ISOLATIONISM IN ACTION: THE NINETEENTH CENTURY

As a result of the isolationist nature of its foreign policy during the nineteenth century, there was a severe restriction on treaty commitments that would bind the United States *politically* to other states. In fact, one prominent historian has pointed out that the United States made no treaties of alliance between the treaty with France in 1778 and the Declaration of the United Nations in 1942.[32] A survey of American agreements, however, would show that the United States did, in fact, enter into a number of agreements on political matters with other states.[33] For example, the United States enacted agreements on extradition, navigation of the seas, treatment of nationals, and amity and friendship. None of these agreements could be construed as "entangling" alliances, however; instead they served primarily to facilitate amicable trade relations with other states.

A summary of the kind of agreements made by the United States from its founding to the twentieth century—and, for comparison, from 1947 to 1960—is displayed in Table 1.1.[34] The column of data for the 1778–1899 period confirms the large emphasis upon economic ties and the limited political ties in the early history of the nation.

Agreements on amity and commerce and claims (largely economic) constitute about 70 percent of the agreements. Even the agreements with more direct political elements, such as those dealing with consular activities and extradition, are largely routine matters for fostering good relations with other states, rather than highly controversial political issues. Only those pacts that deal with boundary issues and territorial concessions (e.g., the Louisiana Purchase, the purchase of Alaska, the Oregon Treaty, or the Gadsden Treaty) might be placed in the more controversial category. Even those, however, still comprise less than 10 percent of all commitments. The single alliance was the treaty with France, which was ultimately allowed to lapse in 1800.[35]

By contrast, the data for 1947–1960—the initial period of America's active entry into global affairs—show a strikingly different pattern of commitments. First, the sheer number of agreements are markedly different from one period to the next—from just over 600 in a 120-year period to over 4,900 in a 14-year period. While economic agreements (amity and commerce) still constituted the largest single type of agreement (about 60 percent), alliances and multilateral commitments now constituted about 30 percent of all agreements. To be sure, these alliances ties were broadly defined—such as setting up military bases, establishing defense pacts and mutual security agreements, and sending military missions to particular nations—but they still demonstrated a much different level and scope of involvement than had occurred in the country's early years. Similarly, the number and kind of multilateral pacts are also distinctive in the two periods. For the more recent period, the number of such pacts were now over ten times greater, and their content reflected a new dimension to such ties. About 10 percent of the multilateral pacts in the immediate post–World War II years were defense commitments; no such level was registered in the earlier period.

In short, then, the comparative data bring into sharp relief the fact that America's global involvement in the late eighteenth century and the entire nineteenth century was very different than in the more recent period. The first 120 years of the Republic produced relatively few international agreements, and even these agreements were largely restricted to fostering amicable relations and sound commercial ties between the new American nation and the rest of the world.

An illustration or two from these earliest agreements will more fully demonstrate the limited extent of any political commitments in these early pacts. Under the Treaty of Amity and Commerce between the United States and Sweden, both parties committed themselves to neutrality in case of war and agreed to help each other's ships at sea if they were subject to attack by third parties.[36] Similar kinds of commitments were made in treaties with Prussia, Tripoli, Tunis, and others in the early years of the Republic. Even a subsequent Treaty of Peace and Friendship between the United States and Tripoli (November 4, 1796, and January 3, 1797) emphasized the common effort to facilitate freedom of shipping for the two contracting parties more than the political bonds between the nations. Document 1.1 excerpts the main elements of the pact to illustrate this point more fully.

This type of treaty hardly bound the United States to other societies in any large degree. Instead, such treaties further typify the essential kind of international commitment that the young nation wanted: agreements to facilitate and enhance commerce. Further, commercial ties covered virtually all areas of the world, ranging from Europe to South America to the Far East, where agreements were made with Japan, China, and Siam, among numerous others. In essence, Washington's principle that political ties should be avoided while economic ties were facilitated was generally honored in the first century of the United States.

A brief survey of the diplomatic history of the United States during the nineteenth century gives further evidence of a commitment to the principles of Washington and Monroe. For example, President James K. Polk, in his first annual address to the Congress on December 2, 1845, reemphasized the tenets Monroe had set down twenty-two years earlier: "It should be distinctly announced to the world as our settled policy, that no future European colony or dominion shall, with our consent, be planted or established on any part of the North American continent."[37] While Polk did not explicitly relate the ongoing dispute with the British over the Oregon Territory with his reaffirmation of Monroe's policy, the inference (in the view of at least one noted diplomatic historian) was quite clear.[38] Similarly, Polk expressed concern over rumors that the British were about to obtain land in the Yucatan. In a message to Congress (April 29, 1848), Polk said that the "United States would not permit such a deal, even with the consent of the inhabitants."[39]

During this same period the United States concluded the Clayton-Bulwer Treaty, which stipulated that neither Britain nor the United States would ever "obtain or maintain for itself any exclusive control" over a canal across the isthmus at Panama and that "neither will ever exert or maintain fortification commanding the same, or in the vicinity thereof, or fortify, or colonize, or assume, or exercise any dominion over Nicaragua, Costa Rica, the Mosquito Coast, or any

---

DOCUMENT 1.1   TREATY OF PEACE AND FRIENDSHIP
BETWEEN THE UNITED STATES AND TRIPOLI

Article 1.

There is a firm and perpetual Peace and friendship between the
United States of America and the Bey and subjects of Tripoli of
Barbary, made by the free consent of both parties, and guaranteed by
the most potent Dey & regency of Algiers.

Article 2.

If any goods belonging to any nation with which either of the
parties is at war shall be loaded on board of vessels belonging to the
other party they shall pass free, and no attempt shall be made to take
or detain them.

Article 3.

If any citizens, subjects or effects belonging to either party shall
be found on board a prize vessel from an enemy by the other party,
such citizens or subjects shall be set at liberty, and the effects
restored to the owners.

Article 6.

Vessels of either party putting into the ports of the other and
having need of provissions [sic] or other supplies, they shall be
furnished at the market price. And if any such vessel shall so put in
from a disaster at sea and have occasion to repair, she shall be at
liberty to land and reembark her cargo without paying any duties.
But in no case shall she be compelled to land her cargo.

Article 7.

Should a vessel of either party be cast on the shore of the other,
all proper assistance shall be given to her and her people; no pillage
shall be allowed; the property shall remain at the disposition of the
owners, and the crew protected and succoured till they can be sent to
their country.

Article 8.

If a vessel of either party should be attacked by an enemy within
gunshot of the forts of the other she shall be defended as much as
possible. If she be in port she shall not be seized or attacked when it
is in the power of the other party to protect her. And when she
proceeds to sea no enemy shall be allowed to pursue her from the
same port within twenty four hours after her departure.

Article 9.

The commerce between the United States and Tripoli,—the
protection to be given to merchants, masters of vessels and seamen,—
the reciprocal right of establishing consuls in each country, and the
privileges, immunities and jurisdictions to be enjoyed by such
consuls, are declared to be on the same footing with those of the
most favoured nations respectively.

DOCUMENT 1.1 TREATY OF PEACE AND FRIENDSHIP
BETWEEN THE UNITED STATES AND TRIPOLI (CONTINUED)

Article 11.

As the government of the United States of America is not in any
sense founded on the Christian Religion—as it has in itself no
character of enmity against the laws, religion or tranquility of
Musselmen,—and as the said States never have entered into any war
or act of hostility against any Mehomitan nation, it is declared by the
parties that no pretext arising from religious opinions shall ever
produce an interruption of the harmony existing between the two
countries.

Article 12.

In case of any dispute arising from a violation of any of the
articles of this treaty no appeal shall be made to arms, nor shall war
be declared on any pretext whatever. But if the Consul residing at the
place where the dispute shall happen shall not be able to settle the
same, an amicable referrence shall be made to the mutual friend of
the parties, the Dey of Algiers, the parties hereby engaging to abide
by his decision. And he by virtue of his signature to this treaty
engages for himself and successors to declare the justice of the case
according to the true interpretation of the treaty, and to use all the
means in his power to enforce the observance of the same.

Source: Excerpted from Hunter Miller, ed., *Treaties and Other International Acts of the
United States of America.* Volume 2 (Washington, D.C.: U.S. Government Printing Office,
1931), pp. 364–366.

part of Central America."[40] While this pact was later viewed as a mistake by some because it gave some standing to the British in the
hemisphere, it did allow continued involvement by the United States
in the political affairs in Latin America. Consistent with the prescriptions of the Monroe Doctrine, it also tried to regulate European affairs in the area.[41]

Late in the nineteenth century, during the presidency of Grover
Cleveland, American policymakers again invoked the principles of
the Monroe Doctrine to support Venezuela's claim against the British
over a boundary dispute between British Guiana and Venezuela. On
July 29, 1895, Secretary of State Richard Olney sent a note to the Brit-
ish stating that they were violating the Monroe Doctrine and that the
United States could not permit any weakening of this policy. The
British, with good reason, rejected this interpretation. President
Cleveland responded angrily, asked Congress for funds to establish
a boundary commission to investigate the dispute, and got them

quickly, thus fueling war fever over this relatively minor issue.[42] The incident, too, illustrates the continuing influence of the Monroe Doctrine on American foreign policy throughout much of the nineteenth century.[43]

ISOLATIONISM IN ACTION: THE TWENTIETH CENTURY

Despite the appeal of imperial expansion for some American leaders, global isolationism and noninvolvement continued to be the guiding principle toward much of European affairs. Only when moral principle justified interventionist policy into European affairs, as the case of World War I surely illustrates, as we will discuss shortly, was isolationism temporarily abandoned. Even then, though, interventionism was largely a last resort and was justified in strong moral tones by the Wilson administration. By contrast, several social, economic, and political actions, largely directed toward Europe, illustrate the preferred isolationist sentiment that continued to dominate American thinking and policy in the early decades of the twentieth century.

In social policy, perhaps the most notable development in the early twentieth century was the passage of the National Origins Act of 1924. This legislation restricted "new" immigration from Southern and Eastern Europe and forbade immigration from the Orient. The act was largely a reaction to the "red scare" and the fear of aliens that had shaken the country, and it represented an attempt to control foreign influences within the United States through more stringent regulation of immigration. In economic policy, the Smoot-Hawley Tariff of 1930 imposed high tariff barriers on foreign goods. Such protectionist legislation was yet a further attempt to isolate the United States from the effects of global economic influences. Further, in the words of one analyst, "the belief...that the Depression stemmed from forces abroad against which the United States had to insulate itself...also gave a 'protective' tariff an irresistible symbolic appeal."[44] In the political arena, the isolationist impulse was equally pronounced. After American involvement in World War I, a "return to normalcy" was the dominant theme. This theme implied a more isolationist and pacifist approach toward world affairs and was manifested in American rejection of membership in the League of Nations established after World War I, its refusal to recognize the Soviet Union (until 1933) and other regimes of which it disapproved, its attempt to outlaw international war with the signing of the Kellogg-Briand Pact in 1928, and its effort to limit global armament through a series of conferences in the 1920s and again in the early

1930s. In addition, a strong pacifist movement emerged, with over fifty peace societies developing across the country in the 1920s. The efforts to eliminate international war were viewed as partial reparation for involvement in World War I and as an effort to prevent such involvement in the future. Thus, international reform was wholly consistent with domestic reform in the minds of many Americans.[45]

In Latin America, however, isolationism and noninvolvement were not the guiding foreign policy principles in the new century. Instead, the 1904 Roosevelt Corollary to the Monroe Doctrine further refined the meaning of that doctrine and expanded U.S. involvement in the Western Hemisphere. As a means of blunting possible European intervention into the affairs of some Western Hemisphere states that had not paid their debts, President Theodore Roosevelt extended the meaning of the Monroe Doctrine to include American intervention, if necessary, to protect the region.

In a letter to the Congress on December 6, 1904, Roosevelt outlined his rationale for this addition to the Monroe Doctrine:

> Chronic wrongdoing, or an impotence which results in a general loosening of the ties of civilized society, may in America, as elsewhere, ultimately require intervention by some civilized nation, and in the Western Hemisphere the adherence of the United States to the Monroe Doctrine may force the United States, however reluctantly, in flagrant cases of such wrongdoing or impotence, to the exercise of an international police power. Our interests and those of our southern neighbors are in reality identical. They have great natural riches, and if within their borders the reign of law and justice obtains prosperity is sure to come to them. While they thus obey the primary laws of civilized society they may rest assured that they will be treated by us in a spirit of cordial and helpful sympathy. We would interfere with them only in the last resort and then only if it became evident that their inability or unwillingness to do justice at home and abroad had violated the rights of the United States or had invited foreign aggression to the detriment of the entire body of American nations.[46]

Ironically, the Monroe Doctrine, which had been initiated to prevent intervention from abroad, was now used to justify American intervention in the Western Hemisphere.

This policy was quickly implemented in 1905 by American intervention into the Dominican Republic to manage its economic affairs and to prevent any other outside interference. Similar financial and military interventions followed on the basis of this experience. The United States became involved in the affairs of the Dominican

Republic, Haiti, Nicaragua, and Mexico with intervention in each of these countries throughout the early years of the twentieth century. American forces occupied the Dominican Republic from 1916 to 1924, Haiti from 1915 to 1934, Nicaragua from 1912 to 1933, and Mexico for a time in 1914. In addition, the United States established a protectorate over Panama from 1903 to 1939 and over Cuba from 1898 to 1934.[47]

In recent decades the Monroe Doctrine has hardly lost its relevance for American policy. In 1954 the United States supported a coup that overthrew the government of the Jacobo Arbenz Guzman regime in Guatemala after Arbenz had initiated domestic reform programs and had received arms shipments from the Soviet bloc. Both the fear of communism in the Western Hemisphere and the tradition of the Monroe Doctrine figured prominently in this action.[48] After Fidel Castro seized power in Cuba in 1959, a U.S.-backed force of Cuban exiles was organized and trained to topple the Castro regime. In April 1961 the abortive Bay of Pigs invasion ended in disaster but was defended as an attempt to stop the spread of communism in the Western Hemisphere. In 1962 the American blockade against Cuba after the discovery of Soviet missiles in that country was again justified by this doctrine. In his address to the nation during the Cuban Missile Crisis, President Kennedy noted how these missiles violated "the traditions of this nation and the Hemisphere."[49] In April 1965, when communists were allegedly seizing power in the Dominican Republic, President Lyndon Johnson sent in some 23,000 U.S. and Organization of American States (OAS) forces to protect American citizens and to restore a government more favorable to the United States.

By the late 1970s and into the early 1990s, the tenets of the Monroe Doctrine continued to shape American foreign policy in the Western Hemisphere. In September 1979, when the presence of 2,000 to 3,000 Soviet combat troops was revealed in Cuba, Senator Richard Stone of Florida cited the Monroe Doctrine as one reason the troops had to be removed. Secretary of State Cyrus Vance echoed the sentiments of this doctrine when he said that the presence of these forces would not be tolerated. When successful political revolutions occurred in El Salvador and Nicaragua in 1979, the United States immediately became concerned that these revolutions would produce "Soviet beachheads" at America's backdoor in the Western Hemisphere. Quick efforts were made to bolster the new moderate government in El Salvador with large amounts of economic and military assistance to meet the challenge from a guerrilla force, the Farabundo Marti National Liberation Front (FMLN).

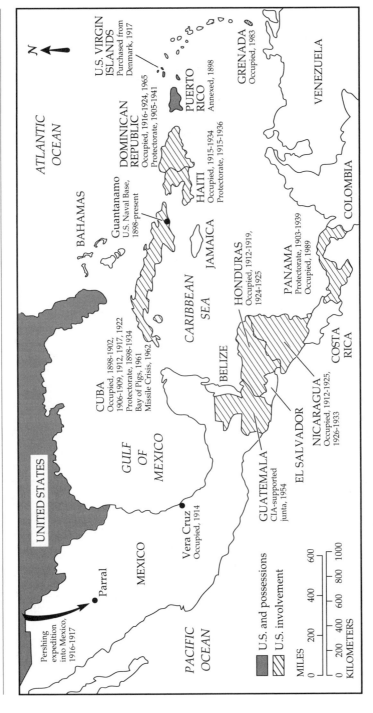

MAP 1.1   U.S. Involvements in Central America and the Caribbean, 1898–1990

Source: The involvement data for 1898–1939 are taken from the map in Walter LeFeber's *The American Age* (New York: W.W. Norton and Company, 1989), p. 233. The subsequent American involvements have been added by the author.

UNITED STATES

Parral

Pershing expedition into Mexico, 1916–1917

MEXICO

PACIFIC OCEAN

Vera Cruz
Occupied, 1914

GULF OF MEXICO

ATLANTIC OCEAN

BAHAMAS

CARIBBEAN SEA

BELIZE

GUATEMALA
CIA-supported junta, 1954

EL SALVADOR

NICARAGUA
Occupied, 1912-1925, 1926-1933

HONDURAS
Occupied, 1912-1919, 1924-1925

COSTA RICA

PANAMA
Protectorate, 1903-1939
Occupied, 1989

COLOMBIA

JAMAICA

CUBA
Occupied, 1898-1902, 1906-1909, 1912, 1917, 1922
Protectorate, 1898-1934
Bay of Pigs, 1961
Missile Crisis, 1962

Guantanamo
U.S. Naval Base, 1898-present

HAITI
Occupied, 1915-1934
Protectorate, 1915-1936

DOMINICAN REPUBLIC
Occupied, 1916-1924, 1965
Protectorate, 1905-1941

PUERTO RICO
Annexed, 1898

U.S. VIRGIN ISLANDS
Purchased from Denmark, 1917

GRENADA
Occupied, 1983

VENEZUELA

N

MILES
0   200   400   600

0   200   400   600   800   1000
KILOMETERS

■ U.S. and possessions
▨ U.S. involvement

By contrast, the Reagan administration challenged the new Marxist-led Sandinista government in Nicaragua and, by late 1981, had initiated a covert operation to support the contras, a counter-revolutionary force committed to the overthrow of that new Nicaraguan government. When the funding for the contras was stopped by the U.S. Congress from late 1984 to late 1986, Reagan administration officials devised a scheme to continue supporting the contra rebels by secretly selling arms to Iran and transferring part of the proceeds to the Nicaragua rebels. This operation became known as the Iran-contra affair (see Chapter 5). Through continued American support for the contras and diplomatic efforts by the United States, but especially by the Central American states, a free election was arranged for February 1990 in Nicaragua. In this election, the U.S.-backed candidate, Violetta Chamorro, in a stunning upset to many observers, defeated the incumbent Sandinista leader, Daniel Ortega, for the presidency of Nicaragua. A government that was more consistent with U.S. interests was once again in power, and the Monroe Doctrine seemed intact.

In Panama, the U.S. worried about the corrupt regime of Manuel Antonio Noriega and its implication for American influence in that country. General Noriega, who had ruled Panama since the violent death of General Omar Torrijos in 1981, reportedly made huge profits from the drug trade that went through Panama and became increasingly repressive in the treatment of his citizens, going so far as cancelling an election result in May 1989 that did not go in his favor. The Reagan administration sought and obtained an indictment on drug smuggling in Miami and undertook various unsuccessful efforts to oust Noriega from power through American economic and diplomatic actions. A military coup covertly supported and encouraged by the Bush administration in October 1989 also failed when the U.S. suddenly limited its level of involvement. Then, in December 1989, the United States employed a military force totaling about 24,000 to overthrow the Noriega regime. The effort was successful, and Noriega was finally captured and brought to the United States to stand trial on drug trafficking charges.

While the effort to stabilize El Salvador, Nicaragua, and Panama has proved costly, the imperative to keep the Western Hemisphere free of outside powers and to keep the Monroe Doctrine alive continues largely unabated. Likewise, the American view, since at least the Theodore Roosevelt administration, that it could use its power to establish order in this region also is alive and well as the most recent intervention into Panama demonstrates.

MORALISM IN AMERICAN FOREIGN POLICY

The founding of the United States with a unique set of values, and the nation's development in the context of political isolationism, yielded another important dimension of America's foreign policy: a highly moralistic approach to world affairs.[50] Americans never felt very comfortable with international politics (especially power politics as practiced in Europe), and they had largely honored the imperative to stay away from foreign entanglements. This policy of political noninvolvement generated a certain self-righteousness when the country occasionally did become involved in international politics. As political scientist John Spanier and others have argued, distinct American attitudes developed toward such important political concepts as the balance of power, war and peace, and force and diplomacy.[51] More generally, the role of moral values (as opposed to political interests) became an important feature of American policymaking. Furthermore, this moralistic fervor was reflected in policy by the great moral "crusades" the United States undertook in the late nineteenth and twentieth centuries, when it did begin to abandon its global isolationist posture.

The balance-of-power concept, which dominated policymaking in Europe since the inception of the nation-state system there, is predicated on several key assumptions. First, it assumes that all states are interested in preventing large-scale war and in preserving the existence of at least the major states in the international system. Second, it is based on the view that all states are fundamentally motivated in their foreign policy behavior by power considerations and national interests. Third, it assumes that states are willing and able to join alliances (and to change alliances) to prevent the dominance of any one state. Fourth, it assumes that there will be few domestic political constraints preventing states from acting in the political arena.[52] The essence of the balance-of-power concept is the adroit use of diplomacy and bargaining, but it maintains that force and violence can—and should—be used to perpetuate the system.

Until recently, the United States has tended to reject virtually all the assumptions of balance-of-power politics.[53] American society has maintained that foreign policy should be motivated not by interests and power considerations but by moral principles; domestic values have been seen as the sole basis for foreign policy behavior. As Henry Kissinger, a critic of American antipathy toward power politics, has observed: "It is part of American folklore that, while other nations have interests, we have responsibilities; while other nations

are concerned with equilibrium, we are concerned with the legal requirements of peace."[54]

The views of war and peace and force and diplomacy in American society follow from its views of power politics. Because they have
rejected the balance-of-power concept, most Americans would find
little comfort in Karl von Clausewitz's dictum that war is "the continuation of political activity by other means."[55] Instead, Americans
have generally perceived war and peace as dichotomous: either war
or peace exists. Intermediate conditions in which limited force is
used (e.g., uses of military force to settle border disputes or short-
term interventions to achieve some limited objectives, such as the
liberation of Kuwait from the Iraqis in February 1991 by the U.S.) are
not wholly understandable or tolerable to most Americans. When
war does break out, and the country does have to get involved, an
all-out effort should be made to win the war. If the cause is sufficiently important in the first place, should not the effort be complete
and total? Likewise, if the cause is not important, why should U.S.
forces be committed at all?

The continued power of this view of war and peace is illustrated
by public reaction to two recent "limited wars" engaged in by the
United States. For many Americans, the conduct of the Korean and
Vietnam wars was perceived as extraordinarily frustrating because
an all-out military effort was not undertaken. Instead, a mixture of
military might and diplomacy was employed.

The U.S. view of force and diplomacy parallels the attitudes toward peace and war. Americans generally believe that when a nation
resorts to force, its use should be sufficient to meet the task at hand.
There should be no constraints of "politics" once the decision to use
force has been made. As a consequence, combining force and diplomacy (as in the balance-of-power approach) is not understandable to
large segments of the American public because it appears to compromise the country's moral position. Again, the Korean and Vietnam
wars illustrate this point. In both instances, "talking and fighting"
were not well understood or well received by many Americans. Similarly, the efforts by Henry Kissinger and Richard Nixon to combine
force and diplomacy (a policy of "coercive diplomacy") were criticized by both the political right and the political left because they
suggested a certain amoralism in American foreign policy efforts.

American diplomacy, too, has historically been heavily infused
with this moral tradition. Eminent historian Dexter Perkins has
noted that this kind of moralism produced a certain "rigidity" in
dealing with other states. Diplomacy, by its very nature, requires
some compromise on competing points. However, when "every

question is to be invested with the aura of principle, how is adjustment to take place?"[56] Similarly, Spanier has noted that, given the moralism so prevalent in American policymaking, it has traditionally been difficult for Americans to understand how compromise is possible. If a state has moral righteousness on its side, how can compromise be necessary?[57]

MORALISM AND INTERNATIONAL INVOLVEMENT

This moralist tradition was manifested in four important instances prior to 1947, when the United States involved itself in political conflict on a global scale.[58] On each of these occasions—the War of 1812, the Spanish-American War, World War I, and World War II—the justifications for involvement were alleged moral violations by adversaries.

The first instance when isolationism was abandoned in the name of moral principle was the War of 1812. When the U.S. Congress finally voted a declaration of war against Great Britain in June 1812, it did so only after various efforts to avoid involvements with the dominant European powers of the time—France and England—and only after what it perceived as continuous violations of an important principle of international law: freedom of the seas for neutral states.[59] Under a series of Orders in Council, and as part of its ongoing effort to limit Napoleon's power and enhance its own, the British government barred American commerce from France or any continental ports that barred the British. Further, it barred any neutral vessel that had not passed through a British port or paid British customs duties from carrying on commerce. U.S. ships violating such standards were subject to seizure. (France, under Napoleon, enacted similar restrictions on neutral shipping with his Continental System of commerce, but, for a variety of reasons, the U.S. responded with greater hostility to the British strictures.[60]) Such British actions infuriated the U.S., and American leaders characterized them as blatant violations of freedom of the seas. In addition to the seizure of American vessels, the British went further in their effort to control the seas through the practice of impressment. This practice involved seizing sailors off American vessels and forcing them into the British navy (because they were alleged to be deserters from the Royal Navy). Impressment further challenged America's freedom of commerce and the seas and was seen as besmirching U.S. national honor. While America's involvement in the War of 1812 proved costly and ultimately unpopular and the final results largely confirmed the status quo, it does suggest the potency of moral principle in guiding early American action.[61]

In the Spanish-American War of 1898, a variety of moral arguments was advanced to justify American actions: the harsh Spanish treatment of the Cubans, the sinking of the American battleship *Maine,* and the personal affront to President William McKinley by the Spanish ambassador in a private letter. (The ambassador portrayed McKinley as a "bidder for the admiration of the crowd" and as a "common politician.")[62] Few arguments for American participation were advanced on the basis of how it might affect the national interest; instead, moral arguments provided the dominant rationale.[63]

American participation in World War I in 1917–1918 was also cast in terms of the same kind of moral imperative, rather than the demands of the balance of power in Europe. Only for sufficient ethical cause did the United States feel compelled to enter this European conflict. In this case, the moral justification was provided by Germany's violation of the principle of freedom of the seas and the rights of neutrals through its unrestricted warfare campaign on the open sea.[64]

The outrage that developed in 1915 with the sinking of the British passenger ship, the *Lusitania* (and later, the *Sussex*), with the accompanying loss of American lives, provided sufficient reason to abandon isolationism temporarily for the affairs of the world. The proximate events that precipitated U.S. entry into the war, however, were the German announcement of its unrestricted submarine warfare in February 1917 and the Zimmermann telegram by Germany to Mexico, which sought to get that country into war with the United States.[65] Even as the United States embarked on this course, the need for continued moral justification was reflected in the elegant slogans devised to boost American participation. It was to be a "war to end all wars" and a campaign to "make the world safe for democracy."

U.S. participation in World War II from 1941 to 1945 again reflected the need for moral justification for the country's foreign policy behavior. Although the United States was assisting the Allies before its formal involvement, U.S. reentry into world conflict could only be justified in terms of some moral violation. The Neutrality Act of 1939, for example, had reduced the restrictions on arms sales and allowed the United States to supply France and Britain. The destroyers for bases deal with Great Britain—in which the United States gained naval and air bases in Newfoundland and some Caribbean islands in exchange for fifty destroyers—occurred in September 1940.[66] In March 1941, moreover, the Congress passed the Lend-Lease Act as another way to help the Allies.[67] Nevertheless, it was not until the Japanese bombing of Pearl Harbor, Hawaii, on December 7, 1941, "a date which will live in infamy" as President Franklin Roosevelt described it, that the United States was accorded a wholly satisfactory reason for plunging the country into the conflict.[68] Then the United States, consistent with its attitude, felt compelled to seek "absolute victory," as Roosevelt said. A total war effort was mounted, which ultimately led to the unconditional surrender of the Japanese in September 1945, only a few months after the victory in Europe had been secured.

IMPLICATIONS FOR U.S. INVOLVEMENT

As these four instances demonstrate, the United States has been re-luctant to give up its isolationism and has done so only for heady moral reasons. It has traditionally viewed such international actions only in terms of violation of clearly established principles of interna-tional law, rather than in terms of the requirements of power politics as many other states have done. As a consequence, American activi-ties in the world of power politics have been decidedly few in the past and have been entered into only in special circumstances. In short, America's particular conception of moralism dramatically af-fected the extent to which it entered into world politics.

After each of the first three involvements, the United States gen-erally moved back to its favored position of isolationism; none brought about a basic change in American foreign policy orientation. (The impact of World War II was considerably different, and Chapter 2 discusses its impact on our foreign policy approach.) After the War of 1812, for example, the immediate reaction was the reaffirmation of the policy of noninvolvement in European affairs by the Americans and the call for no European involvement in Western Hemisphere af-fairs via the Monroe Doctrine of 1823.

The strong American impulse toward isolationism was perhaps most vividly demonstrated in the rejection of the idealistic foreign policy proposed by President Woodrow Wilson at the end of World War I. Wilsonian idealism, as it came to be called, attempted to shake the U.S. from its isolationist moorings and become a continuing par-ticipant in global affairs. Wilsonian idealism, largely born out of the president's personal beliefs, consisted of several key tenets. First, moral principle should be the guide to U.S. actions abroad. Second, the Anglo-American values of liberty and liberal democratic institu-tions are worthy of emulation and promotion worldwide. Indeed, they are necessary if world peace is to be realized. Third, the old or-der based upon balance of power and interest politics must be replaced by an order based upon moral principles and cooperation by all states against international aggression. And fourth, the U.S. must continue to take an active role in bringing about these global reforms.[69] For Wilson, then, moralism would serve as a continuing guide to global involvement, but the interests of humankind and global reform would take precedence over any narrowly defined national or state interest.

The most complete statement of the new world that Wilson envisioned was probably summarized in the Fourteen Points that he offered to a joint session of Congress in January 1918, and which became the basis for the Paris Peace Conference at the end of World War I.[70] This new order would ban secret diplomacy and foster international trade among nations. It also emphasized self-determination and democracy for nations and set forth several specific requirements for resolving nationality and territorial issues in Central Europe at that time. (A summary of Wilson's Fourteen Points is presented in Document 1.2.) Point XIV of this plan, however, was particularly notable—and ultimately troubling to many Americans—because of its explicit rejection of isolationism. This point called for the establishment of a collective security organization—a League of Nations—that would rid the world of balance-of-power politics and create a world order based on universal principles. The League was to be an organization that would exploit the cooperative potential among states and emphasize the role of collective (i.e., universal) action to stop warfare and regulate conflict. As such, it would require each participant to be involved in the affairs of the international system. If the U.S. were to join such an organization, it would be permanently involved in global politics and would be an active participant in this global reform effort.

While his collective security proposal would have moved the U.S. away from isolationism, it also would have imposed a highly moral cast to that involvement and to global politics generally. In a real sense, Wilson's idealism (or moralism) was not far from the isolationism that was ultimately embraced by the United States, as one of Wilson's harshest critics put it. Moralism (or Wilsonianism) and isolationism were largely the same side of the coin, with one more extreme than the other, and were equally divorced from political reality. In this analyst's view, then, both were detrimental to American foreign policy: "Both [isolationism and Wilsonianism] have a negative relation to the national interest of the United States outside the Western Hemisphere. . . . Wilsonianism applies the illusory expectations of liberal reform to the whole world, isolationism empties of all concrete political content the realistic political principle of isola-

DOCUMENT 1.2   WILSON'S FOURTEEN POINTS

I. Open covenants of peace, openly arrived at. . . .

II. Absolute freedom of navigation upon the seas. . . .

III. The removal, so far as possible, of all economic barriers and the establishment of an equality of trade conditions among all the nations. . . .

IV. Adequate guarantees given and taken that national armaments will be reduced to the lowest point consistent with domestic safety.

V. A free open-minded, and absolutely impartial adjustment of all colonial claims. . . .

VI. The evacuation of all Russian territory and such a settlement of all questions affecting Russia. . .[and] an unhampered and unembarassed opportunity for the independent determination of her own political development and national policy. . . .

VII. Belgium. . .must be evacuated and restored without any attempt to limit the sovereignty which she enjoys in common with all other free nations.

VIII. All French territory should be freed and the invaded portions restored, and the wrong done to France by Prussia in 1871 in the matter of Alsace-Lorraine, which has unsettled the peace of the world for nearly fifty years, should be righted. . . .

IX. A readjustment of the frontiers of Italy should be effected along clearly recognizable lines of nationality.

X. The peoples of Austria-Hungary. . .should be accorded the freest opportunity of autonomous development.

XI. Rumania, Serbia, and Montenegro should be evacuated; occupied territories restored; Serbia accorded free and secure access to the sea; and the relations of the several Balkan states to one another determined by friendly counsel along historically established lines of allegiance and nationality. . . .

XII. The Turkish portions of the present Ottoman Empire should be assured a secure sovereignty, but the other nationalities. . . under Turkish rule should be assured. . .[an] opportunity of autonomous development, and the Dardanelles should be permanently opened as a free passage to the ships and commerce of all nations. . . .

XIII. An independent Polish state should be erected. . .[with] political and economic independence and territorial integrity. . . guaranteed by international covenant.

DOCUMENT 1.2 WILSON'S FOURTEEN POINTS (CONTINUED)

XIV. A general association of nations must be formed under specific covenants for the purpose of affording mutual guarantees of political independence and territorial integrity to great and small states alike.

Source: Taken from a speech by President Woodrow Wilson to a joint session of the U.S. Congress as reported in *Congressional Record*, January 8, 1918, p. 691.

---

tion and transforms it into the unattainable parochial ideal of automatic separation."[71]

Although Wilson's plan for a League of Nations did become a reality for a time, it did so without the participation of the United States; the Versailles peace treaty failed to pass the U.S. Senate by the necessary two-thirds vote. On two of three different roll calls, the treaty failed even to obtain majority support in the upper chamber of the U.S. Congress.[72] Despite America's longstanding rejection of balance-of-power politics, it remained unwilling to increase its global involvement in order to destroy this system. Instead, the United States reaffirmed its isolationist beliefs, reverted to "normalcy" in the 1920s, and remained in that posture throughout the 1930s as well.

The return to isolationism was also manifested in another way in the interwar years. As the situation in Europe began to polarize and conflict seemed once again imminent, the United States passed a series of neutrality acts in 1935, 1936, and 1937. These acts sought to prevent the export of arms and ammunition to belligerent countries and to restrict travel by American citizens on the vessels of nations involved in war.[73] The ultimate aim was to reaffirm U.S. noninvolvement and to reduce the prospects of America's being drawn into war through these means. Although President Roosevelt had, by 1939, asked for and received some alterations in the neutrality acts of the past,[74] it was not until the Japanese attack that the United States was again fully shaken from its isolationist stance.

CONCLUDING COMMENTS

The twin traditions of isolationism and moralism are the essence of America's past in foreign policy,[75] and they continue to influence the country's orientation to the world to this day. These traditions, however, have been altered in various ways in response to the shock of World War II, the substantial destruction of the major European powers of France, Britain, and Germany, and by the emerging Soviet challenge. Nonetheless, their importance for understanding American foreign policy in post–World War II circumstances remains—even now, when the United States has found that it can no longer remain aloof from international politics.

In the next five chapters, we will highlight the changes in America's value orientation to meet the circumstances of the post–World War II decades, demonstrating how the emphasis on isolationism and moralism has changed but continues to influence the various administrations and their policies. In Chapter 2 we will specifically examine the global political and economic factors that shook the U.S. from its isolationist moorings and propelled it into global politics. At the same time, we shall see how moralism as a guide to policy remained largely intact.

NOTES

1. Harold D. Lasswell, *Politics: Who Gets What, When, How* (New York: Whittlesey House, 1936), p. 3.

2. Ibid. Emphasis in original.

3. Robert A. Dahl, *Modern Political Analysis*, 2nd ed. (Englewood Cliffs, NJ: Prentice-Hall, Inc., 1970), pp. 4–6. Also see, Christian Bay, *The Structure of Freedom* (New York: Atheneum Publishers, 1965), pp. 20–21, for another discussion of the definition of politics.

4. David Easton, *The Political System* (New York: Alfred A. Knopf Inc., 1953), p. 90. Emphasis added.

5. Milton Rokeach, *Beliefs, Attitudes and Values* (San Francisco: Jossey-Bass, Inc., 1968). pp. 124, 159–160.

6. We shall use the terms *values* and *beliefs* interchangeably throughout this book. These concepts (along with attitudes), while distinct, are very closely related to one another, as discussed in Rokeach, *Beliefs*, pp. 113, 159–160.

7. See Milton Rokeach's discussion under "Attitudes" in the *International Encyclopedia of the Social Sciences* (New York: The Macmillan Company and the Free Press, 1968), pp. 449–457. The quotations are from pp. 450 and 454, respectively. Emphasis in original.

8. A recent book which surveys the research done within the context of these various factors to explain foreign policy is Lloyd Jensen, *Explaining Foreign Policy* (Englewood Cliffs, NJ: Prentice-Hall, Inc., 1982).

9. For a discussion of how the political culture concept can be used to explain a nation's behavior, see Gabriel Almond and Sidney Verba, *The Civic Culture* (Boston: Little, Brown & Co., 1963). A discussion of American political culture is in Donald J. Devine, *The Political Culture of the United States* (Boston: Little, Brown & Co., 1972). The approach that we adopt falls more generally within the societal and belief system determinants of foreign policy. For a good summary

discussion of these approaches—and some recent research on them—see Lloyd Jensen, *Explaining Foreign Policy* (Englewood Cliffs, NJ: Prentice-Hall, Inc., 1982), pp. 45–105.

10. A. F. K. Organski, *World Politics* (New York: Alfred A. Knopf Inc., 1968), p. 87.

11. Kenneth W. Terhune, "From National Character to National Behavior: A Reformulation," *Journal of Conflict Resolution* 14 (June 1970): 259. For more discussion of Terhune and others on national character, see Howard Bliss and M. Glen Johnson, *Beyond the Water's Edge: America's Foreign Policies* (Philadelphia: J. B. Lippincott Co., 1975), pp. 93–98.

12. See, for example, Seymour Martin Lipset, *The First New Nation* (Garden City, NY: Anchor Books, 1967); Russel B. Nye, *This Almost Chosen People* (East Lansing, MI: Michigan State University Press, 1966); John G. Stoessinger, *Crusaders and Pragmatists* (New York: W. W. Norton and Company, 1979), pp. 3–7; Edmund Stillman and William Pfaff, *Power and Impotence: The Failure of America's Foreign Policy* (New York: Vintage Books, 1966), pp. 15–59; Paul A. Varg, *Foreign Policies of the Founding Fathers* (East Lansing, MI: Michigan State University Press, 1963), pp. 1–10; and John Spanier, *American Foreign Policy Since World War II*, 9th ed. (New York: Holt, Rinehart and Winston, 1982), pp. 1–14. The last work is perhaps the best brief treatment of this and other topics in this chapter. Its utility here will be readily apparent.

13. This characterization was made by Professor Frank A. Cassell, chairman, Department of History, University of Wisconsin—Milwaukee, in a 1989 Independence Day interview. See Jerry Resler, "Living On: U.S. as Model Would Please Founder," *Milwaukee Sentinel*, July 4, 1989, part 4, p. 1.

14. Quoted in Robert W. Tucker and David C. Hendrickson, "Thomas Jefferson and Foreign Policy," *Foreign Affairs* 69 (Spring 1990): 136.

15. George F. Kennan recently made this point about the ideological roots of American society by noting the isolated development of the United States and the Soviet Union. This development in relative isolation from the rest of the world produced a strong sense of righteousness. See his "Is Détente Worth Saving?" *Saturday Review*, March 6, 1976, pp. 12–17. For others who would judge America as an ideological society, see, for instance, Nye, *This Almost Chosen People*, and Stillman and Pfaff, *Power and Impotence*. Stanley Hoffmann would not entirely agree. See his *Gulliver's Troubles, or the Setting of American Foreign Policy* (New York: McGraw-Hill, 1968), pp. 114–117.

16. Lipset, in *The First New Nation*, uses the values of equality and achievement as the basis of his analysis.

17. This description, as noted in Spanier, *American Foreign Policy*, p. 7, was true for most Americans but not all. Some were clearly excluded from the political process: blacks, women, Indians, and the many who were propertyless.

18. On Locke's view of the goals and limits of government, see John Locke, *Two Treatises of Government*, portions of which are reprinted in William Ebenstein, *Great Political Thinkers: Plato to the Present*, 3rd ed. (New York: Holt, Rinehart and Winston, 1965), pp. 404–408 in particular. Also see the discussion of classical liberalism in Everett C. Ladd, Jr., "Traditional Values Regnant," *Public Opinion* 1 (March/April 1978): 45–49; and Charles W. Kegley and Eugene R. Wittkopf, *American Foreign Policy: Pattern and Process*, 4th ed. (New York: St. Martin's Press, 1991), pp. 249–250.

19. These values are discussed in Ladd, "Traditional Values Regnant," and some evidence is presented on the current American commitment to these values and beliefs.

20. Tucker and Hendrickson, "Thomas Jefferson and Foreign Policy," p. 139. For a discussion of how Jefferson's views were shared by other early leaders, see pp. 143–146. On Jefferson's difficulty in actually making this distinction work, see pp. 146–156.

21. See Spanier, *American Foreign Policy*, pp. 6 and 12. Many others, of course, agree with this assessment of the role of isolationism and moralism. See, for instance, Varg, *Foreign Policies*, and Dexter Perkins, *The American Approach to Foreign Policy* (Cambridge, MA: Harvard University Press, 1962).

22. Dexter Perkins, *Hands Off: A History of the Monroe Doctrine* (Boston: Little, Brown & Co., 1941), pp. 3–26. For a vivid picture of how one prominent American viewed Europe, see Daniel J. Boorstin, *America and the Image of Europe: Reflections on American Thought* (New York: Meridian Books, 1960), p. 21, in which he quotes Thomas Jefferson while traveling in France: "For this whole chapter in the history of man is new. . . . Before the establishment of the American States, nothing was known to history but the man of the old world, crowded within limits either too small or overcharged, and steeped in the vices which that situation generates." This passage is also cited in Stillman and Pfaff, *Power and Impotence*, p. 16.

23. See Cecil V. Crabb, Jr., *Policy-Makers and Critics: Conflicting Theories of American Foreign Policy* (New York: Frederick A. Praeger, Inc., 1976), pp. 1–33, for an extended discussion of this isolationist tradition.

24. See ibid., pp. 715, for a discussion of several different dimensions of isolationism in America's past.

25. "Washington's Farewell Address," *Annals of The Congress of the United States*, 4th Cong., 2nd Sess., 1786–1797, p. 2877.

26. Ibid.

27. Ibid., p. 2878. Emphasis in original.

28. Albert Bushnell Hart, *The Monroe Doctrine: An Interpretation* (Boston: Little, Brown & Co., 1916), pp. 20–68.

29. These themes are succinctly discussed in Evarts Seelye Scudder, *The Monroe Doctrine and World Peace* (Port Washington, NY: Kennikat Press, 1972), pp. 15–20. The quote is at p. 19. Emphasis in original.

30. "President's Message," *Annual of the Congress of the United States*, 18th Cong., 1st Sess., 1823–1824, pp. 22–23. Emphasis added.

31. Several scholars have emphasized how the Monroe Doctrine, more than any other policy statement, formalized and solidified the U.S. isolationist tradition in world affairs—at least toward Europe. See, for instance, Perkins, *The Evolution of American Foreign Policy*, 2nd ed. (New York: Oxford University Press, 1966), pp. 33–38; Nye, *This Almost Chosen People*, p. 184; and Spanier, *American Foreign Policy*, p. 6.

32. Thomas A. Bailey, *The Man on the Street: The Impact of American Public Opinion on Foreign Policy* (New York: Macmillan, Inc., 1948), p. 251.

33. A survey of all international agreements during the early history was undertaken using the listing compiled by Igor I. Kavass and Mark A. Michael, *United States Treaties and Other International Agreements, Cumulative Index 1776–1949* (Buffalo, NY: William S. Hein and Company, Inc., 1975), pp. 3–130. For the latter period, the data source was Igor I. Kavass and Adolf Sprudzs, *United States Treaties Cumulative Index 1950–1970*, Volume 2 (Buffalo, NY: William S. Hein and Company, Inc., 1973), pp. 11–444, and some additional agreements from the first source for the years 1947–1949 at pp. 526–615.

34. The table was constructed using the source listed in note 33. The category labels were largely derived from the descriptions of the agreements given in

the first source. For manageability and convenience, agreements in different years in the 1778–1899 period were segmentally categorized (e.g., 1778–1799, 1800–1850, etc.), and the overall results were collapsed and categorized. For the second part of the table (1947–1960), the same categories were used. While the content of the categories is relatively self-evident, the alliance, amity and commerce, and multilateral categories deserve some comment. The alliance category consisted primarily of formal military commitments, but it also included establishing military bases, signing mutual security agreements, and sending military missions to other countries. The amity and commerce category included a wide array of commercial, health and sanitation, technical cooperation, educational, aviation, and postal agreements, among others, and commitments for friendly relations with other states. The multilateral category included all agreements that were designated as such by the source. The actual content of those pacts covered a wide array of issues, but the multilateral designation was retained to show the degree to which the United States committed itself to groups of other states during this period. Finally, some agreements overlapped the categories, and some judgments were made to place them into one category rather than another. Others categorizing the pacts might likely come up with a different classification and slightly different results. It is unlikely, however, that the general pattern of the results would be changed.

35. Perkins, *The Evolution of American Foreign Policy*, p. 30, reports that the French alliance was not renewed in that year.

36. The treaty text is given in Hunter Miller, ed., *Treaties and Other International Acts of the United States of America*, vol. 2 (Washington, D.C.: U.S. Government Printing Office, 1931), pp. 123–150.

37. Thomas A. Bailey, *A Diplomatic History of the American People* (New York: F. S. Crofts & Co., 1942), p. 238.

38. Ibid.

39. Hart, *Monroe Doctrine*, p. 115.

40. Robert H. Ferrell, *American Diplomacy: A History* (New York: W. W. Norton & Company, Inc., 1975), p. 231.

41. Ibid., pp. 231–232. For the controversy over whether the Clayton-Bulwer Treaty really regulated European involvement in the Western Hemisphere, see Hart, *Monroe Doctrine*, pp. 122–125; and Bailey, *Diplomatic History*, pp. 292–295. The Hay-Pauncefote Treaty of 1901 annulled the Clayton-Bulwer Treaty and enabled the United States to become the sole guarantor of the canal. See Ferrell, *American Diplomacy*, p. 400.

42. For a discussion of the various challenges to the Monroe Doctrine in the latter half of the nineteenth century, see Scudder, *Monroe Doctrine*; and Hart, *Monroe Doctrine*.

43. See Perkins, *The Evolution of American Foreign Policy*, pp. 35–36, on this point and on the general applicability of the Monroe Doctrine and its declining influences as well (pp. 32–36).

44. Robert Dallek, *The American Style of Foreign Policy* (New York: Alfred A. Knopf, Inc., 1983), p. 110. The discussion here is based upon pp. 92–122. Dallek also discusses the competing motivations that shaped policy during the interwar years and how these motivations often appear to contradict one another.

45. Ibid., pp. 96–97, in which Dallek discusses the various implications of the pacifist movements in this time period.

46. *Congressional Record*, December 6, 1904, p. 19.

47. Ferrell, *American Diplomacy*, pp. 395–415. The American occupations and protectorates in the Caribbean are outlined by Walter LaFeber, *The American Age: United States Foreign Policy at Home and Abroad since 1750* (New York: W. W. Norton & Company, 1989), p. 233.

48. Walter Lefeber, *Inevitable Revolutions: The United States in Central America* (New York: W. W. Norton and Company, 1984), pp. 111–126, especially pp. 118–123. Clearly, however, Lefeber does not fully accept this interpretation of events in Guatemala in the early 1950s.

49. President Kennedy's address to the nation can be found in Robert F. Kennedy, *Thirteen Days* (New York: Signet Books, 1969), pp. 131–139. The quoted passage is at p. 132.

50. See Dexter Perkins, *American Approach*, pp. 72–97, for a cogent discussion of moralism in American foreign policy.

51. See Spanier, *American Foreign Policy*, pp. 9–11; and Stoessinger, *Crusaders and Pragmatists*, pp. 5–7.

52. A discussion of the assumptions, aims, and means of the balance of power can be found in Edward V. Gulick, *Europe's Classical Balance of Power* (Ithaca, NY: Cornell University Press, 1955), pp. 3–91.

53. Changes in American policymakers' attitudes and beliefs toward a balance-of-power system occurred dramatically during the years Henry Kissinger was responsible for formulating American policy. This will be discussed in Chapter 4.

54. Henry A. Kissinger, *American Foreign Policy*, expanded ed. (New York: W. W. Norton & Company, 1974), pp. 91–92.

55. Carl Von Clausewitz, *On War*, ed. and trans. Michael Howard and Peter Paret (Princeton: Princeton University Press, 1976), p. 87. Spanier, *American Foreign Policy*, p. 10, also raises this point and discusses the dichotomous view of war and peace upon which we draw.

56. Perkins, *American Approach*, p. 77.

57. Spanier, *American Foreign Policy*, p. 11.

58. These instances are discussed in George F. Kennan, *American Diplomacy 1900–1950* (New York: Mentor Books, 1951); Robert Endicott Osgood, *Ideals and Self-Interest in America's Foreign Relations* (Chicago: The University of Chicago Press, 1953); and Farrell, *American Diplomacy*, pp. 123–153.

59. Harry L. Coles, *The War of 1812* (Chicago: The University of Chicago Press, 1965), pp. 1–37; and Farrell, *American Diplomacy*, pp. 136–141.

60. For some hint as to why the target over these violations of freedom of the seas was Britain rather than France, see Coles, *The War of 1812*, pp. 11–23.

61. Farrell, *American Diplomacy*, p. 142.

62. Kennan, *American Diplomacy 1900–1950*, p. 14; and Farrell, *American Diplomacy*, p. 353.

63. For an informative discussion of the impact of popular sentiment on this conflict, see Kennan, *American Diplomacy 1900–1950*, pp. 15–16.

64. Ferrell, *American Diplomacy*, pp. 456–462; and Kennan, *American Diplomacy 1900–1950*, pp. 50–65.

65. Ferrell, *American Diplomacy*, pp. 468–469.

66. Ibid., pp. 556–558.

67. P.L. 77–11, March 11, 1941, 55 Stat 31.

68. Speech by President Franklin D. Roosevelt to a joint session of Congress. The quotation can be found in the *Congressional Record*, 77th Cong., 1st Sess., Volume 87, December 8, 1941, p. 9519.

69. On Wilson's beliefs, see John G. Stoessinger, *Crusaders and Pragmatists: Movers of Modern American Foreign Policy*, 2nd ed. (New York: W. W. Norton & Company, 1985), pp. 8–27; and Michael H. Hunt, *Ideology and U.S. Foreign Policy* (New Haven: Yale University Press, 1987), pp. 125–136, especially at pp. 129–135.

70. For a listing of the Fourteen Points and a discussion of the Paris Conference, see Ferrell, *American Diplomacy*, pp. 482–492. The depiction of the new order draws upon Hunt, *Ideology and U.S. Foreign Policy*, p. 134.

71. Hans J. Morgenthau, "The Mainsprings of American Foreign Policy" in James M. McCormick, ed., *A Reader in American Foreign Policy* (Itasca, IL: F. E. Peacock Publishers, Inc., 1986), p. 46.

72. Robert Farrell, *American Diplomacy: The Twentieth Century* (New York: W. W. Norton & Company, 1988), p. 153.

73. See the text of the Neutrality Act of 1935 (August 31, 1935) or the Neutrality Act of 1936 (February 29, 1936) for a full treatment of the restrictions on arms exports and travel by Americans. Both are reprinted in Nicholas O. Berry, ed., *U.S. Foreign Policy Documents, 1933–1945: From Withdrawal to World Leadership* (Brunswick, OH: King's Court Communications, Inc., 1978), pp. 25–27, 32.

74. See the Neutrality Act of 1939 (November 4, 1939), reprinted in ibid., pp. 58–60.

75. See Howard Bliss and M. Glen Johnson, *Beyond the Water's Edge: America's Foreign Policies*, Chap. 4, for a discussion of other values that have shaped the American style. Also see Hoffmann, *Gulliver's Troubles*, Chaps. 5 and 6.

CHAPTER 2 AMERICA'S GLOBAL INVOLVEMENT AND THE EMERGENCE OF THE COLD WAR

"It is logical that the United States should do whatever it is able to do to assist in the return of normal economic health in the world.... Our policy is directed not against any country or doctrine but against hunger, poverty, desperation, and chaos. Its purpose should be the revival of a working economy in the world so as to permit the emergence of political and social conditions in which free institutions can exist." **SECRETARY OF STATE GEORGE C. MARSHALL, AN ADDRESS AT HARVARD UNIVERSITY, JUNE 5, 1947**

"It is clear that the main element of any United States policy toward the Soviet Union must be that of a long-term, patient but firm and vigilant containment of Russian expansive tendencies." **"MR. X" [GEORGE KENNAN], "THE SOURCES OF SOVIET CONDUCT," JULY 1947**

World War II thrust the United States fully into global affairs. By the end of 1941, it had fully committed itself to total victory, and its involvement was to prove crucial to the war effort. Because of the central importance of the United States to allied success and its substantive involvement in international affairs, the U.S. found it difficult to change course in 1945 and revert to the isolationism of the past. To be sure, the first impulse was in this direction. Calls were heard for massive demobilization of the armed forces, cutbacks in the New Deal legislation of President Franklin Delano Roosevelt, and other efforts toward political and economic isolationism.[1] However, at least three sets of factors militated against such a course and propelled the United States in the direction of global power: (1) the global political and economic conditions of 1945 to 1947; (2) the decision of leading political figures within the United States to abandon isolationism after World War II; and, most important, (3) the rise of an ideological challenge from the Soviet Union.

In this chapter, we first examine these factors and how they led to the abandonment of isolationism and the adoption of globalism by the United States. In turn, we set forth the military, economic, and political dimensions of this new globalist involvement—summarized under the rubric of the containment doctrine—and discuss how this involvement became both universal in scope and highly moral in content. As we shall show in the following chapter, moreover, the containment doctrine produced a distinct set of foreign policy values, beliefs, and actions on the part of the United States.

THE POSTWAR WORLD AND AMERICAN INVOLVEMENT

The international system that the United States faced after the defeat of Germany and Japan was considerably different from any that it had faced in its previous history. The traditional powers of Europe were defeated or had been ruined by the ravages of war; the global economy had been significantly weakened by that war; and a relatively new power equipped with a threatening ideology, the Soviet Union, had survived the war, arguably in better shape than any other European power. The United States was in a relatively strong political, economic, and military position. Such conditions seemed to imply the need for sustained U.S. involvement despite its isolationist past. Yet, a decision for such involvement was made neither quickly nor automatically; rather, it seemed to come about over the course of several years and largely through the confluence of several complementary factors. We begin our discussion, therefore, with a brief description of three of these factors and suggest how they interacted with one another to move the United States toward sustained global involvement.

THE GLOBAL VACUUM: A CHALLENGE TO AMERICAN ISOLATIONISM

The first important factor that contributed to America's decision to move away from isolationism was the political and economic conditions of the international system immediately after World War II. The land, the cities, and the homes, along with the economies, of most European nations had been devastated by the war. Sizeable portions of the land had been either flooded, scorched from battle, or confiscated for military operations. Even the land that remained for cultivation was in poor condition. Hunger was widespread, and a black market in food flourished. The industrial sectors of these nations, along with the major cities, were badly damaged or in total ruins. London, Vienna, Trieste, Warsaw, Berlin, Rotterdam, and Cologne, among others, bore the scars of war. Millions of people were homeless, too. By one estimate, five million homes had been destroyed, with many more millions badly damaged. In a word, Europe was a "wasteland."[2]

European economies were weak, in debt, and driven by inflation. Britain, for example, had to use up much of its wealth to win the war and was left with a debt of about $6 billion at its end. The country had to rely upon American assistance to remain solvent.[3] France, the Netherlands, Belgium, and other European states were in no better shape. Each had to rely, in varying degrees, upon American assistance to meet its financial needs. Foreign and domestic political problems also confronted these states. Several British and French colonies were demanding freedom and independence. In Syria, Lebanon, Indochina, and later in Tunisia, Morocco, and Algeria, for instance, indigenous movements were seeking independence from France. The British were confronted by independence efforts in India, Burma, Ceylon, and Palestine, among others. Britain faced domestic austerity, while the French struggled at home with governmental instability and worker discontent. With such problems at home and abroad, neither of these states was in a position to assert a very prominent role in postwar international politics.

The conditions in Germany and Italy further contributed to the political and economic vacuum in Europe. Both of these powers had been defeated, and Germany was divided and occupied. Italy had a huge budget deficit in 1945–1946 (300 billion lire by one estimate) as well as an extraordinarily high rate of inflation. Germany, too, was in debt, owing nearly nine times more than at the beginning of World War II.[4] Overall, then, Europe, which for so long had been at the center of international politics and for so long had shaped the global order, was ominously weak, both politically and economically. None of the traditional European powers seemed able to exert its traditional dominance in global politics.

In contrast to this portrait of Europe, the United States was healthy and prosperous. Its industrial capacity was intact, and its economy was still booming. In the middle 1940s, the U.S. had growing balance-of-trade surpluses and huge economic reserves. For example, while Europe had trade deficits of $5.8 billion and $7.6 billion in 1946 and 1947, the U.S., in those same years, had trade surpluses of $6.7 billion and $10.1 billion. Furthermore, American reserve assets—about $26 billion in 1948—were substantial and were increasing.[5]

The military might of the United States, too, seemed preeminent at that time. American troops occupied Europe and Japan. The nation had the world's largest navy. ("The Pacific and the Mediterranean had become American lakes," in the words of one historian.[6]) And, of course, the United States alone had the atomic bomb. In this sense, the United States seemed to have the capacity to assume a global role. Moreover, the international environment seemed highly conducive to both the possibility and the necessity for America to play a dominant role in global affairs.

AMERICAN LEADERSHIP AND GLOBAL INVOLVEMENT

A second factor that encouraged the United States to abandon its isolationist strategy was the change in world view among American leaders during and immediately after the Second World War. Most importantly, President Franklin Roosevelt had long concluded that America's response to global affairs after World War I had been ill-advised and that such a response should not guide American policy after World War II.[7] Instead, Roosevelt had decided that continued American involvement in global affairs was necessary and, early on in the war, had revealed his vision of world order in the postwar period.

The first necessity in Roosevelt's plan was the total defeat and disarming of the adversaries, with no leniency shown toward aggressor states. Second, there must be a renewed commitment on the part of the United States and others to prevent future global economic depressions and to foster self-determination for all states. Third, there must be the establishment of a global collective security organization with active American involvement. Finally, above and beyond these efforts, the allies in war must remain allies in peace in order to maintain global order.[8]

This last element of the plan was the core of Roosevelt's global blueprint.[9] American involvement in world affairs and its cooperation with the other great powers were essential. Indeed, Roosevelt's design envisaged a world in which this postwar cooperation among the four principal powers (U.S., Great Britain, U.S.S.R., China) would yield a system in which they acted as the "Four Policemen" to enforce global order. In other words, unlike Wilson's League of Nations, where all states would act to stop warfare and regulate conflict, only the great powers would have this responsibility. Such a vision bore a striking and unmistakable resemblance to traditional balance-of-power politics, although Roosevelt was unwilling to describe it in such terms.

To make this global design a reality, two major tasks confronted Roosevelt's diplomatic efforts during the war. One was directed toward building wartime cooperation, which would continue after the war. The other was directed toward jarring the United States from its isolationist moorings and positioning the country in such a way that it would retain a role in postwar international politics. To realize the first goal, the building of cooperation with the Soviet Union was deemed essential. Roosevelt, unlike some of his advisors and some State Department officials, believed that cooperation with the Soviet Union was possible after the end of World War II. He believed that the Soviet Union was motivated, in the shorthand of Daniel Yergin, more by the "Yalta Axioms" (the name is taken from the 1945 wartime conference in which political bargains were struck between East and West) than by the "Riga Axioms" (the name is taken from the Latvian capital city from which a U.S. mission "issued constant warning against the [Soviet] international menace" in the 1920s and 1930s.[10] In the Yalta view, the Soviet Union was much like other nations in terms of defining its interests and fostering its goals based upon power realities (the Yalta Axioms) rather than being driven primarily by ideological considerations (the Riga Axioms). As Yergin contends, "Roosevelt thought of the Soviet Union less as a revolutionary vanguard than as a conventional imperialist power, with ambitions rather like those of the Czarist regime."[11] Because of this perceived source of their policy, he judged that the Grand Alliance would be able to continue on a "businesslike" level as long as each party would come to recognize the interests of the others. Moreover, since the Soviet Union would be concerned about the reconstruction of its economy and society after the devastation of the war, it would have further incentives to seek postwar stability and peace.

To facilitate postwar cooperation with the Soviets, Roosevelt made a concerted effort throughout the war to foster good relations with them. The United States extended Lend-Lease assistance to the Soviet Union (albeit not as rapidly as the Soviet Union wished) and agreed to open up a second front against the Germans to relieve the battlefield pressure placed on them (albeit not as soon as the Soviet Union wanted). Through the several wartime conferences—Teheran, Cairo, Moscow, and Yalta—Roosevelt gained an understanding of the degree of Russian insecurity regarding their exposed western borders and the need to take this factor into account in dealing with them. At the same time, though, he became increasingly convinced that he could work with "Uncle Joe" Stalin and that political bargains and accommodations with the Soviets were possible.

Among the wartime conferences, the one that bears most directly upon postwar arrangements was the Yalta Conference held in that Crimean resort during February 1945. Not only did this conference achieve agreement on a strategy for the completion of the war effort, but it also appeared to achieve agreements on the division and operation of postwar Europe. Such agreements were important since they signaled continued American interest and involvement in global affairs—specifically Europe's—but they also signaled that the competing interests of states were subject to negotiation and accommodation. Spheres of influence and balance-of-power politics were expressly incorporated into these agreements, and the major powers were to possess the greatest amount of importance in fulfilling them.[12]

Specifically, Roosevelt, Stalin, and British Prime Minister Winston Churchill agreed to zones of occupation of Germany by the Americans, British, French, and Russians. Second, they provided some territorial concessions to the Soviets at the expense of Poland. (In turn, Poland was to receive some territory from Germany.) Third, the wartime leaders allowed an expansion of the Lublin Committee, which was governing Poland, to include some Polish government officials who were in exile in London as a way of dealing with the postwar government question in Poland. Fourth, they proclaimed the Declaration of Liberated Europe, which specified free elections and constitutional safeguards of individual freedom in the liberated nations. And, finally, the conferees produced an agreement on the

Soviet Union's joining the war against Japan and the veto mechanism within the Security Council of the United Nations.[13]

In light of subsequent events, Roosevelt has been highly criticized for the bargains that were made at Yalta. The Soviets got several territorial concessions and were able in the space of a few short years to gain control of the Polish government as well as other Eastern European governments. Roosevelt's judgment on this matter was that only by taking into account the interests of the various parties (including the Russians) was a stable postwar world possible. Moreover, he also appeared to take into account the Soviet sense of insecurity along their western border in making some of these arrangements. Finally, and perhaps more important than these other considerations, Soviet troops already occupied these Eastern European states.[14] Any prospects of a more favorable outcome for the Western states appeared to be more in the realm of hope than a real possibility. Despite these criticisms, the Yalta agreements do mark the beginning of an American commitment to global involvement beyond the wartime period. In addition, with the agreement on the operation of the Security Council and the subsequent conference on the United Nations Charter in San Francisco during April 1945, the United States was rather quickly moving itself toward global involvement.

THE RISE OF THE SOVIET CHALLENGE

This commitment to international involvement was no less true for President Roosevelt's successor, Harry S. Truman, and his principal foreign policy advisors. But this commitment was expanded and solidified by the rise of the Soviet ideological challenge that developed by late 1946 and early 1947.

Although Truman's foreign policy approach was not nearly as well developed as that outlined by Roosevelt's postwar plan, there was no inclination on the part of President Truman to reject continued American involvement in the world. Three sets of factors seem to have shaped his commitment to involvement: (1) his Wilsonian idealism, (2) the wartime situation existing when he assumed office, and (3) the views of his principal foreign policy advisors.

Truman, prior to assuming the presidency, had displayed a commitment to an international role for the United States. In particular, he agreed with Woodrow Wilson that America should participate in world affairs, particularly through a global organization. As a consequence, Truman worked in the Senate to gain support for the emer-

MAP 2.1 EUROPE DIVIDED BETWEEN EAST AND WEST AFTER WORLD WAR II

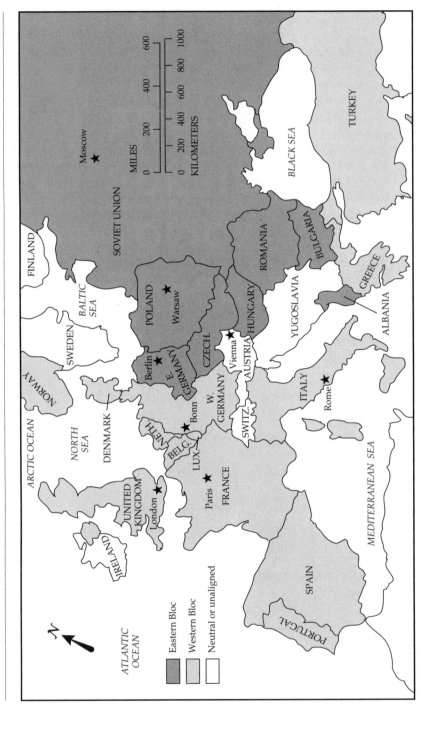

gent United Nations. At the same time, and like Wilson, he tended to see the United States as a moral force in the world and was somewhat suspicious of the postwar design epitomized by the Four Policemen plan.[15] Nonetheless, he supported and worked to put Roosevelt's plan into practice.

Second, Truman's commitment to global involvement was aided by the circumstances at the time he became president. President Roosevelt died just after the Yalta agreements on postwar Europe had been concluded, just prior to the United Nations Conference in San Francisco, and just before the Allies were ultimately successful in World War II. As a result, Truman felt the Yalta agreements had to be implemented, the United Nations needed to become a reality, and the war had to be won. In all of these areas, President Truman forged ahead along the lines of his predecessor.

Truman's closest advisors were also influential in reinforcing the commitment to a global role for the United States. In particular, such key advisors as Admiral William Leahy, Ambassador Averell Harriman, Secretary of State Edward Stettinius, and Secretary of War Henry Stimson all counseled for a continuance of a leading role for the United States.[16] Later, such men as Secretary of State James Byrnes, Under Secretary of State (and later Secretary of State) Dean Acheson, and Secretary of the Navy James V. Forrestal became Truman's key policy advisors. These new advisors also tended to favor an active global involvement, especially with their less favorable view of the Soviet Union, although, according to historian Ernest May, "their prejudices and predispositions can serve as only one small element" in the change of American policy toward the Soviet Union.[17]

Nevertheless, the issue soon became less one of whether there should be American global involvement and more a question of the degree of that involvement. Fueled by negative assessments of the Soviet Union by seasoned diplomatic observers, Truman's advisors increasingly focused upon the threat posed by international communism generally and by the Soviet Union specifically.[18] In time, the shape of America's postwar global role became largely a consequence of the perceived intentions of Soviet ideology.

In the first months after assuming office, President Truman followed Roosevelt's strategy for peace and American involvement by trying to maintain great-power unity. As he said: "I want peace and I am willing to work hard for it: . . . to have a reasonably lasting peace, the three great powers must be able to trust each other." Likewise, he remained faithful to the requirements of the Yalta agreements and tried to cajole Stalin to do the same by telling Soviet Foreign Minister Molotov to "carry out your agreements."[19]

But by the time of the Potsdam Conference (July 1945), President Truman was increasingly urged to be tough with the Soviets, while still seeking postwar cooperation. Although the accommodation that came out of Potsdam over German reparations and German boundaries, as well as other agreements, were deemed tolerable, American officials ultimately came away uneasy over the future prospects of Soviet-American relations.[20] Subsequent meetings in London (September 1945) over peace treaties for Finland, Hungary, Romania, and Bulgaria, and in Moscow (December 1945), over adherence to the Yalta accords, reinforced this uneasiness and continued to highlight the growing suspicion between the United States and the Soviet Union.[21]

The end of 1945 and early months of 1946 seemed to mark a watershed in Soviet-American relations.[22] By this time, the American public, Congress, and the president's chief advisors were increasingly lobbying for tougher action against Soviet noncompliance with the Yalta agreements and with its efforts to undermine governments in Eastern Europe. Coupled with these domestic pressures were ominous statements by Stalin and Churchill about American and Soviet intentions toward the world.

In a speech on February 9, 1946, Joseph Stalin emphasized the incompatibility of capitalism and communism and the inevitability of war between the capitalist states. Additionally, he warned the Soviet people of the enormous sacrifices that would have to be made and the need to be aware of the possibility of war. In the assessment of two prominent diplomatic historians, Stalin was suggesting that "war was inevitable as long as capitalism existed," and "that future wars were inevitable until the world economic system was reformed, that is, until communism supplanted capitalism. . . . "[23] Such a view was alarming to American policymakers because of its grave implications for future Soviet-American cooperation.

On March 5, 1946, Winston Churchill made his famous "iron curtain" speech at Westminster College in Fulton, Missouri, in which he called for "a fraternal association of the English-speaking peoples" to provide global order since "from Stettin in the Baltic to Trieste in the Adriatic, an iron curtain has descended across the Continent."[24] This speech marked a frontal attack on the Soviet Union, and, like Stalin's February speech, suggested the impossibility of continued Soviet-American cooperation in the postwar world because of the differing worldviews of the two nations. Importantly, too, President Truman seemed to be giving some legitimacy to such a view, since he accompanied Churchill to Missouri.[25]

At about the same time as these two important speeches were delivered, George F. Kennan, an American diplomat serving in Moscow at the time, sent his famous "long telegram" to Washington. In this lengthy message, Kennan highlighted the fundamental incompatibility between the Soviet Union and the capitalist states, the ruthlessness of Soviet tactics, and the need for a more vigorous approach by the United States to conteract Soviet intentions and behavior. As he put it in his concluding section of the telegram:

> ...we have here a political force committed fanatically to the belief that with US there can be no permanent modus vivendi, that it is desirable and necessary that the internal harmony of our society be disrupted, our traditional way of life be destroyed, the international authority of our state be broken, if Soviet power is to be secure....Finally, it is seemingly inaccessible to considerations of reality in its basic reactions. For it, the vast fund of objective fact about human society is not, as with us, the measure against which outlook is constantly tested and reformed, but a grab bag from which individual items are selected arbitrarily and tendentiously to bolster an outlook already preconceived.[26]

In essence, this view of the Soviet Union has come to be summarized as the Riga Axioms (in contrast to the Yalta Axioms, which President Roosevelt had adopted). Ideology, and not the realism of power politics, was the important determinant of Soviet conduct.

These statements by Stalin and Churchill and the circulation of Kennan's long telegram within the Washington bureaucracy increased the clamor for a changed policy toward the Soviet Union. They produced a "get tough" policy on the part of the United States. And they permanently changed the role of the United States in global affairs.

AMERICA'S GLOBALISM: THE TRUMAN DOCTRINE AND BEYOND

The immediate response to these calls for a "get tough" policy was reflected in American policy over Soviet troops remaining in Iran in March 1946. Under the Tripartite Treaty of Alliance signed by Iran, the Soviet Union, and Great Britain in January 1942, Allied forces were to be withdrawn from Iranian territory within six months after hostilities had ended between the Allies and the Axis Powers. By March 2, 1946—six months after the surrender of Japan—all British and American forces had indeed withdrawn from Iran, but Soviet forces had not. Instead, the Soviets were sending additional troops into Iran, were continuing to meddle in Iranian politics, and apparently had designs on Turkey and Iraq from their Iranian base.[27]

Under such circumstances, the American leadership decided to stand firm on the withdrawal of Soviet forces. Secretary of State James Byrnes and British Foreign Minister Ernest Bevin gave important speeches that made the West's position clear. In a late February speech, Secretary Byrnes asserted:

> We have joined our allies in the United Nations to put an end to war. We have covenanted not to use force except in the defense of law as embodied in the purposes and principles of the [UN] Charter. We intend to live up to that covenant.
>
> But as a great power and as a permanent member of the Security Council *we have a responsibility to use our influence to see that other powers live up to their covenant. . . .*
>
> We will not and we cannot stand aloof if force or threat of force is used contrary to the purposes and principles of the Charter. We have no right to hold our troops in the territories of other sovereign states without their approval and consent freely given. . . .[28]

Later, on March 16, Secretary of State Byrnes reiterated American resolve in another speech by repeating some of the themes from the earlier address. In addition, though, Byrnes urged an extension of the expiring military draft and called for the adoption of universal military service in the future. The target of such proposed measures was unmistakable.

Faced with British and American resolve and with an imminent UN Security Council session on the Iranian issue, the Soviet Union began to seek a negotiated solution. In early April 1946, an agreement was reached that called for the withdrawal of all Soviet forces from Iran by the middle of May 1946.[29]

Thus, when America adopted a tougher policy line toward the Soviet Union, it was able to achieve results. Despite the initial success of this firmer course in early 1946, the real change in America's policy toward the Soviets (and ultimately toward the rest of the world) was not fully manifested until a year later.

The occasion for the formal pronouncement of this sharp turn in policy, from one of accommodation to one of confrontation, was the question of aid to Greece and Turkey to combat threats to their security. The Greek government was under pressure from a communist-supported national liberation movement, while Turkey was under political pressure from the Soviet Union and its allies over control of the Dardanelles (the straits that provide access to the Mediterranean from the Soviet Union's Black Sea ports) and over territorial concessions to the Soviets in Turkish-Soviet border areas.[30] Because the British, in February 1947, had indicated to the Americans that they could no longer aid these countries, the burden apparently fell to the Americans if Greece and Turkey were to remain stable. Accordingly, President Truman decided to seek $400 million in aid for these Mediterranean states.

The granting of aid itself was not a sharp break from the past, since the United States had provided assistance in 1946.[31] What was dramatic about the aid request were its *form, rationale, and purpose.* The form of the request was a formal speech by President Truman to a joint session of Congress on March 12, 1947. The rationale for the request was even more dramatic: a need to stop the expansion of global communism. And the purpose was equally startling: to commit the United States to a global strategy against this communist threat.

In his speech, in which he announced what has come to be known as the Truman Doctrine, the president first set out the conditions within Greece and Turkey that necessitated assistance. Then he more fully outlined the justification for his policy and identified the global struggle that the United States faced. The United States, he said, must *"help free peoples to maintain their free institutions and their national identity against aggressive movements that seek to impose upon them totalitarian regimes."* Moreover, such threats to freedom affect the security of the United States: "*. . . totalitarian regimes imposed upon free peoples, by direct or indirect aggression, undermine the foundations of international peace and hence the security of the United States."* At this juncture in history, President Truman continued, the nations of the world face a decision between two ways of life: one free, the other unfree; one based "upon the will of the majority," the other based upon "the will of a minority"; one based upon "free institutions," the other based upon "terror and oppression." The task for the United States, therefore, is a clear one, he concluded:" *. . . we must assist free peoples to work out their own destinies in their own way."* The challenge to the Soviet Union was now clearly drawn. The Cold War had begun.[32]

The specific policy that the United States was to adopt in this struggle with the Soviet Union was the containment strategy. This term was first used in an anonymously authored article in *Foreign Affairs* magazine in July 1947. (Its author was quickly identified, though, as George F. Kennan, by then the head of the Policy Planning Staff at the Department of State in Washington, and the article actually grew out of his "long telegram" sent to the State Department a year earlier.) According to Kennan, the appropriate policy to adopt against the Soviet challenge was "a long-term, patient but firm and vigilant containment of Russian expansive tendencies." Specifically, he called for the "application of counter-force at a series of constantly shifting geographical and political points," against Soviet action. By following such a policy, the United States may, over time, force "a far greater degree of moderation and circumspection...and in this way to promote Soviet tendencies which must eventually find their outlet in either the break-up or the gradual mellowing of Soviet power."[33] Although Kennan was not precise in stating what the substance of the counterforce or containment should be, the immediate response of American policymakers was to embark upon a series of sweeping military, economic, and political initiatives from 1947 through the mid-1950s to control international communism.[34]

ELEMENTS OF CONTAINMENT: REGIONAL SECURITY PACTS

The first, and probably principal, initiative was the establishment of several regional politico-military alliances. In Latin America, the *Rio Pact* (formally known as the Inter-American Treaty of Reciprocal Assistance) was signed in September 1947 by the United States and twenty-one other American republics. In Western Europe, the *North Atlantic Treaty Organization* (NATO) was set up in April 1949 by the United States, Canada, and ten (later increased to thirteen) Western European nations. In Asia, two important pacts were established: the *ANZUS Treaty* of September 1951 and the Southeast Asia Collective Defense Treaty of September 1954. The former treaty involved the United States, Australia, and New Zealand, while the latter included the United States, the United Kingdom, France, Australia, New Zealand, Pakistan, the Philippines, and Thailand and formed what became known as the *Southeast Asia Treaty Organization* (SEATO). For the SEATO treaty, a protocol was added to provide security protection for South Vietnam, Cambodia, and Laos. (This protocol would become most important in light of America's subsequent involvement in the Vietnam War.)[35] Map 2.2 visually portrays these organizations and the areas covered by each and summarizes the principal goals of each organization and the nations that comprise its membership.

One other collective security organization, the *Central Treaty Organization* (CENTO), was also established during this time period. The United States, however, was not a direct member. This organization evolved out of a bilateral pact of mutual cooperation between

Iraq and Turkey (the so-called Baghdad Pact of February 1955) and was formally constituted in 1959 with the inclusion of the United Kingdom, Pakistan, and Iran. Through an executive agreement with Turkey, the United States pledged to support the security needs of CENTO members and to provide various kinds of assistance. In addition, the United States actively participated in CENTO meetings and assisted their joint undertakings. Because of this active involvement in the operation of the organization by the United States and because of its indirect pledge of support, CENTO was actually another link in the global security arrangements that were initiated by the United States in the immediate postwar years. All of these defense agreements had provisions that provided for assistance when confronted by armed attacks, threats of aggression, or even internal subversion in the case of SEATO. For the ANZUS, SEATO, Rio, and CENTO pacts, however, the response is not automatic. Instead, in the main, each of the signatories agreed "to meet the common danger in accordance with its constitutional processes." The exception among these pacts is the NATO one. This pact differs in the degree of commitment by the parties to an automatic response, and, as it developed, its manner of operation. The NATO agreement called for a more automatic armed response on the part of the signatories to an attack. As Article 5 states:

> The Parties agree that an armed attack against one or more of them in Europe or North America shall be considered an attack against them all, and consequently they agree that, if such an armed attack occurs, each of them... will assist the Party or Parties so attacked forthwith, individually, and in concert with the other Parties, such action as it deems necessary, including the use of armed force, to restore and maintain the security of the North Atlantic area.[36]

The members of NATO also established an integrated military command structure and called for the commitment of forces to NATO (although the forces remained under ultimate national command) by each of the member states. In both of these ways, then, NATO proved the most important of the regional security pacts established, since it involved the area of greatest concern for American interests and because Europe was regarded as the primary area of potential Soviet aggression.

In addition to the regional military organizations that were set up, a series of bilateral defense pacts were established in Asia to combat Soviet and Chinese aggression. Bilateral pacts were completed with the Philippines (1951), Japan (1951), the Republic of Korea (1953), and the Republic of China (Taiwan—1954). These pacts

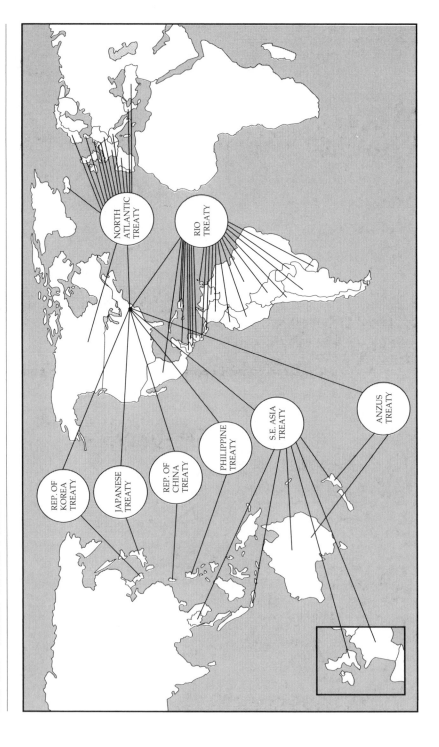

Map 2.2   United States Collective Defense Arrangements

MULTILATERAL PACTS

RIO TREATY, OR THE INTER-AMERICAN TREATY OF RECIPROCAL ASSISTANCE (22 NATIONS)

A treaty signed September 2, 1947, which provides that an armed attack against any American state, "shall be considered as an attack against all the American States and . . . each one . . . undertakes to assist in meeting the attack. . . ."

Membership: United States, Mexico, Cuba, Haiti, Dominican Republic, Honduras, Guatemala, El Salvador, Nicaragua, Costa Rica, Panama, Colombia, Venezuela, Ecuador, Peru, Brazil, Bolivia, Paraguay, Chile, Argentina, Uruguay, and Trinidad and Tobago

NORTH ATLANTIC TREATY (16 NATIONS)

A treaty signed April 4, 1949, by which "the Parties agree that an armed attack against one or more of them in Europe or North America shall be considered an attack against them all; and . . . each of them . . . will assist the . . . attacked by taking forthwith, individually and in concert with the other Parties, such action as it deems necessary, including the use of armed force . . . ."

Membership: United States, Canada, Iceland, Norway, United Kingdom, Netherlands, Denmark, Belgium, Luxembourg, Portugal, France, Italy, Greece (joined in 1952), Turkey (1952), Federal Republic of Germany (1955), and Spain (1982).

ANZUS TREATY (3 NATIONS)

A treaty signed September 1, 1951, whereby each of the parties "recognizes that an armed attack in the Pacific Area on any of the Parties would be dangerous to its own peace and safety and declares that it would act to meet the common danger in accordance with its constitutional processes."

Membership: United States, New Zealand, and Australia

SOUTHEAST ASIA TREATY (7 NATIONS)

A treaty signed September 8, 1954, whereby each party "recognizes that aggression by means of armed attack in the treaty area against any of the Parties . . . would endanger its own peace and safety" and each will "in that event act to meet the common danger in accordance with its constitutional processes."

Membership: United States, United Kingdom, France, New Zealand, Australia, Philippines, and Thailand

BILATERAL PACTS

PHILIPPINE TREATY

A treaty signed August 30, 1951, whereby each of the parties recognizes "that an armed attack in the Pacific Area on either of the Parties would be dangerous to its own peace and safety" and each party agrees that it will act "to meet the common danger in accordance with its constitutional processes."

Membership: United States and the Philippines

JAPANESE TREATY

A treaty signed January 19, 1960 (replacing the original security treaty of September 8, 1951), whereby each party "recognizes that an armed attack against either Party in the territories under the administration of Japan would be dangerous to its own peace and safety and declares that it would act to meet the common danger in accordance with its constitutional provisions and processes."

Membership: United States and Japan

REPUBLIC OF KOREA TREATY

A treaty signed October 1, 1953, whereby each party "recognizes that an armed attack in the Pacific area on either of the Parties . . . would be dangerous to its own peace and safety" and that each party "would act to meet the common danger in accordance with its constitutional processes."

Membership: United States and the Republic of Korea

REPUBLIC OF CHINA TREATY

A treaty signed December 2, 1954, whereby each of the parties "recognizes that an armed attack in the West Pacific Area directed against the territories of either of the Parties would be dangerous to its own peace and safety . . ." and that each "would act to meet the common danger in accordance with its constitutional processes." The territory of the Republic of China is defined as "Taiwan (Formosa) and the Pescadores."

Membership: United States and the Republic of China

Source: U.S. Department of State, Bureau of Public Affairs, September 1977 and April 1981.

resulted from two major political events that occurred in Asia in the late 1940s and early 1950s. The first concerned political developments in China; the second concerned the war that broke out in Korea.

By October 1949 Mao Zedong had won the civil war in China and had declared the establishment of the People's Republic of China. He quickly sought close ties with the leader of the communist world (the Soviet Union), and the United States soon viewed the communist movement as increasingly powerful and challenging to U.S. and Western interests. As a result, the United States refused to recognize Mao's regime and discouraged other states from doing so. (Indeed, formal diplomatic relations would not develop until three decades later, in 1979.) Instead, the U.S. continued to support its ally in the Chinese civil war (Chiang Kai-shek, who had fled to the island of Taiwan) and recognized the government of the Republic of China as the official government of all China. The United States also began to deploy its Seventh Fleet in the Taiwan Straits to discourage any attempts by the mainland to invade Taiwan or, conversely, for the island government to seek to invade the mainland.[37]

The second major upheaval in Asia was the Korean War, which lasted from 1950 to 1953. In June 1950 North Korea attacked South Korea. In response, American forces were dispatched to South Korea under United Nations auspices to fight a protracted war. During this war, Chinese communist "volunteers" assisted the North Koreans. The involvement of both communist powers raised concern over the aggressive intentions of these states and served as further motivation for the establishment of defense pacts in the area. The Korean War is discussed in more detail below since it is often cited as the first real test of containment and the event that brought the Cold War to fruition.[38]

With the bilateral treaties of the early 1950s, the mosaic of global security was largely completed. Moreover, a quick look at Map 2.2 indicates that the United States was quite successful in forming alliances in most areas that were not directly under Soviet control.

Nevertheless, two prominent regions, Africa and the Middle East, were still not directly covered by these security arrangements. Here, too, however, some elements of containment were evident. In Africa, for instance, the European colonial powers still held sway, and thus the region was largely under the containment shield through these allied states.[39] The security efforts in the Middle East region were more complex. Although the Middle Eastern regimes at this time were mainly traditional monarchies, stirrings of nationalism and pan-Arabism within Egypt under Gamal Abdel Nasser and their diffusion throughout the region made treaty commitments difficult. Added to these factors were America's close ties to Israel and the festering Arab-Israeli conflict. Despite these hindrances, the United States did initiate one important security proposal to the nations in this volatile area. This proposal came to be labeled the Eisenhower Doctrine.

This doctrine arose from a speech given by President Eisenhower to a joint session of Congress over perceived trouble in the Middle East and the need for the United States to combat it. "If power-hungry Communists should either falsely or correctly estimate that the Middle East is inadequately defended, they might be tempted to use open measures of armed attack," President Eisenhower declared. To combat this eventuality, he asked Congress for the presidential authority to extend economic and military assistance as needed and "to use armed forces to assist any such nation or group of such nations requesting assistance against armed aggression from any country controlled by international communism."[40] The security commitments were now truly global in scope.

ELEMENTS OF CONTAINMENT: ECONOMIC AND MILITARY ASSISTANCE

The second set of initiatives to implement the containment strategy focused upon economic and military assistance to friendly nations. From the late 1940s through the middle and late 1950s, substantial aid (reaching over $10 billion in 1953) was provided to an ever-expanding set of nations throughout the world. While the initial goal of these assistance efforts was to foster the economic well-being of the recipient societies, the ultimate rationale, especially after 1950, became strategic and political in content: to ensure the stability of those states threatened by international communism and to build support for anti-communism on a global scale. Three important programs reflect the kinds of assistance initiated by the United States during this period as well as its change in orientation over time: (1) the Marshall Plan, (2) the Point Four program, and (3) the mutual security concept.[41]

The Marshall Plan is the best known of the assistance efforts that the United States began in the postwar period. The plan was proposed in a speech by Secretary of State George Marshall at the Harvard commencement exercises in June 1947. Marshall called for the Europeans to draw up a plan for economic recovery and pledged American economic support to implement such an effort. As a consequence of this speech and subsequent European-American consultations, President Truman asked Congress for $17 billion over a four-year period from 1948 to 1952 to revitalize Western Europe. The enormity of such an aid commitment became apparent when it is compared to the approximately $1 billion of assistance offered to Eastern Europe after the collapse of the Iron Curtain in 1989 and 1990. Its size is also reflected in the fact that Marshall Plan aid constituted about 1.2 percent of the GNP of the United States at the time. Over recent years, the amount of U.S. development assistance has constituted well under 0.5 percent of the GNP and constituted only 0.15 percent of the GNP in 1989.[42]

The rationale for the Marshall Plan was the rebuilding of the economic system of Western Europe. As a key trading partner for the United States, a healthy Europe was important to the economic health of America. Beyond these economic concerns, though, there were political concerns. If Europe did not recover, the region might well be subject to political instability and perhaps communist penetration and subversion. According to Gilbert Winham's imaginative analysis of the decision making over the Marshall Plan, this "threat" dimension became particularly important in the late stages of deliberations on the plan (February through April 1948, just prior to its enactment).[43] In this sense, by the time of its formal passage by Congress, the European Recovery Program, or Marshall Plan, had clear elements of the containment strategy even though its initial motivations were primarily economic.

While the Marshall Plan proved remarkably successful in fostering European recovery, President Truman also envisioned a larger plan of assistance for the rest of the world. His Point Four program was announced in his inaugural address of January 20, 1949. (The name was derived from the fact that this was the fourth major point in his suggested courses of action for American policy.) The aim of this program was to develop on a global scale the essentials of the Marshall Plan, which was then underway in Western Europe. Unlike the Marshall Plan, though, Point Four was less a cooperative venture with participating states and more a unilaterial effort on the part of the United States, although America's allies might also become involved. In essence, the program was to provide industrial, technological, and economic assistance to the underdeveloped nations of the world. As President Truman announced:

> We must embark on a bold new program for making the benefits of our scientific advances and industrial progress available for the improvement and growth of underdeveloped areas. . . . I believe that we should make available to peace-loving peoples the benefits of our store of technical knowledge in order to help them real-

ize their aspirations for a better life. And, in cooperation with other nations, we should foster capital investment in areas needing development.[44]

In this sense, the Point Four program was an imaginative and substantial commitment to global economic development by the United States.

While Point Four had some of the same ambitious economic, and undoubtedly political, motivations as the Marshall Plan, the program never really received sufficient funding authorization from the Congress.[45] Instead this strategy of global assistance was rather quickly replaced by a new approach that was more explicitly political in content, the mutual security concept. The mutual security approach emphasized aiding nations to combat communism and to strengthen the security of the United States and the "free world." In addition to the change in rationale for aid, the kind of assistance also changed by the early and middle 1950s from primarily economic and humanitarian aid to military assistance. While economic aid was not halted during this period, its purpose changed. Economic assistance was more likely given to bolster the overall security capability of friendly countries.

These changes in aid policy can be explained by the deepening global crisis that the United States perceived in the world. Tensions between the Soviet Union and the United States were rising over Soviet actions in Eastern Europe and its potential actions toward Western Europe. The Korean War had broken out, apparently with Soviet compliance. Subsequently, the Chinese communists entered this conflict, again evoking concern over communist intentions. Domestically, there was an increased sense of communist threat, led by the verbal assaults of Senator Joseph McCarthy of Wisconsin on various individuals and groups for being "soft on communism" and more. All in all, America's national security was perceived to be under attack, and this required some response.

The first real manifestation of this new aid strategy was the Mutual Defense Assistance Act of 1949.[46] This act, signed after the completion of the NATO pact and after the Soviets had tested an atomic bomb, provided for military aid to Western Europe, Greece, Turkey, Iran, South Korea, the Philippines, and the "China area." The strategic location of these countries is quite apparent; most bordered the Soviet Union or mainland China. Although the amount of aid called for in this act was relatively small, its significance lay in the fact that it was the initial effort in military aid by the United States.

A later act, the Mutual Security Act of 1951, marked the real beginning of growth in military assistance amounts. Equally important, the introductory language of the act dramatically illustrated the

FIGURE 2.1   PATTERNS IN FOREIGN AID, 1945–1970
(NET GRANTS AND CREDITS)

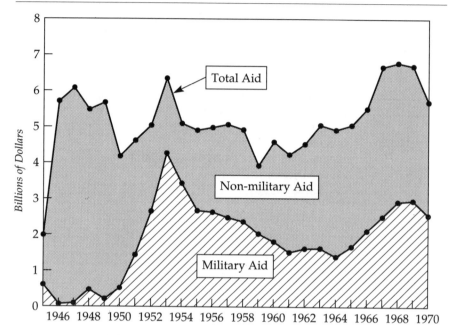

Source: *The Statistical History of the United States from Colonial Times to the Present* (New York:
Basic Books, Inc., 1976), pp. 274 and 872.

linkage between this new aid policy and American security. The aim
of this act was:

> to maintain the security and to promote the foreign policy of the
> United States by authorizing military, economic, and technical as-
> sistance to friendly countries to strengthen the mutual security
> and individual and collective defenses of the free world, [and] to
> develop their resources in the interest of their security and inde-
> pendence and the national interest of the United States. . . .[47]

With successive mutual security acts like these, American global
assistance, and particularly military assistance, increased sharply.
Furthermore, the number of recipient countries also began to grow.
As Figure 2.1 shows, military assistance came to dominate the total
assistance effort. Even with the addition of food aid under Public
Law 480 in 1954 and with the inclusion of some technical and devel-
opmental assistance to particular countries (e.g., Yugoslavia and Po-

land),[48] the proportion of military assistance was often greater than non-military assistance until about 1960. By that time, a new approach to aid, one motivated more explicitly by development considerations, was already being contemplated and was finally implemented under the Kennedy administration in 1961 with the establishment of the Agency for International Development (AID).

In general, though, the political rationale dominated aid policy and the choice of aid recipients prior to the emergence of AID. Nations that were "neutral" or "nonaligned" in the Cold War struggle between the United States and the Soviet Union were viewed skeptically and were not likely to receive economic or military assistance from the United States.[49] Instead, aid was intended to save America's friends from Soviet (and Chinese) communism.

ELEMENTS OF CONTAINMENT: THE DOMESTIC COLD WAR

The third element in the containment strategy was primarily domestic. Its aim was to make the American people aware of the Soviet threat and to change American domestic priorities to meet it. In essence, this aspect of containment might be labeled the domestification of the Cold War.

One important document, completed by the National Security Council in April 1950, and entitled NSC-68, summarizes the goals of this effort and provides a good guide to the subsequent domestic (and international) changes that occurred to meet the perceived communist threat. NSC-68 was the result of a review of American foreign and domestic defense policies by State and Defense Department officials under the leadership of Paul Nitze. What makes NSC-68 distinct from the other elements of containment is its emphasis upon a domestic response to the Cold War. But it is useful for another reason: since it remained classified until 1975, it gives us a unique picture of the thinking of American officials without the restraining effects that domestic political considerations of the moment might produce.

The document itself is a rather lengthy statement that begins by outlining the nature of the current international crisis between the Soviet Union and the United States and then goes on to contrast the foreign policy goals of Washington and Moscow in much the same vein as the Truman Doctrine, albeit in much harsher language. (Document 2.1 excerpts portions of NSC-68 that depict these alternate views of the world.)

DOCUMENT 2.1   EXCERPTS FROM NSC-68, APRIL 14, 1950

Fundamental Design of the United States
The fundamental purpose of the United States is laid down in the Preamble of the Constitution. . . . In essence, [it] is to assure the integrity and vitality of our free society, which is founded upon the dignity and worth of the individual.

Fundamental Design of the Kremlin
The fundamental design of those who control the Soviet Union and the international communist movement is to retain and solidify their absolute power, first in the Soviet Union and second in the areas now under their control. In the minds of the Soviet leaders, however, achievement of this design requires the dynamic extension of their authority and the ultimate elimination of any effective opposition to their authority. . . . The United States, as the principal center of power in the non-Soviet world and the bulwark of opposition to Soviet expansion, is the principal enemy whose integrity and vitality must be subverted or destroyed by one means or another if the Kremlin is to achieve its fundamental design.

Nature of the Conflict
The Kremlin regards the United States as the only major threat to the achievement of its fundamental design. There is a basic conflict between the idea of freedom under a government of law, and the idea of slavery under the grim oligarchy of the Kremlin. . . . The idea of freedom, moreover, is peculiarly and intolerably subversive of the idea of slavery. But the converse is not true. The implacable purpose of the slave state to eliminate the challenge of freedom has placed the two great powers at opposite poles. It is this fact which gives the present polarization of power the quality of crisis.

The assault on free institutions is world-wide now, and in the context of the present polarization of power a defeat of free institutions anywhere is a defeat everywhere. . . .

In a shrinking world, which now faces the threat of atomic warfare, it is not an adequate objective merely to seek to check the Kremlin design, for the absence of order among nations is becoming less and less tolerable. This fact imposes on us, in our own interests, the responsibility of world leadership. It demands that we make the attempt, and accept the risks inherent in it, to bring about order and justice by means consistent with the principles of freedom and democracy. . . . Coupled with the probable fission bomb capability and possible thermonuclear bomb capability of the Soviet Union, the intensifying struggle requires us to face the fact that we can expect no lasting abatement of the crisis unless and until a change occurs in the nature of the Soviet system.

Source: *A Report to the National Security Council, April 14, 1950*, pp. 5–9. Declassified on February 27, 1975, by Henry A. Kissinger, Assistant to the President for National Security Affairs.

An example of how Soviet policy is characterized in the document makes this point as well:

> The Kremlin's policy toward areas not under its control is the elimination of resistance to its will and the extension of its influence and control. . . . The means employed by the Kremlin in pursuit of this policy are limited only by considerations of expediency. Doctrine is not a limiting factor; rather it dictates the employment of violence, subversion, and deceit and rejects moral considerations.[50]

The report goes on to assess the relative strengths and weaknesses of the Soviet Union and the United States. At this juncture, NSC-68 is germane to our analysis because it notes two arenas that were perceived as particularly vulnerable to Soviet challenge: U.S. military capability and American moral capabilities. The U.S. military, it contended, was inferior to that of the Soviets in number of "forces in being and in total manpower." Furthermore, the amount of U.S. defense spending was relatively low, about 6–7 percent of the GNP, as compared to more than 13 percent for the Soviet Union. Moral capabilities were also vulnerable. The Soviets might well seek to undermine America's social and cultural institutions by infiltration and intimidation:

> Those that touch most closely our material and moral strength are obviously the prime targets, labor unions, civic enterprises, schools, churches, and all media for influencing opinion. The effort is not so much to make them serve obvious Soviet ends as to prevent them from serving our ends, and thus to make them sources of confusion in our economy, our culture and our body politic.[51]

In its conclusion, NSC-68 suggested that the United States follow a policy of rapidly building up the political, economic, and military strength of the free world to meet the Soviet threat. While several specific recommendations were made for strengthening alliance relationships and for increasing economic and military assistance abroad, important domestic policy recommendations were also emphasized.

For example, NSC-68 called for a rapid buildup of the American military establishment to counteract the Soviet challenge. But beyond this important general demand, it went one step further to propose a new policy on military budgeting, stating that it might be necessary in the future to meet defense and foreign assistance needs by the reduction of federal expenditures in other areas.[52] In effect, this policy was to place defense spending as the number one priority in the budgeting process of the U.S. government. Instead of defense being a residual category of the budget, it was to become the focal point of future allocation decisions. The rest of the budgetary items would become residual categories.

NSC-68 had one other significant statement on military planning. In the body of the report (and not specifically in its recommendations), the document called for the United States to "produce and stockpile thermonuclear weapons in the event they prove feasible and would add significantly to our net capability."[53] Although this reference is relatively oblique in the context of the entire report, it was significant in terms of timing. During this period, the Truman administration was embroiled in a policy debate on whether to go forward with the building of the H-bomb.

The other major area of domestic policy recommendations was the development of internal security and civilian defense programs. NSC-68 contended that the government must "assure the internal security of the United States against dangers of sabotage, subversion, and espionage." It must also "keep the U.S. public fully informed and cognizant of the threats to our national security so that it will be prepared to support the measures which we must accordingly adopt."[54] In essence, there should be efforts to protect the American people against subversion and to gain their support for Cold War policies.

To a considerable degree, these recommendations became American policy in the early 1950s, sparked, as we shall see, by American involvement in the Korean War. Defense expenditures took off to over 10 percent of the GNP in the early 1950s and generally stayed about 8 percent throughout the 1960s. Similarly, defense spending as a percentage of the federal budget rose sharply in the 1950s to over 50 percent and remained over 40 percent for all the years through the Johnson administration. A parallel growth pattern occurred in the size of the American armed forces, with the number of people under arms reaching over 22/1000 population in the early 1950s and remaining above 14/1000 population throughout the heart of the Vietnam War years. Figure 2.2 provides a summary view of these trends during the 1946–1968 period.[55] Additionally, the H-bomb program was given the go-ahead, and nuclear weapons became a part of defense strategy.

Efforts to ensure internal security were undertaken, too. As we have already noted, Senator Joseph McCarthy initiated his campaign against "communists" within the government. Even aside from his unswerving attacks, questions were raised among the public about communist subversion within America. The various investigations by the House Un-American Activities Committee of the 1950s and

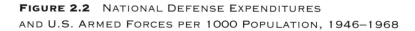

FIGURE 2.2 NATIONAL DEFENSE EXPENDITURES
AND U.S. ARMED FORCES PER 1000 POPULATION, 1946–1968

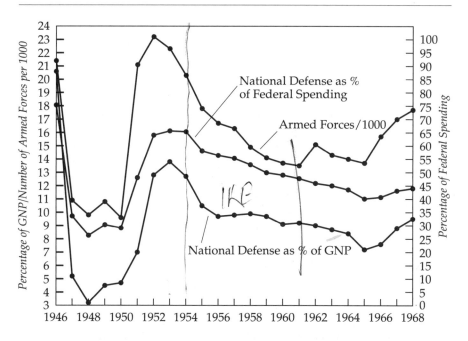

Sources: The data for national defense as a percentage of federal spending and GNP are taken
from Alice C. Moroni, *The Fiscal Year 1984 Defense Budget Request: Data Summary* (Washington, D.C.:
Congressional Research Service, 1983), p. 13. Total National Defense data, rather than only Department
of Defense data, are used here. The two totals are usually very close (p. 14). The armed forces
percentages were calculated from total population (Part 1, p. 8) and armed forces (Part 2, p. 1141) data in
U.S. Bureau of the Census, *Historical Statistics of the United States, Colonial Times to 1970*, Bicentennial
Edition, Parts 1 and 2 (Washington, D.C.: U.S. Government Printing Office, 1975).

1960s reflect this growing concern with possible Soviet penetration.
FBI and CIA activities in this area were also prevalent, as the Church
Committee investigations of intelligence activities were to reveal in
the mid-1970s. Furthermore, efforts to employ loyalty oaths also reflected this trend toward national security consciousness. In short,
political attacks from the schoolrooms to the boardrooms produced a
sense of widespread fear about veering too far from the mainstream
on foreign policy issues. To a remarkable degree, a foreign policy
consensus was the result of this Cold War effort. Foreign policy de-

bate became a casualty of the political environment. Moreover, when debate did occur, it was more often on foreign policy tactics rather than on fundamental strategy.[56]

THE KOREAN WAR: THE FIRST MAJOR TEST OF CONTAINMENT

Although the events in Greece and Turkey stimulated the emergence of the containment policy in 1947, the first major test of this policy, and what brought the Cold War fully into existence, occurred in Korea in 1950. On June 25, 1950, North Korea attacked South Korea, and this attack quickly engaged the Soviet Union, the People's Republic of China, and the United States in a confrontation on the Korean peninsula. For the United States, it also provided the raison d'être for fully implementing the various elements of the containment strategy outlined above.

AMERICAN INVOLVEMENT IN KOREA

A brief description of the situation on the Korean peninsula, the origins of the conflict, and the extent of U.S. involvement illustrate that conflict's significance for American postwar policy. Korea had been annexed by the Japanese in 1910 and was finally freed by American and Soviet forces at the end of World War II. By agreement between the two countries, Korea was then temporarily divided along the 38th parallel, with Soviet forces occupying the north and U.S. forces occupying the south. Despite several maneuvers by both sides, this division assumed a more permanent cast when a UN-supervised election in the south resulted in the establishment of the Republic of Korea on August 15, 1948, and when the adoption of a constitution in the north resulted in the creation of the Democratic People's Republic of Korea on September 9, 1948.[57] Each regime claimed to be the government of Korea, and neither would recognize or accept the legitimacy of the other. While both Soviet and American occupying forces left in 1948 and 1949, respectively, the struggle between the two regimes (with the support of their powerful allies) was not finished.

This struggle soon erupted into sustained violence in mid-1950. When the North Koreans attacked South Korea, their powerful allies were quickly brought into this conflict. Indeed, the United States viewed this attack on South Korea as Soviet-inspired and Soviet-directed.[58] Thus, the U.S. had little recourse but to respond and to

MAP 2.3 THE KOREAN WAR, 1950–1953

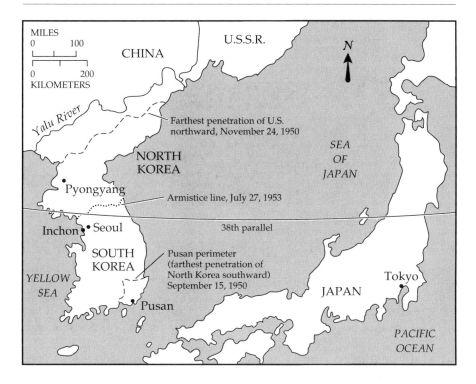

make the containment doctrine a reality. Within days, President Harry Truman ordered American air and naval support for the beleaguered Korean troops and also dispatched the Seventh Fleet to patrol the Formosa Strait to prevent communist Chinese actions against the nationalist government on Taiwan. In addition, Truman sought and quickly obtained United Nations Security Council condemnation of the attack and support for a collective security force to be sent to aid the South Korean forces under U.S. direction. (The UN action was made possible by the Soviet Union's boycott of UN Security Council sessions because the China seat had not been given to the communist government led by Mao Zedong. As a result, the Soviet Union was unable to exercise its veto.) Although some fourteen other nations ultimately sent forces to aid the South Koreans, the bulk of the war effort was carried out by the Americans.[59] Indeed, the commander of all UN and U.S. forces in Korea was General Douglas MacArthur.

Initially, the American-led effort in Korea fared badly. Allied troops were driven to a small enclave around Pusan in southeast Korea, and the North Koreans were on the verge of overrunning the entire peninsula. In September 15, 1950, however, General MacArthur executed his Inchon landing behind North Korean lines, and, within a matter of weeks, his forces proceeded across the 38th parallel into North Korea. While this invasion was brilliant as a strategic move, the Chinese became alarmed as MacArthur's forces moved ever more northward, coming within miles of the Chinese border.[60]

While the Chinese had warned the West indirectly through India in September 1950 that it would not "sit back with folded hands and let the Americans come to the border,"[61] that warning was not believed by U.S. policymakers. Beginning as early as mid-October 1950, Chinese People's Volunteers began crossing into North Korea to aid that government's forces. By late November 1950, Chinese forces totaling over 300,000 fought alongside the North Koreans against the UN and U.S. forces. The massive Chinese intervention drove allied forces back across the 38th parallel, the "temporary" dividing line between North and South Korea. Stalemate ensued.

General MacArthur proposed that the United States forces carry the war into China as a way to resolve the conflict. Because President Truman had ordered him not to make public statements without administration approval and because the administration policy was to limit the conflict, Truman fired General MacArthur for insubordination. This action caused an outpouring of support for MacArthur and a vilification of President Truman.[62] By and large, the American people continued to support the proposition that once a war was undertaken, it should be fought to be won; it should not be limited by political constraints. The Truman administration felt otherwise. As General Omar Bradley, chairman of the Joint Chiefs of Staff, put it: "So long as we regarded the Soviet Union as the main antagonist and Western Europe as the main prize" a massive invasion of China "would involve us in the wrong war at the wrong place at the wrong time and with the wrong enemy." In other words, involvement in the land war in Asia would lead "to a larger deadlock at greater expense" and would do little to contain Soviet designs on Western Europe.[63]

By July 1951, truce talks were arranged, and fighting ceased for the most part by the end of the year. An armistice, however, did not come about for another year and a half, as a prolonged controversy developed over the repatriation of prisoners of war, and as an American election occurred with Korea as an important issue. An uneasy peace eventually did result with the establishment of a demilitarized zone between North and South Korea. The first test of containment, however, brought numerous lessons for American policymakers for the course of the Cold War.[64]

KOREA AND IMPLICATIONS FOR THE COLD WAR

Political scientist Robert Jervis argues that the American involvement in Korea "shaped the course of the cold war by both resolving the incoherence which characterized U.S. foreign and defense efforts in the period 1946–1950 and establishing important new lines of policy."[65] It resolved that incoherence by moving the United States to match its perceived sense of threat from the Soviet Union and international communism with policy actions consistent with that threat. New policy actions were undertaken in at least three different areas, and the political rhetoric of the late 1940s became the policy reality of the 1950s.

The first policy effect of the Korean War was to produce a sharp increase in the American defense budget and the militarization of NATO. While NSC-68 had called for such military increases, they did not result until U.S. involvement in this war and were largely sustained after it. Note from Figure 2.2 how high military spending (either as a percentage of the GNP or as a percentage of the budget) remained throughout much of the 1950s. Similarly, the establishment of an integrated military structure of NATO and the eventual effort to rearm West Germany followed directly on the heels of American involvement in Korea. The threat of Soviet expansionism had been made real with the actions in Asia.

A second effect of the Korean War was that it brought home to American policymakers the need to have large armies and to take action against aggression wherever it appeared. Limited wars, too, may be necessary, even if they arouse unpopular responses at home.[66] In this view, if the U.S. did not confront aggression in one dispute, questions would be raised about American resolve in other disputes that might arise. Indeed, the Korean experience had already raised this doubt. After all, Secretary of State Dean Acheson had seemed to indicate in a speech in January 1950 that the Korean peninsula was not within the "defense perimeter" in Asia.[67]

A third effect of the Korean War was to solidify the American view that a Sino-Soviet bloc promoting communist expansion was a reality and that there was a need to combat it. The Chinese intervention on the side of the North Koreans illustrated the extent to which China was controlled by the Soviet Union. Indeed, the view that Sino-American hostilities were intense and that "China and Russia were inseparable were products of the war."[68] Moreover, the various bilateral pacts in Asia were established after the Korean War was underway. In sum, then, the outbreak of the Korean War and American involvement in it were to bring about a correspondence between U.S. policy beliefs and its actions in a most dramatic way.

CONCLUDING COMMENTS

In Chapter 1, we noted that isolationism and moralism were America's twin pillars from the past. The Cold War period and the containment policy appear to represent a sharp break from this heritage, at least with respect to isolationism. On one level, of course, the United States did abandon isolationism for a policy of globalism.[69] On another level, America's globalism was largely a unilateralist approach on the part of the United States, a strategy of going it alone in the world, or at least attempting to lead other nations of the world in a particular direction. In other words, much as the original isolationism was unilaterialist, so, too, was the containment policy. It was a strategy by the United States to reshape the global order through its own design and largely through its own efforts.

The heritage of moralism is more readily evident in the Cold War period and in the containment policy. The universal campaign that the United States initiated was highly consistent with its past. Moral accommodation with the values of Russian communism, or any communism, was simply not acceptable. In fact, some even sought to "roll back" communism rather than just contain it. Like the efforts in America's past (the War of 1812, the Spanish-American War, World War I, and World War II), then, the containment strategy represented an all-out attempt—in this case, to confront the moral challenge from the Soviet Union and all it represented. Moralism was alive and well in the post–World War II world and served as the primary justification for American policy once again.

In the next chapter, we examine more fully the values and beliefs that shaped the U.S. approach to the world during the height of the Cold War. A Cold War consensus among American leaders and the public was developing in the late 1940s and the early 1950s, and the Korean War only served to solidify it. This consensus, which we discuss more fully in Chapter 3, provided the rationale for the complete implementation of the containment policy during the rest of the 1950s and 1960s and guided U.S. policy during the subsequent decades until it was challenged by several key international events.

NOTES

1. Joseph Weeks, *The Fifteen Weeks* (Chicago: Harcourt, Brace and World, Inc., 1955), pp. 89–99.

2. The term is from Richard Mayne's Chapter 2 title in his *The Recovery of Europe 1945–1973* (Garden City, NY: Anchor, 1973), pp. 27–52. The discussion here draws upon this chapter as well as p. 14 on the extent of decolonization.

3. Ibid., pp. 39–40.

4. Ibid.

5. Stephen E. Ambrose, *Rise to Globalism: American Foreign Policy 1938–1976* (New York: Penguin Books, 1976), p. 16. A good discussion of the economic strength of the United States in the immediate postwar period can be found in Joan Edelman Spero, *The Politics of International Economic Relations*, 2nd ed. (New York: St. Martin's Press, 1981), pp. 23–30, 33–41. The economic data cited are from Spero, p. 36.

6. Ambrose, *Rise to Globalism*, p. 16.

7. John Lewis Gaddis, *The United States and the Origins of the Cold War 1941–1947* (New York and London: Columbia University Press, 1972), p. 1. See also Daniel Yergin, *Shattered Peace: The Origins of the Cold War and the National Security State* (Boston: Houghton Mifflin Company, 1977), pp. 42–68.

8. Gaddis, *Origins of the Cold War*, p. 2.

9. Yergin, *Shattered Peace*, pp. 43–46.

10. Ibid., pp. 17–68. The quote about Riga is at p. 19.

11. Ibid., p. 55.

12. See the discussion of the Yalta agreements in Robert H. Ferrell, *American Diplomacy: A History* (New York: W. W. Norton & Company, Inc., 1975), pp. 594–603.

13. Ferrell, *American Diplomacy: A History*, pp. 594–603.

14. James Lee Ray, *Global Politics*, 2nd ed. (Boston: Houghton Mifflin Company, 1983), p. 30.

15. Yergin, *Shattered Peace*, pp. 71–73.

16. Ibid. Also see Gaddis, *Origins of the Cold War*, pp. 200–206.

17. Ernest R. May, *"Lessons" of the Past* (New York: Oxford University Press, 1973), pp. 20–22. The quotation is from p. 22.

18. See ibid., pp. 22–32, for a discussion of the views of these diplomatic assessments and their impact on Truman and his advisors.

19. Harry S. Truman, *Year of Decision* (New York: Doubleday & Co., Inc., 1955), p. 99. The earlier passage is quoted in Gaddis, *Origins of the Cold War*, p. 232.

20. For a recent description and assessment of the Potsdam Conference, see Charles L. Mee, Jr., *Meeting at Potsdam* (New York: M. Evan & Co., Inc., 1975).

21. Gaddis, *Origins of the Cold War*, pp. 263–281.

22. Ibid., pp. 282–312.

23. The first quote is from Walter Lafeber, *America, Russia, and the Cold War 1945–1975*. (New York: John Wiley & Sons, Inc., 1976), p. 39, and the second is from Gaddis, *Origins of the Cold War*, p. 299.

24. The text of the speech can be found in Robert Rhodes James, ed., *Winston S. Churchill: His Complete Speeches 1897–1963*, vol. VII: 1943–1949 (New York: Chelsea House Publishers, 1974), pp. 7285–7293.

25. Yergin, *Shattered Peace*, p. 176.

26. George F. Kennan, *Memoirs 1925-1950* (Boston: Little, Brown & Co., 1967), p. 557.

27. The discussion draws upon Jones, *The Fifteen Weeks*, pp. 48-58, especially pp. 48-49.

28. Quoted in ibid., p. 54. Emphasis in original.

29. Ibid., p. 56. Jones does point out that the Soviets apparently got some concessions for their withdrawal.

30. Lafeber, *America, Russia, and the Cold War*, pp. 50-59, provides a useful description of the situation in Greece at this time, while Jones, *The Fifteen Weeks*, pp. 59-77, describes the situations in Greece and Turkey during 1946 and 1947.

31. These characteristics of the Truman Doctrine are from Lafeber, *America, Russia, and the Cold War*, p. 53.

32. The "Truman Doctrine" speech can be found in *House Documents, Miscellaneous*, 80th Cong., 1st Sess., Volume 1 (Washington, D.C.: U.S. Government Printing Office, 1947), Document 171. Emphasis added here. John Lewis Gaddis in his book, *Strategies of Containment* (New York: Oxford University Press, 1982), pp. 65-66, asserts that the Truman Doctrine was not so much meant as a call to attack "communism" as it was to attack "totalitarianism" in general. Truman's reference to two ways of life referred to totalitarian versus democracy. Only later did the commitment to contain communism really develop. See his "Was the Truman Doctrine a Real Turning Point?" *Foreign Affairs* 52 (January 1974): 386-402.

The source of responsibility for the Cold War and its exact date of origin are topics of great debate among scholars. Some argue that the Cold War was initiated by the Soviet Union, with its expansionist policies in Eastern Europe; others contend that the United States was responsible, with its attempt to use its great power to restructure global order; still others see a more complex process of mutual causation.

When the Cold War began is also controversial. Did it begin in 1947 (as we tend to argue) or was it put into place much later (e.g., with the outbreak of the Korean War)? Our intention is not to resolve this issue, but rather to make the reader aware of the controversy surrounding the Cold War concept. Besides Gaddis and Yergin, some other literature to consult on this topic includes the following: Gar Alperovitz, *Atomic Diplomacy: Hiroshima and Potsdam* (New York: Random House, 1965); D. F. Fleming, *The Cold War and its Origins, 1917-1970* (New York: Doubleday & Co., Inc., 1961); and Howard Bliss and M. Glen Johnson, *Consensus at the Crossroads: Dialogues in American Foreign Policy* (New York: Dodd, Mead & Co., Inc., 1972). More recent discussions on the Cold War and containment can be found in John Lewis Gaddis, "Containment: A Reassessment," *Foreign Affairs* 55 (July 1977): 873-887; Eduard Mark, "The Question of Containment: A Reply to John Lewis Gaddis," *Foreign Affairs* 56 (January 1978): 430-441; Robert Jervis, "The Impact of the Korean War on the Cold War," *The Journal of Conflict Resolution* 24 (December 1980): 563-592; and Charles S. Maier, ed., *The Origins of the Cold War and Contemporary Europe* (New York: New Viewpoints, 1978).

33. George Kennan has reprinted his July 1947 article from *Foreign Affairs* entitled "The Sources of Soviet Conduct" in his *American Diplomacy 1900-1950* (New York: Mentor Books, 1951). The quoted passages are at pp. 99 and 105 in the latter volume. It has also been reprinted in *Foreign Affairs* 65 (Spring 1987): 852-868.

34. George Kennan, in his *Memoirs 1925-1950*, pp. 354-367, contends that the implementation of containment by such sweeping actions was not what he had intended. He envisioned a more limited, more measured response than

what resulted. Also see his views on the Truman Doctrine at pp. 313–324. A more recent summary of Kennan's views on containment are available in "Containment Then and Now," *Foreign Affairs* 65 (Spring 1987): 885–890.

35. A brief description of the development of these organizations, and the charter of each one, can be found in Ruth C. Lawson, *International Regional Organizations: Constitutional Foundations* (New York: Praeger, 1962). The subsequent discussion of CENTO is also based upon this source.

36. *NATO Handbook* (Brussels: NATO Information Service, 1980), p. 14.

37. On the evolution of American strategy policy toward China and Asia in the late 1940s and early 1950s, see Thomas H. Etzold, "The Far East in American Strategy, 1948–1951," in Thomas H. Etzold, ed., *Aspects of Sino-American Relations Since 1784* (New York: New Viewpoints, 1978), pp. 102–126. On the sending of U.S. forces into the Taiwan Straits, see the discussion below in the text on the Korean War.

38. On the Korean War, see Allen S. Whiting, *China Crosses the Yalu* (Stanford: Stanford University Press, 1960); and John W. Spanier, *The Truman-MacArthur Controversy and the Korean War* (New York: W. W. Norton & Company, 1965). On the importance of the Korean War in really instigating the containment policy and producing the Cold War, see Gaddis, "Was the Truman Doctrine a Real Turning Point?" and Jervis, "The Impact of the Korean War on the Cold War."

39. In fact, the original NATO pact (subsequently altered in January 1963) covered "the Algerian Departments of France" in its security network. In this limited sense, a small part of Africa was originally included in NATO. See Article 6 of the NATO charter in ibid., p. 14, on this point.

40. The speech by President Eisenhower can be found in *House Documents, Miscellaneous,* 85th Cong., 1st Sess., Volume 1 (Washington, D.C.: U.S. Government Printing Office, 1957–1958), Document 46. The first quote is from this document. The latter quote is from Public Law 85-7, which was passed on March 9, 1957, to put the Eisenhower Doctrine into effect.

41. This section draws largely upon the fine summary of American foreign aid policy between 1945 and 1964 presented in *Congress and the Nation 1945–1964* (Washington, D.C.: Congressional Quarterly, Inc., 1965), pp. 160–186.

42. The text of Secretary of State Marshall's address can be found in the *New York Times,* June 6, 1947, p. 2. The Soviet Union and Eastern European states were invited to participate in the Marshall Plan under the original formulation. While Poland and Czechoslovakia had shown some initial interest, the Soviet Union quickly vetoed their efforts. See Ferrell, *American Diplomacy,* pp. 634–635. The percentage of GNP for the Marshall Plan was calculated from data presented in U.S. Bureau of the Census, *Historical Statistics of the United States, Colonial Times to 1970,* Bicentennial Edition. Parts 1 and 2 (Washington, D.C.: U.S. Government Printing Office, 1975). Aid effort over time by the United States can be found in the yearly reports by *Development Co-Operation* (Paris: Organization for Economic Cooperation and Development). The datum for 1989 is from Joseph C. Wheeler, *Development Co-Operation* (Paris: Organization for Economic Cooperation and Development, December 1990), p. 91.

43. Gilbert Winham, "Developing Theories of Foreign Policy Making: A Case Study of Foreign Aid," *The Journal of Politics* 32 (February 1970): 41–70. For other case studies of the Marshall Plan, see Morton Berkowitz, P. G. Bock, and Vincent Fuccillo, *The Politics of American Foreign Policy* (Englewood Cliffs, NJ: Prentice-Hall, Inc., 1977), pp. 20–38; and Jones, *The Fifteen Weeks,* pp. 239–256.

44. President Truman's inaugural address can be found in *Senate Documents, Miscellaneous*, 81st Cong., 1st Sess., Volume 1 (Washington, D.C.: U.S. Government Printing Office, 1949), Document 5.

45. See Robert A. Pastor, *Congress and the Politics of U.S. Foreign Economic Policy 1929–1976* (Berkeley: University of California Press, 1980), p. 269.

46. *Congress and the Nation 1945–1964*, p. 166.

47. The Mutual Security Act of 1951 can be found as Public Law 82-165, passed on October 10, 1951.

48. Aid was given to some countries to bolster their economies and their political will to retain some independence from Moscow. See *Congress and the Nation 1945–1964*, pp. 161–162.

49. Secretary of State John Foster Dulles was particularly noted for the suspicion with which he viewed the actions of neutral or non-aligned states in international politics.

50. *A Report to the National Security Council, NSC-68*, Washington, D.C., April 14, 1950, p. 13.

51. Ibid., p. 34. The quoted phrase on military strength is at p. 31, and the information on spending is at p. 25 in NSC-68.

52. Ibid., p. 57. On this point and others on NSC-68, see John C. Donovan, *The Cold Warriors: A Policy-Making Elite* (Lexington, MA: D. C. Heath and Company, 1974), pp. 81–96.

53. *A Report to the National Security Council, NSC-68*, p. 39.

54. Ibid., p. 63. These passages are actually from an earlier report, NSC 20/4, in NSC-68.

55. Similar data are reported in James L. Payne, *The American Threat* (College Station, TX: Lytton Publishing Company, 1981), p. 291. For an extended treatment of what the authors call the "militarization of American foreign policy" over the post–World War II decades, see Charles W. Kegley and Eugene R. Wittkopf, *American Foreign Policy: Pattern and Process*, 4th ed. (New York: St. Martin's Press, 1991), pp. 72–111.

56. See Howard Bliss and M. Glen Johnson, *Beyond the Water's Edge: America's Foreign Policies* (Philadelphia: J. B. Lippincott Co., 1975), pp. 3–10, for a discussion of the "costs of consensus" and for another set of assumptions comprising the postwar consensus.

57. For various accounts of the Korean War, and upon which we relied for this summary, see John G. Stoessinger, *Why Nations Go to War*, 5th ed. (New York: St. Martin's Press, 1990), pp. 55–83, especially at p. 61; Spanier, *The Truman-MacArthur Controversy and the Korean War*, especially pp. 23–26; Young W. Kihl, *Politics and Policies in Divided Korea: Regimes in Contest* (Boulder, CO: Westview Press, 1984), pp. 27–42; and Whiting, *China Crosses the Yalu*.

58. Stoessinger, *Why Nations Go to War*, p. 61 and Spanier, *The Truman-MacArthur Controversy*, pp. 23–26, for example.

59. Stoessinger, *Why Nations Go to War*, p. 67.

60. See the chronology of events in Whiting, *China Crosses the Yalu* and in John E. Mueller, *War, Presidents, and Public Opinion* (New York: John Wiley & Sons, Inc., 1973), among others, upon whom we rely.

61. As quoted in Whiting, *China Crosses the Yalu*, p. 93.

62. On the firing and its implications for American foreign policy, see Spanier, *The Truman-MacArthur Controversy and the Korean War*.

63. Bradley is quoted in Robert H. Ferrell, *American Diplomacy: The Twentieth Century* (New York: W. W. Norton & Company, 1988) at pp. 284–285.

64. Mueller, *War, Presidents and Public Opinion*, pp. 25–27.

65. Jervis, "The Impact of the Korean War on the Cold War," p. 563.

66. These effects are derived from ibid.

67. In a speech to the Press Club on January 12, 1950, Secretary of State Dean Acheson had indicated that the U.S. "defensive perimeter runs along the Aleutians to Japan and then goes to the Ryukyus. We hold important defense position in the Ryukyu Islands, and these we will continue to hold.... The defensive perimeter runs from the Ryukyus to the Philippine Islands." Korea thus was outside this defense line. See Dean Acheson, *Present at the Creation* (New York: W. W. Norton & Company, 1969), p. 357.

68. Jervis, "The Impact of the Korean War on the Cold War," p. 584.

69. For an extended discussion of the following argument in a similar vein, see Edmund Stillman and William Pfaff, *Power and Impotence* (New York: Vintage Books, 1966), but especially at pp. 15, 58–59.

CHAPTER 3 THE COLD WAR CONSENSUS AND CHALLENGES TO IT

"Let every nation know, whether it wishes us well or ill, that we shall pay any price, bear any burden, meet any hardship, support any friend, oppose any foe to assure the survival and success of liberty."
PRESIDENT JOHN F. KENNEDY, INAUGURAL ADDRESS, JANUARY 20, 1961

"In honor of the men and women of the armed forces of the United States who served in the Vietnam War. The names of those who gave their lives and of those who remain missing are inscribed in the order they were taken from us." INSCRIPTION ON THE VIETNAM VETERANS MEMORIAL, WASHINGTON, D.C.

From the Cold War environment, and the initial encounter of the Korean War, an identifiable foreign policy consensus developed among the American leadership and the public at large. This consensus was composed of a set of beliefs, values, and premises about America's role in the world and served as an important guide for U.S. behavior during the heart of the Cold War period (the late 1940s to the late 1960s). In the first part of this chapter, we shall undertake to (1) identify the principal components of the Cold War consensus, (2) illustrate how strongly the key values of this consensus were held within American society, and (3) provide a brief description of how the Cold War evolved in the first three decades after the end of World War II. In particular, we will show how the Cold War consensus largely prevailed in shaping American policymaking during this period, but that the Cold War interactions between the United States and the Soviet Union also reflected both periods of hostility and periods of accommodation. In the second half of the chapter, we will discuss how the Cold War consensus was to come under challenge during the 1960s from a variety of sources: (1) a changing international environment, particularly in the Third World, Eastern Europe, and Western Europe, which made implementing the containment policy more difficult; (2) the American domestic environment, particularly as a result of the Cuban Missile Crisis and the Vietnam War, which made policymaking more difficult; and (3) the emergence of new political leadership in the late 1960s and 1970s with alternate views for achieving global order even in the face of Soviet and communist challenge. In sum, both anti-communism and containment, as the cornerstones of American foreign policy, would be modified but not abandoned as the United States entered the 1970s. And some of the chill of the Cold War would be removed.

KEY COMPONENTS OF THE COLD WAR CONSENSUS

Lincoln P. Bloomfield has compiled an extensive listing of the U.S. foreign policy values in his book, *In Search of American Foreign Policy.*[1] Table 3.1 reproduces a portion of his list, and it shall serve as a starting point for our discussion of the Cold War consensus.

First of all, Bloomfield reminds us of the dichotomous view most Americans held of the world—one group of nations led by the United States and standing for democracy and capitalism, the other group led by the Soviet Union and standing for totalitarianism and socialism. Even this dichotomy was not wholly accurate because the

---

TABLE 3.1 THE AMERICAN POSTWAR CONSENSUS
IN FOREIGN POLICY

---

1. Communism is bad; capitalism is good.

2. Stability is desirable; in general, instability threatens U.S. interests.

3. Democracy (our kind, that is) is desirable, but if a choice has to be made, stability serves U.S. interests better than democracy.

4. Any area of the world that "goes socialist" or neutralist is a net loss to us, and probably a victory for the Soviets.

5. Every country, and particularly the poor ones, would benefit from American "know-how."

6. Nazi aggression in the 1930s and democracy's failure to respond provides the appropriate model for dealing with post-war security problems.

7. Allies and clients of the United States, regardless of their political structure, are members of the Free World.

8. The United States must provide leadership because it (reluctantly) has the responsibility.

9. "Modernization" and "development" are good for poor, primitive, or traditional societies—and they will probably develop into democracies by these means.

10. In international negotiations the United States has a virtual monopoly on "sincerity."

11. Violence is an unacceptable way to secure economic, social, and political justice—except when vital U.S. interests are at stake.

12. However egregious a mistake, the government must never admit having been wrong.

Source: Excerpted from *In Search of American Foreign Policy: The Humane Use of Power* by Lincoln P. Bloomfield. Copyright © 1974 by Oxford University Press, Inc. Reprinted by permission.

United States came to define the "free world" not in a positive way— by adherence to democratic principles of individual liberty and equality—but in a negative way—by adherence to the principles of anti-communism. Thus the "free world" could equally include the nations of Western Europe (including the dictatorships of Spain and Portugal through the mid-1970s) and the military regimes of Central and South America, because they embraced anti-communism. Such an "alliance" provided a ready bulwark against Soviet expansion.

While a substantial part of such a "free world" structure was grounded in this abiding concern over Soviet expansion, a second concern also permeated this thinking: U.S. attitudes toward stability and change. During this period, change in the world was viewed suspiciously. It tended to be seen as communist-inspired and, therefore, something to be opposed. Stability was always the preferred global condition.

Change was feared because it might lead to enhanced influence (and control) for the Soviet Union. This gain in influence could occur directly (by a nation's formal incorporation into the Soviet bloc) or indirectly (by a state's adopting a neutral or nonaligned stance in global affairs). As a consequence, Americans also tended to be skeptical of new states following the nonaligned movement initiated by Prime Minister Nehru of India and President Tito of Yugoslavia, among others. At this time, such a movement represented a loss for America's effort to rally the world against revolutionary communism.

Change was even more troublesome for the United States when it appeared in a nationalist and revolutionary environment. While the U.S. tended to have philosophical sympathy for such nationalist and anti-colonialist efforts, the global realities, as viewed by American policymakers, often led them to follow a different course. J. William Fulbright, at that time senator from Arkansas and chairman of the Senate Foreign Relations Committee, described this dilemma for America when dealing with forces of nationalism and communism in a revolutionary setting:

> . . . we are simultaneously hostile to communism and sympathetic to nationalism, and when the two become closely associated, we become agitated, frustrated, angry, precipitate, and inconstant. Or, to make the point by simple metaphor: loving corn and hating lima beans, we simply cannot make up our minds about succotash.[2]

The resultant American policy, as Fulbright goes on to state, was often to oppose communism rather than to support nationalism.

This fear of change was manifested in yet a more dramatic way: the several American military interventions (either directly or through surrogates) in the 1950s and 1960s to prevent communist gains. A few instances will make this point. In 1950, of course, U.S. military forces were sent to South Korea to assist that government from the attack by the North Koreans. In 1953, the United States was involved in the toppling of Prime Minister Mohammed Mossadegh of Iran and the restoration of the Shah. In 1954, the CIA assisted in the overthrow of the Jacobo Arbenz Guzman government in Guatemala because of the fear of growing communist influence there. In

1958, President Eisenhower ordered 14,000 marines to land in Lebanon to support a pro-Western government from possible subversion from Iraq, Syria, and Egypt.

The early 1960s saw the occurrence of three more interventions for a similar reason. In April 1961, the Bay of Pigs invasion of Cuba by Cuban exiles was attempted without success. This effort was designed to topple the communist regime of Fidel Castro, who had seized power in 1959, and was planned and organized by the CIA. In 1965, President Lyndon Johnson ordered the marines to land in Santo Domingo, Dominican Republic, to protect American lives and property from a possible change in regimes there. Communist involvement in this unrest was the rationale. Finally, of course, the prolonged involvement in Vietnam, beginning in a substantial way in the early 1960s (although having a history back to at least 1946), was justified by the desire to prevent the fall of South Vietnam, and subsequently all of Southeast Asia, to the communists.[3]

Beyond these direct interventions, the military was used in another way as an important instrument of American policy during the heart of the Cold War period. Two foreign policy analysts, Barry M. Blechman and Stephen S. Kaplan, provide some useful data on this topic in their examination of the "armed forces as a political instrument." According to these analysts, *"[a] political use of the armed forces occurs when physical actions are taken by one or more components of the uniformed military services as part of a deliberate attempt by the national authorities to influence, or to be prepared to influence, specific behavior of individuals in another nation without engaging in a continuing contest of violence."*[4] Thus, the movement of a naval task force to a particular region of the world, troops put on alert, a nonroutine military exercise begun, and the initiation of reconnaissance patrols can all be illustrations of this use of armed forces when accompanied by specific political goals toward another country.

Using these criteria, then, Blechman and Kaplan identified 215 incidents from 1946 to 1975. For the period that marked the height of the Cold War (1946–1968), 181 incidents occurred. Table 3.2 shows the breakdown of these incidents from Truman through Johnson. President Eisenhower used these military instruments most frequently (although he was in office longer than the other presidents), but Presidents Kennedy and Johnson had the highest average use of these types of military instruments during their tenures. Further, Latin America and Asia were the most frequent areas of these incidents for all the presidents since Truman. For President Truman, as one might suspect, Europe commanded the greatest attention in the use of this kind of military force.

TABLE 3.2 USE OF AMERICAN MILITARY FORCE DURING FOUR
ADMINISTRATIONS, 1946–1968 (CATEGORIZED BY REGIONS)

Administration	Latin America	Europe	Middle East and North Africa	Rest of Africa	Asia	Total
Truman	5	16	7	1	6	35
Eisenhower	18	6	13	2	19	58
Kennedy	17	6	4	2	11	40
Johnson	13	11	6	5	13	48
Regional totals	53	39	30	10	49	

Source: Calculated by the author from Barry M. Blechman and Stephen S. Kaplan, *Force Without War: U.S. Armed Forces as a Political Instrument* (Washington, D.C.: The Brookings Institution, 1978), pp. 547–552. See the text for a definition of what constitutes an incident in which military force is used.

Overall, then, even though the number of direct military interventions is relatively limited, the use of military armed forces as a political instrument was quite frequent during the period of the Cold War consensus. Moreover, Blechman and Kaplan conclude that "when the United States engaged in these political-military activities, the outcomes of the situations at which the activity was directed were often favorable from the perspective of U.S. decisionmakers at least in the short term."[5] In the long term though, Blechman and Kaplan are less optimistic; nevertheless, this consequence of the Cold War consensus appeared to be popular among policymakers.

Thus, violence came to be justified to defend American interests. Challenges to national security (increasingly defined as global security) were not to go unmet. Instead, the confrontation of potential aggressors was essential to world peace. The so-called "Munich syndrome," the fear of appeasing an aggressor as Chamberlain had done with Hitler, became another theme of American Cold War thinking. In short, the use of historical analogies as a guide to present policy was an important source of this kind of response to aggression.[6]

Given the nature of the perceived global struggle, a final important theme emerged from this postwar consensus. The U.S. came to believe that it alone could solve the problems of the poor and emerging nations through the application of its technological skills.[7] Additionally, the U.S. tended to offer itself as the model to achieve development and democracy. Such a policy came to be viewed as a markedly paternalistic one and one that some states viewed warily. Thus large-scale development efforts were initiated, particularly in the 1960s, to pursue this ideal. This policy, however, led to frustration for Americans when development did not occur as rapidly as envisioned or democracy did not result. Nonetheless, this belief during the 1950s and 1960s seems to summarize nicely the general value orientation that the U.S. employed to achieve its view of global order and to oppose the strategy of the Soviet Union.

THE PUBLIC AND THE COLD WAR CONSENSUS

Bloomfield's listing provides an excellent summary of the Cold War consensus, but it does not convey how deeply held these views were among the American public during the late 1940s and 1950s. Fortunately, some limited public opinion survey data are available and provide additional support for Bloomfield's generalizations.[8] In particular, these survey results depict prevailing American attitudes toward the perceived threat from international communism, the use of American troops to combat it abroad, and, more generally, how the public thought relations should be conducted with the Soviet Union.

Table 3.3 summarizes the results to a survey question asked on three different occasions in 1950 and 1951: "In general, how important do you think it is for the United States to try to stop the spread of communism?" On average, 80 percent of the American public identified the stopping of communism as a "very important" goal of the United States and another 8 percent said that this goal was "fairly important." Only 5 percent of the American public saw the stopping of communism as "not important." When the public was asked a similar question two years earlier about the threat of communism spreading to specific regions and countries, the results were virtually the same (Table 3.4). Between 70 and 80 percent of the public agreed with the statement that if Western Europe, South America, China, or Mexico were to go communist, it would make a difference to the United States.

The public also was quite willing to use American force to stop the spread of communism, even if it meant going to war. In two surveys, one in 1951 and another in 1952, the public was asked the following: "If you had to choose, which would you say is more important—to keep communism from spreading, or to stay out of

TABLE 3.3   ATTITUDES TOWARD STOPPING THE SPREAD
OF COMMUNISM, 1950–1951

In general, how important do you think it is for the United States to try to
stop the spread of communism in the world—very important, only fairly
important, or not important at all?

Survey Date	Very Important	Fairly Important	Not Important	Don't Know
January 1950	77%	10%	5%	8%
April 1950	83	6	4	7
June 1951	82	7	4	7

Source: Eugene R. Wittkopf, *Faces of Internationalism: Public Opinion and American Foreign Policy* (Durham, NC: Duke University Press, 1990), p. 169.

another war?" Less than 30 percent of the public chose to stay out of war, and about two thirds of the public was quite willing to take action to stop the spread of communism. Further, when the public was asked about the use of American forces to stop communist attacks against particular countries or regions, the response was usually overwhelmingly favorable. For communist attacks against the Philippines, the American-occupied zone in Germany at the time (and what eventually became West Germany), or Formosa (Taiwan) in Asia, the public favored going to war with the Soviet Union if these attacks occurred (Table 3.5). Similarly, the public favored using force if Central or South America were attacked by another country (Table 3.6). Indeed, the public appeared willing to sustain a worldwide effort to stop communism, including the use of armed forces.

Short of force, the American public also expressed support for efforts to stop communism. They were generally quite willing to provide economic and military assistance to countries threatened by international communism. In surveys by the National Opinion Research Center between January 1955 and January 1956, the average level of support for using economic aid to help countries opposing communist aggression was about 81 percent. Similarly, support for the use of military assistance, according to six surveys in 1950 and 1951, averaged 57 percent among the American public.[9]

Finally, the public remained highly suspicious of dealing with the Soviet Union in any political way during the height of the Cold War. In ten different surveys between April 1948 and November

TABLE 3.4 ATTITUDES TOWARD THE THREAT
OF COMMUNISM, 1948

Question Wording A: Do you think it makes much difference to the United
States whether the countries in Western Europe go communist or not?

Question Wording B: Do you think it makes much difference to the United
States whether Germany goes communist or not?

Question Wording C: How about China? [Do you think it makes much
difference to the United States whether China goes communist or not?]

Question Wording D: And how about the small countries in South America?
[Do you think it makes much difference to the United States whether they go
communist or not?]

Question Wording E: Do you think it makes much difference to the United
States whether China goes communist or not?

Question Wording F: How about Mexico—Do you think it would make much
difference to our country whether or not Mexico were to go communist?

Question Wording G: And how about the countries in South America? [Do you
think it makes much difference to our country whether they go communist or
not?]

Region/Country	Survey Date	Question Wording	Yes	No	Don't Know
Western Europe	July 1948	A	80%	10%	10%
Germany	July 1948	B	80	9	11
China	July 1948	C	73	14	13
South America	July 1948	D	70	15	15
China	Nov. 1948	E	71	17	12
Mexico	Nov. 1948	F	82	8	10
South America	Nov. 1948	G	80	8	12

Source: Eugene R. Wittkopf and James M. McCormick, "The Cold War Consensus: Did It Exist?"
Polity 22 (Summer 1990), p. 633.

1953, the American public was asked to respond to the following
question: "How do you feel about our dealings with Russia—Do you
think the United States should be more willing to compromise with
Russia, or is our present policy about right, or should we be even
firmer than we are today?" About 60 percent of the respondents
chose a response that called for the U.S. to "be even firmer." A policy
of "compromise" never enjoyed more than a 10 percent level of sup-

TABLE 3.5 ATTITUDES TOWARD THE USE OF TROOPS
TO RESPOND TO COMMUNIST ATTACKS, 1950

Do you think the United States should or should not go to war with Russia if
any of these things happen?

	Survey Date	Should	Should Not	No Opinion
1. Communist troops attack Philippines	July 1950	82%	9%	9%
2. Communist troops attack the American zone in Germany	July 1950	80	12	9
3. Communist troops attack Formosa	July 1950	58	25	16

Source: Eugene R. Wittkopf, *Faces of Internationalism: Public Opinion and American Foreign Policy* (Durham, NC: Duke University Press, 1990), p. 178.

port in the surveys. When the American public was asked its views on trading with the Soviet Union or about working out "a business arrangement to buy or sell more goods to each other," a majority occasionally supported such a position even during the height of the Cold War.[10] In this sense, the public appeared to be supportive of some contact with the Soviet Union, but that contact was to be primarily one that the U.S. had historically fostered with other states—a commercial relationship.

PATTERNS OF INTERACTIONS DURING THE COLD WAR, 1946–1972

Even with these deeply held views that constituted the Cold War consensus and the evident hostility between the United States and the Soviet Union, the Cold War interactions between these two states were not played out in a straight-line fashion of either increasing or decreasing levels of hostility. Instead, the Cold War was largely a series of ebbs and flows, from periods of greater to lesser hostilities and from periods of greater to lesser advantage by one power over the other. Neither party gained all the goals that had motivated this conflict, but neither party was able to vanquish the other. As these nations changed in their capabilities, and as the international system

TABLE 3.6 ATTITUDES TOWARD THE USE OF TROOPS
IN CENTRAL AND SOUTH AMERICA, 1947–1954

Question Wording A: Suppose some country attacked one of the countries in South America. Would you approve or disapprove of the United States sending armed forces along with other American countries to stop the attack?

Question Wording B: Suppose some big country attacks a South American nation. Would you approve or disapprove of the United States using its armed forces to help stop the attack?

Question Wording C: How about South America—Would you approve or disapprove of the United States using its armed forces to help stop any attack on a country in South America?

Question Wording D: Suppose some country in South or Central America does set up a communist government. Would you favor trying to get them out, even if we have to use armed force?

Survey Date	Question Wording	Favorable Response	Not Favorable	Don't Know/ Not Qualified/ No Opinion
June 1947	A	72%	12%	16%
April 1949	B	62	19	19
September 1949	C	50	30	20
June 1954	D	65	26	9

Source: Taken from a portion of Table IV in Eugene R. Wittkopf and James M. McCormick, "The Cold War Consensus: Did It Exist?" *Polity* 22 (Summer 1990), p. 641.

changed, the nature of the Cold War changed, and the first major attempt at accommodation occurred by the early 1970s.

Zbigniew Brzezinski has nicely captured these ebbs and flows in U.S.-Soviet relations over the height of the Cold War and has categorized them into six different phases through 1972.[11] Chronology 3.1 summarizes these phases along four dimensions: the relative international standing of these rivals in each phase, their relative military capabilities toward each other, their relative economic capabilities toward each other, and the relative stability of their domestic political environments.

As the chronology suggests, the early phase of the Cold War, as discussed in Chapter 2, was marked by uncertainty in the relationship between the two powers. By the 1948–1952 period, however, the Soviet Union was in a more assertive policy pattern, and the United

---

CHRONOLOGY 3.1 SIX PHASES OF THE COLD WAR, 1945–1972

PHASE I 1945–1947 Preliminary Skirmishing
1. International Standing U.S. advantage
2. Military Power probably a Soviet advantage
3. Economic Power overwhelming U.S. advantage
4. Domestic Policy Base uncertainty in both

PHASE II 1948–1952 Soviet Union Assertive
1. International Standing U.S. advantage
2. Military Power marginal Soviet advantage?
3. Economic Power decisive U.S. advantage
4. Domestic Policy Base U.S. advantage

PHASE III 1953–1957 United States Assertive
1. International Standing U.S. advantage
2. Military Power U.S. advantage
3. Economic Power U.S. advantage
4. Domestic Policy Base U.S. advantage

PHASE IV 1958–1963 Soviet Union Assertive
1. International Standing declining U.S. advantage
2. Military Power uncertain U.S. advantage
3. Economic Power U.S. advantage
4. Domestic Policy Base probable U.S. advantage

PHASE V 1963–1968 United States Assertive
1. International Standing marginal U.S. advantage
2. Military Power clear U.S. advantage
3. Economic Power U.S. advantage
4. Domestic Policy Base declining U.S. advantage

PHASE VI 1968–1972 Soviet Union Assertive
1. International Standing roughly equal
2. Military Power marginal U.S. advantage?
3. Economic Power U.S. advantage
4. Domestic Policy Base Soviet advantage

Note: The year 1972 was added to the end of phase VI, since the article used as a source was written in that year.

Source: Zbigniew Brzezinski, "How the Cold War Was Played," *Foreign Affairs* 51 (October 1972), pp. 203–204. Reprinted by permission of FOREIGN AFFAIRS, October 1972. Copyright 1972 by the Council on Foreign Relations, Inc.

States was largely relegated to responding to the Soviet challenge, whether that challenge occurred in Eastern Europe with the fall of Czechoslovakia, Hungary, and Poland and the Berlin blockade of 1948–1949, or in Asia with the establishment of communism in China and the outbreak of the Korean War. Hostility and conflict were sharp and intense.

By the 1953–1957 phase, though, the United States was in a better position to respond to this challenge. Indeed, in Brzezinski's estimation, the United States was preeminent on numerous fronts—politically, militarily, economically, and domestically—during these years. U.S. military capability was enhanced with a large-scale increase in its long-range nuclear bomber fleet, its adoption of a nuclear strategy of massive retaliation, and the conventional arms buildup in Western Europe. The American economy was expanding, and the gap in the strengths of the two economies was widening. The United States was in a strong position politically, too, and was largely able to work its political will in international affairs through the several alliance structures that it had created globally.

Even during this period of American ascendancy and intense rivalries between the two emerging superpowers, though, some nascent efforts at accommodation were attempted. After Stalin's death in 1953, President Dwight Eisenhower made a conciliatory speech to the Soviet Union, which responded with some informal contacts. In 1955, an Austrian State Treaty was agreed upon, in which Soviet and American troops would be withdrawn from that country. Austria became a neutral demilitarized state in Central Europe, and tensions were reduced somewhat in that region of the world.[12] In July of that same year, the "spirit of Geneva" blossomed with a summit conference among the leaders of the United States, the Soviet Union, France, and Great Britain.[13] Similarly, Soviet Premier Nikita Khrushchev, at the Twentieth Party Congress, renounced the inevitability of war among the capitalist states—an important Stalinist tenet—and raised the prospect that some longer term accommodation with the West might be possible.[14] "Peaceful coexistence" had entered the lexicon of American-Soviet diplomacy, but rivalries were still intense.

In the next phase of the Cold War, roughly about 1958 and beyond, hostilities heated up once again. The Soviet Union attempted to engage in a truly global policy and expanded its activities in Europe, the Middle East, Africa, Asia, and even in the Western Hemisphere. Soviet Premier and Communist Party Secretary Nikita Khrushchev proclaimed his nation's support for "national liberation struggles" around the world and attempted to place the United States on the defensive in numerous trouble spots. In Europe, for example, the United States and the Soviet Union confronted each other over the future of Berlin in 1958–1959 and 1961.[15]

In November 1958, the Soviet Union proposed to sign a separate peace treaty with the East German government, ending its control over the Soviet sector of Berlin and allowing the East Germans to control access to the British, French, and American sectors of Berlin.

(Since Berlin was located about 100 miles inside East Germany, it was particularly vulnerable to such action.) Its aim was to establish a "free city" of West Berlin, albeit under the ultimate control of the East German government, and to eliminate Western influence there. The Soviet Union did not act immediately, however. Instead, it served notice that the Soviet Union would give the West six months to solve this problem before it effected a change in status for Berlin. The United States viewed this declaration as an ultimatum and stood firm to resist it, although some accommodation by the West as to the number of military forces in Berlin were proposed. The Soviet deadline passed without incident, however, and no immediate change in the status of Berlin occurred. By mid-1959, the crisis over Berlin was further moderated when President Eisenhower invited the Soviet leader to visit the United States for an "informal conversation" on numerous matters, including Berlin. The first American visit by a Soviet leader served to provide a brief thaw in the Cold War.

In 1961, the Berlin issue was raised anew by Khrushchev with a newly elected American president, John F. Kennedy. The demands by the Soviets were essentially the same, a peace treaty that would include giving East Germany control over access to Berlin, an end to all access rights by the Western allied powers, and the establishment of West Berlin as a "free city" within East German territory. President Kennedy responded by indicating U.S. determination to defend West Berlin and undertook several actions to demonstrate that resolve. He called for an increase in military spending by the United States, the ordering to active duty of certain reserve units, and stepped-up efforts in procuring new conventional weapons. Premier Khrushchev answered with "one of the most belligerent speeches of his career" and spoke determinedly about the Soviet Union's intention to resist this "military hysteria" in the United States.[16] In a matter of days, on August 13, 1961, the Soviet Union and the East German government began to seal off East Berlin from the West by building a wall of wire, and eventually of mortar. The Berlin Wall was a response to the actions of the U.S. and its allies in Berlin and to the extraordinary flow of East German refugees to West Berlin. Moreover, the Berlin Wall, which stood until November 9, 1989, came to serve as a prominent symbol of the Cold War and the deep ideological and political gulf that existed between East and West.

In the developing world, three other confrontations occurred that reflected how the East versus West dimension dominated global politics during this period. In the central African Republic of the Congo (now called Zaire), the U.S. and the U.S.S.R. found themselves supporting opposite sides in a civil war that erupted after that nation gained independence from Belgium in June 1960. Both powers sent in considerable resources to bolster their allies as the Cold War was played out in an arena far from either power's territory. The United Nations eventually assumed a major role in this dispute and attempted to diffuse it through the sending of peacekeeping forces. In the Western Hemisphere, a similar phenomenon took place. With Fidel Castro's successful revolution in Cuba and his eventual declaration that he was a Marxist-Leninist, another series of confrontations between East and West were played out. The first occurred with the Bay of Pigs invasion in April 1961, and the second was played out in the Cuban Missile Crisis of October 1962. In Asia, the United States and the Soviet Union were deeply involved in the civil war in Laos. The United States pressed for the status quo—a neutral government in Laos—while the Soviet Union backed forces attempting to overthrow that regime. In this instance, and unlike the outcomes over Berlin and Cuba, a Declaration and Protocol on the Neutrality of Laos was received in July 1962.[17]

In the next phase, the Cold War reached its climax with the occurrence of the Cuban Missile Crisis and its aftermath and the escalation of the Vietnam War. During this period, the United States once again asserted its globalist posture and challenged the Soviet Union and its allies. Changes in governments from Brazil to Algeria and from Ghana to Indonesia produced a global environment more favorable to U.S. interests. Yet, as Brzezinski contends, this "new phase did not involve a return to the mutual hostility of the fifties."[18] Instead, more efforts at accommodation persisted. The negotiation of the Limited Test Ban Treaty in 1963 and the Nuclear Non-Proliferation Treaty in 1968, the opening of a "hot line" between Washington and Moscow, the beginning of a more differentiated strategy toward Eastern Europe on the part of the United States, and the continuance of superpower summitry—all suggested that the tenor of the Cold War was changing. Many of these events, and several international changes, had a profound impact on the stability of the Cold War consensus. We shall discuss them in more detail in the last portion of this chapter.

The final phase in Brzezinski's description of how the Cold War evolved is dated from 1969, with Richard Nixon's assumption of the presidency, and ends roughly with the Moscow Summit of 1972. At that summit, the Strategic Arms Limitation Talks (SALT I) produced two important nuclear arms pacts—an agreement limiting offensive arms and an agreement limiting defensive arms (the Anti-Ballistic Missile Treaty). The significance of these agreements lay in the mutual recognition by each superpower of the destructive capacity of its nuclear arsenal and the need to address this common dilemma. Equally significant, this summit, and indeed this entire period, recognized the essential equivalence of the U.S. and the U.S.S.R. in international affairs. (Note that in Chronology 3.1 neither power dominates across all four policy arenas as had largely been the case previously.) As a result, agreements for greater political, economic, and social cooperation were struck in addition to the military accords. The intense chill of the Cold War was replaced by the spirit of détente ("relaxation of tensions") between the superpowers. Although this period of détente proved to be somewhat short-lived (lasting only until about 1979), the values and beliefs of the Cold War consensus were now well on their way to being seriously challenged.

CHALLENGES TO THE COLD WAR CONSENSUS

While this East versus West approach as reflected in the Cold War consensus provided the basic prism for viewing international politics during the administrations from Truman through Johnson, it did begin to meet resistance. The predominant challenge came from the changing world environment—a world that was increasingly multipolar rather than bipolar. New power centers began to appear within the communist world, among the Western allies, and between the developed world and the Third World.[19] Other serious challenges to the postwar consensus were over the limits of American power as exercised in the Cuban Missile Crisis in October 1962, but even more so over America's Vietnam policy, particularly from 1965 to the early 1970s. While these latter two challenges were initiated abroad, their impact was profoundly manifested at home. In particular, Vietnam policy produced a full-blown domestic debate over the conduct of American foreign policy and is often cited as having signaled the death knell of the Cold War consensus.

THE SINO-SOVIET SPLIT

The policy split between the People's Republic of China and the Soviet Union, the two largest communist powers, challenged the Cold War assumption about the basic unity of international communism and the degree to which communism was directed from Moscow. Throughout the height of the Cold War, the United States had treated communism as a monolithic movement that everywhere took its orders from the Soviet Union. When these two powers became increasingly antagonistic toward one another in the late 1950s and early 1960s, the West, and the U.S. in particular, were challenged to rethink their assumption about communist unity.

In many ways, the Sino-Soviet split should not have been surprising to U.S. policymakers. Both historical rivalries and social-cultural differences had long characterized Soviet-Chinese relations. Historically, the Soviet Union had always wanted to gain access to and control over Asia, and, in turn, had always feared the growth of Chinese influence. Likewise, the Chinese had always perceived the Russians as an "imperialist" power and as a threat to their sovereignty and territorial integrity. Territorial disputes date back at least to the signing of the Treaty of Nerchinsk in 1659 and continued into the nineteenth and twentieth centuries as the disintegration of China took place at the hands of outside powers—including the Russians.[20]

On a cultural level, too, deep suspicions have always permeated Soviet and Chinese views of each other. The Soviets viewed the "Mongols" from the East with grave concern, while the Chinese saw the Soviet commissars with similar apprehension. To the Chinese, the Soviets were "foreigners" and "barbarians," intent upon destroying the glories of Chinese culture and society. Although the other "imperialist" powers were driven from China with Mao's successful revolution of 1949, the Soviets never left. Their continued presence reinforced the hostility on the part of the Chinese toward the Soviets.

Despite these profound suspicions of each other, a formal alliance was forged between the Soviet Union and the People's Republic of China in 1950. This pact raised the belief in official Washington that past differences were resolved rather than temporarily shelved. In fact, mutual self-interest apparently dictated this formal tie. The China of Mao Zedong, although successful in its domestic revolution, was still weak and hardly independent. The Soviets, badly in need of global partners in a world of capitalist powers, had much to gain by allying with their new ideological partner.[21] In a world that both China and the U.S.S.R. viewed as hostile to communist states, an alliance of these two large socialist regimes seemed essential.

But new differences between the two communist giants quickly began to arise and were superimposed on the disputes of the past. The new difficulties were mainly economic and ideological. Although the Soviet Union provided economic aid and technological assistance to China, neither was sufficient. Such low aid levels frustrated the Chinese aim of self-sufficiency, a goal that the Soviet Union did not share. Furthermore, the Soviet Union refused to help the Chinese build an independent nuclear force. This singular technological failure had been identified by some as the catalyst for the re-emergence of the Sino-Soviet split.[22]

On an ideological level, Mao's brand of communism, unlike what Soviet Premier Nikita Khrushchev was enunciating, did not call for a policy of "peaceful coexistence" with the West.[23] Nor did it call for emulating the Soviet model of heavy industrialization as the road to modernization and socialism. Further, the Soviets and the Chinese disagreed over the de-Stalinization movement, engaged in a rather continuous debate over the degree of diversity allowable among communist states and parties, and adopted differing views on the nature of the worldwide revolutionary movement.[24] In short, Mao's proclamations on the "correct" interpretation of Marxism-Leninism were increasingly perceived as direct challenges to Soviet leadership of the communist world.

By the late 1950s and into the early 1960s, the traditional Sino-Soviet split emerged full blown once again. With these two powers at odds with each other, American officials slowly began to recognize this global reality and the need for a policy that did not homogenize the communist powers.

DISUNITY IN THE EAST AND WEST

A second fissure in America's view of the communist world as wholly unified occurred in Eastern Europe. While the differences that emerged within the military alliance between the Soviet Union and its Eastern European neighbors—the Warsaw Pact—were nowhere as severe as the Sino-Soviet split, they again suggested that some change was needed in the unidimensional way in which the U.S. viewed and approached the communist world during the Cold War.

Uprisings in the German Democratic Republic (East Germany) in 1953 and Poland in 1956, outright revolt in Hungary later in 1956, and the call for "communism with a human face" in Czechoslovakia by 1968—all signaled a changed Eastern Europe. Considering also Yugoslavia's long-standing independent communist route, Albania's departure from the Warsaw Pact in 1968, and Romania's break with Eastern Europe over the recognition of the Federal Republic of Germany (West Germany) in 1967, Eastern Europe was hardly the model of alliance unity. It soon became apparent to American observers that exploiting the internal differences within the Eastern bloc was yet another way of moving these nations away from Soviet control. Furthermore, Eastern European nations themselves sought to expand economic advantage through diplomatic contact and recognition.[25] Failure to seize available economic and political opportunities could prove highly dysfunctional for the long-term American policy of combating international communism. Yet such opportunities would be lost if the world were conceptualized and treated only through the strict East Bloc versus West Bloc dichotomy.

But fissures in this unified East versus unified West definition of global politics were not confined to disharmony among the communist states. If the Soviet Union faced challenges from the People's Republic of China and Eastern Europe, America faced severe challenges within its own NATO alliance. By the early 1960s, the United States could no longer automatically expect the Western European states to follow its foreign policy lead. More accurately, no longer could the United States dictate Western policy. With the economic recovery of France and West Germany and the emergence of the European Common Market, a number of European states wanted to exercise a more independent role in world affairs—or at least not be so subservient to American policy prescriptions.

The best example of this fissure within the Western bloc was the foreign policy pursued by France under President Charles de Gaulle (1958–1969), the undisputed leader of this challenge to U.S. leadership. Under de Gaulle's guidance, France sought to restore some of its lost glory by reducing its strong linkage with the United States, weakening overall American influence over Western European affairs, and improving ties with the Soviet Union and Eastern Europe. De Gaulle's ultimate goal, in fact, was to break the "hegemonic" hold of both the Soviet Union and the United States on Europe and to establish a "community of European states" from the "Atlantic to the Urals."[26] In this global design, France would be able to reassert its central role in European politics.

To accomplish this, de Gaulle undertook a series of initiatives to reduce American influence on the continent and to weaken Soviet control as well. In 1958, shortly after gaining the French presidency, de Gaulle reportedly proposed a three-power directorate for the NATO alliance. Under this proposal, policy decisions within the Western alliance could only result with the unanimous consent of the United States, Great Britain, and France. In effect, such a proposal would allow a veto by France over NATO policy. Second, de Gaulle, despite American objections, continued with his plan to develop an independent French nuclear force, the *force de frappe*, and refused to join American and British (and later, German) plans for an integrated nuclear force. Third, and perhaps most dramatically, de Gaulle announced that France was withdrawing from the military structure of NATO in 1966. This last act was probably the single most potent challenge to Western unity. The appearance of political divisions within the NATO structure became a reality with de Gaulle's military withdrawal.

Both the Kennedy and Johnson administrations favored a strong, unified Europe, closely allied to the United States. De Gaulle did not favor such prominent U.S. involvement in European affairs. Instead, President de Gaulle took a series of actions to reshape Western European politics more in accord with his views and as a further means of frustrating American dominance. Thus he sought to reshape the European Common Market, increase French-German ties (at the expense of American-German relations), and isolate Great Britain from European affairs. De Gaulle attempted to reduce the supranational components of the Common Market—the power of the European Commission, for example—and to increase the emphasis on intergovernmental components within the organization. In effect, he wanted to allow the member states, especially France, more control over Common Market policy. To accomplish this, he proposed the Fouchet Plan, which was both a broadening of coverage of the Common Market concept to include political, cultural, and defense activities within a European union and a lessening of centralized control. Although this plan was ultimately rejected, it caused considerable controversy and division within the European Community.

President de Gaulle on two different occasions (1963 and 1967) vetoed British entry into the Common Market. Both vetoes were blows to American prestige, since the U.S. had pushed hard for British membership. The first veto was a particular affront because de Gaulle blamed his veto on the fact that Britain was too closely tied to the United States and might well be a surrogate for the Americans in European affairs. In essence, Britain was not sufficiently independent of the Americans to be admitted into European membership.

In yet a third step to combat American influence in Europe and to increase European independence, de Gaulle sought, largely unsuccessfully, to forge a strong alliance between France and West Germany. His strategy, once again, was to break the close ties between the United States and the Federal Republic. In the main, he was rebuffed by German Chancellor Konrad Adenauer and his successor, Ludwig Erhard, although he did manage to put into effect a German-French Treaty of Friendship in January 1963. Even the utility of the treaty as a lever against German-American ties was weakened, however, because a preamble that was strongly pro-American was added to the pact by the German Bundestag.[27]

BRIDGES ACROSS EAST AND WEST

Although de Gaulle's actions did not represent the only source of dissension within the Western alliance, they did represent the most consistent pattern of moving away from the bipolar world of the Cold War. But de Gaulle's challenge to a bipolar world did not stop with these actions toward America and Western Europe. He also opened up a series of contacts with Eastern Europe and took policy steps clearly at odds with the bloc-to-bloc relations of the previous decade. Such actions alarmed the Americans because de Gaulle was operating unilaterally and outside the policy of the Western Alliance; they undoubtedly pleased the Eastern Europeans because they granted these nations some legitimacy in the eyes of the West; and they probably caused a mixed reaction among the Soviets because, while granting recognition to Eastern Europe, they had the potential effect of undermining Warsaw Pact unity.

De Gaulle's strategy toward Eastern Europe was first to increase social, cultural, and economic ties and then to proceed toward political accommodation. For instance, educational exchanges between France and Eastern Europe were increased dramatically in the early to middle 1960s. Tourism between France and the East was increased. Trade relations were expanded, too. (In actual trade totals, though, German, British, and Italian trade increased more than did French trade with Eastern Europe during the 1960s.) More importantly, however, France initiated political contacts at the highest levels of government with the Eastern Europeans.

In the first part of his campaign to "build bridges" to the East, de Gaulle sent his Minister of Foreign Affairs, Couve de Murville, to several Eastern European countries. This action was dramatic in itself and was in response to the numerous political officials from Eastern Europe who had visited France. But even more dramatic was de Gaulle's decision to visit Eastern Europe himself. He subsequently made official visits to the Soviet Union in June 1966, Poland in September 1967, and Romania in May 1968. Additionally, he had accepted invitations to visit Czechoslovakia, Hungary, and Bulgaria, although these trips were not made before he left office.[28] The significance of these visits cannot be overstated. Since Western policy was not to yield any official diplomatic recognition to the Eastern European governments because of their failure to recognize West Germany, de Gaulle's behavior was a sharp break with the past.

Throughout these visits, differences between France and Eastern Europe were still evident over the question of Germany (with the Eastern Europeans continuing to call for the recognition of the East

German regime and de Gaulle steadfast in his support of the Federal Republic). Nevertheless, mutual calls for reconciliation were made. Moreover, de Gaulle's characterization of Europe's division into blocs as "artificial" and "sterile" epitomized his continuing effort to break the political divisions of the Cold War.[29] His effort gave impetus to greater contact between Eastern and Western Europe. For instance, the Federal Republic's Ostpolitik was slowly nurtured during this period under the chancellorship of Kurt Kiesinger (1966–1969) and began to reach fruition under Willy Brandt's leadership in 1969. French initiatives were important harbingers of changes in the politics of the European continent. For the Americans, these initiatives once again demonstrated the difficulties of conducting policy based on bipolarity in a world that was multipolar.

THE NONALIGNED MOVEMENT

In the post–World War II years, another major political force was unleashed: the desire for independence by colonial territories, especially throughout Asia and Africa. In fact, over ninety nations were granted or achieved political independence from the colonial powers from 1945 through 1980. Sixteen states became independent in the years 1945–1949, ten states in the 1950–1959 period, forty-three in 1960–1969, twenty-six in 1970–1979, and seven states between 1980 and 1990 (see Chronology 3.2).[30] This surge of independence started in Asia and northern Africa. Pakistan, India, and the Philippines, among others, gained independence in the late 1940s, while Tunisia, Cambodia, Morocco, Libya, and Malaysia, among others, gained their sovereignty by the middle 1950s. The decolonization of the African continent occurred mainly in the early 1960s, although Ghana and Guinea led the way by gaining independence in the late 1950s. By the end of the 1960s, in fact, some sixty-eight new nations were part of the international system, and this process continued into the 1970s, albeit at a slower pace.

This decolonization movement proved to be a third major challenge to the bipolar approach that was at the base of American foreign policy during the Cold War years. These new states generally refused to tie themselves into the formal bloc structures of the Cold War, preferring instead to follow an independent, nonaligned foreign policy course. Moreover, these new states actually started a nonaligned movement to demonstrate their independence.

The founder of this nonaligned movement was Jawaharlal Nehru of India, who as early as 1946 had stated that India "will follow an independent policy, keeping away from the power politics of groups aligned one against another."[31] He continued his efforts for this

---

CHRONOLOGY 3.2   THE GROWTH OF NEW NATIONS 1945–1990

Nations Gaining Independence 1945–1949

Bhutan	India	Korea, North	Pakistan
Burma	Indonesia	Korea, South	Philippines
Germany, East	Israel	Laos	Sri Lanka
Germany, West	Jordan	Lebanon	Taiwan

Nations Gaining Independence 1950–1959

Ghana	Libya	Morocco	Tunisia
Guinea	Malaysia	Sudan	Vietnam
Cambodia			

Nations Gaining Independence 1960–1969

Algeria	Equatorial	Maldives	Somalia
Barbados	Guinea	Mali	Swaziland
Benin	Gabon	Malta	Tanzania
Botswana	Gambia	Mauritania	Togo
Burkina Faso	Guyana	Mauritius	Trinidad and
Burundi	Ivory Coast	Nauru	Tobago
Cameroon	Jamaica	Niger	Uganda
Central African	Kenya	Nigeria	Western Samoa
Republic	Kuwait	Rwanda	South Yemen
Chad	Lesotho	Senegal	Zaire
Congo	Madagascar	Sierra Leone	Zambia
Cyprus	Malawi	Singapore	

Nations Gaining Independence 1970–1979

Angola	Dominica	Papua New	Seychelles
Bahamas	Fiji	Guinea	Solomon Islands
Bahrain	Grenada	Qatar	Suriname
Bangladesh	Guinea-Bissau	St. Lucia	Tonga
Cape Verde	Kiribati	St. Vincent and	Tuvalu
Comoros	Mozambique	the Grenadines	United Arab
Djibouti	Oman	São Tomé and	Emirates
		Príncipe	

Nations Gaining Independence 1980–1990

Antigua and	Brunei	St. Kitts and	Zimbabwe
Barbuda	Namibia	Nevis	
Belize		Vanuatu	

Source: The dates of independence for the new nations from 1945 to 1989 were taken from Bruce Russett and Harvey Starr, *World Politics: The Menu for Choice* (New York: W. H. Freeman and Company, 1989), pp. 593–599.

---

movement once he reached power in India, and he then proceeded to help organize the Conference of Afro-Asian States held at Bandung, Indonesia, in 1955. This conference is sometimes cited as the initial effort toward the development of a nonaligned movement, since it was the first time that former colonial territories met without the presence of European powers. However, the tone of the debate and the principles adopted have been criticized recently as not fully reflecting the principles of nonalignment.[32]

The more formal institutionalization of this movement was the Belgrade Conference in September 1961. Spurred on by the organizational efforts of such leaders as Tito of Yugoslavia, Nasser of Egypt, Nkrumah of Ghana, and Sukarno of Indonesia, as well as Nehru, this conference of twenty-five nations produced a statement of principles for those nations seeking a "third way" in world politics. Several critical passages in the Declaration of the Belgrade Conference of Heads of State and Government of Nonaligned Countries are worth quoting because they demonstrate the rejection of the bloc politics of the Cold War and outline the policy course that these states wanted to pursue:

> The participating countries consider...that the principles of peaceful existence are the only alternative to the cold war and to a possible general nuclear catastrophe. The non-aligned countries represented at this Conference do not wish to form a new bloc and cannot be a bloc. They sincerely desire to cooperate with any Government which seeks to contribute to the strengthening of confidence and peace in the world.... They consider that the further extension of the non-committed area of the world constitutes the only possible and indispensable alternative to the policy of total division of the world into blocs, and intensification of cold war policies. The non-aligned countries provide encouragement and support to all peoples fighting for their independence and equality.[33]

In effect, these states not only wanted to reject bloc politics, they also wanted to expand the areas of the world that were part of the nonaligned movement. They saw their contribution to world peace as directly opposite to the way world politics had been conducted up to that time—taking an active part in world affairs through their own initiatives and in their own way without going through coordinated actions of a bloc of states. More specifically, these states rejected military alliances with, or military bases for, the superpowers so that the politics of the Cold War could be extended through such intermediary states. In this sense, nonalignment did not mean noninvolvement or total rejection of global politics, but it did mean the rejection of the way international politics had been played during the Cold War.[34]

This movement proved highly successful, and adherents to its beliefs rapidly increased in number. In the space of less than a decade, the membership had doubled, with fifty-three nations attending the Third Summit Meeting in Lusaka, Zambia, in September

1970.[35] These new members came primarily from colonial territories as they gained their independence in the early to middle 1960s. Essentially, then, the new participants in world politics were joining the ranks of the nonaligned. These states wanted neither to infringe upon their newly gained independence by the formal incorporation into the East-West bloc structures nor to return to the influence of their former colonial powers, the nations which largely composed these blocs. The United States thus found that the new states would not join in its efforts against international communism.

At the same time, the United States was always a bit skeptical of the nonaligned movement and its degree of independence in world politics. Indeed, a continuous debate existed from the movement's inception over how "nonaligned" the movement was. The organization's policy pronouncements have often been more critical of the actions of the West than of the East, and it was typically more critical of capitalism than of socialism. Further, several prominent nations within the organization had close ties with the Soviet Union. Cuba, Vietnam, and Afghanistan, among others, could hardly be viewed as "nonaligned" in global politics during the entire history of this movement.

Despite this anamoly within the nonaligned movement, the movement itself provided yet another reason for American policymakers to conclude that global politics would not conform to their image of East versus West; they were further confronted with the need to consider their policy toward this new and powerful movement and, ultimately, toward international politics in general.

THE MISSILES OF OCTOBER: THE FIRST CRISIS OF CONFIDENCE

The last two important challenges to America's Cold War consensus are summarized under the heading of two major foreign policy events: the Vietnam War and the Cuban Missile Crisis. Although these two episodes are foreign policy events, their impact was as much domestic as it was foreign, and they profoundly affected American domestic thinking about the world. These episodes brought home to American leaders and to the American people—in most dramatic fashion—the limits of the United States in influencing the Soviet Union and the Third World areas. Both events illustrate the limited extent to which American beliefs and values were able to create the global design envisioned by the Cold War consensus.

The Cuban Missile Crisis of October 16–28, 1962, was the closest that the United States and the Soviet Union had come to nuclear confrontation since the advent of atomic power. Cuba, under the leadership of Fidel Castro since 1959, had by this time declared itself a "Marxist-Leninist" state and had sought assistance from the Soviet Union against alleged American intrigues. The crisis centered on the introduction of "offensive" intermediate-range ballistic missiles into Cuba by the Soviet Union during the fall of 1962. Such Soviet actions were in violation of its stated commitment to introduce only "defensive weapons" into Cuba.

Upon the discovery of the "offensive" weapons on October 16, 1962, President John F. Kennedy set out to devise an appropriate strategy to remove these missiles from territory only ninety miles from American shores. After a week of highly secret deliberations through his Executive Committee of the National Security Council, President Kennedy finally announced on October 22, 1962, that a naval quarantine of 800 miles around Cuba would be set up to interdict the further shipment of these weapons. Furthermore, President Kennedy threatened the Soviet Union with a nuclear response if the missiles in Cuba were used against the United States. In addition, a series of other measures, ranging from actions through the Organization of American States and the United Nations to bilateral contacts with the Soviet Union, were undertaken to remove the missiles already in place. After another week of tense confrontation and diplomatic exchanges of notes, an agreement was worked out for the removal of the missiles by the Soviet Union under United Nations supervision. The United States, in turn, pledged that it would not attempt to overthrow the Castro regime in Cuba.

This episode had several important lessons for the future of Soviet-American relations. First, the crisis fully brought home to both Soviet and American leaders (and their populaces) that nuclear anniliation was a real possibility. Mutual assured destruction was no longer an abstract theory. While the United States may have been relatively safe from Soviet nuclear attacks in the 1950s, the development of intercontinental missiles, and even the intermediate range missiles that had been placed in Cuba, demonstrated that this condition no longer existed. Americans were now vulnerable to Soviet nuclear power, just as the Soviets were to the U.S. nuclear arsenal.

Mutual survival was more important than the unilateral interests of either country. Despite their avowed antipathy toward one another, then, neither the Soviet Union nor the United States would want to back the other into a corner where all-out war (and nuclear holocaust) or surrender were the only options. This caution was also reflected in the various personal accounts of the decision making during the crisis and in the importance that was attached to "placing ourselves in the other country's shoes."[36]

Such caution also yielded a second lesson: both the United States and the Soviet Union were capable of evaluating in a rational way their national interests and global consequences. This lesson was especially important for American policymakers. Because of the Cold War consensus, Americans tended to view skeptically the decision making of the Soviet Union. Being so consumed by Marxist-Leninist ideology, would the Soviets be able to assess the costs and the consequences of their actions and respond prudently? The answer was clearly yes, as reflected in the outcome of the crisis and in the subsequent scholarly research on this event.[37] Rational policymaking with the Soviet Union might just be possible.

Finally, and most importantly, the episode suggested that the Soviet Union and the United States were going to be major participants in international relations for a long time and that each state might just as well devise policies that would acknowledge the interests and rights of the other. Neither superpower would be able to dislodge the other from its place in world politics. For the Americans, any vision of "rolling back communism" was illusory at best; for the Soviets, any vision of capitalist collapse was similarly myopic. Thus the Americans and the Soviets learned that accommodation with their major adversary was possible—and necessary—for mutual survival. In this sense, and somewhat ironically, the nuclear showdown over the missiles in Cuba has been cited as the beginnings of détente between the Soviet Union and the United States.

In sum, then, the Cuban Missile Crisis—even with the Soviet humiliation over the removal of its missiles from Cuba—challenged the Cold War view that the Soviet Union or communism could be quickly and easily dislodged from global politics. A foreign policy based solely upon this assumption was therefore likely to remain frustrating and self-defeating. (Although this point is difficult to demonstrate, the Soviet Union probably learned similar lessons about the United States.) At the same time, and equally important, the Cuban Missile Crisis illustrated the possibility of negotiating with an implacable foe—even over the most fundamental of questions—and accommodating a world of different political and social systems.

THE VIETNAM DEBACLE

American involvement in Vietnam began at the end of World War II and lasted for almost thirty years, until the evacuation of American embassy personnel from Saigon at the end of April 1975. That involvement spanned six administrations, from President Truman to President Ford, and was largely guided by the values and beliefs of the Cold War consensus. This involvement, however, produced the most divisive foreign policy debate in the history of the Republic, and it ultimately produced a major foreign policy defeat for the United States as well. At home, the most important outcome of the Vietnam War was that it signaled a halt to the Cold War foreign policy approach—at least until the emergence of the Reagan administration in the 1980s. Before we assess the overall impact of Vietnam, let us present a brief sketch of American involvement there.

THE ORIGINS OF INVOLVEMENT, 1945–1963

Although President Roosevelt gave the first hints of American interest in Indochina (an area that is now Cambodia, Laos, and Vietnam) when he indicated a preference for an international trusteeship arrangement at the end of World War II, the events of the immediate postwar years and the rise of the Cold War propelled the U.S. in a different direction. While the Truman administration had serious reservations about identifying itself with colonialism, Soviet actions toward Eastern Europe, communist success in China, and uncertainty about the political leanings of Ho Chi Minh, the leader of the Vietnamese independence movement, ultimately tipped the U.S. to assume "a distinctly pro-French 'neutrality.' " As a result, the United States began clandestinely providing economic and military assistance to France in the late 1940s in its war against the Vietminh (the followers of Ho Chi Minh).[38] In addition, the Truman administration was not prepared to lose another country to communism or to forfeit the valuable raw materials of the region, such as rubber, oil, tin, and tungsten. French domination was, therefore, preferred to "Commie domination of Indochina," as Secretary of State Dean Acheson later put it.[39]

After the outbreak of the Korean War, which seemed to confirm Washington's suspicions about Soviet global intentions, American involvement deepened, as did the war in Indochina against the French. Over $133 million of military hardware was committed to the French for Indochina, and another $50 million was sent in economic and technical assistance to the governments that the French has established in Indochina. Throughout the rest of the Truman administration, the United States provided more and more military and economic assistance. In fiscal year 1951, military aid totaled $426 million and economic aid was an additional $22 million, while in fiscal year 1952, the amounts reached $520 million for the former and $25 million for the latter. Such aid constituted 40 percent of the total costs of the ongoing war of the French against the insurgents in Indochina.[40] Most importantly, perhaps, by now the Truman administration had begun to commit American prestige into a war that was still fought by the French.

The Eisenhower administration took the rationale for American involvement in Vietnam one step further by invoking much of the language of the Cold War over the conflict there and by continuing to increase assistance to the non-communist and French-backed Vietnamese government. President Eisenhower and his assistants, for example, invoked diplomatic and strategic language tying American security to what happened in Southeast Asia and regularly used language of the Cold War to describe the threat posed by the Vietminh. In a 1954 news conference, President Eisenhower referred to the "falling dominoes" in Southeast Asia, and Secretary of State John Foster Dulles hinted at the role of the Chinese communists in causing the unrest in Indochina.[41]

Yet, the Eisenhower administration did not go much beyond providing economic and military assistance throughout its years in office. In fact, it explicitly ruled out the use of American force to rescue the French from defeat at the decisive battle of Dien Bien Phu against the Vietminh in 1954, and instead sought to achieve a negotiated outcome between the French and the Vietminh at a 1954 Geneva conference on Indochina.[42] The results of that conference were incomplete at best. They called for an armistice between the parties, a temporary division of the country at the 17th parallel, and elections in 1956 to unify the country. The United States neither signed these accords nor endorsed them, and the all-Vietnam elections scheduled for 1956 were never held. Nonetheless, these accords did purchase some breathing room for the non-communist forces in Vietnam, and the United States promptly proceeded to help such forces.

Indeed, the United States quickly became the principal supporter of the non-communist government of Premier (later President) Ngo Dinh Diem in South Vietnam. Diem, who had been invited back to Vietnam to form a government in mid-1954, was largely opposed by the French and hence came to be identified as "America's Mandarin." Moreover, President Eisenhower and Secretary of State Dulles believed Diem represented the best prospect for developing a non-communist Vietnam. Between 1955 and 1961 the United States provided $1 billion in aid to Diem. By 1961, South Vietnam was the fifth largest recipient of U.S. foreign assistance.[43]

Even with this massive assistance, the stability of that government was still precarious. On the one hand, the Diem regime in South Vietnam still had not rallied much domestic support. Instead, the regime had become even more authoritarian as it sought to main-

MAP 3.1   Vietnam, 1954–1975

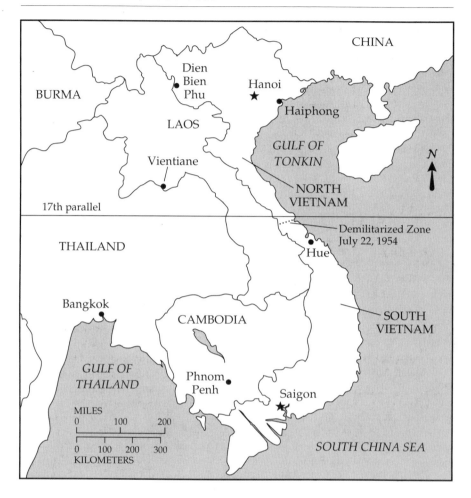

tain its hold on power. On the other hand, North Vietnam had decided to change its tactics from a "political struggle" to an "armed
struggle" in its effort to achieve a united Vietnam. And in another
important development, the National Liberation Front for South
Vietnam, the Vietcong, was officially founded in 1960, with its membership rising to 300,000 within one year.

Upon taking office, therefore, President Kennedy expanded the
military and economic assistance to South Vietnam and contemplated sending in American military forces to prevent the fall of
South Vietnam to communism. Yet, he did not quite take that step.

Instead, he incrementally enlarged the number of American military "advisors" in South Vietnam from 685 when he took office to about 16,000 by the time of his assassination.[44] Still, President Kennedy appeared to commit the U.S. to the defense of South Vietnam, although, by one account, he did not give an "unqualified commitment to the goal of saving South Vietnam from Communism."[45] Nonetheless, President Kennedy's actions had taken the U.S. further down the path to military involvement and may well have continued in that direction if he had remained in office.[46]

AMERICAN MILITARY INVOLVEMENT IN VIETNAM

It was, however, President Lyndon Johnson who fully changed the U.S. involvement in South Vietnam from a political to a military one. He both broadened and deepened the American commitment to preserve a non-communist South Vietnam and was ultimately the one who decided to send American military forces into Vietnam.

As the stability of the South Vietnamese government worsened (some nine changes of government occurred from the time of the coup against President Diem in November 1963 until February 1965) and as North Vietnamese and Vietcong successes increased, the Johnson administration sought a new strategy to hold on to South Vietnam.[47] As early as February 1964, American clandestine operations were underway against North Vietnam. Ultimately, these actions led to attacks by the North Vietnamese upon two American destroyers, the *Maddox* and the *C. Turner Joy* in the Gulf of Tonkin, off the North Vietnamese coast in August 1964. These actions were quickly used by the Johnson administration to seek congressional approval of American military forces in Southeast Asia.[48] In a matter of hours, Congress approved the Gulf of Tonkin Resolution, which authorized the president to take "all necessary measures" in Southeast Asia (see Chapter 7).

For the Johnson administration, this resolution became the equivalent of a declaration of war, and retaliatory air strikes were quickly ordered. By December 1964, U.S. air attacks against North Vietnamese infiltration routes through Laos had begun. By February 1965, "Operation Rolling Thunder," a bombing strategy to weaken North Vietnam's resistance and bring it to the negotiating table, was initiated. By March 1965, the first American ground troops landed, and a rapid buildup in these forces was ordered in July of that year.[49] Indeed, the number of forces continued to escalate until they ultimately reached over a half million American soldiers by late 1968.

Despite this vast commitment of men and materiel, the war continued to go badly for the South Vietnamese and the United States. The Tet offensive (named after the occurrence of the lunar new year), perhaps more than any other event, brought this home to Americans. This offensive consisted of widespread attacks by the North Vietnamese and the Vietcong over a six-month period beginning at the end of January 1968. While the offensive was ultimately a military failure for the North Vietnamese costing them tens of thousands of lives, it was a political success in that it showed the vulnerability of South Vietnam, despite years of war. Moreover, the impact of this offensive within the U.S. was immediate, with a sharp drop in the American public's optimism about the war.[50] Additionally, the political pressure on President Johnson became so severe that, in March 1968, he voluntarily withdrew from considering a reelection campaign.

President Richard Nixon, elected as Johnson's successor in part on a commitment to change Vietnam policy, adopted a different strategy. He began to decrease American military involvement through a policy of "Vietnamization" of the war—a policy whereby the South Vietnamese military would replace American soldiers in the war—and also pursued the peace negotiations (begun originally in mid-1968 in Paris) through both open and secret channels. The Vietnamization program proceeded fairly quickly, but a negotiated settlement proved more difficult.

With this policy, American forces in Vietnam were reduced from about 543,000 shortly after President Nixon took office to about 25,000 by the end of his first term in office.[51] As part of this Vietnamization strategy, the Nixon administration undertook an invasion of Cambodia in April 1970, with the expressed purpose of wiping out the North Vietnamese sanctuaries in order to accommodate the departure of American forces and to bolster the South Vietnamese government against further attack. To many Americans, though, this action appeared to be a widening of the war. Protest erupted across the U.S., and tragedy struck on two college campuses (Kent State University and Jackson State) where student protestors were killed. Further opposition to the war resulted.

After one final North Vietnamese offensive in the spring of 1972 had been repulsed, and after further American bombing of the North near the end of the negotiations, a settlement was finally arranged. After continuous involvement by the U.S. since 1965 and the loss of over 58,000 American lives and countless Vietnamese, a cease-fire agreement, formally called "The Agreement on Ending the War and Restoring the Peace," was signed on January 27, 1973.[52] The agreement called for the withdrawal of all Americans and the return of prisoners of war. In addition, it allowed the North Vietnamese to keep their military forces in South Vietnam and left open the question of the future of South Vietnam. On balance, the agreement was less a "peace with honor," as it was portrayed at the time, and more a mechanism for enabling the U.S. to leave Vietnam.[53]

Although the cease-fire reduced the level of fighting and provided a way for the United States to extricate itself from Vietnam, it did not totally end the war nor end the American involvement in Vietnam. The end of American involvement really came two years later, during the Ford administration. With the fall of Saigon and the final evacuation of all American personnel, the American involvement in Vietnam finally ceased on April 30, 1975. It ended with a humiliating defeat for a policy based on preventing communist success in that Southeast Asian country. This defeat produced searching policy reflection at that point; but even before, the basic premises of America's Vietnam involvement had come under scrutiny and intense debate.

SOME LESSONS FROM VIETNAM

Several political and military explanations have been offered for the American defeat. Some have focused, for example, on the military tactics that the U.S. used in responding in Vietnam. The use of a policy of "graduated response" did not allow the U.S. to take maximum advantage of its military capabilities. Others point to the failure to adjust the military strategy to the nature of the unconventional war in Vietnam and the futility of the "search-and-destroy" approach against the adversary.[54] Still others point to the political problems associated with the war. The "legitimacy" of the South Vietnamese government remained a problem, and its degree of domestic support weakened its efforts.[55] By contrast, the determination and will of the North Vietnamese was much greater than many had suggested. Even under the pressure of intensive bombing and high casualties, they continued to fight. Yet another explanation focuses on the loss of support for the war back home. Both the American public and the Congress ultimately were unwilling to sustain support for the war. Some no longer supported the war because they believed that it was not being prosecuted fully, while others did so because they no longer believed that it was moral or ethical to engage in this conflict. Hence this foreign policy defeat, and various explanations for it, produced a significant reexamination of the Cold War consensus and was largely responsible for ultimately undermining it.

TABLE 3.7   THE DOMINO THEORY IN SOUTHEAST ASIA

Basic Value Imperative: Contain the influence of Communist China

Axiom 1: If South Vietnam falls, then wars of liberation are encouraged in Southeast Asia.

Axiom 2: If wars of liberation occur, then other countries will go communist.

Axiom 3: If Southeast Asia goes communist, then Communist China will gain influence.

Policy Prescription: South Vietnam must be defended.

American policy toward Vietnam, of course, was guided by an elegant, albeit simple, theory about Southeast Asia. Dubbed the "domino theory" after President Eisenhower's reference as early as 1954, this theory was derived directly from the assumptions of the Cold War consensus. The theory contended that change is a function of "wars of liberation," inspired by communist forces (in this case, the Chinese communists). Success of one of these wars of liberation would eventually produce wars in neighboring countries. In time, the whole region would be lost to the communist movement. As a consequence, preventing the fall of one of the "dominoes" (i.e., South Vietnam) was essential to prevent the collapse of the whole region to international communism. Table 3.7 summarizes the assumptions and the important deduction of the domino theory as applied to Southeast Asia and South Vietnam.[56]

The domino theory made many assumptions consistent with the Cold War consensus: the world was divided between communists and anti-communists; change is inspired by communist forces; American security is directly threatened by political change in Third World areas; and the United States has the responsibility for maintaining global order. Virtually all of these assumptions—and the overall utility of the domino theory—were challenged in the domestic debate that developed over Vietnam policy.

The first consequence of such domestic turmoil was the questioning of the U.S. role in the world. Should the U.S. be responsible for political activity everywhere in the world—especially in a country half a world away with only the most tangential relationship to American national security? Was the American public willing to support and legitimize such actions? Was the public willing to support a policy that had only the most lofty goals in international affairs? The

FIGURE 3.1 THE "MISTAKE" QUESTION ON VIETNAM

Percentages of responses to the question: "In view of the developments since we entered the fighting in Vietnam, do you think the U. S. made a mistake sending troops to fight in Vietnam?" (Gallup Organization data)

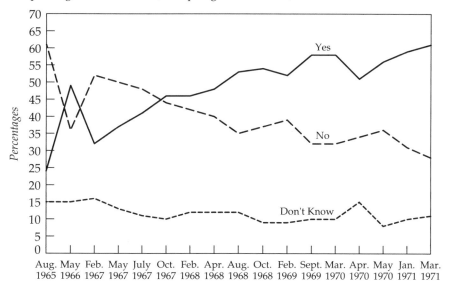

Source: Adapted from a portion of Table 3.3 in John E. Mueller, *War, Presidents and Public Opinion* (New York: John Wiley & Sons, Inc., 1973), pp. 54-55.

American public's response to these questions was generally a re-sounding "No." There were limits to American power; there were limits to America's responsibility; there were limits to how much globalism the American public would tolerate. The role of the United States would need to be much more limited in scope.

The Vietnam experience had a second consequence for Ameri-can foreign policy. Foreign policy goals became a source of public de-bate. Public opinion challenged the leadership policy on Vietnam. By 1968 and early 1969, a majority of the American public viewed Viet-nam as a "mistake."[57] (See the public opinion data in Figure 3.1.) In the Congress, too, divisions were apparent between "liberals" and "conservatives" and between "hawks" and "doves" on foreign pol-icy matters.[58] Such divisions stood in sharp contrast to the situation just a few years earlier, when "liberals" and "conservatives," despite their differences on domestic matters, stood together on foreign pol-icy issues. After the Vietnam experience, no such harmony was evident. Foreign policy matters had now become a subject for domestic debate.

The third consequence followed from the first two. The value and belief consensus that had guided the conduct of foreign policy since the end of World War II was shattered. No longer could the American foreign policy elite depend upon general support for their foreign policy goals and actions. Moreover, the foreign policy elite was divided among itself about the relative role of the United States in the world.

CONCLUDING COMMENTS

More than any other action, the Vietnam War appears responsible for ultimately shattering the Cold War consensus and producing a reassessment of America's approach to international affairs. Moreover, the public, as well, had seemingly changed its views from what it had embraced in the 1950s. While the threat of communism remained real to many Americans in the post-Vietnam era, Americans were no longer as enthusiastic about using economic and military aid or American soldiers to combat it. Furthermore, the public was much more favorable to greater accommodation with the Soviets and less inclined to confrontation with them.[59]

Thus, Vietnam, coupled with these other Cold War challenges, produced a foreign policy vacuum at home. The nation was ready for new ideas to deal with the rest of the world. A unique opportunity existed for succeeding presidents to develop a new foreign policy approach. Each new administration for the next two decades attempted to initiate this new change of direction. In the following chapters, we survey the realist and idealist approaches of the Nixon and Carter administrations, a modified Cold War approach by the Reagan administration, and a pragmatic approach by the Bush administration, and we evaluate their relative success in shaping a new direction in U.S. foreign policy.

NOTES

1. Lincoln P. Bloomfield, *In Search of American Foreign Policy: The Humane Use of Power* (New York: Oxford University Press, Inc., 1974).

2. J. William Fulbright, *The Arrogance of Power* (New York: Vintage Books, 1966), p. 77. His conclusion on American policy choice in this dilemma is on p. 78.

3. See the Rusk-McNamara Report to President Kennedy in *The Pentagon Papers, New York Times Edition* (New York: Bantam Books, Inc., 1971), p. 150, for a statement of American objectives in Southeast Asia.

4. Barry M. Blechman and Stephen S. Kaplan, *Force Without War* (Washington, D.C.: The Brookings Institution, 1978), p. 12. The examples are from p. 13. Emphasis in original.

5. Ibid., p. 517. Their skepticism over the long term is at p. 532.

6. As Ernest May points out, however, American policymakers have often used historical analogies badly by preparing for the last war. See his *"Lessons" of the Past*, especially his discussion of the Korean War and Truman's use of the 1930s as the analogue for U.S. policy, pp. 81–86.

7. On this "skills thinking" in the American approach to foreign policy, see Stanley Hoffmann, *Gulliver's Troubles, or the Setting of American Foreign Policy* (New York: McGraw-Hill, 1968), pp. 148–161.

8. I am indebted to Eugene R. Wittkopf for sharing these public opinion poll results with me. A more complete analysis of public opinion during the Cold War years is presented in Eugene R. Wittkopf and James M. McCormick, "The Cold War Consensus: Did It Exist?" *Polity* (Summer 1990), pp. 627–653. This section draws upon this research.

9. Ibid., p. 635.

10. Ibid., p. 648.

11. Zbigniew Brzezinski, "How the Cold War Was Played," *Foreign Affairs* 51 (October 1972): 181–204. Our subsequent discussion of these phases is drawn from his work and from the others cited below (see note 12).

12. See John Lewis Gaddis, *The Soviet Union and the United States: An Interpretative History* (New York: John Wiley & Sons, Inc., 1978), pp. 214–215; and Seyom Brown, *The Faces of Power* (New York: Columbia University Press, 1983), p. 92.

13. Gaddis, *The Soviet Union and the United States: An Interpretative History*, p. 215.

14. Paul Marantz, "Prelude to Détente: Doctrinal Change Under Khrushchev," *International Studies Quarterly* 19 (December 1975): 510.

15. Brown, *The Faces of Power*, pp. 138–145.

16. Ibid., pp. 222–233. The quotes are at p. 229, with the second one from Khrushchev directly.

17. Ibid., p. 214.

18. Brzezinski, "How the Cold War Was Played," p. 194.

19. In his review and critique of Henry Kissinger's approach to international politics, Richard Falk identifies some of these characteristics as the basis for the growth of multipolarity and shows how they fit into Kissinger's foreign policy design. See Richard Falk, "What's Wrong with Henry Kissinger's Foreign Policy," *Alternatives* 1 (March 1975): 86. An earlier analysis of the "challenge to consensus" can be found in Howard Bliss and M. Glen Johnson, *Beyond the Water's Edge: America's Foreign Policies* (Philadelphia: J. B. Lippincott Co., 1975), pp. 1–26. Their analysis focuses primarily on the impact of Vietnam.

20. For an informative discussion of these historical antipathies, see Harrison E. Salisbury, *War Between China and Russia* (New York: W. W. Norton & Company, 1969), pp. 13–52. Also see John G. Stoessinger, *Nations in Darkness: China, Russia, and America*, 3rd ed. (New York: Random House, 1978), pp. 212–218; and Robert C. North, *The Foreign Relations of China*, 2nd ed. (Encino and Belmont, CA: Dickenson Publishing Company, Inc., 1974), pp. 112–122, for two other lucid discussions of this dispute.

21. Stoessinger, *Nations in Darkness*, pp. 214–215.

22. For the centrality of military issues in the Sino-Soviet split, see North, *The Foreign Relations of China*, pp. 41–46, 121.

23. Ibid., pp. 116–120.

24. These issues and others are discussed in Donald S. Zagoria, *The Sino-Soviet Conflict 1956–1961* (Princeton, NJ: Princeton University Press, 1962).

25. The extent of these East-West contacts is analyzed in Josef Korbel, *Détente in Europe: Real or Imaginary?* (Princeton, NJ: Princeton University Press, 1972).

26. For a summary of de Gaulle's vision of European and global politics, see ibid., 40–60; Alfred Grosser, *French Foreign Policy Under DeGaulle* (Boston: Little, Brown & Co., 1965), especially pp. 13–28; Edward A. Kolodziej, *French International Policy under DeGaulle and Pompidou* (Ithaca, NY: Cornell University Press, 1974); Edward A. Kolodziej, "Revolt and Revisionism in the Gaullist Global Vision: An Analysis of French Strategic Policy," *The Journal of Politics* 33 (May 1971): 448–477; Roy C. Macridis, "The French Force de Frappe," and William G. Andrews, "DeGaulle and NATO," in Roy Macridis, ed., *Modern European Governments: Cases in Comparative Policy Making* (Englewood Cliffs, NJ: Prentice-Hall, Inc., 1976), pp. 75–116. These sources were used for our discussion here.

27. On this point, see Josef Joffe, "The Foreign Policy of the German Federal Republic," in Roy C. Macridis, ed., *Foreign Policy in World Politics*, 5th ed. (Englewood Cliffs, NJ: Prentice-Hall, Inc., 1976), p. 141.

28. This discussion draws upon Korbel, *Détente in Europe*, pp. 40–60.

29. Ibid., p. 58.

30. The number of newly independent states from 1945–1980 was calculated from Appendix B, "Characteristics of States in the Contemporary International System," in Bruce Russett and Harvey Starr, *World Politics: The Menu for Choice* (San Francisco: W. H. Freeman and Company, 1981), pp. 575–583. For the period from 1981–1990, the same appendix in the third edition of this book was used, pp. 593–599.

31. Richard L. Park, "India's Foreign Policy," in Roy C. Macridis, ed., *Foreign Policy in World Politics*, 5th ed. (Englewood Cliffs, NJ: Prentice-Hall, Inc., 1976), p. 326.

32. On this point, see the discussion in Peter Willetts, *The Non-Aligned Movement: The Origins of a Third World Alliance* (London: Frances Pinter Ltd., 1978), p. 3.

33. These passages are drawn from more extensive extracts from the Belgrade Declaration, which are presented in Roderick Ogley, ed., *The Theory and Practice of Neutrality in the Twentieth Century* (New York: Barnes and Noble, Inc., 1970), pp. 189–194. The quoted passages are at pp. 191 and 192.

34. For two important discussions of the notion of nonalignment, see Cecil V. Crabb, Jr., *The Elephants and the Grass: A Study of Nonalignment* (New York: Frederick A. Praeger, 1965); and Willetts, *The Non-Aligned Movement*, especially pp. 17–31.

35. See Table 1.1 in Willetts, *The Non-Aligned Movement*, for a summary of the various non-aligned conferences and their membership.

36. Robert F. Kennedy, *Thirteen Days* (New York: Signet Books, 1969), p. 124.

37. See, for example, the study of Ole R. Holsti, Richard A. Brody, and Robert C. North, "The Management of International Crisis: Affect and Action in American-Soviet Relations," in Dean G. Pruitt and Richard C. Snyder, eds., *Theory and Research on the Causes of War* (Englewood Cliffs, NJ: Prentice-Hall, Inc., 1969), pp. 62–79.

38. George C. Herring, *America's Longest War: The United States and Vietnam.* (New York: Alfred A. Knopf Inc., 1986), pp. 7–10. The quote is at p. 10.

39. Quoted in ibid., p. 15.

40. These data are primarily from Leslie H. Gelb with Richard K. Betts, *The Irony of Vietnam: The System Worked* (Washington, D.C.: The Brookings Institution, 1979), p. 46. But also see Herring, *America's Longest War: The United States and Vietnam*, pp. 18 and 19, for the first two pieces of data.

41. Gelb with Betts, *The Irony of Vietnam: The System Worked*, pp. 50 and 51.

42. See the chapter on "The Decision Not to Intervene in Indochina, 1954," in Morton Berkowitz, P. G. Bock, and Vincent J. Fuccillo, *The Politics of American Foreign Policy* (Englewood Cliffs, NJ: Prentice-Hall, Inc., 1977), pp. 54–74. Also see *The Pentagon Papers*, pp. 13–22; Herring, *America's Longest War: The United States and Vietnam*, pp. 41–42; and Timothy J. Lomperis, *The War Everyone Lost—and Won* (Washington, D.C.: CQ Press, 1984), p. 48, on the Geneva Accords.

43. On the role of the United States in backing Diem and the "America's Mandarin" label, see Stanley Karnow, *Vietnam: A History* (New York: The Viking Press, 1983), pp. 206–239. On the level of support, see Herring, *America's Longest War: The United States and Vietnam*, p. 57.

44. The information in this paragraph and the previous one is from *The Pentagon Papers*, pp. 76, 78, and 83.

45. Ibid., p. 107.

46. See Richard K. Betts, "Misadventure Revisited," in James M. McCormick, ed., *A Reader in American Foreign Policy* (Itasca, IL: F. E. Peacock Publishers, Inc., 1986), p. 100, for this assessment.

47. On the changes in Vietnamese governments, see Lomperis, *The War Everyone Lost—and Won*, p. 62.

48. See *The Pentagon Papers* at pp. 236–237 for the chronology of events in 1964. For the controversy of what really happened in the Gulf of Tonkin, see Herring, *America's Longest War: The United States and Vietnam*, pp. 119–123.

49. *The Pentagon Papers*, pp. 308–309 and pp. 459–461.

50. Lomperis, *The War Everyone Lost—and Won*, pp. 76–79. On the Tet offensive, also see Karnow, *Vietnam: A History*, pp. 515–566.

51. Ibid., p. 82. On the Cambodian invasion, see pp. 83–85.

52. According to the fact sheet issued by the Vietnam Veterans Leadership Program of Houston, Inc., 57,704 deaths occurred in the Vietnam War. The number of names inscribed on the Vietnam Veterans War Memorial in Washington, D.C., however, is 58,132. On the last "Easter invasion," see Lomperis, *The War Everyone Lost—and Won*, pp. 87–90.

53. Ibid., p. 94, for terms of the negotiated settlement; and Herring, *America's Longest War: The United States and Vietnam*, pp. 255–256, for this assessment of it.

54. On these explanations, ibid., pp. 276–278.

55. See Lomperis, *The War Everyone Lost—and Won* for a thorough examination of the national legitimacy question. For many lessons of Vietnam, see Gelb with Betts, *The Irony of Vietnam: The System Worked*, pp. 347–369.

56. I am indebted to Professor Cleo Cherryholmes of Michigan State University for originally providing me with this formalization of the domino theory over 20 years ago.

57. See Table 3.3 on public opinion survey results on support and opposition to the Vietnam War in John E. Mueller, *War, Presidents and Public Opinion* (New York: John Wiley & Sons, Inc., 1973), pp. 54–55.

58. For one summary of the literature on domestic policy/foreign policy divisions among liberals and conservatives, see Bruce Russett, "The Americans' Retreat from World Power," *Political Science Quarterly* 90 (Spring 1975), pp. 1–21, especially pp. 14 and 15.

59. Wittkopf and McCormick, "The Cold War Consensus: Did It Exist?" discusses the public's view in the post-Vietnam period.

CHAPTER 4 NIXON'S REALISM AND CARTER'S IDEALISM IN AMERICAN FOREIGN POLICY

''...the United States will participate in the defense and development of allies and friends, but... America cannot—and will not—conceive all *plans, design* all *programs, execute* all *the decisions, and undertake* all *the defense of the free nations of the world.''* **PRESIDENT RICHARD M. NIXON, "U.S. FOREIGN POLICY FOR THE 1970s," FEBRUARY 18, 1970**

''...we are now free of that inordinate fear of communism which once led us to embrace any dictator who joined us in that fear....It is a new world that calls for a new American foreign policy—a policy based on constant decency in its values and on optimism in our historical vision.'' **PRESIDENT JIMMY CARTER, COMMENCEMENT ADDRESS AT THE UNIVERSITY OF NOTRE DAME, MAY 1977**

With the breakdown of the Cold War consensus seemingly finalized by America's agonizing defeat in the Vietnam War, succeeding administrations attempted to bring forth new foreign policy perspectives to replace this shattered world view. In this chapter, we discuss the values and beliefs that the Nixon and Carter administrations brought to U.S. foreign policy. Each relied upon considerably different value perspectives to inform foreign policymaking. The Nixon administration, primarily through its secretary of state and national security advisor, Henry A. Kissinger, sought to employ a "power politics" or "realist" approach to U.S. policy, while the Carter administration tried to employ a "global politics" or "idealist" approach.[1] Neither approach, however, succeeded in producing a new foreign policy consensus; instead, each met with substantial criticism and resistance. In its own way, however, each approach contributed to a more differentiated worldview on the part of the U.S. foreign policy.

REALISM AND IDEALISM AS FOREIGN POLICY CONCEPTS

Realism and idealism are two concepts that require some discussion before we proceed.[2] Each has been widely used to describe the behavior of individuals and states in the study of foreign policy. Each is an *ideal type*, a phenomenon in which individuals and states are closer to one approach than the other but do not match either perfectly. Earlier post–World War II presidents (e.g., Truman or Eisenhower) may have combined elements of realism and idealism, but none matched these characteristics as well as Nixon and Carter in their foreign policy behavior. In this sense, realism and idealism serve as important ways to think about the foreign policy actions of these administrations even if these concepts do not fully describe them.

The realist approach is based upon several key assumptions about world politics: (1) the nation-state is the primary actor in world politics; (2) interest, defined as power, is the primary motivating force for the action of states; (3) the distribution or balance of power (predominantly military power) at any given time is the key concern that states must address; and (4) the quality of state-to-state relations (and not the character of domestic politics within another state) is the primary consideration that should shape how one nation responds to another. Since for the realist human nature is ultimately flawed, efforts at universal perfection in global politics are myopic, shortsighted, and ultimately dangerous. Instead, moral considerations in foreign policy are largely derived from what is good for the state and for its place in international politics.

In this view, foreign policy is a highly conflictual process among states, with each state seeking to further its interests and with each warily monitoring the activities of others. Balance-of-power politics predominates because all states are concerned about the relative distribution of power at any one time, and all states are trying to maximize their own power and standing in international affairs.

The idealist approach starts with a different set of assumptions: (1) the nation-state is only one, among many, participants in foreign policy; (2) values, rather than interests, are predominant in shaping foreign policy responses; (3) the distribution of power is only one of many values of concern to the idealist, with social and economic issues equally as important as military ones; and (4) overall global conditions, not state-to-state relations, dominate foreign policy considerations. For the idealist, human nature can be changed and efforts at universal perfection is a laudable goal. Universal values should be the basis of action.

In this view, foreign policy should be a cooperative process between states and groups. Joint efforts ought to be undertaken to address the universal problems facing humankind, whether they be political, military, economic, or social. International institutions (e.g., international and regional organizations) are crucial to shaping global politics, and balance-of-power politics are largely to be eschewed.

REALISM AND THE NIXON ADMINISTRATION

The Nixon administration adopted a foreign policy approach more closely approaching the realist tradition than earlier post–World War II presidents. Its approach was based upon the principles of the balance of power and was to be anchored in a global equilibrium among the United States, the Soviet Union, and the People's Republic of China (and, later, Japan and Europe). This realist perspective was to enable the United States to play a more limited global role and to utilize substantial amounts of regional power (and power centers) to foster American interests worldwide. At the same time, it would allow the United States to remain an important, even dominant, participant in global affairs. One should keep in mind that this new realism in foreign policy was precipitated by the events of Vietnam (see Chapter 3). Indeed, the Nixon administration was as much consumed by the events there as it was in reordering superpower relations. Both factors pointed the U.S. in the direction of a different approach to foreign policy, however.

THE NIXON APPROACH TO FOREIGN POLICY

The essential elements of President Richard Nixon's approach to the world were described in his State of the World Address to the Congress in early 1970.[3] In that statement, he outlined his conception of how to build a new "structure of peace" in the world. Three principles shaped the "Nixon Doctrine" and were driven in no small measure by the desire to shape a role for the U.S. after America's departure from Vietnam:

1. Peace would require a partnership with the rest of the world.
2. Peace would require strength to protect U.S. national interests.
3. Peace would require a willingness to negotiate with all states to resolve differences.

What these principles meant was that the role of the United States was to be diminished and its power was to be shared with others in terms of preserving world order. Such a design also meant that the United States would act to protect its interests and would do so primarily through the use of military might. Furthermore, the United States would welcome the opportunity to negotiate with other states to resolve outstanding differences.

Such a conception was some distance from the postwar consensus, which had put so much stock in the ability of the United States to carry the burden of the responsibilities in the "free world." In addition, President Nixon made two other important observations in this speech. First of all, he recognized that the world was multipolar: "Today, the nature of that world has changed—the power of individual Communist nations has grown, but international Communist unity has been shattered." Second, he acknowledged the power of nationalism in the developing world. Moreover, he implied that this nationalism should not be equated with the increase in communist penetration: "Once, many feared that they [the new nations] would become simply a battleground of cold-war rivalry and fertile ground for Communist penetration. But this fear misjudged their pride in their national identities and their determination to preserve their newly won sovereignty."

Other dimensions of this policy design were foreshadowed in a *Foreign Affairs* article that Richard Nixon had written for the April

1967 issue, almost two years before he took office.[4] He emphasized two main points: (1) the importance of bringing the People's Republic of China back into the world community; and (2) the more limited role for the United States in regional disputes in the future. The United States, Nixon wrote, "cannot afford to leave China forever outside the family of nations. There is no place on this small planet for a billion of its potentially most able people to live in angry isolation." At the same time, Nixon argued that a policy of "firm restraint" must be employed to persuade Beijing to accept the "basic rules of international civility."

Further, Nixon foreshadowed a change in American policy toward regional conflict: "Other nations must recognize that the role of the United States as world policeman is likely to be limited in the future." If U.S. assistance is requested, it must come only after a regional collective effort has been attempted and failed and only when a collective request is made to the United States. Unlike the Vietnam experience, direct intervention by the U.S. must be reduced or limited.

In all, then, this design pointed to a different foreign policy approach for the United States and represented a sharp break with the postwar consensus.

HENRY KISSINGER AND WORLD ORDER

While President Nixon's statements outlined the key components of a new policy approach, the new national security advisor, and later secretary of state, Henry Kissinger, provided a more complete exposition of what the policy design would look like in practice. To appreciate Kissinger's approach, we must begin with his basic philosophy of international politics, which was developed from a number of years of academic writing and from practical foreign policy experience in previous administrations.

For Henry Kissinger the essential problem in the postwar world was a structural one: the lack of a legitimate international order.[5] Both the United States and the Soviet Union had tended to think of the world in terms of absolutes and had tried to impose their own views of world order in international politics. Neither had succeeded. As a result, a "revolutionary" and multipolar international system emerged. This system was characterized by (1) the emergence of many states and new centers of power; (2) the growth of vast new technologies, which had created great disparities in power; and (3) the appearance of a diversity of political purposes by these states. All these forces made it difficult to establish or maintain any legitimate order. Thus, according to Kissinger, the most important challenge confronting the United States was "to develop some concept of order in a world which is bipolar militarily but multipolar politically."

To create such order, Kissinger argued, the United States must think more along the lines of balance-of-power politics. While America's idealism of the past should not be abandoned, the requirements of global equilibrium should give some "perspective" to such idealism. The United States should not be afraid to pursue its interests; it should not be afraid to pursue equilibrium; and it should not be afraid to think in terms of power.[6]

What Kissinger proposed was an international order in which stability was a fundamental goal—in contrast to absolute peace, a goal so essential in America's past. Only by achieving a stable international system would international peace really become possible. Kissinger himself pointed to the dangers of blindly seeking peace without the concern for international stability:

> Whenever peace—conceived as the avoidance of war—has been the primary objective of a power or a group of powers, the international system has been at the mercy of the most ruthless member of the international community. Whenever the international order has acknowledged that certain principles could not be compromised even for the sake of peace, stability based on an equilibrium of forces was at least conceivable.
>
> Stability, then, has commonly resulted not from a quest for peace but from a generally accepted legitimacy. "Legitimacy"... should not be confused with justice. It means no more than an international agreement about the nature of workable arrangements and about the permissible aims and methods of foreign policy.[7]

In short, the achievement of stability—in which competing powers recognize the rights of one another—held the best prospect for achieving international peace because no state would attempt to impose its views on the international system.

To achieve stability and an equilibrium of forces, the legitimacy of states and of the international system had to be recognized. A prerequisite for such legitimacy was for states to accept the rights and interests of other nations and contain their revolutionary fervor. Henry Kissinger (and President Nixon) therefore proposed a "structure of peace" that would be composed of a "pentagonal" balance of power among the United States, the Soviet Union, the People's Republic of China, Western Europe, and Japan. The emphasis first would be to gain some accommodation among the first three, with Western Europe and Japan added later to this global design.

An important requirement of this design was that deviations from respecting the rights and interests of other states would not go

FIGURE 4.1 THE PRINCIPAL PARTICIPANTS IN THE
BALANCE-OF-POWER SYSTEM CONCEPTUALIZED
BY NIXON AND KISSINGER

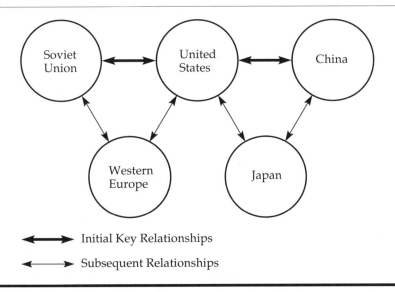

unpunished. If, for example, a state took actions outside its "traditional area of interest," other states should take action to demonstrate that violations of the required "norms of international conduct" would not be tolerated. For instance, if the Soviet Union provided economic or military support to revolutionary forces in Angola—an area where it had no historical tie—as it did in 1975, some response must be made. The response could take the form of reducing the quality of the bilateral relationship between the United States and the Soviet Union (e.g., reducing trade or the prospects of future arms negotiations) or in the multilateral relationship in the third area itself (e.g., giving direct assistance to the factions opposing the Soviet-backed group in Angola). Whichever strategy is employed, some action must be taken. The intent of such action is to bring home to the offending state the limitations of acceptable international behavior and demonstrate that attempts at expansion (and the upsetting of international stability) would not go unpunished. In this way, conflict itself would contribute to stabilizing the international order.

This approach to violations of acceptable norms of international behavior came to be known as the "linkage" in the operation of the

Kissinger system. Put differently, this concept meant that the character of behavior in one foreign policy arena (e.g., completing bilateral trade agreements) was inevitably linked to the character of behavior in another foreign policy arena (e.g., aiding insurgents in a Third World nation). It is significant to note that the Nixon-Kissinger approach did *not* link foreign and domestic arenas. For Nixon and Kissinger, linkage did not mean, for example, predicating the completion of arms agreements on changes in domestic conditions within the Soviet Union. Nonetheless, the importance of this concept to the Nixon-Kissinger approach should not be minimized; it was indeed at the heart of their foreign policy strategy.

By getting all states to accept the legitimacy of the rights and interests of one another and by employing the notion of linkage, Kissinger believed that the United States would go a long way toward achieving the stability that he sought. In the short run, the success of this strategy meant the abandonment by the United States, the Soviet Union, and the People's Republic of China of their universal goals of transforming international politics to their own ends. Furthermore, it meant that a policy of cooperation would be mixed with a policy of competition in the relationship among these states. This approach, which became labeled "détente," or relaxation of tension between the superpowers, was an attempt to build some predictability into international politics. In the long run, if this approach could be institutionalized, a global order, based upon balance-of-power principles, would be a reality.

DOMESTIC VALUES AND FOREIGN POLICY

Aside from bringing a policy of accommodation with adversaries to American foreign policy, Henry Kissinger also challenged four other precepts of past American approaches to the world. He believed that diplomacy (or the "statesman" as he labeled him in his essay on the subject"[8]) was the key to the resolution of disputes and to the operation of international politics. As he said, "negotiation is the mechanism of stability because it presupposes that maintenance of the existing order is more important than any dispute within it." Moreover, he was willing to negotiate outstanding differences between states as the principal means of achieving stability. As we suggested in Chapter 1, such reliance on diplomacy was directly at variance with America's traditional approach to global politics.

But Kissinger's challenge to the past did not stop with his heavy reliance on diplomacy; he also took a different attitude toward the use of force and the combining of force with diplomacy. His attitude may best be summarized as, "Negotiate when possible, use force when necessary." Furthermore, Kissinger believed in the use of relative levels of force in efforts to achieve foreign policy goals. Such an attitude toward force and the use of degrees of force was, again, wholly at odds with America's past. Recall our discussion in Chapter 1, where we noted that Americans were not disposed to such distinctions. Force and diplomacy were rarely bedfellows in the minds of many, and when force was used, all-out force was the standard.

Kissinger challenged the postwar consensus and America's traditional approach in two other significant ways. His view was that domestic values should not dominate American foreign policy. Policy should not become excessively moralistic; when it does, policy becomes dangerous, especially in a pluralistic world.[9] America should be guided by its historical values, but it should seek to evoke them in the world rather than try to impose them on the world.

In this same vein, Kissinger wanted a clear demarcation between the operation of domestic politics and foreign policy. He viewed these two arenas as separate and distinct. The imposition of standards of conduct across these two areas should be minimal. In particular, Kissinger did not want the U.S. Congress imposing conditions on the ability of a nation's "statesman" to operate in the international system. Thus, he vigorously opposed the imposition of restraints on trade with the Soviet Union because of its treatment of Jews who sought to emigrate. While human rights standards were perfectly acceptable in domestic politics, these standards were, he believed, unacceptable in the conduct of foreign policy. Put differently, the domestic policies of a nation mattered less to Kissinger than the way that nation treated the United States in foreign policy. The principal guide to American foreign policy should be the condition of relations *between* the two nations, not the domestic conditions *within* another nation. In essence, Kissinger was acting in a way consistent with the traditional European and balance-of-power view of international politics. His view becomes more understandable if one recalls that he was born in Germany and his initial exposure to international politics was largely in the 1930s, before his emigration to the United States.[10]

THE NIXON-KISSINGER WORLDVIEW IN OPERATION

Many of the foreign policy beliefs of Henry Kissinger and Richard Nixon became policy for the United States. This section illustrates the correspondence between their views on world order, the use of force and diplomacy, and the role of domestic values and American foreign policy actions from 1969 through 1976.[11] It will also offer some important criticisms that arose concerning this realist approach to foreign policy.

DEVELOPING SINO-SOVIET-AMERICAN DÉTENTE

Almost immediately upon assuming office, National Security Advisor (and later Secretary of State) Henry Kissinger and President Nixon set out to establish the model of world order that they proposed. By November 1969, the first discussions with the Soviet Union over nuclear accommodation were under way. The Strategic Arms Limitation Talks (SALT) were initiated in Geneva and proceeded through several sessions before agreement was reached in 1972. At the Moscow Summit in May 1972, President Nixon and Soviet President Leonid Brezhnev signed the SALT I accords. These accords consisted of two agreements. One, the Interim Agreement on Offensive Strategic Arms, called for limitations on the offensive nuclear weapons that the Soviet Union and the United States were allowed; the other, the Anti-Ballistic Missile Treaty, called for limitations on the development of defensive nuclear weapons systems by the two superpowers. These pacts signaled the first agreements to stabilize a structure of world order between the two superpowers and to institute a stable "balance of terror" between them. They became synonymous with the notion of détente. Document Summary 4.1 provides greater details on both of these agreements and the other agreements at the summit.

The Moscow Summit meetings produced more than military accommodation between the U.S. and the U.S.S.R.; it also produced a series of political, economic, and social/cultural arrangements. A political agreement ("Basic Principles of Relations between the United States and the Union of Soviet Socialist Republics") was reached in which the principle of linkage was presumably institutionalized, because each country pledged not to take advantage of the other, either "directly" or "indirectly." An economic commitment was made to improve trade relations between the two countries, and a joint commission was established for that purpose. Four social/cultural agreements were also signed in Moscow. These agreements called for U.S.-Soviet cooperation on protecting the environment, enhancing medical science and public health cooperation, undertaking joint space activities (including the 1975 Apollo-Soyuz flight), and science

DOCUMENT SUMMARY 4.1   MAJOR AGREEMENTS FROM THE
MOSCOW SUMMIT, MAY 1972

POLITICAL AGREEMENT
Basic Principles of Relations between the United States and the Union of Soviet Socialist Republics
This agreement committed both countries to conduct their relations on a basis of peaceful coexistence while recognizing their differences in ideology and in social systems. It also committed them to "do their utmost to avoid military confrontations and to prevent the outbreak of nuclear war" and "to recognize that efforts to obtain unilateral advantage at the expense of the other, *directly* or *indirectly,* are inconsistent with these objectives."

MILITARY AGREEMENTS
Strategic Arms Limitation Talks—SALT I Accords
• Anti-Ballistic Missle (ABM) Treaty
  This treaty limited each country to two ABM sites within its territory. One in each country would be around its capital and another around a land-based missile site. It also limited the number of ABM launchers for each of those sites. In effect, the agreement severely restricted this defensive kind of nuclear weapons system. The agreement was of limited duration.
• Interim Agreement on Strategic Offensive Arms
  This five-year interim agreement limited the number of land-based and sea-based intercontinental missile launchers to 1,054 and 710 for the United States and 1,618 and 950 for the Soviet Union. In addition, the United States could possess 44 ballistic missile submarines and the Soviet Union 62.
Agreement on Prevention of Incidents at Sea
This agreement provided for procedures to prevent incidents at sea between the Soviet and American navies and in the air space of their navies at sea.

ECONOMIC AGREEMENTS
Commitment to a U.S.–U.S.S.R. Trade Agreement
No formal agreement was made, but a joint communique committed the two countries to achieve this goal "in the near future."
Creation of a U.S.–Soviet Joint Commercial Commission
The purpose of this commission was to explore ways to increase commerce between the two countries.

SOCIAL/CULTURAL AGREEMENTS
Agreement on Cooperation in the Area of Medical Science and Public Health
Agreement on Cooperation in the Exploration and Use of Outer Space
Agreement on Science and Technology
Agreement on Cooperation in Environmental Protection

Source: Abstracted from the agreements and the joint communique, from the *Department of State Bulletin,* June 26, 1972, pp. 898–899, 918–917.

and technology.[12] The essence of détente with the Soviet Union was in place with these 1972 agreements because broad avenues of cooperation were opened in the context of a relationship that was still competitive. An important part of the three-pronged global order seemed to be operating.

These agreements, moreover, were signed at the same time that the United States was bombing Hanoi, the North Vietnamese capital, and blockading Haiphong, its principal harbor, in its continuing effort to bring "peace with honor" over the war in Vietnam. Thus, the effort to stabilize global relationships among the strong went forward even at a time of sharp U.S.-U.S.S.R. disagreement over policy in Asia. Much as Kissinger desired, negotiated efforts to achieve global stability proved more important than any existing conflict in the world. To Kissinger, the Soviet Union appeared willing to submerge ideological conflict in Asia for a larger attempt at world order.

Similar efforts at achieving global stability were initiated with the other major player in the Kissinger-Nixon design: the People's Republic of China. In late 1970, Premier Zhou Enlai gave the first hints of an interest in establishing contact with the United States.[13] The United States responded quickly and positively. By mid-year 1971, Henry Kissinger made a secret trip to Peking in order to pave the way for a visit by an American president to that long-isolated country. On July 15, 1971, President Nixon appeared on American radio and television with the shock announcement that he had been invited to the People's Republic of China, he had accepted the invitation, and would go there as soon as arrangements could be worked out. Nixon visited China in February 1972 and, by any analysis, enjoyed a huge success.

The Shanghai Communique resulted from this meeting and was issued from that Chinese city on February 28, 1972.[14] While the communique reflected the differing worldviews of the two nations, it did provide areas of global and bilateral commonalities. See Document Summary 4.2 for a summary of the areas of agreement and disagreement in the communique. For instance, it reflected some movement on the question of Taiwan by both sides, confirming that there was only "one China"; it opposed "hegemony" in the world (a not-so-subtle strategy by the U.S. to use the "China card" to influence Soviet behavior); it called for efforts at normalization of relations (although full diplomatic relations would not be achieved until the Carter administration); and it opened up trade and other contacts between the American and Chinese peoples. Overall, the content of the communique did not provide the areas of cooperation that the Moscow meeting would, but it had the seeds of such cooperation.

DOCUMENT SUMMARY 4.2 KEY ELEMENTS OF THE SHANGHAI COMMUNIQUE, FEBRUARY 27, 1972

AREAS OF DISAGREEMENT

Competing Worldviews
The U.S. side stated: Peace in Asia and peace in the world requires efforts both to reduce immediate tensions and to eliminate the basic causes of conflict. The United States will work for a just and lasting peace; just, because it fulfills the aspirations of peoples and nations for freedom and progress; secure, because it removes the danger of foreign aggression. The United States supports individual freedom and social progress for all the peoples of the world, free of outside pressure or intervention.

The Chinese side stated: Wherever there is oppression, there is resistance. Countries want independence, nations want liberation, and the people want revolution—this has become the irresistible trend of history. All nations, big or small, should be equal; big nations should not bully the small and strong nations should not bully the weak. China will never be a superpower and it opposes hegemony and power politics of any kind.

The Taiwan Question
The Chinese side reaffirmed its position:. . . .the Government of the People's Republic of China is the sole legal governmemt of China; Taiwan is a province of China which has long been returned to the motherland; the liberation of Taiwan is China's internal affair in which no other country has the right to interfere.

The U.S. side declared: The United States acknowledges that all Chinese on either side of the Taiwan Strait maintain there is but one China and that Taiwan is a part of China. The United States Government does not challenge that position. It reaffirms its interest in a peaceful settlement of the Taiwan question by the Chinese themselves.

AREAS OF AGREEMENT

Anti-hegemony Clause
Neither [country] should seek hegemony in the Asia-Pacific region and each is opposed to efforts by any other country or group of countries to establish such hegemony.

Both sides are of the view that it would be against the interests of the peoples of the world for any major country to collude with another against other countries, or for major countries to divide up the world into spheres of interest.

Normalization of Relations
The two sides agreed that it is desirable to broaden the understanding between the two peoples. . . .

Both sides view bilateral trade as another area from which mutual benefit can be derived, and agreed that economic relations

---

DOCUMENT SUMMARY 4.2   KEY ELEMENTS OF THE SHANGHAI
COMMUNIQUE, FEBRUARY 27, 1972 (CONTINUED)

---

based on equality and mutual benefit are in the interest of the
peoples of the two countries. . . .
    The two sides expressed the hope that the gains achieved during
this visit would open up new prospects for the relations between the
two countries. They believe that the normalization of relations
between the two countries is not only in the interest of the Chinese
and American peoples but also contributes to the relaxation of
tension in Asia and the world.

Source: "Text of Joint Communique Issued at Shanghai, February 27," *Department of State
Bulletin*, March 20, 1972, pp. 435–438. The substantive elements are quoted directly from the
communique.

Nonetheless, it was remarkable in a more profound sense: after more
than thirty years, formal contact between harsh adversaries was begun. The Asian component of the Kissinger-Nixon global design
seemed to be falling into place as well.

The last component of this détente strategy was the Final Act of
the Conference on Security and Cooperation in Europe signed in
Helsinki, Finland, on August 1, 1975.[15] It was signed after President
Nixon had left office, but while Henry Kissinger still dominated policy, and it signaled efforts at expanding détente from involving only
the superpowers to including all European states.

The conference itself was composed of thirty-five countries from
Eastern and Western Europe and the United States and Canada. The
Final Act (or the Helsinki Accords as they are sometimes called) was
a "political statement," rather than a legally binding treaty of international law. It was composed of three "baskets" of issues, with each
basket containing provisions for enhancing cooperation among the
signatory nations. The first basket dealt with principles of conduct
toward one another and ways to reduce military tension among
them; the second dealt with efforts to enlarge cooperation in economic, technological, and environmental arenas; and the third dealt
with a series of measures for fostering closer social/cultural interaction among them. Document Summary 4.3 summarizes these "baskets" more fully. The Final Act, however, was not viewed as an end
in itself; instead, it was seen as the beginning point of an evolving
cooperative process in Central Europe, much as the Moscow and
Shanghai agreements of 1972 were viewed. In this sense, the "relaxation of tensions" and the stability of the international order that

---

DOCUMENT SUMMARY 4.3   A DESCRIPTION OF THE THREE
"BASKETS" OF THE HELSINKI ACCORDS, AUGUST 1, 1975

BASKET 1   *The Declaration of Principles on Political Relations among the States*
This basket contains ten principles to guide the conduct of relations among the thirty-five signatory countries. These principles range from respect for "sovereign equality," the "inviolability of frontiers," and "respect for human rights and fundamental freedoms" to "cooperation among states," "the peaceful settlement of disputes," and "nonintervention in the affairs of states." This basket also contains a series of proposals (called "confidence-building measures" or "CBMs") that states should undertake to contribute to stability in Europe.

BASKET 2   *A Call for Economic, Scientific, Technical, and Environmental Cooperation among the States*
This basket contains a series of recommendations for enhancing East-West cooperation in all of these areas. Efforts should be undertaken, for example, to encourage industrial cooperation, reduce trade barriers, promote joint scientific research, and support environmental cooperation.

BASKET 3   *A Call for Humanitarian Cooperation between East and West*
This basket calls for the "freer movement of people, ideas, and information" between East and West. The reunification of families, binational marriages, and freer travel should be encouraged; greater exchange of information should be allowed; and cultural and educational cooperation should be promoted.

Source: Abstracted from "Conference on Security and Cooperation in Europe," *Department of State Bulletin*, September 26, 1977, pp. 404–410.

Nixon and Kissinger had envisioned expanded to all of Central Europe with the Helsinki Accords.

FORCE AND DIPLOMACY IN THE THIRD WORLD

Two major events demonstrate the importance of the combined use of force and diplomacy to the Nixon-Kissinger foreign policy approach. The first involved negotiations over ending the Vietnam War, and the second entailed the use of "shuttle diplomacy" on the Middle East. From the outset of Kissinger's tenure as national security advisor, he saw negotiations as the key to the resolution of the Vietnam War.[16] A two-track system of secret and open negotiations was put into effect immediately. These negotiations, however, did not produce quick results. In addition, the process of the war itself continued to deteriorate from the American perspective, and protests at home continued to increase. In any attempt to get the negotiations back on track, force, and in this case the escalation of force, needed to be added to the diplomatic track. For Kissinger and Nixon, force could be used to demonstrate resolve on their bargaining position and to prod their adversary to serious negotiations.

On at least three occasions, the use of escalating force was combined with the ongoing Vietnam negotiations in efforts to produce diplomatic results. First, in April 1970, Kissinger and Nixon agreed to an American "incursion" into Cambodia, a neutral country—essentially widening the war (although secret bombing attacks had previously been undertaken). This action was taken to demonstrate U.S. resolve on the issue and as a way to move the Vietnamese toward serious negotiations. Second, about two years later (May 1972), when negotiations were again stalled, the bombing and blockading of Hanoi and Haiphong were used for the same expressed goal. Kissinger apparently had some doubts about the blockading of Haiphong because it might wreck the upcoming Moscow Summit and the signing of the SALT I accords. Although he believed that a more intensive bombing campaign might be sufficient to show resolve, he ultimately acquiesced in the policy decision by the president.[17] Third, force and diplomacy were combined in the so-called "Christmas bombing" of December 1972. After Kissinger had so solemnly announced that "peace is at hand" in October 1972, and that only a few details were left to negotiate, the final negotiations abruptly hit a snag. As a consequence, President Nixon initiated the bombing of North Vietnam as a way to reopen negotiations and to bring about the successful completion of the Paris agreements. While there is some dispute over the extent to which Kissinger concurred with the bombing decision from the outset, he did not publicly challenge it. Instead, he went on record as supporting it.[18] Further, debate remains over how much impact the bombing had on altering the terms of the settlement. In the words of one historian, George C. Herring, "the bombing did not produce a settlement markedly different from the one that the United States had earlier rejected.... The changes were largely cosmetic, enabling each side to claim that nothing had been given up."[19] In any event, and as we noted in Chapter 3, by late January 1973, a Vietnam disengagement was signed in Paris.

The other major illustrations of the importance of diplomacy as the keystone of American policy for Kissinger and Nixon (and, later, President Gerald Ford) occurred in the Middle East. After the Yom

Kippur War of October 1973, and the imposition of the oil embargo by the Arab oil states, Kissinger used his considerable diplomatic skills to negotiate a series of disengagement pacts among Egypt, Syria, and Israel. These agreements began to untangle the Middle East conflict, but they had, perhaps, more importance in turning the oil spigot back on for the United States. The negotiations were to demonstrate to Arab states (and particularly the Arab oil states) that the U.S. was serious about resolving the Middle East conflict.

Intermittently, over a period of months from 1973 through 1975, Henry Kissinger "shuttled" between Cairo, Tel Aviv, and Damascus to hammer out two disengagement agreements over the Sinai Peninsula between Egypt and Israel and one over the Golan Heights between Syria and Israel. Such diplomatic actions brought into sharp relief the central role that negotiations placed upon the "statesman." Although his further efforts were ultimately stalled by intransigence on both sides, even his efforts to that point illustrated how diplomacy could be a powerful tool in moving toward international order.

HUMAN RIGHTS AND FOREIGN POLICY ACTION

Finally, there indeed appeared to be a separation between American domestic values and American foreign policy actions during the tenure of Kissinger and Nixon. This separation was perhaps best illustrated in policy toward authoritarian and totalitarian regimes. Kissinger and Nixon were reluctant to bring to the attention of the Chilean and Greek juntas their concerns about violations of human rights because of the overriding importance of such states to establishing global order. Similarly, U.S. policy toward South Africa continued tacit support for that regime, despite its apartheid policy of legally separating races in social and political life. Strategic considerations became an important motivating force for the Nixon administration once again.

Toward totalitarian regimes, Kissinger seemed to operate on a similar dichotomy. For instance, he opposed giving any official Washington recognition to Aleksandr Solzhenitsyn when he was expelled from the Soviet Union, just as he opposed the Jackson-Vanik Amendment to the Trade Act of 1974. This amendment essentially made free emigration policy a requirement for any U.S. trading partner seeking most-favored-nation status. Because the Soviet Union enforced a restrictive emigration policy, most-favored-nation trading status was denied them. Domestic politics in any state were to be subordinated to the requirements of international politics. To the extent that domestic situations within another state were to be ad-

MAP 4.1   ISRAEL AND ITS NEIGHBORS

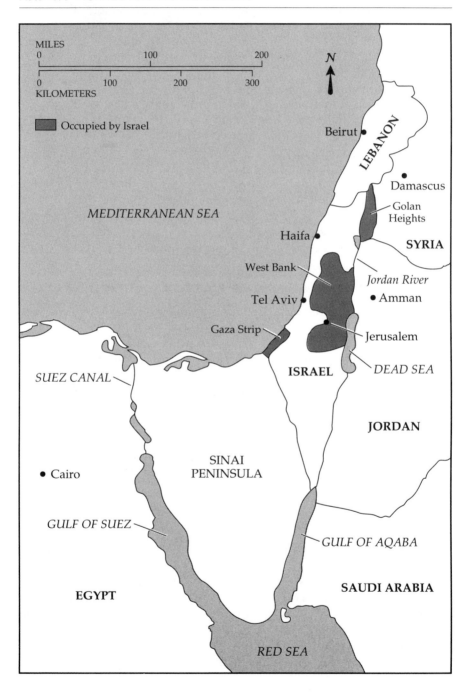

dressed, these were to be done through "quiet diplomacy"—secret representations to the offending regime.

CRITICISMS OF THE NIXON-KISSINGER APPROACH

Despite the policy successes that Nixon and Kissinger brought to U.S. foreign policy in the 1970s, their foreign policy approach was subject to criticism both for the content of its policy and for its style of policymaking. These criticisms came from analysts on both the left and the right sides of the political spectrum, and even from the foreign policy establishment.

On the left, the most telling critique was offered by political scientist Richard Falk in an essay aptly entitled "What's Wrong With Henry Kissinger's Foreign Policy?"[20] His criticisms focused upon the lack of moral content in Kissinger's policy and its irrelevance to the last quarter of the twentieth century. Kissinger's concern with order and stability in international politics ignored the more important questions of peace and justice in global affairs. The most pressing issues of international politics were not power and domination, as Kissinger emphasized, but hunger, poverty, and global inequality, which Kissinger did not. Yet, his policy approach had no direct way to deal with these important concerns.

Instead, his global order was predicated upon preserving the nation-state system and attempting to manage that system by moderating conflict among a few strong Northern Hemisphere states. Such a view represents the "underlying conceptual flaw in Kissinger's approach," according to Falk.[21] This "cooperative directorate among great powers" that Kissinger envisioned was shortsighted in more fundamental ways as well:

> It accepts as inevitable the persistence of large-scale misery and repression. It enables the disfavored many to be kept under control by the favored few. The global structure of control that Kissinger envisages and endorses tempts change-minded groups to adopt some variant of "desperate politics" to achieve their goals of liberation from social, political and economic oppression.[22]

The anti-revolutionary nature of Kissinger's policies and his indifference to the character of domestic regimes with which it dealt further eroded the prospect for meaningful global reform through his foreign policy. Although Kissinger emphasized the stopping of "revolutionaries" of the right or left, his policy was mainly directed at controlling those from the left. In this sense, his policy approach was little different than the staunch anti-communism of an earlier era. His "tendency to remove the moral question from the sphere of international diplomacy"[23] enhanced his ability to gain support within the United States from liberals and conservatives alike, but it did not add to the moral character of U.S. policy.

Former senator and presidential nominee George McGovern also criticized the Nixon-Kissinger approach for its outdated pentagonal design and for its lack of moral character in the 1972 campaign address. McGovern argued that the "five-corner, balance of power thesis attempts to force onto the contemporary world a naive prenuclear view dating back to the 19th century and before."[24] The United States ought to stand for more than that narrow vision, and it ought to reflect "our attitudes towards ourselves, towards our country, and towards the rest of mankind." McGovern's proposed "New Internationalism" would use American power to achieve "elemental human dignity" and to support a new kind of interventionism in which the U.S. provides "agricultural and technical assistance . . . the building of roads and schools . . . the training of skilled personnel, in concert with other nations and through multilateral institutions."[25]

On the right, ironically, the Kissinger approach was also criticized for its moral relativity. In particular, political conservatives viewed the policy of détente as morally bankrupt because it gave legitimacy and equality to regimes to which the United States had not done so in the past. Indeed, the opening to the People's Republic of China was particularly troubling, since the U.S. had never recognized or interacted with the regime of Mao Zedong. Suddenly, this situation changed almost over night. While the change was not as abrupt with the Soviet Union, the effect was largely the same.

William Buckley, a leading conservative spokesman, put this criticism in a slightly different way. He argued that the détente policy was based upon an "ideological egalitarianism" that implied that there were no fundamental differences between the American, Soviet, and Chinese societies. As he noted in a televised interview with Henry Kissinger, the Chinese had been most often described as "warlike," "ignorant," "sly," and "treacherous" in a 1966 American poll in the U.S. One month after President Nixon's return from China in 1972, however, the description had changed dramatically. Now, the Chinese were most often described as "progressive," "hard-working," "intelligent," "artistic," "progressive," and "practical."[26] Yet, the regime in Beijing (at that time), had hardly changed its policy at all; only American policy had changed. Détente, therefore, had the effect of reducing the ideological distinction between the U.S. and these communist states almost overnight.

A third criticism from the right, and hardly divorced from the other two, is that détente is a strategy that connotes a "no win" strategy against communism. By accepting the legitimacy of these other key states and by working with them, these states are perpetuated, not undermined, which presumably had been the U.S. aim for three decades.

The détente policy of the Nixon-Kissinger years was criticized from yet another quarter. Former undersecretary of state in the Kennedy and Johnson administrations George Ball, writing near the end of Kissinger's time in office, did not see the policy as particularly new or as necessarily advantageous to the U.S. for three reasons.[27] First, ever since World War II, the United States and the West had tried to obtain better relations with the Soviet Union. Indeed, America's initiatives of the late 1960s and early 1970s were largely grounded in earlier Western European efforts. Second, the results of détente were not all that advantageous to the West. While the SALT accords were useful, the other agreements struck with Moscow produced few tangible results and may have been too high a price to pay for SALT. After all, SALT was in the bilateral interests of both countries. Third, the détente policy approach had not produced the kind of superpower cooperation envisaged in the "Basic Principles" agreement at the 1972 Moscow Summit. The Soviets, for example, had not been cooperative in resolving the Middle East conflict, or at least Kissinger had not been able to engage them in such cooperation.

Finally, Ball also charged that the style of policymaking by Nixon and Kissinger in the pursuance of their foreign policy agenda was inappropriate for a great power and for a democratic society. Kissinger's "lonely cowboy" approach to policymaking limited the foreign policy agenda that could be pursued. The result was "a policy that ignore[d] relations with nations that happen. . .to be outside the spotlight, and. . .encourage[d] a practice of haphazard improvisation."[28] Further, this "policy of maneuver," by the "Master Player," as Ball characterized the approach, was built on secrecy and personalism that was hardly consistent with a democratic society. Policies, and their rationales, must be fully explained to the American public—something that Nixon and Kissinger were not wont to do.

In short, opponents appeared on both the political right and the political left to charge that the Nixon-Kissinger "power politics" strategy was fundamentally amoral and inconsistent with America's past, and that its style of decision making challenged democratic traditions at home. Despite these fundamental criticisms, America's approach to the world had come full circle during the eight years of Nixon-Ford and Kissinger. American policy had indeed moved away from both moralism and isolationalism; instead it had embraced the basic elements of realism. From an initial postwar moral crusade, driven largely by fervent anti-communism, the United States had now adopted an approach driven by the principles of pragmatism and "power politics." Support for this approach was to wane rather quickly, and the 1976 presidential election was fought, at least in part, on the morality of American foreign policy. That election produced a new president—one committed to a foreign policy based on moral standards.

IDEALISM AND THE CARTER ADMINISTRATION

Jimmy Carter ran for president in 1976 on the theme of making American foreign policy compatible with the basic goodness of the American people. He came to office pledged to restore integrity and morality to American policy. With those fundamental concerns, President Carter introduced a policy approach that was closer to the idealist "ideal type" than earlier postwar presidents. His approach sought to change the focus of America's policy abroad away from a singular emphasis on adversaries, and especially the Soviet Union, as the Nixon-Ford-Kissinger approach had done, and toward a policy with a truly global emphasis. Four major policy areas would be emphasized: (1) resolving regional conflicts; (2) improving relations with the Western allies; (3) addressing important global issues such as poverty, hunger, and nuclear proliferation; and (4) focusing on global human rights.[29] Despite his initial idealism, however, by the last year of his term, Carter had reverted to a policy much more consistent with the realist policies of previous postwar presidents.

THE CARTER APPROACH TO FOREIGN POLICY

From the outset, President Jimmy Carter highlighted the importance of domestic values as a guide to American foreign policy. In this sense, his approach was consistent with the moralism so evident in America's historical past and in sharp contrast with the previous two administrations. For his presidency, domestic values were to be preeminent in the shaping of America's foreign policy; the U.S. must "stand for something" in the world. Even more, America should serve as a model for other nations.

In his inaugural address, President Carter stated these beliefs forcefully. He said: "Our Nation can be strong abroad only if it is strong at home. And we know that the best way to enhance freedom in other lands is to demonstrate here that our democratic system is worthy of emulation."[30] He went on to say that the United States would not act abroad in ways that would violate domestic standards. In a similar vein, during his 1977 Notre Dame commencement address, President Carter again emphasized the moral basis of American policy: "I believe we can have a foreign policy that is democratic, that is based on fundamental values, and that uses power and influence which we have for humane purposes."[31]

In addition to emphasizing this moral basis of policy, President Carter also called for a different style of foreign policy—one that would be "open and candid," and not one that was a "policy by manipulation" or based on "secret deals." Such references were apparently to what he saw as the foreign policy style adopted during the years in which Henry Kissinger was at the helm of American foreign policy.

Finally, while the president recognized that moral principle must guide foreign policy, he acknowledged that foreign policy cannot be "by moral maxims." The U.S. would have to try to produce change rather than impose it. In this sense, Carter believed that there were limits to what the U.S. could do in the world. Although these limits would need to be recognized, America could not stand idly by. The U.S. should try to play a constructive and positive role in shaping a new world order. This role should be through an American policy "based on constant decency in its values and on optimism in our historical vision."[32]

CARTER AND GLOBAL ORDER: NEW STATES AND OLD FRIENDS

The focus of the Carter administration also reflected its view of the world. To begin with, its policy would not be simply one of anticommunism inherited from the past. (President Carter said, "we are now free of that inordinate fear of communism which once led us to embrace any dictator who joined us in that fear.") Instead, the Carter administration proposed a policy of global cooperation, especially with the newly influential countries in Latin America, Africa, and Asia, but also with the industrial democracies of the world. The aim of such an effort would be "to create a wider framework of international cooperation suited to the new and rapidly changing historical circumstances."[33] Moreover, this effort sought to move beyond a policy seeking global stability among the strong to a policy that recognized the reality of the new states and their place in the world order.

The philosophical basis for such a policy cannot be attributed only to Carter himself; it also reflects the influence of one of his principal foreign policy advisers, Zbigniew Brzezinski. Writing in *Foreign Policy* in the summer of 1976, and interviewed later by Elizabeth Drew for *The New Yorker* in 1978, Brzezinski echoed these themes.[34] In his view, the greatest danger in the world was international anarchy, not the potential domination of the Soviet Union. America, Brzezinski wrote, was "indispensable" in addressing these issues. "For all its shortcomings, America remains the globally creative and innovative society." The failure of the United States "to project a constructive sense of direction would hence contribute directly to major global economic and political disruption." America must not be afraid of change in the world; in fact, it must seek change in order to confront the new global agenda that faces humankind.

Within this same global context, crucial regional trouble spots of the world were to be important areas of American foreign policy concentration. Efforts at resolving the seemingly intractable problems of the Middle East were to have a high priority in the Carter administration. The festering problems of southern Africa—Rhodesia (now Zimbabwe), Namibia, and South Africa, for example—would need solutions if a more just and peaceful global order were to evolve. Similarly, the problems with Panama and the Canal, and the potential of this issue for generating hostility toward the United States in the Western Hemisphere, also formed part of this strategy of addressing regional conflicts as a stepping-stone to a more stable international order.

A second major focal point within the global approach was the improvement of relations with Western Europe and Japan. This emphasis upon better trilateral relations was again, in part, a response to the previous administration's emphasis on improving relations with adversaries. For instance, Kissinger's much heralded "Year of Europe" for 1973 was essentially stillborn as pressing Middle East problems arose. As a result, fissures began to appear in ties with America's traditional friends. Economic, political, and military differences with its principal postwar allies, therefore, were to be difficult problems for the Carter administration.

Economic fissures were fueled by global inflation and skyrocketing oil prices. The Europeans and the Japanese were concerned about American inflation and its effect on their economies, while the Americans were disappointed with the failure of the Europeans (and especially the Germans) and the Japanese to expand their economies as a means of assisting the rest of the continent out of recession. Similarly, trade imbalances between the Japanese and the Americans were producing increased friction. To the Carter administration, however, better economic coordination among the developed democracies was a necessity for the late 1970s.

Accompanying these economic woes, political differences had emerged. A consistent complaint of the Europeans and the Japanese was that they had been inadequately consulted during the height of détente between the United States and the Soviet Union and during the initial period of rapprochement between the United States and the People's Republic of China. Too often, the allies contended, they were only informed of decisions made by the superpowers. Thus, their status as important U.S. partners seemed to have been undermined. In essence, better political coordination would also be essential to refurbish and strengthen alliance ties.

Finally, the Americans wanted the Europeans and the Japanese to increase their military efforts to confront the increased Soviet defense buildup both in Eastern Europe and East Asia. The Europeans and the Japanese, however, were reluctant to do so given their current domestic economic woes. At the same time, these nations were worried about America's commitment to their defense. Would the Americans have the Europeans and Japanese increase their defenses as a means of lessening U.S. efforts? Better military coordination would be needed as well.

The differences in emphases between this administration and its immediate predecessors were clear: While the Nixon-Ford-Kissinger administrations had come to recognize the legitimacy of the newly independent states, the Carter administration was going to make them the important focal point of American foreign policy; while previous administrations had talked of closer ties with the Europeans and the Japanese, the Carter administration was committed to making those ties a reality.

CARTER AND THE SOVIET UNION

With such a global emphasis, the centrality of the Soviet-American relationship was downgraded. To be sure, détente policy with the Soviet Union would not be abandoned, but it would be placed in a larger context of global issues. In particular, President Carter was committed to joint efforts at strategic arms control; thus, this aspect of the Soviet-American tie would be the continuing and central part of the relationship. The broad comprehensive détente approach of the previous administrations, however, would not be the aim of the

Carter administration. Economic, socio-cultural, and political cooperation could continue, but only on the basis of mutual advantage. What was crucial here was that such cooperation would not be linked to the overall quality of the relationship. In this sense, the "linkage" notion of the past would be jettisoned.[35]

In essence, Carter's approach to the Soviet Union assumed that the world order of the late 1970s and early 1980s would not be achieved merely by harnessing the Soviet-American relationship. Détente had neither produced stability in U.S.-Soviet relations nor addressed the crucial global and regional issues. Instead, it had encouraged a variety of critics at home and abroad and had diverted attention from the important global concerns. In short, the heart of international politics in this period had moved beyond this bilateral relationship, and any vision of an improved world along the Kissinger design was not politically feasible.

Carter's initial approach toward the Soviet Union deeply offended and confused them. This approach offended them because the Soviet Union had long commanded the bulk of America's attention since 1945 and because they had gained superpower status only five years before in the series of Moscow agreements of May 1972. Now this status was apparently being denied them. It confused them because the Soviets saw themselves as the critical nation that could affect conflict in the world, especially in the nuclear age. Despite their centrality to questions of war and peace, the Carter administration seemed to be shoving them aside. The Soviets did not quite know how to react to this new American moralism and globalism as espoused by Jimmy Carter, or to its emphasis on human rights.

CARTER AND HUMAN RIGHTS

The pivotal new focus of the Carter administration was the emphasis on human rights.[36] The role of this policy in the Carter administration can be gleaned from his inaugural address:

> Our commitment to human rights must be absolute. . . . Because we are free, we can never be indifferent to the fate of freedom everywhere. Our moral sense dictates a clear-cut preference for those societies which share with us an abiding respect for individual human rights. We do not seek to intimidate, but it is clear that a world which others can dominate with impunity would be inhospitable to decency and a threat to the well-being of all people.[37]

At his Notre Dame commencement address, too, President Carter reaffirmed this commitment to human rights. Outlining the premises of his foreign policy, he began his presentation by enunciating the central role of human rights once again:

> We have reaffirmed America's commitment to human rights as a fundamental tenet of our foreign policy. . . . We want the world to know that our nation stands for more than financial prosperity.[38]

Such a human rights philosophy was to provide the key moral principle for guiding American foreign policy. The United States would not conduct "business as usual" with nations that grossly and consistently violated the basic rights of its citizens. Instead, America would require states to change their domestic human rights behavior if they wished amicable relations with the United States. While President Carter made it clear that the human rights criterion would not be the only consideration, he also believed "that a significant element in our relationships with other governments would be their performance in providing basic freedoms to their people."[39]

The human rights issue appealed to Jimmy Carter because of his strong personal and religious beliefs about individual dignity, but also because of the issue's strong domestic appeal, especially after Vietnam, Watergate, and revelations about CIA abuses. The "something" that the United States would stand for in the world would now be something that it had historically embraced: the freedom of the individual. At the same time, the human rights issue appealed across the political spectrum and thus would be domestically attractive. Conservatives would like this policy because it would presumably condemn communist nations for their totalitarian practices, while liberals would like it because the United States would now reexamine its policy toward authoritarian states.

Although the human rights campaign tapped American moral traditions, President Carter also believed that it would improve America's standing abroad: "Our country has been strongest and most effective when morality and a commitment to freedom and democracy have been the most clearly emphasized in our foreign policy." Furthermore, President Carter thought that human rights "might be the wave of the future," and he wanted the United States to be involved in it.[40]

THE CARTER WORLDVIEW IN OPERATION

In the main, Carter's initial foreign policy strategy was well received by the American public—especially in light of the traumatic events of the early 1970s. His approach represented a reemergence of American idealism, with a clear emphasis on traditional American values and beliefs. As political scientist Stanley Hoffmann has noted, President Carter "was determined to redefine the national interest to make it coincide with the moral impulse" of the United States.[41] In this sense, Carter succeeded. Coupled with the idealism of the Carter approach, however, was the realization of the limits of American power. While the United States could assist in the shaping of global order, it did not have the power to direct the international system of the 1970s—a system that was so diverse and complex that no nation or set of nations could impose its views of international order. In this sense, the Carter approach was partly compatible with the previous Kissinger approach—the United States must evoke a global order through its actions. However, the focal point of this new order was considerably different from the past.

In this section, we shall evaluate the Carter worldview and its overall success in changing the focus and direction of American foreign policy. Such an analysis will enable us to understand more fully the abrupt change in policy by President Carter in the last year of his presidency.

IMPROVING HUMAN RIGHTS

Almost immediately, the Carter administration faced the problem of clearly defining human rights and establishing a consistent application of this policy on a global basis. What President Carter apparently had in mind originally was the humane treatment of individuals: free from torture and arbitrary punishment for expressing political beliefs. Yet such a policy was not sufficiently defined by his spokespersons.

Early on, the Carter administration seemed to assert a much broader interpretation of human rights policy. In this official description, the human rights policy fell into three main categories, and the United States would engage change in each worldwide:

1. First, the right to be free from governmental violation of the integrity of the person. Such violations include torture; cruel, inhuman, or degrading treatment or punishment; arbitrary arrest or imprisonment. . . .
2. Second, the right to fulfillment of such vital needs as food, shelter, health care, and education. . . .
3. Third, the right to enjoy civil and political liberties such as freedom of thought, religion, assembly, speech, and the press; freedom of movement both within and outside one's country; freedom to take part in government.[42]

In this sense, the human rights notion was broadened to indicate political, economic, and social rights. Nonetheless, according to Lincoln Bloomfield, who dealt with human rights issues on the National Security Council during the last two years of the Carter administration, the priority was still on individual civil and political liberties more than on economic and social rights. After an initial review and refinement of the policy, there seemed to be a slight downplaying of the human rights criterion for foreign policy; human rights would be one consideration in determining U.S. foreign policy toward another nation, and President Carter and Secretary of State Cyrus Vance indicated as much. Secretary Vance cautioned against "mechanistic formulas" for the human rights campaign, and President Carter recognized the limitation of "rigid moral maxims" in his Notre Dame speech.[43] From the initial rush of enthusiasm over human rights, then, a detectable pullback appeared underway.

A second problem also arose. How was the human rights campaign going to be put into effect? How far was the U.S. willing to go to produce human rights change? Was it willing to cut off all contact with the nations allegedly pursuing human rights violations? Was the U.S. going to stop all diplomatic, economic, or military ties to offending states? Or, alternatively, was the U.S. going to continue or modify these ties in line with more responsive behavior by the other nations? After all, was not this a better way to exercise influence over another nation than by stopping all contacts, and thus all means of influence?

Aid—and particularly military aid—was cut off to principal offender nations such as Chile, Argentina, Uruguay, Guatemala, Nicaragua, Vietnam, Cambodia, Uganda, and Mozambique.[44] Economic aid was used to encourage continued human rights improvements for another group of states. But the primary instrument used toward states with poor human rights records was diplomatic "jawboning"—publicly and privately bringing to the attention of the foreign governments American dissatisfaction with their human rights practices.

At the same time, efforts were made to make certain that the United States was fully compliant with existing human rights standards, especially as required by the Helsinki Accords (or more formally, the Statement of Principles of the Conference on Security and Cooperation in Europe) of August 1975. President Carter, for example, removed travel restrictions on American citizens to Cuba, North Korea, Vietnam, and Cambodia.[45] Furthermore, President Carter sought and gained repeal of the Byrd Amendment, which had allowed trade with Rhodesia and which had violated international sanctions over that country's minority and illegal regime. Despite these actions, though, the Carter administration was unable to persuade the Congress to ratify all the components of what came to be called the "International Human Rights Bill." This "bill" consists of three United Nations agreements—the Universal Declaration of Human Rights (1948), the International Covenant on Economic, Social, and Cultural Rights (1966), and the International Covenant on Civil and Political Rights (1966). The U.S. signed all three, but the U.S. Senate had failed to ratify the last two. Further, the Carter administration had failed to get congressional approval for the International Convention on the Elimination of All Forms of Racial Discrimination, and the Covenant on the Prevention and Punishment of the Crime of Genocide.[46]

A third major problem was: To whom should the human rights policy apply? The paradox of the Carter policy was evident when nations saw the U.S. calling for the free exercise of human rights, particularly in the Soviet Union and in Latin America, but, at the same time, saw the U.S. providing economic and military assistance to nations often cited has having serious human rights violations, such as South Korea, the Philippines, and Iran. Juxtaposing the human rights policy against the demands of realpolitik became a central dilemma for the Carter administration and a constant target of attack by its critics.

The apparent problem of selective application was criticized from two different directions. On the one hand, neo-conservative critics, perhaps best represented by Jeane Kirkpatrick, argued that the human rights standards as practiced by the United States against "moderately repressive," but friendly, regimes was, in effect, undermining these states and American global influence. The unintended result of this action might well be the replacement of these imperfect regimes by ones opposed to U.S. interests—for example in Iran and Nicaragua. Whatever the merits of human rights (and Mrs. Kirkpatrick would argue that they are considerable), the requirements of global balance-of-power politics could not be wholly jettisoned.[47] In this sense, quiet efforts—as well as intergovernmental, semigovernmental, and nongovernmental efforts—were necessary to pursue human rights in the international system.[48]

Critics from a different perspective argued that the U.S. human rights policy was yet another way to impose American values on the international system. Moreover, it reflected the naiveté and the lack of political realism that had too often dominated America's moralistic past. In this respect, it was another of America's attempts to dominate global politics. As well intentioned as was the human rights goal, it was inappropriate for the diverse international system and would ultimately be dysfunctional for global order. Such a refrain was heard from Third World leaders and even from some American allies, notably France and Germany.

The overall effect of the Carter administration's human rights campaign is obviously difficult to measure. While the number of countries with an improved human rights record did increase slightly during the Carter years, much greater gains were necessary if global human rights conditions were to be changed substantially. Such a result is as much as admitted in one of the State Department's annual human rights reports to the Congress. The report concludes that "the distance covered is still small in comparison to the distance that remains to be traveled before people throughout the world are secure from the excesses of government power, find opportunities to feed, clothe, and educate their children, and see before them a future of freedom and equality."[49]

To be sure, some tangible instances of improved global human rights were registered by the Carter administration. The Dominican Republic made a turn toward democracy; elections were announced for 1978 in Peru, Ecuador, and Bolivia; improved conditions were evidenced in Colombia, Malaysia, Honduras, Morocco, and Portugal, among others; political prisoners were released in Sudan, Nepal, Indonesia, Haiti, and Paraguay in the first year of the policy; and instances of torture apparently did show a decline.[50] More significantly, perhaps, American prestige in various areas of the world was enhanced. The United States began to stand for particular political values in world affairs. As a result, a more receptive attitude toward American initiatives was forthcoming throughout the world, and especially within the developing world.

Perhaps the greatest demonstration of this human rights impact was in Africa. The black nations of southern Africa, in particular, began to have confidence in the Carter administration and American policy toward that region. Through the vigorous efforts of Andrew Young, President Carter's ambassador to the United Nations, the "front-line" states around white-ruled Rhodesia (Angola, Botswana, Mozambique, Tanzania, Zambia) began to believe that the Carter administration was willing to seek a just solution to the problems of that nation, Namibia, and South Africa itself. Moreover, the pivotal African state of Nigeria also began to express confidence in the American administration by receiving President Carter for an official visit.[51]

President Jimmy Carter, writing in his memoirs, *Keeping Faith*, seemed to place the greatest benefit of his human rights policy on the intangible change of atmosphere and attitude toward individual liberties on a worldwide scale during his years in office. As he notes, "The lifting of the human spirit, the revival of hope, the absence of fear, the release from prison, the end of torture, the reunion of a family, the newfound sense of dignity" were the ultimate measure of the worth of the human rights policy.[52] For him, that was satisfaction enough to have made it worthwhile.

On the negative side, the human rights campaign caused friction with friendly, but human-rights-deficient nations. Relations with Nicaragua, Argentina, Brazil, Iran, and South Korea, among others, were strained by these calls for human rights efforts. Further, the human rights policy contributed to problems in Soviet-American relations. The policy was particularly challenging to détente because it implied an "intervention" into the internal affairs of other states. Nonintervention in internal affairs, by contrast, was the benchmark of the détente approach that evolved under the Nixon-Ford-Kissinger administrations.[53]

Beyond the apparent violation of national sovereignty, the human rights policy threatened the Soviet Union for more fundamental reasons: fostering individual freedom of expression and tolerating diversity directly affronted totalitarian control at home and foreshadowed a weakening of Soviet control over Eastern Europe. Thus, when President Carter wrote a letter to Andrei Sakharov, perhaps the leading Soviet scientist and dissident, or expressed support for Vladimir Bukovsky, the leader of the Helsinki Monitoring Group in the Soviet Union, the tension in East-West relations was exacerbated. While President Carter acknowledged that these kinds of actions "did create tension between us and prevented a more harmonious resolution of some of the other differences," he disputes the claim that the human rights issue singularly affected overall Soviet-American relations: "I cannot recall any instance when the human rights issue was the *direct* cause of failure in working with the Soviets on matters of common interest."[54]

The Soviet Union challenged and attacked Carter's human rights policy. The Soviets contended that the United States was guilty of human rights violations itself because of the lack of economic rights for its citizens—insufficient employment, inadequate health care, and unsatisfactory social welfare benefits. Furthermore, the atmosphere for conducting relations between the United States and the Soviet Union was affected by the human rights campaign, as Foreign Minister Andrei Gromyko implied in April 1977, after initial arms control discussions had broken down."[55]

DEALING WITH THE SOVIET UNION

The essential aim of the Carter administration was to downgrade the dominance of the Soviet-American relationship in the foreign policy of the United States and to concentrate efforts primarily on other areas of the world. As one analyst has aptly put it, the goal was to contain the Soviet Union not by directly confronting it as in the past, but "by drying out the pond of possible Soviet mischief" through resolving global issues.[56] If global problems were addressed, global intrusions by the Soviets would be much less likely, and the Soviet Union would be contained.

Despite the intentions of the Carter administration to deemphasize the Soviet-American relationship, it never really was possible to do this. The distance between the Carter administration's perception of what policy should be and its ability to achieve it was greatest in this particular policy area. Moreover, Carter's failure to establish a clear and consistent policy toward the Soviet Union was probably the greatest shortcoming of his initial foreign policy approach. Ironically—especially in light of his basic approach—the failure to establish such a policy hindered the attempt to give greater priority to other global issues and to achieve more success in those areas.

At least three different reasons may be cited for the overall inconsistency of Carter's policy toward the Soviet Union. First of all, the Soviets would not allow the U.S. to downgrade their centrality to global politics. The Soviet Union's prestige was damaged by the Carter policy. Since the Soviet Union had placed a great effort on achieving superpower military and political parity, and had finally achieved it with the 1972 agreements, it was unwilling to yield to playing second fiddle on global issues. Thus, the Soviets challenged Carter on human rights, but they also attacked him on arms control, despite their desire for it. More importantly, the Soviets challenged Carter's attempt to focus on Third World issues. The Soviets sought to make inroads into the Western Hemisphere, especially in Central America, through Cuba (or so the U.S. believed). The Soviets, too, were not restraining the Vietnamese in Asia and were continuing their military deployments there. Finally, the Soviet Union continued its pressure on Western Europe through an increase in its own military capabilities.[57]

A second factor also contributed to the lack of a consistent policy toward the Soviet Union: a division within the Carter administration itself over how to deal with the Soviet Union. In other words, how convinced was the American leadership that they wanted to move away from a Soviet-focused foreign policy? Such a question particularly focuses upon the competing perspectives of Carter's two top advisors, Secretary of State Cyrus Vance and National Security Advisor Zbigniew Brzezinski. More specifically, it focused on the conflicting views within the thinking of Brzezinski himself. While Secretary Vance appeared to be committed to Carter's globalist perspective and wanted to deal with the Soviets on a piecemeal basis without linkage, Brzezinski, seemed to be of two minds in dealing with the Soviets.[58]

Although Brzezinski was in many ways the originator of the global perspective for the Carter administration, once in office as national security advisor, he seemed to interpret international events through the Soviet-American prism. Brzezinski had formally rejected the notion of "linkage" as the guide to American policy in dealing with the Soviets, yet he adopted a policy stance that seemed markedly close to it. In fact, the first time that the Soviets took significant actions in a "third area"—in the Horn of East Africa—shades of the original Kissinger formula for dealing with the Soviet-American relationship appeared. He wanted to confront the Soviets directly on this matter and to downgrade any remaining elements of the détente relationship.

The issue that precipitated this controversy over the appropriate policy approach to the Soviet Union was the question of Cuban and Russian action in Ethiopia in early 1975. To Brzezinski, these activities in the Horn of Africa should affect the SALT negotiations, and he said so directly.[59] Moreover, he used language strongly reminiscent of linkage in discussing this issue:

> In the nuclear age, we can't have stability unless détente is general and reciprocal. What we have to establish is that the rules of the games have to be the same for both sides. I think that the Horn is a basic test of that. I think if we don't establish some reciprocity and some mutual restraint and don't make it binding, especially in its military favor, then we're going to get a reaction against détente that is going to make some things that are desirable impossible to achieve—such as SALT.[60]

Others within the Carter administration—Secretary of State Cyrus Vance and Secretary of Defense Harold Brown, as well as the President himself—were not willing to go as far as Brzezinski on this issue. While Brzezinski eventually lost out on this debate, it was this kind of dispute over how to deal with the Soviets, and especially how multilateral events were to affect bilateral relations between the two superpowers, that dominated the Carter administration agenda during its first three years.

Beginning with this rather dramatic example over the Horn of Africa, President Carter and his advisors were groping for a coherent policy toward the Soviet Union. Speeches by the president at Wake Forest University and the U.S. Naval Academy demonstrated efforts to pursue a more vigorous foreign policy toward that nation. Nonetheless, a conciliatory policy continued to hold sway throughout 1978.[61] In fact, the same general approach was followed until late 1979 and the Soviet invasion of Afghanistan. Despite the Carter intention of reducing the American fixation on its relationship with the Soviet Union in its foreign policy, the internal policymaking debate among Carter and his advisors had just the opposite effect.

A third factor that made it difficult for the U.S. to move away from the Soviets as dominant in foreign policy matters was the nature of American domestic beliefs. A real dualism existed in the minds of the American public. While Americans supported détente efforts by a wide margin, they were also increasingly wary of growing Soviet power vis-à-vis the United States. Additionally, the American public continued to see the Soviet Union as central to U.S. foreign policy.[62]

Accompanying this dual attitude was a shift away from support for cuts in defense spending, which had been so strong in the immediate post-Vietnam years. By 1977, and especially by 1978, support for more defense spending was increasing, and the public's willingness to favor military force against Soviet incursions was also becoming more evident.[63] Thus, from the viewpoint of domestic politics, the Soviet-American relationship still seemed very crucial, and the Carter administration was no doubt aware of these changing beliefs and the need to accommodate them in the foreign policy arena.

For various reasons, then, the Soviet-American relationship could not be removed from its dominant role in American foreign policy matters despite the initial Carter administration hopes. Moreover, the inability of the administration to integrate fully the primacy of this relationship into its foreign policy design and its "strategic incoherence" when it tried to do so plagued the administration throughout its four years.[64]

ADDRESSING GLOBAL ISSUES

Beyond the all-encompassing issue of human rights, in which the record is mixed, the Carter administration was only marginally successful in dealing with two major global concerns that it had initially identified: arms control and rich-poor issues.

The Carter administration took important initial steps to deal with both nuclear proliferation and conventional arms transfers, but it faltered in its own execution of these policies. Although restraints on nuclear proliferation were enacted into law (the Non-Proliferation Act of 1978), President Carter himself backed away from the requirements of this act in 1980 by selling nuclear fuel to India, despite that country's 1974 nuclear explosion and the potential for proliferation in that region. The requirements of global and regional power politics intruded into this nuclear restraint measure.[65] At the same time, increased international standards on nuclear fuel transfers were developed, and overall nuclear proliferation seemed to slow down. On balance, though, the goal of strong nuclear proliferation control remained elusive.

President Carter also attempted to control and reduce conventional arms transfers by issuing Presidential Directive 13 on May 19, 1977. By this directive, the president said the United States "will henceforth view arms transfers as an exceptional foreign policy implement, to be used only in instances where it can be clearly demonstrated that the transfer contributes to our national security interests." Specifically, the United States would not be the first supplier to introduce newly developed weapons systems into a region of the world; would not permit development or modification of "*advanced* weapons systems *solely for export*"; would not permit coproduction with other countries of significant weapons, equipment, and major components; and, finally, would not permit the retransfer of U.S. weapons to a third party. In addition, new procedures for decision making on arms transfers and a dollar ceiling on the amount of new commitments (with lower amounts in subsequent years) were established.[66]

In reality, though, the conventional arms policy did not effectively control the sophistication or amount of weaponry sent abroad. Although some weapons transfers were curtailed by the Carter directive, significant agreements with Iran, Saudi Arabia, South Korea, and Egypt were not. Moreover, these involved a number of new and modern weapons transfers (F-15 and FX fighter aircraft, AWACS, and TOW tank missiles).[67] Further, U.S. arms sales actually rose from $12.8 billion in 1977 to $17.1 billion in 1980,[68] although the rate of inflation reduced the real amount of growth during this period.

In the strategic nuclear arms control area, the Carter record was only a bit better. Despite numerous fits and starts, SALT II was finally hammered out and signed in Vienna by Jimmy Carter and Leonid Brezhnev in June 1979. However, the measure was never approved by the U.S. Senate and became a hostage of Soviet action toward Afghanistan in late 1979.

Despite initial enthusiasm and rhetoric on closing the rich-poor gap, the overall evaluation of the Carter administration in the areas of aid, trade, and debt relief for poor countries was at best mixed. While the administration did provide greater dollar amounts of aid, especially for the Middle East, foreign assistance reached one of its lowest levels as a percentage of the GNP in the postwar period (about 0.20 percent of the GNP in 1979). Total aid did rebound to 0.27 percent of the GNP in 1980, but the overall record was still relatively poor—especially as compared with the other Development Assistance Committee countries of the Organization for Economic Cooperation and Development (OECD).[69] On a more positive side, the United States increased its multilateral aid from about $1 billion in 1977 to $2.5 billion in 1979.[70] In the trade area, the "Tokyo Round" negotiations reached an agreement on reform of the GATT (General Agreement on Tariffs and Trade) system during the Carter administration, but the poor states were not very satisfied with the results— as witnessed by the fact that almost all of the Third World nations boycotted the April 1979 signing ceremony.[71] A similar result occurred in the debt area. The United States was not very responsive to requests for debt relief or debt rescheduling by the poor states.[72]

RESOLVING THIRD WORLD CONFLICTS

The area of greatest success for the Carter administration in implementing its global design was in addressing Third World conflicts. During his administration, President Carter was able to alleviate, if not resolve, conflict in three different areas of the world: Central America over the Panama Canal, the Middle East between Egypt and Israel, and southern Africa over Rhodesia and Namibia. In addition, he was able to lessen conflict for the U.S. in Asia with the formal establishment of diplomatic relations between the People's Republic of China and the United States.

Perhaps the greatest arena of success was the resolution of the Panama Canal dispute. For over two decades, the United States had negotiated over the transference of the Canal and the Canal Zone to sole Panamanian sovereignty. The failure to resolve this dispute was one of those regional issues that was undermining American influence in Central and South America, and it was one of the issues that President Carter was determined to address during his presidency.

Indicative of the importance of this issue was the fact that the first Presidential Review Memorandum emanating from the Carter administration dealt with the Panama Canal issue.[73] With such a central priority, the American and Panamanian negotiators set out to reach an agreement. In a few months they were successful, and by September 1977 the two treaties that constituted the agreement were ready for an elaborate signing ceremony in Washington. All Latin American countries were invited to witness the signing of these two pacts, and it was a triumphant occasion for the Carter administration.

One of the pacts, the Panana Canal Treaty, called for the total transference of Canal control to Panama by the year 2000, with intermediate stages of transfer during the twenty-two years of the pact. The second agreement, the Neutrality Treaty, would become effective in the year 2000 and was of unlimited duration. This pact stated that the Canal would be permanently neutral, secure, and open to the vessels of all nations in time of peace and war. Moreover, the U.S. and Panama agreed to maintain and defend this neutrality principle. Document Summary 4.4 summarizes these treaties.

While the signing of the treaties was a Carter success, the task of getting them passed by the U.S. Senate proved to be an even greater triumph for his administration.[74] Although the treaties were subjected to modification in the Senate, neither was burdened with an amendment requiring its renegotiation with Panama. Through a long and arduous lobbying effort—even in the face of opposition by the American public—President Carter saw the Neutrality and Panama Canal Treaties passed by identical votes, 68 to 32, on March 16, 1978, and April 18, 1978, respectively.[75]

President Carter viewed these pacts as clearly compatible with his goals of reducing regional conflicts and fostering global justice. Both of these goals, moreover, would minimize anti-American feelings and enhance American prestige and influence abroad.[76]

In the Middle East, a constant regional trouble spot, the initial strategy of the Carter administration was to seek a comprehensive settlement through a Geneva Conference, co-sponsored with the Soviet Union. This approach did not get very far because the Israelis were reluctant to participate and the Arabs demanded maximum Palestinian participation.[77] The Israeli fear was that they would be outvoted in such a conference by the larger number of Arab states and the Soviet Union. Hence the outcome of such a meeting would be far from their liking.

In November 1977, however, President Anwar Sadat of Egypt took a dramatic step to move the peace process along. He announced

---

DOCUMENT SUMMARY 4.4   THE PANAMA CANAL TREATIES,
SEPTEMBER 1977

Panama Canal Treaty
This treaty abrogates any earlier treaty arrangements between the
United States and Panama and allows the United States to operate
the Panama Canal until December 31, 1999. At that time, the control
of the Canal will revert to Panama. The Panama Canal Company will
be dissolved, and the Panama Canal Commission, composed of
Americans and Panamanians, will operate the Canal until its
reversion. The canal administrator will be an American, with a
Panamanian as a deputy until 1990; after 1990, the canal
administrator will be a Panamanian, with an American as a deputy
until the year 2000.

*Treaty Concerning the Permanent Neutrality and Operation
of the Panama Canal*
This treaty enters into effect at the same time as the Panama Canal
Treaty and guarantees that the Canal "shall remain secure and open
to peaceful transit by vessels of all nations on the terms of entire
equality," whether in times of war or peace. Panama and the United
States each "shall have the discretion to take whatever action it
deems necessary, in accordance with its constitutional processes, to
defend the canal against any threat to the permanent regime of
neutrality."

Source: These summaries are drawn from "Text of Treaties" and "Letters of Submittal,"
Department of State Bulletin, October 17, 1977, pp. 438–485 and 496–498, and Department of
State, "Panama Canal: The New Treaties," Deparment of State Publication 8924, November
1977, pp. 7–12.

---

that he was willing to go to Jerusalem to seek peace. Prime Minister
Menachem Begin of Israel quickly issued an invitation for President
Sadat to speak to the Israeli Parliament. On November 19, 1977,
President Sadat landed in Jerusalem for three days of discussions
with the Israelis.[78] The importance of this visit cannot be overstated.
It broke the impasse that had set into the Middle East process since
the shuttle diplomacy of Henry Kissinger; it established the precedent of face-to-face negotiations between Arabs and Israelis; and it
raised hope for real progress.

   Such hopes were soon dashed. Both sides still held strong positions on the fundamental questions of the return of Arab lands and
Israeli security. These concerns would not be easily altered. Moreover, by the summer of 1978 an impasse had set in—despite mediation efforts by President Carter. At this juncture, President Carter
himself took a bold gamble by inviting President Sadat and Prime

---

DOCUMENT SUMMARY 4.5   THE CAMP DAVID ACCORDS
BETWEEN EGYPT AND ISRAEL, SEPTEMBER 1978

Framework for Peace in the Middle East
This framework called for a "just, comprehensive, and durable settlement of the Middle East conflict through the conclusion of peace treaties based upon Security Council Resolutions 242 and 338 in all their parts." (The resolutions called for an exchange of land by Israel—the territories seized in the June 1967 war—for peace with their Arab neighbors—an end to the state of war with Israel.) It consisted of two parts.
The first part of the framework dealt with resolving the conflict over the West Bank of the Jordan and the Gaza Strip, which Israel had seized. This portion called for the establishment of a self-governing authority within these territories "for a period not exceeding five years." By at least the third year of that self-governing authority, "negotiations will take place to determine the final status of the West Bank and Gaza and its relationship to its neighbors and to conclude a peace treaty between Israel and Jordan. . . ." These negotiations will involve representatives from Egypt, Israel, Jordan, and "representatives of the inhabitants of the West Bank and Gaza. . . ."
The second part of the framework called for Egypt and Israel "to negotiate in good faith with a goal of concluding within three months from the signing of this Framework a peace treaty between them." [This treaty was ultimately signed in March 1979 in Washington, D.C. Under this treaty, Israel returned the Sinai Peninsula to Egypt, and Israel and Egypt ended their state of war, recognized one another, and established diplomatic relations.]

Source: This description is drawn from the framework, which was printed in Department of State Publication 8954, *The Camp David Summit* (Washington, D.C.: Office of Public Communications, Bureau of Public Affairs, September 1978).

Minister Begin to Camp David, Maryland—the presidential retreat—for in-depth discussions on the Middle East. As a result of thirteen days of intense negotiations, "A Framework for Peace in the Middle East" was agreed to by the two competing parties and witnessed by President Carter.[79] (Document Summary 4.5 summarizes the key components of this framework.) Both adversaries attributed the success of the Camp David meetings to the personal efforts of Jimmy Carter.

The signing of this Camp David framework on September 17, 1978, was another highlight of the Carter foreign policy. Some real progress had been made in addressing the Middle East conflict. Furthermore, in March 1979, a peace treaty following the Camp David framework was signed between Egypt and Israel. A comprehensive peace settlement, however, ultimately eluded the Carter administration, as all the Arab states except Egypt refused to accept and participate in the Camp David framework. Nonetheless, these Middle East results, too, served as an important achievement in addressing regional conflict with American assistance—a key goal of the Carter approach.

The third region of the world where the Carter administration achieved some success was in southern Africa over the questions of Rhodesia and Namibia. The role of the U.S. was not as direct as in the other two areas, but it was nonetheless important. Specifically, the Carter administration adopted a strong stand for black majority rule in these areas and assisted the British in achieving a successful outcome for Rhodesia (now Zimbabwe). The United States, with the assistance of other Western states, maneuvered the South African government into accepting a UN resolution on the transfer of power in Namibia.[80]

In the case of Rhodesia, the Carter administration ceased trade with the white-dominated government and imposed economic sanctions on it in the first year of its term. It also refused to lift sanctions even when the Ian Smith government and some black leaders had reached an "internal settlement" in 1978 because dissident factions in exile outside the country had not participated in the settlement. By adopting such a measure, despite considerable opposition within the Congress, the United States gave impetus to the British efforts toward a comprehensive settlement involving all parties. Such a settlement was ultimately worked out in the Lancaster House negotiations in London during the fall of 1979, and the agreement was put into effect in 1980.[81] Majority rule was obtained in Zimbabwe, and the Carter administration rightly claimed credit for its role.

The same policy posture was adopted toward South Africa—a firm stance against apartheid and a policy position calling for the transfer of control of Namibia to majority rule. Under U.S. policy pressure and that of other states, South Africa agreed to UN resolution 435 on this transfer. The transfer of power met numerous snags and was not implemented during the Carter years. (In fact, it was not fully implemented until 1990.) Nonetheless, the decision to promote American domestic values of respecting human rights and fostering majority rule won praise for the United States throughout Africa.

Finally, the Carter administration's decision to establish formal diplomatic relations with the People's Republic of China on January 1, 1979, was another major foreign policy success. Although this decision caused some initial difficulties with Taiwan (since relations

MAP 4.2   SOUTHERN AFRICA

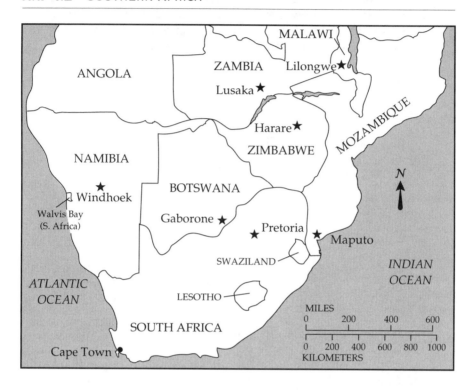

were broken with this regime), it was generally hailed as an important milestone in American foreign policy. Opening relations with
Peking reduced hostilities between two important states and had the
potential of easing conflicts in East Asia. At the same time, though,
this step created another uncertainty in America's approach to its traditional adversary, the Soviet Union, and reinforced the Soviet view
that the Carter administration was more interested in dealing with
other states than with it.

ALLIANCE RELATIONS

In attempting to improve relations with America's friends the Carter
administration was less successful than it was in addressing some
important Third World conflicts. Significant political, economic, and
military decisions were made during his administration, but as President Carter left office, differences in alliance relations were still
quite serious, despite some cooperative efforts.

Yearly economic summit conferences (which had been started in the Ford administration) served as the principal vehicle for trying to coordinate policy between the U.S. and its trilateral friends (i.e., Europe and Japan) during the Carter presidency. At these meetings, agreements were reached for the Europeans and the Japanese to expand their economies through increased governmental spending and for the United States to decrease its dependence on imported oil. Similarly, at a 1979 economic summit, a commitment among the U.S., Japan, Canada, and the European Community to put a quantitative lid on oil imports was agreed to.[82] Still, domestic, economic, and political considerations were still to dash the hopes for full trilateral economic cooperation.

In the military area, two important agreements were reached among the alliance members during the Carter administration. The first dealt with a commitment by all NATO countries to increase their defense expenditures by 3 percent annually through 1984. The second was the Dual Track Decision of 1979 on intermediate nuclear forces for Europe. The deployment decision was contingent upon whether progress occurred in arms control negotiations with the Soviet Union over these kinds of weapons.[83] The increased military expenditure levels were not met by the NATO countries, however, and the new theater nuclear weapons decision met considerable political resistance in Europe, although the deployment eventually did begin in late 1983 and remained until the signing of the Intermediate Nuclear Forces Treaty of December 1987 (see Chapter 5).

Political differences between the Carter administration and its allies remained, too. Most prominently, disputes developed between Western Europe and the United States over America's approach toward the Soviet Union. European concern quickly developed, for example, over the strident human rights campaign during the early part of the Carter administration because it might endanger East-West détente. Also, when the United States adopted a hardline policy toward the Soviet Union over its invasion of Afghanistan, the Europeans were much less willing to go along with such an approach. Alliance unity suffered as a result.

The allies tended to view Carter as unpredictable and not always sensitive to their needs. His on-again, off-again decision making over the development and deployment of the neutron bomb particularly caused alliance problems. Although the neutron bomb was proposed as one way to counterbalance the Soviet buildup in populous Central Europe, it had one troubling feature for many Europeans. This new nuclear weapon would kill more people ("soft targets") than it would destroy property ("hard targets"). Hence, property would be saved even as more and more lives were destroyed. Not only did it cause alliance difficulties over the type of weapon it was and because Europe would be the arena of its primary deployment, but many Europeans felt that their concerns were not sufficiently considered in alliance decision making over this new weapons system.

REALISM IN THE LAST YEAR: A RESPONSE TO CRITICS

By 1979, the Carter foreign policy was already subject to considerable criticism on the grounds that it was inconsistent, incoherent, and a failure. According to one critic, it was leading to a decline in America's standing abroad.[84] While some successes in his global approach might be identified, too many problems were evident, without a clear strategy for dealing with them. A revolution occurred in Iran, replacing the Shah (whom the Carter administration had supported) with a markedly anti-American regime; a revolution was successful in Nicaragua, with the U.S. adopting a policy that pleased neither the Somozistas nor the Sandinistas; the Middle East peace effort was in a holding pattern with Arab rejection of the Camp David framework; and Soviet power was continuing to grow without an American response. On all these fronts, a certain malaise seemed to have set into the Carter foreign policy, marked by indecision and inability to act. For all these reasons, a change in policy direction might well have been anticipated, yet two international events ultimately proved critical to the Carter foreign policy change.

The seizure of American hostages in Iran in November 1979 and the Soviet invasion of Afghanistan a month later were the watershed events in the global approach of the Carter administration.[85] Despite the administration's effort to move away from concentration on the Soviet Union, these two events brought that nation back into focus for America—the former indirectly, because it raised the prospect of Soviet inroads into the Middle East and Southwest Asia; the latter directly, because it projected the Soviet Union into the center of global affairs once again. (Map 6.1 visually portrays the geographical and strategic importance of Iran and Afghanistan in Southwest Asian and Middle Eastern affairs.)

The impact of the Soviet invasion of Afghanistan upon President Carter's view of the Soviet Union was poignantly stated by the president himself in an ABC television interview at the time: "My opinion of the Russians has changed most drastically in the last week than even in the previous $2^{1}/_{2}$ years before that."[86] Thus, in the last year of his administration, President Carter moved away from his global approach and adopted the bilateral approach of the past, with the Soviet-American relationship at the heart of his policymaking. Policy actions, moreover, concentrated on this central concern. While not all the earlier initiatives were jettisoned, the other issue areas that President Carter had earlier identified were given a secondary role.

Most immediately, the Carter administration adopted a series of responses to the Soviet Union over the invasion of Afghanistan. The ratification of the SALT II Treaty was shelved in the U.S. Senate; high technology sales to the Soviet Union were halted; Soviet fishing privileges in American waters were restricted; and a grain embargo was imposed upon the Soviet Union.[87] A little later, Carter announced an American boycott of the 1980 Summer Olympics in Moscow.

Global events now were increasingly interpreted through lenses that focused on their effect on Soviet-American relations. The principal U.S. efforts during this year were to rally its friends to contain the Soviet Union. Moreover, it was during this time period that such global goals as arms transfer controls were downplayed as a signal to the Soviets of American resolve. For instance, discussions were held with the Chinese about providing them with arms. Furthermore, the United States began an effort to shore up its ties in the Persian Gulf and in Southwest Asia. Military aid was quickly offered to Pakistan, and National Security Advisor Zbigniew Brzezinski made a highly publicized trip to the Khyber Pass to illustrate American determination over Afghanistan. Contacts were also made with friendly regimes in the Middle East to gain base and access rights for the United States in case of an emergency. Finally, the development of the U.S. Rapid Deployment Force—an elite military force that could respond quickly to an emergency anywhere in the world—was given a top priority.

As a further signal to the Soviet Union, President Carter in his 1980 State of the Union Address warned the Soviets that "an attempt by any outside force to gain control of the Persian Gulf region will be regarded as an assault on the vital interests of the United States. It will be repelled by use of any means necessary, including military force."[88] Quickly labeled the Carter Doctrine, this statement was highly reminiscent of an earlier era, with its Cold War rhetoric and its reliance on the essential elements of containment. Nonetheless, it accurately set the tone for the final year of the Carter administration and the policy shift that had occurred within the administration.

Policy actions toward Iran, too, reflected this new national self-interest orientation of the Carter administration. Rather than trying to accommodate Third World demands, as had been attempted in previous years, the United States now took a variety of steps, from breaking diplomatic relations, to seizing Iranian assets, to imposing sanctions, and ultimately attempting a military rescue as a means of demonstrating resolve. Such actions also connoted a return to a realist perspective in foreign policy and away from the idealism President Carter had initially tried to pursue. Unfortunately, this strategy failed to yield quick results, and the American hostages were not freed for 444 days, until immediately after President Carter left office on January 20, 1981.

Despite President Carter's attempt to change foreign policy direction, the perception of ineffectiveness continued to haunt his administration. As a consequence, foreign policy, with particular emphasis on the Iranian and Soviet experiences, became an important campaign issue in the 1980 presidential election.[89] Then, however, instead of focusing on a foreign policy that was "good and decent," as in 1976, the Republican challenger to President Carter, Ronald Reagan, called for a policy to "make America great again." Such a policy was surely a call to move away from the idealism of the early Carter years. Yet—and ironically—it was a call to pursue the kind of foreign policy that President Carter himself had tried to initiate in his last year in office.

CONCLUDING COMMENTS

The Nixon and Carter administrations offered different approaches to American foreign policy as the Cold War was challenged. Each approach sought, albeit in different ways, to change the emphasis from the globalism and moralism of that earlier period. The greatest value change the Nixon years brought to U.S. policy was a movement away from the emphasis on moralism and greater acceptance of traditional realism as the basis for actions toward the rest of the world. At least until the last year of its time in office, the Carter administration sought to continue the limited globalism of the Nixon years (defined more with an emphasis on trilateral and Third World relations than upon superpower ties) but to change from the singular moralism of anti-communism to a more comprehensive moralism, best exemplified by its human rights campaign. As we have discussed, though, neither administration succeeded completely, and both faced challenges.

In the next chapter, then, we shall survey yet another approach to American foreign policy in the post-Vietnam era. The administration of Ronald Reagan sought less to impose a new value approach and more to restore an earlier one—best epitomized by the Cold War consensus. While the Reagan administration would continue the moral tones of the Carter administration (although now the target would once again be global communism, not global human rights violations), it would seek to restore an American globalism more reminiscent of an earlier era than that of its immediate predecessors.

NOTES

1. The approach of the Ford administration (1974–1976) is not treated separately here because Henry Kissinger continued to serve as national security advisor (through 1975) and as secretary of state (through 1976).

2. For some discussion of idealism and realism, see, among others, Yale H. Ferguson and Richard W. Mansbach, *The Elusive Quest: Theory and International Politics* (Columbia: University of South Carolina Press, 1988), esp. pp. 40–48; Charles O. Lerche, Jr., and Abdul A. Said, *Concepts of International Politics,* 3rd ed. (Englewood Cliffs, NJ: Prentice-Hall, Inc., 1979), pp. 4–5; and Hans J. Morgenthau, *Politics Among Nations: The Struggle for Power and Peace* (New York: Alfred A. Knopf Inc., 1973), pp. 3–15.

3. Richard M. Nixon, *U.S. Policy for the 1970's, A New Strategy for Peace.* A Report to the Congress (Washington, D.C.: U.S. Government Printing Office, February 18, 1970). The quoted passages are at pp. 2 and 3.

4. Richard M. Nixon, "Asia After Viet Nam," *Foreign Affairs* 46 (October 1967): 111–125. The quoted passages are at pp. 121, 123, and 114.

5. This section draws upon Kissinger's important essay "Contemporary Issues of American Foreign Policy." It is printed as Chapter 2 in Henry A. Kissinger, *American Foreign Policy,* 3rd ed. (New York: W. W. Norton & Company, 1977), pp. 51–97. The quoted passage is at p. 79.

6. Ibid., pp. 91–97.

7. Henry A. Kissinger, *A World Restored: Metternich, Castlereagh and the Problems of Peace, 1812–1822* (Boston: Houghton Mifflin Company, 1957), p. 1.

8. For a description of the characteristics of the "statesman," see Kissinger's essay "Domestic Structure and Foreign Policy," in James N. Rosenau, ed., *International Politics and Foreign Policy,* rev. ed. (New York: Free Press, 1969), pp. 261–275. The quoted passage on the importance of negotiations to stability is at p. 274.

9. Kissinger, *American Foreign Policy,* pp. 120–121.

10. For a further analysis of the dimensions of Kissinger's approach described here, and a strong critique of it, see Falk, "What's Wrong With Henry Kissinger's Foreign Policy," *Alternatives* I (1975): 79–100.

11. Once again, the analysis includes the years through 1976, even though President Ford came to office in August 1974, because Henry Kissinger continued to dominate the foreign policy apparatus as secretary of state.

12. "U.S.-U.S.S.R. Exchanges Programs," *GIST* (Washington, D.C.: Department of State, April 1976).

13. See the excerpts from Henry Kissinger's *White House Years* (Little, Brown & Co., 1979) on China in *Time,* October 1, 1979, pp. 53–58.

14. The Shanghai Communique is reprinted in Gene T. Hsiao, ed., *Sino-American Détente and Its Policy Implications* (New York: Praeger Publishers, Inc., 1974), pp. 298–301.

15. This discussion draws upon "Conference on Security and Cooperation in Europe," *Department of State Bulletin,* September 26, 1977, pp. 404–410. The notion of "baskets" to summarize their work came from the conference itself (p. 405).

16. See his essay in *American Foreign Policy,* expanded ed. (New York: W. W. Norton & Company, 1974), pp. 99–135.

17. See John G. Stoessinger in his *Henry Kissinger: The Anguish of Power* (New York: W. W. Norton & Company, 1976), pp. 62–63.

18. Ibid., p. 73.

19. George C. Herring, *America's Longest War: The United States and Vietnam 1950–1975,* 2nd ed. (New York: Alfred A. Knopf Inc., 1986), p. 255.

20. Falk, "What's Wrong With Henry Kissinger's Foreign Policy?" pp. 79–100.

21. Ibid., p. 98.

22. Ibid., p. 99.

23. Ibid., p. 88.

24. George McGovern, "A New Internationalism," in William Taubman, *Globalism and Its Critics* (Lexington, MA: D.C. Heath and Company, 1973), p. 163.

25. Ibid., p. 167.

26. William F. Buckley, Jr. "Politics of Henry Kissinger," Transcript of *Firing Line* program, originally telecast on the Public Broadcasting System, September 13, 1975, p. 5. Mr. Buckley was quoting from the Gallup Polls.

27. George W. Ball, *Diplomacy for a Crowded World* (Boston: Atlantic Monthly/Little, Brown & Co., 1976), pp. 108–129.

28. Ibid., p. 15. The other quotes are from pp. 13 and 14.

29. This global perspective (and changes in it) is discussed in part in Leonard Silk's brief analysis of an address by Zbigniew Brzezinski, "Economic Scene: New U.S. View of the World," *New York Times,* May 1, 1979, p. D2; and in an address by Cyrus Vance, "Meeting the Challenges of a Changing World," Washington, D.C.: Bureau of Public Affairs, Department of State, May 1, 1979.

30. Jimmy Carter, "Inaugural Address of President Jimmy Carter: The Ever-Expanding American Dream," *Vital Speeches* 43 (February 15, 1977): 258.

31. Jimmy Carter, "Humane Purposes in Foreign Policy," Department of State News Release, May 22, 1977, p. 1 (Commencement Address at the University of Notre Dame).

32. Ibid., p. 2.

33. Ibid., pp. 1 and 5.

34. Zbigniew Brzezinski, "America in a Hostile World," *Foreign Policy* 23 (Summer 1976): 65–96; and Elizabeth Drew, "A Reporter At Large: Brzezinski," *The New Yorker,* May 1, 1978, pp. 90–130. The quotations are from "America in a Hostile World," at p. 91 and p. 94, respectively.

35. See the discussion in Drew, "A Reporter At Large: Brzezinski," over the extent to which linkage was applied, especially pp. 117–121.

36. Although the Carter administration is usually identified with the human rights issue, congressional action on this issue began at least in 1973 with hearings by the International Organizations and Movements Subcommittee headed by Donald Fraser. On this point, see the discussion in Harold Molineu, "Human Rights: Administrative Impact of a Symbolic Policy," in John C. Grumm

and Stephen L. Wasby, eds., *The Analysis of Policy Impact* (Lexington, MA: Lexington Books, D. C. Heath and Company, 1981), pp. 24–25.

37. "Inaugural Address of President Jimmy Carter: The Ever-Expanding American Dream," p. 259.

38. "Humane Purposes in Foreign Policy," p. 2.

39. Jimmy Carter, *Keeping Faith* (New York: Bantam Books, 1982), p. 145.

40. Ibid., pp. 142 and 144.

41. Stanley Hoffmann, "Requiem," *Foreign Policy* 42 (Spring 1981): 3.

42. These descriptions are from *Human Rights and U.S. Foreign Policy* (Department of State Publication 8959, Washington, D.C.: Bureau of Public Affairs, 1978), pp. 7–8. Secretary of State Cyrus Vance had outlined these same categories in a speech to the University of Georgia School of Law on April 30, 1977 *(Department of State Bulletin,* May 23, 1977, pp. 505–508).

43. Lincoln P. Bloomfield, "From Ideology to Program to Policy," *Journal of Policy Analysis and Management* 2 (Fall 1982): 6.

In reality, some nations (Argentina, Brazil, Guatemala, for example) simply rejected American military assistance after attacks on their human rights records by the U.S. See Charles W. Kegley, Jr., and Eugene R. Wittkopf, *American Foreign Policy: Pattern and Process,* 2nd ed. (New York: St. Martin's Press, 1982), p. 595.

45. " The President's News Conference of March 9, 1977," in *Weekly Compilation of Presidential Documents* 13 (March 14, 1977): 328–329.

46. Louis René Beres, *People, States, and World Order* (Itasca, IL: F. E. Peacock Publishers, Inc., 1981), p. 51.

47. These arguments are developed in Jeane J. Kirkpatrick, "Dictatorships and Double Standards," *Commentary* 68 (November 1979): 34–45; and "Human Rights and American Foreign Policy: A Symposium," *Commentary* 79 (November 1981): 42–45.

48. See, for example, the proposal by William F. Buckley, Jr., in his "Human Rights and Foreign Policy," *Foreign Affairs* 58 (Spring 1980): 775–796. Also, see Arthur Schlesinger, Jr., "Human Rights and the American Tradition," *Foreign Affairs* 57 (Winter 1978/79): 503–526, for his view on intergovernmental and nongovernmental organizations.

49. Department of State, *Report on Human Rights Practices in Countries Receiving U.S. Aid.* Submitted to the Committee on Foreign Relations, U.S. Senate and Committee on Foreign Affairs, U.S. House of Representatives (Washington, D.C.: U.S. Government Printing Office, 1979), p. 5.

50. Ibid., pp. 4–5; Bloomfield, "From Ideology to Program to Policy," p. 9; and Warren Christopher, "The Diplomacy of Human Rights: The First Year," Speech to the American Bar Association, February 13, 1978 (Washington, D.C.: Department of State, 1978).

51. See Colin Legum, "The African Crisis," in William P. Bundy, ed., *America and the World 1978* (New York: Pergamon Press, 1979), pp. 633–651.

52. Carter, *Keeping Faith,* p. 150.

53. See, for example, the Helsinki Accords discussed above and summarized in Document Summary 4.3 regarding this principle.

54. The quotations are from *Keeping Faith,* p. 149. Emphasis in original. The support for Bukovsky is cited in Bloomfield, "From Ideology to Program to Policy," p. 9.

55. Christopher S. Wren, "After a Rebuff in Moscow, Détente Is Put to the Test," *New York Times,* April 1, 1977, pp. IA and 8A.

56. Stanley Hoffmann, "Carter's Soviet Problem," *The New Republic* 79 (July 29, 1978): 21. On this point and for a discussion of other Carter difficulties discussed here, see Stanley Hoffmann, "A View From at Home: The Perils of Incoherence," in William P. Bundy, ed., *America and the World 1978* (New York: Pergamon Press, 1979), pp. 463–491.

57. Most significantly, perhaps, the Soviet Union began the deployment of the SS-20s, its intermediate-range ballistic missiles, in the late 1970s.

58. Such a dualism in Brzezinski's thinking about the Soviets probably should not have been unexpected. His academic career had been largely made on the basis of a strong anti-Soviet view. Thus, his concern with global issues was a more recent phenomenon in his thinking.

59. Drew, "A Reporter At Large: Brzezinski," p. 117.

60. Ibid., p. 118.

61. Hedley Bull, "A View From Abroad: Consistency Under Pressure," in William P. Bundy, ed., *America and the World 1978* (New York: Pergamon Press, 1979), pp. 444–445.

62. John E. Rielly, ed., *American Public Opinion and U.S. Foreign Policy 1979* (Chicago: The Chicago Council on Foreign Relations, 1979), pp. 5 and 15.

63. Bruce Russett and Donald R. Deluca, " 'Don't Tread on Me': Public Opinion and Foreign Policy in the Eighties," *Political Science Quarterly* 96 (Fall 1981): 381–399.

64. Hoffmann, "Requiem," p.11.

65. For a summary of the congressional-executive debate on this matter, see "Congress and Nuclear Proliferation Policy," in *Congress and Foreign Policy 1980*, Committee on Foreign Affairs, U.S. House of Representatives (Washington, D.C.: U.S. Government Printing Office, 1981), pp. 89–109.

66. Statement by the President, "Conventional Arms Transfer Policy," *Weekly Compilation of Presidential Documents* 13 (May 23, 1977): 756–757; and Andrew J. Pierre, *The Global Politics of Arms Sales* (Princeton, NJ: Princeton University Press, 1982), pp. 52–54. The quoted passages are at p. 756 in the president's statement. Emphasis in original.

67. Ibid., pp. 52–57.

68. Ibid., p. 57.

69. See James M. McCormick, "The NIEO and the Distribution of American Assistance," *The Western Political Quarterly* 37 (March 1984): 100–101. Also see Roger D. Hansen, Albert Fishlow, Robert Paarlberg, and John P. Lewis, *U.S. Foreign Policy and the Third World Agenda 1982* (New York: Praeger, 1982). The aid as a percentage of the GNP for 1979 is from *The Interdependent*, March 1981, p. 5. Part of the reason for the lower aid levels during the Carter years may be attributed to the fact that Congress did not pass new aid bills for fiscal years 1980 and 1981; instead, it could only agree upon continuing resolutions from the previous legislation.

70. John W. Sewell and John A. Mathieson, "North-South Relations," in Joseph A. Pechman, ed., *Setting National Priorities Agenda for the 1980's* (Washington, D.C.: The Brookings Institution, 1980), p. 524.

71. See Dale Story's "Trade Politics in the Third World: A Case Study of the Mexican GATT Decision," *International Organization* 36 (Autumn 1982): 769. This passage also draws upon Sewell and Mathieson, "North-South Relations," pp. 524–525. For an analysis of the Tokyo Round, see Stephen D. Krasner, "The Tokyo Round: Particularistic Interests and Prospects for Stability in the Global Trading System," *International Studies Quarterly* 23 (December 1979): 491–531.

72. Sewell and Mathieson, "North-South Relations," pp. 524–525.

73. Carter, *Keeping Faith*, p. 157.

74. See the fine case study of congressional decision making on the treaties of William L. Furlong, "Negotiations and Ratification of the Panama Canal" in John Spanier and Joseph Nogee, eds., *Congress, The Presidency, and American Foreign Policy* (New York: Pergamon Press, 1981), pp. 77–106.

75. A New York Times/CBS Poll in April 1978 indicated that Americans opposed the treaties five to three and that those figures had been stable over the previous six months. See this discussion in "Americans' Support for Israel Declines, A Poll Finds," *New York Times*. April 14, 1978, pp. 1A and 10A. President Carter in his discussion of Panama Canal poll results reports a more optimistic picture. See *Keeping Faith*, pp. 159, 162, and 167.

76. Ibid., p. 184.

77. Ibid., p. 292.

78. Ibid., pp. 296–297.

79. Department of State Publication 8954, *The Camp David Summit* (Washington, D.C.: Office of Public Communications, Bureau of Public Affairs, September 1978).

80. See UN Security Council Resolution 435 in *Resolutions and Decisions of the Security Council, Security Council Official Records: Thirty-Third Year* (New York: United Nations, 1979), p. 13, for the resolution that South Africa eventually said that it would work to put into effect.

81. See Henry Wiseman and Alastair M. Taylor, *From Rhodesia to Zimbabwe: The Politics of Transition* (New York: Pergamon Press, 1981).

82. See the declaration of the Tokyo economic summit of June 29, 1979, in *Department of State Bulletin* 79 (August 1979): 8.

83. See the "Final Communique" of the North Atlantic Council Summit of May 1978, *Department of State Bulletin* 78 (July 1978): 10; and David Watt, "The European Initiative," in William P. Bundy, ed., *America and the World 1978* (New York: Pergamon Press, 1979), p. 584, on the agreement to increases in defense expenditures among the allies. See *NATO Review* 28 (February 1980): 24–28, for the official communique from the December 1979 NATO meetings on the intermediate-range missile decision for Europe.

84. For an analysis of the Carter foreign policy from this perspective, see Robert W. Tucker, "America in Decline: The Foreign Policy of 'Maturity,' " in William P. Bundy, ed., *America and the World 1979* (New York: Pergamon Press, 1980). pp. 449–488.

85. The impact of these events on Carter's foreign policy is discussed in Richard Burt, "Carter, Under Pressure of Crises, Tests New Foreign Policy Goals," *New York Times*, January 9, 1980, pp. A1 and A8, upon which we rely.

86. "My Opinion of the Russians Has Changed Most Drastically" *Time* (January 14, 1980), p. 10.

87. These actions are outlined in a speech that President Jimmy Carter gave to the nation on January 4, 1980. The speech can be found in *Vital Speeches of the Day* 46 (January 15, 1980): 194–195.

88. Jimmy Carter, "State of the Union 1980," *Vital Speeches of the Day* 46 (February 1, 1980): 227.

89. Poll results suggested that the failure to quickly secure the release of the American hostages contributed significantly to the electoral defeat of Jimmy Carter in 1980.

CHAPTER 5 THE REAGAN ADMINISTRATION: A RENEWAL OF THE COLD WAR?

"What I am describing...is a plan and a hope for the long term—the march of freedom and democracy which will leave Marxism-Leninism on the ashheap of history as it has left other tyrannies which stifle the freedom and muzzle the self-expression of the people." **PRESIDENT RONALD REAGAN, ADDRESS TO MEMBERS OF THE BRITISH PARLIAMENT, JUNE 8, 1982**

"For our own security, the United States must deny the Soviet Union a beachhead in North America....Will we give the Nicaraguan democratic resistance the means to recapture their betrayed revolution, or will we turn our backs and ignore the malignancy in Managua until it spreads and becomes a mortal threat to the entire New World?" **PRESIDENT RONALD REAGAN, ADDRESS TO THE NATION ON NICARAGUA, MARCH 16, 1986**

Just as the foreign policy of Jimmy Carter was a shift away from the Nixon-Ford-Kissinger years, the foreign policy of Ronald Reagan was intent upon establishing a different course than his predecessor, Carter. Ronald Reagan campaigned for the presidency on the principle of restoring American power at home and abroad, and his foreign policy was aimed at reflecting such power. While Jimmy Carter attempted to move away from the power politics of the Kissinger era and away from a foreign policy that focused directly on adversaries—and particularly the Soviet Union—Ronald Reagan embraced the need for power—especially military power—and the necessity of focusing on the Soviet Union and its expansionist policy. Although the previous administration had mainly followed a global politics perspective, the Reagan administration reverted to a bipolar perspective, with a sharp echo of the containment strategy of three decades earlier. During its second term, however, the Reagan administration sought and successfully obtained some accommodation with the Soviet Union. Hence, the strident manner in which it had challenged the Soviet Union was more muted in the second half of the 1980s.

THE VALUES AND BELIEFS OF THE REAGAN ADMINISTRATION

Ronald Reagan did not bring to the presidency a fully developed foreign policy design, but he did bring to the office a strongly held worldview. For him, the prime obstacle to peace and stability in the world was the Soviet Union, and particularly Soviet expansionism. The principal foreign policy goal of the United States, therefore, was to be the revival of national will to contain the Soviet Union and a restoration of confidence among friends that America was determined to stop communism. Furthermore, the United States must make other nations aware of the dangers of Soviet expansionism.

The ideological suspicion with which President Reagan viewed the Soviet Union was stated rather dramatically at his first news conference in January 1981:

> I know of no leader of the Soviet Union, since the revolution and including the present leadership, that has not more than once repeated, in the various Communist Congresses they hold, their determination that their goal must be the promotion of world revolution and a one-world socialist or Communist state—whichever word you want to use.
> Now as long as they do that and as long as they, at the same time, have openly and publicly declared that the only morality they recognize is what will further their cause: meaning they reserve unto themselves the right to commit any crime; to lie; to

cheat, in order to obtain that, and that is immoral, and we operate on a different set of standards, I think when you do business with them—even at a détente—you keep that in mind.[1]

Indicative perhaps of the lack of fundamental change in the Reagan administration's approach to the Soviet Union throughout its first term was a speech by the president himself in early 1983. Recalling this first news conference, President Reagan assailed the morality of the Soviet Union once again and denounced it as an "evil empire." The United States, in his judgment, remained in a moral struggle with that nation. Referring specifically to the ongoing discussion of the nuclear freeze issue, President Reagan made his point in this way:

> So in your discussions of the nuclear freeze proposals, I urge you to beware the temptation of pride—the temptation blithely to declare yourself above it all and label both sides equally at fault, to ignore the facts of history and aggressive impulses of an evil empire, to simply call the arms race a giant misunderstanding and thereby remove yourself from the struggle between right and wrong, good and evil.[2]

Such a consistently hostile view of the Soviet Union brought to mind comparisons with the U.S. foreign policy orientation of the 1950s, when the Cold War consensus was dominant. It surely stood in contrast to Jimmy Carter's view only four years earlier that "we are now free of that inordinate fear of communism."[3] Instead, President Reagan's view implied the centrality of the Soviet Union and its foreign policy objectives to American actions abroad. Indeed, to many observers, such a posture suggested the emergence of a new Cold War.[4]

President Reagan's choice as secretary of state, General Alexander Haig, shared such a worldview and stated as much in his Senate confirmation hearings in January 1981. While Haig acknowledged the diffusion of power among more than 150 nations, the growing economic interdependence of the industrialized states, and the diversity within the Third World, he contended that these global changes are made more difficult by the "central strategic phenomenon of the post–World War II era: the transformation of Soviet military power from a continental and largely defensive land army to a global offensive army, navy, and air force fully capable of supporting an imperial foreign policy.... Today the threat of Soviet military intervention colors attempts to achieve international civility."[5] Moreover, in outlining the issues that the United States would have to deal with in the 1980s, Haig listed the "management of Soviet power" at the top.

In his first news conference, too, Secretary Haig gave further substance to the centrality of the Soviet Union as a source of global problems and as the focal point for U.S. foreign policy. He identified the Soviet Union as in a "risk-taking mode" through its "Cuban proxy" in the Western Hemisphere and in Africa. Counteracting such behavior would be a high priority for the Reagan administration. Haig also contended that the Soviet Union was the source of international terrorism (the "ultimate abuse of human rights") because it was involved "in conscious policies, in programs, if you will, which foster, support, and expand this activity, which is hemorrhaging in many respects throughout the world today."[6] Thus, controlling Soviet behavior would have the effect of controlling international terrorism as well. In short, if Soviet adventurism were confronted, both global interventionism and global terrorism would be reduced.

Such a Soviet-centric foreign policy was further reflected in the statements of two other principal foreign policy advisors of President Reagan. Secretary of Defense Caspar Weinberger likewise warned of the dangers that the Soviet Union caused in the world and the need to build up United States military might: "We all must come to recognize the threat for what it is and must combine our energies effectively to counter it. Ours is not a mindless quest for military superiority. It is a realistic effort to meet a real threat posed by a society inimical to our own."[7] Similarly, Richard V. Allen, the first national security advisor for the Reagan administration, expressed similar concerns about the Soviet Union: "The only way to deal with the Soviet Union is from a strong position. Only if it is absolutely clear then that we are in the process of fielding weapons of our own will they agree to serious bargaining on their weapons."[8]

The foreign policy orientation of the Reagan administration, therefore, bore a sharp resemblance to the Cold War consensus that we discussed in Chapter 3. The Soviet Union (and international communism) was the central focus and the principal adversary. The world was divided by the Iron Curtain between East and West, rather than along the equator (North and South, which the Carter administration had tried to introduce). The Soviet Union was primarily responsible for global unrest whether it was interventionism or terrorism. All global problems ultimately affected the U.S.-Soviet rivalry (linkage was again accepted on the part of the Reagan administration without any equivocation). And, finally, the United States had the responsibility to lead the free world against the Soviet Union.

The policy prescriptions that were to flow from this perspective also paralleled those of the earlier era: rebuild United States military might, strengthen alliance capabilities (both militarily and economically), expand military assistance to friendly states without undue concern over the internal characteristics of those regimes, and enlarge the global consensus against the Soviet danger.

THE POLICY APPROACH OF THE REAGAN ADMINISTRATION

Despite the ideological cohesion that seemed to permeate the Reagan administration, the translation of that perspective into a working foreign policy was not readily apparent to outside observers. In fact, charges were immediately hurled about that the Reagan administration really had no foreign policy because it appeared to have no coherent strategy for reaching its goals. Critics complained that rhetoric served as policy. Such a failing was particularly accented since the Reagan administration had come into office determined to bring coherence and consistency to foreign affairs, which they charged the Carter administration had failed to do.[9]

Yet this criticism is a bit overstated, since Secretary of State Haig did provide a statement of principles and the underlying rationale for dealing with the world early in his tenure. Describing his approach as a "strategic" one, Secretary Haig asserted that United States foreign policy behavior was based upon four important pillars:

1. The restoration of our economic and military strength.
2. The reinvigoration of alliances and friendships.
3. The promotion of progress in the developing countries through peaceable changes.
4. A relationship with the Soviet Union characterized by restraint and reciprocity.[10]

None of these pillars should be pursued independently, and policy initiatives in any one of these areas must support the others. The glue that would hold these "pillars" together was the Soviet-American relationship because, as Secretary Haig indicated, "Soviet-American relations must be at the center of our efforts to promote a more peaceful world."[11] A survey of Reagan administration behavior in each of these pillars will reveal how the Soviet-American concern came to dominate each one.

REBUILDING AMERICAN STRENGTH

The Reagan administration quickly called for an increase in military spending. It proposed a $1.6 trillion defense buildup over a six-year period (1981–1986). The Reagan goals were quite ambitious: to increase the size of the U.S. Navy to 600 ships, to accelerate the purchase of new aircraft and tanks, to raise military pay to retain good personnel, to increase conventional readiness, to upgrade the Rapid Deployment Force started under the Carter administration, and to embark on a strategic force modernization plan.[12] The strategic modernization plan attracted much of the initial attention in the early part of the Reagan presidency.

The modernization plan was a projected $180 billion effort, which provided for revamping the American nuclear triad, the three-pronged defense system of land-based and sea-based nuclear weapons and intercontinental bombers. First of all, the Reagan administration was committed to the deployment of a new intercontinental missile, the MX, or missile experimental, which would carry up to ten nuclear warheads each. These new missiles would be placed in existing hardened silos. The aim of this project was to strengthen the land-based leg of the strategic triad and close the "window of vulnerability" to Soviet attack that the Reagan administration charged had developed over the years. Second, the Trident II missile developed for deployment in America's ballistic missile submarine fleet would go forward. This effort would upgrade and strengthen the sea-based leg of the triad. Third, the cruise missile (for both land-based and sea-based operations) would continue to be developed and deployed as a further means of improving the strategic forces in those two areas. Land-based theater nuclear forces—which included cruise missiles—for Western Europe would also go forward in compliance with the NATO decision of December 1979. Fourth, the modernization plan called for the development of the B-1 bomber, a project that the Carter administration had canceled in the summer of 1977. This new bomber would replace the aging B-52s, which had constituted the third leg of the triad system. Moreover, the B-1 was intended to last until the Stealth aircraft, a new and technologically superior bomber, became available in the 1990s. The last part of the modernization plan was to upgrade the strategic command and control structure, which is the technical communication structure that provides direction for U.S. nuclear forces.[13] If this structure was not able to withstand a first strike, the strategic retaliatory force would not be very usable in any coherent way.

Such a program as proposed by the Reagan administration called for rapidly increasing defense expenditures. Defense spending quickly passed $200 billion, and projected budgets called for military spending of over $300 billion per year by the middle 1980s.[14] By 1983, Congress approved funding for the production of the MX missile, B-1 bomber, and binary nerve gas.[15] In 1984, President Reagan called for a record defense budget, including the funding of forty more MX missiles, another Trident submarine, thirty-four more B-1 bombers, and more M-1 tanks and F-15 and F-16 fighter aircraft.[16]

In a March 1983 address to the nation, President Reagan added yet another element to America's nuclear arsenal. He called for the U.S. to "embark on a program to counter the awesome Soviet threat with measures that are defensive." Such a system "could pave the way for arms control measures to eliminate...[nuclear] weapons themselves."[17] Formally called the Strategic Defense Initiative (SDI), but more commonly known as "Star Wars"—after the popular motion picture—this proposal was viewed by critics as a further escalation of the arms race. Since defensive systems had seemingly been forestalled with the restrictions in the Anti-Ballistic Missile Treaty of 1972, this new call threatened to have the Americans and the Soviets move toward the building of a new set of weapons. Furthermore, the proposal raised the prospect that new and more destructive offensive weapons might be developed to defeat these new defensive systems. Nonetheless, the SDI proposal was yet another component of the Reagan administration's effort to rebuild America's military might and to confront Soviet power directly.

Table 5.1 summarizes the relative success of the Reagan modernization plan.

REINVIGORATING THE ALLIES

The reinvigoration of the allies meant basically to upgrade the military strength of the West and to support the political leadership of the United States in its global policies. In the military area, the United States wanted the Western Europeans to go forward with the theater nuclear forces decision and the deployment of the 572 Pershing II and cruise missiles scheduled for late 1983. (In fact, by the end of 1983 this aspect of military modernization of the alliance began to become a reality with the deployment of the cruise and Pershing II missiles in Western Europe.[18]) In addition, the United States wanted the Europeans to accept a greater defense burden as a means of counteracting growing Soviet power. Similarly, the United States wanted the Japanese to assume greater military responsibility in the East Asian area with the goal of helping to counter Soviet expansion in that region of the world. The second major thrust of the Reagan approach toward the allies was to seek their political support in policy toward the Soviet Union and regional trouble spots throughout the world. For instance, to respond to a perceived neutralist sentiment in Europe, both Secretary of Defense Caspar Weinberger and

TABLE 5.1 MAJOR WEAPONS SYSTEMS SOUGHT AND OBTAINED BY THE REAGAN ADMINISTRATION, 1981–1988

Weapons System	Policy Goal	Policy Outcome
MX Missile	200 deployed missiles	50 missiles deployed
B-1B Bomber	100 operational bombers	100 bombers approved by Congress
Trident (D5) Missile	Full development of these submarine-launched missiles	Complete Trident program approved by Congress
Intermediate-range missiles in Europe	Deployment of 464 cruise missiles and 108 Pershing II missiles	Deployment started in November 1983
	Treaty to remove all such American and Soviet missiles from Europe	INF Treaty of December 1987 eliminated all intermediate- and medium-range missiles
Strategic Defense Initiative ("Star Wars")	Funding over six years totaling $30 billion	Funding over six years totaled $16 billion

Source: Abstracted from "Reagan Administration National Security Scorecard" in *Nucleus* 10 (Fall 1988), p. 5.

National Security Advisor Richard Allen exhorted the Europeans not to follow this course and to stand firm against the Soviet Union.[19] Likewise, appeals were made for the Europeans to follow the American lead over enacting sanctions against the Soviet Union and Poland after the imposition of martial law in the latter nation. More controversial was the American action to try to stop the Europeans from completing a natural gas pipeline arrangement with the Soviet Union and, later, the American effort to impose sanctions on the Europeans themselves over their failure to follow the American wishes.[20]

Despite these military and political attempts to get the Europeans to see the world from the perspective of the Reagan administration—and to act from it—the Europeans were reluctant to go along. Their objections centered on the narrow bipolar focus of the Reagan approach, with its heavy emphasis on the military component of foreign policy. As a group, the allies (and especially the Europeans) were not convinced that this approach would work, and they were reluctant to jettison East-West détente arrangements of the previous decade to try it. Moreover, this pillar of foreign policy proved more difficult to put into effect than the others. In essence, the Reagan administration found that the rhetoric of renewed anti-communism was easier to enunciate than to make a part of alliance policy.

BOLSTERING FRIENDS IN THE DEVELOPING WORLD

The meaning of the third pillar—a commitment to progress in the Third World—was to reflect a sharp shift in strategy toward American friends in the developing states. As compared to earlier administrations, and especially the Carter years, the Reagan administration changed policy in three distinct ways. First of all, unlike President Carter, who expressed a sympathy for Third World aspirations, the Reagan administration challenged those nations to pull themselves up by their own bootstraps and to seek improvement through the efforts of private enterprise. This view was spelled out by President Reagan himself in a speech given just prior to his attendance at the 1981 summit—a meeting of twenty-two developed and developing states in the Mexican resort of Cancún. President Reagan called for a development strategy that allowed "men and women to realize freely their full potential, to go as far as their God-given talents will take them. Free people build free markets that ignite dynamic development for everyone."[21]

The first major economic development initiative offered by the Reagan administration—the Caribbean Basin Initiative—contained precisely this emphasis on the private sector as the key to global development. While economic assistance to the region would be increased by $350 million, the principal centerpieces of the initiative were preferential trade access to American markets for the Caribbean states and an increase in U.S. investments in these countries. Furthermore, the administration committed itself to seek various measures to encourage private U.S. investment in the Caribbean Basin: congressional approval would be sought to grant tax breaks to American investors; new international insurance facilities through multilateral banks (e.g., Inter-American Development Bank) and the private sector would be sought to protect the new investments; and the United States would work with each country to facilitate private sector development.[22] Thus, the Caribbean Basin Initiative would likely become a model for American development strategy to the poor of the world during the Reagan years.

The second major shift in policy was the increased reliance on military assistance as an "essential" element of U.S. policy. Although the Reagan administration committed itself to economic development, it contended that such modernization could take place only in the context of political stability. To implement this policy, the Reagan administration scrapped the arms transfer policy of the Carter administration and announced one of its own—one more attuned to its philosophical orientation. The new Reagan policy directive stated that the United States would provide military assistance to "its major alliance partners and to those nations with whom it has friendly and cooperative security relationships." The directive goes on to suggest that the United States would not endanger its own security by engaging in unilateral action to restrict the transfer of weapons abroad. Furthermore, the directive concluded that "the realities of today's world demand that we pursue a sober, responsible and balanced arms transfer policy. . . . We will deal with the world as it is, rather than as we would like it to be."[23]

Given the dangers the Reagan administration saw in the world, such a change in policy had the potential of greatly expanding global arms sales. In fact, new aid initiatives were put forward at the outset of the Reagan administration, and arms transfers were now free to assume a greater role in U.S. foreign policy.

The third shift in policy toward the developing world focused on how regional conflicts would be analyzed and acted upon by the United States. Regional conflicts would not be analyzed on the basis of regional concerns only. Conflicts in the developing world had to be recast into the underlying global conflict that the Reagan administration saw in the world. In turn, U.S. actions in these regional disputes must recognize that global reality. Therefore, the emphasis was on how regional conflicts affected U.S.-Soviet relations. The aim was to build a "strategic consensus" against the Soviet Union and its proxies.[24] Only after the Soviet danger posed in these conflicts was addressed could the regional concerns be brought into the resolution of the conflicts.

RESTRAINT AND RECIPROCITY WITH THE SOVIET UNION

The fourth pillar of the Reagan administration focused directly on the Soviet Union. Only if the Soviet Union demonstrated restraint in its global actions would the United States carry on normal and reciprocal relations with it. In this sense, the familiar linkage notion of the Kissinger years was at the heart of any relationship with the Soviet Union. Specifically, Secretary Haig stated that the United States would "want greater Soviet restraint on the use of force. We want greater Soviet respect for the independence of others. And we want

the Soviets to abide by their reciprocal obligations, such as those undertaken in the Helsinki accords." Furthermore, no area of international relations could be left out of this restraint requirement. "We
have learned that Soviet-American agreements, even in strategic
arms control, will not survive Soviet threats to the overall military
balance or Soviet encroachments... in critical regions of the world.
Linkage is not a theory; it is a fact of life that we overlook at our peril."[25]
Confrontation and challenge of the Soviet Union were to be central
components of policy.

THE REAGAN WORLDVIEW IN OPERATION

With these four pillars as the primary guide to U.S. foreign policy, a
brief survey of American actions toward the Soviet Union, Central
America, southern Africa, and the Middle East will illustrate how
the Reagan administration put these principles into action.

POLICY ACTIONS TOWARD THE SOVIET UNION

Because the Soviet Union had exercised neither policy restraint nor
reciprocity in the past, the Reagan administration did not seek to improve relations with the other superpower. Instead, as we have suggested, the U.S. sought to rally other states against it and adopted
several initial measures to prod the Soviet Union to exercise international restraint. First, verbal attacks were made against the Soviet
Union. President Reagan and Secretary Haig attacked the Soviet system as bankrupt and on the verge of collapse, and they continued to
charge the Soviets with fomenting international disorder.[26] Second,
direct actions were adopted to demonstrate American resolve. The
Reagan administration, in addition to its strategic modernization
plan, called for the production and stockpiling of the neutron bomb
within the United States. Most significantly, perhaps, the United
States imposed sanctions upon the Soviet Union and Poland to indicate its dissatisfaction with the imposition of martial law in Poland.
These sanctions included the suspension of all flights to the United
States by Aeroflot, the Soviet national airline, the suspension of li-
censes for exporting electronic equipment and oil and gas equipment to the Soviet Union, the postponing of further discussions on a
long-term grain agreement, and the review of all exchange agreements.[27]

Third, some actions were *not* taken to demonstrate that normal
relations could not occur until the Soviet Union showed restraint. In

this connection, the two most important omissions were the failure to move rapidly on arms control and the failure to engage in summit meetings. In fact, arms control discussions were put on the back burner until the arms buildup was addressed. Additionally, questions of a summit meeting between the Soviet and American leaders were put off with the comment that the conditions were not appropriate and that little valuable discussion would result.

Despite a relationship that was primarily marked by harsh rhetoric and strong action, some initial cooperative elements were still evident. Moreover, they illustrate the anomalies that were present even in a relationship that was marked by such hostilities. For example, on April 24, 1981, President Reagan lifted the grain embargo that President Carter had put into effect after the Afghanistan invasion. While domestic politics played a large part in this decision, it seemed a particularly curious action for an administration so committed to isolating and punishing the Soviet Union. Furthermore, along these same lines, the Reagan administration in its second year in office sought to expand grain sales to the Soviet Union and eventually agreed to a new five-year grain deal.[28] Second, the United States also stated that it would continue to adhere to the SALT I and SALT II limitations if the Soviets would.[29] This stance was adopted even though the former pact had expired in 1977 and the latter had not been ratified by the U.S. Senate. Morever, President Reagan had in his election campaign called SALT II "fatally flawed." Third, despite the political atmosphere, Secretary of State Haig did meet with Soviet Foreign Minister Andrei Gromyko during his visit to the UN General Assembly in the fall of 1981, and the two held a long discussion. Finally, the intermediate nuclear force (INF) talks reluctantly were begun by the Reagan administration during November 1981—much earlier than might have been expected given the overall political climate—and President Reagan also initiated the Strategic Arms Reduction Talks (START), despite the seeming confrontational environment.[30]

By November 1983, neither of these talks had reached any agreement, and the United States went ahead with its deployment of intermediate missiles in Europe.[31] That action had an immediate effect on the already deteriorating relationship between the two superpowers. The Soviet Union walked out of the INF negotiations and, within one month, said that it would not proceed with the separate Strategic Arms Reduction Talks either. Further, the Soviets took a number of other provocative actions over the next few months to show its displeasure with the Reagan administration's policy. It resumed the deployment of SS-20s, their immediate range missiles, and now placed them in East Germany and Czechoslovakia as well as in the Soviet Union. It announced the deployment of more nuclear submarines off the American coasts in retaliation for the new American weapons in Western Europe. And, finally, in a parallel move with what the United States had done in 1980 over Afghanistan, the Soviet Union withdrew from the 1984 Olympic Games in Los Angeles, claiming that their athletes would not be safe there.[32]

The consequence of this barrage of various charges and actions by both superpowers was that Soviet-American relations by the middle of 1984 were "at the lowest level for the entire postwar period."[33] The "restraint and reciprocity" that the Reagan administration had initially set out to achieve had not been accomplished, but the desire to restore that nation to the center of American foreign policy and to build up U.S. defenses were well under way.

POLICY ACTION TOWARD THE THIRD WORLD

In Central America, the response of the Reagan administration toward the unrest in El Salvador reflected its basic foreign policy approach. The administration quickly moved to interpret the ongoing civil war in El Salvador as Soviet and Cuban directed. Calling El Salvador a "textbook case" of communist aggression, the Reagan administration issued a white paper outlining the danger there. The administration contended that:

> the American people and the world community be aware of the gravity of the actions of Cuba, the Soviet Union, and other Communist states who are carrying out what is clearly shown to be a well-coordinated, covert effort to bring about the overthrow of El Salvador's established government and to impose in its place a Communist regime with no popular support.[34]

Furthermore, testifying at a House Foreign Affairs Committee hearing in March 1981, Secretary of State Haig charged that the communist attack on El Salvador was part of a "four-phased operation" aimed at the ultimate control of Central America.[35] Lost in Washington's dramatic rhetoric was the importance of local issues as the source of the civil war in El Salvador. The country had long suffered extreme poverty (one of the lowest per capita income levels in the region), a maldistribution of land and wealth, and the dominance of a political oligarchy. The Reagan administration, while not dismissing such causal factors, did downplay them initially.

Military assistance and the threat of military action were the principal means used to respond to the situation. Military aid totaling $25 million was immediately proposed for the government of El

MAP 5.1   CENTRAL AMERICA

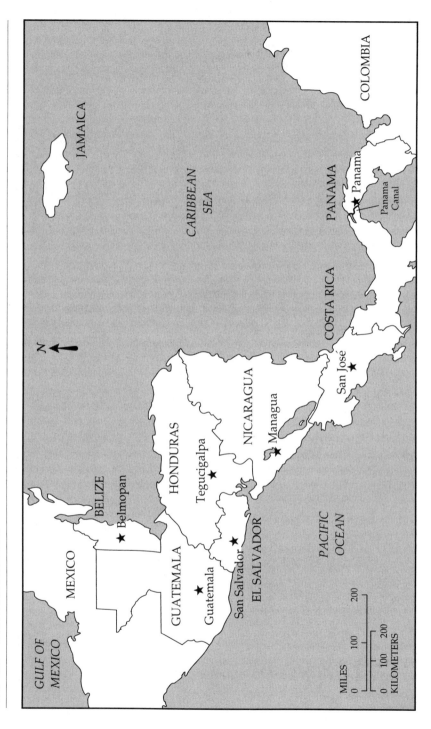

Salvador in its struggle with rebel forces, with more to come. The number of military advisors was increased from twenty-five to fifty-five by the spring of 1981.[36]

A similar policy approach was adopted toward Nicaragua, the Sandinista-led nation of Central America. Charging that the Nicaraguan government was arming the guerrillas in El Salvador, the Reagan administration immediately cut off $15 million of economic aid.[37] Furthermore, press leaks indicated that the Reagan administration was exploring military actions against Cuba and Nicaragua. By 1982, in fact, the Reagan administration apparently had a clandestine operation underway in Honduras; it was supporting rebel forces of Nicaraguans opposed to the Sandinista government.[38]

In keeping with its effort to bolster friends, the Reagan administration took other actions in Latin America. It sought to eliminate American restrictions on military and economic assistance to Chile and Argentina, for example, and it also sought to lift economic aid bans that had been imposed on Paraguay and Uruguay. These actions were taken toward states whose previous human rights records were hardly laudable.[39]

By 1983 and 1984, President Reagan continued to analyze the situation in Central America in East-West terms and proceeded to use some of the harshest rhetoric of his administration to describe the situation. Central America, he charged, "has become the stage for a bold attempt by the Soviet Union, Cuba, and Nicaragua to install Communism by force throughout the hemisphere."[40] Further, President Reagan described the Sandinista government as "a Communist reign of terror," and Nicaragua as "Cuba's Cubans" for its assumed involvement in aiding the Salvadoran guerrillas.[41] And finally, he even quoted directly frrom the Truman Doctrine of four decades earlier to justify the need for American action in the region ("I believe that it must be the policy of the United States to support free peoples . . .").[42] For all these reasons, then, President Reagan continued to seek military assistance for El Salvador and covert and overt aid for the Nicaraguan contras, those forces opposing the Sandinistas.

The hardline policy of containing communism in Latin America was perhaps manifested most dramatically with the American invasion of the Caribbean island of Grenada in October 1983. After Marxist Prime Minister Maurice Bishop was killed on October 19, 1983, and after a more radical group seized control of that nation, the United States agreed to join forces with the five members of the Organization of Eastern Caribbean States "to restore order and democracy" in Grenada. In addition, the action was taken to ensure the safety of between 800 and 1,000 Americans—mostly medical students—and "forestall further chaos."[43]

The American action proved to be swift and effective; within a few days, the control of the island was achieved, the Marxist regime had been replaced, and the return to a Western-style democracy was under way. In short, the action demonstrated the determination of the Reagan administration to use military force, if necessary, and to confront Marxist regimes. Both actions were fully consistent with the Reagan administration's basic foreign policy approach.

In southern Africa, the Reagan administration's actions were consistent as well. The administration adopted a policy of "constructive engagement" toward South Africa and linked any settlement to Namibia (then called Southwest Africa) to the removal of Cuban forces from Angola. These policies were predicated upon several key beliefs. First, South Africa was staunchly anti-communist, and, as such, the United States should not seek a confrontational approach toward it. Second, the conflict in the region really had East-West overtones that could not be overlooked. After all, South Africa was confronted by a Marxist regime in Angola, which was backed by Cuban soldiers and Soviet arms.[44] Third, only when the South Africans felt more confident of American support could the United States try to exert influence upon them to change their apartheid policy and to seek a solution to the question of Namibia. In this region, then, the strategic concern of controlling communism placed a considerably different emphasis upon the regional conflict, especially in comparison to the Carter administration, which had adopted a policy so strongly based upon human rights considerations. Moreover, the basic strategy was to last throughout the Reagan years and was only to achieve some success at the very end of Reagan's second term.

In the Middle East, the strategy was much the same initially. No new initiatives were proposed in the first year and a half to resolve the conflict between the Arabs and Israelis. Nor was there much effort to proceed with the Camp David framework the Reagan administration had inherited. Instead, as elsewhere, the Reagan administration attempted to rally the Arab states against the Soviet Union and to engage the Israelis in a strategic understanding.

In the case of the Arab states, the U.S. initiated a series of military actions. Secretary of Defense Caspar Weinberger, for example, announced the establishment of a new Persian Gulf command, with the Rapid Deployment Force as part of the structure. The United States and several Middle East states conducted negotiations regarding bases and access rights in the region. Egypt, Sudan, Somalia, and Oman agreed to joint military exercises (Operation Brightstar) with the United States in November 1981.[45] The United States adopted a similar strategy toward the Israelis. The United States sought and obtained a military cooperation agreement with Israel through a Memorandum of Understanding.[46]

The most dramatic examples of using military assistance to bolster American influence against the Soviet Union also occurred in this region. The United States agreed to sell technologically advanced aircraft equipment and the Airborne Warning and Control Systems (AWACS) aircraft to Saudi Arabia in October 1981. Likewise, the Reagan administration also agreed to supply forty F-16 fighter aircraft to Pakistan (an arms deal worth more than $3 billion) as part of its strategy for Southwest Asia.[47] On balance, the focus of these measures was to promote the security of these states against the Soviet Union. Any regional differences between them would be submerged into this larger context.

But a global policy emphasis proved short-lived in this volatile region. By the summer of 1982—and wholly as a result of Israel's invasion of Lebanon and its advance all the way to Beirut—the Reagan administration was fully emersed in local issues in the Middle East. The Reagan administration felt compelled to respond to local issues, not global ones. The administration sought to negotiate a ceasefire between the Israelis and the surrounded Palestinian forces in West Beirut and then tried to negotiate a withdrawal of Syrian and Israeli forces from Lebanon itself. Moreover, President Reagan himself moved into a mediator posture with a new initiative (labeled the Reagan Initiative) to serve as a follow-up on the Camp David framework. This initiative called for a Palestinian homeland that would be in federation with Jordan, an end to Israeli settlements in the West Bank, and security for Israel.[48]

On two other occasions in 1982 and 1983, the Reagan administration also became involved in regional disputes in Lebanon, even to the point of deploying American military personnel. One met with success, the other was a dramatic failure. The administration sent a contingent of American Marines into Lebanon in August 1982 as part of an effort to evacuate the Palestine Liberation Organization (PLO) members from Beirut where they had been surrounded by the Israelis. This mission was successfully completed without any major incident. Later, in September 1982, however, the Marines were again dispatched to Lebanon as part of the Multinational Force (MNF), and that effort ultimately proved disastrous.[49]

The role of the MNF was to serve as a "peacekeeping" force between the various Lebanese factions and to facilitate a negotiated settlement among the warring religious groups. The U.S. also hoped that a strong central government could be established that would rid Lebanon of all foreign forces. But these efforts proved elusive. Factional feuding continued, and the role of the MNF became increasingly unclear. In time, the American Marines, encamped at the Beirut airport, became identified with the Lebanese (Christian-dominated) central government of Amin Gemayel and became the target of snipers from the other Lebanese factions. More than this, the Marines became the target of a terrorist bombing on October 23, 1983, and 241 Americans were killed in the attack on their barracks.

Although the Reagan administration originally intended to deal with regional issues in a global context, it became deeply involved in "local issues" in the Middle East without a well-conceived policy. Moreover, this region was to prove as intractable for the Reagan administration as it had for other administrations, but it was also to serve as a point of important policy reversal by the end of the Reagan years in office, as we discuss below.

CHALLENGES TO THE REAGAN APPROACH

Despite the efforts of the Reagan administration to redirect the focus and content of American policy to the Soviet danger, the rest of the world would not so easily yield to its perception. Concern—and at times rejection—over the ideological tone and substance of the Reagan foreign policy came from several different sources. Moreover, these challenges made it difficult for the Reagan administration to continue the ideological consistency that it originally intended and undoubtedly contributed to some modification in it over time.

The Western European states, for example, were reluctant to follow the Reagan administration's lead in dealing with the Soviet Union. The Europeans were concerned with preserving contact with the East, not disrupting it. Thus, the Reagan attempts to isolate the Soviet Union and Poland because of the establishment of martial law in Poland brought only negative diplomatic rebukes from the European Community and individual European states. They did not produce the sanctions toward the Soviets that President Reagan had initiated and had desired. The foreign ministers of both the European Economic Community and NATO issued only statements of disapproval and condemnation.[50] Similarly, the European states would not drop the development of the natural gas pipeline that the Soviet Union planned to build to Western Europe. Nor would the Europeans stop the granting of credits or the sale of equipment to the Soviet Union for the completion of the pipeline.[51]

A second major European issue that challenged American leadership and its policy of confrontation toward the Soviet Union was the question of arms control. While the Europeans were committed to the Dual Track decision of 1979—the deployment of theater nuclear weapons in Western Europe if negotiations on intermediate nuclear arms control were not successful—they were unsure (and uneasy) about President Reagan's commitment to the second half of that decision. With his harsh rhetoric, his strategic modernization plan, his reluctance to proceed very quickly with arms control talks (since rearmament must occur first), President Reagan did not seem to be following a policy of arms restraint. Furthermore, both Secretary of State Haig and President Reagan engaged in some rather loose talk about the possibility of a demonstration nuclear explosion and a limited nuclear war—actions highly threatening to the Europeans.[52]

Indeed, hundreds of thousands of demonstrators filled the streets of London, Rome, Berlin, and Bonn in protest of the Reagan arms policy. In the Federal Republic of Germany, the proposed location for most of the theater nuclear forces, the opposition to the deployment of such weapons during 1983 assisted the Greens, a new anti-nuclear and environmental party, in gaining some seats in the legislatures of the Laender (or state) governments and eventually in the Bundestag (the national parliament) of the Federal Republic.[53]

Third, some European and Latin American states failed to support the American approach to the situation in El Salvador or its policy toward Nicaragua. In fact, early on, France and Mexico proposed to initiate negotiations between the government in El Salvador and the political arm of the rebel movement.[54] Similarly, the international socialist movement, led by Willy Brandt of West Germany, also sought to get negotiations started.

These alliance challenges were paralleled by domestic challenges as well. While the public was willing to support some increase in defense spending at the time the Reagan administration took office, the situation had changed considerably by 1983. By then, public support for increased defense expenditures had hit the lowest level of the past decade. Forty-five percent of the American public indicated that the U.S. was spending too much on the military, and only 14 percent indicated that the U.S. was spending too little. By contrast, in 1981, only 15 percent of the public had indicated that the U.S. was spending too much on defense, while 51 percent indicated that the United States was spending too little.[55]

Like its European counterpart, the nuclear freeze movement within the United States also gained quick public support, with opinion polls consistently showing over 60 percent of the American public supporting a "mutual and verifiable freeze" of nuclear weapons between the Soviet Union and the United States.[56] This movement was able to turn out over 700,000 people to demonstrate in New York City in June 1982—one of the largest single demonstrations in American political history. Its composition reflected the diversity of support for this movement; individuals from a wide variety of political and social backgrounds were involved.[57]

Domestic challenges arose over Central American policy, too. In particular, concern was expressed over potential American involvement in the region, especially now that more American advisors were being sent there. Would American combat forces be sent into the region? Was this involvement the beginning of another Vietnam quagmire in which American involvement would slowly escalate? This kind of fear caused Secretary of State Haig to rule out the use of American troops in Central America.[58] Further, local conditions, such as poverty and inequality, ought to be given greater credence in the political unrest than the Reagan administration was allowing.

POLICY CHANGE: ACCOMMODATION WITH THE SOVIET UNION

In the aftermath of his resounding election to a second term in November 1984 with the largest electoral vote total in American history (525 out of a possible 538) and by one of the largest percentages of the popular vote (59 percent), President Reagan immediately announced that his administration would continue to do "what we've been doing."[59] In reality, some change did occur. While generally not abandoning his hardline approach to Soviet expansionism in Third World areas, President Reagan actually came to embrace a much more accommodationist approach to the Soviet Union in his second term.

SOURCES OF CHANGE

At least three factors contributed to this movement away from the previous hardline approach of the Reagan administration toward the Soviet Union: (1) a change in the policy stance of the American leadership; (2) the emergence of new leadership and "new thinking" in the Soviet Union; and (3) the domestic realities of the arms race between the superpowers. Although it is difficult to specify which of these factors (and presumably others as well) weighed most heavily in this policy change—or to show fully how they interacted with one another—a discussion of each will portray the change in approach from only four years earlier.

Secretary of State George Shultz seemingly signaled the first change in emphasis by the Reagan administration. In a speech in October 1984, he indicated that Soviet behavior in all areas of the world would not automatically be linked to the quality of relations between the Soviet Union and the United States. Unlike former Secretary of State Alexander Haig's characterization of linkage as a fact of life, Shultz said that "clearly linkage is not merely a 'fact of life' but a complex question of policy. There will be times when we must make progress in one dimension of the relationship contingent on progress in others. . . . At the same time, linkage as an instrument of policy has limitations; if applied rigidly, it could yield the initiative to the Soviets, letting them set the pace and the character of the relationship. . . . In the final analysis, linkage is a tactical question; the strategic reality of leverage comes from creating facts in support of our overall design."[60] Later, in early 1985 testimony to the Senate Foreign Relations Committee, Secretary Schultz summarized the goal for the future: "We must learn to pursue a strategy geared to long-term thinking and based on both negotiation and strength simultaneously, if we are to build a stable U.S.-Soviet relationship for the next century."[61]

In his second inaugural address, President Reagan reiterated his post-election commitment to better relations with the Soviet Union, especially in the area of nuclear arms control. He indicated that the U.S. would seek to reduce the cost of national security "in negotiations with the Soviet Union." These negotiations, however, would not focus just on limiting an increase in nuclear weapons, but, he said, "we seek. . . to reduce their numbers."[62] To appreciate how dramatic a change had taken place, recall how this policy stance contrasts with the Reagan administration's initial position on negotiating with the Soviet Union. In 1981, for example, the Reagan administration had indicated that there was really nothing to negotiate with the Soviet Union until that nation changed its behavior and American military might was restored. Further, negotiations had explicitly been rejected as an option in dealing with the other superpower.

A second factor that contributed to the possibility of accommodation between the Soviet Union and the United States was the emergence in 1985 of Mikhail Gorbachev as the General Secretary of the Communist Party of the Soviet Union, and eventually as President of the Soviet Union. Gorbachev's rise to power was critical because he brought with him several important conceptual changes to Soviet foreign policy thinking and a commitment to improving relations with the United States. In fact, he added two major concepts to the political lexicon of the 1980s, *perestroika* and *glasnost*. *Perestroika* referred to the "restructuring" of Soviet society in an effort to improve the economy, while *glasnost* referred to a new "openness" on the part of Soviet society and a movement toward greater democratization within that system.

Such "new thinking" by the Soviet leadership, as Gorbachev himself called it, came to have important implications for Soviet-American relations. In contrast to earlier desires for "nuclear superiority," the Soviet leadership began to embrace the concept of "reasonable sufficiency" as a nuclear weapons strategy in dealing with the West, and it began to recognize the need for greater "strategic stability" in the nuclear balance as well. In such an environment, nuclear arms accommodation between the two superpowers became a viable option. Furthermore, the Soviet leadership indicated that the struggle between capitalism and socialism had changed, and political solutions to outstanding issues, rather than military ones, ought to be pursued.[63] This position, too, invited some thawing in Soviet-American relations following Gorbachev's rise to power.

Yet, a third factor may well have been the most pivotal for both nations: the increasing domestic burden of sustained military spending. The military burden of continued confrontations between these two rivals was distorting and undermining the domestic health of both economies. In the Soviet Union, the basic needs of its people could not be met as more and more resources were spent on the military. Even Gorbachev's hope of restructuring the Soviet system could not really be undertaken as long as military spending consumed so much of the wealth of the society. In the United States, with military budgets exceeding $300 billion per year and federal budget deficits increasing, the health of the economy remained in question. Further, no longer could the Reagan administration count on public support for increased military spending. Opinion polls in 1982 and 1986 showed that the public favored keeping military expenditures about the same. At the same time, though, there did not appear to be great sentiment for defense cuts.[64]

THE RETURN OF SOVIET-AMERICAN SUMMITRY

The most significant manifestations of this changed policy were the reemergence of summitry between American and Soviet leaders and the signing of one important arms control agreement and progress on several others. Moreover, summitry and arms control progress were to go hand in hand with one another during the second term of the Reagan administration.

Ironically, President Reagan, who explicitly rejected talks with the Soviet leadership early on, ultimately held more summits with the Soviet leadership than any other American president in the post–World War II era. In the space of the last four years of his presidency, he held five summits with President Gorbachev of the Soviet Union.[65] Each of these summits proved to be important building blocks for improving Soviet-American ties.

The first summit between President Reagan and General Secretary Mikhail Gorbachev was held in Geneva, Switzerland, on November 19–21, 1985, and was called the "fireside summit" for the backdrop in which the talks were held. No important agreements really emerged from this summit; rather, it was an opportunity for both leaders to get to know each other better and to exchange views on numerous issues, including arms control questions, human rights issues, and regional conflicts. Perhaps the most important outcome of this summit was a commitment by both leaders to have their negotiators pursue more vigorously rapid progress in ongoing strategic offensive and defensive talks, chemical weapons talks, and conventional weapons negotiations and to agree upon a political agenda for future superpower relations. As President Reagan put it in his post-summit statement: "These two days of talks should inject a certain momentum into our work on the issues between us—a momentum we can continue at the meeting we have agreed on for next year."[66]

The second summit was held in Reykjavik, Iceland, on October 11 and 12, 1986, and focused largely on seeking progress on the nuclear arms talks underway between the Soviet Union and the United States. The most significant results of this summit were agreements in principle to reduce all strategic nuclear weapons 50 percent over a five-year period and to limit intermediate-range nuclear forces to 100 warheads for each side.[67] Both of these commitments were significant for advancing work on a strategic arms reduction (START) agreement and on an intermediate nuclear forces (INF) agreement. Within a few months, too, the Soviet Union agreed to separate the INF discussions from the discussions on other nuclear weapons systems. This action ultimately set the stage for the signing of the INF Treaty a year later.

In one area, however, Reykjavik represented a setback in nuclear arms discussions between the two superpowers. In the area of space weapons, the Soviet Union tried to make its acceptance of the 50 percent reduction principle contingent on the U.S. effectively stopping the development of its Strategic Defense Initiative, or "Star Wars," nuclear defensive system. Because no agreement was ultimately reached on this question, the issue continued to cast a pale over whether any agreements would ultimately be completed.

The third and fourth summits, however, answered that concern decisively. The third summit, held in Washington, D.C., on December 8–10, 1987, was President Gorbachev's first visit to the United States and proved to be a dramatic success. It was highlighted by the signing of the INF Treaty (discussed below), a commitment by both sides not to let "Star Wars" prevent the negotiation of a new strategic arms reduction pact, and a mutually shared view by both leaders that they had succeeded in shifting the course of Soviet-American relations in a relatively short period of time.

The fourth summit was held in Moscow from May 29 to June 2, 1988. The agenda for this summit was to exchange instruments of ratification of the new INF Treaty, to seek further progress in strategic arms negotiations, and to discuss other key global issues. It also produced a series of technical agreements on student exchanges, nuclear power research, maritime search and rescue cooperation, fisheries, transportation, and radio navigation, all of which continued to foster more and more cooperation between the two adversaries. Finally, and indicative of the changed relationship between the two nations, President Reagan was allowed to openly criticize the Soviet Union and its lack of freedom and democracy in a major speech at Moscow State University without any rupture in the summit proceedings. As a result, at the end of the summit, President Reagan was moved to note the significant changes in Soviet-American relations: "I think there is quite a difference today in the leadership and in the relationship between our two countries."[68]

The fifth and final Soviet-American summit of the Reagan administration was held in New York City on December 7, 1988, in conjunction with President Gorbachev's visit and speech to the United Nations. The occasion was purposely described by President Reagan as not "a working summit" because there was no set agenda.[69] Instead, it was an opportunity for a final exchange of views before Reagan left office and for the new President-elect, George Bush, to meet the Soviet leader. No substantive agreement was reached at this brief meeting (which was cut shorter still because of Gorbachev's desire to return home to deal with an earthquake in Armenia), but it did continue the ongoing dialogue between the two nations. Still, progress on a START treaty would need to await the new Bush administration.

FROM NUCLEAR ARMS NEGOTIATIONS TO THE INF

The major substantive manifestation of progress in Soviet-American relationships in the second term was the completion of the Intermediate Nuclear Forces (INF) Treaty. This treaty culminated a long series of negotiations that had originally begun in November 1981, broke off in November 1983, and resumed again after a joint Soviet-American agreement to link all nuclear arms negotiations in a set of "New Negotiations" in January 1985.

These "New Negotiations" called for three sets of discussions in the context of one negotiation—one on intermediate nuclear forces, a second on strategic nuclear forces, and a third on defense and space arms. The aim of these new talks was that "all questions [would be] considered and resolved in their interrelationship."[70] At least two reasons existed for these interrelated negotiating tracks and for the new name. First, the Soviet Union was particularly sensitive toward resuming any negotiations after they had broken off talks on the first two topics when the U.S. had begun the deployment of cruise and Pershing II missiles in late 1983. These new and more complex negotiations, however, provided the Soviets with some diplomatic cover in which they could claim that the process was beginning again and not just resuming the old discussions. Second, the Soviet Union wanted to tie any future arms agreement to a limitation on defense and space weapons, the "Star Wars" program that President Reagan had initiated. A "package deal," such as these talks suggest, could accomplish this objective.

Although these discussions started as three separate tracks in one negotiation, in reality each was rather quickly separated. After the 1986 Reykjavik summit, for example, the intermediate nuclear forces talks were quickly separated for accelerated action; after the 1987 Washington Summit, the defense and space talks were downgraded; and after this same meeting, the main outlines of a strategic agreement were adopted. Yet, the only talks to receive fruition during the Reagan years were the intermediate arms talks.

As we have noted, the Intermediate Nuclear Forces Treaty was signed at the 1987 Washington Summit, and the instruments of ratification were exchanged at the first 1988 Moscow Summit.[71] This agreement, summarized in Table 5.2, called for the elimination of all medium-range nuclear weapons within three years and all intermediate-range nuclear weapons within 18 months. It also prohibited the United States and the Soviet Union from ever again possessing such weapons. Further, it provided for a series of on-site

---

TABLE 5.2 KEY COMPONENTS OF THE INTERMEDIATE
NUCLEAR FORCES (INF) TREATY

Treaty Articles
requires the Soviet Union and the United States to eliminate all
intermediate-range missiles within three years of the effective date of the
treaty and all medium-range missiles within 18 months

Memorandum of Understanding on Data Exchange
requires the Soviet Union and the United States to provide each other with
data on the number, location, and character of their intermediate-range and
medium-range nuclear missiles

Elimination Protocol
provides specific guidelines and procedures for the destruction of all missiles,
launchers, support structures, and support equipment for these
intermediate-range and medium-range nuclear missiles

The Inspection Protocol
provides for a wide variety of on-site inspections by each side upon the other
for up to 13 years after the treaty enters into force

Special Verification Commission
establishes this commission for the purpose of resolving immediately any
problem that is identified by either party

Source: Abstracted and adapted from "The INF Treaty: What's in It?" in *Arms Control Update* (Washington, D.C.: Arms Control and Disarmament Agency, January 1988), pp. 4–5.

---

inspections for each party and set out exacting procedures on how
these weapons should be destroyed. Finally, it established a Special
Verification Commission, which would be continuously in session to
deal with any issues that might arise. This stood in sharp contrast to
earlier arms control agreements in which such a commission would
have to be called into session or only meet periodically. Under this
new arrangement, problems or concerns would be immediately addressed by the two parties.

The military significance of this pact has been questioned. Relatively few nuclear missiles were destroyed by this agreement, and
the two superpowers retained a formidable arsenal with which to destroy one another and the world at large. The political significance of
the pact, however, cannot be questioned. The INF Treaty represented the first nuclear arms reduction pact in human history, and it
gave real momentum to arms control and arms reduction for the future. Further, with the incorporation of on-site inspection into the
pact itself, it initiated a new departure in the verification of arms control agreements between the superpowers. Finally, the INF Treaty

demonstrated to the United States and the Soviet Union, and to the world, that serious arms reduction could be undertaken.

POLICY CONTINUITY: THE REAGAN DOCTRINE AND THE THIRD WORLD

Although actions toward the Soviet Union represented an important source of change, policy toward the Third World—and the perceived role of the Soviet Union in causing unrest there—remained an important constant during the second term of the Reagan administration. This continuity was reflected in the formal emergence of the "Reagan Doctrine," a policy of supporting anti-communist movements in various locations around the world, and most dramatically demonstrated by the sustained support of the Nicaraguan contras by the Reagan administration, even as the Congress cut off military support for that operation from 1984 to 1986. This episode, which quickly became known as the "Iran-contra affair," reflected the administration's determination to "stand tall" against perceived communist penetration in Central America. (We discuss this affair in detail later in this chapter.) At the same time, this episode produced a major inconsistency in policy: The Reagan administration secretly abandoned its official policy of an arms embargo toward Iran in an attempt to free American hostages held there. Indeed, this undertaking ultimately proved to be the major foreign policy failure of the Reagan years.

THE REAGAN DOCTRINE

By 1985, the Reagan administration's support for anti-communist forces in the Third World had gained such prominence and permanency that it took on a name of its own—the Reagan Doctrine. Unlike U.S. policy that focused on containing the expansion of communism throughout the post–Cold War years, the Reagan Doctrine espoused "providing assistance to groups fighting governments that have aligned themselves with the Soviet Union."[72] Despite the thaw in relations with the Soviet Union, this strategy was pursued vigorously throughout the second term of the Reagan administration and proved to be the main thread of continuity with the hardline policy of anti-communism that was so prominent in 1981.

What this policy meant in reality was that several anti-communist movements across three continents were to receive both covert and overt American economic and military assistance and po-

litical encouragement in their fights against the communist governments in power. In Asia, for example, the United States continued to
support the Afghan rebels in their battle with the Soviet troops and
the Soviet-backed Kabul government. In Cambodia, the United
States clandestinely funneled aid to groups opposing the government supported by the occupying Vietnamese troops. In Africa, the
Reagan administration persuaded the Congress to repeal its prohibition under the Clark Amendment on aid to forces opposing the Angolan government, and it continued to support rebel leader Jonas
Savimbi and his National Union for the Total Independence of Angola (UNITA) in its fight against the Marxist-supported government
there. In Central America, perhaps the best known example of this
Reagan Doctrine continued as well. The Reagan administration continued to support Nicaraguan contras against the Sandinista regime,
even as Congress diligently attempted to end such aid.

Perhaps a useful indicator of how institutionalized the Reagan
Doctrine had become was the 1985 foreign aid authorization bill.
While that bill included some aid for the Nicaraguan rebels, support
for other anti-communist rebel groups was publically acknowledged
with a $5 million allocation to the Cambodian rebels and a $15 million "humanitarian" allocation to the Afghan people.[73] Further, as alluded to above, the congressional prohibition on aid to rebel forces
in Angola was formally rescinded in this legislation.

POLICY SUCCESS AND THE REAGAN DOCTRINE

At least two policy successes were registered in Third World areas as
a result of reliance on the Reagan Doctrine. Through continued support of the Afghan rebels by the United States and other nations and
through the decision by President Gorbachev to reduce the Soviet
Union's worldwide activity, an agreement on Soviet withdrawal from
Afghanistan was reached in August 1988. Under UN mediation, Afghanistan, Pakistan, the United States, and the Soviet Union signed
an agreement to provide for the total withdrawal of Soviet troops by
February 1989. Pakistan and Afghanistan also agreed not to interfere
in each other's domestic affairs, and the U.S. and the Soviet Union
agreed to serve as guarantors of those commitments.[74]

A similar outcome favorable to the Reagan Doctrine occurred in
southern Africa. Throughout his administration, President Reagan
had supported independence for Namibia from South Africa
through UN-supervised elections, but that commitment to independence was conditioned upon the removal of Cuban troops from
neighboring Angola. As an incentive for such a political settlement,

the Reagan administration had provided support to UNITA in Angola. This strategy finally proved successful in late December 1988, when an agreement was signed among Angola, Cuba, and South Africa calling for a phased withdrawal of all Cuban troops in Angola by July 1991, the withdrawal of South African troops from Namibia by the end of 1990, and the completion of elections in Namibia by the end of 1990.[75]

At least two other policy actions were taken that were consistent with the principles of the Reagan Doctrine and with the principle of confronting challenges from the Third World. Substantial economic and military assistance continued to flow to the government of El Salvador as that government sought to control Marxist-backed forces within its borders. In the Middle East, the Reagan administration responded swiftly and decisively to a terrorist act in West Germany in which Americans were the target. Based upon its intelligence, the American government claimed that Libya was the source of this attack, and President Reagan quickly ordered a retaliatory air strike against Libya in April 1986, including the headquarters of President Muammar al-Qadhafi among its targets. This action appeared to have results. Further Qadhafi-inspired attacks seemed to stop over the next two years. (However, in late 1991 the U.S. government indicted two Libyan intelligence agents over the 1988 bombing of Pan Am flight 103 over Lockerbie, Scotland, in which 270 people were killed.)

THE IRAN-CONTRA AFFAIR, 1984–1986

The one episode that best illustrates the extent to which the administration embraced the Reagan Doctrine was the Iran-contra affair, which lasted from 1984 to 1986. Ironically, this episode also proved to be the major foreign policy failure of the Reagan presidency and raised significant questions about the means that were being used to implement the Reagan Doctrine.

This affair brought together two vexing foreign policy problems for the Reagan administration.[76] The first was over the question of dealing with the Sandinista regime in Nicaragua. The Sandinistas, who had overthrown the Nicaraguan dictator Anastasio Somoza in 1979, were viewed as avowed Marxists by the Reagan administration, intent upon spreading revolution throughout Central America. The administration, of course, was equally intent upon stopping such action. The second was over the question of dealing with Iran and its government led by Ayatollah Khomeini. That government had seized American hostages in November 1979, held them for 444 days, and only released them on the day of President Reagan's inauguration. Hence, the U.S. government was intent upon making certain that such actions would not occur again.

The Reagan administration's policy in dealing with the former problem was to support the Nicaraguan contras fighting against the Sandinistas. In November 1981, President Reagan reportedly signed a secret intelligence finding authorizing U.S. clandestine support for the contras in their efforts against the Sandinistas. The policy toward Iran grew out of an executive order signed by President Carter imposing trade sanctions against Iran and President Reagan's initiation of "Operation Staunch" in the spring of 1983. The latter policy prohibited the sale of U.S. arms to that country and sought to discourage other countries from doing so as well.

Beginning in 1984, however, both policies faltered, and they eventually unravelled by the middle of 1985. The actions of Iran in support of terrorism caused the first challenge to the Reagan administration's policy. As a result of the U.S. presence in a multinational peacekeeping force in Lebanon in 1982 and 1983, anti-American sentiment and terrorism against the U.S. rose significantly. Much of this terrorism, moreover, was supported by the Khomeini government in Iran. In October 1983, terrorists bombed American Marines who were in Lebanon as part of the Multinational Forces. They seized three Americans in Beirut in early 1984. (One hostage was later identified as the CIA station chief in Beirut.) Later, in 1985, they took four more Americans as hostages. The American public, of course, was increasingly clamoring for the administration to do something about the hostage situation, and President Reagan was increasingly impatient with the lack of viable policy options to respond to these events. By the middle of 1985, therefore, Reagan decided to reverse the long-standing—and publically stated—policy of an arms embargo against Iran in an attempt to free U.S. hostages.

Yet the Reagan administration's reversal on policy toward Iran was not done in isolation; it quickly became tied to an attempt to save its policy of aiding the Nicaraguan contras. In a continuing budget resolution in October 1984, the Congress had cut off all American military assistance to the Nicaraguan contras with the passage of the most restrictive version of the Boland Amendment (see Chapter 8). Such action represented a reversal of the Reagan administration's policy and served as a direct challenge to its efforts to get rid of the Sandinistas and to implement the Reagan Doctrine. In light of this congressional reversal, high executive branch officials almost immediately undertook efforts to keep the contras together in "body and soul," as President Reagan had instructed. What ultimately emerged from these efforts was a covert operation by private operatives to raise money and provide support for the Nicaraguan rebels. At least two ways were used to raise money to support the contras: one was through contributions by private individuals and other governments; the other was through the clandestine sale of arms to the Iranian government and the transfer of profits to the Nicaraguan rebels. Importantly, throughout the entire episode and during the investigation afterwards, President Reagan consistently denied that he knew that the arms sales' profits were being transferred to the contras or that the arms sales to Iran were tied solely to the freeing of American hostages held in Lebanon. (According to President Reagan, the larger goal of these arms sales was to seek better ties with the Iranian government.)

The covert arms operation and the contra resupply was codenamed "the Enterprise." It was directed by Lt. Col. Oliver North of the National Security Council staff and located in the basement of the White House. The Enterprise, apparently initiated as early as the summer of 1984, moved into full operation by the middle of 1985 when President Reagan orally approved American participation in an Israeli arms sale of American weapons to Iran, with the U.S. promising to replenish the Israeli stockpile. In August and September 1985, about 500 TOW anti-tank missiles were shipped to Iran. Another Israeli shipment of 18 HAWK anti-aircraft missiles followed in November. A retroactive intelligence finding was approved by President Reagan in December 1985 and reportedly stated that the deal was a straight arms-for-hostages arrangement. (Under current law, an "intelligence finding" is required for any covert operation, and it must generally be shared with the intelligence committees in Congress. See Chapter 10.) According to the investigation of this episode by the Congress, however, "National Security Advisor [John] Poindexter destroyed this Finding a year later because... its disclosure would have been politically embarrassing to the President," and the Congress was never informed.

President Reagan did sign an intelligence finding on January 17, 1986, in which he approved the shipment of arms to Iran and, in effect, lifted the embargo that both he and President Jimmy Carter had imposed on that country. Further, he ordered William Casey, the director of the Central Intelligence Agency, not to inform the intelligence committees of Congress about this action. National Security Advisor John Poindexter, in a memo actually prepared by Lt. Col. Oliver North, recommended to President Reagan "that you exercise your statutory prerogative to withhold notification of the finding to the congressional oversight committees until such time that you deem it to be appropriate." The memo stated that Attorney General

William French Smith had determined "that under an appropriate finding you could authorize the CIA to sell arms to countries outside the provisions of the laws and reporting requirements for foreign military sales." The finding signed by the president also explicitly directed that "due to its extreme sensitivity and security risks, I determine it is essential to limit prior notice, and direct the Director of Central Intelligence to refrain from reporting this finding to the Congress...until I otherwise direct."[77]

The intelligence finding resulted in at least four arms shipments by the United States to Iran. In February 1986, 1,000 TOW anti-tank missiles were sent to Israel for eventual shipment to Iran. In May, HAWK missile parts were sent to Iran, and Lt. Col. North and former National Security Advisor Robert McFarlane went to Tehran for five days, hoping to negotiate the release of American hostages in Lebanon. In July 1986, after one hostage was released, a third shipment of more HAWK spare parts was delivered to Iran. In late October, the final shipment of 500 TOWs was sent to Iran.

Swiss bank accounts were set up to facilitate these transactions, and at least part of the profits from these arms sales were reportedly destined to assist the Nicaraguan contras in their fight against the Sandinistas. Although $16 million was realized in profits from the arms sales, in fact only about $3.8 million was ultimately transferred to support the contras. Further, although three hostages were released from Lebanon during the arms sales period, three more hostages were seized before the affair was disclosed publicly. In this sense, even on this narrow policy goal, the arms sales did little to resolve the question of hostages in Lebanon.

Throughout the period of these arms sales or diversion of funds, these activities were never reported to the Congress as required by the Intelligence Oversight Act and other governing legislation. Indeed, the Congress did not learn formally of this covert operation before November 21, 1986, when CIA Director William Casey briefed the intelligence committees in Congress.

The Iran-contra affair affected both procedural and policy aspects of American foreign policy during the latter years of the Reagan administration. It damaged both the clarity and credibility of the administration's policy and challenged the way the Reagan Doctrine was being carried out. It had a profound effect upon congressional-executive relations and upon public support for foreign policy. The affair also resulted in two separate investigations—one by the executive branch (the Tower Commission, named after its chair, former Senator John Tower of Texas), the other by the Congress (the establishment of special Iran-contra committees in the House and the Senate)—which sought to identify exactly what went on and what changes needed to be made to ensure that similar episodes would not occur in the future. Finally, the foreign policy episode resulted in the appointment of an independent prosecutor to investigate possible wrongdoings and to charge and try the responsible individuals, if necessary.

In general, the congressional investigation found that standard procedures were not followed in making policy decisions, that the Congress was misled, that dishonesty and excessive secrecy pervaded the process, and that the president should have known, if he did not, about the diversion of funds from the arms sales to the Nicaraguan rebels. The executive branch investigation reached many of the same conclusions. Yet, perhaps its major conclusion was put best by a member of the review panel and a former national security advisor, Brent Scowcroft, as the Tower report was being released: "The problem at the heart was one of people, not of process. It was not that the [decision making] structure was faulty; it is that the structure was not used."[78] Some specific recommendations for monitoring intelligence activities in the future are discussed in detail in Chapter 10.

On the policy side, and especially in dealing with Third World policy, the impact of the Iran-contra affair for the Reagan administration was more immediate. First, support for President Reagan declined quickly and dramatically. In a *Newsweek* poll at the time, his approval rating dropped some 17 percentage points from October to December 1986, from 64 percent to 47 percent. Prior domestic popularity had helped the president's ability to work his will on foreign policy, even when the Congress and the public were skeptical of particular foreign policy decisions. Now the American public began to doubt the veracity of the president as well.[79] Second, members of Congress, and especially members of his own Republican party, were no longer willing to embrace President Reagan's leadership on foreign policy so automatically. Third, the policy toward the Sandinistas was seriously weakened. As a result, future funding for the contras proved to be more difficult, although by early 1988, the Congress did approve $48 million in "humanitarian" aid, but only after earlier rejecting military assistance.[80] Fourth, the incentive for further congressional support of other Reagan Doctrine efforts was likely reduced, although it is unclear if any covert actions were actually changed.

The Iran-contra affair produced another foreign policy tragedy by casting a cloud over the integrity of U.S. foreign policy: could Americans trust their president and his appointees to act within the

2336

laws passed by Congress? Several key Reagan administration foreign policy officials and private political operatives working for "the Enterprise" were indicted and convicted of wrongdoings in this affair. In all, at least ten individuals involved in Iran-contra were indicted, including three top Reagan administration officials—former National Security Advisor Robert McFarlane, his successor as national security advisor, John Poindexter, and Lt. Col. Oliver North, who reportedly ran the covert operation. McFarlane, Poindexter, and North were all convicted of offenses, but Poindexter's and North's convictions were later overturned on appeal.

Finally, this episode raised doubts about foreign policy leadership. The various investigations could never fully determine how much President Reagan knew about this activity or how much George Bush, then vice-president and shortly the president-elect, knew about it either. Further, the episode raised anew questions of the utility of covert operation as an instrument of American foreign policy and the relationship of the Congress and the executive in monitoring such operations. In Chapter 10, we revisit this episode from that perspective to show more fully how congressional-executive relations over the use of covert operations were badly damaged by this affair as well.

POLICY CHANGE AND REAGAN: THE PHILIPPINES, THE PLO, AND SOUTH AFRICA

Although policy continuity largely marked the Reagan approach to the Third World, three important modifications are worth noting. The first involved the movement toward democracy under Corazon Aquino in the Philippines in 1985 and 1986. The United States had long supported the government of Ferdinand Marcos, principally because of his anti-communist credentials and because of the need to maintain two strategic U.S. bases on Philippine soil: the naval base at Subic Bay and an air base at Clark Field. Yet Marcos's dismal human rights record and authoritarian rule had long been a source of embarrassment and concern to U.S. policymakers. Consistent with its basic orientation to Third World stability, however, the Reagan administration had largely acquiesced in continued support for the Marcos government.

With the assassination of Senator Benigno Aquino, Jr., the leading politician in the opposition to Marcos, upon his return to the Philippines in August 1983, and the rise in strength of the New People's Army, a Marxist opposition group, and other nationalist opposition groups, the Reagan administration came under increasing pressure to reevaluate its policy. By 1984, that reevaluation had begun and a National Security Council directive undertook to plan for a post-Marcos period.[81] In particular, U.S. officials began to meet with opposition leaders and to pressure the Marcos regime for democratic reform. This initial change in policy was motivated both by the fear of communist insurgency (a pattern consistent with the Reagan Doctrine) and by a commitment to democratic reform. Indeed, the former motivation was used continuously upon President Marcos to stimulate more reform, while the latter was used as a motivation to encourage the opposition.

Under increasing domestic pressures over the investigation of the Benigno Aquino assassination and repressive actions at home, President Marcos suddenly agreed to hold a "snap election" in early 1986 to demonstrate his popularity. Opposing President Marcos on the ballot was Corazon Aquino, wife of the assassinated senator and a political novice. Although Marcos was declared the election winner, accusations of voter fraud were rampant. Opposition groups surrounded the presidential palace and called for Marcos to give up power. At that juncture, the Reagan administration threw its full support behind the opposition candidate, Corazon Aquino, and informed Marcos that he should resign. Within a matter of days, he left the country and took up exile in Hawaii.

The significance of this event for the Reagan administration was that it represented a clear departure from previous policy. Instead of seeking to maintain stability through support for authoritarian rule, it had moved to seek change, even in the face of possible communist gains after the departure of the Marcos regime. Hence, the promotion of human rights and democracy in the Philippines—while fully consistent with traditional U.S. values—seemed at odds with an administration that had previously supported Third World stability as the less dangerous way to thwart potential communist expansion.

A second illustration of changed Reagan administration policy toward the Third World concerned the question of talking with the Palestine Liberation Organization (PLO) in any Middle East peace negotiations. Since 1975, as part of the commitments associated with a second disengagement agreement between Israel and Egypt, the United States had pledged to Israel that it would have no contact with the PLO until at least two conditions were met: (1) the PLO recognized the right of the state of Israel to exist; and (2) the PLO accepted UN Resolutions 242 and 338 as the basis for negotiations in the Middle East.[82] Over the years, a third requirement for any contact between the PLO and the U.S. was added: (3) the PLO would have to renounce the use of terrorism.[83]

With the deteriorating political conditions within the Middle East by the mid-1980s, however, the time was ripe for bold actions to affect change. From 1985, a series of efforts initiated by Secretary of State George Shultz had failed to stimulate discussions between the Arab states and Israel. Further, PLO chief Yasir Arafat and King Hussein of Jordan seemingly had adopted a joint position for such negotiations only to have such an agreement collapse. In December 1987, with the emergence of the *intifada* ("uprising") among Palestinians in the Israeli-occupied territories of the West Bank and the Gaza Strip and the harsh Israeli reaction to those disturbances, the prospects for diplomatic movement looked dim.

In November 1988, the Palestine National Council, the political assembly of the PLO, took a dramatic step to change the situation. First, it declared an independent Palestinian state in the area occupied by Israel and sought recognition from abroad. Second, and most importantly for U.S. policy, it moved to accept the first American condition for discussion between the parties and accepted in part the second condition. On the third condition, however, it only "condemned" terrorism and did not renounce it. By the middle of December 1988, however, Yasir Arafat, head of the PLO, sensing the political values of discussions with the U.S., announced his full acceptance of the three explicit conditions for U.S.-PLO dialogue and his renunciation of terrorism. Within a matter of hours, President Reagan determined that Arafat's statement met American conditions and announced a shift in American policy: "These have long been our conditions for a substantive dialogue. They have been met. Therefore, I have authorized the State Department to enter into a substantive dialogue with PLO representatives."[84]

The shift in policy produced an immediate series of discussions between U.S. and PLO representatives. Although the shift occurred with only days left in office for the Reagan administration, the expectation was that this new opening would facilitate discussion among all parties and perhaps assist in the resolution of the long and seemingly intractable dispute between Israel and its Arab neighbors. Nonetheless, the Reagan administration began once again to focus on "local issues" as the source of regional conflict, a distinctly different approach than what it had adopted at the outset of its years in office. The PLO was seen less in the light of U.S.-Soviet relations and rather more in the context of the Israeli-Arab dispute.

One final area that reflected change for the Reagan administration's policy toward the Third World was South Africa. Although all American administrations, including Reagan's, had long opposed South Africa's policy of apartheid—segregation of the races—the

Reagan administration had followed a policy of "constructive engagement" in which "quiet diplomacy" was seen as the best way to elicit change in that strategically important country. By August 1985, however, the Congress had become impatient with such a strategy and was on the verge of passing a compromise bill that would have imposed economic sanctions on South Africa as a more tangible way to effect change. In a clear reversal of policy, and undoubtedly as an attempt to rescue the initiative from the Congress, President Reagan issued an executive order imposing virtually the same set of sanctions that the Congress had proposed.[85]

In 1986, however, the Reagan administration failed to take any further action against South Africa. The Congress pressed ahead, however, and passed a new, tough sanctions bill, the Anti-Apartheid Act of 1986, over President Reagan's veto. The policy change that President Reagan had originally put into place after congressional prodding in 1985 was now made permanent by an act of Congress in 1986. In this sense, the policy change on the part of the Reagan administration was less decisive than in the earlier two cases.

CONCLUDING COMMENTS

The Reagan administration came to office in 1981 largely committed to restoring the values of the Cold War era as the guide to policy action. It largely succeeded in doing so—by placing the Soviet Union at the center of American foreign policy, by taking actions to challenge the Soviets worldwide, and by attempting to rally the rest of the nations of the non-communist world against the Soviet challenge. During its second term, in one of the most dramatic reversals in American foreign policy, the Reagan administration moved from confrontation to accommodation with the Soviet Union. It quickly sought to improve ties through frequent summit meetings (five in all) and by completing the first nuclear arms reduction treaty (the INF Treaty) by the end of its years in office. In policy toward the rest of the world, however, the Reagan administration continued to pursue a staunch anti-communist policy (a policy soon labeled the Reagan Doctrine) to perceived Soviet inroads. Any record of success in that pursuit, however, was marred by the major foreign policy failure known as the Iran-contra affair.

In the next chapter, we complete our survey of different value approaches of the recent administrations by turning to the Bush administration approach to foreign policy. Although the Bush administration began as one generally committed to the more accommodative and pragmatic approach of the second Reagan term, it quickly faced two major foreign policy challenges: the collapse of communism in Eastern Europe and the rise of blatant aggression in the Middle East. Both events were to have a profound effect on how Bush—and American society—would view the world and what foreign policy values they would pursue in the 1990s.

NOTES

1. "Transcript of President's First News Conference on Foreign and Domestic Topics," *New York Times*, January 30, 1981, p. A10.

2. "Excerpts From President's Speech to National Association of Evangelicals," *New York Times*, March 9, 1983, p. A18.

3. Jimmy Carter, "Humane Purposes in Foreign Policy," Department of State News Release, May 22, 1977, p. 1 (Commencement Address at the University of Notre Dame).

4. See, for example, Robert E. Osgood, "The Revitalization of Containment," William P. Bundy, ed., *America and the World 1981* (New York: Pergamon Press, 1982), pp. 465–502.

5. Alexander Haig, "Opening Statement at Confirmation Hearings" (Washington, D.C.: Bureau of Public Affairs, Department of State, January 9, 1981), p. 2 (Current Policy No. 257).

6. Alexander Haig, "News Conference" (Washington, D.C.: Bureau of Public Affairs, Department of State, January 28, 1981), p. 5 (Current Policy No. 258).

7. Richard Halloran, "Weinberger, in London, Cautions Against Appeasement in Moscow," *New York Times*, October 23, 1981, p. A6.

8. Robert Pear, "Reagan Aide Assails Pacifism in Europe," *New York Times*, March 22, 1981, p. 13. At about this same time, Richard E. Pipes, Soviet foreign policy expert on the National Security Council, was quoted anonymously (although later identified) as saying that there was no alternative to war with the Soviet Union if it did not give up communism. See Hedrick Smith, "Discordant Voices," *New York Times*, March 20, 1981, p. A2.

9. One American diplomat was quoted as saying, "Aside from opposing the Soviets, we don't really have a foreign policy." Hedrick Smith in "Discordant Voices," p. A2, quotes this diplomat.

10. See, for example, the following statements by Alexander Haig and issued by the Department of State, "A New Direction in U.S. Foreign Policy" (April 14, 1981); "Relationship of Foreign and Defense Policies" (July 30, 1981); and "A Strategic Approach to American Foreign Policy" (August 11, 1981)." The four items here are quoted from the last one at p. 2. We shall rely upon this last one for our subsequent analysis here.

11. Ibid. Later section subtitles are from these points.

12. On these plans, see, for example, *Congressional Quarterly Almanac 1981* (Washington, D.C.: Congressional Quarterly, Inc., 1982), pp. 240–241; and Stephen Webbe, "Defense: Reagan Plans Largest U.S. Military Buildup Since Vietnam. . . ." *Christian Science Monitor*, May 1, 1981, pp. 8–9. The latter article puts the buildup at $1.5 trillion.

13. Alexander Haig, "Arms Control and Strategic Nuclear Forces" (Washington, D.C.: Bureau of Public Affairs, Department of State, November 4, 1981). This is Current Policy No. 339 and constituted Secretary Haig's statement before the Senate Foreign Relations Committee on that date. The elements of strategic modernization are drawn from that statement. On the importance of the "command and control" system, see John D. Steinbruner, "Nuclear Decapitation," *Foreign Policy* 45 (Winter 1981/82): 16–28. Also see Osgood, "The Revitalization of Containment," pp. 474–478; and Raymond Aron, "Ideology in Search of a Policy," in William P. Bundy, ed., *America and the World 1981*, pp. 504–508. These articles were also useful for our later survey of policies in the various regions of the world.

14. Defense budget estimates were projected to go to over $350 billion by 1986. See Alice C. Moroni, *The Fiscal Year Defense Budget Request: Data Summary* (Washington, D.C.: Congressional Research Service, February 1, 1983).

15. See the chronology in William P. Bundy, ed., *America and the World 1983* (New York: Pergamon Press, 1984), p. 786. Also see P.L. 98-94.

16. "Deficits Cloud Reagan Budget," *Des Moines Register*, February 2, 1984, p. 8A.

17. "Peace and Security, President Reagan Televised Address to the Nation, March 23, 1983," reprinted in *Realism, Strength, Negotiation: Key Foreign Policy Statements of the Reagan Administration* (Washington, D.C.: Department of State, May, 1984).

18. The centrality of the deployment issue in Soviet-American relations is noted in William P. Bundy, "A Portentous Year," in William P. Bundy, ed., *America and the World 1983*, p. 499.

19. See Halloran, "Weinberger, in London, Cautions Against Appeasement in Moscow"; Pear, "Reagan Aide Assails Pacifism in Europe"; and *Newsweek*, April 6, 1981, p. 37.

20. On June 18, 1982, President Reagan imposed sanctions on American subsidiaries or their licensees that prohibited them from continuing to supply the Soviets for the construction of the gas pipeline. What this did was to affect the Europeans directly. See Josef Joffe, "Europe and America: The Politics of Resentment (Cont'd)," in William P. Bundy, ed., *America and the World 1981* (New York: Pergamon Press, 1982), pp. 573–574.

21. The quotations are drawn from President Reagan's speech to the World Affairs Council of Philadelphia. Portions of it can be found in "Excerpts From Reagan Speech on U.S. Policy Toward Developing Nations," *New York Times*, October 16, 1981, p. A12. The same theme was struck a week later by President Reagan at Cancun, Mexico. See Howell Raines, "President Asserts Meeting in Cancun Was Constructive," *New York Times*, October 25, 1981, p. 1. Also see the detailed discussion of the Reagan approach to the Third World and its difference from the Carter approach in Osgood, "The Revitalization of Containment," pp. 486–495, upon which we also draw.

22. "Caribbean Basin Initiative, *GIST* (Washington, D.C.: Department of State, February 1982).

23. Press release on arms transfer policy, The White House Office of the Press Secretary, July 9, 1981.

24. See the survey of Reagan's foreign policy in the November 9, 1981, issue of *Newsweek*, in which there is "A Tour of Reagan's Horizon," pp. 34–43. The mention of "strategic consensus" for the Middle East is at p. 41, but the concept can be applied to all areas of the world during the Reagan administration.

25. Haig, "A Strategic Approach to American Foreign Policy," p. 3. Emphasis added.

26. See, for example, the "Text of Haig's Speech on American Foreign Policy," *New York Times*, April 25, 1981, p. 4, and his characterization of the Soviet Union. Also see the chronology in Bundy, ed., *America and the World 1981*, p. 728, for President Reagan's comment at his June 16, 1981, press conference in which he says that the Soviet Union "shows signs of collapse." (The quote is from Bundy.) The text of President Reagan's remarks can be found in "The President's News Conference of June 16, 1981," *Weekly Compilation of Presidential Documents* 17 (June 22, 1981): 633.

27. The announcement of the neutron bomb can be found in Leslie H. Gelb, "Reagan Orders Production of 2 Types of Neutron Arms for Stockpiling in the U.S.," *New York Times*, August 9, 1981, p. 1. The president's statement on the imposing of sanctions on the Soviet Union over the Polish situation can be found in *Weekly Compilation of Presidential Documents* 17 (January 4, 1982): 1429–1430.

28. Steven Weisman's "Reagan Ends Curbs on Export of Grain to the Soviet Union," *New York Times*, April 25, 1981, pp. 1, 6, discusses the lifting of the embargo. The expansion of grain sales is reported in John F. Burns, "U.S. Will Permit Russians To Triple Imports of Grain," *New York Times*, October 2, 1981, pp. IA, D14. A five-year grain deal was eventually agreed to in July 1983, Steven R. Weisman, "A New Pact Raises Soviet Purchases of American Grain," *New York Times*, July 29, 1983, pp. A1 and D9. Also see William G. Hyland, "U.S. Relations: The Long Way Back," in William P. Bundy, ed., *America and the World 1981*, pp. 542–543.

29. Bernard Gwertzman, "U.S. Says It Is Not Bound by 2 Arms Pacts With Soviets," *New York Times*, May 20, 1981, p. A11.

30. On the Haig-Gromyko meeting and for prospects on arms control talks, see Bernard Gwertzman, "U.S. and Soviet Agree to Renew Weapons Talk," *New York Times*, September 24, 1981, pp. A1, A10.

31. A discussion of the INF negotiations can be found in Strobe Talbott, "Buildup and Breakdown," in William P. Bundy, ed., *America and the World 1983*, pp. 587–615. On the first deployment, see James M. Markham, "First U.S. Pershing Missiles Delivered in West Germany," *New York Times*, November 24, 1983, p. A14.

32. The cataloguing of these events and other Soviet actions can be found in the "Cooling Trend in Soviet Policy," *Christian Science Monitor*, May 25, 1984, p. 1. On the explanation for the withdrawal from the Olympics, see "U.S.-Soviet Ties Termed 'Worst Ever,' " *Des Moines Sunday Register*, May 27, 1984, p. 1.

33. The comment was by a Soviet official and is quoted in "U.S.-Soviet Ties Termed 'Worst Ever.' " The anomaly in the Reagan administration policy was its deteriorating relations with the Soviet Union, but its warming relations with another communist giant, the People's Republic of China (including a successful trip by President Reagan to that country in April 1984).

34. "Communist Interference in El Salvador" (Washington, D.C.: Bureau of Public Affairs, Department of State, February, 1981), p. I. Special Report No. 80.

35. Testimony of Secretary of State Alexander Haig before the House Foreign Affairs Committee. The quoted phrase can be found in Foreign Assistance Legislation for Fiscal Year 1982, hearing before the Committee on Foreign Affairs, the House of Representatives, 97th Cong., 1st Sess. (Washington, D.C.: U.S. Government Printing Office, 1981), p. 194.

36. See chronology in Bundy, ed., *America and the World 1981*, p. 749.

37. "No More Aid for Nicaragua," *Today*, April 24, 1981, p. 13.

38. In its November 8, 1982, issue, *Newsweek* devoted its cover story to the covert war against Nicaragua. See "A Secret War for Nicaragua," pp. 42–55. American funding of these covert activities eventually became an open secret.

39. See the chronology in Bundy, ed., *America and the World 1981,* p. 751.

40. "Prepared Text of Reagan Speech on Central American Policy," p. 6.

41. Ibid.

42. "Reagan Says Security of U.S. Is At Stake in Central America," p. 6A.

43. The justification for the Grenada invasion is taken from President Reagan's remarks on October 25, 1983. They are reprinted in "Grenada: Collective Action by the Caribbean Peace Force," *Department of State Bulletin* 83 (December 1983): 67.

44. The Reagan administration sought congressional repeal of the Clark Amendment, an amendment passed in 1976 that prohibited aid to forces in Angola. The apparent aim of such an action was to allow the United States to support Jonas Savimbi and his UNITA forces, who were still fighting the Marxist government in Angola. The Congress, however, failed to repeal the amendment as President Reagan had wanted.

45. A chronology of these various actions is presented in William P. Bundy, ed., *America and the World 1981,* pp. 734–735. This chronology, and the subsequent ones in the other volumes of this series, were useful beginning points for unraveling the sequence of events in the Reagan administration.

46. This agreement was quickly suspended by the United States after the Israelis annexed the Golan Heights in December 1981. See Aron, "Ideology in Search of a Policy," p. 517.

47. Juan de Onis, "U.S. and Pakistanis Reach an Agreement on $3 Billion in Aid," *New York Times,* June 16, 1981, pp. A1, A15. On the importance of both the AWACS and Pakistani sales, see Carol Housa, "Arms Sale Test, U.S.-Pakistan Ties," *Christian Science Monitor,* November 12, 1981, p. 3.

48. President Reagan's initiative was proposed in a speech to the nation on September 1, 1982. For a text of the speech, see "Transcript of President's Address to Nation on West Bank and Palestinians," *New York Times,* September 2, 1982, p. A11.

49. The explanations for sending these forces into Lebanon are contained in the reports to the Congress on August 24, 1982, and September 29, 1982, and in the Multinational Force Agreement between the United States and Lebanon of September 25, 1982. All of these are reprinted in *The War Powers Resolution: Relevant Documents, Correspondence, Reports,* Subcommittee on International Security and Scientific Affairs, House Committee on Foreign Affairs, December 1983, pp. 60–63, 74–76.

50. See "Communique by the Common Market," *New York Times,* January 5, 1982, p. A7; and "Text of Declaration on Poland by The Foreign Ministers of NATO," *New York Times,* January 12, 1982, p. A8. Also see John Vinocur, "Bonn Says Sanctions Are Not the Solution," *New York Times,* December 30, 1983, pp. A1, A7.

51. See Andrew Knight, "Ronald Reagan's Watershed Year?" in William P. Bundy, ed., *America and the World 1982* (New York: Pergamon Press, 1983), pp. 511–541.

52. The president's comment is contained in Bernard Gwertzman, "President Says Should Not Waiver in Backing Saudis," *New York Times,* October 18, 1981, p. 1; and the statement by Haig is reported in Gwertzman's "Allied Contin-

gency Plan Envisions a Warning Atom Blast, Haig Says," *New York Times*, November 5, 1981, pp. A1, A9.

53. "Focus on The National Elections in West Germany on March 6, 1983," p. 6, and "Focus on the Results of the National Elections in the Federal Republic of Germany on March 6, 1983," p. 2. Both are published by the German Information Center.

54. Paul E. Sigmund, "Latin America: Change or Continuity?" in William P. Bundy, ed., *America and the World 1981*, p. 636.

55. George Gallup, "Military Budget Boost Loses Support, Poll Hints," *Des Moines Sunday Register*, February 27, 1983, p. 5A.

56. A *Newsweek* poll reported in the magazine's April 26, 1982, issue, p. 24, found that 68 percent of those who had heard of the nuclear freeze movement favored or strongly favored it. A later *Newsweek* poll in January 1983 found that 64 percent of the public supported the nuclear freeze proposal. See *Newsweek*, January 31, 1983, p. 17.

57. The crowd estimates ranged from 500,000 to 700,000 or more. Paul L. Montgomery, "Throngs Fill Manhattan To Protest Nuclear Weapons," *New York Times*, June 13, 1982, pp. 1, 43. For a survey of how the freeze movement reflects a cross section of the American public, see "A Matter of Life and Death," *Newsweek*, April 26, 1982, pp. 20–33.

58. President Reagan rejected the use of U.S. armed forces in a March 1981 interview with Walter Cronkite. Francis X. Clines, "President Doubtful on U.S. Intervention," *New York Times*, March 4, 1981, pp. A1, A22. In a December 1981 interview, Secretary Haig ruled out American troops. See Sigmund, "Latin America: Change or Continuity?" p. 641, for a report on this interview.

59. The quoted passages are from "Transcript of President's News Conference on Foreign and Domestic Issues," *New York Times*, Nov. 8, 1984, p. 13. The discussion here also draws upon Howell Raines, "Reagan Takes 49 States and 59% of Vote, Vows to Stress Arms Talk and Economy," and Hedrick Smith, "Reagan Faces Difficult Task in Leading Divided Congress," *New York Times*, Nov. 8, 1984, p. 1, 10; Brad Knickerbrocker, "Defense & Diplomacy," *Christian Science Monitor*, Nov. 8, 1984, pp. 1, 4; and James McCartney, "Reagan Faces Decisions on Arms Curbs, Nicaragua," *Des Moines Register*, Nov. 8, 1984, p. 7A.

60. George Schultz, "Managing the U.S.-Soviet Relationship over the Long Term," address before the Rand/UCLA Center for the Study of Soviet International Behavior, October 18, 1984, reprinted in *Department of State Bulletin*, December 1984, p. 2.

61. George Shultz, "The Future of American Foreign Policy: New Realities and New Ways of Thinking," in James M. McCormick, ed., *A Reader in American Foreign Policy* (Itasca, IL: F. E. Peacock Publishers, Inc., 1986), pp. 379–392. The quotation is from p. 382.

62. "Text of Inaugural Address," *Des Moines Register*, January 22, 1985, p. 4A.

63. On the changes in Soviet foreign policy, see David Holloway, "Gorbachev's New Thinking," and Robert Levgold, "The Revolution in Soviet Union Foreign Policy," in William P. Bundy, ed., *America and the World 1988/89* 68 (1989), pp. 66–98.

64. John E. Rielly, ed., *American Public Opinion and U.S. Foreign Policy 1987* (Chicago: The Chicago Council on Foreign Relations, 1987), p. 6.

65. For a comparison with the number of summits by other presidents, see Harold W. Stanley and Richard G. Niemi, *Vital Statistics on American Politics* (Washington, D.C.: CQ Press, 1988), pp. 293–294.

66. Taken from "Concluding Remarks: President Reagan, November 21, 1985," reprinted in *Department of State Bulletin,* January 1986, p. 11.

67. "The Reykjavik Meeting," *GIST* (Washington, D.C.: Department of State, December 1986).

68. Steven B. Roberts, "Reagan Says He Was Moved by Contacts with Russians," *New York Times,* June 2, 1988, p. A16. On the third summit, see R. W. Apple, Jr., "Reagan and Gorbachev Report Progress on Long-Range Arms and Mute 'Star Wars' Quarrel," *New York Times,* December 11, 1987, pp. 1 and 10.

69. President Reagan's statement of December 3, 1988, which is reprinted in the *Department of State Bulletin* 89 (February 1989), p. 3.

70. "Joint Statement, Geneva, January 8, 1985," *Department of State Bulletin,* March 1985, p. 30.

71. The complete text of the INF Treaty and its protocols are available in *Arms Control and Disarmament Agreements: Texts and Histories of the Negotiations* (Washington, D.C.: United States Arms Control and Disarmament Agency, 1990), pp. 345–444.

72. Michael Mandelbaum, "The Luck of the President," in William G. Hyland, ed., *America and the World 1985* (New York: Pergamon Press, 1986), p. 408.

73. *Congressional Quarterly Almanac 1985* (Washington, D.C.: Congressional Quarterly, Inc., 1986), pp. 40, 56, and 58.

74. Peter Hayes, ed., "Chronology 1988" *Foreign Affairs: America and the World 1988/89* 68 (1989): 239.

75. For a summary of the accord on Angola and Namibia, see "Angola/ Namibia Accords," *Department of State Bulletin* (February 1989): 10–16.

76. Several sources were used to construct the description of events associated with the Iran-contra affair. Among them were *Report of the Congressional Committees Investigating the Iran-Contra Affair* (Washington, D.C.: U.S. Government Printing Office, November 1987); *Report of the President's Special Review Board* (Washington, D.C.: U.S. Government Printing Office, February 26, 1987); Peter Hayes, ed., "Chronology 1987" *Foreign Affairs: America and the World 1987/88* 66 (1988): 638–676; Peter Hayes, ed., "Chronology 1988" *Foreign Affairs: America and the World 1988/89* 68 (1989): 220–256; Clyde R. Mark, "Iran-Contra Affair: A Chronology," Report No. 86-190F (Washington, D.C.: Congressional Research Service, April 2, 1987); James M. McCormick and Steven S. Smith, "The Iran Arms Sale and the Intelligence Oversight Act of 1980," *PS* 20 (Winter 1987): 29–37. The Reagan quote on keeping the contras' "body and soul together" can be found in *Report of the Congressional Committees Investigating the Iran-Contra Affair,* p. 4, and the quote about Poindexter can be found at p. 7 of this report.

77. The quotations are taken from the intelligence finding and the accompanying memo by Poindexter, which are reprinted in *The Washington Post,* January 10, 1987, p. A10. Most of them are also reported in McCormick and Smith, "The Iran Arms Sale and the Intelligence Oversight Act of 1980," pp. 31–32.

78. David Hoffmann and Dan Morgan, "Tower Panel Details Administration Breakdown, Blames Reagan, Top Aides for Policy Failures," *Washington Post,* February 27, 1987, p. A1.

79. The poll results are in "A Rapid Decline," *Newsweek,* December 15, 1986, pp. 26–27, while in "Reagan's Crusade," *Newsweek,* December 15, 1986, at p. 28, it is reported that "only 10% of a national sample believed that he was telling the truth about the contra funding." This paragraph also draws upon McCormick and Smith, "The Iran Arms Sale and the Intelligence Oversight Act of 1980," pp. 35–36.

80. Peter Hayes, ed., "Chronology 1988" *Foreign Affairs: America and the World 1988/89*, 68 (1989): 249. For some background on contra aid, see Andrew Taylor and Lenore Webb, *"Chronology of Hill-Reagan Tug of War Over U.S. Involvement with Contras,"* *Congressional Quarterly Weekly Report* (March 26, 1988): 806–807.

81. This account of the change in support is based upon Sandra Burton, "Aquino's Philippines: The Center Holds," *Foreign Affairs: America and the World 1986* 65 (1987): 524–537, especially pp. 524–526.

82. Nadav Safran, *Israel: The Embattled Ally* (Cambridge, MA: The Belknap Press, 1978), p. 594.

83. Alan Cowell, "Arafat Urges U.S. to Press Israelis to Negotiate Now," *New York Times*, November 16, 1988, pp. A1 and A10.

84. "U.S. Makes Stunning Move Toward PLO, *Des Moines Register,* December 15, 1988, p. 3A. The results of the Palestine National Council deliberations are discussed in "The P.L.O.: Less Than Meets the Eye," *New York Times*, November 16, 1988, p. A30; and Youssef M. Ibrahim, "Palestinian View: A Big Stride Forward," *New York Times*, November 16, 1988, p. A10.

85. The discussion is based upon *Congressional Quarterly Almanac 1985* (Washington, D.C.: Congressional Quarterly, Inc., 1986), pp. 39, 40, and 85; and *Congressional Quarterly Almanac 1986* (Washington, D.C.: Congressional Quarterly, Inc., 1987), pp. 359–362.

CHAPTER 6 THE BUSH ADMINISTRATION AND THE COLD WAR'S END

"From the Baltic to the Adriatic, an irresistible movement has gathered force—a movement of, by, and for the people. In their peaceful urgent magnitude, the peoples of Eastern Europe have held up a mirror to the West and have reflected the enduring power of our own best values....The changes amount to nothing less than a peaceful revolution." **SECRETARY OF STATE JAMES BAKER, PREPARED ADDRESS TO THE BERLIN PRESS CLUB, DECEMBER 12, 1989**

"Out of these troubled times,...a new world order...can emerge; a new era—freer from the threat of terror, stronger in the pursuit of justice, and more secure in the quest for peace, an era in which the nations of the world, East and West, North and South, can prosper and live in harmony." **PRESIDENT GEORGE BUSH, ADDRESS TO A JOINT SESSION OF THE U.S. CONGRESS, SEPTEMBER 11, 1990**

George Bush was elected president in November 1988, less on a commitment to change the course of U.S. foreign policy than on the American people's desire for continuity in its approach to the world. Bush came to office less an ideologue on foreign policy than Ronald Reagan and more as a pragmatist without a strongly held worldview. In this sense, President Bush's initial foreign policy impulse leaned toward maintaining continuity with the recent past, rather than seeking change. However, his commitment to continuity was challenged by the dramatic events that began at the end of his first year in office: the demise of the Soviet empire; the emergence of new political, economic, and social openness in Poland, Hungary, Czechoslovakia, and East Germany; and the movement toward the reunification of Germany.

By 1990, President Bush had modified the course of American foreign policy away from one driven by the anti-communist principles of the past and toward one driven by the changes in the Soviet Union and Eastern Europe. Iraq's invasion of Kuwait and the American and allied response to it gave further impetus for seeking a new direction for foreign policy. Indeed, shortly after the beginning of the Persian Gulf War, President Bush acknowledged as much when he announced that "we stand at a defining hour" in our foreign policy.[1] The Bush administration began to advance a new rationale for America's global involvement using the old rubric of a "new world order." Yet, the elements of this new order, and how it would be implemented, were not fully spelled out by the administration. As a consequence, the exact direction of U.S. foreign policy by the early 1990s remains in flux.

In this chapter, then, we review the initial commitment of the Bush administration to continuity in policy with the Reagan administration, the dramatic events that challenged such a continuity, and the efforts to build a "new world order" in American foreign policy for the 1990s. We also assess the Persian Gulf War of 1991, which proved to be the major foreign policy challenge of the Bush presidency, and evaluate its implications for the future of American foreign policy.

(Throughout this chapter, when discussing events before the breakup of the Soviet empire in 1989–1990, the use of the term "Eastern Europe" shall refer to those countries that were communist allies of the Soviet Union—East Germany, Poland, Czechoslovakia, Hungary, Romania, Bulgaria—and formed part of the "Soviet bloc." When discussing events after the dramatic changes in those two years, the term "Central Europe" shall refer to these countries, since it is more descriptive of their proper geographical location.)

THE VALUES AND BELIEFS OF THE BUSH ADMINISTRATION

"Pragmatic" and "prudent" (as contrasted with "ideological") have been favorite values used to describe the Bush administration's basic approach to American foreign policy.[2] The Bush administration did not come to office with a grand design or with a "vision thing" (as President Bush himself might say) for reshaping international politics. Instead, the administration's policy approach really reflected the values, beliefs, and temperament of Bush himself, a moderate, middle-of-the-road, professional politician who was well trained in foreign affairs. After all, President Bush came to office with a wealth of foreign policy experience—as former director of the CIA, former American representative to the People's Republic of China, former ambassador to the United Nations, and former vice-president of the United States. Although at various times he claimed to be from Texas, Connecticut, or Maine, Bush had spent most of the previous twenty years deep within the establishment in Washington, and he was fully steeped in the foreign policy emanating from the nation's capital. In this sense, he was aptly prepared for the "give and take" of Washington and global politics. And, indeed, he would be put to the test rather quickly.

THE COMMITMENT TO CONTINUITY: A PROBLEM SOLVER, NOT A VISIONARY

President Bush may describe himself as a policy conservative (and, hence, was comfortable with the foreign policy objectives of the previous administration), but he is more than that. He is a problem solver who can, and does, work well with those with whom he may disagree.[3] His underlying political approach might best be summarized in two brief statements: getting results are more important than claiming ideological victory; getting results are the best way to achieve political success.

Because of his cautious nature and his willingness to pursue pragmatic policies, President Bush's initial impulse was less an effort to initiate his own foreign policy approach and more an effort to assure continuity with the last half of the Reagan administration. To be sure, his initial foreign policy action was to call for a complete policy review in an attempt to separate himself from the previous administration. Yet when that four-month review was completed, the shape of policy looked only modestly different from the policy pursued by the Reagan administration during its second term.

To the extent that the foreign policy values and beliefs of the Bush administration reflect any general principles of foreign policy-making, the tenets of realism (Chapter 4) come the closest to describing them. President Bush essentially wanted to deal with the world as it existed and sought only those changes that would not be too unsettling for the international system as a whole. Further, the Bush administration was much more interested in relations with the strong (e.g., the Soviet Union, China, and Central Europe) than in relations with the weak (e.g., the Third World nations). In this sense, his policy orientation came closer to the balance-of-power approach that Nixon, Kissinger, and Ford brought to U.S. policy than to the staunchly anti-communist, ideological approach of the Reagan years or the strident moralism of the Carter years. While these principles continue to hold sway, the events of late 1989 and 1990 compelled the Bush administration to search for values and beliefs—largely from America's past—to guide U.S. policy in the post–Cold War years.

The personal style of decision making by President Bush gives further reason for asserting that personal values enter into the foreign policy process. Unlike the disengaged style of Ronald Reagan, George Bush is actively involved in policymaking—usually with a relatively small group of advisors. According to observers, he continuously "works the phone" to accomplish his foreign policy objectives. Since he has served around the world and was vice-president for eight years, he does indeed have a close working relationship with leaders from many nations. As such, he is quick to contact them directly and to employ personal persuasion to shape his foreign policy agenda. This personal dimension was most evident during the last half of 1990 and the early part of 1991, as he worked vigorously to put together the anti-Iraq coalition and then to hold it together.

Critics of the Bush administration viewed the president's initial pragmatic and cautious approach as indecisive or deliberate. Most agreed that the designs of policy were nonexistent or, more charitably, still emerging. As Theodore Sorensen, a former Kennedy administration official, put it, the early part of the Bush administration was "all tactics, no strategy." Moreover, he argued that "there is a difference between caution and timidity, and Mr. Bush has been excessively timid in his proposals on arms reductions, ethics, and education." Additionally, "he reacts but rarely initiates."[4] Furthermore, nothing in his early actions suggested that President Bush had a real road map for where he wanted the country to go in either foreign or domestic affairs.

Another analyst, William Hyland, a former official in the Ford administration, was more supportive of the Bush administration's initial deliberateness in foreign policy. "It is the nature of the problems, however, not the style, that has dictated this approach," he contended at the time. Because the international system was in flux at the beginning of the Bush presidency, time and reflection were required. Further, in Hyland's view (and as we discuss below), when some initial decisions were required, the administration "avoided confrontation with wise compromises" in its early days.[5]

Still another foreign policy observer wondered whether the Bush style—at least as practiced in the first year of his presidency—could really adjust American foreign policy to the rapidly changing world. His failure to move rapidly on Soviet-American relations, Central American policy, and Middle East opportunities implies as much. Once again, the Bush administration's style of "pursuing means" and "not envisioning ends" seemed to be the underlying problem.[6] A clear vision of how the world should look and work remained elusive.

Other questions can be raised about his "hands-on" approach to policymaking and the dangers that may result from it. During the Bush administration's decision to support the coup attempt in Panama in October 1989, the president was apparently deeply involved in tactical decision making, perhaps much to his regret. By contrast, and perhaps indicative of his future style, he took a more detached approach to conducting the Persian Gulf War and left most tactical decisions to his military advisors. Even in the latter instance, however, he did not stay too far away from the details, with constant briefings and updates.[7]

Similarly, despite the admiring characterization of the administration's foreign policy advisors as "closely integrated and coherent" and "a parallel-minded team," a danger existed that few dissenters resided within the inner circle of advisors.[8] While the absence of such advisors may have appeared a problem, the personal Bush strategy of consulting widely diminished the potency of this criticism considerably. Nonetheless, the Bush administration, like virtually all previous administrations, was susceptible to the charge that too few contrary opinions were received at the top.

BUSH'S FOREIGN POLICY TEAM: "SENSIBLY CONSERVATIVE"[9]

The foreign policy team that came to Washington, the initial policy review, and the early policy decisions generally lent credence to this pragmatic, cautious—yet realist—description of the Bush administration's approach to foreign policy. The initial Bush foreign policy team, for example, reflected the same kind of pragmatic moderation. Individuals without strong ideological posture and those given to practical solutions to problems were chosen for the key cabinet and national security positions in the administration. Bush's choices for secretary of state, James Baker, and national security adviser, Brent Scowcroft, were individuals with this same kind of commitment to incremental change in global affairs. According to one long-time foreign policy analyst, "The Baker-Scowcroft combination is the most competent-looking pair of people any new president has put in those jobs."[10] They were two individuals who could work well with each other and with the Congress. Indeed, both enjoyed enormous credibility on Capitol Hill.

The other key foreign policy participants in the Bush cabinet largely shared those pragmatic and "sensibly conservative" labels, and possessed governmental experience as well. At the State Department, the two top assistants to James Baker were Lawrence Eagleburger, as deputy secretary of state, and Robert Kimmett, as under secretary of state for political affairs. Eagleburger had been in the foreign service for twenty-seven years and had worked with Kissinger Associates between government appointments. Kimmett had served as an aide both at the Department of Treasury and the National Security Council. Neither would be described as a conservative ideologue.[11] At the National Security Council, Scowcroft's top aide, Robert Gates, was perhaps more conservative than his boss, but he appeared to be a team player. Indeed, President Bush nominated him as CIA director in 1991.

At the Department of Defense, the appointment of Richard Cheney, after the bruising nomination defeat of Bush's first choice, John Tower, reflected a policymaker of the same order as the others. While Cheney, a former member of Congress, had an exceedingly conservative voting record, he was also viewed as pragmatic and reasonable in his approach to policy questions. His experience as chief of staff during the Ford administration demonstrated his pragmatic approach to policymaking particularly well, and his handling of policymaking during the Persian Gulf troop buildup and during the war itself won him high marks from several quarters.

The same held true for the top policymakers at the CIA, Treasury, and as U.S. trade representative. At the CIA, William Webster, Bush's first director and a holdover from the Reagan administration, was generally recognized as a top-flight professional without the ideological fervor of his predecessor, William Casey. At Treasury, Nicholas Brady, a personal friend of the president and a former U.S. senator, came from this same moderate policy tradition, as did Carla

Hills, the new U.S. trade representative. Mrs. Hills had previously worked in the Nixon administration as the secretary of housing and urban development.

THE POLICY APPROACH OF THE BUSH ADMINISTRATION

As a mechanism for looking to the future, President Bush called for a policy review at the very outset of his administration. The review process was centered in the National Security Council system, but it inevitably involved the entire foreign policy machinery. Moreover, it took almost four full months to complete, and its results were announced not through a single document, but through a series of speeches that Bush gave in April and May 1989: a speech to a Polish-American audience in Hamtramck, Michigan, another to a German audience in Mainz, West Germany, and commencement addresses at Texas A&M University, Boston University, and the Coast Guard Academy.[12] These speeches were primarily focused on security questions with the Soviet Union and Eastern Europe. While they generally failed to reveal foreign policy departures from the last years of the Reagan administration, they did convey a positive approach toward future foreign affairs cooperation with other states, particularly for the nations of Europe.

THE POLICY REVIEW: INITIAL IDEAS AND PROPOSALS

The commencement address at Texas A&M University is probably the most important statement about the Bush administration's approach because of the considerable amount of ground it covered in dealing with the Soviet Union and the approaching end of the Cold War. As President Bush said, "We are approaching the conclusion of an historic postwar struggle between two visions: one of tyranny and conflict, and one of democracy and freedom. . . . And now, it is time to move beyond containment to a new policy for the 1990s—one that recognized the full scope of changes taking place around the world and in the Soviet Union itself." His administration, he continued, would "seek the integration of the Soviet Union into the community of nations."

To achieve that aim, however, President Bush outlined a number of changes in Soviet foreign policy that the United States would require. (In reality, these changes were more of a "wish list" than a "requirement list.") First, the Soviet Union must change some of its global commitments. The Soviet Union must no longer arm the Sandinista regime in Nicaragua, and it must no longer threaten the nations of the Western Hemisphere. Further, it must abandon its ties with Libya, respect China's territorial integrity, and return the Soviet-occupied territories to Japan. Second, the Soviet Union must undertake several changes in Eastern Europe. Soviet troops must be reduced there. Since conventional force levels still favored the Warsaw Pact nations, forces should be cut "in proportion to their legitimate security needs." The Brezhnev Doctrine toward Eastern Europe must be abandoned and the Iron Curtain torn down. The Brezhnev Doctrine, named after the former Soviet leader Leonid Brezhnev, reserved to the Soviet Union the right to ensure the maintenance of socialism in any country of Eastern Europe by taking all necessary actions, including military intervention. Third, the Soviet Union must work closely with the West to address several festering regional and global conflicts. The Soviet Union, for example, must cooperate in resolving ongoing Central American, southern African, and Middle Eastern conflicts. It must also demonstrate a substantial commitment to political pluralism and human rights and must join with the United States in "addressing pressing global problems, including the international drug menace and dangers to the environment."

If these actions were undertaken (and many, in fact, became reality during the first two years of the Bush administration), the response of the United States to the Soviet Union would be positive. President Bush indicated that he would seek completion of the START negotiations (although still reserving the U.S. option to deploy nuclear defense systems) and would move toward agreeing on verification procedures in order to permit the implementation of two signed, but unratified, treaties between the U.S. and the Soviet Union limiting the size of nuclear tests. President Bush also proposed a renewal of the "open skies" policy, first enunciated by President Eisenhower, as a way to build trust between the two nations. Under this proposal, the Soviet Union and the United States would allow surveillance flights over one another's territory. Further, if the Soviet Union would establish emigration laws in accordance with international standards, the U.S. would seek a waiver of the requirements of the Jackson-Vanik Amendment for the Soviet Union. (This amendment, passed by the Congress in 1974, withheld most-favored-nation trade status to the Soviet Union because of its restrictions on the emigration of Soviet Jews.) Then, the Bush administration could move toward its expressed goal of placing "trade and financial transactions . . . on a normal commercial basis."

Juxtaposed against this proposed strategy of Soviet-American cooperation, President Bush reaffirmed the commitment to a strong national security strategy for the 1990s, largely consistent with the tradition of the Reagan administration. The United States would continue "to defend American interests in light of the enduring reality of Soviet military power." It would also seek to "curb the proliferation of advanced weaponry; . . . check the aggressive ambitions of renegade regimes; and . . . enhance the ability of our friends to defend themselves." While the precise security strategy to obtain these goals had not yet been fully devised, the Bush administration would base its formulation on two key principles. One was to maintain an effective nuclear deterrent with continued commitments to the deployment of the MX missile, the continued development of the Strategic Defense Initiative ("Star Wars"), and, in something of a departure, the development and deployment of a new, mobile, and single-warheaded missile, the Midgetman. The second principle of this stragegy was a renewed commitment to arms control. The U.S. needed "to maintain an approach to arms reduction that promotes stability at the lowest feasible level of armaments." These reductions, moreover, must occur in both conventional and nuclear weapons.

In the other speeches, President Bush's comments were primarily directed to the future of Eastern Europe. He first applauded the emergence of democracy in Poland, offered various forms of assistance by the U.S. and the international community, and expressed a hope for future changes in Eastern Europe as well. He later expressed American support for the uniting of Europe into a single market in 1992, for the development of new mechanisms of consultation and cooperation with Europe in the future, and for the maintenance of U.S. military forces in Europe "as long as they are wanted and needed to preserve the peace in Europe."

In his Mainz, West Germany, address, President Bush set forth his view of the political future of Europe. On the occasion of the fortieth anniversary of the NATO alliance, Bush said, "Let Europe be whole and free. . . . The Cold War began with the division of Europe. It can only end when Europe is whole." He also outlined four proposals to reach this goal. First, he called for "free elections and political pluralism in Eastern Europe." Second, he called for bringing "*glasnost* [openness] to East Berlin." The Berlin Wall should come down. Third, Eastern and Western Europe must cooperate on environmental issues. Fourth, East and West must work vigorously to reduce the degree of militarization in Central Europe. On balance, this last speech was the most far-reaching in its recommendations, and the most prescient of these four speeches. In large measure, it fore-shadowed the dramatic changes about to unfold in Central Europe.

Missing from these speeches was a strategy for dealing with the rest of the world. None of the speeches focused upon policy toward the Third World exclusively, and none had much to say about relations with the developing world except in the context of superpower ties. Yet, the policy review apparently was not entirely devoid of such a strategy. As was subsequently revealed during the height of the Persian Gulf War, his Pentagon and CIA advisors had given the general direction for dealing with Third World trouble spots in its review of national security policy:

> In cases where the U.S. confronts much weaker enemies, our challenge will be not simply to defeat them, but to defeat them decisively and rapidly. . . . For small countries hostile to us, bleeding our forces in protracted or indecisive conflict or embarrassing us by inflicting damage on some conspicuous element of our forces may be victory enough, and could undercut political support for U.S. efforts against them.[13]

EARLY ACTIONS: A MIX OF MODERATION, CAUTION, AND REALISM

Unlike the bold speeches on the future of Eastern Europe and on ties with the Soviet Union or even the apparent advice on Third World trouble spots, the early policy actions of the Bush administration mainly reflected its impulses of pragmatism and moderation, albeit occasionally mixed with touches of political realism. U.S. policy behavior in four major trouble spots reflected this policy mixture and set the tone for the reaction of the Bush administration to the major political changes that occurred in Central Europe in late 1989 and throughout 1990.

The first instance of the administration's pragmatism and moderation involved policy accommodation with the Congress over future support for the Nicaraguan contras, long a central policy concern of the Reagan administration (see Chapter 5). Realizing that Congress was in no mood to provide further military support, the Bush administration quickly fashioned a bipartisan proposal that provided some support for the contras, which the president wanted, and that committed the U.S. to the ongoing Central American peace, which the Congress wanted.[14] The package called for $50 million of non-military aid to the contras and pledged the Bush administration to employ diplomatic and economic measures to pressure the Sandinistas to open up their political system. Further, in a remarkable feature of this agreement, and in yet another effort to cement congressional-executive cooperation, the Bush administration agreed to allow four congressional committees the right to suspend any aid after November 30, 1989. As a result of this bipartisan agreement on Central America, the aid package was passed overwhelmingly in both chambers of Congress (89–9 in the Senate, 309–110 in the House)—a cooperative executive-congressional action that stood in stark contrast to the partisan and ideological bickering on this issue during much of the Reagan administration.[15] Fortuitously, this policy of moderation paid off for both Congress and the Bush administration. The Sandinista government held to its earlier promise to hold nationwide elections in February 1990, and in a stunning result, the united opposition won a convincing victory over the Sandinistas.

This same kind of policy moderation occurred in dealing with the ongoing civil war among the four parties competing to control the government of Cambodia. In a sharp break with the policy of previous administrations, the Bush administration in the summer of 1990 withdrew its support from the three parties opposed to the Vietnamese-supported government in Cambodia and agreed to have direct talks with the Vietnamese government over the future of Cambodia.[16] This strategy, formulated in cooperation with the Soviet Union, was intended to get all parties to accept a United Nations peace plan for resolving the dispute, first through an internationally supervised cease-fire and then through an internationally supervised election. Once again, this pragmatic approach by the Bush administration produced some success. Within two months of this change in American policy, the four competing parties in Cambodia committed themselves to using the UN framework for settling the conflict.[17]

Policy accommodation, however, was not practiced everywhere by the Bush administration during its first year in office. Its actions toward Panama indicated the willingness to use force to defend American interests and, in effect, to take actions consistent with tenets of political realism. The Panamanian government of General Manuel Antonio Noriega had long been a source of annoyance and trouble for the Reagan administration and, as it turned out, for the Bush administration as well. In February 1988, Noriega, a long time CIA operative, was indicted on drug trafficking charges by a federal grand jury in Florida and was widely reported to be involved in numerous other unsavory international activities. As a result, the Reagan administration decided to impose economic sanctions on Panama and to use those and other economic measures as a way to force Noriega's resignation as the head of government.[18] None of these efforts, however, proved successful.

President Bush was thus faced with the same problem when he took office. He continued economic sanctions but without success. When Noriega nullified the national election results in May 1989—an election in which the opposition apparently won—the Bush administration decided to take several additional steps to force him from power. First, the Organization of American States (OAS) was asked to investigate the election results. After the OAS did so, it issued a resolution condemning the actions of the Noriega government and asking that he step down. The Noriega regime, however, was unresponsive to these OAS efforts. Second, President Bush also took several unilateral actions: he declared that Noriega's hand-picked regime was illegitimate, called for the installation of the democratically elected government, and stated that the American ambassador to Panama, who had previously been called home for consultations, would not return. Earlier, too, he had ordered more American forces into Panama, and, for political effect, the military conducted exercises in Panama. Third, when all of these measures failed to budge Noriega's hold on power, the Bush administration threw its support behind a coup attempt in October 1989. Because the administration viewed the coup's leaders with suspicion, however, it provided only lukewarm support to the effort. The result was a disaster. The coup failed within hours, much to the embarrassment of President Bush.[19] Finally, and as a last resort, President Bush ordered 13,000 American troops into Panama (in addition to the 11,000 already stationed at U.S. bases there) in December 1989. In a matter of days, the invasion was successful, and Noriega was captured and returned to the United States to stand trial on the drug trafficking charges. Even though the invasion was a reflection of American interventionism of the past, the Bush administration opted for the requirement of realist politics in choosing this course of action.

President Bush displayed the same reliance on political realism in his policy toward the People's Republic of China. During May and early June 1989, massive pro-democracy demonstrations calling for reforms within the country occurred in Beijing and other Chinese cities. The Chinese government tolerated these demonstrations for a time, but it finally decided to put them down militarily. In a violent and bloody assault upon the demonstrators in Beijing's Tiananmen Square, the Chinese military killed hundreds, and perhaps thousands, of demonstrators.[20]

The initial reaction of the Bush administration was to condemn the Chinese actions as violations of human rights and throw its support behind the expansion of democracy within China. Indeed, it immediately imposed a series of economic sanctions through an executive order. Arms sales to China were stopped, visits between U.S. and Chinese military officials were suspended, humanitarian and medical assistance was offered to those injured in the military crackdown, and the U.S. immigration service was instructed to be sympathetic to Chinese students in the U.S. wishing to extend their stay.

At the same time, President Bush acknowledged that he wanted to maintain some ties with China, even in the context of continuing repression: "I understand the importance of the relationship with the Chinese people and the Government, it is in the interest of the United States to have good relations."[21] Indeed, the Bush administration sought to discourage legislative sanctions against the Chinese and went so far as to veto legislation that would have allowed Chinese students to stay in the U.S. after their visas had expired. Further, it condoned the meeting of high U.S. government officials with Chinese officials, even though a ban on such visits was presumably still in effect. Secretary of State James Baker met with the Chinese foreign minister on at least two occasions, and National Security Advisor Brent Scowcroft and Deputy Secretary of State Lawrence Eagleburger traveled to Beijing to consult with Chinese officials.

Both of these actions set off congressional protests at home over the commitment of the Bush administration to promoting global human rights and democracy. The response by the administration was largely framed in terms of realist politics, however. Despite the unacceptability of Chinese government actions, the administration reasoned, global realities compelled the United States to pursue a foreign policy that enabled it to have contact with the Beijing government and to attempt to affect its actions. The Chinese government was too critical to global order for the U.S. to isolate itself from that regime, despite its domestic repression. Political realism, not domestic moralism, guided the actions of the Bush administration.

POLITICAL CHANGE AND EASTERN EUROPE

While Nicaragua, Cambodia, Panama, and China demonstrate the mixture of moderation and realism practiced by the Bush administration toward regional trouble spots, the changes in Eastern Europe were to pose a challenge to its policy approach and to U.S. foreign policy generally. Yet, in large measure, the Bush administration pursued the same policy mix, even as the Soviet Empire unraveled, and even as democracy began to take hold in Eastern Europe. Moderate and pragmatic responses, albeit occasionally infused with doses of political realism, were still the governing principles.

The events of 1989 and 1990 can only be described as monumental in that they shook the foundation upon which U.S. foreign policy had been based since the end of World War II and the beginning of the Cold War. In the space of less than two years, the Soviet empire collapsed, with most of the states of Eastern Europe moving from socialist states to capitalist ones and from non-democratic (communist) states to democratic ones; the future of a divided Germany was resolved through reunification by the end of 1990; and the Soviet Union itself initiated several internal democratic reforms. Further, the Soviet Union was threatened with the possibility of disintegration, or at least with deep ethnic divisions, as some of its constituent republics sought independence. In effect, the central issues of the Cold War—a divided Europe and Soviet-American antagonism—were seemingly forever changed by these series of events.

Because the political changes were so substantial, a brief sketch of them is necessary to put American foreign policy in the early 1990s into perspective and to appreciate the policy response of the Bush administration more fully.

THE COLLAPSE OF THE SOVIET EMPIRE

The initial set of changes within Eastern Europe began in Poland in early 1989.[22] In January, initial steps were taken to grant legal status to Solidarity, the banned Polish trade union movement. By April 1989, a sweeping agreement was approved that formally legalized Solidarity but that also committed the communist government to hold free elections in June 1989 and to allow a more open governmental structure within Poland (although one in which the Communist party initially retained significant power). The results of the June 1989 election could not have been a more stunning defeat for the Communist party leadership. Solidarity or Solidarity-backed candidates for parliament won all of the available seats in the lower house and 99 out of 100 seats in the upper house. Such sweeping results immediately raised the prospects of even greater political change within Poland.

Further bargaining between Solidarity and the Polish government ensued, and a Solidarity member, Tadeusz Mazowiecki, was ultimately chosen as the first non-communist prime minister in an Eastern European state since the end of World War II, assuming office in August 1989. The forces for democratic change in that country—and, indeed, in Eastern Europe—had begun. Within little more than a year, the power of the Communist party in Poland was virtually eliminated as the founder of the Solidarity movement, Lech

Walesa, was popularly elected as the president of Poland in November 1990.

In Hungary, a similar evolutionary process occurred. In January 1989, the Hungarian parliament took the first steps to guarantee individual liberties to its citizens. By October 1989, the Hungarian parliament undertook several political reforms: the name of the state was changed from the Hungarian People's Republic to the Republic of Hungary; formal approval of opposition political parties was granted; the basic human rights of all Hungarian citizens were codified; and, most importantly, all references to the "leading role" of the Communist party in the affairs of state were changed in the constitution. Parliamentary elections were subsequently held in March and April 1990, with the Communist party candidates once again faring badly and the conservative democratic parties and their coalition partners capturing most of the seats. A second democratic transformation of a communist country had occurred peacefully.

In Czechoslovakia, the change to democracy was even more rapid and equally nonviolent. The first popular demonstrations occurred later there than in other Eastern European countries. Only in November 1989 did demonstrations demanding the resignation of the Communist party and democratic reform increase in frequency throughout the country. By early December, however, they began to achieve success with the eventual appointment of playwright Vaclav Havel, the leader of Civil Forum, as president in late December 1989. By June 1990, free and democratic parliamentary elections were held in Czechoslovakia, with results consistent with what had occurred in other countries: the Communist party candidates fared poorly and the new democratic opposition candidates did well. The Velvet Revolution, as it came to be called, had succeeded in Czechoslovakia as well.

In East Germany, pressures for democratic reform were also felt by the communist government in power, especially since Erich Honecker, the long-serving Communist party leader, had stood so resolute against change. The real catalysmic change in East Germany was less the institutionalization of such reform (although it did occur) and more the East's ultimate unification with West Germany as we shall discuss below.

The popular call for change was evidenced as early as August 1989, when East Germans began fleeing to West Germany using accesses through Hungary, Czechoslovakia, and Austria. Other East Germans sought asylum in West German embassies in East Berlin and elsewhere as yet other avenues of escape. By October 1989, the number of East Germans seeking asylum numbered almost 11,000.

CHRONOLOGY 6.1   THE DEMOCRATIZATION OF FOUR EASTERN EUROPEAN NATIONS, 1989–1990

POLAND

April 1989—The Communist party of Poland and Solidarity, the Polish trade union movement, agree on the legalization of Solidarity and the holding of a national election in June.

June 1989—The first democratic elections are held, with Solidarity candidates winning virtually all available seats in the upper and lower houses of parliament.

August 1989—Tadeusz Mazowiecki of the Solidarity movement is named the prime minister of Poland, although the presidency is still controlled by the Communist party leader, General Jaruzelski.

October 1989—The Polish government announces the "full introduction of market mechanisms and institutions" during 1990 and 1991.

November 1990—Presidential elections are held, and the founder of Solidarity, Lech Walesa, is elected president. Communist party power has thus been replaced in both parliament and the presidency.

HUNGARY

January 1989—Hungarian parliament initiates legislation to guarantee individual liberties.

June 1989—Communist officials allow opposition groups to negotiate for the establishment of a multiparty system in Hungary.

October 1989—The Communist party is officially disbanded and a new party, the Socialist party, replaces it. The parliament establishes the Republic of Hungary to replace the Hungarian People's Republic. A popular referendum is held on the form of government for the nation.

March–April 1990—Free parliamentary elections are held, with the Communist party candidates badly defeated.

CZECHOSLOVAKIA

November 1989—Massive demonstrations call for the resignation of the Communist party and for democratic reforms.

November–December 1989—A series of changing Communist party governments seek to maintain control, but they are rejected by the populace.

CHRONOLOGY 6.1   THE DEMOCRATIZATION OF FOUR
EASTERN EUROPEAN NATIONS, 1989–1990 (CONTINUED)

December 1989—Popular playwright Vaclav Havel, the leader of Civic Forum, the leading opposition organization, is elected president by the parliament.

June 1990—Free and democratic parliamentary elections are held, with the Communist party candidates faring badly.

EAST GERMANY

September 1989—East Germans begin fleeing the country through Austria, Hungary, and Czechoslovakia and through seeking asylum in West German embassies.

October–November 1989—Massive demonstrations calling for democratic reform occur in Leipzig and other East German cities.

October 1989—Long-time Communist party leader Erich Honecker is forced to resign. The communist government resigns in early November.

November 1989—East Germany opens the Berlin Wall and allows free travel in that divided city.

December 1989—The Communist party gives up its monopoly on political power.

March 1990—Free and democractic elections are held in East Germany with conservative and anti-communist parties gaining power.

October 1990—East and West Germany are reunited into the Federal Republic of Germany.

Source: Peter Hayes, ed., "Chronology 1989" *Foreign Affairs: America and the World 1989/ 90*, 69 (1990): 218–230; Peter Hayes, ed., "Chronology 1990" *Foreign Affairs: America and the World 1990/91*, 70 (1991): 212–222; Elizabeth A. Palmer, "East Bloc Political Turmoil...Chronology of Big Changes," *Congressional Quarterly Weekly Report*, December 9, 1989, pp. 3376–3377; *The 1990 World Book Yearbook* (Chicago: World Book, Inc., 1990); and *Encyclopaedia Britannica 1990 Book of the Year* (Chicago: Encyclopaedia Britannica, Inc., 1990).

Popular demonstrations began in earnest during the rest of October and continued into November. Demonstrations in Leipzig were particularly large and influential in ultimately affecting governmental change. Honecker eventually was forced to step down, and a series of new governments emerged.

By March 1990, free and democratic elections were held in East Germany, with the conservative Alliance for Germany obtaining the greatest percentage of votes. Its success foreshadowed a rapid movement toward reunification, since such a stance was the central plank in the Alliance's election campaign. Importantly, the renamed Communist party (the Party of Democratic Socialism) obtained only 16 percent of the vote in that election. In short, democracy also came to East Germany, although this action was soon eclipsed by its incorporation into the Federal Republic of Germany by the end of 1990.

Nascent democratic movements also were born in other Eastern European states, but their turn to democracy was slower and generally much less complete than in Poland, Hungary, Czechoslovakia, and East Germany. In Bulgaria, long-time Communist party leader Todor Zhivkov resigned in November 1989, and, a month later, he was expelled from the party. By early 1990, democratic reforms were initiated, and national elections held. Here, however, the former Communist (renamed Socialist) party obtained the most support and effectively remained in power. In Romania, sustained demonstrations occurred in mid-December 1989 against the long-ruling regime of Nicolae Ceausescu. They eventually led to violent confrontations and substantial civil strife in an attempt to overthrow the regime. As Ceausescu and his wife attempted to flee, they were captured, given a secret trial, and executed on Christmas Day 1989. By May 1990, free elections were held, although those closely allied with the former communist government obtained the most votes and retained the presidency.

In Yugoslavia, there were similar calls for reforms, and 1989 and 1990 represented considerable maneuvering in the constituent republics over the future. While democratic reforms moved forward, concern was readily voiced over whether the country would hold together or break into its constituent parts. Indeed, in June 1991 two republics, Slovenia and Crotia, unilaterally declared their independence, and clashes between the central government and these republics quickly occurred.

Finally, Albania, long the most Stalinist East European state, also came under pressure for democratic reform. By the end of 1990, opposition political parties were allowed, and the first one was promptly formed. Free and democratic elections were finally held there in late March 1991, but the communist forces remained in power. Protests continued, however, and a caretaker government of communists and non-communists was eventually formed with the promise of new elections by 1992. In late June 1991, Secretary of State James Baker traveled to Tirana, the nation's capital, and was greeted enthusiastically by some 300,000 Albanians. He committed the U.S. to support their efforts at achieving democratic reform and offered a token amount of economic assistance as well.

THE UNIFICATION OF GERMANY

The story of the unification of Germany was the second major Eastern European event of 1989–1990 and the event most directly related to the ending of the Cold War. Germany, which had been consciously divided by the victorious allies at the Yalta Conference in February 1945, and which had existed as two separate states—the German Democratic Republic and the Federal Republic of Germany—from 1949 to 1990 was formally reunited on October 3, 1990.[23] Despite the pace of events elsewhere in Eastern Europe during the previous two years, both the ease and speed of this reunification were still spectacular by any assessment.

The immediate pressures for this reunification were the massive East German emigration to the West that began in August 1989 and the popular demonstrations within East Germany, perhaps epitomized by the Leipzig demonstration of more than 200,000, which called not only for democratic reforms but for one Germany as well. Further, when East German authorities opened the Berlin Wall—the most tangible symbol of a divided city in a divided nation—on November 9, 1989, the calls for political reunification began in earnest.

Despite Soviet President Mikhail Gorbachev's contention on November 15, 1989, that German unification "is not a matter of topical politics," the issue of unification was quickly accepted by both East and West as fully negotiable by early 1990.[24] West German Chancellor Helmut Kohl first proposed a "confederation" of the two Germanys in late November 1989, and the new East German Prime Minister Hans Modrow offered a plan for unification in February 1990. What seemingly might have complicated progress on this reunification was the fact that the major wartime allies—the U.S., France, Britain, and the U.S.S.R.—still retained rights over the future of Germany and, in particular, Berlin. This difficulty was quickly overcome, however. At a February 1990 meeting of the foreign ministers from these four countries and from East and West Germany, a formula was agreed upon for the eventual reunification of Germany. These so-called "two plus four" talks called for the two Germanys to discuss their plans for reunification and then talks with the four allied powers to resolve remaining security matters.

By May 1990, East and West Germany had worked out the terms for completing reunification. Existing borders were agreed upon; an economic union was initiated on July 1, 1990; a treaty setting out the legal and social bases of the new union was signed on August 31, 1990; and formal reunification, under the name of the Federal Republic of Germany, took place on October 3, 1990.[25] Finally, demo-

---

CHRONOLOGY 6.2   THE DIVISION AND REUNIFICATION OF GERMANY, 1945–1990

February 1945—The Yalta Conference decides upon zones of occupation in Germany by the four major allied powers. Eventually, Britain, France, the United States, and the Soviet Union have zones of occupation. Berlin, the German capital, is also divided into these four occupation zones.

September 1949—The Federal Republic of Germany is formed from the Western zones of Germany (occupied by Britain, France, and the U.S.).

October 1949—The German Democratic Republic is established in the Soviet zone of occupied Germany. Berlin remains divided among the four allied powers.

August 1961—The Berlin Wall is built by the Soviet Union and East Germany to keep East and West divided.

December 1972—The Basic Treaty is signed between East and West Germany, calling for two German states in one German nation. The division between the two states remains, even as they begin some social, economic, and political contacts.

August–October 1989—Thousands of East Germans seek to escape to the West through third countries, and thousands of others call for democratic reforms in East Germany.

November 1989—The Berlin Wall is opened by East Germany, and calls for German reunification begin. West German Chancellor Helmut Kohl offers a plan for the confederation of East and West Germany.

February 1990—East German Prime Minister Hans Modrow announces plans for the reunification of the two Germanys. The foreign ministers from the four allied countries and from East and West Germany agree upon the mechanism for discussing the reunification of Germany.

May–August 1990—Social, economic, and legal agreements are reached on reunification between East and West Germany with the economic union initiated on July 1.

September 1990—The four allied powers formally relinquish their rights over Germany and grant full sovereignty to the German state.

---

cratic parliamentary elections across the unified German state were held in December 1990.

Completing the external relations for the unified Germany initially proved a bit more difficult, but these, too, were completed fairly quickly. After much political maneuvering throughout the spring and early summer, the Soviet Union agreed to a Western de-

---

CHRONOLOGY 6.2 THE DIVISION AND REUNIFICATION
OF GERMANY, 1945–1990 (CONTINUED)

October 3, 1990—The formal unification of East and West Germany takes place under the name of the Federal Republic of Germany.

December 2, 1990—Democratic elections are held in the new German state.

Source: Peter Hayes, ed., "Chronology 1989" *Foreign Affairs: America and the World 1989/90* 69 (1990): 218–235; Peter Hayes, ed., "Chronology 1990" *Foreign Affairs: America and the World 1990/91* 70 (1991): 212–226; Elizabeth A. Palmer, "East Bloc Political Turmoil...Chronology of Big Changes," *Congressional Quarterly Weekly Report*, December 9, 1989, pp. 3376–3377; Thomas L. Friedman, "Four Allies Give Up Rights in Germany," *New York Times*, September 13, 1990, pp. A1 and A6; and "One Germany: Next Steps," *New York Times*, July 18, 1990, p. A4.

---

mand that a reunited Germany be allowed to maintain its membership in NATO. Agreement was also reached on the formal withdrawal of East Germany from the Warsaw Pact and on a withdrawal of all Soviet forces from East Germany by 1994. These commitments were formalized in a pact entitled the "Treaty on the Final Provisions Regarding Germany," signed on September 12, 1990.[26] Under this treaty, too, the allied powers renounced their rights and powers over German affairs and granted full sovereignty to the German states over its foreign and domestic affairs. In about fifteen months from the time of the first sustained efforts on the part of East Germans to emigrate to the West and in less than a year from the time that the Berlin Wall has been formally breached, the reunification of Germany had become a reality. The "German question," which had consumed so much of postwar politics between East and West, had seemingly been decided.

POLITICAL CHANGE AND THE SOVIET UNION: BEFORE AND AFTER THE AUGUST 1991 COUP

The Soviet Union itself was not immune to the changes that were sweeping its Eastern European neighbors in the early 1990s. The changes in the Soviet state, however, were not as rapid in 1989 and 1990 as they were elsewhere in Eastern Europe. Instead, reform efforts were undertaken largely within the limits of maintaining a modified socialist system. After a coup attempt by Soviet hardliners against these reforms failed in August 1991, change accelerated. In particular, calls were heard for greater regional autonomy and greater democratization. As a result, the future of the Soviet Union as a unified state seemed in doubt in the immediate aftermath of the coup. By late 1991, moreover, the Baltic republics had achieved independence and a looser confederation among the republics emerged as the new Soviet Union. This devolution of Soviet power from the center to the republics would both challenge and provide new opportunities for U.S. foreign policy in the 1990s.

CHANGES WITHIN THE SOVIET UNION
BEFORE THE COUP

Two kinds of changes occurred within the Soviet Union before the August 1991 coup: (1) efforts at institutionalizing democratic reforms and moving the country from a centrally planned to a market economy; and (2) pressures for independence by some of its constituent republics. Both types of changes were to influence the conduct of global politics generally and the foreign relations between the United States and the Soviet Union in particular.

The efforts at democratic reform within the Soviet Union were essential parts of Mikhail Gorbachev's effort at *glasnost* and *perestroika*, the opening up of Soviet society and restructuring it in a way that would make it more efficient and competitive globally. In March 1989, for example, in the freest election since the 1917 Revolution, voting was held for seats in the new legislative body, the Congress of People's Deputies.[27] Later in the year, an effort was even undertaken—which Gorbachev initially opposed—to eliminate the "leading role" of the Communist party in the Soviet Union. In February 1990, the party adopted a platform that opened up the system to more than one party.[28]

In 1990 more reforms were tried, albeit with mixed success. Democratic local and constituent republic elections were held throughout the country, and the Supreme Soviet, the national legislature of the U.S.S.R., approved new press freedoms and recommended a movement toward a market economy. By the second half of 1990, plans were offered for a 500-day transition to a market economy, but that plan and less dramatic versions of it were ultimately shelved by the end of the year. More ominous still was the sudden resignation of Soviet Foreign Minister Eduard Shevardnadze, a leading proponent of accommodation with the West and reform at home, coupled with his stark warning of impending dictatorship within the Soviet Union. During the last months of 1990 and early 1991, Gorbachev moved toward slowing down and even halting the political and

---

CHRONOLOGY 6.3   POLITICAL CHANGE WITHIN THE SOVIET
UNION, 1985–1991

March 1985—Mikhail Gorbachev is named general secretary of the
Communist party after the death of Konstantin Chernenko.

June 1985—Gorbachev calls for new economic policies and initiates
the process of *perestroika* (restructuring) with an initial economic
reform plan proposed in October 1985.

July–September 1985—Long-time foreign minister Andrei Gromyko is
replaced by Eduard Shevardnadze, a close ally of Gorbachev. Prime
Minister Nikolai Tikhonov retires and is succeeded by Nikolai
Ryzhkov.

June 1986—Gorbachev announces his intention to open up the Soviet
system by establishing a program of *glasnost* (openness), in which
government censorship would be reduced.

November 1986—The Supreme Soviet, the national parliament,
approves legislation that would allow some private enterprise by
Soviet citizens.

July 1988—Gorbachev proposes a restructuring of the Soviet
government: the president would be given more power but would be
chosen by a more representative national parliament; key officials
would have limited terms; multiple candidates would be allowed in
elections; and more authority would be granted to local governing
bodies. The plan is quickly approved by the Communist party and
later by the Supreme Soviet.

March 1989—The first national elections to the new parliament, the
Congress of People's Deputies, are held. Multiple candidates are on
the ballot, and numerous Communist party members are defeated.
Two months later, Gorbachev is elected president of the Soviet Union
by this body.

February 1990—The Central Committee of the Communist Party of the
Soviet Union recommends that Article 6 of the Soviet constitution—
granting the Party a monopoly on power—be changed.

---

economic liberalizations he had undertaken. Many of the internal reforms within the Soviet Union appeared stalled by the middle of
1991, and economic conditions worsened. Still, relations between
the United States and the Soviet Union warmed during this time
period, especially after the 1991 London Summit among the industrial democracies, which promised further economic cooperation
with the Soviet Union, and after the Moscow Summit (July 1991) in

---

CHRONOLOGY 6.3 POLITICAL CHANGE WITHIN THE SOVIET
UNION, 1985–1991 (CONTINUED)

March 1990—Lithuania, a Baltic republic forcefully incorporated into
the Soviet Union in 1940, declares its independence from Moscow
and forms a new non-communist government. This actions sparks
calls for independence in many of the other republics within the
Soviet Union.

October 1990—The "Gorbachev Plan" for economic *perestroika* is
approved by the Supreme Soviet, but it calls for a slower transition to
a market economy than the 500-day Shatalin Plan that was originally
proposed.

December 1990—Eduard Shevardnadze, foreign minister of the
U.S.S.R., resigns his post and warns that reform efforts are being
threatened by reactionary forces and that dictatorship may reemerge
in the Soviet Union.

January 1991—Reform efforts are stalled as Soviet troops are ordered
into several republics to halt independence movements. Several
citizens are attacked and killed in Lithuania.

April 1991—Nine republics of the Soviet Union agree in principle to
sign a new Union Treaty in which more power would be granted to
the republics, although central authority would be retained.

June 1991—Boris Yeltsin, an advocate of more rapid change within the
Soviet Union and an opponent of Gorbachev, is popularly elected as
president of the Russian Republic, the largest republic within the
Soviet Union.

August 18, 1991—The "State Committee for the State of Emergency," a
group of close associates to Gorbachev, seizes power in the Soviet
Union and ousts him from office. Popular opposition, led by Russian
President Boris Yeltsin, quickly develops, and within three days the
coup collapses.

August–September 1991—Gorbachev returns to power, albeit in a
politically weakened condition, while Boris Yeltsin's relative influence
increases. Gorbachev quickly announces the end of the Communist
party's role within the Soviet Union and appoints officials committed
to hastening reform. Virtually all of the Soviet republics demand
autonomy, however, and the future unity of the Soviet Union appears
threatened.

---

which the superpowers signed the Strategic Arms Reduction Treaty
(START).

The other dramatic internal changes within the Soviet Union
were the pressures for independence by several of the constituent republics. The three Baltic states of Lithuania, Latvia, and Estonia took

CHRONOLOGY 6.3 POLITICAL CHANGE WITHIN THE SOVIET
UNION, 1985–1991 (CONTINUED)

September 2, 1991—A proposal is submitted to the Congress of
People's Deputies to create a more confederative Soviet Union in
which political power would be devolved to the constituent republics,
although the central government would maintain military and
security powers.

September 5, 1991—The Congress of People's Deputies approves a new
interim confederative arrangement for the Soviet Union.

Sources: Kay King, ed., "Chronology 1985" *Foreign Affairs: America and the World 1985* 64
(1986): 654; Sara Robertson, ed., "Chronology 1986" *Foreign Affairs: America and the World
1986* 65 (1987): 667–668; Peter Hayes, ed., "Chronology 1988" *Foreign Affairs: America and the
World 1989/90* 68 (1989): 226–230; Peter Hayes, ed., "Chronology 1989" *Foreign Affairs: America and the World 1989/90* 69 (1990): 218–230; Peter Hayes, ed., "Chronology 1990" *Foreign Affairs: America and the World 1990/91* 70 (1991): 212–222; "Gorbachev's Six Years," *The Wall Street
Journal*, August 20, 1991, p. A10; Serge Schmemann, "Gorbachev, Yeltsin, and Republic
Leaders Move to Take Power from Soviet Congress," *New York Times*, September 3, 1991, pp.
A1 and A6; and Serge Schmemann, "Soviet Congress Yields Rule to Republics to Avoid Political and Economic Collapse," *New York Times*, September 6, 1991, pp. A1 and A6.

the boldest steps in this regard by passing various measures declaring their independence or eventual independence from the central
government in Moscow. In addition, other republics, such as Georgia and Armenia and even the largest Soviet republic, Russia, sought
to achieve greater independence. Hence, Gorbachev and the Soviet
leadership were required to devote a considerable amount of time to
holding the U.S.S.R. together. Moreover, Moscow, on several occasions, relied upon economic sanctions and military force in its effort
to keep the country together. For the Bush administration, these independence movements provided another source of concern for U.S.
foreign policy toward the Soviet Union, even as the Cold War was
ending.

AFTER THE COUP: THE DEVOLUTION OF POWER
WITHIN THE SOVIET UNION

While President Gorbachev had sought to produce change in the Soviet Union within the context of maintaining strong central authority, impetus for even greater change occurred in late August 1991. On
the day prior to the signing of the proposed Union Treaty in which
greater power would have, in fact, been dispersed to the constituent
republics, a group of hardline Communist party members and gov-

ernment officials (the "State Committee for the State of Emergency") deposed Mikhail Gorbachev and seized power briefly in the Soviet Union. The "three-day coup" (August 18–21, 1991) collapsed due to massive protests in Moscow led by the popularly elected president of the Russian Republic, Boris Yeltsin; the apparent failure of the KGB to attack the protestors surrounding the Russian parliament building (the so-called "White House"); and the virtual unified international condemnation. Upon his return to power, Gorbachev called the failed coup "a majority victory for *perestroika*" and pledged "to move ahead democratically in all areas."[29]

Ironically, the coup attempt had the effect of pressuring for even greater reform within the Soviet Union, undoubtedly beyond what Gorbachev had initially envisioned. Within a matter of days after Gorbachev had returned to office, his power was effectively curtailed. He felt compelled to abandon his role as general secretary of the Communist party and to call for a disbanding of the party itself because of its role in the coup. Further, he consulted with the president of the Russian Republic, Boris Yeltsin, over the appointment of a number of key political offices and named several key officials from that republic to leadership posts within the central government.

Even more remarkable, this sequence of events immediately stimulated greater demands for independence by many of the fifteen constituent republics and raised doubts about the future of the Soviet Union as a unified state. Within weeks of the coup, the Baltic states (Lithuania, Latvia, and Estonia) obtained their independence and a new transitional confederative arrangement was devised between the central government and most of the republics. Under this interim arrangement, the republics gained more control over several policy areas, and the constituent republics would also play a much larger role in setting the policy of the central government through their participation in a series of interrepublic councils. The central government, however, would continue to have primary responsibility for military, security, and foreign affairs matters. Economic union would also continue to be fostered among the constituent republics, even as each republic would be allowed to pursue its own status with the union. Eventually, a new constitution would be formulated for a new Soviet state structure.[30] As with political change in Eastern Europe, the process of reform within the Soviet Union took on a life of its own, aided ironically by a coup that sought to topple the effort. While the future shape of the Soviet Union was still evolving, it surely would be different than originally constituted after the Bolshevik Revolution of 1917.

AFTER THE COLD WAR: POLICY TOWARD
CENTRAL EUROPE

Throughout the period of these changes in Central Europe and the Soviet Union, the Bush administration policy was largely that of an interested spectator, not an active participant. Its policy approach was to encourage change in Central Europe and in the Soviet Union, but it did not seek to shape events. The policy goal of the Bush administration was summarized in its basic theme of seeking a "Europe whole and free." The administration also was careful to avoid any actions that would embarrass the Soviet Union or the Eastern European governments as they sought to undertake change. Similarly, the U.S. sought to refrain from any actions that might appear as "gloating" over the extraordinary movement to democracy and capitalism in these countries. In these important ways, then, its basic pragmatic and cautionary approach toward U.S. foreign policy was largely being followed, even in a context of dynamic global change.

Perhaps indicative of the policy of caution on the part of the United States was President Bush's restrained reaction on the day the Berlin Wall was opened between East and West—undoubtedly one of the most dramatic moments in recent political history. Although President Bush claimed that he was "elated" by the development, he went on to justify his reserve when he met reporters by indicating that "I'm just not an emotional kind of guy" and that "we're handling this properly with the allies. . . ." Another administration official acknowledged the largely rhetorical nature of U.S. policy and gave some reasons for the measured American reaction to changing events: "I admit that when all is said and done it is a policy largely of stated desires and rhetoric. But what would you have us do? What we are dealing with in Eastern Europe, and to a lesser extent in the Soviet Union, is a revolutionary situation."[31]

POLICY TOWARD CENTRAL EUROPE AND
THE FUTURE OF GERMANY

Once these revolutionary changes were well underway, however, the Bush administration did outline tangible policy actions toward Central Europe, the reunification of Germany, and future relations with the Soviet Union. Toward Central Europe, the principal policy response was to provide some economic assistance to the new democracies and to encourage other European states (and particularly the European Community) to do so as well. In 1989 visits to Poland and

Hungary, for example, President Bush offered aid to both countries, and by the end of that year Congress had approved an aid package that totaled over $900 million. The funds would aid efforts to stabilize the economy, foster private enterprise, provide food aid, trade credits, and environmental funds, and support agricultural programs, technical training, and scholarship and exchanges with the U.S.[32] In November 1990, President Bush visited Czechoslovakia and promised economic assistance to that country as well, and the Congress, in turn, earmarked $370 million to assist the newly developing democracies in Eastern Europe.[33]

Regarding the future of Germany, the Bush administration added elements of realism to its accommodative approach, especially after the collapse of the Berlin Wall in November 1989. Beginning as early as December 1989, the Bush administration adopted the view that German reunification should succeed, that Germany's full sovereignty should be restored, and that other states (including the United States) would necessarily lose some of their rights over German territory. Somewhat later, it also made clear that it would only accept a reunified Germany that allowed the state to remain a full member of NATO.[34] This clear policy position, moreover, proved significant in the final outcome. While the administration was sensitive to Soviet concerns about moving too quickly on European questions and tried to be accommodative, it clearly had decided about the future of Germany and about the kind of Central Europe that it sought.

POLICY TOWARD THE SOVIET UNION: THE MALTA AND WASHINGTON SUMMITS

In bilateral relations with the Soviet Union, and consistent with the administration's overall policy approach, the Bush administration attempted to establish the foundation for a long-term cooperative relationship with the Soviet Union in late 1989 and 1990. During this period, two major summits were held and several agreements reached on fostering and sustaining cooperation across a series of political, military, and economic questions.

The Malta Summit in November 1989 proved to be a watershed conference in ending the Cold War between the United States and the Soviet Union. As President Gorbachev indicated at that summit: "The world leaves one epoch of cold war and enters another epoch" and "the characteristics of the cold war should be abandoned."[35] At that summit, the Bush administration and the Soviet leadership committed themselves to make rapid progress on nuclear and conventional arms control. The Bush administration decided to throw its support behind the internal reforms initiated within the Soviet Union and to assist the Soviet Union in joining the world economy. The administration did so after the Soviet Union had indicated its willingness to accept the ongoing changes in Central Europe and after it had decided that internal reforms within the Soviet Union were consistent with U.S. interests.[36] In a matter of months, the Soviet Union gained observer status in the General Agreements on Tariff and Trade (GATT) with U.S. assistance.[37]

If the Malta Summit set the tone for the end of the Cold War and for future relations between the two superpowers, the June 1990 Washington Summit between Presidents Bush and Gorbachev took several concrete steps to solidify that relationship. Several important agreements signed at this meeting signaled the changed relationship: an agreement was signed calling for the destruction of a substantial portion of each nation's chemical arsenal by the year 2002; two other agreements pledged both parties to accelerate negotiations on the Strategic Arms Reduction Treaty (START) and the Conventional (i.e., non-nuclear) Arms Forces in Europe (CFE) Treaty; and several cultural exchange treaties were also agreed upon during the meeting.[38]

In an unexpected move at this summit, the United States agreed to a treaty that would normalize trade and economic ties with the Soviet Union and grant it most-favored-nation (MFN) status. In effect, this action would allow the Soviet Union greater access to the American market, which it had long sought since the passage of the Jackson-Vanik Amendment to the Trade Act of 1974. The Jackson-Vanik Amendment had denied the Soviet Union MFN status due to its failure to have a policy of free emigration. At the same time, however, the Bush administration placed an important condition on its signing of the treaty; it would not send the treaty for the Senate's advice and consent until the Soviet law on emigration was changed. At the Moscow Summit of July 1991, President Bush announced that he would ask Congress to grant this status to the Soviet Union, since legislation on free emigration passed the Supreme Soviet in May 1991.[39]

In December 1990, the Bush administration did go a step further to aid the Soviet Union, even though this treaty was not yet in effect. It temporarily lifted a portion of the Jackson-Vanik Amendment and approved up to $1 billion in loans to the U.S.S.R. to assist it in meeting that winter's food shortages. President Bush also proposed that the Soviet Union be given a "special association" with the International Monetary Fund and the World Bank in an effort to transform its economy according to market principles and to assist it in meeting the requirements of *perestroika*. In June 1991, the Bush administration granted another waiver in an effort to aid the Soviet economy by offering new agricultural credits totaling $1.5 billion.[40]

Yet another sign of the importance that the Bush administration attached to this new relationship was signaled in its attitude and policy toward the Soviet Union's effort to dissuade the Baltic republics (Lithuania, Latvia, and Estonia) from pursuing independence in the spring of 1990 and the winter of 1990–91. In both cases, the Gorbachev government took punitive measures—economic sanctions and the sending of Soviet troops to these republics. In both instances, the Bush administration decried these actions but did not do much more. (In January 1991, though, the Bush administration postponed a planned summit meeting, ostensibly because of the Persian Gulf War, but undoubtedly due to Soviet action in Lithuania.) In effect, the Bush administration's commitment to political realism surfaced once again.

POLICY TOWARD THE SOVIET UNION: MILITARY AND ECONOMIC COOPERATION

In July 1991, two steps—one military, another economic—were taken by the Bush administration as part of its new policy approach toward the Soviet Union. First, President Bush and President Gorbachev met in London at the end of the yearly economic summit among leaders of the industrial democracies (United States, France, Britain, Canada, Germany, Italy, Japan, and the European Community) and completed work in principle on a Strategic Arms Reduction Treaty (START).[41] (The agreement was formally signed about two weeks later at a hastily arranged summit in Moscow.) Under this agreement, the first in which the long-range nuclear arsenals of the two superpowers would be reduced (not just limited as under the SALT agreements), both sides would trim their nuclear warhead arsenals. The U.S. would reduce its from approximately 12,000 to 10,400, while the Soviet Union would cut its from 10,800 to 8,000. The number of warheads on all nuclear delivery vehicles (land-based missiles, sea-based missiles, and intercontinental bombers), however, would be limited to 6,000 for each side. The total number of these nuclear delivery vehicles would also be reduced from current 1,850 for the U.S. and 2,500 for the Soviet Union to 1,600 for each side. The agreement will be put into place over seven years and last for fifteen years (unless replaced by another agreement). It will also allow twelve types of on-site inspections by each side and will require each side

---

DOCUMENT SUMMARY 6.1 KEY COMPONENTS OF THE
STRATEGIC ARMS REDUCTION TREATY, JULY 1991

Limitations on Numbers of Nuclear Warheads and Delivery Vehicles

	U.S.	U.S.S.R.
Total nuclear delivery vehicles (land-based and sea-based ballistic missiles and intercontinental bombers) allowed	1,600	1,600
Total accountable warheads on all nuclear delivery vehicles allowed	6,000	6,000
Total warheads on land-based or sea-based ballistic missiles allowed	4,900	4,900
Total warheads allowed on mobile land-based missiles	1,100	1,100
Nuclear warheads not covered by the treaty	c. 4,400	c. 2,000

Inspection and Verification Provisions
- Exchange of information between the U.S. and the U.S.S.R. on all strategic offensive weapons would take place prior to treaty signing.
- Twelve types of on-site inspections would be allowed under the agreement.
- Several types of cooperative procedures will be implemented to ensure verification.

Duration and Implementation of the Treaty
The treaty will be implemented over a seven-year period and will last for fifteen years. It may be continued in intervals of five years thereafter.

Source: Eric Schmitt, "Senate Approval and Sharp Debate Seen," *New York Times*, July 19, 1991, p. A5 (including the accompanying table entitled "New Limits on Strategic Weapons"); and Office of Public Affairs, U.S. Arms Control and Disarmament Agency, "Strategic Arms Reduction Talks," *Issues Brief*, April 25, 1991.

---

not to interfere in efforts by the other to monitor compliance. (Fuller details of the treaty are summarized in Document Summary 6.1.) This agreement completed nuclear arms negotiations that had been initiated in June 1982 and represented the end of an era of remarkable change in Soviet-American relations.

The important economic step, also completed after the London economic meetings, involved economic assistance for the Soviet Union by the industrial democracies. While these countries did not provide immediate financial aid to President Gorbachev and the Soviet Union, they did agree upon six different measures to aid efforts at economic reform in that country. The industrial leaders called for "special association" status for the Soviet Union with the International Monetary Fund and the World Bank (much as President Bush had done earlier), encouraged cooperation between the Soviet Union and all international economic institutions, pledged greater technical assistance and cooperation, supported the restoration of trade between the Soviet Union and its Central European neighbors, pledged continued closer contacts between the leaders of the industrial democracies and the Soviet Union, and encouraged governmental financial officials in the West to work closer with their counterparts in the Soviet Union.[42] While these actions may not have gone as far as the Soviet Union had initially hoped, they represented an extraordinary change in the economic relationship among the United States, the West, and the Soviet Union.

In the aftermath of the August coup within the Soviet Union and with the movement to a more confederative state in late 1991, the Bush administration confronted calls to initiate new economic and political ties with the constituent republics and the newly independent Baltic states. The Bush administration did proceed with diplomatic recognition for Lithuania, Latvia, and Estonia, albeit after several European states and the European Community had done so.[43] Further, the administration continued to promise to supply humanitarian aid to the Soviet Union as needed, although it also indicated that this assistance would go to the constituent republics directly.[44] Yet, there were limits as to how far it would go in providing massive economic assistance to the central government. In general, the Bush administration did not deviate from its policy announced after the London Summit, which, in effect, withheld economic aid until significant and sustained policy reforms were carried out.

FORMALIZING THE END OF THE COLD WAR

Toward the end of 1990, the Bush administration made three other important commitments that served as the capstone for the ending of the Cold War in Central Europe and set the stage for European politics for the 1990s and beyond.[45] At the Conference on Security and Cooperation in Europe (CSCE) in November 1990, the United States and its NATO allies and the Soviet Union and its Warsaw Pact allies signed the Conventional Armed Forces in Europe (CFE) Treaty, which provided for a substantial reduction in conventional forces on both sides. Second, these states also signed a declaration on nonaggression between the two sides to officially end the Cold War. Third, the parties to the CSCE (which includes the U.S., Canada, and virtually all European states) signed an agreement to give the CSCE a greater role in future European affairs. Under this "Paris Charter for a New Europe," a secretariat for the organization was established in Prague, biannual summit meetings of the members' leaders will be initiated, and annual meetings of the members' foreign ministers will be scheduled. With this document in place, the aim of the CSCE is to become the central mechanism for dealing with peace and security in Central Europe. It also cemented the end of the Cold War and set the course for a new relationship between the United States and Europe. Finally, and in another important symbol of the end of the Cold War in Central Europe, the Warsaw Pact—the military alliance among the Soviet Union and its former satellites in Eastern Europe—was formally disbanded at the end of March 1991. As domestic violence occurred among the constituent states in Yugoslavia and as domestic change accelerated in the Soviet Union, these new institutional arrangements in Central Europe took on a new significance for peace and stability in the area.

THE SEARCH FOR A NEW WORLD ORDER

With the international politics of the post–World War II period forever altered by the dramatic changes in Central Europe and with Soviet-American political cooperation seemingly now a reality, the Bush administration sought to devise a new direction for international politics generally and for U.S. foreign policy specifically. This direction was first hinted at in an address that President Bush gave to the UN General Assembly in September 1989, but it was more fully outlined in speeches to a joint session of Congress in September 1990 and in his State of the Union Address in January 1991.[46] He summarized the future direction of U.S. foreign policy as an effort to build "a new world order."[47]

President Bush described the new world order in this way: "a new era—freer from the threat of terror, stronger in the pursuit of justice, and more secure in the quest for peace, an era in which the nations of the world, East and West, North and South, can prosper and live in harmony." Such a world would be different from the one that had existed over the past forty-five years. It would be "a world where the rule of law supplants the rule of the jungle, a world in which nations recognize the shared responsibility for freedom and justice, a world where the strong respect the rights of the weak."[48] In his State of the Union Address, President Bush summarized this new world order as a condition "where diverse nations are drawn together in common cause to achieve the universal aspirations of mankind: peace and security, freedom, and the rule of law."[49]

Such a new world order would have specific policy prescriptions for the United States and the nations of the world. As President Bush put it, "America and the world must defend common vital interests. . . . America and the world must support the rule of law. . . . America and the world must stand up to aggression."[50] Yet, President Bush was quick to add that the United States had a special role to play in creating this new world order:

> For two centuries, America has served the world as an inspiring example of freedom and democracy. For generations, America has led the struggle to preserve and extend the blessings of liberty. . . . American leadership is indispensable. . . . we have a unique responsibility to do the hard work of freedom.[51]

The new world order the Bush administration envisioned, in effect, represented a reaffirmation of the traditional values that had shaped the birth of the nation and its foreign policy actions in its earliest years (see Chapter 1). Indeed, the new world order largely was the resurrection of the values that the nation's earlier founders had embraced—namely freedom and democracy—and that made this nation so distinct from the European ones from which the earliest Americans had come.

But, unlike the foreign policy at the beginning of the Republic, this reaffirmation of traditional values was coupled with a profound commitment to sustained American involvement. Indeed, in both tone and emphasis, the new world order of the Bush administration had the ring of the Wilsonian idealism with its initial turn toward the League of Nations and toward collective security at the end of World War I. With the destruction of the old order, the balance-of-power system that had produced World War I, Wilson proposed the substitution of a new and changed international order, one founded on the rule of law and united against aggressive change through the collective actions of the League of Nations. On the face of it, the Bush administration adopted a similar design. With the demise of the old order—the Cold War system from 1947 to 1990—a new world order was envisioned, one grounded in the cooperation of all states and one based upon greater involvement of the collective security actions of the United Nations. President Bush, however, did not appear to portray the same fervor in calling for this new system as did President Wilson, and he continued to embrace the principles of political realism from time to time. Nonetheless, President Bush did see his approach as an important departure from America's recent past (Cold War) behavior.

THE PERSIAN GULF WAR: FIRST TEST OF A NEW WORLD ORDER?

The event that assisted in creating this concept of a new world order—and what ultimately forced the Bush administration to give some definition to it—was the decision by Iraqi President Saddam Hussein to invade Kuwait early on the morning of August 2, 1990. Iraq's action raised the question of whether the initial cooperation between the United States and the Soviet Union could be sustained in another arena and whether the global community could rally around a set of common values. As events unfolded, the first test of the new world order appeared to succeed: Soviet-American cooperation was sustained; the global community was largely supportive of this effort as well; and aggression was stopped.

In some respects, the vigorous response of the Bush administration may have been unexpected by Iraq. Beginning in the middle of the Reagan administration, the United States had sought to better relations with Iraq. Diplomatic relations had been restored in 1984, after being ruptured since the outbreak of the Six-Day War in 1967. The United States also tilted toward Iraq during the Iran-Iraq War, even though the U.S. had sold arms to Iran in a futile effort to get American hostages released from Lebanon. Still, the Reagan administration had its quarrels with Iraq. It was displeased over the Iraqi attack upon the *U.S.S. Stark* in the Persian Gulf in May 1987. Thirty-seven American sailors died, but the U.S. accepted the Iraqi explanation. The Reagan administration also protested strongly in 1988 when Iraq used chemical weapons against its own Kurdish population.[52]

Despite those protests, and in keeping with its realist principles, the Bush administration decided to try to foster better relations with Iraq for both strategic and economic reasons. Iraq's location in the Persian Gulf area was important in efforts at achieving stability in that region, and its considerable oil reserves made Iraq crucial for global energy concerns. Furthermore, Iraq was importing a substantial amount of American agricultural products, which assisted in reducing the large U.S. trade deficit.[53] Consequently, the Bush administration decided to overlook the abysmal human rights record of Saddam Hussein's regime and its effort to develop nuclear weapons capabilities. Incentives, not sanctions, would remain the basic policy approach.

MAP 6.1   THE PERSIAN GULF AND SOUTHWEST ASIA

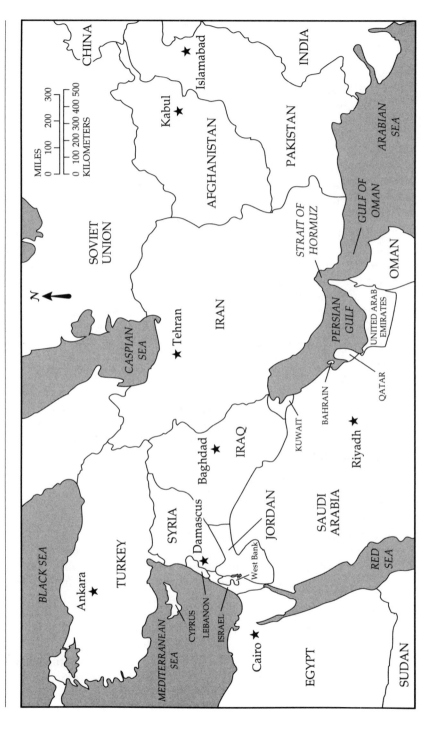

When the Congress sought in early 1990 to enact economic sanctions against the Iraqi regime, the U.S. assistant secretary of state for Near Eastern and Southern Asian Affairs argued against such an option.[54] In the summer of 1990, when Iraq began to complain vigorously that Kuwait was responsible for keeping oil prices low by exceeding its oil quota (and hence hurting the Iraqi economy), called for an OPEC meeting to raise oil prices, and began to threaten an invasion of Kuwait, the Bush administration's policy position did not really change. Indeed, the American ambassador in Baghdad actually seemed to reassure Saddam Hussein of U.S. disinterest in these questions. At a meeting just over a week before the invasion, U.S. Ambassador April Glaspie told Saddam Hussein: "I have direct instructions from President Bush to seek better relations with Iraq," and that "we have no opinion on the Arab-Arab conflicts, like your border disagreement with Kuwait." Furthermore, in testimony on Capitol Hill only days before the intervention, the administration did not issue any warning when asked about a possible Iraqi invasion into Kuwait.[55]

(In testimony to congressional committees after the Persian Gulf War had ended, Ambassador Glaspie provided a different account'of her meeting with Saddam Hussein than the one released by Iraq in September 1990. While acknowledging the veracity of the often-quoted statements, she testified that she also told Hussein that "we would defend our vital interests, we would support our friends in the Gulf, we would defend their sovereigny and integrity." She also told Hussein that Arab-Arab conflicts ought to be settled "in a nonviolent manner, not by threats, not by intimidation, and certainly not by aggression."[56] Glaspie acknowledged in this same testimony, however, that she did not tell Saddam Hussein that the U.S. would use force to defend Kuwait. Further, the diplomatic cable that she sent to the Department of State in late July 1990 reportedly did not indicate a firm stand by the U.S. over potential Iraqi action on the question of Kuwait.[57])

Despite this apparent equivocal attitude toward Kuwait by the Bush administration in the summer of 1990, the response to the Iraqi invasion was immediate, not only by the U.S., but also by other nations and the international community as a whole. The Bush administration, for example, immediately condemned the Iraqi action and called for its withdrawal from Kuwait, froze all Iraqi and Kuwaiti assets in the United States, and imposed a trade embargo on Iraq as well. The European Community and the Arab League condemned the action, too. Most importantly, the Soviet Union joined the United States in condemning this action in a statement issued by

Secretary of State James Baker and Soviet Foreign Minister Eduard Shevardnadze within hours of the invasion.[58] A few weeks later, President Bush and President Gorbachev arranged a meeting in Helsinki, Finland, to deal with this crisis and concluded by issuing a joint statement saying that "Iraq's aggression must not be tolerated."[59] Within a matter of a few weeks, about 100 nations had issued condemnations of Iraq's actions toward Kuwait.

Further, the Bush administration announced on August 8, 1990, that it was sending about 150,000 American forces into Saudi Arabia and the surrounding region for the purpose of helping that country defend its homeland against possible Iraqi aggression. In addition, President Bush outlined four policy goals that the U.S. sought to achieve in taking this action against Iraq: (1) "the immediate, unconditional, and complete withdrawal of all Iraqi forces from Kuwait"; (2) "the resolution of Kuwait's legitimate government"; (3) the protection of American citizens in Iraq and Kuwait; and (4) the achievement of "security and stability" in the Persian Gulf.[60] Two days later, the Arab League also voted to send forces to Saudi Arabia to stop further Iraqi aggression.[61] Within a matter of weeks, at least twenty-eight nations from virtually every continent had sent forces to Saudi Arabia on behalf of this effort to get Iraq out of Kuwait, and other nations (e.g., Germany and Japan) had pledged financial assistance.[62]

The United Nations Security Council also quickly took concerted actions against the Iraqi government over its invasion of Kuwait. Within hours of the Iraqi action, the Security Council voted to condemn the invasion and demanded the immediate withdrawal of Iraq as well. What was remarkable about this action was not only its rapidity, but also the unanimity among the permanent members of the Security Council (the United States, the Soviet Union, Britain, China, and France). Because of the Cold War and the existence of the veto power available to the permanent Security Council members, collective action by the United Nations had always proved difficult in dealing with questions of international peace and security.

This great power unity continued across the next several months as the UN Security Council proceeded to pass eleven other resolutions against Iraq over its invasion of Kuwait. These resolutions really reflected a tightening of the economic and political noose around Iraq in an effort to force it to leave Kuwait. They included the imposition of mandatory economic sanctions against Iraq, the invalidation of Iraq's annexation of Kuwait, a condemnation of Iraq's holding of foreign nationals and diplomats, and the expansion of the embargo to include sea and air embargoes as well.

CHRONOLOGY 6.4   THE PERSIAN GULF WAR, 1990–1991

August 2, 1990—Iraqi forces invade Kuwait and seize control of that nation. The United Nations Security Council condemns the Iraqi action and calls for the unconditional withdrawal of Iraq from Kuwait.

August 2–4, 1990—The United States, France, Britain, and the European Community condemn the invasion and impose economic sanctions against Iraq. The Arab League condemns the Iraqi action as well.

August 8, 1990—President Bush announces that the United States will send American forces to Saudi Arabia to protect that country from Iraqi aggression and to seek to restore independence for Kuwait. Operation Desert Shield begins.

August 10, 1990—The Arab League votes to send forces to defend Saudi Arabia. Over the next few weeks, other countries make similar commitments, and, in all, some twenty-eight nations form the anti-Iraq coalition of military forces in and around Saudi Arabia.

September 9, 1990—Soviet President Mikhail Gorbachev and President George Bush meet in Helsinki, Finland, and issue a joint statement calling for Iraq "to withdraw unconditionally from Kuwait."

August–November 1990—The United Nations Security Council passes ten resolutions calling for economic sanctions against Iraq, authorizing various measures to enforce those sanctions, and condemning its annexation of Kuwait and its holding of foreign nationals and diplomats.

November 8, 1990—President Bush announces that American forces in the Persian Gulf will be increased to enable them to possess an offensive capability.

November 29, 1990—The United Nations Security Council votes to authorize member states to "use all necessary means" to enforce the previously passed UN resolutions, but allows Iraq until January 15, 1991, to comply with the resolutions.

January 12, 1991—The U.S. Senate, by a vote of 52–47, approves a resolution authorizing the president to implement the UN resolutions; the House of Representatives does likewise by a vote of 250–183.

January 16, 1991—The allied coalition forces begin a massive bombing attack against Iraq and occupied Kuwait. Operation Desert Storm begins.

February 23, 1991—A massive ground assault is undertaken by allied forces to expel Iraq from Kuwait.

CHRONOLOGY 6.4   THE PERSIAN GULF WAR, 1990–1991
(CONTINUED)

February 27, 1991—President Bush declares that "Kuwait has been liberated," and calls for a suspension of hostilities by the allied coalition at midnight, February 28.

March 3, 1991—The United Nations Security Council passes a resolution suspending the Persian Gulf War, placing the liabilities for the war upon Iraq. Allied and Iraqi commanders meet in southern Iraq to formalize the cease-fire and set the terms of peace and the procedures for the exchange of prisoners of war.

April 3, 1991—The United Nations Security Council passes a resolution formally ending the Persian Gulf War and requiring Iraq to destroy chemical and biological weapons, renounce terrorism, use a portion of its oil income to repair damage in Kuwait, and accept the "inviolability" of the frontier between Iraq and Kuwait.

Source: Peter Hayes, ed., "Chronology 1990" *Foreign Affairs: America and the World 1990/ 91 70* (1991): 226–232; Andrew Rosenthal, "Bush Calls Halt to Allied Offensive; Declares Kuwait Free, Iraq Beaten; Sets Stiff Terms for Full Cease-fire," *New York Times*, February 28, 1991, p. A1; R. W. Apple, Jr., "U.S. Says Iraqi Generals Agree to Demands 'On All Matters'; Early P.O.W. Release Expected," *New York Times*, March 4, 1991, pp. A1 and A6; "New U.S. Hint about Hussein," *New York Times*, March 4, 1991, p. A6; Paul Lewis, "UN Security Council Drafts Plan to Scrap Most Deadly Iraqi Arms," *New York Times*, March 27, 1991, pp. A1 and A6; Paul Lewis, "UN Votes Stern Conditions for Formally Ending War; Iraqi Response Is Uncertain," *New York Times*, April 4, 1991, pp. A1 and A7; and "UN Conditions," *Des Moines Register*, April 4, 1991, p. 14A.

Finally, after being frustrated in getting an Iraqi response to these UN actions, the Security Council passed its most significant resolution. On November 29, 1990, the council authorized member states "to use all necessary means to uphold and implement" the previous UN resolutions unless Iraq left Kuwait by January 15, 1991.[63] In effect, this resolution authorized the nations of the world to use force to expel Iraq from Kuwait. This call for collective security action was only the second time in which the UN Security Council had authorized such action (the other was over the North Korean invasion of South Korea in June 1950). Unlike that earlier instance, when the Soviet Union was boycotting the Security Council over the failure to allow the People's Republic of China to hold the China seat, this action had the full cooperation of the Soviet Union, although the People's Republic of China did abstain on this vote.

When Iraq failed to leave Kuwait by the January 15 deadline and after the U.S. Congress had given the president the authority to use American forces to implement this last UN resolution, the anti-Iraq

coalition, now totaling over a half million military personnel, initiated a massive bombing attack against Iraq and occupied Kuwait.
With over 2,000 air sorties a day, the allied coalition inflicted massive
destruction and damage, but it initially failed to budge the Iraqis. By
mid-February, Iraq, in negotiations with the Soviet Union, agreed to
withdraw from Kuwait, albeit with conditions attached. The anti-
Iraq coalition, led by the Bush administration, rejected that plan and
imposed a twenty-four-hour ultimatum on February 22, 1991, for the
Iraqis to begin to leave Kuwait.

When Iraq failed to meet this deadline, the allied coalition
mounted a massive ground, air, and sea assault to drive Iraq out.
The assault lasted for 100 hours—just over four days. The results
were devastating for the Iraqis, with the loss of about 4,000 of their
4,200 tanks, the surrender of about 60,000 troops to the allied coalition, 100,000 killed, and perhaps 300,000 wounded. Coalition losses
were surprisingly small, with less than 200 American deaths. On
February 27, 1991, President Bush declared that "Kuwait is liberated"
and announced the suspension of hostilities beginning at midnight
on February 28. On March 3, 1991, the United Nations Security
Council passed a resolution ending the hostilities and placing responsibilities upon the Iraqis for their invasion of Kuwait. On the
same day, the military commanders from both sides met in southern
Iraq to formalize the terms of the military cease-fire and to work out
arrangements for the exchange of prisoners of war.[64] Finally, on April
3, 1991, the United Nations Security Council passed a resolution formally ending the war, but placing stiff conditions on Iraq. Iraq was
required to destroy all of its chemical and biological weapons and
ballistic missile systems that have a range of more than 150 kilometers, pay reparations to Kuwait, reject support for international terrorism, and respect the sovereignty of Kuwait.[65]

Ensuring a lasting peace within Iraq, and the region generally,
proved more difficult than winning the short war. Almost immediately after the coalition victory, rebellions broke out in northern and
southern Iraq.[66] In the north, the Kurdish minority rebelled. When
that rebellion failed to gain any outside assistance, the Hussein regime, still left in power in Baghdad, put it down. That action initiated the flight of thousands of Kurds to Turkey and Iran to avoid
further retaliation. They were persuaded to return only after the U.S.
(and later the UN) offered guarantees of protection against retaliation. In the south, the Shiite population attempted to rebel against
the authorities in Baghdad, but they also failed. Saddam Hussein
thus remained in control, even as the country continued to suffer
from the war's devastation.

Later on, UN inspectors sent to Iraq to examine compliance with the terms of the cease-fire also confronted resistance as they tried to inspect some facilities suspected of producing nuclear materials. As a result, the Bush administration raised new concerns and issued new threats over Iraqi failure to comply with the cease-fire terms. Defectors from Iraq and satellite surveillance activities also raised questions about the level of compliance by Hussein's regime. In addition, even though Secretary of State James Baker had made at least four different trips to the region to seek a compromise approach between Israel and the Arabs, efforts at initiating a Middle East peace conference stalled in the aftermath of the war.[67]

By late July and early August 1991—after two more visits to the region by Secretary Baker and after the completion of the superpower summit in Moscow—the prospects for a U.S.-Soviet sponsored peace conference appeared to improve, however. Several Arab states agreed to participate, and Israel gave its tentative approval as well. All the details, including who would represent the Palestinians, were still to be worked out. Still, some movement in this long-standing dispute did occur, and the outlook for some success seemed better than in many years. In late October 1991, a Middle East peace conference, co-sponsored by the United States and the Soviet Union, was held in Madrid, Spain, among Arab states, Israel, and representatives of the Palestinians.

Despite the problems of establishing a long-term peace in the region after the Persian Gulf War, Iraqi aggression had been stopped. Further, that country seemed unlikely to pose a threat to the region again very soon. In this limited sense, then, the first test of the new world order appeared to have been met.

CHALLENGES TO A NEW WORLD ORDER

Will such an order be sustained and more fully developed in the 1990s and beyond? Are other nations willing to follow what is essentially a U.S. idea, and will the American public support a policy that may well involve continued political, economic, and military actions across several continents, especially as portrayed in the sweeping language of President Bush's original pronouncements? Numerous factors raise serious doubts about such a prospect for the near future, and hence about the degree of change in the direction of policy that President Bush may be able to achieve. Let us briefly mention at least three important factors here.

First, the international community's success in the Iraq-Kuwait crisis may simply have been an aberration. That is, the degree of international cooperation in this crisis was unique in that the Iraqi aggression was so blatant and so dangerous that other states could not fail to respond. What about instances in which the aggression or threats to international order and stability are less well defined? What about other instances where a crucial resource like oil is not involved? Will the international community be willing to be so cooperative in these new instances, or in instances of unresolved international crises (e.g., the Arab-Palestinian-Israeli dispute)?

Second, while Soviet-American cooperation was pivotal in addressing the first post–Cold War crisis and in making the new world order a reality in that instance, will that cooperation continue? Concerns are already evident due to the changes occurring in the Soviet Union, including a short-lived coup in August 1991, independence for several constituent republics, and the redistribution of political power between the center and the republics. With the new Soviet state continuing to evolve and the range of authority for the central government still unclear, will that nation remain a key international participant? The Soviet Union may no longer be as relevant or as necessary for producing a new world order as it was in 1990. Instead, the ethnic divisions within that newly reorganized state may actually become sources of international tensions themselves. Indeed, it is likely that an immediate challenge to the Bush administration's new world order will be stabilizing the relationship with a new and more differentiated Soviet Union and its constituent republics.

Third, will the Bush administration continue to have the domestic political support to sustain such a far-reaching policy as that implicit in the concept of a new world order? While President Bush's domestic and foreign policy support at home has been remarkably high, will the American public demonstrate more and more "fatigue" over the globalism in this policy posture? More importantly, as budget deficits continue to reduce policy flexibility, will latent isolationist sentiment appear once more? Or will economic nationalism arise? Indeed, the public has expressed much greater concern about foreign economic issues and America's economic competitiveness abroad than they have in promoting some of the values implicit in the new world order.[68]

CONCLUDING COMMENTS

As the first post–Cold War and post-Vietnam administration, then, the Bush administration adopted a different course in foreign affairs and offered a new vision of what future global politics should look like. Instead of Soviet-American relations serving as the centerpiece

for American foreign policy—and, indeed, for all of global politics—
as it had for the past forty years, a new international order would be
developed. That order would be based upon a shared set of global
values, would involve cooperation among nations, and would be
grounded in the leadership of the United States.

This new world order, though, raises a more fundamental question about the foreign policy direction of the Bush administration,
and of the United States generally. As we indicated at the outset of
this discussion, President Bush has largely portrayed himself as a
pragmatic foreign policy realist, and many of his actions reflect that
view. Yet the new world order, with its lofty goals for transformation
of the international system embodies a substantial degree of political
idealism. In this sense, the fundamental challenge for the Bush administration, and for U.S. foreign policy in the years ahead, remains
a political and philosophical one. Can the Bush administration successfully combine the requirements of American idealism (moralism)
and realism (globalism) in a way that will provide coherence and
permanence to American foreign policy in the post-Vietnam, and
now the post–Cold War, era? Or will America, having lost the moral
anchor of anti-communism as the basis of its policy, find greater appeal in turning toward some variant of its isolationist tradition as it
deals with the world in the 1990s? As our surveys of recent administrations over the last three chapters have argued, few presidents
have been successful in wholly shaping a new approach to U.S. foreign policy. While the international changes have been more profound during the Bush administration (and thus arguably provide a
greater opportunity for a new foreign policy approach to succeed
than in earlier administrations), numerous domestic and international factors militate against this effort. In this sense, the Bush administration is unlikely to be the exception.

NOTES

1. "Text of President Bush's State of the Union Message to Nation," *New
York Times*, January 30, 1991, p. A8.

2. These concepts are discussed in and drawn from Charles W. Kegley, Jr.,
"The Bush Administration and the Future of American Foreign Policy: Pragma-
tism, or Procrastination?" *Presidential Studies Quarterly* 19 (Fall 1989): 717–731, es-
pecially p. 717. For another analysis of the Bush presidency, see Barbara
Kellerman and Ryan J. Barilleaux, *The President as World Leader* (New York: St.
Martin's Press, 1991), pp. 210–216.

3. See Elaine Sciolino, "Bush Selections Signal Focus on Foreign Policy,"
New York Times, January 17, 1989, p. 1, for this depiction of Bush as a problem
solver and not as a visionary.

4. Theodore C. Sorensen, "Bush's Timid 100 Days," *New York Times,* April 27, 1989, p. 27.

5. William G. Hyland, "Bush's Foreign Policy: Pragmatism or Indecision?" *New York Times,* April 26, 1989, p. 25. The second quote is taken from capsuled summaries of the main themes of the article.

6. The analyst is Charles William Maynes, editor of *Foreign Policy,* who discussed his views in Burt Solomon, "Vulnerable to Events," *National Journal,* January 6, 1990, p. 10. The quote on "means" and "ends" is prior to Maynes's comment but also at p. 10. Also see Kellerman and Barilleaux, *The President as World Leader,* p. 211, for a discussion of this piece and Maynes's view, upon which we also rely.

7. Evan Thomas with Thomas M. DeFrank and Ann McDaniel, "Bush and the Generals," *Newsweek,* February 4, 1991, p. 27.

8. Siolino, "Bush Selections Signal Focus on Foreign Policy," p. 1; and Thomas, "Bush and the Generals," p. 27.

9. The description was made by Charles William Maynes and is quoted in Sciolino, "Bush Selections Signal Focus on Foreign Policy," p. 1.

10. Political analyst I. M. Destler is quoted in John Felton, "Will Bush-Hill Honeymoon Bring Bipartisanship?" *Congressional Quarterly Weekly Report,* February 18, 1989, p. 334.

11. Sciolino, "Bush Selections Signal Focus on Foreign Policy," pp. 1 and 11; Elaine Sciolino, "Lawyer Is Picked for High State Department Post," *New York Times,* January 23, 1989, p. 3; and Clifford Krauss, "In Hot Spots Like Gulf, He's Baker's Cool Hand," *New York Times,* January 3, 1991, p. A4.

12. The National Security Council staff confirmed that there was no publically available summary of the "policy review" and that these speeches summarized the essence of the policy positions of the Bush administration at that time. The speeches that are quoted were supplied by the NSC staff and consisted of the following: "Remarks by the President to the Citizens of Hamtramck," April 17, 1989; "Remarks by the President at Texas A&M University, May 12, 1989; "Remarks by the President at Boston University Commencement Ceremony," May 21, 1989; "Remarks by the President at the Coast Guard Academy Graduation Ceremony," May 24, 1989; and "Remarks by the President at Rheingoldhalle," Mainz, Germany, May 31, 1989.

13. Quoted in Maureen Dowd, "Bush Moves to Control War's Endgame," *New York Times,* February 23, 1991, p. 5. According to NSC staff, no formal report of the policy review was released, only the speeches containing the principal themes.

14. John Felton, "Bush, Hill Agree to Provide Contras with New Aid," *Congressional Quarterly Weekly Report,* March 25, 1989, pp. 655–657.

15. See *Congressional Quarterly Weekly Report,* April 15, 1989, pp. 853–854.

16. Steven Erlanger, "Hanoi's Partial Victory," *New York Times,* July 20, 1990, pp. A1 and A2.

17. Steven Erlanger, "Ending Talks, All Cambodia Parties Commit Themselves to U.N. Peace Plan," *New York Times,* September 11, 1990, p. A3.

18. The following discussion draws upon "U.S. Invasion Ousts Panama's Noriega," and "From U.S. Canal to Invasion...A Chronology of Events," *Congressional Quarterly Almanac 1989* (Washington, D.C.: Congressional Quarterly, Inc., 1990), pp. 595–609 and 606–607, respectively; and Stephen Engelberg, "Bush Aides Admit a U.S. Role in Coup and Bad Handling," *New York Times,* October 6, 1989, pp. 1 and 8.

19. Ibid.

20. Nicholas D. Kristof, "Beijing Death Toll at Least 200; Army Tightens Control of City But Angry Resistance Goes On," *New York Times*, June 5, 1989, p. 1. A summary of the Bush administration's actions over this episode can be found in "Repression in China Leads to Sanctions," *Congressional Quarterly Almanac 1989* (Washington, D.C.: Congressional Quarterly, Inc., 1990), pp. 518–526, which was used here.

21. "President's New Conference on Foreign and Domestic Issues," *New York Times*, June 9, 1989, p. 12.

22. The chronology of events in the next three sections are based upon several sources: Peter Hayes, ed., "Chronology 1989" *Foreign Affairs: America and the World 1989/90* 69 (1990): 213–257; Peter Hayes, ed., "Chronology 1990" *Foreign Affairs: America and the World 1990/91* 70 (1991): 206–248; "East Bloc Political Turmoil . . . Chronology of Big Changes," *Congressional Quarterly Weekly Report*, December 9, 1989, pp. 3376–3377; and the chronologies in *The World Book 1990 Yearbook* (Chicago: World Book, Inc., 1990), and the *Encyclopaedia Britannica 1990 Book of the Year* (Chicago: Encyclopaedia Britannica, Inc., 1990). For the recent changes in Yugoslavia and Albania, see "2 Republics Split From Yugoslavia," *Des Moines Register*, June 26, 1991, pp. 1A and 12A; and Thomas L. Friedman, "300,000 Albanians Pour Into Streets to Welcome Baker," *New York Times*, June 23, 1991, pp. 1 and 4.

23. Serge Schmemann, "Two Germanys Unite After 45 Years with Jubilation and a Vow of Peace," *New York Times*, October 3, 1990, pp. A1 and A9.

24. Quoted in "German-NATO Drama: 9 Fateful Months," *New York Times*, July 17, 1990, p. A6. This piece is a useful chronology of the steps toward reunification, which we also used here.

25. The details of the unification treaty can be found in "Bonn, GDR Sign Unification Treaty," *The Week in Germany*, September 7, 1990, pp. 1–2.

26. " 'Two Plus Four' Treaty Signed; Germany Regains Full Sovereignty," *The Week in Germany*, September 14, 1990, pp. 1–2.

27. On these elections, see Bill Keller, "Soviet Savor Vote in Freest Election Since '17 Revolution," *New York Times*, March 27, 1989, pp. A1 and A6.

28. "Reforms in the Soviet Union," *Des Moines Sunday Register*, February 11, 1990, p. 1C.

29. The quotations are taken, respectively, from "Gorbachev's First Remarks: 'They Failed,' " *New York Times*, August 23, 1991, p. A9, and his first post-coup press conference ("The Gorbachev Account: A Coup 'Against the People, Against Democracy,' " *New York Times*, August 23, 1991, p. A10).

30. See Serge Schmemann, "Gorbachev, Yeltsin and Republic Leaders Move to Take Power from Soviet Congress," *New York Times*, September 3, 1991, pp. A1 and A6; "Excerpts from Soviet Congress: Time for Drastic Changes," *New York Times*, September 3, 1991, p. A7; and Serge Schmemann, "Soviet Congress Yields Rule to Republics to Avoid Political and Economic Collapse," *New York Times*, September 6, 1991, pp. A1 and A6.

31. The president and the "senior Bush Administration policy maker" are quoted in Thomas L. Friedman, "U.S. Worry Rises Over Europe's Stability," *New York Times*, November 10, 1989, p. 10.

32. "Poland, Hungary Aid Launched in 1989," *Congressional Quarterly Almanac 1989* (Washington, D.C.: Congressional Quarterly, Inc., 1990), pp. 503–504.

33. Janet Hook, "101st Congress Leaves Behind Plenty of Laws, Criticism," *Congressional Quarterly Weekly Report*, November 3, 1990, p. 3709.

34. Karl Kaiser, "Germany's Unification," in William P. Bundy, ed., *America and the World 1990/91* 70 (1991), pp. 179–205.

35. The quotations are from "Transcript of the Bush-Gorbachev New Conference in Malta," *New York Times*, December 4, 1989, p. A12. Also see Andrew Rosenthal, "Bush and Gorbachev Proclaim A New Era for U.S.-Soviet Ties; Agree on Arms and Trade Aims," *New York Times*, December 4, 1989, pp. A1 and A10; and Frances X. Clines, "Economic Pledges Cheer Soviet Aides," *New York Times*, December 4, 1989, p. A11.

36. "As Iron Curtain Falls, Superpowers Thaw," *Congressional Quarterly Almanac 1989* (Washington, D.C.: Congressional Quarterly, Inc., 1990), pp. 477–484.

37. Peter Hayes, ed., "Chronology 1990" *Foreign Affairs: America and the World 1990/91* 70 (1991): 208.

38. See "Text of the Statement on Long-Range Arms," "Summary of U.S.-Soviet Agreement on Chemical Arms," and "The Other Agreements in Brief," *New York Times*, June 2, 1990, p. 8.

39. Ibid. and R. W. Apple, Jr., "Bush Vows to Put Soviets in Group Favored in Trade," *New York Times*, July 31, 1991, pp. A1 and A4.

40. Andrew Rosenthal, "Bush, Lifting 15-Year-Old Ban, Approves Loans for Kremlin to Help Ease Food Shortages," *New York Times*, December 13, 1990, pp. A1, A6 and "Bush Extends Credits to Soviet Union," *Congressional Quarterly Weekly Report*, June 15, 1991, p. 1605.

41. R. W. Apple, Jr., "Superpower Weapons Treaty First to Cut Strategic Bombs," *New York Times*, July 18, 1991, pp. A1 and A6; Thomas L. Friedman, "Bush and Gorbachev Close Era in U.S.-Soviet Relations, *New York Times*, July 18, 1991, p. A8; Eric Schmitt, "Senate Approval and Sharp Debate Seen," *New York Times*, July 19, 1991, p. A5 (including accompanying table entitled "New Limits on Strategic Weapons"); and Office of Public Affairs, U.S. Arms Control and Disarmament Agency, "Strategic Arms Reduction Talks," *Issues Brief*, April, 25, 1991.

42. Steven Greenhouse, "7 Offer Moscow Technical Help," *New York Times*, July 18, 1991, pp. A1 and A8, and "Excerpts from Talks by Gorbachev and Major: Investing and Accepting," *New York Times*, July 18, 1991, p. A6.

43. Andrew Rosenthal, "Baltics Recognized," *New York Times*, September 3, 1991, pp. A1 and A8.

44. Clifford Krauss, "U.S. And Britain Will Send Some Food Aid to Republics," *New York Times*, August 30, 1991, p. A10.

45. James Baker "The Gulf Crisis and CSCE Summit," *Dispatch* 1 (November 19, 1990): 273–274; Pat Towell, "Historic CFE Treaty Cuts Arms, Marks the End of Cold War," *Congressional Quarterly Weekly Report*, November 24, 1990, pp. 3930–3932; and "CSCE Summit in Paris Shapes 'New Europe,' " *The Week in Germany*, November 23, 1990, p. 1. The end of the Warsaw Pact was officially announced as March 31, 1991. See "The End of an Alliance," *New York Times*, March 26, 1991, p. A1.

46. See George Bush, "Outlines of a New World of Freedom," an address before the 44th session of the UN General Assembly, New York City, September 25, 1989, and "Toward a New World Order," an address before a joint session of the Congress, September 11, 1990. Both of these addresses were made available by the Department of State, Bureau of Public Affairs, Washington, D.C. The other discussion of the new world order appears in "Text of President Bush's State of the Union Message to Nation," *New York Times*, January 30, 1991, p. A8.

47. President Bush's national security advisor, Brent Scowcroft, is given credit for developing this phrase and the strategy behind it. See Andrew Rosenthal, "Scowcroft and Gates: A Team Rivals Baker," *New York Times*, February 21, 1991, p. A6.

48. "Toward a New World Order," p. 2.

49. "Text of President Bush's State of the Union Message to Nation," p. A8.

50. "Toward a New World Order," p. 2.

51. "Text of President Bush's State of the Union Message to Nation," p. A8.

52. *The Middle East*, 7th ed. (Washington, D.C.: Congressional Quarterly, Inc., 1990), pp. 164–165.

53. John H. Kelly, "US Relations with Iraq," statement before the Subcommittee on Europe and the Near East of the House Foreign Affairs Committee, April 26, 1990.

54. Ibid., p. 3.

55. The first quoted passage is cited in Tom Matthews, "The Road to War," *Newsweek*, January 28, 1991, p. 56, while the second quoted passage is from Elaine Sciolino with Michael R. Gordon, "U.S. Gave Iraq Little Reason Not to Mount Assault," *New York Times*, September 23, 1990, p. 1. The entire *Newsweek* report (pp. 54–65) provides a useful background for the evolution of the crisis, and it was used for this section on the administration testimony on Capitol Hill just prior to the invasion.

56. Ambassador Glaspie is quoted in Thomas L. Friedman, "Envoy to Iraq, Faulted in Crisis, Says She Warned Hussein Sternly," *New York Times*, March 21, 1991, pp. A1 and A7.

57. The question on fighting over Iraq was asked by Congressman Lee Hamilton (D-Indiana) in Glaspie's testimony on Capitol Hill. The testimony and the controversy over her cable are both described in Russell Watson with Margaret Garrand Warner and Thomas M. DeFrank, "Was Ambassador Glaspie Too Gentle With Saddam?" *Newsweek*, April 1, 1991, p. 17.

58. Peter Hayes, ed., "Chronology 1990" *Foreign Affairs: America and the World 1990/91* 70 (1991): 228.

59. The joint statement is reprinted in "US-USSR Statement" *Dispatch* 1 (September 17, 1990): 92.

60. George Bush, "The Arabian Peninsula: US Principles," an address to the nation from the Oval Office of the White House, August 8, 1990, provided by the Department of State, Bureau of Public Affairs, Washington, D.C.

61. See "How the Arab League Voted in Cairo," *New York Times*, August 11, 1990, p. 4.

62. The most commonly cited number of countries in the anti-Iraq coalition in public descriptions was twenty-eight nations, but see Steven R. Bowman, "Iraq-Kuwait Crisis: Summary of U.S. and non-U.S. Forces," Washington, D.C.: Congressional Research Service, The Library of Congress, December 27, 1990, in which slightly more nations are identified as having contributed some contingents of forces.

63. UN Security Council Resolution 678 (1990), reprinted in Marjorie Ann Brown, "Iraq-Kuwait: U.N. Security Council Resolutions—Texts and Votes," Washington, D.C.: Congressional Research Service, The Library of Congress, December 4, 1990. This source provides complete texts and a summary of the previous eleven UN resolutions, while "U.N. Resolutions on Iraq," *New York Times*, February 16, 1991, p. 6, provides a summary of them. The latter source was used for the earlier discussion.

64. Andrew Rosenthal, "Bush Calls Halt to Allied Offensive; Declares Kuwait Free, Iraq Beaten; Sets Stiff Terms for Full Cease-fire," *New York Times*, February 28, 1991, p. A1; R. W. Apple, Jr., "U.S. Says Iraqi Generals Agree to Demands 'On All Matters'; Early P.O.W. Release Expected," *New York Times*, March 4, 1991,

pp. A1 and A6; and "New U.S. Hint About Hussein," *New York Times*, March 4, 1991, p. A6. The estimates on Iraqi casualties were made well after the war was ended and were acknowledged to have perhaps a 50 percent error factor. See Patrick E. Tyler, "Iraq's War Toll Estimated by U.S.," *New York Times*, June 5, 1991, p. A5, and "The Reluctant Warrior," *Newsweek*, May 13, 1991, p. 22 for Iraqi and American battle death estimates.

65. Paul Lewis, "UN Votes Stern Conditions for Formally Ending War; Iraqi Response Is Uncertain, *New York Times*, April 4, 1991, pp. A1 and A7, and "UN Conditions," *Des Moines Register*, April 4, 1991, p. 14A.

66. On the outbreak of these rebellions, see, among others, "Apocalyse Near," *Newsweek*, April 1, 1991, pp. 14–16.

67. On these matters, see Paul Lewis, "Iraqis Fire To Bar U.N.'s Inspectors," *New York Times*, June 29, 1991, pp. 1 and 5; "Feed Iraqis, Starve Saddam," *New York Times*, July 1, 1991, p. A10; and Pamela Fessler, "Baker Calls Both Sides Earnest, But Hill Remains Skeptical," *Congressional Quarterly Weekly Report*, May 25, 1991, p. 1389.

68. See John Rielly, ed., *American Public Opinion and U.S. Foreign Policy 1991* (Chicago: Chicago Council on Foreign Relations, 1991).

PART II THE PROCESS OF POLICYMAKING

Now that the reader is generally familiar with the basic values and beliefs that have shaped American policy over time, we shift our focus to policymaking itself. In Part II, we examine in some detail the policymaking process and how various institutions and groups—the executive, the Congress, several bureaucracies, political parties, interest groups, and the public at large—compete to promote their own values in American policy abroad. In this section, our goal is to provide essential information on who the principal foreign policymakers are, what their relative influence within the decision-making process is, and how their power has changed in the postwar period. In this way, the student may be better able to understand how and why particular values, beliefs, and policies are adopted by the United States toward the rest of the world.

Chapters 7 and 8 examine the institutional competition between the two most important participants in the foreign policy process: the president and the Congress. While each branch of government has constitutionally prescribed power over particular aspects of the formulation and conduct of foreign policy, each shares responsibilities with the other in shaping America's foreign policy. Because these institutions share responsibilities, conflict inevitably occurs regarding who should hold sway over the process. Chapter 7 explains why the values and beliefs of the executive branch often dominate the foreign affairs machinery of the American government. Chapter 8 discusses the post-Vietnam and post-Watergate efforts of the Congress to reassert some of its constitutional prerogatives and to engage more fully in a foreign policy partnership with the executive.

Chapters 9 and 10 focus upon the bureaucratic structures within the executive branch that compete for policy influence. At least three reasons justify this emphasis upon bureaucracies in analyzing American foreign policy: first, the growth of executive institutions associated with foreign affairs (e.g., the National Security Council, the Department of State, and the Department of Defense) and the expansion of policy activities by other bureaucracies not normally viewed as participants in foreign policymaking (e.g., the Department of the Treasury, the Department of Agriculture, and the Department of Commerce); second, the emergence of competition among bureaucracies over policy options (e.g., the National Security Council versus the Department of State) and the importance of this competition in understanding policy; and third, the ability of some bureaucracies to dominate policy, not always with adequate control by the executive branch, the Congress, or the public at large (e.g., the Central Intelligence Agency). Chapter 9 examines the role of the Department of State, the National Security Council, and some economic departments in the policy process, while Chapter 10 examines the impact of the Department of Defense and the intelligence community. In the latter chapter, we also explain how policymaking has been coordinated among these various bureaucracies by the president through a system of interagency groups.

The final participants in the foreign policy process are political parties, interest groups, and public opinion. Political parties seek to influence foreign policymaking by gaining control of the machinery of government—the presidency, the Congress, and the bureaucracy. Interest groups and public opinion attempt to influence foreign policymaking, indirectly rather than directly, by influencing these institutions. Chapter 11 discusses the role of political parties and interest groups and their impact on foreign policy. In the first part of this chapter, we outline the bipartisan tradition that the Democrats and Republicans have often claimed to follow in policymaking and demonstrate how this tradition has eroded significantly in the last two decades. Further, we show how the two parties are moving farther apart on foreign policy as ideological differences become stronger. In the second half of Chapter 11, we identify the myriad types of interest groups that attempt to influence foreign policy. To illustrate how influence has been exercised by interest groups, we focus in particular on two types that, perhaps, have enjoyed the greatest success in the postwar period: economic interest groups and ethnic interest groups. Finally, Chapter 12 is devoted to a discussion of the role of public opinion in the foreign policymaking process. While we highlight several factors that limit the influence of public opinion, we also demonstrate that the public can and does affect the actions of policymakers in foreign policy.

CHAPTER 7 THE PRESIDENT AND THE MAKING OF FOREIGN POLICY

". . . the President alone has the power to speak or listen as a representative of the nation." JUSTICE GEORGE SUTHERLAND, *UNITED STATES* V. *CURTISS-WRIGHT CORPORATION*, 299 U.S. 304 (1936)

"General Noriega's reckless threats and attacks upon Americans in Panama created an imminent danger to the 35,000 American citizens in Panama. As President, I have no higher obligation than to safeguard the lives of American citizens. And that is why I directed our Armed Forces to protect the lives of American citizens in Panama and to bring General Noriega to justice in the United States." PRESIDENT GEORGE BUSH, ADDRESS TO THE NATION, DECEMBER 20, 1989

During his 1989 Senate confirmation hearings, Secretary of State James Baker asserted that "in the saloons of the old West...you never shoot the piano player. And Dean Acheson wrote that in foreign policy, the President was the piano player."[1] Baker then appealed for a "kinder and gentler Congress" in foreign policy, and one where the president would play the tune. Eight years earlier in the same setting, Alexander Haig echoed this theme more formally: "...the Constitutional and traditional responsibility of the President for the conduct of foreign affairs must be reaffirmed...the authoritative voice must be the President's."[2] Recently, former Presidents Jimmy Carter and Gerald Ford also reiterated this long-standing view of American foreign policy. Carter said that there is "only one clear voice" in foreign policy, and that is the president's; Ford endorsed this view by adding that the Congress is too large and too diverse to handle foreign policy crises.[3] Indeed, presidential dominance is usually the principal way to describe U.S. foreign policymaking.

In the past two decades, however, the U.S. Congress has increasingly played a larger role in the making of American foreign policy. Congressional resurgence began in the early 1970s, fueled by the Vietnam and Watergate experiences, and resulted in several initiatives that sought to curb executive prerogatives in foreign affairs. That assertiveness continued in the 1980s with major roles for the Congress in shaping Central American, Middle Eastern, and Soviet-American policy. As the 1990s began, congressional initiatives did not diminish. Indeed, the debate between these two branches over the control of U.S. foreign policy persists.

In this chapter and the following one, we examine the struggle between the president and the Congress to make American foreign policy. The analysis explores three main themes: (1) why and how the executive has dominated the foreign policy process; (2) why and how the Congress has tried to curb presidential power recently; and (3) what is likely to be the relationship between the president and the Congress in the future.

CONSTITUTIONAL POWERS
IN FOREIGN POLICY

Under the Constitution, both the legislative and executive branches of government have been delegated specific foreign affairs powers. Each branch, too, was directed to *share* some foreign policy responsibility with the other. This arrangement ensured that the Congress and the president would each serve as a check on the actions of the other in foreign policy, much as the two branches do in domestic policy. Throughout the history of the Republic, however, the division of these foreign policy powers between the legislature and the executive has not always been clear. Indeed, political disputes have often arisen over it. In order to appreciate American foreign policymaking more fully, we begin our analysis by identifying the foreign policy powers of each branch and the areas of dispute between them.

PRESIDENTIAL POWERS

Under Article II of the Constitution, the president is granted several foreign policy powers. First, the president is granted the power to be chief executive. ("The Executive Power shall be vested in a President" and "he shall take Care that the Laws be faithfully executed.") The president is granted the power to command the armed forces. ("The President shall be Commander in Chief of the Army and Navy of the United States.") The president is also granted the power to be the chief negotiator and the chief diplomat. ("He shall have Power, by and with the Advice and Consent of the Senate, to make Treaties, . . . shall appoint Ambassadors, . . . and he shall receive Ambassadors and other public Ministers. . . . ") The president, in short, is to wear at least three different hats in foreign policy: chief executive, chief diplomat, and commander in chief of the armed forces. With this power, the president seemingly possesses the constitutional mandate to dominate foreign affairs.

This delegation of foreign policy powers to the executive branch in our Constitution represented a marked change from the arrangements under the earlier Articles of Confederation. During that period, prior to 1787, the Congress controlled foreign policy through its Committee on Foreign Affairs. Such a process, however, did not work very well. Indeed, according to one study, *''the mismanagement of foreign affairs by Congress''* during those years contributed to the holding of the Constitutional Convention and the eventual strengthening of the foreign policy powers of the presidency.[4] In addition to this preference for a strong executive in the Constitution, the Founders also believed that emergency powers resided in the office to take quick action if necessary, even though it is not explicitly stated in the Constitution and even though restrictions were placed on the presidency. This view was consistent with John Locke's "Of Prerogative" (in *The Second Treatise of Government*), which essentially stated that the executive could resort to exceptional powers in an emergency and to exercise self-preservation.[5] In Federalist No. 70, one of a series of newspaper articles written to promote ratification of the Constitution, Alexander Hamilton also noted that the presidency, as a one-person office, possessed "decision, activity, secrecy, and dispatch"—qualities associated with sound government and tied to quick action in foreign affairs.[6] Such beliefs, coupled with the constitutional powers granted to the executive, adds credence to the view that the Founders expected the president to dominate foreign affairs in the American system.

CONGRESSIONAL POWERS

Under Article I of the Constitution, however, the Congress is also granted several foreign policy powers. The Congress has the right to make and modify any laws and to appropriate funds for the implementation of any laws. ("No money shall be drawn from the Treasury, but in Consequence of Appropriations made by Law.") The Congress has the right to provide for the national defense and to declare war. (The Congress is authorized to "provide for the common Defence . . .; To declare War . . .; To raise and support Armies . . .; To provide and maintain a Navy.") The Congress is also delegated the responsibility to regulate international commerce ("To regulate commerce with foreign nations") and to use the implied powers (the right to "make all Laws which shall be necessary and proper" for carrying out its other responsibilities).

Constitutional scholar Louis Henkin has argued that the Congress has even more powers, what he calls the "Foreign Affairs Powers." These are powers that are not explicitly derived from the Constitution, but derive from the fact that the United States has sovereignty and nationhood. Thus, Congress enjoys additional authority to support legislation to regulate and protect "the conduct of foreign relations and foreign diplomatic activities in the United States." These undefined powers also allow congressional legislation in such areas as immigration, the regulation of aliens, the authorization of international commitments, and the extradition of citizens to other states. Moreover, Henkin rather boldly concludes that today there is no matter in foreign affairs "that is not subject to legislation by Congress."[7] In this sense, Congress has a constitutional mandate to be involved in foreign policy, just as the executive branch does.

"THE TWILIGHT ZONE" AND FOREIGN POLICY

The nation's Founders, always suspicious of concentrated power, thus delegated separate foreign policy responsibilities to each branch, but they went further by checking the power of each branch

TABLE 7.1 SOME FOREIGN POLICY POWERS SHARED BETWEEN THE PRESIDENT AND THE CONGRESS

PRESIDENT	CONGRESS
Warmaking "Commander in Chief of the Army and Navy of the United States"	the power "to declare war"; "to raise and support armies"; to "provide for the Common Defence"
Commitment making "He shall have Power...to make Treaties"	"provided two thirds of the Senators present concur"
Appointments "He shall nominate...and shall appoint Ambassadors"	"by and with the Advice and Consent of the Senate"

as well: they shared some foreign policy powers between them. While the president is the chief executive of the United States, the Congress decides what laws are to be enforced; while the president may command the armed forces, the Congress decides whether wars should be initiated; and while the president may negotiate treaties, the Congress (or, more accurately, the Senate) must give its advice and consent. (Table 7.1 shows three areas of shared foreign policy powers as outlined in Articles I and II of the Constitution.) As a result, virtually all of the presidential powers in foreign affairs are "checked" by congressional prerogatives, and presidential dominance is considerably less than what might be inferred from any initial examination of the Constitution. Even as strong a proponent of executive power as Alexander Hamilton was led to conclude that the president under the Constitution would have less substantive foreign affairs powers than the King of England.[8]

The constitutional ideal of shared foreign policy powers is easier to describe than it has been to put into effective operation. Often, the actions of one branch seemingly cross over into the responsibilities of another branch. The president will rely upon the commander-in-chief power to initiate conflict with another nation, even though only the Congress has the power to declare war. The Congress will seek to restrict the deployment of troops into a particular region, even though the president has the power to direct the deployment of armed forces. What has emerged, in the words of former Supreme Court Justice Robert Jackson, has been "a zone of twilight in which [the president] and Congress may have concurrent authority, or in which its distribution is uncertain."[9]

Owing to constitutional ambiguity, the result of this shared responsibility has been an historical tension over who ultimately controls foreign policy. Historian Arthur Schlesinger, Jr., in his book, *The Imperial Presidency,* describes the division between the two branches as "cryptic, ambiguous, and incomplete."[10] Constitutional scholar Henkin notes that "the constitutional blueprint for the governance of our foreign affairs has proved to be starkly incomplete, indeed skimpy."[11] Edward S. Corwin, the noted scholar on constitutional and presidential power, has provided the most often cited summary of this dilemma: The Constitution has really provided "an invitation to struggle for the privilege of directing American foreign policy."[12]

THE GROWTH OF EXECUTIVE DOMINANCE IN FOREIGN AFFAIRS

Indeed, a struggle has resulted, but the presidency seems to have emerged as more successful than the Congress over the history of the Republic.[13] Only in recent years has the legislative branch attempted to wrest some foreign policymaking from the executive branch. In the main, though, the president has been the one to dominate foreign affairs matters due to several key factors:

1. Important executive precedents
2. Supreme Court decisions
3. Congressional deference and delegation
4. The growth of executive institutions
5. International situational factors

While these factors are the results of long-term trends, several are particularly associated with the rise of American globalism in the post–World War II years. We now turn to examine each of these factors in detail.

HISTORICAL PRECEDENTS

An important first factor that contributed to executive dominance of foreign affairs consists of those actions taken by the various presidents throughout history. By assuming that they possessed control of foreign policy over particular issues and by taking action, the early presidents set a pattern for how future executives would act. In this regard, the actions of the first president, George Washington, were particularly pivotal, since he put into effect the meaning of the Constitution "in response to events."[14] In turn, then, Washington set foreign policy precedents in at least four important areas: the right of the president to represent the United States abroad, the right to negotiate international agreements, the right to recognize other states, and the right to initiate the conduct of foreign policy. Other early presidents followed Washington's lead and were to give the presidency preeminence in these foreign policy areas.

THE ROLE OF WASHINGTON AND OTHER EARLY PRESIDENTS   In the area of representing the United States abroad, President Washington made it clear that the executive would be that representative. He sent personal emissaries to represent him in negotiations abroad and simply informed the Congress of his actions. In 1791, for instance, President Washington informed the Senate that Gouverneur Morris, who was in Great Britain at that time, would confer with the British over their adherence to the treaty of peace. A short time later, Washington sent his friend Colonel David Humphrey to Spain and Portugal as his personal representative.[15] By such actions, Washington established the principle that the president would conduct relations with other states.

In a similar vein, President Washington provided another precedent by declining to share important diplomatic information with the House of Representatives when negotiating the Jay Treaty. Although his rationale was that the House had no standing in the treaty process, the implications of his actions went further. In Corwin's view, the allowance of this precedent broadened presidential power so that "a President feels free by the same formula to decline information even to his constitutional partner in treaty-making...."[16]

President Washington established another important precedent: the executive would be the one to recognize other states. When Washington received Edmond Genêt ("Citizen Genêt"), the first minister to the United States from the French republic, he went a long way toward legitimizing that nation's revolutionary government. Similarly, when Genêt seemingly violated his power, it was up to Washington to send him home.[17]

Finally, President Washington also established the precedent of executive initiation of foreign policy. In unilaterally declaring neutrality between France and Britain in 1793, he began the process of presidential direction for foreign policy matters. The Congress, after this declaration, was left primarily to try to recover lost ground. In effect, what Congress did was to pass a neutrality act in conformity with Washington's wishes.[18] (President Monroe followed a similar approach with his unilateral declaration of the Monroe Doctrine in 1823. Few options were left to the Congress except to follow his lead.)

By these actions of sending emissaries abroad and receiving representatives from other states, President Washington gave meaning to the constitutional power of appointing and receiving ambassadors. In effect, the executive power in this area came to eclipse any congressional prerogative. When President Washington followed the Hamiltonian notion of inherent executive power by initiating foreign policy actions, he seemed to imply that the powers of the executive derived from the fact that the United States was a sovereign state and that the president was the representative of that sovereignty. In short, President Washington gave meaning to the characterization of the presidency by a future chief justice of the United States, John Marshall: "The President is the sole organ of the nation in its external relations, and its sole representative with foreign nations."[19]

Other early presidents followed Washington's lead of a strong executive carrying on relations with other states. For instance, President John Adams used his executive power to extradite an individual under the Jay Treaty without congressional authorization. Likewise, Adams vigorously defended his right to recognize other states. President Thomas Jefferson, although a proponent of legislative dominance in the affairs of state, still exercised considerable individual control over the Louisiana Purchase. Still later, President James Monroe refused to relinquish the president's right to recognize other governments, especially with regard to several Latin American states. The result, as Corwin concludes, was to "reaffirm the President's monopoly of international intercourse and his constitutional independence in the performance of that function."[20] This presidential preeminence in the recognition of and negotiation of relations with other states continued through the rest of the nineteenth century and into the twentieth century. As a result, the president's right to recognize and to negotiate with states is little challenged to this day.

PRESIDENTS AND WARMAKING   Another area in which actions by early executives set a precedent was in warmaking. Although the Congress was granted the right to declare war under the Constitution, to what extent could the executive use military force without the explicit authorization of the legislative branch? Put differently, how far could the president go under the commander-in-chief clause of the Constitution before it intruded on the constitutional prerogative to declare war?

Early presidents generally were quite careful about extending the meaning of the commander-in-chief clause. Only in the case of attacks upon Americans or American forces did the president occasionally provide immediate military responses. As Arthur Schlesinger points out, however, even in those instances, the early presidents were quite meticulous in involving the Congress in any actions.[21] When President Thomas Jefferson was faced with the question of using force against Tripoli because of its attacks upon American shipping, he sent U.S. frigates to the Mediterranean, but he limited them to defensive action only. After the frigates had responded to an attack, Jefferson sent a message to Congress declaring that his actions were "in compliance with constitutional limitations on his authority in the absence of a declaration of war."[22]

By the 1840s, however, some transformation in this commander-in-chief clause was already evident. President James K. Polk was instrumental in using his power as head of the armed forces to precipitate a declaration of war against Mexico. By moving American troops into land disputed with Mexico—resulting in a Mexican attack upon these forces—President Polk was able to obtain a declaration of war from the Congress.[23] By using his constitutional power as commander in chief, President Polk was able to force the Congress's hand on the war powers.

The boldest precedents with the commander-in-chief clause came during the presidency of Abraham Lincoln. Combining the powers granted under this clause with the executive power to take care that the laws are carried out, President Lincoln effectively made the "war power" his own, as Corwin has said. Because of the Civil War, President Lincoln, without consulting the Congress, "proclaimed a blockade of the Southern ports, suspended the writ of habeas corpus in various places, and caused the arrest and military detention of persons 'who were represented to him' as being engaged in or contemplating 'treasonable practices....' "[24] In addition, Lincoln enlarged the army and navy, pressed into service the state militias, and called into service 40,000 volunteers. Despite outcries that the president was going beyond his limits, neither the Congress nor the courts challenged him. In fact, the former body gave approval to his actions after the fact, and the Supreme Court upheld his actions in the *Prize* cases by a narrow margin of 5–4.[25] While these presidential actions were taken in the context of a civil war (and their transference to foreign wars was debatable), the expansion of the presidential power in warmaking was not lost on future presidents.

While congressional acquiescence to Lincoln's actions did not produce any expansion of the warmaking power by his immediate successors, it did establish important precedents for later commanders in chief.[26] The dispatch of troops to China by President William McKinley in 1900, the interventions by Presidents Theodore Roosevelt and William Howard Taft in the Caribbean in the early 1900s, and even the sending of American forces to Korea (albeit with a UN resolution) were done without congressional authorization.

Furthermore, the several interventions by the United States during the height of the Cold War (Lebanon, Bay of Pigs, Dominican Republic, and Vietnam) were done without the benefit of congressional actions before the fact. Lyndon Johnson was able to boast that there was a large body of precedent for his Vietnam policy by citing the actions of previous commanders in chief. On one occasion, for instance, President Johnson was able to cite 125 cases in which previous presidents took military action to protect American citizens. On another occasion, he was able to cite 137 cases in which earlier chief executives had unilaterally employed force to protect U.S. citizens.[27] Later on during the Vietnam War, President Nixon justified the Cambodian invasion of 1970 by stating: "I shall meet my responsibility as Commander-in-Chief of our Armed Forces to take the action necessary to defend the security of our American men."[28]

The pattern has continued throughout the 1980s and into the 1990s as well. In 1982, President Reagan initially sent American troops into Lebanon as a "peacekeeping force" without congressional approval and justified that action through the commander-in-chief clause of the Constitution. (Only after some American lives were lost in this deployment did the Congress insist on applying the requirements of the War Powers Resolution, a congressional resolution requiring congressional notification and involvement when the president uses force. See Chapter 8.) In April 1986, President Reagan unilaterally initiated a retaliatory attack against Libya over that country's involvement with a terrorist attack upon Americans in West Berlin. In December 1989, President Bush approved the U.S. intervention into Panama and justified it on the basis of his "constitutional authority with respect to the conduct of foreign relations," his responsibility "to protect American lives in imminent danger," and as commander in chief of American military forces.[29] In August 1990 and beyond, President Bush once again used a similar kind of constitutional rationale for sending some American military personnel into Saudi Arabia to protect that country from Iraq's Saddam Hussein, who had seized Kuwait. When the president actually decided to use force against Iraq over its seizure of Kuwait, he did seek congressional authorization, as we discuss below.

According to critics, then, the commander-in-chief clause had been transformed into a presidential power not only to conduct a war already begun, but to *initiate* a conflict if necessary. The growth of this executive precedent has caused the Congress to react strongly to an apparent incursion into its area of responsibility. As we shall discuss in the next chapter, the War Powers Resolution was passed in an attempt to curb executive warmaking, but it has been far from successful.

PRESIDENTS AND FOREIGN COMMITMENTS   A final area of executive precedent was in the making of foreign policy commitments. Instead of relying on the treaty as the basic instrument of making commitments to other states, presidents have come to rely on the so-called executive agreement as a principal means of establishing bonds with other nations. By such precedent, the treaty power of the Congress has been eroded, and congressional involvement in this aspect of foreign policymaking has been weakened. In this way, once again, the president has enhanced his ability to make and carry out foreign policy by executive action only.

The executive agreement is an agreement made by the president or a representative of the president, usually without congressional involvement, with another country. Its most important distinction from a treaty is that it does not require the advice and consent of the Senate, yet it has the same force of law as a treaty. An executive agreement actually may take one of two forms. One type is based solely on the constitutional power of the president; the other type is based on congressional legislation authorizing or approving the president's making a commitment with another nation. The former relies upon powers granted in Article II, and especially the commander-in-chief clause. An example would be the agreement made by the United States for use of naval facilities in Bahrain in 1971. A State Department official testified before Congress that the "President, as Commander in Chief, has constitutional authority to make arrangements for facilities for our military personnel." The latter type, the so-called statutory executive agreement, relies on some precise piece of earlier congressional authorization or a treaty. An example would be the agreement with Portugal for military rights on the Azores in 1971, which was based upon a 1951 Defense Agreement between the two countries in accordance with the NATO Treaty.[30]

Overall, the statutory executive agreement is the more prevalent form of executive agreement and the more controversial.[31] While the statutory agreement allows the Congress to be involved procedurally

TABLE 7.2 Treaties and Executive Agreements, 1789–1988

Years	Treaties	Executive Agreements	Percent of Total as Executive Agreements
1789–1839	60	27	31%
1839–1889	215	238	57
1889–1929	382	763	67
1930–1939	142	144	50
1940–1949	116	919	89
1950–1959	138	2,229	94
1960–1969	114	2,324	95
1970–1979	173	3,040	95
1980–1988	136	3,094	96
Totals/Overall %	1,476	12,778	90%

Source: The agreement data from Michael Nelson, ed., *Congressional Quarterly's Guide to the Presidency* (Washington, D.C.: Congressional Quarterly, Inc., 1989), p. 1104. Column 3 was calculated by the author.

in the agreement process, the extent of substantive congressional involvement remains an important question. It is not always clear that the Congress was fully aware of the considerable discretion that it was affording the president in making commitments abroad or how far statutory authority was expanded to cover a contemplated executive agreement. In some instances, the Congress may be providing legislation that might later be viewed as a "blank check" for presidential action.

Table 7.2 provides some data on the use of executive agreements (including both the statutory agreement and the "pure" constitutionally based agreements in one category) and treaties over the history of the Republic. As these data show, the executive agreement—instead of the treaty—was used moderately at first, but its use has grown dramatically in the last century or so.[32] By the 1889–1929 period, the number of executive agreements was almost twice that of the treaty form. By comparison, the executive agreement in the post–World War II period has virtually exploded in usage, dwarfing the treaty mechanism as the principal instrument of commitment abroad. Over the history of the nation, about 90 percent of all agreements have been executive in nature, but the differences between the pre-1950 period and the post-1950 period are substantial. Prior to 1950, only about 70 percent of all agreements took the form of executive agreements; but after 1950, about 95 percent took that form.

Despite the limited use of the executive agreement in the first century of the Republic, important commitments were still made via this route. For instance, the agreement between the British and the Americans to limit naval vessels on the Great Lakes (the Rush-Bagot Agreement of 1817) was done through an exchange of notes by executive representatives of both governments. Later, President McKinley agreed to the terms for ending the Spanish-American War by executive agreement. President Theodore Roosevelt entered into a secret agreement with Japan over Korea and into a "Gentlemen's Agreement" in 1907 to restrict Japanese immigration into the United States.[33]

In the modern era, the executive agreement was used frequently and for important commitments. The actions of President Franklin Roosevelt set the pattern for recent presidents. Roosevelt, for instance, completed the Destroyer-for-Bases deal of 1940 with an executive agreement. Similarly, the Yalta Agreement of 1945 was completed through this mechanism. President Harry S. Truman followed this pattern with the Potsdam Agreement, also by executive agreement. Later, President Truman made an oral commitment to defend the newly independent state of Israel in 1948 and started a pattern of support for this nation through executive declaration.[34]

Following these initiatives, the other postwar executives proceeded to make numerous important political and military commitments through the executive agreement. As a Senate Foreign Relations subcommittee investigation revealed in the late 1960s and early 1970s, numerous political, military, and intelligence commitments (some verbal and some secret) were extended to a diverse group of nations—including, among others, Thailand, Laos, Spain, Ethiopia, and the Philippines—through executive action only. The Congress was kept almost entirely in the dark about these commitments.[35]

A later analysis has also documented the extent to which important foreign military commitments have taken the form of executive agreements in the postwar years.[36] The commitment of military missions in Honduras and El Salvador in the 1950s, pledges to Turkey, Iran, and Pakistan over security in 1959, the permission by the British to use the island of Diego Garcia for military purposes in the

1960s, and the establishment of a military mission in Iran in 1974 were all done by executive agreement. Further, the analysis revealed that some "understandings" and arrangements with nations are handled by executive agreements. For instance, a message by President Nixon to aid the reconstruction of North Vietnam as part of a peace effort was handled in this way, and an "understanding" regarding the role of American military personnel in the Israeli-Egyptian disengagement agreement of 1975 was as well. Similarly, the Offensive Arms Pact of the Strategic Arms Limitation Talks (SALT I) took the form of an executive agreement. Various pledges at the superpower summits or presidential meetings have also taken this form, although the Congress can still become involved if changes in the status of a nation under a treaty or convention is committed (to most-favored-nation trading status for the Soviet Union, for example) or additional funding of some program is made (increased foreign aid for El Salvador, for instance).

In sum, executive precedents in several different areas—negotiating with and recognizing other states, initiating conflicts or interventions toward other nations, and making unilateral commitments abroad—have given operational meaning to the delegation of executive foreign policy powers as outlined in Article II of the Constitution. In some instances, too, these precedents have expanded presidential authority in foreign policy well beyond what the Founders envisioned. As a result, precedents alone have contributed significantly to making the president the chief executive, the chief diplomat, and, if necessary, the chief warmaker in the conduct of foreign policy. Yet this factor has not been the only one that has allowed American presidents to dominate foreign policymaking.

SUPREME COURT DECISIONS

The Supreme Court has also aided the executive in gaining ascendancy in the foreign policy arena. With few exceptions, the Court's decisions have supported presidential claims to dominance over foreign policy matters. Four important court cases from the early twentieth century will illustrate the extent to which the Supreme Court has deferred to the president in matters dealing with international politics, even prior to America's extensive global involvement after World War II. Several cases from the last two decades will illustrate how the principles from these earlier cases and precedents have been upheld to the present day. Since 1970, moreover, there have been only two notable cases in which the Court has not upheld the president's wishes on foreign policy questions.

THE *CURTISS-WRIGHT* CASE   The most important, and far-sweeping, grant of presidential dominance over foreign policy was set forth in the Supreme Court's decision in *U.S.* v. *Curtiss-Wright Export Corporation et al.* (1936).[37] In effect, this case gave special standing to the executive in foreign policy matters. A brief summary of the issues in dispute will make this clear.

The case dealt with a joint congressional resolution that authorized the president to prohibit "the sale of arms and munitions of war . . . to those countries engaged . . . in armed conflict" in the Chaco region of South America if he determined that such an embargo would contribute to peace in the area. On May 28, 1934, President Franklin Roosevelt issued such a proclamation and put the resolution into effect. Later, in November 1935, he revoked this resolution with a similar proclamation. As a result of the original proclamation, however, the Curtiss-Wright Corporation was indicted on a charge that it conspired to sell fifteen machine guns to Bolivia beginning in May 1934.

Several issues were raised by the corporation in denying any wrongdoing in this matter. Curtiss-Wright contended that the joint resolution was an invalid delegation of legislative power, that the joint resolution never became effective because of the failure of the president to find essential jurisdictional facts, and that the second proclamation (lifting the ban) ended the liability of the company under the joint resolution.[38] While the Court rejected all of the arguments, its reasoning on the first was the most important for enlarging presidential power in foreign affairs.

The Court held that the delegation of power to the executive—to apply the embargo or not—was not unconstitutional because the issue dealt with a question of external, not internal, affairs. In these two areas, the Court said, the powers of delegation are different. In internal affairs, the federal government can only exercise those powers specifically enumerated in the Constitution (and such implied powers as are necessary and proper), but in the external area, such limitations do not apply. Because of America's separation from Great Britain, and as a result of being a member of the family of nations, the United States possesses external sovereignty and the powers associated with it. "The powers to declare and wage war, to conclude peace, to make treaties, to maintain diplomatic relations with other sovereignties, if they had never been mentioned in the Constitution, would have vested in the federal government as necessary concomitants of nationality."[39]

Most importantly, the Court held that the president was the representative of that sovereignty (". . . the President alone has the power to speak or listen as a representative of the nation"). Therefore, the executive's powers in foreign affairs go beyond the actual Constitutional delegation of power. Furthermore, the president is to be granted considerable discretion in the exercise of these powers as compared to the domestic arena. As the Court said, "It is quite apparent that if, in the maintenance of our international relations, embarrassment—perhaps serious embarrassment—is to be avoided and success for our aims achieved, congressional legislation which is to be made effective through negotiation and inquiry within the international field must often accord to the President a degree of discretion and freedom from statutory restriction which would not be admissible were domestic affairs alone involved."[40]

In light of such a view and numerous precedents that the decision cites, the Court held that the joint resolution was not an unlawful delegation of legislative power. Most importantly, the decision established that foreign policy and domestic policy were different arenas, with a special position for the president in the former. In sum, the *Curtiss-Wright* case made clear that the president's power in foreign policy could not be gleaned only from constitutional directives; there were "extra-constitutional" powers—tied to the sovereignty of the United States and the executive's role as the representative of that sovereignty. Subsequent cases and legal analyses have challenged this interpretation, but they have not fully undermined the notion of the executive's primacy in foreign affairs.[41]

MISSOURI V. HOLLAND   An earlier Supreme Court decision clarified, and actually enlarged, the treaty powers given to the executive. In *Missouri v. Holland* (1920), the Court held that the treaty powers could not be limited by any "invisible radiation" of the Tenth Amendment to the Constitution.[42] Put differently, the power of the president in making treaties with other nations was ensured against any intrusion by states' rights advocates.

The particulars of the case will once again point to the significance of the Court's decision. The dispute involved the constitutionality of the Migratory Bird Act, which was passed by the Congress pursuant to a treaty between the United States and Great Britain. Missouri contended, however, that this act was void because Article I of the Constitution did not delegate the regulation of such birds to the Congress; therefore, this power was reserved to the states by the Tenth Amendment. In two earlier cases, moreover—before the treaty was signed—two U.S. district courts had voided such a congressional act. But now the Court decided differently, mainly because of the intervening treaty. Mr. Justice Holmes in his opinion for the majority wrote:

> Acts of Congress are the supreme law of the land only when made in pursuance of the Constitution, while treaties are declared to be so when made under the authority of the United States. We do not mean to imply that there are no qualifications to the treaty-making power; they must be ascertained in a different way. It is obvious that there may be matters of the sharpest exigency for the national well being that an act of Congress could not deal with but that a treaty followed by such an act could, and it is not lightly to be assumed that, in matters requiring national action, "a power which must belong to and somewhere reside in every civilized government" is not to be found.[43]

Mr. Justice Holmes argued further that the regulation of migratory birds was best left to the federal government. Although he acknowledged that the Constitution was silent on this issue, such silence was not sufficient to support the claim made by the state of Missouri. In addition, Mr. Justice Holmes held that "a treaty may override" the powers of the state.[44]

In sum, *Missouri* v. *Holland* was highly significant for the powers of the president. It legitimized the president's role of using the treaty process to add to the constitutional framework of the nation; it arguably reduced the implied powers of the states and the Congress, since those powers could be overridden through the treaty power; and it began a series of twentieth century Court decisions giving special deference to the president in foreign affairs.

THE *BELMONT* AND *PINK* CASES The third and fourth important Supreme Court decisions, one prior to World War II and the other during the war, dealt with the legal status of executive agreements.[45] The decisions in these cases gave the president another means of enhancing these foreign policy powers.

U.S. v. *Belmont* (1937) involved whether the federal government could recover the bank account of an American national, August Belmont, who owned obligations belonging to a Russian company before the establishment of the Soviet Union. The bank account in question was held in the state of New York. The federal government tried to reclaim this account because under the Litvinov Agreement—which established diplomatic relations between the U.S. and the Soviet Union—all Soviet accounts had been assigned to the U.S. government. While the federal district court held that the federal government could not claim such accounts since the property existed in New York, not the Soviet Union, the Supreme Court held otherwise. Mr. Justice Sutherland argued that the external powers of the U.S. must be exercised without regard to the constraint of state law or policies, and no unjust confiscation of property would occur as a result.

U.S. v. *Pink* (1942) also dealt with the legitimacy of the Litvinov Agreement and involved some of the same issues as the *Belmont* case. It was an action brought by the U.S. government against the New York State Superintendent of Insurance to acquire the remaining assets of the First Russian Insurance Company. When the Soviet Union was established, all properties—wherever located—were nationalized. Under the Litvinov Agreement, as we noted, all such assets were assigned to the American government. Superintendent Pink claimed, however, that the nationalization action had "no territorial effect" and that the U.S. government action was improper.[46] The Supreme Court held otherwise, and Justice Douglas stated the Court's view in this forceful passage:

> We hold that the right to the funds or property in question became vested in the Soviet Government as the successor to the First Russian Insurance Co.; that this right has passed to the United States under the Litvinov Assignment; and that the United States is entitled to the property as against the corporation and the foreign creditors.[47]

These cases are important because the Litvinov Agreement between the United States and the Soviet Union was an executive agreement. Thus, these decisions have been interpreted as giving legitimacy to executive agreements as the law of the land—without any congressional action. Once again, then, the president's hand in the conduct of foreign affairs was strengthened. Moreover, Louis Henkin argues, the language and reasoning in the *Belmont* and *Pink* cases were sufficiently general to apply to any executive agreement and to ensure its supremacy over any state law.[48]

Recent Court Decisions   Several recent cases reflect the extent to which the Supreme Court and other federal jurisdictions continue to defer to the prerogatives of the executive in the conduct of foreign policy, often at the expense of the Congress. Document Summary 7.1 arrays these cases to show how they have reinforced the president's treaty power, the commander-in-chief power, and the executive authority over foreign affairs over the last decade and a half.

The first two cases affirmed the treaty powers of the president and, in effect, reduced congressional standing in dealing with foreign policy. One case dealt with the constitutionality of President Carter's decision to transfer the Panama Canal back to Panama, the other dealt with his breaking of the Mutual Defense Treaty with Taiwan as part of the process of establishing diplomatic relations with the People's Republic of China. In *Edwards* v. *Carter*, sixty members of Congress charged that both houses of Congress must approve any

DOCUMENT SUMMARY 7.1 PRESIDENTIAL FOREIGN POLICY POWERS AND THE COURTS: SOME RECENT DECISIONS

AFFIRMATION OF TREATY POWERS

Edwards v. *Carter* [580 F. 2d 1055 (D.C. Cir. 1978)]
This case involved the constitutionality of the transfer of the Panama Canal from the U.S. to Panama. The members of Congress who brought the suit claimed that property could not be transferred through treaty, but instead needed the approval of both houses of Congress, according to Article IV, Section 3, Clause 2 of the Constitution.

The court of appeals decided that property can be transferred internationally through the treaty power.

Goldwater et al. v. *Carter* [444 U.S. 996 (1979)]
This case concerned the constitutionality of President Carter's termination of the Mutual Defense Treaty with Taiwan. Several members of Congress, led by Senator Barry Goldwater, contended that the termination of the treaty should be subjected to approval by a two-thirds majority in the Senate.

The Court held for the Carter administration because the issue was "political" in nature between the branches, because it was not ripe for judicial action since no confrontation had occurred between the two parties, and because the president possessed the "well-established authority to recognize, and withdraw recognition from, foreign governments."

AFFIRMATION OF COMMANDER-IN-CHIEF CLAUSE

Crockett v. *Reagan* [720 F. 2d 1355 (D.C. Cir. 1983), certiorari denied 467 U.S. 1251 (1984)]
The case involved a suit by 29 members of Congress challenging the presence of U.S. military advisors in and military assistance to El Salvador and the failure of the Reagan administration to comply with the War Powers Resolution and the warmaking powers of the Congress.

The court ruled that the case was a nonjusticiable political question and one in which it could not resolve the factual issues in dispute.

Conyers v. *Reagan* [765 F. 2d. 1124 (D.C. Cir. 1985)]
Eleven members of Congress claimed that the U.S. invasion of Grenada by the executive branch was unconstitutional because it violated the war powers of the Congress.

The district court held that it lacked jurisdiction. The District of Columbia Appeals Court held that the matter was moot, since the invasion had ended. It dismissed the suit.

Lowry v. *Reagan* [676 F. Supp. 333 (D.D.C. 1987)]
This case was brought by 110 members of Congress who wanted the

---

DOCUMENT SUMMARY 7.1   PRESIDENTIAL FOREIGN POLICY
POWERS AND THE COURTS: SOME RECENT DECISIONS (CONTINUED)

---

president to report to the Congress under the provisions of the War
Powers Resolution concerning the role of American forces in the
Persian Gulf.

The district court dismissed the case because it involved a
political question between the Congress and the executive and
because it involved a dispute within the Congress as well.

AFFIRMATION OF EXECUTIVE POWERS

INS v. Chadha [462 U.S. 919 (1983)]
After the House of Representatives vetoed the Immigration and
Naturalization Service's suspension of a foreign student's deportation
under a "legislative veto" provision contained in the legislation, the
student challenged the power of the House to overrule the INS and
the constitutionality of the "legislative veto."

The Court held that the one-house legislative veto was
unconstitutional because it violated the presentment clause of Article
I of the Constitution. That is, every bill passed by the Congress must
"be presented to the President" for his action.

Source: The cases were drawn from the discussions in Warren Christopher, "Ceasefire
between the Branches: A Compact in Foreign Affairs," in James M. McCormick, *A Reader in
American Foreign Policy* (Itasca, IL: F. E. Peacock Publishers, Inc., 1986); Jean E. Smith, *The
Constitution and American Foreign Policy* (St. Paul: West Publishing Company, 1989); and the
cases themselves.

---

transference of property, according to Article IV of the Constitution.
Such action cannot be taken, they claimed, by self-executing treaties
(such as the Panama Canal Treaty). The District of Columbia Court
of Appeals held otherwise, arguing that the property clause in the
Constitution is distinguishable from other grants of congressional
power. The Supreme Court left this decision stand by refusing to
hear the case. In *Goldwater et al. v. Carter,* several senators charged
that President Carter could not terminate the defense treaty with Taiwan without either a two-thirds majority of the Senate or a majority
of both houses of Congress. The Supreme Court, however, divided
along several lines. Four justices held that the case was "nonjusticiable" because it involved a political issue, another said that it was not
ready for court action since Congress, as a body, had taken no formal
action to challenge the president, and another said that the president
acted constitutionally.[49] The upshot of this ruling, as it had been in

the earlier one, was to dismiss the challenge to the president and his treaty powers.

Because the "political question" doctrine has been used frequently by the courts in several recent cases, we need to say a brief word about the meaning of this doctrine, why it has been invoked in several foreign policy challenges, and its implications for presidential power over foreign affairs. While the basis for the doctrine is not well developed or wholly understood in constitutional law, the doctrine seemingly has been invoked under several different circumstances by the court: when the court believed it lacked the authority to decide the case because the constitutionally prescribed activities of another branch of government were involved, when the effective remedy involved a political remedy that would favor one branch of government over another, and when the court wanted to avoid a question brought before it.[50] When it has been invoked in foreign policy cases, it has usually implied that a *political* (not a constitutional) dispute exists between two branches of government, normally the Congress and the presidency, and hence is not subject to judicial remedy. The upshot of such rulings, as *Goldwater et al.* v. *Carter* illustrates, is often implicitly to support or strengthen the hand of the president in foreign affairs.

Three cases in the 1980s and one in 1990 challenged the president's commander-in-chief powers, and these cases produced the same result as efforts to challenge the president's power over the Vietnam War a decade earlier. Several attempts were made to challenge the constitutionality of that conflict, but in virtually all instances the court refused to hear these cases since it judged them to deal with a political question between the two branches.[51] Much the same reasoning prevailed in the cases dealing with presidential actions in El Salvador, Grenada, and the Persian Gulf.

In *Crockett* v. *Reagan*, 29 members of Congress contended that the sending of U.S. military advisors and military aid to El Salvador was a violation of the War Powers Resolution and the Foreign Assistance Act. The former required presidential reporting to Congress of American forces sent abroad; the latter restricted aid to countries engaged in human rights violations (see Chapter 8). The lower court held that the issue was nonjusticiable because the issue was a "political question" between the branches and because it could not determine all the facts in the case. In *Conyers* v. *Reagan*, 11 members of Congress, led by John Conyers of Michigan, charged that the executive branch had gone beyond its powers and had usurped Congress's warmaking powers in sending U.S. forces to invade Grenada. The district court dismissed the case by asserting that it lacked jurisdiction, and the appeals court held the issue as moot, since the invasion had ended. In *Lowry* v. *Reagan,* 110 members of Congress wanted the president to report to the Congress under the War Powers Resolution because of the activity of American forces in the Persian Gulf during the Iran-Iraq War. Once again, the district court dismissed the case as a political matter between the two branches, and no further action was taken.[52] Finally, in a suit brought in late 1990 by 54 members of Congress challenging President Bush's right to go to war against Iraq without a congressional declaration of war, a federal district court in Washington ruled against the members. The judge held that the issue was not "ripe" for decision because the Congress as a body had not taken a formal stand on whether it wanted President Bush to seek a congressional authorization. While leaving the door open for such a decision if the Congress acted and rejecting the executive claim that the courts could not intrude into this dispute, the judge's ruling did not formally restrict executive power in this area.[53]

In the area of executive power, too, the court has largely been deferential to the president. (The one notable exception in the postwar years was the court's refusal to support President Truman's seizure of the steel mills during the Korean War.)[54] In the 1980s, the most important case reaffirming this principle was *Immigration and Naturalization Service* v. *Chadha* (1983). In that case, the Supreme Court declared the "one-house legislative veto" unconstitutional. A legislative veto was a procedural device that Congress used to control more fully the actions of the executive in carrying out policy. When this device was employed by the legislative branch, the Congress would explicitly incorporate in a piece of legislation a provision that allowed the Congress to stop or modify the executive's subsequent implementation of the statute by simply declaring its objection. The legislative branch could register its "veto" of executive action in one of two ways: (1) by passing a single chamber veto resolution (either Senate or House) or (2) by a two-house veto resolution (a concurrent resolution), depending upon how the original legislation was written. The most important point is that neither kind of resolution allowed the executive to approve or disapprove the action. In other words, when the legislative veto was incorporated within an act of Congress, the legislative branch could pass legislation and then could, unilaterally, monitor and modify the implementation of that legislation by the executive branch.

The particulars of the *Chadha* case will make clear how a legislative veto operates. The case involved an East Indian student who was born in India and held a British passport. He overstayed his student nonimmigrant visa and was ordered deported by the INS. He appealed the deportation, and his deportation was suspended by immigration authorities. By a provision that was incorporated into previous immigration legislation, however, the Congress (either the House or the Senate) could pass a simple majority resolution objecting to this suspension of the deportation order. In this case, the House of Representatives did so; in effect, the House called for Chadha's deportation promptly. Chadha appealed the House's action, and ultimately the court of appeals ruled in his favor, declaring that the "legislative veto" was unconstitutional because it violated the principle of the separation of powers between the branches. To clear up the matter, the Immigration and Naturalization Service then petitioned the Supreme Court to hear the case.

Once the case reached the Supreme Court, a majority of the justices held that the "legislative veto" in the earlier legislation was invalid for an important constitutional reason: it violated the presentment clause of the Constitution.[55] That is, "every Bill which shall have passed the House of Representatives and the Senate, shall, before it becomes a Law, be presented to the President of the United States" for consideration. Such a presentment did not occur in this case, because the House acted unilaterally to rescind the action of the executive branch. Since the *Chadha* decision dealt only with the "one-house" legislative veto, the Supreme Court expanded its decision about two weeks later by declaring the "two-house" legislative veto unconstitutional as well.[56]

At the time of the *Chadha* decision, at least fifty-six statutes, including several important foreign policy statutes, contained one or more such provisions.[57] Since the legislative veto was a prominent device used by the Congress in the 1970s and early 1980s to reign in executive power in foreign affairs, the *Chadha* decision has had some impact on the extent of congressional resurgence, as we shall discuss in Chapter 8.

Finally, although the president has usually gotten his way with the courts, at least two important Supreme Court decisions occurred in the 1970s in which he did not. The basis for deciding against the president in these cases was less an effort to reduce his foreign policy powers and more an effort to maintain some fundamental American freedoms. In *New York Times* v. *United States* (1971), or the *Pentagon Papers* case as it is more familiarly known, the Court held that the executive's claims of national security could not stop the publication of these volumes chronicling American involvement in Southeast Asia. First Amendment freedoms proved to be more persuasive than any immediate national security needs. In *United States* v. *Nixon* (1974), the case that decided that President Nixon must turn over tape recordings and records dealing with the Watergate investigation, the Supreme Court held that "neither the separation of powers nor the confidentiality of executive communications barred the federal courts from access to presidential tapes needed as evidence in a criminal case." At the same time, the Court was less than precise over whether specific claims of "national security" would have led to another result. As Chief Justice Burger put it, the president did not "claim. . . [a] need to protect military, diplomatic, or sensitive national secrets."[58]

CONGRESSIONAL DEFERENCE AND DELEGATION

A third factor that has added to the presidential preeminence in foreign policy has been the degree of congressional support for presidential initiatives, particularly in the post–World War II period. In addition, the Congress has sometimes gone further than giving its support to the executive; it has, on occasion, delegated some of its foreign policy prerogatives to the president. A brief survey of this factor will illustrate how the president's foreign policy control has been strengthened by congressional support and how it has met some challenge recently.

CONGRESSIONAL LEADERSHIP   Legislative support for the president in foreign policy can be evidenced in the statements and policy actions of members of both houses of Congress. This support was often couched in a commitment to bipartisanship in the conduct of foreign policy; "politics must stop at the water's edge" was a frequent postwar refrain. This tradition of bipartisanship probably can be dated to the pledge of Senator Arthur Vandenberg, chairman of the Senate Foreign Relations Committee, to support President Harry Truman in his foreign policy efforts in the immediate post–World War II years. The Vandenberg Resolution, for example, worked out in close consultation with the Department of State and passed in June 1948, called upon the executive branch to proceed with the development of the North Atlantic Treaty and with reforms of the United Nations. What it also did, however, was to usher in an era of congressional-executive cooperation in the making of foreign policy. Throughout this era, and running to this day, the president has generally taken the initiative, and the Congress has (as it did in the case of the Vandenberg Resolution) often legitimized an executive program.[59]

Leaders of the Congress, and particularly leaders of the foreign affairs committees in both the House and the Senate, have often—

until very recently—viewed their role primarily as carrying out the president's wishes in the foreign policy area. Thomas (Doc) Morgan, long-time chairman of the House Foreign Affairs Committee, stated this view directly: "Under the Constitution, the President is made responsible for the conduct of our foreign relations. . . ." He saw himself as "only the quarterback, not the coach of the team." Moreover, congressional scholar Richard Fenno reports that Chairman Morgan saw his committee, "in *all* matters, as the subordinate partners in a permanent alliance with the executive branch. And as far as he is concerned, the group's blanket, all-purpose decision rule should be: support all executive branch proposals."[60]

Morgan's successor as chairman of the House Foreign Affairs Committee, the late Clement J. Zablocki, despite his activism for congressional reform, still adopted this bipartisan approach. According to committee staff and State Department officials, Congressman Zablocki attempted to work with the executive, generally trying to get the president's program through the committee.[61] At the same time, Zablocki allowed liberal critics ample opportunity to express their views. Further, despite his own moderate-to-conservative beliefs, Zablocki continued to express support—albeit not always enthusiastically—for such congressional initiatives as the nuclear freeze and the ending of covert aid to the Nicaraguan rebels.[62]

Senator J. William Fulbright, chairman of the Senate Foreign Relations Committee for fifteen years, also enunciated this commitment to bipartisanship in foreign affairs—at least until 1965. As Chairman Morgan had done, Senator Fulbright relied upon a football analogy to express this support and deference for the president: "No football team can expect to win with every man his own quarterback. . . . The Foreign Relations Committee is available to advise the President, but his is the primary responsibility."[63] While this bipartisanship by Fulbright and the Senate Foreign Relations Committee waned with the deepening American involvement in Vietnam during the 1960s, the tradition of support for the president by the Committee was not entirely abandoned by subsequent leaders. Nonetheless, by the early 1980s, Senator Charles Percy, former chairman of the Senate Foreign Relations Committee, lamented the "partisan gap" that had developed over foreign policy and renewed the call for bipartisanship "if the United States is to maintain a leadership role in the world."[64]

By the early 1980s, and continuing to the present, any real semblance of policy cooperation between the Congress and the executive had broken down; the congressional leadership was not as willing to follow the lead of the president. Speakers of the House of Representatives, Thomas P. O'Neill, Jr., and James C. Wright, Jr., clashed bitterly with the Reagan administration over Central American policy. The sending of American forces into Lebanon and the exchange of arms for hostages with Iran and transfer of profits to the Nicaraguan contras (the so-called Iran-contra affair) further weakened the notion of congressional support for executive action (see Chapter 5). The establishment of two committees in 1987 to hold hearings on executive decision making during the Iran-contra affair reflects the suspicion with which the Congress held the president's explanation of this whole episode. Throughout these years of confrontation, calls for bipartisanship and for greater executive prerogatives in foreign affairs were never quite quelled by congressional debate over alleged executive abuses.

Sensing the need to renew the foreign policy process between Congress and the executive, President Bush called for the establishment of the "old bipartisanship" in his inaugural address. Some congressional leaders were responsive to this initiative. Proposals were made for increasing consultation between the White House and the Congress by holding monthly meetings to review foreign policy issues, for congressional changes in the foreign aid bill to allow greater presidential flexibility in implementing it, and even for changing the restrictiveness of the War Powers Resolution.[65] While none of these could immediately undo the suspicions of the recent past, these actions indicate that congressional leaders are inclined to defer to presidential leadership on foreign policy.

The chair of the House Foreign Affairs Committee, Dante Fascell, generally applauded this call for bipartisan renewal, but he also wanted the democratic process to work. A moderate Democrat who often found himself in agreement with the Reagan and Bush policies on Central America, Fascell has been described as an effective builder and manager of political coalitions—a fact that should allow him to promote bipartisanship if he so chooses. In his view, "a bipartisan foreign policy does not mean a unilateral decision by the president, rubber-stamped by the Congress." Yet, "if it gets to the point where consensus is asked for and consensus is reached on a specific policy decision, which the president will undertake, then obviously there is a responsibility for the congressional leadership to do what it can to drive that policy." If such a consensus is not reached, though, Fascell favored letting the "democratic process take over."[66]

LEGISLATIVE BEHAVIOR   Although the bipartisanship call by congressional leaders is one indicator of legislative deference to presidential wishes on foreign policy matters, congressional action on executive branch proposals is an even better one. Aaron Wildavsky, in a 1966 article on the presidency, documented the level of congressional support for presidential initiatives and contended that:

> In the realm of foreign policy there has not been a single major issue on which Presidents, when they were serious and determined, have failed. The list of their victories is impressive: entry into the United Nations, the Marshall Plan, NATO, the Truman Doctrine, the decisions to stay out of Indochina in 1954 and to intervene in Vietnam in the 1960s, aid to Poland and Yugoslavia, the test-ban treaty, and many more.[67]

Moreover, Wildavsky goes on to demonstrate that on presidential proposals to the Congress during the 1948 to 1964 period of his study, the president prevailed about 70 percent of the time in defense and foreign policy matters but only 40 percent of the time on domestic matters.[68] Thus, the president not only is successful on foreign policy matters with Congress but is 75 percent more effective on foreign policy matters than on domestic policy matters. In this sense, the Congress has been highly supportive of the president's wishes on issues beyond the water's edge.

Other studies have shown that this extraordinary support for the president's priorities in foreign policy has remained even into the 1970s and beyond, a period sometimes described as producing a congressional "revolution" in foreign affairs. LeLoup and Shull, for instance, demonstrate that congressional approval of presidential foreign policy initiatives remained high for the period of 1965 to 1975, although the average level of support had decreased to about 55 percent, as compared to 70 percent for the 1948 to 1964 period.[69] Similarly, a considerable difference remained between congressional approval of foreign policy versus domestic policy issues advanced by the president (55 percent compared to 46 percent on average). Further, when LeLoup and Shull categorized the domestic policy questions into social welfare, agriculture, government management, natural resources, and civil liberties, presidential proposals in the foreign and defense area still received greater congressional support than any of the other individual issues.[70] Fleisher and Bond, in a study through the first term of the Reagan administration, found that presidential foreign policy success remained substantial in both the House and the Senate through the Reagan administration, although Nixon and Ford did not obtain as much support as did some of the other administrations. Similarly, Carter and Reagan did not do as well in the House as they did in the Senate, compared to earlier presidents.[71]

TABLE 7.3 PRESIDENTIAL VICTORIES ON FOREIGN POLICY VOTES IN THE CONGRESS: FROM TRUMAN TO BUSH

Administration	House		Senate	
Truman	68%	(N = 78)	77%	(N = 110)
Eisenhower	85	(N = 94)	88	(N = 217)
Kennedy	89	(N = 47)	88	(N = 109)
Johnson	86	(N = 111)	81	(N = 231)
Nixon	75	(N = 85)	80	(N = 181)
Ford	59	(N = 46)	76	(N = 106)
Carter	75	(N = 180)	85	(N = 215)
Reagan	64	(N = 275)	84	(N = 325)
Bush (through 1989)	41	(N = 29)	78	(N = 45)

Note: Entries are the percentage of presidential victories on congressional foreign policy votes upon which the president took a position.

Source: Calculated by the author from congressional roll calls made available by the Inter-University Consortium for Political and Social Research. The president's position was based upon *Congressional Quarterly Almanac* (various years) assessments for Eisenhower through Reagan and was determined for Truman by a survey of *Congressional Quarterly Almanac* and presidential papers in collaboration with Eugene R. Wittkopf of Louisiana State University.

In our own calculation of the degree of presidential success from Truman to Bush on foreign policy voting in the Congress, we also found that the recent presidents have been enormously successful in votes on which they took a position. Table 7.3 shows the results of these calculations. Overall, presidential success has been slightly greater, on average, in the Senate than in the House, but both chambers have been supportive of presidential policies. In the Senate, presidents averaged an 82 percent success rate; in the House, they did almost as well at 80 percent. (Both figures exclude the single-year results for the Bush administration.)[72]

In still another study, analyzing the impact of the president on the voting behavior of individual members of Congress, political scientist Aage Clausen found a high degree of congressional deference to the executive's positions on foreign policy issues. In his *How Congressmen Decide*, Clausen reported that legislative voting on "international involvement" issues showed a considerably different pattern than did legislative voting on issues involving agricultural assistance, social welfare, government management, and civil liberties during the years 1953–1964 and 1969–1970. Only on foreign policy questions did "presidential influence" significantly help to explain congressional action in both the House and the Senate. Moreover, this factor did better than region, constituency influence, and party.[73] Here again, then, we find that the role of the president is pivotal in the actions of the Congress, especially as they relate to foreign policy matters.

CHANGING LEGISLATIVE BEHAVIOR?   Foreshadowing our discussion of congressional resurgence in the next chapter, some evidence exists that congressional support for the president on foreign policy matters has waned in recent years. Political scientist Lee Sigelman has shown that when one examines "key votes" the degree of support for the president has declined in recent years, especially since 1973 and especially among the opposition party to the president in power.[74] Moreover, he suggests that despite what Wildavsky and others had contended earlier, the difference in congressional support for presidential initiatives on foreign policy versus domestic policy on key votes was never very great from 1957 to 1972 (74 percent versus 73 percent) and has only slightly widened from 1973 to 1978 (60 percent versus 57 percent).[75] In this sense, the argument about greater congressional support on foreign policy matters than on domestic matters is not demonstrable when key votes are examined. Nonetheless, the support by the Congress for the president's foreign policy agenda even on key votes was still very high at least until 1973.

LeLoup and Shull and our own analyses provide additional evidence that executive success with Congress has weakened somewhat in recent years. LeLoup and Shull demonstrate that the congressional approval of foreign policy initiatives for Nixon and Ford was considerably lower than for the other three presidents in their analysis (Eisenhower, Kennedy, and Johnson).[76] In this sense, the degree of congressional deference to executive proposals began to wane in the 1970s. Table 7.3 shows a similar pattern for recent administrations, too. This weakening of presidential success, however, is confined more to the House than to the Senate. Note that President Ford's success rate was only 59 percent in the House, Carter's higher at 75 percent, but Reagan's at only 64 percent. In the Senate, by contrast, Carter and Reagan are actually at about the same rate as the earlier administrations, although Ford's success rate is a bit lower. Finally, President Bush's success rate is lower in both chambers in comparison to other administrations. His rate is especially low in the House and just a bit below the others in the Senate. Some caution is necessary in concluding too much about the Bush rate, however, since it is based upon only a few votes during his first year in office.

In contrast to Clausen's study noted above, more recent assessments of specific foreign policy issues show that partisanship and ideology are good predictors of congressional behavior. Analyses of congressional voting patterns on the anti-ballistic missile issue in the late 1960s and early 1970s, the Panama Canal Treaties in the late 1970s, the call for a nuclear freeze and the B-1 bomber debate of the 1980s demonstrate that ideology in particular was a potent factor in explaining individual members' votes, seemingly more important than presidential influence.[77]

Finally, Aaron Wildavsky has now acknowledged the substantial change in relations between the Congress and the White House. In a 1989 study, co-authored with Duane Oldfield, Wildavsky now contends that his earlier argument was "time and culture bound." As the public and the political parties have become more ideological, the building of bipartisan support for the president has become much more difficult in the current era. Yet, Oldfield and Wildavsky argue that the president still has other means of exercising his power, much as our survey here suggests.[78] In this sense, the foreign policy debate has become more politicized than in the past.

In the aggregate, then, while we can surely conclude that there has been some change in congressional deference to the executive, overall presidential success remains pronounced. Nonetheless, as we shall demonstrate in Chapter 8, specific areas of foreign policy did elicit changes in congressional procedures in dealing with the executive.

LEGISLATIVE DELEGATION Congress has not only shown this deference by its approval of presidential actions, but it has occasionally gone even further in granting some of its powers to the executive. Most notably, this delegation of its foreign policy powers has occurred in authorizing the president to use armed forces as he sees fit, in affording the president discretion in the distribution of foreign aid, and in implementing trade policy abroad. In effect, these delegations transferred some congressional responsibility to the executive.

This transference of power in the post–World War II period has been most dramatic in the use of armed forces at the president's discretion. In the Formosa Resolution in January 1955, the Congress granted to President Eisenhower the power to use armed forces to defend Quemoy and Matsu from attack by the Chinese communists as well as to protect Formosa and the Pescadores. The language was quite sweeping in its tone: "the President of the United States is authorized to employ the Armed Forces of the United States *as he deems necessary....*"[79]

As we noted in Chapter 2, the Congress also granted to President Eisenhower a broad mandate to deal with the threat of international communism in the Middle East. Popularly called the Eisenhower Doctrine, this congressional resolution granted to the president the right "to use armed forces to assist any such nation or group of nations requesting assistance against armed aggression from any country controlled by international communism" in the Middle East.[80] Once again, what was so remarkable about this resolution was the broad grant of power given to the executive in the warmaking area.

Perhaps the most famous grant of warmaking power by the Congress to the executive was the Gulf of Tonkin Resolution, approved by the House on a vote of 416–0 and in the Senate by 89–2 in August 1964. This resolution granted to the president the right "to take all necessary steps, including the use of armed forces, to assist any member or protocol state of the Southeast Asia Collective Defense Treaty requesting assistance."[81] Moreover, the determination as to when to use these forces was left to the president, but with this prior congressional approval. This resolution was eventually viewed as the "functional equivalent" of a declaration of war by the Johnson administration and was used to expand American involvement in Vietnam and Southeast Asia in the 1960s.[82]

Beyond these rather dramatic examples in the warmaking area, the Congress has had a tendency to grant to the executive considerable discretion in implementing various statutes. In the latest foreign assistance legislation, for example, the president is still afforded latitude in authorizing development assistance "on such terms and conditions as he may determine," in providing economic support funds "on such terms and conditions as he may determine...to promote economic or political stability," and to provide military assistance in a similar fashion that "will strengthen the security of the United States." While this legislation also has imposed considerable restrictions on the executive, considerable residual presidential authority still remains.[83]

In the 1988 trade bill, too, the president's prerogatives were reaffirmed in implementing this legislation. The president was authorized to enter into tariff agreements, both bilaterally and multilaterally. He can also change the U.S. tariff schedules "if the President determines such action to be in the interest of the United States." While the legislation gave more power to the U.S. trade representative in implementing many of the provisions, this representative would still be responsible to the president.[84] In this sense, too, the power of the executive office in this increasingly crucial area remains substantial.

Part of this discretion is understandable in that individual cases might arise that the Congress would not be able to foresee or, alternately, that Congress might not have the time or inclination to handle expeditiously. In this sense, presidential discretion was reasonable, since the presidential responsibility was to execute the law. At the same time, such discretion inevitably has led to a greater concentration of foreign policy power in the hands of the president—usually at the expense of the legislative branch.

THE GROWTH OF EXECUTIVE INSTITUTIONS

A fourth reason for presidential dominance in foreign policy has been the expansion of executive institutions. Since the end of World War II, the foreign policy machinery of the president has grown quite substantially, while the capacity of the Congress has grown only modestly. As a result, presidential control of the foreign policy apparatus and foreign policy information has increased sharply, leaving the Congress at a distinct disadvantage in both areas.

With congressional passage of the National Security Act of 1947, the foreign policy machinery of the executive branch was both consolidated and enlarged.[85] This act provided for the establishment of the National Security Council, the Central Intelligence Agency, and the organization of the separate military forces under the National Military Establishment (later the Department of Defense). In addition, the civilian position of the secretary of defense was mandated to head this National Military Establishment, and the Joint Chiefs of Staff was formally organized by statute to advise the secretary of defense.

All of these new agencies and individuals ultimately were to assist the president with the conduct of foreign policy. The National Security Council, for instance, composed of the president, vice-president, secretary of state, secretary of defense, and others that the president may designate, was "to advise the president with respect to the integration of domestic, foreign, and military policies relating to the national security. . . ."[86] This council to the executive enabled him to make foreign policy with little involvement on the part of the other branches of government, and even without much involvement on the part of the rest of the executive branch. Moreover, as the National Security Council system has evolved—especially with the enhanced role of the national security advisor in more recent administrations—executive control of the foreign policy machinery became firmly entrenched in the office of the president. One indicator of the growth of the National Security Council system is the size of the staffs under each succeeding president in the postwar years.

Under President Truman, for instance, National Security Council personnel numbered twenty in 1951. This total increased to twenty-eight in 1955 under President Eisenhower, grew to fifty in 1962 under President Kennedy, remained at fifty in 1966 under President Johnson, rose to seventy-five under President Nixon, decreased to sixty-four under President Carter in 1979, and again declined to sixty-two in 1982 under President Reagan and to sixty-one in 1990 under President Bush. Thus, while the size of the National Security Council staff has fluctuated over time, it has surely grown from its initial years.[87] More importantly, it has grown in power and influence in the actual formulation of foreign policy within the executive branch (see Chapter 9).

The Central Intelligence Agency was established by the National Security Act for the purpose of developing intelligence estimates and for advising and making recommendations to the National Security Council. The agency also was to assist in coordinating the activities of other intelligence agencies within the U.S. government. Further, the CIA was "to perform such other functions and duties related to intelligence affecting the national security as the National Security Council may from time to time direct."[88] This last function was used as the rationale for "covert actions" by the American government as the CIA developed.

The National Security Act also begat the National Military Establishment in 1947. Under this provision of the act, the Departments of the Army, Navy, and Air Force came into existence, with the secretary of defense heading this overall organizational arrangement. By 1949, amendments to the act created the present Department of Defense to replace the National Military Establishment. Moreover, the secretary of defense, who was the head of this new cabinet department, was required to be a civilian and to be "the principal assistant to the President in all matters relating to the national security."[89]

Finally, the 1947 Act provided for the creation of the Joint Chiefs of Staff. This group would consist of the Army and Air Force chiefs of staff, the chief of naval operations, and the chairman of the Joint Chiefs.[90] Their duties would consist of preparing strategic plans and forces, formulating military policies, and advising the president and the secretary of defense on military matters.

By one congressional act, then, the president was provided with an intelligence advisor (the director of the CIA), a military advisor (the Joint Chiefs of Staff), and a national security advisor (the secre-

tary of defense). In addition, the president was provided with a bureaucratic mechanism for gathering intelligence (the Central Intelligence Agency), for making policy (the National Security Council),
and for carrying out the military options (the National Military Establishment). All of these forums were in addition to the existence of
the Department of State and the secretary of state, traditionally the
principal foreign affairs bureaucracy and its spokesperson.

Later in the postwar period, some additional agencies were established to assist the president, and others assumed a larger role in
foreign policy matters. Three new agencies illustrate how the executive branch continued to gain greater control over various aspects of
foreign policy. In 1961, the Agency for International Development
(AID) was established by Congress to coordinate the distribution of
foreign assistance abroad.[91] In the same year, the Arms Control and
Disarmament Agency (ACDA) was mandated by the Congress to coordinate arms control activities.[92] The director of ACDA was to be the
principal advisor to the president on these foreign policy questions.
In 1963, the Office of the Special Trade Representative was created by
an executive order, and the duties of the individual who would be
U.S. trade representative have been institutionalized and expanded
in subsequent trade acts passed by the Congress.[93] The U.S. trade
representative, for instance, now has the responsibility for directing
all trade negotiations and for formulating trade policy as well. Finally, the other bureaucracies within the executive branch that have
become increasingly involved in international affairs include the Departments of Commerce, Treasury, Agriculture, and Justice, among
others.[94] In short, with all of these agencies in place, the president,
and the executive branch in general, were in a better institutional position to shape foreign policy than its traditional rival, the Congress.

Such structural and hierarchical arrangements have markedly
aided the president and his advisors in gathering information and in
making rapid foreign policy decisions. It is estimated that, at any one
time, over 35,000 people within the executive branch are working on
matters related to foreign policy.[95] With all of these people ultimately
answerable to the president, and with all of these sources of information, centralized and quick decision making can *usually* result.
Thus, the executive can *usually* respond quickly to an international
situation, ranging from the use of military force or negotiating arms
control to the distribution of foreign assistance. As we note in Chapters 9 and 10, however, bureaucratic politics can and does impede the
assumed efficiency of the executive branch. The discerning student
needs to keep this important exception in mind as we discuss the bureaucracies of the executive.

By contrast, the Congress *usually* does not enjoy such advantages, and a number of its bureaucratic, procedural, and informational arrangements have been criticized. Congress is a large and often unwieldy body with 535 members who are sometimes described as parochial, not national or international, in their outlook. As constituency service has become an increasingly important mechanism for political survival, national and foreign policy interests suffer. Congress has a cumbersome bureaucratic system with numerous committees and subcommittees claiming foreign policy responsibilities, thus hindering quick foreign policy decision making. Since the Congress does not enjoy many large, independent information sources on foreign policy matters, it has been often highly dependent upon the executive branch. Further, many complain that the size of congressional staffs has been inadequate to do the necessary background work on foreign policy questions.

While several of these criticisms about Capitol Hill are accurate, since the 1970s others have been and are being addressed by reforms within Congress. Members are becoming more expert on foreign policy, and foreign policy issues can actually work to a member's advantage within a constituency, especially as the boundary between domestic and foreign policy question erode (e.g., agricultural trade policy for a Midwestern member of Congress). Information sources have expanded, too. The General Accounting Office (GAO), an arm of the U.S. Congress, now has a National Security and International Affairs Division with eleven distinct subdivisions to investigate and to provide evaluations to members of the House and the Senate. The Congressional Research Service, a department within the Library of Congress, was expanded under the Legislative Reform Act of 1970 and now has a separate division, the Foreign Affairs and National Defense Division, to work on foreign policy analyses for members of Congress. The Office of Technology Assessment is also a creation of the 1970s and another source of current information on highly specialized topics for the Congress.[96]

INTERNATIONAL SITUATIONAL FACTORS

The final set of factors affects all of the previous ones. Throughout the greater portion of the years since World War II, the United States has made foreign policy within a Cold War environment. Such a perceived dangerous environment had the effect of muting foreign policy debate over long-term goals and, instead, focused on short-term tactics (see Chapter 2). Another consequence, given the dangerous global situation, was a tendency by both the Congress and the

American public to defer to the executive on foreign policy matters. If an emergency arose, the president, not the Congress, could react immediately. If decisions had to be made about the use of force or diplomacy, the president, not the Congress, had to be prepared to act quickly. Furthermore, with the advent of nuclear weapons and instantaneous global communication, centralized control of the foreign policy machinery seemed more necessary than ever.[97]

More generally, the president was often the most admired person among the American people, and this admiration was transferred to trust in his conduct of foreign affairs.[98] As a result, there was a tendency to defer to the executive, with the assumption that the "president knows best."[99]

In the 1970s and 1980s, these assumptions were questioned by both the Congress and the public. After the Watergate episode, the credibility of President Nixon suffered greatly, and President Ford's reputation in turn was hurt by his pardoning of the former president over the Watergate matter. Later on, President Carter's foreign policy capabilities were diminished by his inability to deal effectively with the Iran hostage crisis. In the 1980s, President Reagan had a similar difficulty, at least with regard to his Central American policy. Despite Reagan's overall popularity among the public and several addresses to the American people appealing for their support and that of their representatives in Congress, he was not able to obtain support for his contra aid policy in Central America. Public opinion polls consistently showed opposition to this aspect of his foreign policy throughout his term. Similarly, although President Bush has enjoyed substantial popular support, he has had to fight vigorously with Congress over his policy toward China after the Tiananmen Square massacre of June 1989, had to employ his veto power to stop a restrictive trade policy toward Japan, and had to spar with Congress over his right to conduct American policy unilaterally toward Iraq over its seizure of Kuwait. Further, with the rapidly changing events in Central Europe and the Middle East, and with no evident consensus on what American policy should be in the world, the president is likely to have less automatic support for his foreign policy agenda from the American people or its representatives.

CONCLUDING COMMENTS

Historical precedents and Supreme Court decisions continue to serve as important reservoirs of presidential domination of foreign policymaking. Similarly, the capacity of the executive branch to control the foreign policy bureaucracy and the demands of global events for rapid decision making are usually allies of the president in his remaining preeminent in the making of American foreign policy. While some legislative deference and delegation of power to the executive continues, these sources of executive strength began to change over the last two decades. Increasingly, these have become sources of challenge to presidential power in foreign policy.

In Chapter 8, we shall more fully examine the role of the Congress in foreign policymaking. In particular, we shall focus upon the major areas in which the Congress has tried to reassert its prerogatives and, at the same time, has sought to reduce the degree of executive dominance. After that analysis, we then turn to discuss how to address the inevitable policymaking conflict between these two branches.

NOTES

1. "Excerpts from Baker's Testimony Before Senate Committee," *New York Times,* January 18, 1989, p. 10.
2. Alexander M. Haig, Jr., "Opening Statement at Confirmation Hearings" (Washington, D.C.: Bureau of Public Affairs, Department of State, January 9, 1981), p. 3. Current Policy No. 257.
3. "The MacNeil-Lehrer Report," Public Broadcasting Service, February 10, 1983.
4. See Cecil V. Crabb, Jr., and Pat M. Holt, *Invitation to Struggle: Congress, the President, and Foreign Policy* (Washington, D.C.: Congressional Quarterly Press, 1980), p. 34. Emphasis in original. They cite two earlier studies on this point: "Foreign Affairs and the Articles of Confederation," in Paul A. Varg, *Foreign Policies of the Founding Fathers* (East Lansing, MI: Michigan State University Press, 1963), pp. 46–66; and Albert C. V. Westphal, *The House Committee on Foreign Affairs* (New York: Columbia University Press, 1942), pp. 14–15.
5. See John Locke, *The Second Treatise of Government* (Oxford: Basil Blackwell, 1966), pp. 81–86. The view here is taken from Arthur M. Schlesinger, Jr., *The Imperial Presidency* (Boston: Houghton Mifflin Company, 1973), p. 8, who claims that the Founders were well acquainted with Locke's "Of Prerogative." For a contrary view, see David Gray Adler, "The Constitution and Presidential Warmaking: The Enduring Debate," *Political Science Quarterly* 103 (Spring 1988): 1–36. At p. 32, he argues that: "There is not a scintilla of evidence whatever that the Framers intended to incorporate the Lockean Prerogative in the Constitution." Note, however, that Adler's argument is directed more narrowly to the warmaking power than to the foreign policy prerogatives of the executive in general, as we discuss here.
6. Jacob E. Cooke, ed., *The Federalist* (Middletown, CT: Wesleyan University Press, 1961), p. 472. No. 70 is at pp. 471–480.
7. Louis Henkin, *Foreign Affairs and the Constitution* (Mineola, NY: The Foundation Press, Inc., 1972). The quotations are at pp. 74 and 76.

8. In Federalist No. 69, which can be found in Cooke, ed., *The Federalist,* pp. 462–470.

9. Quoted in Louis Henkin, "Foreign Affairs and the Constitution," *Foreign Affairs* 66 (Winter 1987/88), p. 285, from *Youngstown Sheet & Tube Co. v. Sawyer* (1952).

10. Schlesinger, *The Imperial Presidency,* p. 2.

11. Henkin, "Foreign Affairs and the Constitution," p. 287.

12. Edward S. Corwin, *The President: Office and Powers 1787–1957* (New York: New York University Press, 1957), p. 171.

13. For a brief description of the "pendulum theory" of foreign policy powers between the president and the Congress, see Thomas M. Franck and Edward Weisband, *Foreign Policy by Congress* (New York: Oxford University Press, 1979), pp. 5–6.

14. Henkin, "Foreign Affairs and the Constitution," p. 290.

15. Corwin, *The President,* p. 206.

16. Ibid., p. 182.

17. Henkin, "Foreign Affairs and the Constitution," p. 291.

18. Arthur Schlesinger, Jr., "Congress and the Making of American Foreign Policy," *Foreign Affairs* 51 (October 1972): 82.

19. Quoted in Corwin, *The President,* p. 177.

20. Ibid., p. 188.

21. Schlesinger, "Congress and the Making of American Foreign Policy," pp. 83–87.

22. Johnny H. Killian, ed., *The Constitution of the United States: Analysis and Interpretation* (Washington, D.C.: Congressional Research Service, 1987), p. 338.

23. Schlesinger, "Congress and the Making of American Foreign Policy," p. 86.

24. Corwin, *The President,* p. 229.

25. For a discussion of the *Prize* cases, see *Guide to the U.S. Supreme Court* (Washington, D.C.: Congressional Quarterly, Inc., 1979), pp. 187–189.

26. Schlesinger, "Congress and the Making of American Foreign Policy," pp. 89–91. Also see pp. 91–95 for the interventions mentioned and others executed by presidents without congressional authorization.

27. Francis D. Wormuth, "Presidential Wars: The Convenience of 'Precedent,' " in Martin B. Hickman, ed., *Problems of American Foreign Policy,* 2nd ed. (Beverly Hills, CA: Glencoe Press, 1975), p. 96.

28. Richard M. Nixon, "Cambodia: A Difficult Decision," *Vital Speeches of the Day* 36 (May 15, 1970): 451. This speech was originally delivered to the American public on April 30, 1970.

29. Taken from the "Letter to the Speaker of the House and the President Pro Tempore of the Senate on United States Military Action in Panama," *Weekly Compilation of Presidential Documents,* 25 (December 25, 1989), p. 1985.

30. These two examples are drawn from the testimony of U. Alexis Johnson, under secretary of state for political affairs, and reported in "Department Discusses Agreements on Azores and Bahrain Facilities," *Department of State Bulletin* (February 28, 1972), pp. 279–284. The quoted passage is at p. 282. Johnson did add that the Congress would have to approve the rental payment for the use of the Bahrain facilities.

31. For some evidence illustrating that the bulk of the executive agreements in the postwar period have been pursuant to statute, see Loch Johnson and James M. McCormick, "The Making of International Agreements: "A Reappraisal of Congressional Involvement," *The Journal of Politics* 40 (May 1978): 468–478.

32. The agreement data are from Michael Nelson, ed., *Congressional Quarterly's Guide to the Presidency* (Washington, D.C.: Congressional Quarterly, Inc., 1989), p. 1104. Louis Fisher, *The President and Congress: Power and Policy* (New York: Free Press, 1972), p. 45, reports similar data through 1970.

33. Schlesinger, *The Imperial Presidency*, pp. 86–88.

34. On this point, see "National Commitments," Senate Report 91-129, 91st Cong., 1st Sess., April 16, 1969, p. 26.

35. The series of hearings on American commitments with other countries were held in 1969 and 1970 by a subcommittee of the Committee on Foreign Relations (Subcommittee on United States Security Agreements and Commitments Abroad), chaired by Senator Stuart Symington of Missouri. A summary of these hearings, popularly known as the Symington Subcommittee, is reported in "Security Agreements and Commitments Abroad," Report to the Committee on Foreign Relations of the United States Senate by the Subcommittee on Security Agreements and Commitments Abroad, December 21, 1970.

36. Loch Johnson and James M. McCormick, "Foreign Policy by Executive Fiat," *Foreign Policy* 28 (Fall 1977): 117–138.

37. 299 U.S. 304 (1936).

38. Ibid., p. 314.

39. Ibid., p. 318.

40. Ibid., p. 319, 320. The "extra-constitutional" description below is from Henkins, *Foreign Affairs and the Constitution*, p. 22.

41. See Adler, "The Constitution and Presidential Warmaking: The Enduring Debate," pp. 30–36. See especially his discussion of the steel seizure case and *Reid* v. *Covert* at p. 32 as particular challenges to this broad "extra-constitutional" interpretation of presidential power.

42. 252 U.S. 433.

43. Ibid.

44. Ibid.

45. 301 U.S. 324 (1937) and 315 U.S. 203 (1942).

46. Jean Edward Smith, *The Constitution and American Foreign Policy* (St. Paul: West Publishing Company, 1989), p. 127.

47. 315 U.S. 234 (1942).

48. Henkin, *Foreign Affairs and the Constitution*, p. 185.

49. Warren Christopher, "Ceasefire Between the Branches: A Compact in Foreign Affairs," in James M. McCormick, *A Reader in American Foreign Policy* (Itasca, IL: F. E. Peacock Publishers, Inc., 1986), pp. 253–254.

50. This discussion is gleaned and simplified somewhat from Henkin, *Foreign Affairs and the Constitution*, pp. 210–215. The "political doctrine" question is more complicated than this brief summary conveys and remains a complex issue of constitutional law.

51. See, for example, *Atlee* v. *Richardson* 411 U.S. 911 (1973).

52. The discussion is drawn from *Crockett* v. *Reagan* 720 F. 2d 1355 (1983); *Conyers* v. *Reagan* 765 F. 2d 1124 (1985); and *Lowry* v. *Reagan* 676 F. Supp. 333 (D.D.C. 1987).

53. Neil A. Lewis, "Lawmakers Lose War Powers Suit," *New York Times*, December 14, 1990, p. A9.

54. *Youngstown Sheet and Tube Co.* v. *Sawyer*, 343 U.S. 579 (1952).

55. These details are taken from the *Chadha* decision and from David M. O'Brian, *Constitutional Law and Politics*, vol. 1 (New York: W. W. Norton & Company, 1991), p. 355.

56. Frederick M. Kaiser, "Congressional Control of Executive Actions in the Aftermath of the *Chadha* Decision," *Administrative Law Review* 36 (Summer 1984): 242.

57. These statutes are listed in Appendix I of *INS* v. *Chadha* 462 U.S. 919 (1983).

58. Quoted in Smith, *The Constitution and American Foreign Policy,* from the decision itself at p. 169. The earlier quotation is from Smith's analysis at the same page.

59. On the Vandenberg Resolution, see James A. Robinson, *Congress and Foreign Policy-Making,* rev. ed. (Homewood, IL: The Dorsey Press, 1967), pp. 44–46. Also see Table 2-1 at p. 65, which shows the small degree of congressional initiation in foreign policy and the considerable degree of executive influence within the Congress.

60. Richard F. Fenno, Jr., *Congressmen in Committees* (Boston: Little, Brown & Co., 1973), p. 71.

61. Interview, House Foreign Affairs Committee, Washington, D.C., June 1982, and Department of State, Washington, D.C., October 1981.

62. John Felton, "Foreign Affairs Committee Changes Seen Under Fascell," *Congressional Quarterly Weekly Report* 41 (December 10, 1983): 2622–2623. In fact, Zablocki was the principal sponsor of nuclear freeze resolutions in the House in 1982 and 1983.

63. Fenno, *Congressmen in Committees,* p. 163.

64. Charles H. Percy, "The Partisan Cap," *Foreign Policy* 45 (Winter, 1981–82): p. 15.

65. On the "perpetual crisis in executive-legislative relations" during the Reagan years and on these proposals to improve this situation in the Bush years, see John Felton, "Will Bush-Hill Honeymoon Bring Bipartisanship?" *Congressional Quarterly Weekly Report* (February 18, 1989), pp. 332–337. The quotations are from p. 335.

66. The description of Fascell is taken from Felton, "Foreign Affairs Committee Changes Seen Under Fascell," pp. 2622–2623. Despite Fascell's bipartisan inclination, one should not infer that he would be unwilling to challenge the executive. Fascell led the fight to suspend the testing of new anti-satellite weapons, favored by the Reagan administration, back in 1984. (See "Congressional Leader Urges Suspension of Space-Weapons Tests," *Des Moines Register,* May 21, 1984, p. 4A.)

67. Aaron Wildavsky, "Two Presidencies," *Trans-action* 3 (December 1966): 8.

68. Ibid.

69. Lance T. LeLoup and Steven A. Shull, "Congress Versus the Executive: The 'Two Presidencies' Reconsidered," *Social Science Quarterly* 59 (March 1979): 707.

70. Ibid., pp. 712–713.

71. Richard Fleisher and Jon R. Bond, "Are There Two Presidencies? Yes, But Only for Republicans," *The Journal of Politics* 50 (August 1988): 747–767. Table 1 at p. 754 is the source of these conclusions.

72. These results were calculated from roll call data made available through the Inter-University Consortium of Political and Social Research. (The Consortium bears no responsibility for the analyses and interpretations reported here.) Foreign policy votes were identified for the Eisenhower through Bush years on which the president took a position, based upon *Congressional Quarterly Almanac* assessments, and the president's success or failure was calculated across each

administration. The foreign policy votes for the Truman years were identified from the roll call data, and Truman's position was determined by an assessment of available *CQ Almanacs* and presidential papers. The assistance of Eugene Wittkopf of Louisiana State University in identifying all the foreign policy votes and in determining Truman's position on these particular votes is appreciated. A more detailed discussion of the data collection process is reported in James M. McCormick and Eugene R. Wittkopf, "Bipartisanship, Partisanship, and Ideology in Congressional-Executive Foreign Policy Relations, 1947–1988," *The Journal of Politics* 52 (November 1990): 1077–1100.

73. Aage R. Clausen, *How Congressmen Decide: A Policy Focus* (New York: St. Martin's Press, 1973), pp. 192–212, 222–230. Clausen qualifies this conclusion by stating that presidential influence "appears to be effective only on congressmen of the same party as the president" (p. 209).

74. See Lee Sigelman, "A Reassessment of the Two Presidencies Thesis," *The Journal of Politics* (November 1979), pp. 1195–1205, especially pp. 1200–1201. Drawing upon *Congressional Quarterly,* Sigelman defined a key vote as one involving "a matter of major controversy," "a test of presidential or political power," or "a decision of potentially great impact on the nation and lives of Americans." The number of such votes ranged between 10 and 36 for the years of his study (p. 1199).

75. Ibid., pp. 1200–1201.

76. LeLoup and Shull, "Congress Versus the Executive: The 'Two Presidencies' Reconsidered," p. 710.

77. See Robert A. Bernstein and William Anthony, "The ABM Issue in the Senate, 1968–1970: The Importance of Ideology," *American Political Science Review* 68 (September 1974): 1198–1206; James M. McCormick and Michael Black, "Ideology and Voting on the Panama Canal Treaties," *Legislative Studies Quarterly* 8 (February 1983): 45–63; James M. McCormick, "Congressional Voting on the Nuclear Freeze Resolutions," *American Politics Quarterly* 13 (January 1985): 122–136; Richard Fleisher, "Economic Benefit, Ideology, and Senate Voting on the B-1 Bomber," *American Politics Quarterly* 13 (April 1985): 200–211; and James M. Lindsay, "Parochialism, Policy, and Constituency Constraints: Congressional Voting on Strategic Weapons Systems," *American Journal of Political Science* 34 (November 1990): 939–960.

78. Duane M. Oldfield and Aaron Wildavsky, "Reconsidering the Two Presidencies," *Society* 26 (July/August 1989): 54–59. The quotation is at p. 55.

79. See P.L. 85-7, in *United States Statutes At Large,* vol. 69 (Washington, D.C.: U.S. Government Printing Office, 1955), p. 7. Emphasis added.

80. P.L. 85-7, in *United States Statutes at Large,* vol. 71 (Washington, D.C.: U.S. Government Printing Office, 1958), p. 5.

81. P.L. 88-408.

82. See the testimony by Under Secretary of State Nicholas Katzenbach in "U.S. Commitments to Foreign Powers," *Hearings* before the Committee on Foreign Relations, 90th Cong., 1st Sess., August 16, 17, 21, 23, and September 19, 1967, p. 82.

Two other resolutions were passed by Congress in 1962 "expressing the determination of the United States" to use armed forces if necessary to stop Cuban aggression and to defend Berlin. Neither resolution, however, expressly granted the presidential discretion that the other three resolutions did. See P.L. 87-733 (October 3, 1962) and H. Con. Res. (October 10, 1962).

83. These passages are taken from the Foreign Assistance Act of 1961, as amended, and reported in *Legislation on Foreign Relations Through 1985* (Washington, D.C.: U.S. Government Printing Office, April 1986). The quoted passages are at pp. 32, 141, and 129, respectively.

84. The quoted passage is from P.L. 100-418 at 102 Stat. 1143. A summary of the bill is in *Congressional Quarterly Almanac 1988* (Washington, D.C.: Congressional Quarterly, Inc., 1989), pp. 209–215.

85. P.L. 253, in *United States Statutes At Large*, vol. 61, part 1, 80th Cong., 1st Sess., pp. 495–510.

86. Ibid., p. 496. The membership of the National Security Council has changed slightly over time. This membership represents the current required composition, although the president may invite other members to participate.

87. These data are taken from the Budget of the United States Government for the appropriate years.

88. P.L. 253, p. 498.

89. Ibid., p. 500.

90. The commandant of the Marine Corps was not included in the original makeup of the Joint Chiefs of Staff. Beginning in 1956, he was afforded the opportunity to participate in Marine Corps matters considered by the group. It was not until 1978, however, that the commandant was granted full membership on the Joint Chiefs of Staff. See John Norton Moore and Robert F. Turner, *The Legal Structure of Defense Organization*. Memorandum prepared for the President's Blue Ribbon Commission on Defense Management, January 15, 1986, p. 49.

91. See P.L. 87-194.

92. See P.L. 87-297.

93. *U.S. Government Manual 1989/1990*, July 1, 1989, p. 95.

94. For a discussion of the role of some of these bureaucracies in the foreign policy process, see Chapter 9.

95. Charles W. Kegley, Jr., and Eugene R. Wittkopf, *American Foreign Policy: Pattern and Process*, 3rd ed. (New York: St. Martin's Press, 1987), p. 340.

96. For a discussion of these services for Congress, see *Executive Legislative Consultation on Foreign Policy: Strengthening Foreign Policy Information Sources for Congress* (Washington, D.C.: U.S. Government Printing Office, February 1982), pp. 27–37; Evelyn Howard, *The Congressional Research Service* (Washington, D.C.: Congressional Research Service, August 14, 1989); and General Accounting Office, *National Security and International Affairs Division: Organization and Responsibility* (Washington, D.C.: U.S. Government Printing Office, 1989).

97. Other discussions related to this and other factors described here can be found in Henry T. Nash, *American Foreign Policy: Changing Perspectives on National Security*, rev. ed. (Homewood, IL: The Dorsey Press, 1978), pp. 155–165; and John Spanier and Eric M. Uslaner, *Foreign Policy and the Democratic Dilemmas*, 3rd ed. (New York: Holt, Rinehart and Winston, 1982), pp. 44–67.

98. For some evidence on how admired presidents have been in the postwar period, see John E. Mueller, *War, Presidents and Public Opinion* (New York: John Wiley & Sons, Inc., 1973), pp. 179–195.

99. The phrase is taken from Daniel Yankelovich, "Farewell to 'President Knows Best,' " in William P. Bundy, ed., *America and the World 1978* (New York: Pergamon Press, 1979), pp. 670–693, who discusses this deferential tradition in the American public and its decline in the middle 1970s.

CHAPTER 8 CONGRESSIONAL PREROGATIVES AND THE MAKING OF FOREIGN POLICY

"Congress' role in foreign policy must be recognized, not dismissed, if the benefit of its council is to be realized and if public support is to be secured and maintained. . . . Congress is the partner, not the adversary of the executive branch, in the formulation of policy." **REPORT OF THE CONGRESSIONAL COMMITTEES INVESTIGATING THE IRAN-CONTRA AFFAIR, NOVEMBER 1987**

"Article I, section 8 of the Constitution provides that the Congress clearly has the authority and duty to decide whether the Nation should go to war. . . .It is essential to comply with the Constitution and to commit the nation that Congress give its consent before the President initiates a large-scale military offensive against Iraq. I think the Founding Fathers had a great deal of wisdom when they put this provision in the Constitution." **SENATOR SAM NUNN, DURING THE PERSIAN GULF DEBATE, JANUARY 11, 1991**

The unrest at home over America's involvement in Vietnam, the perceived growth in the foreign policy powers of the president, and the weakening of executive authority as a result of the Watergate incident—all contributed to efforts by the legislative branch to reassert its foreign policy prerogatives in the early 1970s. The Congress achieved some success in placing limitations on the foreign policy powers of the president in four principal ways:

1. Requiring the executive to report all commitments abroad
2. Limiting the war powers of the president
3. Placing restrictions on foreign policy funding
4. Increasing congressional oversight of the executive branch in foreign policymaking

By the early 1990s, several of these limitations had become institutionalized practices between the Congress and the president, but the struggle continues.

In this chapter, we review several of the foreign policy restrictions enacted by the Congress in the 1970s and 1980s, assess how well they have worked in each area, and discuss how they have affected congressional-executive relations in American foreign policymaking.

COMMITMENT MAKING

The first area of congressional resurgence in the 1970s was in executive commitment making. This kind of attempt to rein in executive power was not particularly new, since a similar effort had been undertaken in the 1950s, but it did prove to be more successful than that earlier one. The two efforts differed in several ways: the earlier effort took the form of a proposed constitutional amendment restricting the kind of treaties and executive agreements the president might initiate; the later effort focused upon requiring the president to report to the Congress on commitments already made. The earlier effort was led by congressional conservatives, the later by congressional liberals.

THE BRICKER AMENDMENT

The 1950s effort at curbing the president was motivated by America's increasing global involvement and was led by Senator John Bricker of Ohio. In a series of constitutional amendments, Bricker proposed that any treaty or executive agreement that infringed upon the constitutional rights of American citizens shall be unconstitutional and that the Congress shall have the right to enact appropriate legislation to put into effect any treaty or executive agreement made by the president. Bricker was concerned that the United Nations Treaty and other international agreements might commit the United States to particular domestic actions and, thus, reduce congressional or state prerogatives under the Constitution. Bricker did not want actions to obtain constitutional legitimacy because a treaty or agreement had been agreed to by the president.[1] In effect, then, this amendment was designed to alter the constitutional principle established in *Missouri v. Holland* (Chapter 7), to stop self-executing treaties from occurring, and to ensure a larger congressional role in implementing all treaties and executive agreements domestically.

Several votes were taken in the Senate on these various amendment proposals. All failed. One ballot in 1954, however, came close to passage, failing by only one vote to obtain the necessary two-thirds majority needed to pass such a constitutional amendment in the Senate. Similar proposals were made throughout the mid-1950s, but support waned and President Eisenhower's opposition remained.

THE CASE-ZABLOCKI ACT

With the escalating involvement in Vietnam, primarily through presidential initiative, and with the revelations of secret commitments to a variety of other nations during the 1950s and 1960s, the congressional liberals of the 1970s were prepared to enact some limitations on executive commitments abroad.[2] In June 1969, the Senate passed a "sense of the Senate" resolution stating that the making of national commitments should involve the legislative as well as the executive branch (The National Commitments Resolution).[3] When the executive branch went ahead with executive agreements with Portugal and Bahrain, another "sense of the Senate" resolution was passed stating that agreements with these states for military bases or for foreign assistance should take the form of treaties.[4]

Although these resolutions provided an avenue for venting congressional frustration over executive actions abroad, they were largely symbolic, since they did not legally bind the executive branch to alter its previous policies. Nevertheless, these actions in the late 1960s and early 1970s foreshadowed stronger legislative measures in several different areas over the next few years.

By the middle of 1972, the Congress did pass the first significant piece of legislation in the commitment-making area, the Case-

Zablocki Act, named after Senator Clifford Case (R-New Jersey) and Congressman Clement Zablocki (D-Wisconsin). This law required the executive branch to report all international agreements to the Congress within sixty days of their entering into force. (Classified agreements would be transmitted to the House Foreign Affairs Committee and the Senate Foreign Relations Committee under an injunction of secrecy.[5]) Later, in 1977, this act was amended and strengthened to require that all agreements made by all agencies within the executive branch must be reported to the Department of State within twenty days for ultimate transmittal to the Congress under the provision of the original act.[6]

Even with this reporting arrangement (further strengthened under the Foreign Relations Authorization Act of 1979), the Congress has enjoyed only mixed success in obtaining all agreements in a timely fashion. While a large number of agreements (both public and classified) have been reported to the Congress, the number of late transmittals to the Congress has remained quite substantial. In 1976, for example, 39 percent of all agreements were reported late; by the first half of 1978, the percentage had dropped to 32 percent.[7] By 1981, over 26 percent of all agreements were still transmitted to the Congress beyond the sixty-day period. By 1988, reporting had improved, but one fifth of all agreements were still reported late.[8] Moreover, while some agencies other than the Department of State had contributed to the tardiness of agreements in 1977, the bulk of the late agreements in 1981 had emanated from the department itself. By 1988, both the Department of State and other agencies had contributed about equally to the tardiness in reporting. Table 8.1 provides a summary of the agreements that were reported late in 1981 and 1988.

Late reporting or non-reporting is a concern for Congress not only because it is inconsistent with the procedural requirements of the current legislation, but also because it could affect the substance of policy as well. Although one can readily acknowledge that the late reporting of some executive agreements dealing with administrative details (e.g., water and electricity agreements for American bases in the Philippines) may not be terribly problematic, other executive agreements (e.g., intelligence agreements with other countries) may. The failure of the Congress to know about the latter type of agreements in a timely fashion may well preclude that body from taking any action or even staying current on present policy. Procedurally or substantively, prompt reporting of commitments abroad are necessary in order for Congress to continue to play a role in foreign policy-making.

TABLE 8.1 LATE REPORTING OF INTERNATIONAL AGREEMENTS BY THE EXECUTIVE BRANCH TO THE CONGRESS, 1981 AND 1988

	Number 1981	Number 1988	Percent of Total 1981	Percent of Total 1988
Agreements transmitted to Congress	368	412	100.0%	100.0%
Agreements reported after 60 days	99	79	26.9	19.1
—Late from the Department of State	69	39	18.8	9.5
—Late from other agencies to the Department of State	30	40	8.2	9.7

Source: Constructed from the information provided in *International Agreements,* Communication from the President of the United States, House Document 97-148, 97th Cong., 2nd Sess., February 24, 1982, and *Report on International Agreements Transmitted to the Congress after Expiration of the Sixty-Day Period Specified in the Case-Zablocki Act,* from the House Foreign Affairs Committee for 1988.

BEYOND CASE-ZABLOCKI

While the Case-Zablocki Act was only a reporting requirement, it did signal congressional determination to participate in agreement making. In fact, some members of Congress, not satisfied with just the reporting requirement, sought to go further in strengthening the legislative role in this entire process. Various attempts were made by members of the House and the Senate to give the Congress the right to reject a commitment made by the executive branch within a prescribed period of time (usually sixty days). In the Senate, for example, Senator Sam Ervin (D-North Carolina) introduced several measures that would have allowed both houses to veto any executive agreement within sixty days. Senator John Glenn (D-Ohio) introduced a similar bill that would have allowed only the Senate the right of disapproval of these executive agreements.[9]

Similar measures were introduced in the House. Perhaps the most intriguing and prominent one on this topic was that advanced by Congressman Thomas (Doc) Morgan (D-Pennsylvania), then Chairman of the House Foreign Affairs Committee. He proposed in the Executive Agreements Review Act of 1975 that both houses of Congress have the right of disapproval of executive agreements, but only for those involving "national commitments," mainly those agreements regarding the introduction of American military personnel or providing military training or equipment to another country.[10]

In other words, this legislation attempted to involve the Congress in the review of only "significant" executive agreements and did not burden itself with routine or trivial ties between states. Despite such congressional initiatives through the middle 1970s, none of these proposals became law.

The reform effort that came closest to going beyond the simple reporting of executive agreements was that undertaken by Senator Dick Clark (D-Iowa) on behalf of his Treaty Powers Resolution in 1976 and later. Under this resolution:

> the Senate may...refuse to authorize and appropriate funds to implement those international agreements which, in its opinion, constitute treaties and to which the Senate has not given its advice and consent to ratification.[11]

In other words, the Senate would be able to reject any measure it thought should have been a treaty and, instead, had been done by executive action.

While the Clark resolution was eventually reported out of the Senate Foreign Relations Committee on a tie vote in 1978 after narrowly surviving a vote to delete it, the resolution was replaced on the Senate floor by a weakened substitute measure offered by Senator John Glenn.[12] Nonetheless, the existence of this resolution did set the stage for the passage of some reform procedures between the Congress and the executive that were incorporated into the Foreign Relations Authorization Act for Fiscal Year 1979, passed in October 1978.[13] Under the provisions of this act, the president must now report yearly to the Congress on each agreement that was late (i.e., beyond the sixty-day reporting period) in being transmitted to the Congress; the Secretary of State must now determine what arrangements constitute an international agreement; and oral agreements must now be "reduced to writing."[14] In effect, this act further strengthened the original idea behind the Case-Zablocki Act without necessarily going beyond it.

At the same time, the Department of State worked out an informal arrangement with the Senate Foreign Relations Committee for periodic consultation regarding which international agreements should take the form of treaties. This procedure was arranged through an exchange of letters between the Senate Committee and the Department of State in July 1978, in conjunction with the Senate's consideration of a (non-binding) resolution, formally called the International Agreements Consultation Resolution.[15] This resolution, eventually passed by the Senate in September 1978, explicitly pointed to "agreed procedures with the Secretary of State."[16]

In sum, although the Congress nurtured the beginning of a resurgence in the commitment-making area, it was unwilling to go very far. Except for the informal consultation agreement by the Senate, the Congress did not venture much beyond the reporting mechanism for trying to control agreement making by the executive. More extensive legislative action, however, would be taken in controlling the war powers and the foreign policy purse strings.

WAR POWERS

Frustrated over the use of the commander-in-chief and executive clauses of the Constitution to intervene abroad, the Congress took strong action to limit the warmaking ability of the president. The first important action was the 1970 congressional repeal of the 1964 Gulf of Tonkin Resolution, which had allowed the president a virtual free hand in conducting the Vietnam War.[17] Although the repeal was more symbolic than substantive, the Congress was beginning to assert its role in warmaking. Yet the executive branch still claimed it had the power to continue the war even without the resolution.

Spurred on by the Nixon administration's indifference to the repeal of the Gulf of Tonkin Resolution, the Congress proceeded to work on a proposal that would limit the warmaking powers of the president more generally. The resulting War Powers Resolution, passed over President Nixon's veto in November 1973, remains by far the most significant congressional attempt to reassert its control over committing American forces abroad.[18]

KEY PROVISIONS OF THE WAR POWERS RESOLUTION

This resolution includes several important provisions that require presidential consultation and reporting to Congress on the use of U.S. forces abroad, that limit the time of deployment of such forces, and that provide the Congress a mechanism for withdrawing these forces prior to this time limit. These provisions are worth summarizing in detail.[19]

First, the president is authorized to introduce United States Armed Forces "into hostilities or into situations where imminent involvement in hostilities is clearly indicated by the circumstances" under only three conditions: "(1) a declaration of war, (2) specific statutory authorization, or (3) a national emergency created by attack upon the United States, its territories, or its armed forces." The significance of this provision is that, for the first time, the Congress specified the conditions under which the president could use armed forces. Previously, and excepting a declaration of war, presidential power to use force was more discretionary and ambiguous.

Second, the president "in every possible instance shall consult with Congress" before sending American forces into hostilities or anticipated hostilities and "shall consult regularly with Congress" until those forces have been removed. Put differently, the resolution expected the Congress to be involved in the process from beginning to end.

Third, for those circumstances in which forces are introduced without a declaration of war, the president is required to submit a written report to the Speaker of the House and the president pro tempore of the Senate within forty-eight hours of deploying American forces, explaining the reasons for the introduction of troops, the constitutional and legislative authority for taking such actions, and the "estimated scope and duration of the hostilities or involvement." Further, the president is directed to "report to the Congress periodically on the status of such hostilities or situation as well as on the scope and duration of such hostilities or situation" at least every six months, if troops remain that long.

Fourth, and perhaps its core feature, the resolution places a time limit on how long these forces may be deployed. The resolution specifically authorizes the president to use American forces for no longer than sixty days unless there has been a declaration of war or a specific congressional authorization to continue the use of such forces beyond this period. An extension of thirty days is possible, according to the resolution, if the president certifies that military requirements precluded troop withdrawal within the sixty-day period.

Finally, the congressional resolution includes a provision that allows the Congress to withdraw the troops prior to the expiration of the sixty-day limitation. By passing a concurrent resolution (a resolution in both houses but without presidential approval) by a simple majority, the Congress can specify that the troops be withdrawn from the hostilities immediately. Moreover, the resolution provides time limits on the hearings in committee on such a resolution and requires that a vote must be taken expeditiously. In other words, safeguards were provided so that the concurrent resolution would not become tied up within the Congress without ever reaching a vote.

The clear intent of this war powers legislation was to stop the president from introducing American troops abroad and getting them mired into a conflict without a clear resolution. Put more simply, it was to reduce the possibility of future Vietnams. At the same time, the intent of the resolution was also to reassert the expressed war powers of the Congress under Article I of the Constitution. Despite these combined aims, the resolution would not prevent the president from taking military action if and when necessary; instead, the War Powers Resolution would promote the sharing of responsibility between the executive and legislative branches for dispatching American military personnel abroad.

Despite its obvious legal requirements, the War Powers Resolution also had another important purpose: it served as a political and psychological restraint on presidential warmaking. Under this legislation, the president would have to calculate whether the Congress and the American public would support the sending of American forces to foreign lands. In addition, the president would also have to provide a formal justification for the military action and might well have to submit to formal congressional scrutiny.

PRESIDENTIAL COMPLIANCE

The record of presidential compliance with the requirements of this resolution is at best mixed. Some of the reporting requirements and the time limitation on troop deployments specified in the War Powers Resolution have been adhered to since 1973, but controversy continues to surround the precise situations requiring its applicability, the extent and manner of presidential compliance with all aspects of the resolution, and its overall effectiveness in curbing the expansion of executive power in this area. In addition, the *Chadha* decision on the congressional veto, as noted in Chapter 7, has presumably made the concurrent resolution provision of this law unconstitutional.

Over the last five administrations (through the middle of 1991), twenty-two reports have been forwarded to the Congress in accordance with the procedures of the War Powers Resolution. President Gerald Ford submitted four reports to the Congress under the resolution: one for the evacuation of Vietnam refugees from Da Nang in early April 1975, another for the evacuation from Cambodia in mid-April 1975, a third for the evacuation from Saigon at the end of April 1975, and a fourth over the use of force to free the crew of the *Mayaguez* in May 1975. President Jimmy Carter sent one report in April 1980, after the abortive attempt to rescue the American hostages in Iran.

The most frequent reporting has been done by President Ronald Reagan. Fourteen different reports were sent by President Reagan, including American participation in the Multinational Force and Observers (MFO) in the Sinai Peninsula in accordance with the

Egyptian-Israeli Peace Treaty, the deployment of American forces to Lebanon on two different occasions, the dispatch of two Airborne Warning and Control Systems (AWACS) planes and other aircraft to Sudan, and the deployment of 1,900 members of the U.S. Army and Marines, supplemented with Navy and Air Force personnel to the Caribbean island of Grenada in October 1983.[20] Among other reports sent to the Congress by Reagan were those outlining the use of American military forces in the attack upon Libya in retaliation for a Libyan-sponsored terrorist attack against Americans, the U.S. attack on Iranian vessels in the Persian Gulf, and the U.S. attack upon an Iranian airliner, also in the Persian Gulf.[21]

Up to mid-1991, President Bush had filed three reports to Congress. The first was on the occasion of providing U.S. air patrol support in December 1989 to the Corazon Aquino government in the Philippines to assist her in restoring order and in protecting the lives of U.S. citizens. The second was after his sending of 24,000 American forces to invade Panama and to capture General Manuel Noriega in December 1989. The third was his report to Congress in August 1990 after his ordering of American forces into Saudi Arabia after the seizure of Kuwait by Iraq.[22] Chronology 8.1 summarizes the presidential reporting to the Congress in accordance with the War Powers Resolution.

CONTINUING CONTROVERSIES

Despite these reports, the Congress has been dissatisfied with the kind of executive notification and with the extent of reporting. None of the five presidents since the passage of the War Powers Resolution has fully complied, and each has viewed it as unconstitutional. This reservation about the applicability of the resolution to their foreign policy actions is evidenced by the fact that presidents carefully phrase their reports to the Congress. In virtually every report that the five presidents have sent forward, they have used the same language. They are providing the report "in accordance with my desire that Congress be fully informed on this matter, and consistent with the War Powers Resolution."[23] In no report, however, did the president acknowledge that he was *complying* with the War Powers Resolution. Further, only in his report on the *Mayaguez* incident in 1975 did President Ford cite the operative section [section 4 (a)(1)] of the resolution in his report (and, hence, acknowledge his compliance with the resolution), but only after the military conflict had ceased.[24]

Beyond the kind of reporting, the failure to report some instances has also weakened the comprehensiveness of the resolution.

CHRONOLOGY 8.1 THE WAR POWERS RESOLUTION AND
PRESIDENTIAL REPORTS TO THE CONGRESS

FORD ADMINISTRATION (1974–1977)

April 4, 1975—Evacuation of Americans and other nationals from Da Nang to "safer areas" of Vietnam

April 12, 1975—Evacuation of American personnel and other nationals from Cambodia

April 30, 1975—Evacuation of American personnel and other nationals from Vietnam

May 15, 1975—American military action over the seizure of the American merchant vessel *Mayaguez* by Cambodian forces

CARTER ADMINISTRATION (1977–1981)

April 26, 1980—American military action over the abortive attempt to rescue American hostages in Iran

REAGAN ADMINISTRATION (1981–1989)

March 19, 1982—American military participation in the Multinational Force and Observers in the Sinai Peninsula to implement the peace treaty between Egypt and Israel

August 24, 1982—American military forces to Lebanon to assist in the evacuation of the Palestine Liberation Organization

September 29, 1982—American military forces to Lebanon as part of the Multinational Force

August 8, 1983—Dispatch of AWACS and F-16 aircraft to Sudan for use in coordination with the government of Chad

August 30, 1983—Further report on the American forces in Lebanon, including the deaths of two U.S. Marines

October 25, 1983—Deployment of American military personnel to Grenada

March 26, 1986—U.S. use of missiles against Libyan forces after an attack in the Gulf of Sidra

April 16, 1986—U.S. air and naval strikes upon Libya in response to terrorist activities against Americans

September 23, 1987—U.S. helicopter attack on an Iranian landing craft after it was seen laying mines in the Persian Gulf

October 10, 1987—U.S. helicopter attack on Iranian vessels after being fired upon

---

CHRONOLOGY 8.1 The War Powers Resolution and
Presidential Reports to the Congress (continued)

October 20, 1987—U.S. attack on an Iranian offshore oil platform in the Persian Gulf after an Iranian silkworm missile attack against a U.S.-flagged tanker

April 19, 1988—U.S. destruction of two Iranian offshore oil platforms and an attack on Iranian vessels in the Persian Gulf after the *U.S.S. Samuel B. Roberts* hit a mine laid by Iran

July 4, 1988—After the *U.S.S. Vincennes* and *U.S.S. Elmer Montgomery* fired upon two Iranian vessels in the Persian Gulf and the *Vincennes* shot down an Iranian airliner, believing it to be a military aircraft

July 14, 1988—Following the firing upon two Iranian vessels in the Persian Gulf by American helicopters after an attack

BUSH ADMINISTRATION (1989–   )

December 2, 1989—The use of American combat air patrols in the Philippines to assist the government of Corazon Aquino in restoring order and protecting American lives

December 21, 1989—The deployment of 11,000 U.S. forces to Panama for the purpose of protecting American lives, defending democracy, apprehending Manuel Noriega, and maintaining the Panama Canal Treaties

August 9, 1990—The deployment of American forces to Saudi Arabia to protect that nation after Iraq had seized Kuwait

Source: Compiled by the author from reports in "War Powers Resolution," *Hearings,* Committee on Foreign Relations, United States Senate, 95th Congress, July 13–15, 1977, pp. 332–337; *The War Powers Resolution: Relevant Documents, Correspondence, Reports,* Subcommittee on International Security and Scientific Affairs of the House Committee on Foreign Affairs, December 1983, pp. 40–66, 84–85; Ellen C. Collier, "War Powers Resolution: Presidential Compliance," Congressional Research Service Issue Brief, April 25, 1989, and February 16, 1990; and *Weekly Compilation of Presidential Documents* 25 (December 25, 1989), pp. 1984–1985, and 26 (August 13, 1990), pp. 1225–1226.

President Richard Nixon, for instance, was charged with failure to report to the Congress when U.S. forces were used to evacuate Americans from Cyprus during the ethnic conflict on that island nation in 1974. President Jimmy Carter raised the ire of Representative Paul Findley for his failure to report to the Congress after placing some American forces on alert and for sending U.S. transport aircraft to Zaire during secessionist activities in that country in May 1978.[25]

In the early 1980s, President Reagan became embroiled in controversy with the Congress over the applicability of the War Powers
Resolution in two different areas of the world: Central America and
the Middle East. After President Reagan indicated in early 1981 that
he was going to increase the number of American military advisors
in El Salvador, questions were raised over whether the War Powers
Resolution procedures needed to be invoked. Congressman Clement
Zablocki, chairman of the House Foreign Affairs Committee at the
time, sought clarification from Secretary of State Alexander Haig.[26]

The executive's position was that these U.S. military personnel
were not being introduced into hostilities, nor were they in a situation where "imminent hostilities might occur," as the War Powers
Resolution required. Until such circumstances prevailed, this resolution did not apply.[27] Although the Congress took no further action at
that time, the House of Representatives, as American presence in
Central America was increasing, did pass a measure prohibiting U.S.
military from combat operations in that region. The measure did,
however, contain an important stipulation: it was not meant to infringe upon the president's authority as commander in chief.[28]

American military involvement in Nicaragua and Honduras also
raised questions about the War Powers Resolution. The U.S. government provided support for the Nicaraguan contras against the Sandinista regime, and the U.S. military engaged in joint maneuvers
with the Honduran government.[29] Neither was formally reported under the requirements of the resolution, and both episodes further
muddied the water over what had to be reported to the Congress.

A similar situation arose over the applicability of the War Powers
Resolution to American involvement in Lebanon. President Reagan's
position had been that American forces, first dispatched there in
1982, were on a "peacekeeping mission" at the request of the Lebanese government and that they were not in hostilities or in any immediate danger. By the fall of 1983, however, Congress was unwilling
to accept that position, especially after two Marines were killed on
August 29, 1983. Instead, Congress sought to start the sixty-day
clock under the War Powers Resolution. To head off this time limit on
American forces in Lebanon, President Reagan proceeded to work
out a compromise agreement over the U.S. military presence in Lebanon. The resulting legislation, the Multinational Force in Lebanon
Resolution (October 1983), authorized the president to use American
forces in Lebanon for eighteen months. For the first time, however,
the Congress had specifically imposed the requirements of the War
Powers Resolution upon the president (as of August 29, 1983). Additionally, the legislation attempted to restrict how American forces

would be used. In this sense, congressional participation in the dispatch of American forces was reaffirmed, but "executive flexibility" was preserved.[30]

Even final passage of this compromise was in dispute because both the president and the secretary of state raised doubts over executive adherence to all provisions of the resolution. The crucial issue was the infringement on the commander-in-chief clause of the Constitution. Finally, however, through private presidential assurance, the passage of the resolution was secured. Nonetheless, President Reagan continued to raise doubts about the constitutionality of parts of the legislation even as he signed it.[31]

After President Reagan ordered American troops onto the island of Grenada in October 1983, and after he had sent his report to the Congress, the Senate still proceeded to pass an amendment to a debt ceiling bill declaring that the conditions of the War Powers Resolution became effective on October 25, 1983. Therefore, the troops could not stay there longer than sixty days without specific authorization. A few days later, the House of Representatives passed exactly the same measure.[32] This quick legislative action was intended to demonstrate that the Congress was interested in protecting its prerogatives in the warmaking area and that the president was bound by the War Powers Resolution.

In his second term, President Reagan also failed to report some instances that may be covered by the War Powers Resolution, and President Bush has met with some controversy in this area as well. The Reagan administration, for instance, did not report to the Congress on the U.S. Navy's interception of an Egyptian airliner carrying the hijackers of the *Achille Lauro* in 1985 or on the sending of U.S. Army assistance to the Bolivian government in anti-drug efforts in 1986. More recently, President Bush failed to report to the Congress on sending American military advisors to the Andean countries of Colombia, Bolivia, and Peru as part of a new anti-drug strategy.[33]

The "prior consultation" requirement has caused even greater difficulty between the Congress and the executive branch. Members of Congress have generally held that the president has not really *consulted* with them before using American military forces but has often merely *informed* them of his intended action.[34] The executive branch, however, has contended that it has generally consulted with the Congress and has kept the Congress informed of its actions.

The evidence is at best mixed based upon the limited instances available. President Ford, for example, "advised" members of the congressional leadership on his plans for the evacuation from Southeast Asia in 1975. President Reagan held a meeting with congressional leaders before the actual invasion of Grenada in 1983, but after he had signed the order; and President Reagan also met with congressional leaders after ordering the air strike against Libya in 1986. President Bush met with congressional leaders only seven hours before the invasion of Panama was to begin to inform them of his decision.[35]

In other instances when presidents have chosen not to consult with the Congress, they have defended their actions by pointing to the need for secrecy in carrying out the operation, the limited time available for consultation, and the inherent presidential power to act. When President Jimmy Carter, for instance, was confronted by Congress over his failure to consult prior to the Iran rescue mission in 1980, his legal counsel offered this staunch defense of presidential authority:

> His inherent constitutional power to conduct this kind of rescue operation, which depends on total surprise, includes the power to act before consulting Congress, if the President concludes, as he did in this case, that to do so would unreasonably endanger the success of the operation and the safety of those to be rescued.[36]

In 1989, when President Bush failed to consult the Congress over his use of American aircraft to assist Corazon Aquino's government against an insurrection in the Philippines, his National Security Advisor, Brent Scowcroft, defended his action by stating:

> I can assure you that the President is committed to consultations with Congress prior to deployments of U.S. Forces into actual or imminent hostilities in all instances where such consultations are possible. In this instance, the nature of the rapidly evolving situation required an extremely rapid decision very late at night and consultation was simply not an option.[37]

What remains at issue between the Congress and the president in the consultation area are three crucial questions.[38] First, when should consultation take place? That is, what kind of situations require discussions with Congress? Since the War Powers Resolution does not spell out all such circumstances, ambiguity remains. Second, what actions by the executive constitute consultation? Is informing or meeting with members of Congress on a presidential decision sufficient? Or does the course of action still need to be in doubt for full consultation? Third, with whom should the executive branch consult? Is consultation (in whatever meaning) with the congressional leadership sufficient? Or should only certain foreign policy committees be involved in the process? Congress and the executive have differing views on these items, and they have yet to be resolved.

THE PERSIAN GULF WAR AND THE WAR POWERS RESOLUTION

The Persian Gulf War of 1990–1991 sparked yet another confrontation between the Congress and the president over the War Powers Resolution and, ultimately, the war powers of the Congress. The outcome of this controversy seemed to have enhanced the standing of the Congress in protecting its war powers prerogatives, even as it continued to raise doubts about the applicability and utility of the War Powers Resolution.

As noted above, President Bush sent a report to Congress regarding his August 1990 decision to send American forces to Saudi Arabia to protect that country from further Iraqi aggression after the seizure of Kuwait. He did not acknowledge compliance with the War Powers Resolution, or even its applicability to the situation. Congressional members on Capitol Hill did not object, and they did not take any action to start the sixty-day clock under the War Powers Resolution.

In November 1990, however, when President Bush announced that he was enlarging the American presence in the Persian Gulf to include an "offensive capability" against Iraq, congressional clamor did begin. Several members of Congress complained that the president needed to seek congressional authorization if he contemplated going to war. Calls were heard from both Republicans and Democrats that Congress should come back into a special session after the election to take up this issue. The president denied that any authorization was necessary and, instead, insisted that he had the necessary presidential powers. Some leaders wanted to wait for a presidential request and until the new 102nd Congress was seated in January 1991.[39]

Controversy continued, however. Opinion pieces appeared in elite newspapers challenging the president's interpretation of his powers, and public opinion polls indicated that the president ought to seek congressional support. Fifty-four members of Congress filed a suit in district court claiming that the president needed congressional authorization to use force. Hearings in the House and Senate Armed Services Committees, the Senate Foreign Relations Committee, and the House Foreign Affairs Committee debated the wisdom of continuing sanctions against Iraq versus going to war. To add further fuel to the issue between the Congress and the president was the fact that the Bush administration had asked for—and received—authorization from the United Nations to use force against Iraq, if necessary. UN Security Council Resolution 678, passed on November 29, 1990, authorized member states "to use all necessary means to uphold and implement" the previously passed resolutions calling for Iraq to leave Kuwait after January 15, 1991.[40] Yet no such request was made of the Congress.

Finally, in early January 1991, after he sensed that he would be successful, President Bush changed his mind and requested that authorization from the Congress.[41] After a soul-searching debate in both chambers, the House voted by a margin of 250–183 and the Senate by a margin of 52–47 to grant such authorization. More specifically, the Authorization for Use of Military Force Against Iraq Resolution authorized the president to use U.S. military forces to implement the twelve UN Security Council resolutions that had been passed in 1990 if all diplomatic and peaceful means had been exhausted by the U.S. government. It also made mention of the War Powers Resolution by noting that this Iraq resolution constituted a specific statutory authorization as prescribed in that act and that nothing in the new resolution "supersedes any requirement of the War Powers Resolution."[42] Finally, the resolution required the president to report to Congress every sixty days on whether Iraq was complying with the applicable UN Security Council resolutions. While the resolution did not declare war explicitly, it was the functional equivalent because the president could use force if the stipulation had been met that all diplomatic and peaceful means had been tried.

To proponents of congressional prerogatives in foreign policy, the very act of the president's requesting congressional authorization was significant. It acknowledged the role of the Congress in the use of force abroad and may set a precedent for future American involvements. Further, the president's signing of this authorization with the explicit references to the War Powers Resolution incorporated into it was significant. Since all presidents had denied its constitutionality, President Bush's signing of the Iraqi resolution without challenging this section was a glimmer of hope that the War Powers Resolution may have come to assume some legitimacy. Still, the failure of the War Powers Resolution to be adhered to prior to this showdown between the Congress and the president in January 1991 continued to leave lingering doubts about its legal impact on the war-making power.

REFORMING THE WAR POWERS RESOLUTION

In addition to these continuous controversies and the failure of full compliance by the executive, a more fundamental question about the War Powers Resolution concerns its constitutionality in whole or part. President Nixon, in his veto message in 1973, questioned the constitutionality of that portion of the War Powers Resolution dealing with the withdrawal of troops prior to the sixty-day limitation via a concurrent resolution and the imposition of a sixty-day limit on the use of such troops. In the *Chadha* decision, the Supreme Court seemingly resolved part of this question by invalidating the use of the concurrent resolution or the "legislative veto" by the Congress. Indeed, the Congress acknowledged as much by subsequently passing legislation in late 1983 requiring a joint resolution for any withdrawal of troops prior to the sixty-day period.[43] (A joint resolution requires the approval of a majority of both houses of Congress *and* the president, unlike the concurrent resolution, which requires only congressional action.) The constitutionality of the sixty-day time limit in the War Powers Resolution—often identified by the executive branch as a direct challenge to presidential powers in foreign affairs—has yet to be resolved by the Supreme Court or even to be directly challenged there. Yet this imposition of a time limit remained the major reason for every president since Nixon to question the constitutionality of the entire resolution.

Although some recommendations have been made to change the War Powers Resolution to resolve these concerns, no effort has been successful. Numerous proposals were offered in 1988, for example, and extensive hearings were held in the House and the Senate, sparked by the use of American force in the Persian Gulf in 1987–1988. Some members of Congress proposed the repeal of the resolution, others suggested strengthening the consultation procedures, and still others would have dropped the sixty-day limitation and required an affirmative congressional vote on the use of force by the president.[44] Barring a real constitutional crisis in which the executive fails to comply in any fashion with the resolution, the prospects for reform are slim. Nonetheless, the resolution seems to have served its purpose: it has limited the executive branch's use of military force without involving the Congress in some fashion, it has prevented long-term military involvements by the executive (such as the Vietnam War had been), and it probably has made the president more circumspect and cautious in his foreign military actions than before its 1973 enactment.

CONTROLLING THE PURSE STRINGS

A third area of congressional response has been to use its funding power (the "purse strings") to reduce executive discretion and to increase congressional direction of American foreign policy. Legislative funding provisions were used in the 1970s and 1980s to achieve a number of broad foreign policy objectives: (1) to reduce American military involvement abroad, (2) to cut off covert actions in the Third World, (3) to allow congressional review of the sale of weapons and the transference of nuclear fuels to other countries, (4) to specify the trading relations with other nations, and (5) to limit the transfer of American economic and military assistance to countries with gross violations of human rights. In several instances, specific countries were identified by the Congress and restrictions imposed upon them as a means of shaping foreign policy. Specific human rights restrictions were applied to the transfer of military assistance to El Salvador, for example, and, for a time, the Congress cut off all funding for the Nicaraguan contras as a means of changing the Reagan administration's policy toward that country. Finally, "earmarking" of foreign assistance funds has become a particularly popular mechanism as Congress sought to affect foreign affairs.

CUTTING OFF FUNDS

At one extreme, the Congress sought to eliminate funding for foreign policy actions that it opposed. The Congress, for instance, attempted on several occasions to restrict funding for military activities in Southeast Asia during the late 1960s and early 1970s, but with remarkably little success. During the years 1966 to 1972, for example, the Congress cast ninety-four roll calls on questions relating to American involvement in Southeast Asia.[45] Only a few of these votes succeeded in changing American policy. Senator Frank Church (D-Idaho) was able to get a defense appropriation bill amended to bar the "introduction of U.S. ground combat troops into Laos or Thailand" in 1969, and he, along with Senator John Sherman Cooper (R-Kentucky), was also able to get an amendment passed to bar "U.S. military operations in Cambodia after July 1, 1970." While the House of Representatives in 1969 and 1970 generally agreed to the prohibition on ground combat troops in those countries, it was unwilling to adopt greater restrictions on U.S. activities in that region of the world.

In 1971, Senator Mike Mansfield (D-Montana) was able to get an amendment adopted to stop American involvement after the release of American prisoners of war, but the House rejected it. A similar amendment by Senator Edward W. Brooke (R-Massachusetts) passed the Senate in 1972 only to be deleted by the House in the conference committee. In sum, during the height of American involvement in Vietnam, members of Congress tried, but generally failed, to use the powers of the purse to direct foreign policy.

By 1973, however, the situation had changed. At this juncture, the Congress succeeded in passing a sweeping measure that stopped funding for military activities "in or over or from off the shores of North Vietnam, South Vietnam, Laos, or Cambodia" on or after August 15, 1973."[46] Later, in 1975, when President Ford asked the Congress to approve assistance to Vietnam shortly before its fall, the Congress refused.[47]

At about the same time, the Congress began both to eliminate and to restrict funding as a means of shaping American policy in southern Europe and southern Africa. In 1975, the Congress cut off military and economic aid to Turkey because of its invasion of Cyprus earlier in that year.[48] (In that invasion, Turkey had used American-supplied weapons in violation of statutory requirements that they not be used for offensive purposes.) In 1976, the Congress attached the Clark Amendment to the Arms Export Control Act.[49] This amendment prohibited American assistance to any group involved in the Angolan civil war. The aim of this legislation was to stop American covert assistance to the National Front for the Liberation of Angola and the National Union for the Total Liberation of Angola, who were both fighting the Soviet- and Cuban-backed Popular Movement for the Liberation of Angola.

Congressional restrictions continued in the 1980s. A few illustrations will demonstrate this point. The Congress attached a human rights reporting requirement to the International Security and Development Cooperation Act of 1981 as a condition for continued military assistance to El Salvador.[50] Under the provisions of that law, the executive was required to certify every six months that progress was being made in that country toward improving human rights, continuing social and economic reform, and creating democratic political institutions. These reporting requirements were continued through 1983, when their renewal was pocket vetoed by President Reagan at the end of the congressional session. Although some members of Congress sought legal relief from this pocket veto, the federal court held that President Reagan had acted properly.[51] Nonetheless, subsequent aid legislation for El Salvador imposed a human rights provision. In 1983, the Congress succeeded in placing one further restriction on military aid to El Salvador. Thirty percent of all military aid for fiscal 1984 (about $19.5 million) was to be withheld until those accused of murdering four U.S. churchwomen in December 1980 were brought to trial and a verdict rendered.[52] These funds were subsequently released in May 1984, after the trial was completed.[53]

In the 1990 foreign assistance debate, similar circumstances arose over providing military aid to El Salvador. In the aftermath of the 1989 murder of six priests and two others at a university in that country, the Congress contemplated withholding 30 percent of all such funds to the Salvadoran government. Unlike in 1983, however, it finally opted only for requiring the Bush administration to report on the status of the investigation there.[54]

In another prominent attempt to guide American foreign policy in Central America, the Congress passed a series of Boland Amendments—named after Edward Boland (D-Massachusetts), chair of the House Intelligence Committee at the time—from 1982 to 1986 as a means of restricting or preventing the Reagan administration from aiding the Nicaraguan contras, who were fighting the Sandinista government at the time. Attached to defense appropriation bills and to continuing resolutions for funding the overall operations of the U.S. government, each of the amendments through 1986 became increasingly restrictive in specifying how funds could be used by the executive branch in assisting the contras.

The first Boland Amendment prohibited the use of funds "for the purpose of overthrowing the Government of Nicaragua or provoking a military exchange between Nicaragua and Honduras," and was in effect from December 1982 through September 30, 1983. The second Boland Amendment, passed by the Congress in November 1983, capped the amount of funding at $24 million. Importantly, too, it prohibited the use of any funds "for the purpose of or which would have the effect of supporting, directly or indirectly, military or paramilitary operations in Nicaragua." In the third Boland Amendment, the Congress cut off all funds in October 1984 for military or paramilitary operations. It also included a provision for $14 million in military aid to the contras, but withheld releasing these monies until the 99th Congress acted after February 28, 1985. By that date, the president would need to certify that Nicaragua was threatening its neighbor, and the Congress would have to approve the release of funds.[55]

Although a resolution releasing funds failed to pass the Congress in April 1985, both Houses approved a humanitarian aid package of $27 million in the summer of 1985. Restrictions remained, however, on the use of any aid for military or paramilitary operations. Not until October 1986, moreover, did Congress change its mind on the Boland Amendment and provide $100 million in military and nonmilitary assistance in Central America. As the Iran-contra investigation was to reveal (see Chapter 5), however, violations of the Boland restrictions had already taken place during the two-year period (1984–1986) when no military assistance to the contras was allowed.

EARMARKING OF FUNDS

Congress may also shape foreign policy through earmarking funds for specific purposes. In a real sense, the examples that we have discussed above regarding the use of funds for specific purposes in Central America or southern Africa, or, more accurately, the prohibition on the use of such funds for other purposes in those regions, are "earmarks" by the Congress. Yet, the more common use of the term refers to "specific amounts of foreign aid for individual countries."[56] In the fiscal year 1990 foreign aid bill, for example, $2.8 billion out of $3.2 billion for the Economic Support Fund was earmarked to eleven countries, while nine countries received $4.5 billion out of $4.7 billion in military aid funds. Table 8.2 shows which countries received these earmarked funds. While earmarking has its critics, it is a principal way for Congress to shape foreign policy.

TRADE AND AID REQUIREMENTS

By the 1970s, and continuing into the 1980s, the Congress sought other vehicles to ensure greater legislative participation in U.S. foreign policy. Trade and foreign aid legislation proved to be readily available mechanisms. Increasingly, the Congress sought to add amendments to such legislation in order to work its will in foreign policymaking.

Amendments to four important bills serve to illustrate this kind of action. To the Trade Act of 1974, the Congress added two important sections: the Jackson-Vanik and Stevenson amendments.[57] The Jackson-Vanik Amendment, named after Senator Henry Jackson (D-Washington) and Congressman Charles Vanik (D-Ohio), provided that the United States could grant most-favored-nation status only to those countries that fostered a free emigration policy and did not impose "more than a nominal tax" on citizens wishing to emigrate. Without mentioning any country by name, the clear intent of the amendment was to prohibit the Soviet Union from gaining that status. The action proved successful, as the Soviet Union rejected this

TABLE 8.2   EARMARKED FOREIGN ASSISTANCE FUNDS
IN FISCAL YEAR 1990

	Economic Aid	*Military Aid*
Israel	$1.2 billion	$1.8 billion
Egypt	$815 million	$1.3 billion
Turkey	——	$500 million
Pakistan	$230 million	$230 million
Greece	——	$350 million
Poland	$251 million	——
Philippines	$160 million	——
Jordan	$35 million	$48 million
Morocco	$20 million	$43 million
Sub-Saharan Africa	——	$30 million
Ireland	$20 million	——
Cyprus	$15 million	——
West Bank/Gaza Strip	$12 million	——
Soviet Armenia	$5 million	——

Source: Adapted from "Most Aid Earmarked," *Congressional Quarterly Weekly Report*, January 20, 1990, p. 198.

provision as an intrusion on its national sovereignty. The Stevenson Amendment, sponsored by Senator Adlai Stevenson (D-Illinois), was a more direct affront to the Soviet Union. By limiting the amount of credit available to the Soviet Union from the United States to no more than $300 million this amendment effectively reduced the potential for expanded trade between the two countries. Once again, congressional restrictions were proving very important in shaping American policy, and particularly in the emerging détente relationship between the United States and the Soviet Union.

A second area in which the Congress attached an amendment to afford itself a greater role in foreign policy was the passage of the Nelson-Bingham Amendment to the 1974 Foreign Assistance Act.[58] Under this amendment, introduced by Senator Gaylord Nelson (D-Wisconsin) and Congressman Jonathan Bingham (D-New York), the Congress had the right to review for twenty days any intended arms sale of $25 million or more. Moreover, the Congress reserved the right to reject such a sale by passing a concurrent resolution of disapproval. In the International Security Assistance and Arms Export Control Act of 1976, this provision was modified to allow congressional review of any offer to sell defense articles or services totaling $25 million or more or any major defense equipment of $7 million or more.[59] The time limit for congressional review was extended from twenty to thirty days. The right of the Congress to reject such a sale by concurrent resolution was maintained. By a "gentleman's agreement," in the words of *Congressional Quarterly Almanac*, the Ford administration agreed to an additional twenty-day period of "informal notification"—a policy that was continued by the Carter, Reagan, and Bush administrations.[60]

In the same security assistance legislation (and in earlier legislation on economic assistance), the Congress added human rights considerations in dealing with other states.[61] Neither security assistance nor economic assistance would be granted to any nation whose government "engages in a consistent pattern of gross violations of internationally recognized human rights." Similar provisions were added to U.S. funding for the multilateral banks, such as the World Bank, the Inter-American Development Bank, the African Development Fund, and the Asian Development Bank.[62]

In 1978, the Congress passed the Nuclear Non-Proliferation Act to allow congressional input into this new and important area of trade policy. This act specified a number of important conditions for the transference of nuclear material to other nations: the safeguards established by the International Atomic Energy Agency (IAEA) must be applied to exported material, no exports could be used by the recipient nation to produce nuclear weapons, and the material could not be transferred to another nation without American approval. Furthermore, provisions were included that the U.S. must cease transference to a nation that exploded a nuclear bomb, that did not continue to adhere to IAEA safeguards, and that did not discourage a non-nuclear state from producing a nuclear bomb. In addition, the Congress reserved the right to reject the transference of nuclear fuel to another nation by passing a concurrent resolution of disapproval.[63]

In 1988, the Congress passed the Omnibus Trade and Competitiveness Act and incorporated a stringent trade retaliation provision in the bill known as "Super 301." (The name referred to the section of the trade bill that incorporated these measures.) This provision required the U.S. trade representative to identify countries (with Japan as a principal target) that have employed "a consistent pattern of import barriers and market distorting practices" and to impose sanctions against them if negotiations to remove such practices fail over a year and a half period.[64] Such a provision also indicated the Congress's concern about the direction of U.S. trade policy and its increasing reluctance to leave so much discretion to the president, at least in this one critical area of trade policy. Since its enactment, three countries—Japan, India, and Brazil—have been publicly identified as violating Super 301, and Japan and Brazil were subsequently dropped from the list after some progress in negotiations.[65]

In sum, then, the Congress increasingly uses the funding power and its commerce powers to affect American foreign policy. Moreover, these vehicles will likely remain important ones in the 1990s, and their use will continue to take a variety of forms, such as cutting off funds, earmarking them, or imposing some form of restrictions on use.

CONGRESSIONAL OVERSIGHT

The fourth area of congressional resurgence is in the area of oversight. Oversight refers to the Congress's reviewing and monitoring of executive branch action—in this case, of foreign policy actions. In general, oversight has expanded because Congress now has placed more and more reporting requirements on the executive branch, and congressional committees have increased their review activities as well. In particular, the resurgence in activity by key congressional committees—the Foreign Affairs and Armed Services Committees in the House, the Foreign Relations and Armed Services Committees in the Senate—have contributed to greater foreign policy oversight.[66]

EXPANSION OF REPORTING REQUIREMENTS TO THE CONGRESS

The major mechanism of renewed congressional oversight of foreign policy has been the expansion of reporting requirements placed upon the executive branch. That is, the executive branch must file a written report on how some aspect of American foreign policy was carried out. As we have already noted, important pieces of foreign policy legislation already incorporate this kind of requirement (e.g., the Case-Zablocki Act or the War Powers Resolution), but the extent of such reporting requirements goes beyond these specific instances. At present, approximately 600 foreign policy reporting requirements exist, a threefold increase from the early 1970s. Moreover, these reporting requirements are used "as a tool to oversee executive branch implementation of foreign policy" and are the "workhorses of congressional oversight."[67]

Three main types of reports are required of the executive branch: periodic or recurrent reports, notifications, and one-time reports. The periodic report directs the executive branch to submit particular information to the Congress every year, every six months, or even quarterly.[68] During the 1970s, for example, amendments were added to the Foreign Assistance Act that required an annual assessment of human rights conditions around the world. This report is usually forwarded to the Congress early in each calendar year and is an important source of information on human rights globally. Similarly, the Arms Control and Disarmament Agency must submit an annual report to the Congress on its activities of the previous year. This report "shall include a complete and analytical statement of arms control and disarmament goals, negotiations, and activities and an appraisal of the status and prospects of arms control negotiations and of arms control measures in effect."[69] A third example of these periodic reports by the executive branch is the one on the foreign policies pursued by member countries of the United Nations, required in the State Department authorization legislation. The aim of the report is to assess how these policies comport with the policies and interests of the United States.

A second kind of report is a notification. These reports, by far the most frequent form of reporting, require the executive branch to inform the Congress that a particular foreign policy action is contemplated or has been undertaken. The notifications on executive agreements or on the use of military force fall into this category, but a series of notifications on arms sales, arms control measures, and foreign assistance constitute the bulk of these kinds of reports. Perhaps the most frequent notification occurs with changes in funding levels of foreign assistance toward particular countries. Under current law, the executive branch must notify Congress whenever it "reprograms" economic or military assistance funds in a country from one program or project to another. The number of these economic notifications has been extraordinarily large in recent years. In fiscal year 1984, some 718 notifications were sent to the Congress; in fiscal year 1985, the number rose to 849; and in fiscal year 1986, the total was 744. By contrast, military reprogramming notifications are much less frequent, averaging only about 10 per year. Part of the reason for the lesser number is simply the lesser amount of reprogramming in military aid. Another reason, however, is that reprogramming to several countries may be incorporated into one report.[70]

The third type of report, the one-time report, calls upon the executive branch to examine a particular issue or question. While these reports are probably the most infrequent, they can be very useful in helping the Congress understand an issue or attempt to shape future policy on a question. In the 1986 Anti-Apartheid Act, the Congress called for ten one-time reports. Reports were sought on the degree to which the U.S. depended upon South Africa for minerals, the kind of programs available to help black South Africans, and the efforts that the U.S. undertook to obtain international cooperation to end apartheid.[71]

These differing kinds of reports are, of course, more than informational and more than recordkeeping on the part of the Congress; they also can have a policy effect. The reports alert Congress to changes or potential changes in administration policy and may well set off "fire alarms" in some quarters of the House and the Senate. For instance, reports provided on proposed new arms sales to Arab states or to Israel may elicit reactions from different segments of the Congress. Reports on new covert operations in various corners of the world may have a similar effect. As a result, such proposals are stillborn or change dramatically before enactment by the Congress. On the other hand, even a one-time report can prove to be significant. Because the Department of State is required to report annually on global human rights conditions, members of Congress may be able to use that information in an attempt to impose new strictures on a country or to lift past restrictions. In either case, the reporting was important for the policy process.

THE SENATE FOREIGN RELATIONS COMMITTEE

The Senate Foreign Relations Committee has generally been quite active in the monitoring of the foreign policy actions of the president in the post–World War II period. A principal reason for this activism emanates from the constitutional and oversight responsibilities of the committee itself and from its prestigious position in the Congress. Not only does the Senate Foreign Relations Committee have responsibility for monitoring foreign affairs activities, but it also is required to advise on and consent to treaties and presidential nominations for various diplomatic posts.[72] The committee also has been viewed as the most prestigious in the Senate (and perhaps in the Congress) and provides a ready forum for those members seeking to shape foreign policy and national politics. The committee provides valuable foreign policy experience for those members who entertain presidential ambitions, for instance, and a number of committee members over the years have actively sought the presidential nomination of their party.

A second reason for the active role of the committee has been the quality of leadership at least in the immediate post–World War II period. Particularly prominent among recent committee chairmen was Senator J. William Fulbright (D-Arkansas). His penetrating hearings on American involvement in Vietnam contributed significantly to the national debate on that issue and to America's eventual withdrawal from Vietnam.[73] Further, his active involvement in the numerous reform efforts by the Congress in the late 1960s and early 1970s assured the committee's prominence in the shaping of the nation's foreign policy.

The subsequent chairmen in the 1970s and 1980s, however, did not attain the same stature as Fulbright, and the prestige and activism of the Senate Foreign Relations Committee began to wane.[74] Senators John Sparkman (D-Alabama) and Frank Church (D-Idaho) led the committee only for short periods in the 1970s, but the committee already demonstrated signs of a decline in its role from the earlier decades. Under the leadership of Senator Charles Percy (R-Illinois) from 1981 to 1984, the committee continued in this same vein. Senator Percy was largely supportive of the policies of the Reagan administration as he led the committee, although he placed arms control higher on his list of priorities than the administration had. Yet he faced a committee deeply divided between left and right, and effective consensus and decision making on the committee became difficult. On balance, then, he had little more success than his immediate predecessors in reestablishing the prominence of the Senate Foreign Relations Committee.

His successor, Senator Richard Lugar, a conservative Republican from Indiana, initially indicated his support for the administration, too ("I think it is fair to say that I share the basic assumptions of the President and the Secretary of State in regard to foreign policy."[75]), but he also announced his intention to begin committee hearings on a general review of American foreign policy. Such a review was much in keeping with the more activist role of this committee. Indeed, Lugar was credited with leading the committee effectively "by charting a course and sticking with it, working behind the scenes to build consensus through compromise and patient prodding."[76] As a consequence, the committee was able to exert influence on several issues, including passage of South African sanctions and the ouster of Ferdinand Marcos in the Philippines.

The Democrats regained control of the committee after the 1986 election, and Senator Claiborne Pell (D-Rhode Island) moved up to the chairmanship. Although a competent and respected member of the Senate, Pell has not been particularly outspoken or assertive in running the committee. Committee initiatives lately have been scarce, and it has been dominated with intra-committee quarrels of the right and the left. As a result, visibility of the Senate Foreign Relations Committee has declined under his leadership and, by one analysis, "is even beginning to suffer by comparison with the House Foreign Affairs Committee."[77]

THE HOUSE FOREIGN AFFAIRS COMMITTEE

The House of Representatives, by contrast, did not have a foreign policy committee with a similar reputation. The Committee on Foreign Affairs (called the Committee on International Relations in the middle 1970s) was seen as less prestigious than the Senate Foreign Relations Committee and some other committees in the House.[78] Unlike the other House committees, too, Foreign Affairs was less likely to directly assist the constituency or biennial reelection goals of a member of the House. It was also less prominent than the Senate Foreign Relations Committee as a springboard to national prominence on foreign policy matters. Furthermore, the House Committee on Foreign Affairs had a rather limited agenda, confined mainly to the preparation of the foreign assistance bill, and lacked the wide sweep of responsibilities that the Senate Foreign Relations Committee had.[79]

By the 1970s, however, the House Foreign Affairs Committee underwent a series of changes that produced a considerable resurgence of activity. The oversight function increased rather sharply as a result. As congressional analyst Fred Kaiser reports in a 1973 survey ranking committees by the number of oversight hearings and meetings, the House Foreign Affairs Committee ranked third behind Appropriations and Government Operations, and it was more than three times as active in oversight as the average of all committees in the lower chamber. Further, an analyst with the Congressional Research Service (CRS) is quoted by Kaiser as saying that "International Relations [House Foreign Affairs] and Foreign Relations use the Foreign Affairs Division significantly more than any other committees use any other CRS Division."[80] This view was also confirmed in a Congressional Research Report that demonstrated that the total amount of research time spent by CRS for the House Foreign Affairs

Committee was greater than for any other committee in the Congress. Finally, Kaiser documents the increase in the use of field investigations, the GAO, and what he calls "Extra-Committee Oversight Activities" by House Foreign Affairs.[81]

This newfound zeal for oversight derives from the changing composition of the committee, the structural changes in the committee system within the House of Representatives, and a resurgent interest in foreign policy matters.[82] In the 1970s, the committee increasingly was composed of younger, more liberal members of the House, who viewed foreign policy matters as an important part of their legislative activities. Often elected in opposition to the Vietnam War, these new members were more determined than ever to make American foreign policy accountable to the House. Moreover, this trend of the committee being more liberal than the House as a whole continues to the present day.[83]

Structural reforms within the House have also assisted the oversight process. In an effort to open up the congressional process, limitations were placed on the authority of the committee chairs in the appointment of subcommittee chairs (they were now elected by the committee caucus) and in the number of subcommittees that any member could chair (the number was limited to one).[84] As a result, more liberal members of the committee emerged as subcommittee chairs. In addition, because of some jurisdictional changes, the House Foreign Affairs Committee (and consequently its subcommittees) gained more review power over international economic issues.[85] One manifestation of this enlarged agenda was a change from primarily regional subcommittees to functional ones for a brief time. Although the committee eventually settled on a combination of functional and regional subcommittees, the pattern of increased responsibility was set in motion.[86]

Another congressional reform of the 1970s also aided the House Foreign Affairs Committee. The committee and subcommittee staffs were enlarged and placed formally under the chairs of the particular committees or subcommittees. While these changes regarding the subcommittee chair's control of his or her staff were already in place on this committee, the rule changes in the House formalized them, and the subcommittee staffs grew.[87] One important consequence of these changes has been the significant increase in committee and subcommittee hearings by Foreign Affairs. While these hearings are both oversight and legislative in nature, the sheer volume increase conveys the increase in attentiveness by this committee to its foreign policy responsibilities. As Table 8.3 shows, the number of hearings by the Foreign Affairs Committee has grown dramatically since the

TABLE 8.3 COMMITTEE AND SUBCOMMITTEE HEARINGS OF THE HOUSE FOREIGN AFFAIRS COMMITTEE, 80TH–99TH CONGRESSES

Congress	Committee Hearings	Subcommittee Hearings	Totals
80th (1947–1948)	218	45	263
81st (1949–1950)	250	46	296
82nd (1951–1952)	160	100	260
83rd (1953–1954)	159	122	281
84th (1955–1956)	164	60	224
85th (1957–1958)	158	123	281
86th (1959–1960)	141	170	311
87th (1961–1962)	151	139	290
88th (1963–1964)	135	187	322
89th (1965–1966)	120	243	363
90th (1967–1968)	127	191	318
91st (1969–1970)	91	267	358
92nd (1971–1972)	76	251	327
93rd (1973–1974)	97	198	295
94th (1975–1976)	143	355	498
95th (1977–1978)	218	560	778
96th (1979–1980)	240	531	771
97th (1981–1982)	240	462	702
98th (1983–1984)	210	398	608
99th (1985–1986)	241	377	618

Source: Committee on Foreign Affairs, *Survey of Activities*, 97th Cong. (Washington, D.C.: U.S. Government Printing Office, 1983), pp. 263–264, and *Survey of Activities*, 99th Cong. (Washington, D.C.: U.S. Government Printing Office, 1987), p. 253.

94th Congress and remained high throughout the years of the Reagan administration.

Thus, the House Foreign Affairs Committee has played a larger role in both the formulation and review of American foreign policy since the 1970s. Moreover, that role is likely to continue, as evidenced by recent committee action. Some of its members, such as Lee Hamilton (D-Indiana), Sam Gejdenson (D-Connecticut), Michael Barnes (D-Maryland), and Stephen Solarz (D-New York) were outspoken in criticizing the Reagan administration's defense and Central American policies, proved to be key players in the Iran-contra investigation, and played a key role in monitoring Middle East policy development as well. Under the Bush administration, the activism of the committee has not abated. The whole committee and its subcommittees continue to be active participants in the oversight process, matching and perhaps even surpassing its Senate counter-part, as noted above. Indeed, the House Foreign Affairs Committee continues to exercise a more independent and influential role in the monitoring and shaping of foreign policy than at any time during its postwar history.

THE ARMED SERVICES COMMITTEES

The House and Senate Armed Services committees have also en-joyed a bit of a renaissance in their foreign policy oversight activities in recent years. Throughout the 1950s and 1960s, both committees were often regarded as committees largely supportive of the Penta-gon's point of view on policy matters. One study focusing on data to 1970 found that these committees relied upon the Department of De-fense for its information about military matters and "usually ratified administration proposals." Another analysis described their role up to the early 1970s as both an "advocate" and as an "overseer," with the House Armed Services Committee less of an overseer and more of an advocate than the Senate Armed Services Committee.[88]

Much of what we described as happening with the House For-eign Affairs Committee has also happened with the Armed Services committees. With the changes in rules in the Congress, the leader-ship, and congressional procedures in the 1970s, the extent of legisla-tive oversight of defense policy changed as well, albeit modestly at first. By the 1980s, the activities increased even more with the emer-gence of what one political scientist has called the "outside game" in defense policymaking.[89] Because the Congress as a whole was in-creasingly more interested in scrutinizing defense policy, the com-mittees had to examine legislative policy more carefully as well if they were to retain any legitimacy. While this did happen, one con-cern is that the committees' responsibilities will be eroded with con-tinued Congress-wide involvement.

Both Armed Services committees have also benefited from more assertive leadership. In the House, Les Aspin (D-Wisconsin) gained the chairmanship of the Armed Services Committee by leaping over other members with greater seniority and by offering a policy pos-ture that tended to be more critical of Pentagon requests than that of previous leaders. In the Senate, Sam Nunn (D-Georgia), a moderate-to-conservative southerner, has not automatically proven to be a sup-porter of the military. He, too, has demonstrated a willingness to challenge the Department of Defense with his own defense plans.

Two recent episodes reveal the enhanced power of the Armed Services committees and their chairs in the U.S. Congress, especially in comparison to the foreign policy committees in both chambers. The first centered on the debate over the interpretation of the ABM Treaty during the funding for the Strategic Defense Initiative ("Star Wars") in 1987. Even though the Foreign Relations Committee held hearings on this matter, it was Senator Sam Nunn who proved particularly prominent in challenging the Reagan administration's new interpretation of the treaty. Under that interpretation, tests would be allowed for "space-based anti-missile weapons without violating the treaty."[90] In a series of dramatic speeches on the Senate floor in March 1987, however, Senator Nunn successfully challenged that view and succeeded in convincing the Congress to limit the testing of SDI in a way consistent with the traditional interpretation of the ABM Treaty.

The second prominent episode was over Operation Desert Shield, the Bush administration's action to protect Saudi Arabia and other Gulf states from Iraq in late 1990 and early 1991. In a series of dramatic hearings in November 1990, the Senate Armed Services Committee challenged administration policy on proceeding too quickly to war. Moreover, a number of prominent former government officials called for the continuance of economic sanctions rather than moving toward the military option. While the Senate Foreign Relations Committee also held hearings, its work paled in significance to that of the Senate Armed Services Committee. In the House, too, the Armed Services Committee, led by Congressman Aspin, had more sustained hearings on this operation than did the House Foreign Affairs Committee. In this House committee, though, the sentiment of the committee appeared more supportive of the administration's policy than in the Senate chamber.

In short, as these policy episodes illustrate, and with the end of the Cold War, these individuals and the members of the two Armed Services committees will increasingly play a more active role in attempting to shape defense policy. They no longer can be expected to be merely reflective of the Pentagon's wishes.

CONGRESSIONAL CHANGE AND FUTURE FOREIGN POLICYMAKING

Has the congressional resurgence initiated in the 1970s produced a permanent change in the foreign policy relationship between the Congress and the executive than had developed in the immediate postwar period? Congressional-executive scholars Thomas Franck, Edward Weisband, and I. M. Destler believe so.[91] They point to the structural and procedural arrangements that the Congress now has put in place for dealing with foreign policy, the various pieces of legislation giving Congress more political clout, the larger foreign policy staffs on Capitol Hill and constituencies among the American public, and the adjustments that the executive has made in his relationship with Congress (albeit, perhaps, grudgingly). All these point to a changed congressional-executive relationship in foreign policy by the late 1970s and the early 1980s.

The evidence from the rest of the 1980s and the early 1990s does not alter this view. The Reagan administration was locked in heated policy battles with the Congress on several foreign policy fronts during its time in office. Most prominent, of course, was the six-year struggle with the Congress over the funding of the Nicaraguan contras. Indeed, the Iran-contra affair was a direct result of the policy restrictions imposed by the Congress. The Reagan administration also fought with Congress over its reinterpretation of the Anti-Ballistic Missile (ABM) Treaty as it sought to proceed with the Strategic Defense Initiative, the reflagging of Kuwaiti vessels in the Persian Gulf and congressional war powers, the imposition of economic sanctions on South Africa over its apartheid policy, and the congressional initiatives on international trade policy, among others.[92] These debates were substantive in content, with the Congress concerned over the precise policy the executive was proposing, but they were also procedural, with the Congress concerned about the manner in which policy was formulated.

The Bush administration, too, has sparred with the Congress over both substance and procedure in foreign policymaking. Despite a call for a renewal of the "old bipartisanship," President Bush used his veto power four times in his first year to alter foreign policy legislation with which he did not agree—an extraordinarily high usage of the veto on foreign policy legislation in such a short time. He felt compelled to veto a bill that placed trade restrictions on the joint development of a jet fighter with the Japanese; foreign aid legislation with funding for a UN family-planning agency; a State Department authorization bill that included an amendment imposing criminal penalties on administration officials who sought to support, even indirectly, foreign policy goals inconsistent with U.S. law; and legislation that would have enabled Chinese students to remain in the country after their visas had expired.[93] In all instances, President Bush was successful, but this rancor indicated the continuing intensity of the congressional-executive rivalry in foreign affairs.

Such conflict has been lamented by a number of high officials, and they point to the difficulties of conducting foreign policy with the Congress constantly intruding on, or at least limiting, the president's freedom of action. A principal complaint, for instance, is that coherent foreign policy cannot result with this continuous struggle between Congress and the president. This view was most forcefully expressed recently not by a member of the executive branch, but by a former member of the Senate, John Tower of Texas: "Five hundred and thirty-five Congressmen with different philosophies, regional interests and objectives in mind cannot forge a unified foreign policy that reflects the interests of the United States as a whole."[94] A former member of the House Foreign Affairs Committee, Charles Whalen of Ohio, expressed similar reservations about the new assertiveness of the Congress, and particularly the House. He argued that the legislative branch may have gone too far in its zeal for reform.[95] Both Tower and Whalen argued for repeal of some of these "reforms" to make foreign policymaking more effective.

As he was about to leave office, President Reagan also complained bitterly about the micromangement of U.S. foreign policy through the use of "the blunt instrument of legislation."[96] He criticized the trade policy that the Congress enacted, its passage of restrictions on intelligence activities, its earmarking of foreign assistance, and its efforts to regulate arms sales abroad. In essence, the charge was that the Congress had gone beyond its appropriate role and that it had reduced the president's flexibility in the conduct of U.S. foreign policy.

CONGRESSIONAL REFORM AND POLICY IMPACT

A key question, of course, is how disruptive congressional actions have been to presidential attempts at guiding foreign policy. More generally, have these reforms been particularly debilitating to American foreign policy, and are the reforms worth the foreign policy costs that have been incurred?

For several reasons, the substantive impact of the various reforms on American foreign policy have been much less widespread than might be anticipated by only examining the original legislation. First, the measures have been used relatively infrequently. Despite the arms sales review procedures, for instance, no arms deal has actually been denied the executive branch since 1974, although the composition and timing of other deals may have been altered. The one arms deal that came closest to rejection was the AWACS sale to Saudi Arabia in October 1981. After an overwhelming vote disapproving the sale in the House (301–111), the Senate failed to disapprove the sale by a close vote, 48–52.[97] The human rights requirements did not markedly change the economic or security assistance policies of the subsequent administrations, although they did result in the cutting off of aid to a few nations (e.g., Argentina, Chile) and the rejection of aid by some others (e.g., Brazil). When necessary, legislative loopholes were often found for strategically important states. In the 1970s, for example, exceptions were made for Iran, South Korea, and the Philippines. In the 1980s, El Salvador and Pakistan continued to receive large amounts of aid despite sordid human rights records. Finally, the Congress has not used some powers granted to it under the Nuclear Non-Proliferation Act. In 1980, for example, it had the opportunity to stop the transference of nuclear fuel to a country (India) that had exploded a nuclear device, but it failed to do so. The House passed a resolution disapproving of this sale by a vote of 298 to 98, but the Senate, by a vote of 46–48, rejected the resolution.[98]

The apparent weak public record should not be pushed too far, however. Some significant actions have been taken by the Congress to stop executive action, and some administrations have been dissuaded from pursuing some policy options because of evident congressional opposition. In the first category, the Jackson-Vanik and Stevenson amendments and the cutoff in military aid to the Nicaraguan contras stand out. Both amendments had an impact on trade and détente relations with the Soviet Union, and the Jackson-Vanik Amendment continues to be a source of discussion in Soviet-American relations to this day. The cutoff of contra aid was not completed through any new authority granted to the Congress; rather it was enacted through the regular appropriation process. Nonetheless, it is reasonable to argue that the Congress was emboldened to challenge the executive more vigorously because of the new executive-legislative environment. In the second category, at least proposed arms deals with Jordan had to be withdrawn in the period from 1983 to 1985 because of congressional opposition, and apparently some covert operations were abandoned because of votes of opposition within the congressional intelligence committees.[99] In this sense, the presence of new procedures, even if the Congress did not formally stop an action, had a tangible effect on policy.

A second factor that weakens this newly legislated congressional authority in foreign affairs is that much of this legislation has "escape clauses" for the president. If, for example, the president certifies that an arms sale must go forward for national security reasons, the president may proceed despite a congressional rejection. In 1984, this waiver procedure was invoked—even though the Congress had not acted—for the purpose of sending 400 Stinger anti-aircraft missiles to Saudi Arabia during the escalating war between Iran and Iraq.[100] The most-favored-nation requirement in the Trade Act of 1974 also has an escape clause allowing the president the right to grant such a status if he so wishes. Indeed, this clause has been used since 1980 to grant such status to the People's Republic of China. The human rights requirements in the economic assistance legislation also can be waived if the executive branch certifies that the aid will reach "needy people" in the recipient nation "and if either house of Congress didn't approve the waiver within thirty days."[101] Finally, the 1988 Trade Act allows the president to waive retaliation against trading partners engaging in unfair practices by citing national security or national economic conditions, although obstacles exist to using such a waiver.[102]

A third reason for the limited impact of these congressional reforms focuses on the legislative veto, declared unconstitutional by the Supreme Court in *Immigration and Naturalization Service* v. *Chadha*.[103] Several of the important congressional reforms in foreign policymaking—the War Powers Resolution, the arms sales amendment, and the Nuclear Non-Proliferation Act—incorporate this veto provision. While the removal of this veto power does not wholly paralyze congressional participation in any of these areas, it does make it more difficult to halt presidential action quickly. The president would still be restricted to sending troops abroad for sixty days, for example, but, as noted earlier, the Congress could not remove them before this time period without a joint resolution. In effect, then, this kind of legislation would require a two-thirds majority to override an expected presidential veto, not just a simple majority under the concurrent resolution procedure.

Similar difficulties would confront efforts at stopping an arms sale, halting the sale of nuclear fuel, or cutting off aid on human rights grounds. What has occurred is that the procedures for reporting an arms sales, for instance, have continued, but now a joint resolution would be needed to stop a sale that the Congress did not support. In short, the elimination of the legislative veto has meant a weakening of the foreign policy capability of the Congress in the short run, but the reporting and review mechanisms still remain available.

A fourth factor also reduces the substantive effect of the congressional reforms of the 1970s and the 1980s. Despite the Congress's desire to assert its role in foreign affairs, it still perceives limits as to how far it should go in restricting the executive. Many members of Congress still rely upon the president for the initiation and the execution of foreign policy. What the Congress seeks is to be involved in the formulation of policy (in conjuction with the president), with the implementation of policy left to the executive branch. At the same time, according to foreign policy staff, Congress is unlikely to turn back to an earlier era of congressional acquiescence, but is is equally unlikely to pass many restrictions on presidential power.[104] Instead, Congress will remain alert to exercise its prerogatives in foreign affairs without seeking to direct international matters unilaterally.

CONCLUDING COMMENTS

As Chapters 7 and 8 have emphasized, the Congress and the president share foreign policymaking powers under the Constitution, and hence foreign policy is likely to remain a "contest" between them for the foreseeable future. Neither side is likely to yield its foreign policy prerogatives, not is any structural change ultimately going to alter the inherent constitutional dilemma between these two branches. Instead, as Arthur Schlesinger, Jr., correctly noted some years ago, the problem is "primarily political,"[105] and will undoubtedly require efforts at cooperative solutions in procedural, rather than legislative, remedies. Greater consultation and institutional respect for the role of the other seem the best prescription for dealing with the continuing debate between the president and the Congress. Indeed, a recent proposal for a "new compact" between the branches emphasizes both of these dimensions rather than any new legislation.[106]

While these two institutions are the preeminent actors in foreign policymaking, they are not the only ones involved in the process. Within the executive branch in particular, several important foreign policy bureaucracies—the Department of State, the Department of Defense, the National Safety Council, the intelligence community, and several economic bureaucracies—can and do affect the formulation of American foreign policy. The next two chapters analyze these key bureaucracies and begin to offer a more complete picture of the foreign policy process.

NOTES

1. See Michael Nelson, ed., *Congressional Quarterly's Guide to the Presidency* (Washington, D.C.: Congressional Quarterly, Inc., 1989), pp. 512–513; and *Congressional Quarterly's Guide to Congress*, 3rd ed. (Washington, D.C.: Congressional Quarterly, Inc., 1982), pp. 303–304.

2. See "Security Agreements and Commitments Abroad," Report to the Committee on Foreign Relations of the United States Senate by the Subcommittee on Security Agreements and Commitments Abroad, December 21, 1970.

3. The text of the resolution can be found in the *Congressional Record*, 91st Cong., 1st Sess., June 25, 1969, p. 17245.

4. The text of the amended resolution can be found in "Agreements with Portugal and Bahrain," Senate Report No. 92-632, 92nd Cong., 2nd Sess., February 17, 1972, p. 1.

5. See P.L. 92-403.

6. See section 5 of P.L. 95-45 for the text of the amendment offered by Senator Clifford Case.

7. The data are from Report of the Comptroller General of the United States, "Reporting of U.S. International Agreements by Executive Agencies Has Improved," Report 1D-78-57, October 31, 1978, p. 22.

8. The late reporting by agencies in 1977 is given in ibid., p. 23, while the data for 1981 were derived from "International Agreements," Communication from the President of the United States, February 24, 1982, House Document 97-148, 97th Cong., 2nd Sess., pp. 1–12. This report was furnished by the executive in accordance with the requirements of the Foreign Relations Authorization Act, Fiscal Year 1979. The information for 1988 was taken from *Report on International Agreements Transmitted to the Congress After Expiration of the Sixty-Day Period Specified in the Case-Zablocki Act*, which was provided by the House Foreign Affairs Committee.

9. For a brief review of the Ervin bill, see Marjorie Ann Browne, *Executive Agreements and the Congress*, Issue Brief Number 1B75035 (Washington, D.C.: Congressional Research Service, The Library of Congress, 1981), p. 7. The Glenn bill was S. 1251, 94th Cong., 1st Sess., introduced on March 20, 1975.

10. See H.R. 4439, 94th Cong., 1st Sess., introduced on March 6, 1975.

11. The section of the Treaty Powers Resolution (S. Res. 434) quoted is from the *Congressional Record*, 94th Cong., 2nd Sess., April 14, 1976, p. 10967. Also see a later version of the Treaty Powers Resolution (5. Res. 24), in the *Congressional Record*, 95th Cong., 1st Sess., January 10, 1977, p. 696.

12. See "Foreign Relations Authorization Act, Fiscal Year 1979," Senate Report 95-842, 95th Cong., 2nd Sess., May 15, 1978, pp. 50–55. The Committee vote is discussed at p. 3. For action on the floor, see *Congressional Quarterly Almanac 1978* (Washington, D.C.: Congressional Quarterly, Inc., 1979), p. 413.

13. See Section 708 of P.L. 95-426, October 7, 1978.

14. Ibid. These reforms are also summarized in "Reporting of U.S. International Agreements by Executive Agencies Has Improved," p. 8.

15. The letters are reproduced in "International Agreements Consultation Resolution," Senate Report 95-1171, August 25, 1978, pp. 2–3. These letters are also cited in Thomas M. Franck and Edward Weisband, *Foreign Policy by Congress* (New York: Oxford University Press, 1979), p. 151, and notes 110–111.

16. The *Congressional Record*, 95th Cong., 1st Sess., Volume 124, Part 21, September 8, 1978, p. 28545.

17. P.L. 91-672. For the executive claim of not needing the Gulf of Tonkin Resolution to continue the war, see *Congress and the Nation*, Volume III, 1969–1972 (Washington, D.C.: Congressional Quarterly, Inc., 1973), p. 947.

18. The entire text of the resolution can be found in the *New York Times*, November 8, 1973, p. 20, or in a variety of recent congressional reports. See, for instance, *The War Powers Resolution: Relevant Documents, Correspondence, Reports,*

Subcommittee on International Security and Scientific Affairs, House Committee on Foreign Affairs, December 1983, pp. 1–6.

19. The following analysis is based upon the text of the War Powers Resolution (P.L. 93-148). A section-by-section analysis of the resolution is provided in Robert A. Katzmann, "War Powers: Toward a New Accommodation," in Thomas E. Mann, ed., *A Question of Balance* (Washington, D.C.: The Brookings Institution, 1990), pp, 46–49.

20. The cases of presidential reports to the Congress under the War Powers Resolution were taken from "War Powers Resolution," Hearings, before the Committee on Foreign Relations, 95th Cong., July 13, 14, and 15, 1977, pp. 332–337; and from *The War Powers Resolution: Relevant Documents, Correspondence, Reports,* pp. 40–66, 84–85.

21. The reporting by the Reagan administration in the 1986–1988 period is taken from Ellen C. Collier, "War Powers Resolution: Presidential Compliance," Congressional Research Service Issue Brief 81050, February 16, 1990.

22. For reporting during the Bush administration, see ibid., and the *Weekly Compilation of Presidential Documents* 26 (August 13, 1990), pp. 1225–1226.

23. This language is taken from President Bush's report on the Panama invasion, which is printed in *Weekly Compilation of Presidential Documents* 25 (December 25, 1989), p. 1985.

24. Katzmann, "War Powers: Toward a New Accommodation," p. 65.

25. Jeffrey Frank, "Vietnam, Watergate Bred War Powers Act . . . Controversy Still Surrounds Law's Effects," *Congressional Quarterly Weekly Report,* October 1, 1983, p. 2019.

26. Zablocki's letter is reprinted in *The War Powers Resolution: Relevant Documents, Correspondence, Reports,* p. 51.

27. See the reply to Zablocki by Richard Fairbanks, former assistant secretary of state for congressional relations, in ibid., pp. 52–54.

28. "House Votes To Bar Fighting Forces in 2 Latin Nations," *Des Moines Register,* May 24, 1984, pp. 1A, 10A; and "House Votes To Aid El Salvador, Denies Nicaraguan Rebels," *Des Moines Register,* May 25, 1984, pp. 1A, 15A.

29. Collier, "War Powers Resolution: Presidential Compliance," pp. 9–10.

30. See, for example, President Reagan's reports to the Congress of September 29, 1982, and of August 30, 1983, reprinted in *The War Powers Resolution: Relevant Documents, Correspondence, Reports,* pp. 62–63, 65–66. The complete text of the Lebanon resolution is also reprinted there at pp. 78–81. The quoted phrase is from Congressman Zablocki in John Felton, "Ten Years Later, the Debate Was Familiar," *Congressional Quarterly Weekly Report,* October 8, 1983, p. 2097.

31. See President Reagan's statement as he signed the Lebanese resolution into law, reprinted in "Resolution on Lebanon Signed Into Law," *Congressional Quarterly Weekly Report,* October 15, 1983, p. 2142. Alse see John Felton, "Reagan Pledges Preceded War Powers Votes," *Congressional Quarterly Weekly Report,* October 8, 1983, pp. 2095–2096.

32. Steven V. Roberts, "O'Neill Criticizes Reagan Moves; Senate Invokes War Powers Act," *New York Times,* October 29, 1983, pp. 1, 4; and Richard Whittle, "Congress Examines Causes, Costs of Grenada Operation," *Congressional Quarterly Weekly Report,* November 5, 1983, p. 2292. The debt ceiling bill in the Senate eventually did not pass, however.

33. Collier, "War Powers Resolution: Presidential Compliance," pp. 6 and 14.

34. Katzmann, "War Powers: Toward a New Accommodation," p. 61.

35. Ellen C. Collier, "The War Powers Resolution: Fifteen Years of Experience," Congressional Research Service, August 3, 1988, pp. 29–31; and Collier, "War Powers Resolution: Presidential Compliance," p. 3.

36. "Legal Opinion of May 9, 1980, by Lloyd Cutler, Counsel to Former President Carter, on War Powers Consultation Relative to the Iran Rescue Mission," reprinted in *War Powers Resolution: Relevant Documents, Correspondence, Reports,* p. 50.

37. Collier, "War Powers Resolution: Presidential Compliance," p. 5.

38. Collier, "War Powers Resolution: Fifteen Years of Experience," pp. 27–29.

39. Adam Clymer, "Congress in Step," *New York Times,* January 14, 1991, p. A11.

40. UN Security Council Resolution 678 (1990), reprinted in Marjorie Ann Browne, "Iraq-Kuwait: U.N. Security Council Resolutions—Texts and Votes," Washington, D.C.: Congressional Research Service, Library of Congress, December 4, 1990.

41. Clymer, "Congress in Step," p. A11.

42. "Text of Congressional Resolution on the Gulf," *New York Times,* January 14, 1991, p. A11.

43. Collier, "The War Powers Resolution: Fifteen Years of Experience," pp. 9–11.

44. Katzmann, "War Powers: Toward a New Accommodation," pp. 66–69; Committee on Foreign Affairs, *Congress and Foreign Policy 1988* (Washington, D.C.: U.S. Government Printing Office, 1989), p. 9; and Collier, "The War Powers Resolution: Fifteen Years of Experience," pp. 45–50.

45. The analysis of voting during the 1966–1972 period is drawn from "Congress Took 94 Roll-Call Votes On War 1966–72," *Congress and the Nation,* Volume III, 1969–1972 (Washington, D.C.: Congressional Quarterly, Inc., 1973), pp. 944–945. The quoted passages are from this source.

46. See P.L. 93-126 of October 18, 1973.

47. *Congressional Quarterly Almanac 1975* (Washington, D.C.: Congressional Quarterly, Inc., 1976), pp. 306–315.

48. See Keith R. Legg, "Congress as Trojan Horses? The Turkish Embargo Problem, 1974–1978," in John Spanier and Joseph Nogee, eds., *Congress, The Presidency, and American Foreign Policy* (New York: Pergamon Press, 1981), pp. 107–131, and especially the chronology of events at pp. 108–109 for the passage of the arms embargo.

49. See Section 404 of P.L. 94-329. 90 Stat. 757.

50. See Section 728 of P.L. 97-113.

51. On the pocket veto and the congressional legal challenge, see John Felton, "President's El Salvador Veto Sparks Uproar Among Critics," *Congressional Quarterly Weekly Report,* December 3, 1983, p. 2524; Diane Granat, "33 Democrats Challenge Reagan Pocket Veto," *Congressional Quarterly Weekly Report,* January 7, 1984, p. 14; and "Pocket-Veto Ruling," *Congressional Quarterly Weekly Report,* March 17, 1984, p. 639.

52. See P.L. 98-151. A description of the law is provided by John Felton, "Omnibus Bill Includes Foreign Aid Programs," *Congressional Quarterly Weekly Report,* November 19, 1983, pp. 2435–2436.

53. Chris Hedges (with a report from Julia Malone), "Guilty Verdict in Salvador," *Christian Science Monitor,* May 25, 1984, p. 10.

54. John Felton, "Hill Sidesteps a Confrontation Over Continuing Arms Aid," *Congressional Quarterly Weekly Report,* November 25, 1989, pp. 3258–3259;

and John Felton, "After Bush Veto, Hill Retreats to Save Foreign Aid Bill," *Congressional Quarterly Weekly Report*, November 25, 1989, pp. 3260–3261.

55. For congressional action in 1983, see John Felton, "House Quashes Covert Nicaraguan Aid," *Congressional Quarterly Weekly Report*, July 30, 1983, pp. 1535, and his "White House Gets Better Half of a Covert Aid Compromise," *Congressional Quarterly Weekly Report*, November 26, 1983, p. 2486. For 1984, see "House Votes To Aid El Salvador, Denies Nicaraguan Rebels," pp. 1A, 15A; "House OK's Compromise Spending Bill," *Des Moines Register*, October 11, 1984, pp. 1A, 3A; and Martin Tolchin, "Conferees Agree on Spending Bill, Ending Deadlock," *New York Times*, October 11, 1984, pp. A1, A2.

56. "Most Aid Earmarked," *Congressional Quarterly Weekly Report*, January 20, 1990. For some recent controversy over earmarking, see John Felton, "Dole Takes on Israeli Lobby, Proposes Cutting U.S. Aid," *Congressional Quarterly Weekly Report*, January 20, 1990, pp. 196, 198.

57. See sections 402 and 613 of the Trade Act of 1974 (P.L. 93-618).

58. See Section 36 of P.L. 93-559.

59. See Section 36h of P.L. 94-329. The dollar totals were subsequently raised to $50 million and $14 million, respectively. See John Felton, "Hill Weighs Foreign Policy Impact of Ruling," *Congressional Quarterly Weekly Report*, July 2, 1983, p. 1330.

60. See *Congressional Quarterly Almanac 1981* (Washington, D.C.: Congressional Quarterly, Inc., 1982), p. 132.

61. The economic aid legislation was the International Development and Food Assistance Act of 1975 (P.L. 94-161). The human rights provision can be found at Section 116. In the International Security and Arms Export Control Act, the human rights provision is Section 502b.

62. See P.L. 95-118, Section 701, and P.L. 94-302, Section 28. Also see the discussion of this human rights legislation in Lars Schoultz, "Politics, Economics, and U.S. Participation in Multilateral Development Banks," *International Organization* 36 (Summer 1982): 537–574.

63. These and other provisions of the act are summarized in *Congressional Quarterly Almanac 1978* (Washington, D.C.: Congressional Quarterly, Inc., 1979), pp. 350–356. Also see P.L. 95-242.

64. Quoted from the bill's conference report in Pietro S. Nivola, "Trade Policy: Refereeing the Playing Field," in Thomas E. Mann, ed., *A Question of Balance* (Washington, D.C.: The Brookings Institution, 1990), p. 238.

65. Clyde H. Farnsworth, "U.S. Drops Japan from Target List," *New York Times*, April 28, 1990, pp. 17 and 19.

66. We do not mean to imply that other committees are not involved with foreign policy issues, but rather that these are the principal foreign policy authorizing committees. Other committees in the House and the Senate that deal with foreign policy would include Appropriations, Governmental Affairs (Senate), Government Operations (House), Judiciary, and Select Intelligence, among others. It is important to note that the Foreign Operations subcommittees of the House and Senate Appropriations committees are extraordinarily important in appropriating foreign policy funding. Indeed, some would contend that they do more today to shape policy than the authorizing committees.

67. Ellen C. Collier, "Foreign Policy by Reporting Requirement," *The Washington Quarterly* 11 (Winter 1988), pp. 81 and 77. This article is the source for the subsequent discussion as well.

68. The types of reports and the description of each is taken from ibid.

69. Committee on Foreign Affairs and Committee on Foreign Relations, *Legislation on Foreign Relations Through 1985* (Washington, D.C.: U.S. Government Printing Office, April 1986), p. 907. The requirement for a report on member countries of the United Nations can be found at p. 956.

70. The data on reprogramming reports were obtained from staff members of the House Committee on Foreign Affairs. A more complete description of re-programming reporting is available in James M. McCormick, "A Review of the Foreign Assistance Program," memo prepared for the Office of the Honorable Lee Hamilton.

71. Collier, "Foreign Policy by Reporting Requirement," p. 80.

72. A good source to get some idea of the range of activities of the Senate Foreign Relations Committee is the legislative activities reports. See, for example, the *Legislative Activities Report of the Committee on Foreign Relations,* United States Senate, 170th Anniversary 1816–1986 (Washington, D.C.: U.S. Government Print-ing Office, January 1986).

73. *Congressional Quarterly's Guide To Congress,* p. 289.

74. Ibid., p. 289. On the problems of the committee and the difficulties faced by Percy as chair, see Richard Whittle, "Foreign Relations Committee Searches for Renewed Glory," *Congressional Quarterly Weekly Report,* March 14, 1981, pp. 477–479.

75. Bernard Gwertzman, "Senator Planning Sweeping Hearing on Foreign Policy," *New York Times,* December 9, 1984, p. 20.

76. Helen Dewar, "Senate Foreign Relations Panel Founders," *Washington Post,* October 10, 1989, p. A12.

77. Ibid.

78. Foreign Affairs is not ranked as the most popular committee in the House; it still ranks behind Ways and Means and Appropriations as a desirable committee assignment. See Fenno, *Congressmen in Committees,* pp. 16–20. For a different ranking, see Randall B. Ripley, *Congress: Process and Policy,* 2nd ed. (New York: W. W. Norton & Company, 1978), p. 166.

79. See Fenno, *Congressmen in Committees,* pp. 15–151, on the importance of the Senate Foreign Relations Committee. On the limited responsibilities of the House Foreign Affairs agenda, see ibid., pp. 213–215.

80. See Fred Kaiser, "Oversight of Foreign Policy: The U.S. House Commit-tee on International Relations," *Legislative Studies Quarterly* 2 (August 1977): 259.

81. Fred M. Kaiser, "The Changing Nature and Extent of Oversight: The House Committee on Foreign Affairs in the 1970s," paper presented at the 1975 Annual Meeting of the Midwest Political Science Association, Chicago, Illinois.

82. Fred M. Kaiser, "Structural Change and Policy Development: The House Committee on International Relations," paper presented at the 1976 An-nual Meeting of the Midwest Political Science Association; and Fred M. Kaiser, "Structural and Policy Change: The House Committee on International Rela-tions," *Policy Studies Journal* 5 (Summer 1977): 443–451.

83. Interviews with majority and minority staff in June 1982 revealed that they view the committee as more liberal than the House as a whole. Also see James M. McCormick, "The Changing Role of the House Foreign Affairs Com-mittee in the 1970s and 1980s," *Congress & The Presidency* 12 (Spring 1985), pp. 1–20.

84. *Origins and Development of Congress* (Washington, D.C.: Congressional Quarterly, Inc., 1976), p. 159.

85. Kaiser, "Structural and Policy Change: The House Committee on Inter-national Relations," p. 446.

86. For a recent listing of the subcommittees and for a brief history of the House Foreign Affairs Committee, see *Survey of Activities, 99th Congress* (Washington, D.C.: U.S. Government Printing Office, 1987).

87. Kaiser, in "Structural Change and Policy Development" pp. 21–22.

88. The first study is one by Carol Goss cited in Edward J. Laurance, "The Congressional Role in Defense Policy: The Evolution of the Literature," *Armed Forces & Society* 6 (Spring 1980): 437; the second is "Armed Services Committees: Advocates or Overseers?" *Congressional Quarterly Weekly Report*, March 25, 1972, pp. 673–677.

89. See James M. Lindsay, "Congress and Defense Policy: 1961 to 1986," *Armed Forces & Society* 13 (Spring 1987): 371–401, for a discussion of these committees in the 1970s and 1980s. As he correctly notes, the Defense subcommittees of the House and Senate Appropriations committees are equally important, or even more important, players on defense policy issues.

90. "Congress Reinforces Strings on SDI Program," *Congressional Quarterly Almanac 1987* (Washington, D.C.: Congressional Quarterly, Inc., 1988), p. 196. Also see pp. 195–199. The speeches by Senator Nunn on the Senate floor can be found in *Congressional Record*, March 11, 1987, pp. S2967–2986; *Congressional Record*, March 12, 1987, pp. S3090–3095; and *Congressional Record*, March 13, 1987, pp. S3171–3173.

91. Franck and Weisband, *Foreign Policy by Congress*, pp. 6–9; and I. M. Destler, "Dateline Washington: Congress as Boss?" *Foreign Policy* 42 (Spring 1981): 167–180.

92. Committee on Foreign Affairs, *Congress and Foreign Policy 1988*, and Committee on Foreign Affairs, *Congress and Foreign Policy 1987* (Washington, D.C.: U.S. Government Printing Office, 1989).

93. "Bush's Dozen Vetoes," *New York Times*, June 16, 1990, p. 8; and "State Department Bill Clears, But Faces Bush's Veto," *Congressional Quarterly Weekly Report*, November 18, 1989, p. 3189.

94. John G. Tower, "Congress Versus the President: The Formulation and Implementation of American Foreign Policy," *Foreign Affairs* 60 (Winter 1981/82): 233.

95. Charles W. Whalen, Jr., *The House and Foreign Policy: The Irony of Congressional Reform* (Chapel Hill, NC: The University of North Carolina Press, 1982).

96. The occasion of President Reagan's remarks were a speech at the University of Virginia on December 16, 1988, as summarized and quoted in *Congress and Foreign Policy 1988*, p. 9.

97. *Congressional Quarterly Almanac 1981*, vol. 37 (Washington, D.C.: Congressional Quarterly, Inc., 1982), pp. 136, 138.

98. See "Congress and Nuclear Nonproliferation Policy," in *Congress and Foreign Policy—1980* (Washington, D.C.: U.S. Government Printing Office, 1981), pp. 89, 98. On human rights and foreign aid, see James M. McCormick and Neil J. Mitchell, "Human Rights and Foreign Assistance: An Update," *Social Science Quarterly* 70 (December 1989): 969–979.

99. On the halting of arms sales, see Bruce W. Jentleson, "American Diplomacy: Around the World and Along Pennsylvania Avenue," in Thomas E. Mann, ed., *A Question of Balance* (Washington, D.C.: The Brookings Institution, 1990), p. 161, and on the stopping of covert operations, see Gregory F. Treverton, "Intelligence: Welcome to the American Government," in Thomas E. Mann, ed., *A Question of Balance* (Washington, D.C.: The Brookings Institution, 1990), p. 91.

100. See Section 361 of P.L. 94-329. For the Saudi exception, see "U.S. To Send Saudi Arabia 400 Missiles," *Des Moines Register*, May 28, 1984, pp. 1A, 11A.

101. Norman J. Ornstein and David W. Rohde, "Shifting Forces, Changing Rules, and Political Outcomes: The Impact of Congressional Change on Four House Committees," in Robert L. Peabody and Nelson W. Polsby, *New Perspectives on the House of Representatives*, 3rd ed. (Chicago: Rand McNally, 1977), p. 259. This description, however, was before the *Chadha* decision.

102. Nivola, "Trade Policy: Refereeing the Playing Field," p. 238.

103. See Felton, "Hill Weighs Foreign Policy Impact of Ruling," pp. 1329–1330, for an assessment of the Supreme Court ruling on the legislative veto for foreign policy, and 462 U.S. 919 (1983).

104. These views are based on interviews with staff of the House Foreign Affairs Committee (June 1982), officials of the Department of State who deal with congressional relations (October 1981), and some participant observation in the House of Representatives in 1986 and 1987.

105. Schlesinger, "Congress and the Making of American Foreign Policy," *Foreign Affairs* 51 (October 1972): 106.

106. On a proposal for a foreign policy "compact" between the two branches, see Warren Christopher, "Ceasefire Between the Branches: A Compact in Foreign Affairs," *Foreign Affairs* 60 (Summer 1982): 989–1005.

CHAPTER 9 THE DIPLOMATIC AND ECONOMIC BUREAUCRACIES: DUPLICATION OR SPECIALIZATION?

"The conflict between the president's assistant for national security affairs and the secretary of state, and more broadly between the National Security Council staff and the State Department, has been one of the most persistent, contentious organizational problems afflicting the United States government." ARTHUR CYR, "HOW IMPORTANT IS NATIONAL SECURITY STRUCTURE TO NATIONAL SECURITY POLICY?" *WORLD AFFAIRS*, FALL 1983

"Our strategic goal is to open markets, not close them; to create an ever-expanding multilateral trading system based upon equitable and enforceable rules. As a global power, we prefer to use multilateral negotiations to achieve this end. But we will also engage in bilateral efforts, and take selective unilateral actions, where they can be effective in opening foreign markets to U.S. goods and services." UNITED STATES TRADE REPRESENTATIVE-DESIGNATE CARLA ANDERSON HILLS AT HER CONFIRMATION HEARINGS BEFORE THE SENATE COMMITTEE ON FINANCE, JANUARY 27, 1989

Although the president may dominate the Congress's role in the foreign policy process, he cannot act alone. The president needs information and advice from assistants and the various foreign affairs bureaucracies within the executive branch to formulate policy. The president also needs the aid of the executive branch to implement any foreign policy decision. Thus, while the president may ultimately choose a foreign policy option, such as economic sanctions or the use of force against Iraq, for example, the decision process and the implementation of that choice are greatly influenced by the bureaucratic environment.

The variety of agencies with an interest in foreign policy can be surprising. While we may think of the Department of Agriculture as primarily concerned with domestic farm issues, it may well seek to promote the granting of foreign trade credits with the Soviet Union to help American farmers. While the Department of Treasury may monitor the money supply at home, it also advises the president on the need for a shift in the value of the U.S. dollar against the German mark to improve American trade abroad. While the Justice Department may be interested in controlling the use of illegal drugs at home, it has an interest in drug production in other countries as well. In short, the principal foreign policy bureaucracies that we often think of (and even those we may not immediately think of) compete to get the "president's ear" on international issues and to shape an outcome favorable to their bureaucracy. Understanding the process of domestic bureaucratic politics has increasingly become critically important for understanding foreign policy decision making.

BUREAUCRATIC POLITICS AND FOREIGN POLICYMAKING

The "bureaucratic politics" approach to foreign policymaking stands in contrast to the earlier discussions emphasizing the values and beliefs of American society as a whole, the values of particular presidents and administrations, and even the effects of institutions like Congress and the presidency on U.S. foreign policy. This approach views the emergence of policy from the interactions among the various bureaucracies competing to shape the nation's actions. Policy thus becomes less the result of the values and beliefs of an individual political actor in the process (although each can surely have an effect) and more the result of the interaction process among several bureaucracies. Put differently, policymaking is the result of the "pulling" and "hauling" among the competing institutions.[1] Compromise within bureaucracies and coalition-building across them thus become important ways in which policy ultimately emerges. In this sense, the *process* of policymaking becomes an important mechanism to arrive at the *substance* of policy.

While the bureaucratic politics model has long been used to study domestic policy, its sustained application to foreign affairs is a relatively recent phenomenon. Its use in the study of American foreign policy is usually dated to the imaginative work by political scientist Graham Allison on the Cuban Missile Crisis and to a more general work by political analyst Morton Halperin in which he used this approach to study various facets of the policy process.[2] These two pioneering analyses sparked a more general interest in this approach, and it has now become a particularly important mode of analysis.

Recently, for example, the Reagan administration's arms control policy was analyzed using this approach. The basic message was that the policy decisions were more often the result of domestic bureaucratic squabbles among key officials and institutions than anything else.[3] Another analysis of the Reagan administration's foreign policy reached a similar conclusion: Much of its foreign policy decision making could be described as "bureaucratic tribal warfare."[4] The bureaucratic politics approach is important to foreign policy analysis today and offers yet another useful perspective on the making of American foreign policy.

In this chapter and the next one, therefore, we examine the key foreign policy bureaucracies within the executive branch, describe each one's role in the policy process, and assess its policy influence in relation to the others. We analyze four central foreign policy bureaucracies in detail: the Department of State, the National Security Council, the Department of Defense, and the intelligence community. We will also survey the increasing role of several other bureaucracies—e.g., the Department of Commerce, the Department of the Treasury, and the Department of Agriculture—and examine their role in shaping the foreign economic policy of the United States. In last part of Chapter 10, we try to bring this discussion together by showing how the individual foreign policy bureaucracies coordinate with one another through the process of forming interagency groups (IGs). Throughout both chapters, we discuss a crucial question of the bureaucratic politics approach: How are foreign policy choices the result of interdepartmental coordination and interdepartmental rivalries?

THE DEPARTMENT OF STATE

The oldest cabinet post and the central foreign policy bureaucracy in the American government is the Department of State. The department was established originally in 1781 under the Articles of Confederation as the Department of Foreign Affairs and became the Department of State in 1789 by an act of Congress shortly after the election of George Washington.[5] Over its 200-year history, the department has evolved into a large and complex bureaucracy with a variety of functions. It must advise the president on foreign policy, represent the U.S. government abroad, and implement the policy decisions that emanate from Washington, D.C.

THE STRUCTURE OF STATE AT HOME

Structurally, the State Department is arranged in a hierarchical fashion. At one level, it has five regional bureaus (European and Canadian Affairs, African Affairs, Inter-American Affairs, East Asian and Pacific Affairs, and Near Eastern and South Asian Affairs); at another level, it has several functional bureaus (Economic and Business Affairs, Human Rights and Humanitarian Affairs, Politico-Military Affairs, Intelligence and Research, International Organization Affairs, Public Affairs, Consular Affairs, etc.).[6] Each of these bureaus is headed by an assistant secretary of state, who is likely to represent his or her bureau within interagency groups, with other foreign affairs bureaucracies, with the secretary of state, or with testimony before a congressional committee or subcommittee. At the highest levels of the State Department bureaucracy are the administrative offices. They consist of the secretary of state, deputy secretary of state, and the under secretary of state for political affairs—the top three ranking positions—plus the under secretaries of state for economic and agricultural affairs, international security affairs, and management (Figure 9.1).

In addition, three other agencies are attached to the Department of State in semi-autonomous fashion to complete the diplomatic apparatus of the U.S. government. These are the Arms Control and Disarmament Agency, the U.S. Information Agency (for a time under the Carter administration and a portion of the Reagan administration known as the International Communications Agency), and the International Development Cooperation Agency, with its principal affiliate the Agency for International Development. Each has important, specialized foreign policy responsibilities, which we will outline briefly.

FIGURE 9.1   THE STRUCTURE OF THE DEPARTMENT OF STATE

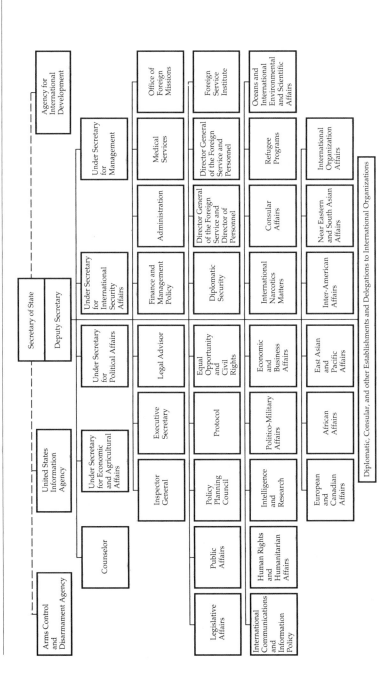

Source: *U.S. Government Manual 1990/1991*, p. 423.

The Arms Control and Disarmament Agency (ACDA) was established by Congress in 1961 and has the responsibility for fostering global arms restraint, seeking arms control agreements with other states, and monitoring compliance with agreements in effect. Although its origins were tied to seeking nuclear weapons restraint, it is also involved in efforts at restraining conventional arms within developed nations and between developed and developing nations. This agency, for instance, has been deeply involved in the Strategic Arms Limitation Talks (SALT) of the 1970s, the Strategic Arms Reduction Talks (START) of the 1980s and 1990s, the Intermediate Nuclear Forces (INF) Treaty of 1987, and the Conventional Forces in Europe (CFE) discussions of the 1990s. The impact of this agency on arms control policy is dependent upon how much confidence the president and his key advisors place in this bureaucracy. During the Carter administration, for example, ACDA had an important role to play in policy formulation. For the Reagan administration, however, more direction for arms control policy came from the White House and less from this agency. Indeed, the Reagan administration had initial suspicions about this agency and the need for arms limitation. By its second term, however, arms control became more crucial for the Reagan administration, and the relative role of this bureaucracy increased, albeit with substantial guidance from the White House. For the Bush administration, the reliance upon the White House and the National Security staff for arms control policy implied a lesser dependence on ACDA.

The United States Information Agency (USIA) has responsibility for disseminating information about American political and social developments to other nations of the world and for coordinating cultural and educational exchange programs. The agency publishes eleven periodicals for distribution abroad, broadcasts to an estimated 120 million people weekly in forty-eight different languages through the Voice of America (VOA), operates Radio Marti's broadcasts to Cuba, and supports "American Centers" in over fifty countries. These American Centers are U.S. government-sponsored facilities in which a library, exhibits, and lectures on American life are available. In some countries, USIA cooperates with a local national committee to establish Binational Centers that highlight the activities of both societies.[7] With all these activities, the United States Information Agency attempts to promote a positive picture of the United States to other nations and peoples.

The third semi-autonomous bureaucracy within the Department of State structure is the Agency for International Development (AID). This agency is an integral part of the International Development Cooperation Agency, an umbrella organization that coordinates the activities of several development units, including the Overseas Private Investment Corporation, the Trade and Development Program, the Development Coordination Committee, the Food for Peace Program, and U.S. participation in multilateral development banks and other international organizations and programs. Much of the foreign assistance program to other countries is conducted by this agency. Finally, the director of AID heads the International Development Cooperation Agency, and thus serves as the president's and the secretary of state's principal advisor on international development activities.[8]

THE STRUCTURE OF STATE ABROAD

The State Department also has the responsibility to represent America abroad through U.S. missions, usually located in the capital city, and with consulates in other major cities of a host country. As of September 1990, the United States had about 300 embassies, missions, consular agencies, consulates general, and other offices abroad. It also had eleven missions at the headquarters of various intergovernmental organizations (e.g., the United Nations, the European Community, and the International Civil Aviation Organization). In all, the United States conducts diplomatic relations with over 150 nations; there are only seven nations with whom the U.S. does not presently have diplomatic relations: Angola, Cambodia, Cuba, Iran, Iraq, North Korea, and Vietnam. In one of the newest diplomatic openings, relations with Albania, after a fifty-two-year rupture, were reestablished in March 1991.

A U.S. embassy is headed by an ambassador, who is the personal representative of the president. The ambassador is assisted by the Deputy Chief of Mission (DCM), who is largely responsible for conducting the day-to-day operation of the embassy staff. While the embassy is staffed with political, economic, consular, and administrative foreign service officers from the Department of State, it also has representatives from other executive departments as well. The composition of the U.S. mission in Venezuela in a recent year illustrates this diversity (Figure 9.2).

The country team for Venezuela consists of an agricultural counselor from the Department of Agriculture, a public affairs counselor from USIA, a commercial counselor from the Department of Commerce, a defense attaché from the Department of Defense, and an advisory military group from the Department of Defense as well as State Department personnel. Other agency representatives are also present, including the Drug Enforcement Agency and the Internal Revenue Service. In addition, officials from the Central Intelligence

FIGURE 9.2 THE STRUCTURE OF A U.S. MISSION ABROAD—VENEZUELA

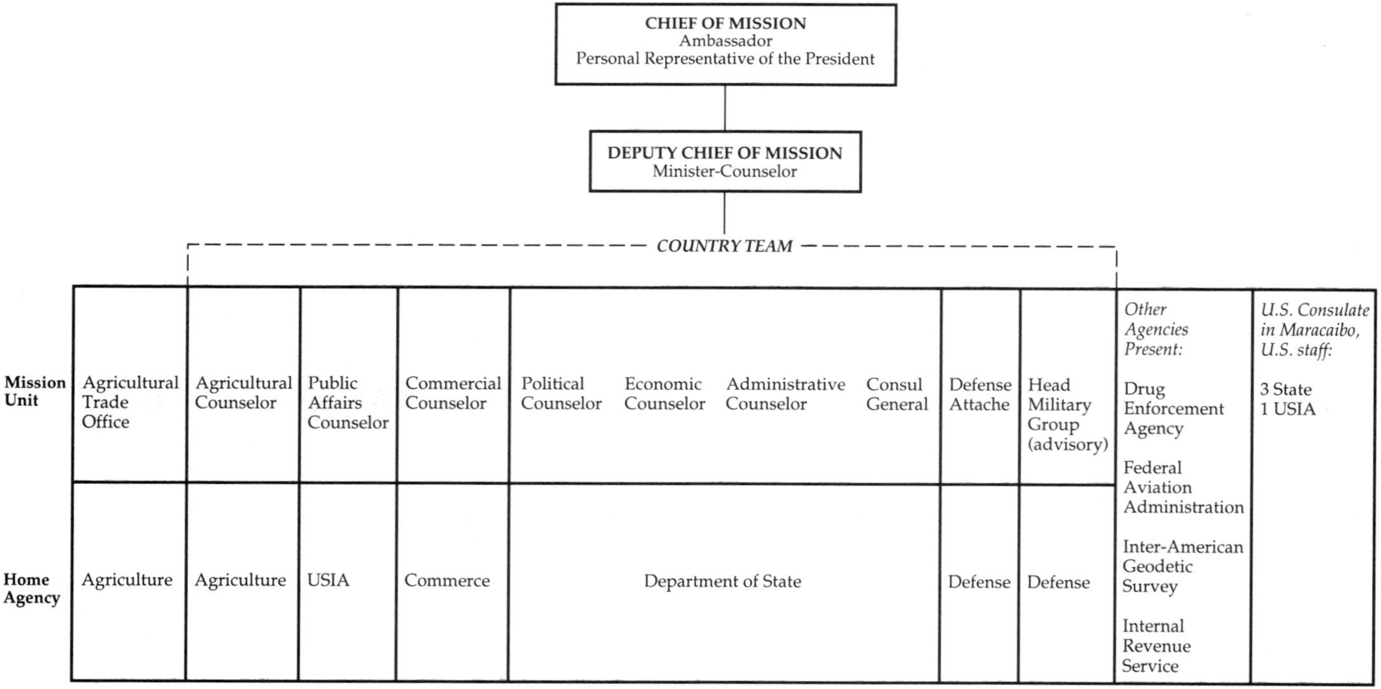

CHIEF OF MISSION
Ambassador
Personal Representative of the President

DEPUTY CHIEF OF MISSION
Minister–Counselor

— — — — — COUNTRY TEAM — — — — —

Mission Unit	Agricultural Trade Office	Agricultural Counselor	Public Affairs Counselor	Commercial Counselor	Political Counselor	Economic Counselor	Administrative Counselor	Consul General	Defense Attache	Head Military Group (advisory)	Other Agencies Present:	U.S. Consulate in Maracaibo, U.S. staff:
Home Agency	Agriculture	Agriculture	USIA	Commerce		Department of State			Defense	Defense	Drug Enforcement Agency Federal Aviation Administration Inter-American Geodetic Survey Internal Revenue Service	3 State 1 USIA

Source: U.S. Department of State, "Foreign Relations Machinery," *Atlas of U.S. Foreign Relations* (Washington, D.C.: Bureau of Public Affairs, October 1982), p. 6.

Agency are often represented in the country team, using a "cover" of some other position. While numerous departments and agencies are represented within a single U.S. mission abroad, the actual size of the mission will primarily be a function of the size of the nation in which the U.S. mission is located and the perceived political and strategic importance of that nation. In Venezuela, for example, 108 Americans were employed in the U.S. mission in Caracas and the consulate in Maracaibo in June 1985. By contrast, the U.S. embassy staff totaled 266 in London and only 21 in Brazzaville, the People's Republic of the Congo.[9]

As this overview indicates, the structure of the Department of State (and its affiliated agencies) appears to be quite large and complex. Yet, in reality, the department itself is one of the smallest bureaucracies within the executive branch. In 1986, the State Department had only about 24,000 full-time employees—14,000 Americans and 10,000 foreign nationals. (By contrast, the Defense Department had about 1 million civilian employees at the same time.) Furthermore, the annual budget of the Department of State— about $2 million—is one of the smallest within the government, and especially small when compared with other foreign affairs sectors of the government.[10]

THE WEAKENED INFLUENCE OF STATE

Despite its role as the principal foreign policy bureaucracy, and the one that will usually offer the nonmilitary option for conducting foreign policy, the Department of State has been criticized for its ineffectiveness in both policy formulation and policy implementation.[11] As a consequence, it has not played the dominant role in recent administrations that its central diplomatic position might imply. In this sense, the *policy influence* of the Department of State is comparatively less than that of other foreign policy bureaucracies in the U.S. government. The factors that have reduced the policy influence of the State Department range from its increasing budget problems as compared to other bureaucracies, the kind of personnel within the department's bureaucracy, and ultimately the relationships among the secretary of state, the department as a whole, and the White House. Let us examine these factors.

THE PROBLEM OF RESOURCES   The first problem that the Department of State faces in the competition to influence foreign affairs and to carry out its responsibilities is one of resources. The small operating budget of the department has been a perennial problem over the last decade, with the Congress reluctant to fund all of its needs. By contrast, the funding for the Department of Defense and the intelligence community continued to increase dramatically, reaching record levels for both departments (see Chapter 10).

To be sure, the Department of State's budget has increased from about $700 million in 1979 to about $2.2 billion currently, but the effects of inflation, newly directed congressional mandates for establishing new departmental bureaus, and the expansion of foreign affairs responsibilities worldwide have caused a real problem. Moreover, the Congress has not always been responsive to its needs. In fact, Secretary of State George Shultz became so frustrated with the situation that he commented in February 1987 that State's budget problems were "a tragedy" and that, as a result, "America is hauling down the flag. . . . We're withdrawing from the world." By November 1987, the department was even hinting that 1,200 jobs would have to be eliminated and several embassies and consulates around the world would need to be closed because of these mounting budget problems.[12] While such draconian measures were not ultimately necessary, funding issues remain a key concern and even a preoccupation of the Department of State as it tries to carry out its present worldwide responsibilities.[13]

The implications of these funding problems for policymaking are numerous. First, State Department personnel are not adequately compensated or supported under such circumstances. Salaries are relatively low (compared to similar positions in the private sector), and salary increases are small. As a result, top quality staff becomes more difficult to keep and less easy to recruit. Indeed, concerns have been expressed that the quality of the new recruits does not match that of earlier years. Second, budget restraints also mean that individuals are asked to carry greater and greater workloads, and, inevitably, the quality of their work suffers. Third, because other executive agencies tend to be better funded than State, morale also suffers. Finally, America's foreign policy representation around the world potentially pays a price in this environment. The information collection and implementation aspects of the department cannot be as complete with limited personnel and staff. All in all, then, the continuing budget problem for the Department of State reduces both the incentives and the capacities for it to compete with other bureaucracies in shaping U.S. foreign policy.

THE PROBLEM OF SIZE   A second problem of the Department of State as it attempts to compete with other bureaucracies is its size. It is, at once, too large and too small. It is too large in the sense that there are "layers and layers" of bureaucracy through which policy reviews and recommendations must pass. At the present time, for example, there are five geographic and eighteen functional bureaus involved in policymaking. A policy recommendation must go through the appropriate regional and functional bureaus before it can reach the "Seventh Floor," where the executive offices of the department are located. As a consequence, the structure of State's bureaucracy is said to hinder its overall effectiveness and reduce the efficiency with which policy recommendations can be developed.

At the same time, the department has been criticized as too small, because it is dwarfed by the other bureaucracies in terms of political representation in the principal foreign policymaking forums. (For example, note the size of the military representation in the National Security Council or the relative size of other bureaucracies in the interagency process discussed below.) Staff does not often carry the same domestic political clout as other large bureaucracies. Consider the lobbying power of the Departments of Defense, Commerce, Treasury, or even Agriculture; all these agencies have large and vocal constituencies to argue their policy position with the American people, the Congress, and, ultimately, the president. By contrast, the Department of State lacks a ready constituency within the American public to offer support and political lobbying within the Congress.[14] The State Department must, therefore, lobby by itself through the testimony of its officials during congressional hearings, through its informal contacts with congressional staff, through the use of legislative action programs (LAPs), and through the interagency process. Suffice it to say, these avenues have not readily yielded political success for the Department of State.

THE PERSONNEL PROBLEM   A third problem of the Department of State focuses on its personnel and the environment in which they operate. Foreign service officers, reserve foreign service officers, and civil service personnel comprise the principal officials of the department. Primary policy responsibility, however, rests with the approximately 4,200 foreign service officers (FSOs) in the department.[15] These officers have sometimes been depicted as an "Eastern elite," out of touch with the country and determined to shape policy in line with their own foreign policy views. According to this line of criticism, many of these foreign service officers share the same educational background (e.g., Princeton, Harvard, Yale, Johns Hopkins, Fletcher School of Law and Diplomacy), overrepresent the Eastern establishment, and adopt a rather inflexible attitude toward global politics. Several careful analyses of the foreign service officer corps challenges some of these stereotypes, and vigorous mid-career ("lateral entry") and minority recruitment efforts have been undertaken to address them as well.[16] Nonetheless, this personnel image remains prevalent and reduces the effectiveness of the Department of State.

At least two attendant perceived personnel problems also persist among members of Congress, the foreign affairs bureaucracy, and the public at large. One is the charge of "clientelism."[17] That is, in an FSO's zeal to foster good relations with the country in which he or she is serving, the officer becomes too closely identified with the interests of that state, sometimes at the expense of American interests and the requirements of American domestic politics. While the criticism is largely overdrawn, it becomes an important staple of members of Congress or the executive branch who want to avoid relying too closely on the recommendations of the State Department.

A second problem is the level of expertise the State Department personnel and FSOs possess on increasingly specialized issues. While these individuals are undoubtedly capable generalists, the level of specific knowledge on technical subjects and some reluctance to recruit outside experts have led to the charge that the quality of work is inadequate:

> Critics complain the State Department studies are long and too descriptive and often unsatisfactory. Based heavily on intuition, and almost never conceptual, many of the analyses are unaccompanied by reliable sources and information, or reflect the FSO's lack of adequate training and expertise; papers are so cautious and vague as to be of little use to policymakers who long ago concluded that such "waffling" constitutes the quintessential character of the "Fudge Factory at Foggy Bottom."[18]

THE SUBCULTURE PROBLEM   Accompanying this kind of personnel problem is a related one. Even if the individuals themselves are not the source of the problem for the Department of State, the *environment* of the department creates a personnel problem. In the view of political scientist Andrew Scott, a bureaucratic "subculture" has developed in the State Department that emphasizes the importance of "trying to *be* something rather than...trying to *do* something."[19] "Don't rock the boat" is the dominant bureaucratic refrain. Because of these institutional norms, obtaining regular promotions and ensuring career advancements have become more important than creating sound, innovative policy. As Scott has also noted: "Subcultural norms discourage vigorous policy debate within the Department. ...The Department is not inclined toward vigorous exploration of policy options and it is not inclined to let anyone else do the job for it."[20] Put differently, policy recommendations become incremental, not innovative.

THE PRESIDENT AND THE SECRETARY OF STATE   A fourth problem of the Department of State focuses on its relationship with the president and the secretary of state.[21] Postwar presidents and secretaries of state have often not made extensive use of the department for policy formulation. Instead, presidents have tried to be their own "secretary of state" or have relied on key advisors for foreign policy advice rather than on the appointed secretary of state. For these reasons, the policymaking power of the secretary of state may be more apparent than real. Even when the secretary of state has enjoyed the confidence of the president for formulating policy, he has sometimes chosen not to widely involve the department itself, but to rely upon a few key aides. Because of these patterns, the State Department's role has once again been diminished.

Although President John Kennedy initially sought to use the Department of State for foreign policy, he ultimately came to rely upon his formal and informal advisors within the bureaucracy and the White House.[22] His secretary of state, Dean Rusk, did not enjoy a central role in the formulation of policy. President Kennedy's successor, Lyndon Johnson, made greater use of Secretary Rusk than did Kennedy, but he ultimately came to rely upon his national security advisor, first McGeorge Bundy, then Walt Rostow, for key foreign policy advice.[23]

Other presidents have followed a similar pattern. President Richard Nixon did not view Secretary of State William Rogers as his key foreign policy advisor; instead, National Security Advisor Henry Kissinger was the primary architect of foreign policy during those years. President Carter initially tried to create a balance in policymaking between Secretary of State Cyrus Vance and National Security Advisor Zbigniew Brzezinski, but he ultimately depended more on Brzezinski for shaping his response to global politics. In fact, Vance resigned in April 1980, after losing a policy dispute over the wisdom of attempting to rescue the American hostages in Iran.

President Reagan came to office committed to granting more control of foreign policy to the secretary of state—first Alexander Haig and then George Shultz—but here, too, recent evidence suggests that at least three of Reagan's national security advisors, William Clark, Robert McFarlane, and John Poindexter, were quite influential in policymaking at the expense of the secretary of state.[24] Indeed, Secretary Shultz testified to the Congress that on one of the major foreign policy initiatives he was generally kept in the dark. He knew little about the Iran arms deal—and opposed what he knew—and was not aware of the diversion of funds to the Nicaraguan contras. After the Iran-contra affair became public, Shultz gained more control of foreign policy than had previous secretaries of state in some time. Nonetheless, he was still involved in protracted bureaucratic battles to put his stamp on policy.

Two post–World War II presidents did rely upon their secretaries of state for policy formulation, but they did not go beyond them to enlist the full involvement of the department itself. Dean Acheson and George Marshall, secretaries of state under President Harry Truman, were primarily responsible for making their own foreign policy without much input on the part of the department.[25] Similarly, John Foster Dulles, secretary of state under President Dwight Eisenhower, was given wide latitude in the formulation of foreign policy.

The Bush administration, in essence, tried to combine these various policy patterns. Formal control of foreign policymaking was given to the national security advisor, not to the secretary of state, but President Bush still maintained substantial control for himself. (Because of President Bush's experience in serving as U.S. representative to the United Nations, director of the CIA, and the American representative to the People's Republic of China, he viewed foreign policy as a particular area of expertise.) Yet, Secretary of State James A. Baker had more regular policy contact with Bush than virtually any other advisor. The political ties and personal friendship between Bush and Baker, spanning over thirty years, account for much of this contact. Both came from relatively privileged families, both started together in local politics in Texas in the 1960s and 1970s, both have relied upon one another for their political success, and both share an ideology of pragmatism and prudence as a guide to foreign policy. As a result, Secretary Baker has been described as "first among equals" in the Bush White House, and he has regular and continuous contact, talking with President Bush "as many as a dozen times a day."[26]

Secretary Baker also has qualities that complement Bush's style, adding to his potential for policy impact. Baker, for instance, is viewed as a good "tactician" and as detail-oriented, both qualities that can greatly aid Bush's more long-range, strategic style of decision making. Yet, Baker's policy influence should not be overemphasized.[27] President Bush views himself as trained and experienced in foreign affairs and a bit of his own secretary of state. He seeks to place his own imprint on policy, albeit tempered with the advice of Baker and others, but to rely on others for its full implementation.

Under any of these arrangements—where the secretary of state was primarily responsible for foreign policy, where the president relied upon other advisors for policymaking, or where the president tried to be his own secretary of state—the Department of State's role in the formulation of foreign affairs has been reduced in comparison with the influence of other executive institutions or key individuals.

THE PRESIDENT AND THE DEPARTMENT   Another aspect of the problem between the Department of State and the president was summarized by a former foreign service officer, Jack Perry, in this way: " . . . the Foreign Service does not enjoy the confidence of our presidents." Too often, foreign service officers are perceived as potentially "disloyal" to the president. Instead, they are seen as being loyal "either to the opposition party or else to the diplomat's own view of what foreign policy should be."[28]

This degree of suspicion between State and the president is reflected in the increased percentage of ambassadorships that go to political friends, mainly large campaign contributors with limited foreign policy experience. As a result, the opportunities available for career foreign service officers, whose aspirations may be to gain ambassadorships to cap their long service to the Department of State, are reduced. From President Kennedy to President Carter, the appointment of political friends ranged from 27 percent to 39 percent (Figure 9.3). During the Reagan administration's two terms, just under 40 percent of all ambassadors were political appointees, not career diplomats.[29] Often, these appointments are made to the critical foreign posts, such as Britain, Mexico, and Canada, and these ambassadors feel much freer to circumvent the State Department in shaping policy or to go their own way. By using "backchannels" to the White House or following their own views, they effectively reduce the role of the Department of State and even alienate the career personnel within an embassy.

The pattern of political appointments has become even more pronounced with the Bush administration. Through the end of 1989, about 57 percent of President Bush's appointments has come from campaign contributors and his political friends, a decidedly higher figure than for the previous five presidents (Figure 9.3). As a result, less than half of all ambassadorial appointments are career foreign service officers. U.S. ambassadors appointed to the Netherlands, Italy, Spain, and Australia, for example, were large campaign contributors, almost entirely lacking in foreign policy experience. The problem with such appointments is not only that they reduce the role of the Department of State, but that their inexperience may be

FIGURE 9.3 CAREER FOREIGN SERVICE OFFICERS AND POLITICAL FRIENDS AS AMBASSADORS, PRESIDENTS KENNEDY TO BUSH

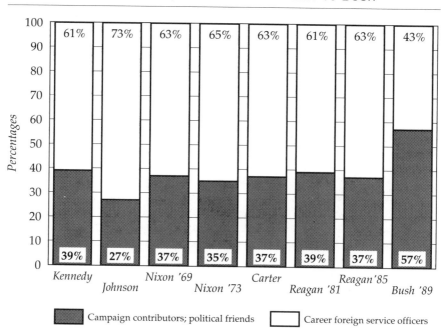

Note: Figures are the percentages of nominations for ambassadors from both career foreign service officers and political friends during the first ten months of each administration.

Source: *The New York Times*, November 7, 1989, p. A8. Copyright © 1989 by the New York Times Company. Reprinted by permission.

damaging to the conduct of U.S. foreign policy. One senator described such appointments as "ticking time bombs moving all over the world."[30]

A second way in which this suspicion is reflected is in the increased use of political appointees within the State Department itself and in weighing political loyalties in appointing foreign service officers as ambassadors abroad. A recent tactic was to engage in a "purge" of bureaus and personnel that were perceived as not fully committed to the administration's policy. The Bureau of Inter-American Affairs suffered this fate early in the Reagan administration because it was not fully in tune with the priorities of the White House. The assistant secretary of state of this bureau was replaced with a career diplomat perceived as more loyal to the administration's goal, albeit lacking in Latin American experience. When that appointment began to waver on policy, he was ultimately replaced by a political appointment who was a staunch conservative and wholly committed to the policy of aiding the Nicaraguan contras. Ambassadors to several Central American countries (El Salvador, Nicaragua, and Honduras) from the Carter administration were fired or transferred because they were not viewed as fully committed to a marked change in policy for the region. They were replaced by "foreign service officers with reputations as good generalists willing to follow orders and not raise troubling questions."[31]

The Bush administration has also employed a number of political appointees, particularly at the top of the State Department bureaucracy. The four key political operatives for Secretary Baker came from outside the department, and one of them is responsible for screening all papers that reach the secretary. By one account, the department's attitude "has evolved from deep hostility to ambivalence" toward Baker and these appointees. The career foreign service people "felt altogether shut out for a time, and to some extent they still are."[32] They are, however, pleased that Secretary Baker is personally close to the president because if they can break through to the leadership they can play a greater role in policymaking.

On balance, though, increasing numbers of political appointees, both as ambassadors and as key departmental leaders, and the use of apparent political tests within the department have eroded the role of the career official in policymaking. In a slightly different context, one former foreign service officer has said it best. "Creeping politicization has corrupted foreign service professionalism, and it has hindered American diplomacy.[33]

THE PUBLIC'S VIEW   A final reason for the Department of State's weakened influence is related to the earlier ones: the department has never really enjoyed a sound reputation among the American public. Beyond the view that the State Department is out of step with the nation as a whole, the department has continued to suffer from the attacks launched by Senator Joseph McCarthy in the 1950s. At one juncture, Senator McCarthy said that the State Department was "thoroughly infested with Communists" and that it contributed to the "loss" of China to communism.[34] Further, the public has not generally been very concerned about the state of American diplomacy in general or the Department of State in particular.[35] While the negative public image has waned over the decades, it, along with the other restraints evident within the department, has produced a certain caution in policy choices advanced by State Department personnel.

THE NATIONAL SECURITY COUNCIL

The bureaucracy that has enlarged its role in the foreign policy process over the last four decades has been the National Security Council (NSC) and its staff. It has grown from a relatively small agency with solely a policy coordinating function to one with a separate bureaucratic structure and major policymaking function. Its head, now designated as the assistant to the president for national security affairs (or the national security advisor), is viewed as a major formulator of U.S. foreign policy, often surpassing the influence of the secretary of state and the secretary of defense.

Because of this evolution, an important distinction ought to be kept in mind as we discuss two different, but related, bureaucratic arrangements operating under the National Security Council label. One bureaucratic arrangement refers to the "NSC system" and focuses on the departmental memberships on the National Security Council itself and the subsequent interagency committees established by the president to coordinate policymaking across the existing bureaucracies. That coordination process remains intact and is the focus of the last portion of Chapter 10. The other bureaucratic arrangement, and one that has become more commonly discussed lately, refers to the "NSC staff" (or simply "the NSC"), the separate bureaucracy that has developed over the years and that has increasingly played an independent role in U.S. foreign policymaking.[36] The following discussion focuses on the growth of that bureaucracy and its policymaking role.

THE DEVELOPMENT OF THE NSC BUREAUCRACY

As originally constituted under the National Security Act of 1947, the National Security Council was to be a mechanism for coordinating policy options among the various foreign affairs bureaucracies. By statute, members were to be limited to the president, vice-president, secretary of state, and secretary of defense, with the director of Central Intelligence and the chairman of the Joint Chiefs of Staff as advisors. These members, along with others that the president might choose to invite, met to consider policy options at the discretion of the president.[37] Over time, the NSC system has evolved with a set of interdepartmental committees to support the National Security Council itself. Table 9.1 portrays the usual composition of the National Security Council under the Bush administration.

Under the original legislative mandate, the assumption was that the *staff* of the NSC was to be small and its responsibilities focused

TABLE 9.1 COMPOSITION OF THE NATIONAL SECURITY COUNCIL

Statutory Members of the NSC
    President
    Vice-President
    Secretary of State
    Secretary of Defense

Statutory Advisors to the NSC
    Director of Central Intelligence
    Chairman, Joint Chiefs of Staff

Other Attendees
    Chief of Staff to the President
    Assistant to the President for National Security Affairs
    Secretary of Treasury
    Attorney General
    Others as invited

Source: U.S. Army War College, Carlisle Barracks, Pennsylvania, December 1989, and "National Security Council Organization," National Security Council mimeo, April 17, 1989.

largely on facilitating coordinating activities among the various foreign affairs departments. Indeed, the NSC staff originally had only three major components: the Office of the Executive Secretary, a Secretariat, and a unit simply called "The Staff." The executive secretary and the secretariat were the permanent employees of the NSC and generally undertook the actual coordinating activities of the council. "The Staff... initially consisted wholly of officials detailed on a full-time basis by the departments and agencies represented on the Council" and was assisted by full-time staff as well.[38] Their responsibilities focused on preparing studies on various regional and functional questions. Nonetheless, the staff members continued to maintain and coordinate their work with the respective departments from which they were drawn. Coordination across departments appeared to be more important than any independent assessment they might undertake.

    Presidents Truman and Eisenhower used the NSC as a coordinating body. Because President Truman had relatively strong secretaries of state, and because he tended to employ them for policy advice, he used the National Security Council meetings primarily as an arena for the exchange of ideas (often not attending the meetings himself until the outbreak of the Korean War). President Eisenhower, by contrast, met with the National Security Council on almost a weekly basis and relied upon it for decision-making discussions. (By one account, Eisenhower attended 306 out of 338 NSC meetings during his presidency.) Actual policy decisions, however, seemed to have been made outside this forum, especially as Secretary of State John Foster Dulles gained decision-making influence.[39] For neither of these presidents, though, was the NSC staff the independent policy influencer that it was to become.

Under Eisenhower, however, the structure and staff of the National Security Council bureaucracy began to change and gain some greater definition. Eisenhower, for instance, created the post of special assistant to the president for national security affairs for Robert Cutler and named him the "principal executive officer" of the NSC.[40] The staff structure was also revamped and enlarged and the mandate and duties of the NSC itself expanded. Most notably, President Eisenhower stated that members of the NSC were "a corporate body composed of individuals advising the President in their own right, rather than as representatives of their respective departments and agencies." In a later revision, however, he indicated that "the views of their respective departments and agencies" ought to be stated as well.[41] While Cutler and the NSC staff continued to perform their coordinating role, President Eisenhower's statements were the first hints of a more independent policy role for the NSC bureaucracy and its staff. Such a view of the NSC bureaucracy would eventually become a reality during the succeeding administrations.

THE RISE OF THE NATIONAL SECURITY ADVISOR

By the time of the Kennedy administration, the role of the National Security Council began to change and a more prominent role for the national security advisor ("special assistant for national security affairs") had begun to emerge. Now more reliance was placed by the president on key ad hoc advisors, including the national security advisor, but not on the NSC as such. In fact, few meetings of the council were held during the Kennedy years. Instead, the national security advisor began to emerge as a source of policymaking rather than as only a policy coordinator. Indeed, through Kennedy's reorganization of the NSC staff, the national security advisor had a number of previous staff responsibilities consolidated into his office. As a result, McGeorge Bundy became the first national security advisor to serve in such a policy-formulating and policy-coordinating capacity.[42]

This role was enhanced even more during the administration of President Lyndon Johnson. Walt W. Rostow, successor to Bundy as national security advisor in the later years of President Johnson's term, and a small group of advisors (the "Tuesday Lunch" group) played an increasingly large role in the formulation of American foreign policy, and especially Vietnam policy.[43] As during the Kennedy years, the national security advisor gained influence during the Johnson years, but the NSC as a decision or discussion forum actually declined in importance.

Not until the administration of President Richard Nixon was the full implication of this changed decision-making style most apparent.[44] With the appointment of Henry A. Kissinger as national security advisor, a transformation in foreign policymaking became evident. Henry Kissinger, an academic and a consultant to previous administrations, was familiar with, and critical of, the bureaucratic machinery of government. In large measure, he saw the bureaucracy as an impediment to effective policymaking and as hindering the job of the ''statesman.''[45]

Through his considerable personal skills, Kissinger was able to reorganize the decision-making apparatus of the foreign policy bureaucracies in a way that allowed him to dominate all the principal decision machinery. He accomplished this transformation through the development of a series of interdepartmental committees flowing from the National Security Council system. These committees included representatives from the other principal foreign policy bureaucracies, but, at the same time, they excluded those institutions from ultimate authority for making policy recommendations. In fact, Kissinger set up a Senior Review Group, which he himself chaired, for examining all policy recommendations before they were sent to the NSC and the president.[46] Even when Kissinger became secretary of state (as well as national security advisor) in September 1973, and after Gerald Ford became president in August 1974, this pattern of National Security Council staff dominance continued.

THE NATIONAL SECURITY ADVISOR IN THE CARTER AND REAGAN ADMINISTRATIONS

Under President Jimmy Carter, the initial impulse was to reduce the role of the national security advisor and his staff (partly in reaction to the role that Henry Kissinger had played in the previous eight years) and to place more responsibility for foreign policy in the hands of the secretary of state. The elaborate NSC committee system developed during the Kissinger years was initially pared back to only two committees.[47] More accurately, President Carter's goal was to balance the advice coming to the president from the secretary of state and the national security advisor. Ultimately, however, the national security advisor, Zbigniew Brzezinski, was able to play a more dominant role in

the shaping of foreign policy and to work his will in the policy process due to the force of his personality, his strong foreign policy
views, and the challenge of global events (e.g., the seizure of American diplomats in Iran in November 1979 and the Soviet invasion of
Afghanistan in December 1979).[48] This development only continued
the pattern of moving away from the Department of State and toward the national security advisor in the formulation of American
foreign policy.

Under the Reagan administration, a reversion to the earlier pattern of collegial policymaking was once again attempted. President
Reagan's first secretary of state, Alexander Haig, came to office determined to restore the dominance of the Department of State (and especially the secretary of state) and to make himself the "vicar" of
foreign affairs. In part to facilitate this reversion to the earlier model
of policymaking, a relatively inexperienced foreign policy analyst,
Richard Allen, was appointed by President Reagan to be the national
security advisor. In this environment, it seemed possible that the
secretary of state could reassert his authority as the dominant force
in the shaping of policy.

Although Secretary of State Haig achieved some initial success
in shaping the foreign policy of the Reagan administration, he failed
to dominate the process. As friction developed among the White
House staff (i.e., the national security advisor), the secretary of defense, and the secretary of state over a variety of policy matters ranging from U.S. policy in the Middle East to America's policy toward its
Western European allies, Haig's influence was eroded. With a newly
appointed national security advisor, William Clark, who was closer
personally and ideologically to President Reagan, Secretary Haig's
days turned out to be numbered. When Clark tilted against Haig
over European and Middle East policy, Haig was replaced as secretary of state by George Shultz in June 1982. Power seemed to be
shifting more perceptibly back to the White House and the national
security advisor.

Shultz initially appeared to be given some latitude in policymaking, but his role was soon eclipsed by that of National Security Advisor William Clark. A series of events reflected this shift in decision
making. The White House set up a new arms control group, chaired
by Clark himself, superseding the interagency group that had been
led by the Department of State. On Clark's initiative, a presidential
commission, with Henry Kissinger as chairman, was established to
review Latin American policy, further eroding State Department
control in that area. President Reagan was persuaded to announce
his Strategic Defense Initiative ("Star Wars") largely at the behest of

Clark and his deputy, Robert McFarlane, and without any systematic policy review within the national security system. Finally, the removal of the ambassador to El Salvador, the firing of the assistant secretary of state for Inter-American Affairs, and the change in the president's personal representative to the Middle East—and the replacement in all instances with individuals tied to the White House or the National Security Council—all illustrate the shift in policy process toward the NSC and away from the Department of State.[49] By one assessment, Clark "became the most influential foreign policy figure in Reagan's entourage" in a very short time.[50]

The shift was so perceptible that Shultz complained bitterly about his treatment. Normally a quiet, conservative, "team player" in the Reagan administration, Shultz reportedly complained directly to the president that he could not do his job effectively if foreign policy decisions were made without his participation.[51]

Under Robert McFarlane, Clark's successor as NSC advisor, Shultz gained a bit of influence, because McFarlane was not personally close to President Reagan and because McFarlane felt constrained by the president's insistence on "cabinet-style" government. Nevertheless, crucial national security decision directives were still issued by McFarlane's office, often without prior departmental clearance.[52] In this way, the national security advisor and his staff continued to play a large role in policy formulation.

Only in the latter portion of Reagan's second term was the NSC displaced from policy dominance. The principal reason for this change was the domestic political fallout from the Iran-contra affair, which had been publicly revealed in November 1986. While this affair in one sense demonstrated the extent to which the NSC had dominated policymaking (after all, the episode seemed to be directed entirely by individuals within the NSC), it also showed the dangers of such a procedure. Both investigations of this affair—the presidential inquiry, known as the Tower Commission, and the report of the two congressional committees—cited the dangers of allowing the National Security Council staff to run covert operations without presidential accountability, faulted the poor operation of the NSC system under the Reagan administration, and recommended reforms both in the actions of individuals and in the decision-making system itself.[53] Further, after the firing of John Poindexter as national security advisor, and as the Iran-contra affair unraveled, Poindexter's two successors—first Frank Carlucci and then Colin Powell—were much more inclined to serve as policy coordinators than as policy formulators. As a result, Secretary of State George Shultz increasingly dominated the policy process.

Even as Shultz exerted influence over policy in the latter portion of the Reagan administration, however, the rivalry with Secretary of Defense Caspar Weinberger remained. Their competition was both personal and political and had developed over a number of years. Indeed, political analyst Hedrick Smith characterized their rivalry as that between an elephant and a terrier. Shultz sought to move cautiously but attempted to dominate everything, while Weinberger sought to move quickly and sharply on a variety of fronts. Whether on arms control policy, the role of the U.S. military in Lebanon, retaliatory actions against terrorists, or Central American policy, their disputes proved legend.[54] Shultz prevailed more often than not, but his struggle still indicated the problem that the secretary of state faced, even in an administration committed to a "cabinet-style" government.

THE NSC AND THE NATIONAL SECURITY ADVISOR IN THE BUSH ADMINISTRATION

At least by formal design, the Bush administration returned to a more familiar pattern of NSC dominance of foreign policymaking. In National Security Directive 1 (NSD-1), President Bush placed National Security Advisor Brent Scowcroft and his deputy at the head of the foreign policymaking machinery by appointing them chairs of the two key coordinating committees of the NSC system—the NSC/Principals Committee and the NSC/Deputies Committee (see Chapter 10 for details on these committees).[55] As heads of these two committees, the NSC and its staff were in a strong position to dominate the Departments of State and Defense in the shaping of policy. Further, the national security advisor, albeit in consultation with the secretaries of state and defense, was given responsibilities for establishing appropriate interagency groups to develop policy options as the need arises.

The extent to which the national security advisor can actually dominate policy, of course, ultimately remained open to question, especially with James Baker as secretary of state. Baker's close personal ties to the president and his ready access to Bush raise some doubt about Scowcroft's ultimate role. With his previous experience in this role as national security advisor and his experience in bureaucratic politics, Scowcroft seems to be fairing quite well. He has put together a staff that has generally been applauded, and it undertook a broad review of American policy early on in Bush's term. Because Scowcroft does not seek the limelight, and because he is content to allow Secretary Baker to do more of the public relations side of foreign policy (e.g., congressional relations and trips abroad), some contend that Scowcroft can succeed as the principal molder and the real "mover and shaker" of American foreign policy within the foreign policy hierarchy.[56]

Another advantage that Scowcroft possesses (and other recent national security advisors possessed) is the elaborate bureaucratic structure that has evolved over the years. Figure 9.4 shows the structure of the National Security Council staff under President Bush. The NSC bureaucracy now has regional (e.g., Asian Affairs, African Affairs) and functional (e.g., International Economic Affairs, Arms Control) divisions and several important leadership positions. These positions start with the assistant to the president for national security affairs and his deputy, but they also include an executive secretary, a legal advisor, a legislative affairs advisor, and a counselor. As the NSC organizational structure imitates that of the Department of State, it is a direct and often successful competitor with that bureaucracy. Compare Figures 9.1 and 9.4 and note how similar the structures of the two organizations are.

The increasing importance of the NSC staff in foreign policy-making also reveals itself in the significance attached to the individuals appointed to its key positions. Indeed, an important gauge of the direction of American foreign policy can be gleaned from the kind of staff people appointed to the various divisions within the NSC organization and the foreign policy views that they possess. Moreover, these positions now rival and even surpass the importance of similar positions at the Department of State and the Department of Defense, and comparisons of the quality of the personnel at the NSC and other bureaucracies are now continuous.

WHY TWO DEPARTMENTS OF STATE?

With the National Security Council and the Department of State competing for influence, the foreign policy apparatus of the United States has actually evolved into what political scientist Bert Rockman calls two Departments of State.[57] There are now "regular" channels (through the Department of State) and "irregular" channels (through the National Security Council) for foreign policymaking. And, as we have suggested, the irregular processes have been in ascendancy within the executive branch over the past three decades. But why have these irregular channels come to dominate the foreign policy process?

Rockman offers several insightful reasons for their prominence.[58] System overload is the first one that he suggests. Overload refers to

FIGURE 9.4 THE STRUCTURE OF THE NATIONAL SECURITY COUNCIL STAFF UNDER PRESIDENT BUSH

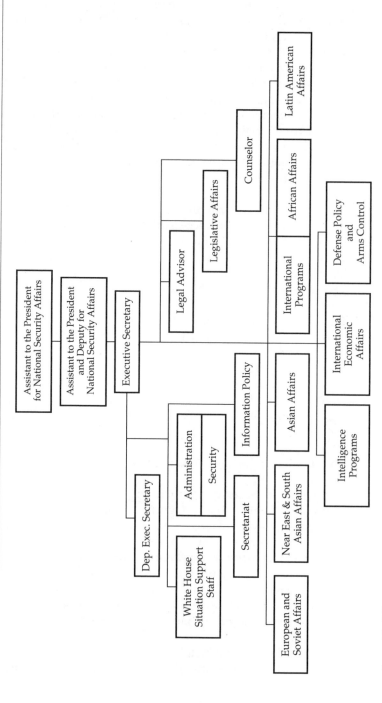

Source: The White House Press Office for Foreign Affairs, June 1991.

the tremendous amount of information and policy analyses available to the president from the various regular bureaucracies. Thus, the national security staff provides a ready arena for coordinating and distilling such a volume of material for the president—something that a single formal bureaucracy would probably be unable to do. As Rockman acknowledges, however, while overload might account for the coordination of policy within the NSC, it does not actually explain the decision-making growth of the NSC system. For this explanation, he looks to institutional and organizational arrangements within the foreign policy bureaucracies and the political culture within Washington.

Because the bureaucracies have their own parochial interests to protect, political advantage is often sought by one institution over another. A favorite tactic is the use of the press leak to undermine some unfavorable policy or position, especially in politically conscious Washington. This approach, moreover, is particularly endemic to the personnel in the regular channels, who believe that they are being left out of the decision process or who have, inevitably, divided loyalties—to the president on the one hand, and to their institutions on the other. Individuals in the irregular channels, however, would be less prone than disgruntled departmental officials to "go public" over a policy dispute, bound as they are to the president by appointment and ideology. Therefore, to protect his policy options, the president would prefer the confidentiality of his White House staff and the NSC system.

Along with the political rivalries, the regular channels (i.e., the Department of State) have institutional norms and bureaucratic subcultures that would be more prone to deflect (or "bury") innovative policy ideas that diverge too greatly from the status quo. By contrast, the irregular channels, presumably more committed to innovation and more committed to translating the president's views into policy, would be receptive to new ideas and might well be the catalyst of policy change themselves. In this way, too, the president's preferred position can be put into effect more quickly. Yet, as the Iran-contra affair shows us, this zealotry has a price. After all, the "irregular" channels of John Poindexter and Oliver North from the National Security Council system carried out this activity because, they contended, they were doing what they perceived as the president's will.

Finally, the political culture of Washington only exacerbates these bureaucratic tendencies. Because the nation's capital operates on "bureaucratic politics" (the competition among departments), the president is constantly in danger of becoming only an arbitrator between agencies rather than a policymaker if he cannot control this infighting. Since the ties between the White House and the departments are never as strong as between the White House and its immediate staff, there is a tendency to develop an "us versus them" relationship between these two groupings and to attempt to isolate the departments. In short, numerous incentives exist for the executive to feel more confident making foreign policy through his staff rather than through regular departments, including the Department of State.

SOME ECONOMIC BUREAUCRACIES AND FOREIGN POLICYMAKING

In the next chapter, we focus on two bureaucracies that deal with military or quasi-military (covert operations) aspects of policymaking. Our discussion in this chapter has focused upon two key foreign affairs bureaucracies that deal with political aspects of policymaking. A third aspect of the foreign policymaking bureaucracy, however, focuses upon economic questions. While those bureaucracies are often avoided or given cursory treatment in books on foreign policy, they are increasingly crucial to the actions of the United States abroad.[59] As more international policy questions address issues of international economics and finance such as trade, debt policy, or investment, American foreign policymaking becomes, more than ever, economic policymaking.

Several bureaucracies usually thought of as dealing with domestic policy only have actually emerged over the past four decades to assume important roles in shaping America's foreign economic policy. To illustrate both the breadth and the growth of these bureaucracies, we will identify several of them, describe the principal ways in which they contribute to foreign policymaking, and discuss some issues with which they have been associated recently. The four economic bureaucracies that we discuss are the Office of the U.S. Trade Representative, the Department of Commerce, the Department of the Treasury, and the Department of Agriculture. Some are more pivotal than others, and we shall try to specify their importance in the discussion.

THE USTR AND THE COMMERCE DEPARTMENT   The Office of the U.S. Trade Representative has been charged with developing and administrating all trade policy for the United States, and the head of that office, the U.S. trade representative (USTR), has been designated as the chief negotiator for virtually all trade activities. Although this office was created by executive order in 1963, its powers and responsibilities were enhanced in the 1970s and 1980s. By an executive reorganization plan in 1980, for example, its negotiating responsibilities were enhanced and its staff size doubled to about 80. With the passage of the Omnibus Trade and Competitiveness Act of 1988, the powers of the Office of the USTR were reaffirmed, and the USTR was given primary responsibility for undertaking trade retaliation actions against unfair trading partners of the United States. In effect, the Office of the USTR has become the "lead agency" for all international trade negotiations, and its representative now chairs all interagency groups on trade matters.[60]

Like the Office of the USTR, the Department of Commerce also benefited from the 1980 executive reorganization act and gained a wider mandate in formulating and implementing U.S. trade policy. It now has the principal responsibility for administering all import-export programs of the United States.[61] Two of the six major divisions within the department, moreover, are now directly involved in these tasks. They are the International Trade Administration and the Bureau of Export Administration, each headed by an under secretary of commerce.[62]

The International Trade Administration has the responsibility for all U.S. trade policy (except agricultural products) and for assisting the U.S trade representative in all trade negotiations. These activities range from formulating and implementing foreign economic policy, shaping all import policies, and promoting and developing American markets around the world. It also has the responsibility for operating the U.S. and Foreign Commercial Service, which aids American businesses seeking to export. Through some 68 district and branch offices within the United States and 124 posts abroad, this agency conducts a variety of activities to showcase U.S. products.[63]

Another important new function of the Department of Commerce is the enforcement of antidumping and countervailing duties statutes. (Prior to 1980, the Department of the Treasury had such responsibilities.) Antidumping statutes deal with monitoring imports from other countries to make certain goods being sold in the United States are not below "fair market value," while countervailing duties statutes focus on whether production costs have been subsidized in a foreign country, hence making them less costly in the U.S market.[64] In either instance, if such a determination were made, the department could recommend retaliation. Import duties, for example, could be added to the products in question. With the rise of the American trade deficit to $170 billion or more in recent years and with the rising tide of protectionism worldwide, monitoring American imports and recommending policy changes have become crucial aspects of American foreign economic policy.

While both the USTR and the Department of Commerce have gained some bureaucratic influence recently and have been working to open up foreign markets to American products, they have enjoyed limited policy success. The best-known recent example involves trade policy toward Japan. Both of these bureaucracies have taken a strong stand to pressure that country to open its markets. They have, however, met resistance not only from the Japanese, but from other bureaucracies within the executive as well. Even the Department of the Treasury, a seemingly natural ally on economic policy, takes a more cautious approach. As one Treasury official said: "We take a very broad macroeconomic view of U.S.–Japan relations. We don't worry much about specific products and industries." Another said: "We rely importantly on Japanese investment capital to help finance our trade and current account deficits."[65] The policy position of USTR and Commerce has also met resistance from those foreign affairs bureaucracies that examine the issue from a political-military perspective. The State and Defense departments, which both look at the political-military implications of pressuring Japan too much, are reluctant to endorse the stronger position of the USTR and the Department of Commerce. In this sense, while these two bureaucracies are increasingly important in foreign policy, they are still working to make their mark. As a result, the Department of Commerce remains a "subordinate power in the...foreign economic formulation councils of U.S. government," and the USTR is still "upstaged" by other bureaucracies.[66]

THE TREASURY DEPARTMENT   The economic bureaucracy that has enjoyed more foreign policy success has been the Department of the Treasury. The department has been described as the "*enfant terrible* of U.S. international economic policymaking," and it now dominates the rest of the bureaucracy on foreign economic questions. Its growth in policy influence has been attributed by one leading analyst to a variety of factors: the relative decline of American economic power globally, the increased recognition that external economic policies affect us at home, a renewed interest by policymakers in achieving economic goals by the United States, legislation granting the Treasury Department a greater global economic policy responsibility, and the enhanced role of the Secretary of the Treasury in economic policymaking, among others. Further, "the Treasury Department has undisputed control of U.S international monetary policy..., international financial policy..., and international tax policy," with only the Department of State as equally interested in the range of foreign economic policy.[67]

While Treasury has an elaborate bureaucratic structure in which various divisions could potentially have an impact on foreign economic policymaking, the center of its activity is the Office of the Assistant Secretary for International Affairs. This division, composed of 18 different offices with about 200 staff economists, has responsibility for conducting financial relations with industrial nations and with the International Monetary Fund, overseeing U.S. participation in various multinational lending institutions, evaluating foreign investments within the U.S. and American investments abroad, and analyzing economic data on a global scale.[68]

The foreign economic policymaking clout of Treasury can be gleaned from three initiatives taken by the department in the 1980s: the Plaza Pact of 1985, a five-nation agreement to lower the value of the dollar; the 1985 Baker Plan on international debt reform; and the Brady Plan of 1989, another proposal on international debt. The first initiative, the Plaza Pact, sought to reduce the value of the dollar against other leading currencies as a means of helping the U.S. and world economies. The pact took its name from the Plaza Hotel in New York, where representatives of the U.S., Japan, West Germany, France, and Great Britain met. These representatives agreed that "further orderly appreciation of the main non-dollar currencies against the dollar is desirable" and that their governments would encourage this kind of an outcome.[69] Because the dollar had risen in value against other currencies during the 1980s, the value of American goods increased, making them more expensive for other nations to buy. One result was that America's trade deficit increased dramatically. As a consequence, the United States was most interested in obtaining a decline in the value of the dollar. This effort was almost entirely a Treasury operation and really challenged the prevailing Reagan administration policy, which opposed U.S. government intervention in the market.[70]

The Baker Plan was a proposal offered by the U.S. secretary of the treasury at the 1985 annual meeting of the World Bank and the International Monetary Fund to address the burgeoning international debt crisis. It called for commercial banks to assist fifteen particularly indebted nations (e.g., Mexico, Argentina, Brazil in Latin America; Nigeria and Morocco in Africa; and the Philippines in Asia) by pledging to provide $20 billion in new loans through 1988 and for international lending institutions (e.g., the World Bank, and the Inter-American Development Bank) to provide $9 billion more. In exchange, the debtor nations would be asked to follow "anti-inflationary fiscal and monetary policies."[71] They would also be asked "to strengthen their private sectors, mobilize more domestic savings, facilitate investment, liberalize trade, and pursue market-oriented approaches to currencies, interest rates, and prices."[72] Once again, this kind of proposal represented a departure from past Reagan administration policy, and it demonstrated, too, that the Treasury Department was taking the lead on foreign economic policy.

The third example of the Treasury Department's policy, the Brady Plan of 1989 (named after President Bush's treasury secretary, Nicholas Brady), was devised within the department by an under secretary.[73] Unlike the Baker Plan, which proposed that poor countries grow their way out of debt, the Brady proposal was a debt-reduction proposal. Under this design, the commercial banks in rich countries would be encouraged to write off a portion of debt owed by Third World countries under a variety of schemes. One idea was to have international monetary institutions (e.g., the World Bank or the IMF) provide funding to poor countries, which, in turn, would buy back a portion of their debt from commercial banks at a reduced price. Another proposal would offer international guarantees to commercial banks for a portion of the debt owed by a country if those banks would write off a portion as well. Still a third idea, advanced before the Brady proposal, was for some form of "debt-equity swaps," where commercial banks get some property or asset within a country or get repaid in local currency for debt owed in dollars.

THE AGRICULTURE DEPARTMENT   A fourth important economic bureaucracy with direct foreign policy responsibilities is the U.S. Department of Agriculture (USDA). This department enters into the foreign policy arena through its involvement with agricultural trade and agricultural aid. Under several pieces of legislation, the USDA has the responsibility to monitor agricultural imports (and to suggest quotas if necessary) and to promote the export of American agricultural products. Under Public Law 480 (PL-480), the Agricultural Trade Development and Assistance Act, the USDA has primary responsibility for providing food aid to needy countries throughout the world.[74]

The principal agency for carrying out these foreign agricultural responsibilities is located in the International Affairs and Commodity Programs division, which is headed by an under secretary of agriculture. The Foreign Agriculture Service (FAS) is involved in formulating and implementing both agricultural trade and aid policy. On the trade side, the FAS is comprised of an elaborate system of agricultural attachés posted at about sixty American embassies abroad (but with responsibilities for about 110 countries worldwide) and an extensive staff of agricultural experts in Washington. These individuals have a wide array of duties, including observing the agricultural policies of host countries abroad, monitoring agricultural imports at home and making recommendations for quotas when necessary, analyzing agricultural trade patterns and trade prospects worldwide, and promoting American agricultural exports at home and abroad. Over the last decade, the FAS has also been authorized to open agricultural trade offices abroad as yet another way to promote American exports. To date, fifteen offices have been set up in key foreign markets. It also operates, in conjunction with the Commodity Credit Corporation (CCC) in USDA, the CCC's Export Credit Guarantee program, the Export Enhancement Program, and the sale of surplus commodities. These various programs represent further efforts to build markets abroad. On the aid side, the FAS plays a central role in managing the PL-480 program. This program provides both loans and grants in the form of food assistance, and it offers various incentives to help developing countries meet their food needs and develop their agricultural sectors.

At least two other USDA offices exist to promote trade and aid in agricultural products. The first is the Agricultural Trade and Development Mission Program, established by Congress in 1987. The primary duty of this program is to develop public- and private-sector trade missions abroad. The second is the Office of International Cooperation and Development, which, in collaboration with the Agency for International Development, works to share U.S. agricultural knowledge with other countries and to foster global cooperation.

According to a recent analysis, the policy impact of the USDA on international agricultural trade is mixed. On the one hand, the Foreign Agricultural Service has a "major input when agricultural trade matters are concerned" in the policymaking process, and its clout has increased "as U.S. agricultural trade has expanded."[75] In addition, President Bush's appointment of Clayton Yeutter as his first secretary of agriculture added further clout to the USDA in shaping agricultural policy. Yeutter had a sustained interest in trade policy (as a former U.S. trade representative) and was a strong believer in free trade in agriculture.[76] Indeed, the U.S. position in the Uruguay Round of the General Agreements on Tariffs and Trade (GATT) negotiations calling for dramatically lower agricultural subsidies and the elimination of trade barriers worldwide was indicative of his approach.

On the other hand, the impact of the USDA should not be over-stated. In the deliberations of the farm bill, which establishes domes-tic and international policy on agriculture every five years, "the trade policy apparatus is pretty much excluded from the process" during congressional deliberations.[77] Further, the Department of State, the Department of Commerce, the Office of Budget and Management, and the National Security Council have increased their interest and expertise in agricultural trade policy and, thus, are in a position to challenge the role of the Department of Agriculture.[78]

CONCLUDING COMMENTS

As this review of the Department of State, the National Security Council, and several economic bureaucracies demonstrates, the process of foreign policymaking is much more complex than is often realized, and more actors are involved in the process than we imme-diately think. Although the Department of State may be often identi-fied as the center of U.S. foreign diplomacy, the National Security Council has increasingly assumed a larger role in the shaping of American foreign policy. Similarly, while political and military issues are also often assumed as the pivotal ones in the foreign policy arena, economic issues are increasingly claiming more attention. Hence, the role of economic bureaucracies has been enlarged.

Although the foreign policy bureaucracies discussed so far are important to policymaking, other bureaucracies cannot be left out of this discussion. In the next chapter, therefore, we complete this sur-vey of the foreign affairs bureaucracies by looking at the Department of Defense and the bureaucracy known as the intelligence commu-nity. In that chapter, we shall also take a closer look at the structural and procedural arrangements used by the two most recent presi-dents to coordinate the policymaking process among these various bureaucracies within the executive branch.

NOTES

1. Graham Allison, *Essence of Decision: Explaining the Cuban Missile Crisis* (Boston: Little, Brown & Co., 1971), p. 144. It is also at p. 158, where Allison quotes from Roger Hilsman's *To Move a Nation* (Garden City, NY: Doubleday Pub-lishing, 1964), p. 6.

2. Allison, *Essence of Decision: Explaining the Cuban Missile Crisis* and Mor-ton H. Halperin, with the assistance of Priscilla Clapp and Arnold Kanter,

Bureaucratic Politics and Foreign Policy (Washington, D.C.: The Brookings Institution, 1974).

3. Strobe Talbott, *Deadly Gambits: The Reagan Administration and the Stalemate in Nuclear Arms Control* (New York: Vintage Books, 1985).

4. The phrase is from the subtitle of Chapter 15 in Hedrick Smith, *The Power Game: How Washington Works* (New York: Ballantine Books, 1988), p. 558.

5. *Department of State Completes 200 Years* (Washington, D.C.: United States Department of State, Bureau of Public Affairs, 1982), p. 1.

6. *U.S. Government Manual 1989/1990*, July 1, 1989, pp. 433–437, provides a succinct description of the various bureaus and their responsibilities within the State Department. The *Manual* is an indispensable source for quick reference on virtually all government agencies.

7. Ibid., pp. 723–730, and *Atlas of United States Foreign Relations* (Washington, D.C.: United States Department of State, Bureau of Public Affairs, December 1985), pp. 12–13.

8. See Appendix A, "Major Changes in the AID Organizational Structure," in AID's *Administrative and Management Problems in Providing Foreign Economic Assistance*, Hearing before a subcommittee of the Committee on Government Operations, House of Representatives, 97th Cong., 1st Sess., October 6, 1981, p. 423; the *U.S. Government Manual 1989/1990*, July 1, 1989, pp. 730–739; *U.S. Government Manual 1990/1991*, July 1, 1990, p. 428; and *Key Offices of Foreign Service Posts: Guide for Business Representatives* (Washington, D.C.: Department of State, September 1990) for the subsequent discussion of U.S. representation abroad. On the restoration of Albanian-U.S. relations, see "U.S. and Albania Re-establish Diplomatic Ties After 52 Years," *New York Times*, March 16, 1991, p. 3.

9. Ibid., pp. 432–439, and *Atlas of United States Foreign Relations*, pp. 8–14.

10. Ronald I. Spiers, "Diplomacy, the Foreign Service, and the Department of State" (Washington, D.C.: United States Department of State, Bureau of Public Affairs, March 1986), p. 1.

11. Among some readings that criticize the effectiveness of the Department of State are the following: I. M. Destler, *Presidents, Bureaucrats, and Foreign Policy* (Princeton, NJ: Princeton University Press, 1974), pp. 154–190; John Franklin Campbell, "The Disorganization of State," in Martin B. Hickman, ed., *Problems of American Foreign Policy*, 2nd ed. (Beverly Hills, CA: Glencoe Press, 1975), pp. 151–170; Robert Pringle, "Creeping Irrelevance At Foggy Bottom," *Foreign Policy* 29 (Winter 1977/78): 128–139; Andrew M. Scott, "The Department of State: Formal Organization and Informal Culture," *International Studies Quarterly* 13 (March 1969): 1–18; and Andrew M. Scott, "The Problem of the State Department," in Martin B. Hickman, ed., *Problems of American Foreign Policy*, pp. 143–151.

12. Elaine Sciolino, "Austerity at State Dept. and Fear of Diplomacy," *New York Times*, November 15, 1987, pp. 1 and 8; and John M. Goshko, "State Dept. Budget Faces New Cuts," *The Washington Post*, April 27, 1987, p. A6. The quoted passages are from the latter.

13. On the continuing budget concerns, see Ronald I. Spiers, "The 'Budget Crunch' and the Foreign Service" (Washington, D.C.: United States Department of State, Bureau of Public Affairs, May 1988); and James Baker, "U.S. Foreign Policy Priorities and FY 1991 Budget Request" (Washington, D.C.: United States Department of State, Bureau of Public Affairs, February 1990).

14. On this point, see Henry T. Nash, *American Foreign Policy: Changing Perspectives on National Security* (Homewood, IL: The Dorsey Press, 1978), p. 139. Also, see Nash's excellent discussion on the problems of State from which our overall discussion benefited.

15. Spiers, "Diplomacy, the Foreign Service, and the Department of State," p. 1.

16. David Garnham, in particular, has looked at one of these stereotypes about the Department of State. While he finds that the background characteristics of FSOs differ from those of the general population, he reports that the FSOs do not differ from other groups in American society in psychological flexibility. Overall, he judges that this elitism has not negatively affected the conduct of U.S. foreign policy. See his "State Department Rigidity: Testing a Psychological Hypothesis," *International Studies Quarterly* 18 (March 1974): 31–39; and "Foreign Service Elitism and U.S. Foreign Affairs," *Public Administration Review* 35 (January/February 1975): 44–51.

17. Duncan L. Clarke, "Why State Can't Lead," *Foreign Policy* 66 (Spring 1987): 134

18. Ibid., pp. 133–134. "Foggy Bottom" refers to the area of Washington, D.C., where the Department of State and several executive agencies are located. Indeed, it is so familiar to Washington residents that it has its own subway stop named "Foggy Bottom."

19. Scott, "The Problem of the State Department," p. 146. Emphasis in original.

20. Scott, "The Department of State: Formal Organization and Informal Culture," p. 6.

21. Nash, *American Foreign Policy: Changing Perspectives,* p. 139.

22. See I. M. Destler, "National Security Advice to U.S. Presidents: Some Lessons from Thirty Years," *World Politics* 24 (January 1977): 148–149, 153–154, 156–157. Also see I. M. Destler, *Presidents, Bureaucrats, and Foreign Policy,* pp. 96–99, for some differing views on how much President Kennedy wanted to rely upon the Department of State for foreign policy formulation.

23. Ibid., pp. 157–158, for a discussion of the extent of Rostow's duties and for a sense of how the secretaries of state and defense were involved in the process.

24. Smith, *The Power Game: How Washington Works,* pp. 558–562; and Theodore C. Sorenson, "The President and the Secretary of State," *Foreign Affairs* 66 (Winter 1987/88): 231–248. But also see Leslie H. Gelb, "McFarlane Carving His Niche," *New York Times,* March 28, 1984, p. B10.

25. Nash, *American Foreign Policy: Changing Perspectives,* p. 100.

26. The quotes are from Maureen Dowd and Thomas L. Friedman, "The Fabulous Bush and Baker Boys," *The New York Times Magazine,* May 6, 1990, p. 36. The other analyses used to assess the close ties between Bush and Baker and the enhanced role of the national security advisor under Bush were John Newhouse, "Profiles (James Baker)," *The New Yorker,* May 7, 1990, pp. 50–82; and Bernard Weinraub, "Bush Backs Plan To Enhance Role of Security Staff," *New York Times,* Feburary 2, 1989, pp. 1 and 6.

27. Dowd and Friedman, "The Fabulous Bush and Baker Boys," p. 64.

28. Jack Perry, "The Foreign Service in Real Trouble, But It Can Be Saved," *Washington Post National Weekly Edition,* January 16, 1984, p. 21.

29. John M. Goshko, "Appointing Loyalists as Envoys," *Washington Post,* April 28, 1987, pp. A1, A16. The data for the other presidents is taken from Elaine Sciolino, "Friends as Ambassadors: How Many Is Too Many?" *New York Times,* November 7, 1989, pp. A1 and A8.

30. Sciolino, "Friends as Ambassadors: How Many Is Too Many?" p. A8.

31. John M. Goshko, "Clout and Morale Decline," *Washington Post,* April 26, 1987, p. A12.

32. Newhouse, "Profiles (James Baker)," p. 76.

33. Perry, "The Foreign Service in Real Trouble, But It Can Be Saved," p. 21.

34. Cited in Campbell, "The Disorganization of State," p. 155.

35. Perry, "The Foreign Service in Real Trouble, But It Can Be Saved," p. 22.

36. I am grateful to Smith, *The Power Game: How Washington Works*, p. 589, for drawing this distinction between the two. "The NSC" is his term.

37. Membership on the National Security Council has varied slightly by statute over time, but these are the ones that have remained continuously on the council.

38. James S. Lay, Jr., and Robert H. Johnson, "Organizational History of the National Security Council during the Truman and Eisenhower Administrations," Report prepared for the Subcommittee on National Policy Machinery, August 11, 1960, p. 8.

39. Destler, "National Security Advice to U.S. Presidents: Some Lessons from Thirty Years," pp. 148–151, 153–159. Also see Nash, *American Foreign Policy: Changing Perspectives*, pp. 140, 172–174. On Truman's and Eisenhower's attendance of NSC meetings, see Lay and Johnson, "Organizational History of the National Security Council during the Truman and Eisenhower Administrations," pp. 5 and 24.

40. Ibid., p. 26. The characterization of Cutler as "the principal executive officer" is Lay and Johnson's.

41. Ibid., p. 30, and footnote 61.

42. For a discussion of how President Kennedy transformed the role of the national security advisor with Bundy, see I. M. Destler, "National Security Management: What Presidents Have Wrought," *Political Science Quarterly* 95 (Winter 1980/81): 578–580; and Bromley K. Smith, "Organizational History of the National Security Council During the Kennedy and Johnson Administrations," Monograph written for the National Security Council, February 1987.

43. See Townsend Hoopes, *The Limits of Intervention* (New York: David McKay, 1968) for a discussion of the important influence of Rostow on LBJ, especially at pp. 20–22 and 59–62. For the identity, and a critique, of the "Tuesday Lunch" group, see Irving Janis, *Groupthink* (Boston: Houghton Mifflin Company, 1972), pp. 101–135.

44. Destler, "National Security Management: What Presidents Have Wrought," p. 580.

45. Henry A. Kissinger, "Domestic Structure of Foreign Policy," in James N. Rosenau, ed., *International Politics and Foreign Policy*, rev. ed. (New York: Free Press, 1969), pp. 261–275, especially pp. 263–267.

46. See the diagram of the "Kissinger National Security Council System," in Nash, *American Foreign Policy: Changing Perspectives*, p. 197.

47. Elizabeth Drew, "A Reporter At Large: Brzezinski," *The New Yorker* (May 1, 1978), p. 94, reports that the initial National Security Council under Brzezinski consisted of only two committees: the Policy Review Committee and the Special Coordination Committee.

48. See the discussion of Brzezinksi's role in Chapter 4. Also see Zbigniew Brzezinski, *Power and Principle: Memoirs of the National Security Advisor, 1977–1981* (New York: Farrar, Straus, Giroux, 1983).

49. On the disputes that precipitated Haig's firing, see Steven R. Weisman, "Aides List Clashes," *New York Times*, June 26, 1982, pp. 1 and 5; and Leslie H. Gelb, "A Year in Office, Shultz Still Mapping His Way Through Diplomacy's Thicket," *Milwaukee Journal*, August 7, 1983, Accent on the News section, p. 2. Also see "Disappearing Act at Foggy Bottom," *Time*, August 8, 1983, p. 28.

50. Smith, *The Power Game: How Washington Works,* p. 593. The characterization of Clark's role in pushing the Strategic Defense Initiative is from pp. 594–599.

51. See "Shultz: No More Mr. Nice Guy?" *Newsweek,* August 22, 1983, p. 17; and "Schultz Peeved, Magazine Says," *Des Moines Register,* August 15, 1983, p. 8A. For Secretary of State Shultz's denial of the report, see "Aide Denies Shultz Losing His Influence," *Des Moines Register,* August 16, 1983, pp. 1A, 2A.

52. Leslie H. Gelb, "McFarlane Carving His Niche," *New York Times,* March 28, 1983, p. B10.

53. *Report of the President's Special Review Board (Tower Commission Report)* (Washington, D.C.: U.S. Government Printing Office, February 26, 1987); and *Report of the Congressional Committees Investigating the Iran-Contra Affair* (Washington, D.C.: U.S. Government Printing Office, November 1987).

54. Smith, *The Power Game: How Washington Works,* pp. 570–576.

55. Weinraub, "Bush Backs Plan To Enhance Role of Security Staff," pp. 1 and 6, and National Security Council statement, "National Security Council Organization," mimeo, April 17, 1989, 3 pp.

56. John Barry with Margaret Garrard Warner, "Mr. Inside, Mr. Outside," *Newsweek,* February 27, 1989, p. 28; and R. W. Apple, Jr., "A Mover and Shaker Behind Bush Foreign Policy," *New York Times,* February 6, 1989, p. 3.

57. Bert A. Rockman, "America's Departments of State: Irregular and Regular Syndromes of Policy Making," *The American Political Science Review* 75 (December 1981): 911–927.

58. Ibid., pp. 914–918. While this section draws upon Rockman's explanations, some of my own interpretations are added to his insights.

59. Two books that address these economic bureaucracies and that have influenced the following discussion are Charles W. Kegley, Jr., and Eugene R. Wittkopf, *American Foreign Policy: Pattern and Process,* 4th ed. (New York: St. Martin's Press, 1990); and Howard J. Wiarda, *Foreign Policy Without Illusion* (Glenview, IL: Scott, Foresman/Little Brown Higher Education, 1990).

60. See Stephen D. Cohen, *The Making of United States International Economic Policy,* 3rd ed. (New York: Praeger, 1988), p. 67, for the characterization of the USTR and other background information. The *U.S. Government Manual 1989/1990,* July 1, 1989, pp. 94–95, was also a source.

61. Cohen, *The Making of United States International Economic Policy,* p. 69.

62. *U.S. Government Manual 1989/1990,* July 1, 1989, p. 146.

63. Ibid., pp. 154–155.

64. Cohen, *The Making of United States International Economic Policy,* p. 70; and Kegley and Wittkopf, *American Foreign Policy: Pattern and Process,* p. 400.

65. These officials are quoted in Robert Pear, "Confusion Is Operative Word in U.S. Policy Toward Japan," *New York Times,* March 20, 1989, p. 6.

66. Cohen, *The Making of United States International Economic Policy,* pp. 70 and 230, respectively.

67. The quotation passages and the set of factors to explain Treasury's growth in influence are from ibid., pp. 60, 61, and 64.

68. Ibid., p. 62, and *U.S. Government Manual 1989/1990,* p. 492.

69. The quote is from Robert D. Hormats, "The World Economy Under Stress," in William G. Hyland, ed., *American and the World 1985* (New York: Pergamon Press, 1986), p. 469. Another source used here was Congressman Lee Hamilton, "The Decline of the Dollar," *Washington Report,* February 25, 1987.

70. The estimate of Treasury involvement is from Cohen, *The Making of United States International Economic Policy,* p. 215, in which he cites an unattributed interview with a Treasury Department official (note 14, p. 219).

71. S. Karene Witcher, "Baker's Plan to Relieve Debt Crisis May Spur Future Ills, Critics Say," *The Wall Street Journal,* November 15, 1985, p. 1.

72. Hormats, "The World Economy Under Stress," p. 474.

73. It was devised by Under Secretary David C. Mulford. See John R. Cranford, "Members Press for Details on Brady Proposal," *Congressional Quarterly Weekly Report,* March 18, 1989, p. 572, for this point and some examples of how the plan would work; and John R. Cranford, "Brady Signals Shift in Policy Toward Debt Reduction," *Congressional Quarterly Weekly Report,* March 11, 1989, pp. 510–513, for an earlier discussion of the plan.

74. The discussion and what follows mainly draws upon *U.S. Government Manual 1989/1990,* July 1, 1989, pp. 104, 122–129, supplemented with Cohen, *The Making of United States International Economic Policy,* pp. 70–71. I am also indebted to my colleague, Ross B. Talbot, for sharing his insight on agricultural policy-making.

75. H. Wayne Moyer and Timothy E. Josling, *Agricultural Policy Reform: Politics and Process in the EC and the USA* (New York: Harvester Wheatsheaf, 1990), pp. 124 (note 6) and 120.

76. George Athan, "Yeutter Likely to Push for Free Trade, Exports," *Des Moines Register,* December 15, 1988, pp. 1A and 11A.

77. Moyer and Josling, *Agricultural Policy Reform: Politics and Process in the EC and the USA,* p. 124 (note 6).

78. See Raymond F. Hopkins and Donald J. Puchala, *Global Food Interdependence: Challenge to American Foreign Policy* (New York: Columbia University Press, 1980), pp. 110–115, for a discussion of tensions between the Department of State and the USDA and the expansion of agricultural capacities in other bureaucracies in the 1970s.

CHAPTER 10 THE MILITARY AND INTELLIGENCE BUREAUCRACIES: PERVASIVE OR ACCOUNTABLE?

"The formulation of U.S. defense policy is at once a debate—concerning extremely complex judgments as to military threats, requirements, strategies, and technologies—and a tug of war—between powerful and often unseen interests in the defense establishment." **RICHARD A. STUBBING WITH RICHARD A. MENDEL, *THE DEFENSE GAME*, 1986**

"The [Central Intelligence] Agency does not make national policy but implements it, and the Clandestine Service is the Agency's action arm. It does not seek danger but accepts the necessary risks of its mission." **CIA RECRUITMENT BROCHURE ON THE CLANDESTINE SERVICE**

This chapter continues the discussion of the bureaucracies and foreign policy by examining the Department of Defense and the intelligence community. Each of these bureaucracies has enjoyed an ascendancy in power over the post–World War II years, but both now have also come under closer scrutiny as the post–Cold War years have begun. Our discussion highlights those changes over time and assesses each bureaucracy's relative position in the 1990s. Further, this chapter explains the mechanism that the executive branch uses to coordinate policymaking across the various bureaucracies that we discuss in the first part of this chapter and in Chapter 9. While each bureaucracy can have a separate impact on foreign policy, their combined effect, or the success of one bureaucracy over another, is manifested most directly through the national security interagency or interdepartmental coordination process that all recent presidents have relied upon.

THE DEPARTMENT OF DEFENSE

The Department of Defense (DOD) may well be thought of as a bureaucracy that only implements policy, but, in fact, the DOD contributes substantially to the formulation of foreign policy decisions. Its power has grown extensively over the years, but the extent of its role in foreign policy formulation is still widely debated. Some would argue that it is but one bureaucracy within the foreign policy apparatus, albeit a powerful one.[1] Others would argue that it has a pervasive effect on American foreign policymaking—often surpassing the competing bureaucracies within the executive branch.[2] Still others would go even further; they suggest that it is the beginning point for the "military-industrial complex" that is woven into American society (see Chapter 11).[3] Yet another view, especially today, is that the military and its role ought to be changed substantially with the advent of the post–Cold War era and dramatic changes in Eastern Europe. Whichever view is adopted by the reader, there can be little doubt that the Department of Defense has increased its foreign policymaking influence over the years and, even in the face of changes in the 1990s, is likely to remain influential for the foreseeable future.

THE STRUCTURE OF THE PENTAGON

This perceived influence of the DOD begins with its considerable size and presence in the foreign policy decision-making apparatus of the government. As Figure 10.1 shows, the Pentagon (located across

FIGURE 10.1   THE STRUCTURE OF THE DEPARTMENT OF DEFENSE

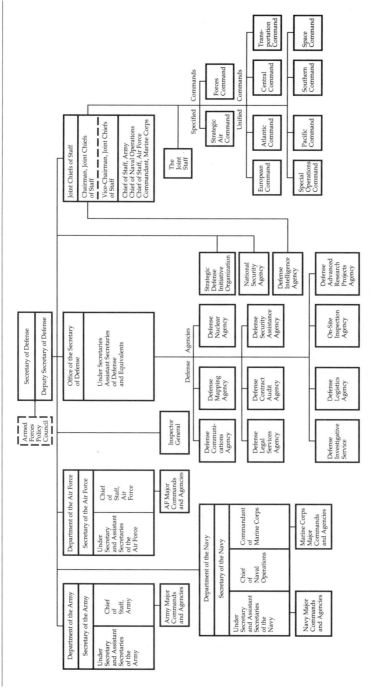

Source: Directorate for Organizational and Management Planning, Office of the Secretary of Defense, *Organization and Functions Guidebook* (Washington, D.C.: Department of Defense, August 1988), p. 4.

the Potomac River from the nation's capital in Arlington, Virginia, and named for the shape of DOD's headquarters) is a large and complex bureaucracy organized into key major divisions. These major divisions are further subdivided into a variety of departments, agencies, and offices that potentially affect many areas of American life.

The Department of Defense is linked to the American public through defense contracts, through domestic and foreign jobs for U.S. corporations, and through the number of men and women serving in the military services. In fiscal year 1988, for example, over $142 billion in prime defense contracts were awarded within the U.S., with every state sharing in those awards, which fostered thousands of jobs. In 1990, the DOD itself employed about one million civilian and two million military personnel. The defense budget now totals more than $300 billion in spending authority.[4] Even with projected cuts in the defense budget (the so-called "peace dividend") as a result of the dramatic changes in Eastern Europe in 1989 and 1990, the pervasiveness of military expenditures and involvement in American life will remain, especially with the recent successes of the military in the Persian Gulf War.

In terms of foreign policy formulation, three sectors of the Department of Defense are pivotal: (1) the Office of the Secretary of Defense (OSD); (2) the Joint Chiefs of Staff (JCS); and (3) the secretary of defense. The Office of the Secretary of Defense is the newest and potentially the greatest source of influence in affecting foreign policy formulation. It is the staff arm of the secretary of defense and is composed of a variety of offices and agencies that deal with the management of the department and the development of foreign policy recommendations. Among its mandated duties are the responsibility to "conduct analyses, develop policies, provide advice, make recommendations, and issue guidance on Defense plans and programs." It also has the responsibility to "develop systems and standards for the administration and management of approved plans and programs."[5] As OSD has grown over the years, this office has become the principal focus for policy development and administration within the DOD.

The policy planning importance of this office can be illustrated by examining the policy section within OSD, which is headed by an under secretary of defense for policy. Within this section are offices for International Security Affairs, International Security Policy, Trade Security Policy, Planning and Resources, and Net Assessment. Each of these offices is headed by an assistant secretary of defense, and each has an important stake in policy development.

Two middle-level offices within OSD will illustrate the increased policy formulation role of the DOD as a whole: the Office of International Security Affairs (ISA) and the Office of International Security Policy. The former, in particular, gained prominence during the Vietnam War period when it was instrumental in offering policy advice.[6] Moreover, its responsibilities today cover such issues as security assistance, military assistance advisory groups and missions abroad, international economic and energy activities, and the oversight of agreements with other nations, excluding the NATO countries.[7] ISA has gained such prominence in policymaking that it has been labeled the "little State Department," because it is said to provide the political component to the military analysis of the Pentagon. The ISA, however, seemed to have declined in influence from Nixon to Carter through some structural and procedural realignments.[8]

More recently, the Office of International Security Policy has assumed a larger role for policy influence within the DOD. This bureau's responsibilities include policy development on NATO and European affairs, including nuclear and conventional forces, strategic and theater arms negotiations, nuclear proliferation questions, and oversight of existing agreements.[9] During the Reagan administration, the assistant secretary of defense for international security policy was particularly prominent in speaking out on arms policy. Richard Perle often took the lead in shaping policy on the question of deploying intermediate-range nuclear missiles in Europe in the early 1980s and in developing the U.S. bargaining position on both intermediate-range and long-range nuclear forces at the arms control talks in Geneva, Switzerland. Indeed, his role in these negotiations and in policy development generally was so substantial that it has been chronicled at book length and in great detail by a political analyst, a rarity for a middle-level official in the foreign policy bureaucracy.[10]

Although these offices have not obtained the same notoriety in the Bush administration, their role in policy formulation has become more routinized over the years. At the same time, the importance of these two offices, or any other in the Department of Defense, will ultimately be a function of how the secretary of defense, or even the president, wants to use them to shape foreign policy.

THE JOINT CHIEFS OF STAFF

Other important policy advisors within the Department of Defense are the Joint Chiefs of Staff (JCS). The JCS, composed of the chief of staff of the Army, the chief of Naval Operations, the chief of staff of the Air Force, the commandant of the Marine Corps, and the chairman of the Joint Chiefs, have been described as "the hinge between the most senior civilian leadership and the professional military."[11] The responsibility of the JCS is to provide the president and the secretary of defense with strategic planning and to coordinate the integration of the armed forces for use if necessary. In addition, the JCS recommends to the president and the secretary of defense the military requirements of the United States and how they are to be accomplished. Finally, the chairman of the Joint Chiefs, appointed by the president with the advice and consent of the Senate, is the primary military advisor to the secretary of defense, the National Security Council, and the president.

Despite its statutory foreign policy duties, the Joint Chiefs of Staff probably have been less effective in shaping American policy than the civilian side of the Pentagon. One important reason is that the Joint Chiefs have enjoyed only mixed favor with both presidents and secretaries of defense since 1947.[12] In fact, some presidents and secretaries have been at odds with the JCS and have tried to reduce their policy impact.

President Eisenhower, for instance, was determined to "balance the budget and restrict military spending"—something the JCS did not favor.[13] With Eisenhower's own vast military experience in World War II, he did not see the need to rely upon the JCS for advice and assistance, especially after it had publicly criticized his policy. Under President Kennedy, the situation for the JCS only worsened, as Secretary of Defense Robert McNamara attempted to streamline and modernize the management and operation of the Pentagon. In addition, any initial confidence that President Kennedy might have placed in the JCS quickly eroded over what he perceived as bad policy advice on the Bay of Pigs invasion in April 1961.[14]

Relations between the JCS and later postwar presidents improved somewhat. During the Johnson administration, relations warmed a bit—especially after the disaffection and, ultimately, the resignation of Secretary of Defense McNamara in 1967—when the chief executive increasingly became dependent upon the JCS for policy advice on the Vietnam War. Even before this occurrence, however, there is some evidence of President Johnson's more favorable tilt toward the DOD, if not directly the Joint Chiefs, in foreign policy-making.[15] Under Presidents Nixon and Ford and during the years when Melvin Laird was Secretary of Defense, the Joint Chiefs were clearly in the ascendancy in terms of influence, even though they did not apparently shape the critical policy positions during those years.[16]

Under the Carter administration, the situation changed once again, with less reliance on their input. Moreover, major policy decisions on troop withdrawals from Korea and the scrapping of the B-1 bomber were done with minimal JCS involvement.[17] By contrast, the Reagan administration appeared to be more receptive to the views of the JCS. At one point in his administration, President Reagan reportedly sent written praise to the Joint Chiefs for their policy advice.[18] Despite such praise, policymaking for the Reagan administration was largely located elsewhere within the executive branch and within the Department of Defense.

A second important factor that has often reduced the policy impact of the Joint Chiefs of Staff is the commitment that each member has toward his own service.[19] That is, each JCS member has the responsibility of managing his own military service in addition to his advisory responsibilities to the president and the secretary of defense through the Joint Chiefs arrangement. As a result, in the estimate of one defense analyst, this service responsibility consumes an important portion of the Joint Chiefs' time and diminishes their foreign policy formulation role. The divided loyalties among JCS members, moreover, produces policy differences among the Joint Chiefs themselves, and policy recommendations reflect a compromise position that may be defended less vigorously by all of the members.[20]

Criticisms of the JCS's recommendations have been particularly harsh. President Jimmy Carter's secretary of defense, Harold Brown, for instance, characterized the advice from the JCS as "worse than nothing." Another former high-ranking Pentagon official labeled it as "a laughingstock." Yet a third official—a former aide to Brown—said the advice was like a "bowl of oatmeal." Despite President Reagan's praise of the JCS, Secretary of Defense Caspar Weinberger rejected or ignored the advice of the Joint Chiefs on such major issues as the basing mode for the MX and on the requirements of the Rapid Deployment Force.[21] Perhaps even more telling regarding the weakened influence of the JCS was President Reagan's failure to even remember the name of the chairman of the Joint Chiefs during a major portion of his administration. When testifying during the Iran-contra trial of John Poindexter, President Reagan was asked if he recognized the name of John Vessey, chairman of the JCS during much of his term in office. While he said that the name sounded "very familiar," he could not be certain as to who he was.[22]

In 1986, however, the Congress reorganized the Joint Chiefs of Staff in a manner to provide more political impact for the staff as such and to reduce the clout of the individual services in policy recommendations. One key change was to give more power to the chairman of the Joint Chiefs of Staff in policy formulation and recommendation. The chairman (and not the Joint Chiefs as such) was designated as the president's primary military advisor and was given the responsibility for providing the executive with a range of military advice on any matter requested. In addition, the chairman was given statutory responsibility for preparing strategic military plans, future military contingency plans, and budget coordination within the military. Finally, the chairman was provided greater control over the JCS and a vice-chairman to assist him.[23]

The other key change was in the command structure. Once again, the unified commanders, those responsible for coordinating the four different services operating under their command in a particular region of the world, were given more authority. Under the previous arrangement, the individual services retained substantial authority. Under this reorganization, greater integration of forces was envisioned and greater authority was placed in those directing multi-service operations.

As a result of these organizational changes and its appointment of General Colin Powell as chairman of the Joint Chiefs of Staff, the Bush administration seemed to have signaled that it wants the JCS to play a greater role on its national security decision-making team. Powell was formerly the national security advisor during the last year of the Reagan administration and was well versed in national security policy and the policymaking process. He has been described as a "military intellectual" and as a person who takes a "pragmatic and collegial approach" to policymaking. In this sense, he is likely to fit in well with the rest of the key staff appointments made by President Bush, and his views are likely to get a full hearing. The JCS's newfound status in the Bush administration is also reflected in the fact that the chairman of the JCS sits on a new executive defense committee established by the secretary of defense.[24] Furthermore, General Powell played a key role in shaping the U.S. response to Iraq's intervention into Kuwait and the resulting American buildup in Saudi Arabia and the Persian Gulf. By one assessment, Powell was "responsible for shaping the U.S. military response in the Gulf," and his strategy of deploying "maximum force" was fully endorsed by President Bush.[25]

THE SECRETARY OF DEFENSE

The third, and perhaps most important, policy advisor within the Defense Department is the secretary of defense. Over the postwar years, the secretary's role in policymaking has been enhanced considerably. As the secretary's control of the department increased through the reform acts of 1953 and 1958, and as the confidence of presidents in their secretaries of defense rose, the influence of this office in foreign policy was enlarged.[26] Two analyses challenge this view and note that the powers of the secretary of defense are less than the responsibilities of the office, and that the relative influence of the secretary can be easily overstated.[27] While noting the cautionary signs that have been raised over the power of the secretary of defense, a good case can be made that on particular issues and in recent administrations the secretaries of defense have often commanded as much influence as the secretaries of state. A brief survey of the most important occupants of this post seems to support this view.

The most influential of the fifteen secretaries of defense since 1947 has been Robert McNamara, who was secretary of defense throughout President Kennedy's years in office and for most of President Lyndon Johnson's years. With his close ties to both presidents, McNamara, more than any other cabinet officer, exercised policy influence.[28] Given a wide mandate to modernize the Pentagon, McNamara was also allowed substantial latitude in shaping America's strategic nuclear policy. Moreover, he was the spokesperson who announced the change in strategic doctrine in two important areas: (1) the nuclear strategy toward the Soviet Union and (2) the defense strategy for NATO.

In the former area, McNamara moved the U.S. nuclear strategy from one of "massive retaliation," in which the United States reserved the right of engaging in an all-out nuclear attack in response to an act of aggression by the Soviet Union, to one of "mutual assured destruction" (MAD). He changed direction primarily because he had little choice; objective conditions between the U.S. and the Soviet Union were changing. As the Soviet Union obtained nuclear capacity, and as it gained the ability to attack the U.S. directly, a new nuclear doctrine was necessary, since massive retaliation was no longer available solely to the U.S. Under the MAD strategy, both the United States and the Soviet Union would jointly target each other's cities, and each would have the capacity to retaliate even after absorbing a first strike from the other. Thus, the incentive would be for each side not to engage in any initial attack. A state of nuclear deterrence would occur.

McNamara did, however, briefly consider another, more controversial, strategy before adopting MAD. In June 1962, in a commencement address at the University of Michigan, he proposed a counterforce strategy, or a "no-cities" doctrine. This strategy would target Soviet military sites in a nuclear exchange and save cities in both countries from attack. In theory, it afforded some bargaining time for the superpowers, even in the context of a nuclear exchange. In one sense, of course, it was appealing; however, it quickly met with questions at home and abroad. Instead of deterring each state, the strategy also opened up the possibility of a first-strike nuclear attack by either side, since there was now some incentive for each one to use its weapons before they were destroyed. Further, any stability in the relationship was contingent upon the Soviets and the Americans both adopting such a strategy. Within a year, therefore, McNamara moved away from this strategy to one of "assured destruction" and eventually "mutually assured destruction."[29] Indeed, MAD has prevailed to this day as the dominant U.S. nuclear strategy, although it has been criticized as both immoral and unstable in recent years.[30]

With regard to NATO defense, McNamara was instrumental in developing the strategy of flexible response for the U.S. and its European allies. This strategy called for the use of both conventional and nuclear forces to respond to any Soviet or Warsaw Pact aggression in Central Europe. Once again, the notion behind this strategy was to move away from simply a reliance upon an all-out nuclear response and instead to use conventional (i.e., non-nuclear) forces and short-range, intermediate, and long-range nuclear weapons in maintaining stability in Central Europe. This strategy remained a core element of America's defense posture for several decades, although as Central Europe is transformed in the 1990s it has come under serious review lately.

McNamara exercised a "one-man" rule within the Defense Department and was quite successful in furthering his goals during the two presidencies.[31] Indeed, he was able to "dominate the decision process" virtually throughout his tenure.[32] Only after he began to have serious doubts about the military action of the Johnson administration in Vietnam and testified about those doubts before the Senate Foreign Relations Committee did McNamara's star begin to fade. By late 1967, he also became embroiled in a policy dispute with the president over the deployment of an anti-ballistic missile (ABM) system against the Soviet Union. Despite his objections, he lost the bureaucratic battle and was forced to announce the development of a limited ABM system to protect the U.S. from the Chinese. In a matters of months, he stepped down, but his important policy role became an example for succeeding secretaries of defense.

His successor in the Nixon administration was Melvin Laird, a veteran congressman from Wisconsin. Although Laird was not President Nixon's first choice for secretary of defense, he proved to be more than satisfactory in his five years in office. His influence on policy was different from McNamara's. Unlike his predecessor, Laird did not try to reshape Pentagon operations or to introduce a new American strategy; instead, his aim was to bolster military morale and to hold the line on the defense budget without any cutbacks in the essential elements. In this respect, he was quite successful, even faced with a strong bureaucratic challenge from National Security Advisor Henry Kissinger.[33]

Two other secretaries of defense during the Nixon-Ford years were James Schlesinger and Donald Rumsfeld. Schlesinger was instrumental in the enunciation of a new strategic doctrine by the United States. The counterforce strategy would be one in which the U.S. would "develop a capacity to launch a limited or surgical nuclear attack against such military targets as missile silos or airfields."[34] He was also instrumental in pushing for the improvement of conventional forces, thus reshaping this aspect of national security policy.

Donald Rumsfeld's influence as secretary of defense rested on his close personal relationship with President Ford. As a result, he was able to reduce the level of cuts in the defense budget and to put into effect a budget plan that would eventually raise the level of defense spending in the late 1970s.[35] Despite his evident skill in preserving DOD interests, he, like many of the other cabinet members, was overshadowed by the influence of Henry Kissinger in the larger policymaking process.

Harold Brown, who served during the Carter administration, continued a pattern of secretaries of defense increasingly influential on foreign and defense policymaking. Originally one of the "whiz kids" in the DOD under Robert McNamara, this former university president and scientist was able to shape Pentagon policy toward his own views and toward those of the president. On such controversial issues as the B-1 bomber, the Panama Canal treaties, and SALT II, Secretary Brown was quite successful in getting the military to follow his lead.[36] In turn, he was able to work well with the White House on such contentious policy questions. According to one close observer, he proved to be particularly adept at bureaucratic infighting and developed good rapport with President Carter because of his technical expertise and substantial knowledge of defense matters. Furthermore, Brown enjoyed good relations with Zbigniew Brzezinski, the national security advisor to the president, who came to dominate policy during much of the Carter administration.[37]

Caspar Weinberger, secretary of defense until the last year of the Reagan administration, was an equally influential participant in the foreign policy process. Aided by strong support from President Reagan, Weinberger was able to achieve virtually all his requests for a conventional and strategic military buildup. Only by 1983 were the secretary and the Department of Defense denied all that they had requested in defense spending. At that juncture, Weinberger agreed to an $11 billion reduction in his defense budget request for fiscal year 1984. Nonetheless, the proposed defense budget still totaled over $273 billion and continued to increase in real terms (i.e., controlling for inflation) over fiscal year 1983, although Congress eventually did reduce the budget.[38] By fiscal year 1985, the Department of Defense's budget authority reached the highest in real terms for any period in the 1980s, a total of $295 billion. While this amount was below what he had requested, Weinberger was highly successful in increasing defense spending from fiscal year 1981 through fiscal year 1985. On average, defense spending in real terms increased over 9 percent a year during this period. In the subsequent years under Weinberger's tenure, he was not as successful. The defense budget actually declined in real terms about 3.5 percent a year from fiscal year 1986 through fiscal year 1988. Nonetheless, Weinberger had been able to move the defense budget from less than $200 billion per year to nearly $300 billion per year in a very brief period of time.[39]

Weinberger's political influence lay in his close ties with President Reagan and with the president's second national security advisor, William Clark.[40] Because Weinberger, Reagan, and Clark shared the same philosophical views about the world, the secretary of defense enjoyed a considerable amount of initial favor at the White House, and his views received a favorable reception. This influence proved to be the case even in his early months in office, when he was involved in some substantial bureaucratic infighting with Secretary of State Alexander Haig over the general direction of American foreign policy. With Clark's successor at NSC, Robert McFarlane, Weinberger's influence may actually have increased, owing to McFarlane's deference to the Reagan "cabinet-style" of government.

With the arrival in 1982 of George Schultz at the Department of State, however, Weinberger's influence was challenged. As noted in Chapter 9, their rivalry, both personal and professional, was legendary and the source of several analyses.[41] They disagreed on arms control policy: Weinberger opposed virtually all efforts in this direction, while Schultz wanted to move the president toward some intermediate nuclear forces and strategic weapons agreements. Before his resignation, Weinberger reportedly urged the president to scrap previous arms control agreements and deploy a partial missile defense system—a modified "Star Wars" proposal. Weinberger and Schultz disagreed publicly and privately on the use of the American military in Lebanon, too. In a reversal of traditional roles, Secretary of State Schultz urged the use of American forces, while Secretary of

Defense Weinberger opposed their use in that troubled country. They disagreed on the policy process. Each sought to meet privately with the president and to exclude the other, and each sought to reduce the impact of the other in policy debates. Partially out of frustration over his waning policy influence—unlike his successful early years in the administration—Weinberger resigned and returned to private life near the end of 1987. His successor, Frank Carlucci, assumed a lower profile in the policy process in the final year of the Reagan administration.

President Bush's first nominee for secretary of defense, John Tower, a former senator from Texas, was turned down by the Senate in a cloud of allegations and rumors over Tower's drinking and womanizing. Bush's second nominee for secretary of defense, Richard "Dick" Cheney, was hailed by friends and adversaries as "bright, articulate, fair, unflappable, and eminently likable."[42] While Cheney's policymaking clout did not seem to match that of his immediate predecessors, he proved to be a competent manager of the DOD, where he quickly put together a plan to reduce the size of the U.S. military for the post–Cold War era; and an articulate spokesman for the military on Capitol Hill, where he previously served as a representative from Wyoming in the U.S. House for six terms, and with the public during the Persian Gulf War. In fact, during the crisis immediately after Iraq's intervention into Kuwait, and then during the conduct of the war itself, Cheney's stature rose appreciably.[43] Along with General Colin Powell, he had the primary responsibility for negotiating the initial commitment of U.S. forces to Saudi Arabia in August 1990, consulting with Congress over more arms sales to Saudi Arabia, and developing the shape of U.S. foreign policy in the region.

Future defense budgeting will once again become a divisive domestic issue, and the secretary of defense will be at the center of the debate. Although sentiments for retaining relatively high defense expenditures developed quickly after the success in the Persian Gulf War, others continue to call for the renewal of the "peace dividend" because of the changes in Soviet-American relations. Secretary Cheney initially proposed a five-year plan to reduce the size of the U.S. military, and he will face increasing domestic pressure to carry out this plan. Those who want to spend more on domestic programs and use the "peace dividend" to pay for them will surely argue for the implementation of this plan or even more dramatic ones. Those who point to the success in the Persian Gulf War will argue for maintaining or making gradual adjustments in America's military capabilities, even in the post–Cold War era. Who will be successful in this debate? While the debate will undoubtedly continue for some time, one thing seems certain: the role of the Department of Defense in shaping U.S. foreign policy will continue to be tested in the 1990s.

THE INTELLIGENCE AGENCIES

The last important structure within the foreign affairs bureaucracy of the American government that we will discuss is the intelligence community. The growth of America's intelligence apparatus owes much to the Cold War. Yet even as we enter the post–Cold War period, the role of intelligence has hardly diminished. Indeed, in an increasingly complex and interdependent world, the ability for the government to sort out effectively the global political, economic, and social conditions may be more important than ever. With continued incidents of global terrorism (e.g., the destruction of Pan American flight 103), the rise of states with aggressive aims (e.g., Iraq), and the occurrences of potential ecological disaster worldwide (e.g., the destruction of the rainforests in Brazil), sound intelligence work remains as necessary as, maybe even more necessary than, at the height of the Cold War.

While the intelligence community is often associated with the Central Intelligence Agency (CIA), it is really much more comprehensive than that single agency. There are intelligence units within the Department of Defense, the Department of Energy, the Department of the Treasury, the Federal Bureau of Investigation, and the Department of State. Each of these intelligence units concentrates on various aspects of information gathering and intelligence analysis. The Defense Intelligence Agency (DIA), for example, operates within the Defense Department, as do the intelligence agencies within each branch of the military services.[44] Furthermore, the Department of Defense has another intelligence agency associated with it, the National Security Agency (NSA). This agency has responsibility for monitoring global communications through satellites and computer technology spread across the country and the world. A summary portrait of this extensive intelligence community is presented in Figure 10.2.

The exact size and budget of the intelligence community is difficult to estimate, shrouded as it is in secrecy within the Department of Defense budget, but some estimates are available. By one account in the early 1970s, the intelligence community consisted of about 150,000 individuals with a budget in excess of $6 billion annually. In 1980, the total budget was estimated at over $10 billion. During the

FIGURE 10.2 THE INTELLIGENCE COMMUNITY

Source: *Factbook on Intelligence* (Washington, D.C.: Central Intelligence Agency, September 1987), p. 20.

Reagan administration, spending on intelligence reportedly "sharply increased...for the CIA and other intelligence activities."[45] Indeed, by the 1990s, the budget has increased threefold from the 1980s, according to one report. The Bush administration apparently asked Congress for $30 billion in funding for intelligence activities during fiscal year 1991, and that figure represented only a "moderate increase" from 1990.[46]

As Figure 10.2 illustrates, the director of central intelligence (DCI) stands at the center of the intelligence community. The exact responsibilities of the DCI and each agency within the intelligence community have been spelled out in an executive order issued by President Reagan in December 1981 and which remains in effect under the Bush administration.[47] This order established that the DCI was responsible for developing the intelligence program and its budget and for directing the collection of all intelligence throughout the various agencies. In general, the DCI was given much greater control over intelligence matters than in the original National Security Act of 1947 or the Central Intelligence Act of 1949.

Under this order, too, the director of central intelligence was specifically designated the primary advisor to the president and the National Security Council on intelligence. Further, the order provided that the National Security Council could establish "such committees as may be necessary to carry out its functions and responsibilities under this Order."[48] The Reagan administration formed the Senior Interagency Group, Intelligence (SIG-I) to advise the NSC on intelligence matters. The membership on the committee varied from time to time, but it was mainly composed of the following: the director of central intelligence, the national security advisor, the deputy secretary of state, the deputy secretary of defense, the chairman of the Joint Chiefs of Staff, the deputy attorney general, the director of the FBI, and the director of the National Security Agency. This committee, under the leadership of the director of central intelligence, was to be the principal intelligence group within the U.S. government and was to oversee the collection of intelligence matters and the implementation of any intelligence decisions by the National Security Council. Later in the Reagan administration, the National Security Planning Group, a smaller and more select group of the National Security Council, assumed responsibility for monitoring covert intelligence activities.[49]

The Bush administration has established a different arrangement. It appears to rely upon the NSC Deputies Committee and an NSC Policy Coordination Committee on intelligence (both described in detail in the next section) for monitoring intelligence activities.

The latter interagency committee has initial responsibility over intelligence activities and is chaired by an individual appointed by the director of the CIA, while the Deputies Committee, headed by the deputy national security advisor, has been given particular responsibility in the area of covert operations within the national security system. President Bush's directive on the organization of the National Security Council system explicitly calls, moreover, for "a representative of the Attorney General" to be in attendance when this committee discusses covert actions.[50]

RELATIVE INFLUENCE IN POLICYMAKING

The impact of the CIA in policymaking stems from its central role in providing information about international issues and in evaluating different foreign policy options. Its exact influence in the policy process is admittedly hard to determine because of the secrecy surrounding its role and its activities. Nonetheless, because decision makers are heavily dependent upon the intelligence community for information about policy, its influence is undoubtedly quite substantial. Even some of its severest critics, such as Marchetti and Marks, hinted at the quality of CIA intelligence estimates. As they point out, the CIA has often served as a counterweight to the influence of the military planners in debates between the president and the Congress on comparative U.S.–U.S.S.R. strength levels. These estimates were not always successful in shaping policy and were subject to abuse on occasion. Further, they note the success of the agency in gathering intelligence leading to the showdown with the Soviet Union over missiles in Cuba in 1962.[51] Another analyst points to the accuracy of the CIA's estimates during the early policymaking on Southeast Asia—although its recommendations were not always followed by presidents and their advisors.[52] Similarly, the CIA reportedly assessed the situation in the Middle East correctly just prior to the outbreak of the Six-Day War in 1967, but policymakers were unable to take effective action to prevent its occurrence.[53] Finally, the intelligence estimates of the state of the Soviet Union and its economy have become important staples of policymakers in Washington. For example, in the early 1990s the intelligence community painted a grim picture of the Soviet economy, characterizing it as in a "near crisis," and indicated that some modest decline in Soviet military spending had occurred.[54] Such estimates are profoundly important in assisting policymakers in deciding on the degree of U.S. support to provide for *perestroika* in the U.S.S.R.

Other threads of evidence also have emerged that suggest the policy influence of the CIA in several different global areas. Prior to the fall of the Shah of Iran in 1979, for example, the CIA reportedly exercised considerable influence over U.S. relations with Iran. More recently, the CIA gained a pivotal role in the shaping of American policy toward Nicaragua. Because the CIA assisted in establishing the Nicaraguan contras (the forces opposed to the Sandinista regime) and because those forces were a key element in American policy toward Nicaragua throughout much of the 1980s, the intelligence community enjoyed a leading role in the formulation of policy. Both the Department of State and the Department of Defense deferred to the intelligence community on this issue for a time. The result was that policy was largely left to the CIA and to key White House allies.[55] Even after the Congress cut all American assistance to the contras in October 1984, we now know in light of the Iran-contra investigation that the CIA and National Security Council operatives, such as John Poindexter and Oliver North, remained active in supporting the contras.

At the same time, the CIA has been a source of severe criticism by presidents for the quality of its intelligence and policymaking recommendations. President Kennedy, in particular, lost confidence in the CIA over its policy recommendations that led to the ill-fated Bay of Pigs invasion.[56] As a result, Kennedy was later reluctant to accept fully the agency's intelligence advice and options on Southeast Asia and the Cuban Missile Crisis. Instead, he sought advice from other agencies and individuals to assist him in policymaking. Later in the 1960s, the CIA was criticized over the loss of the intelligence ship *U.S.S. Liberty* during the Six-Day War in the Middle East and the capture of the navy spy ship *Pueblo* by the North Koreans in 1968.[57] In the early 1970s, the intelligence community again came under attack for its failure to evaluate accurately the likelihood of the Yom Kippur War between Israel and her neighbors in October 1973.[58]

The quality of intelligence developed by the CIA came under criticism in the late 1970s, too. For instance, questions were raised over intelligence failures at the time that the Shah of Iran was losing power in 1978. About that time, President Carter was moved to send off a sharply worded memo to his key advisors: "I am not satisfied with the quality of political intelligence. Assess our assets and as soon as possible give me a report concerning our abilities in the most important areas of the world. Make a joint recommendation on what we should do to improve your ability to give me political information and advice."[59] Indeed, an "Iran Postmortem" report on intelligence lapses over the Iranian revolution of 1979 was prepared for the CIA by political scientist Robert Jervis. The report noted a myriad of problems in assessing the internal situation of that country and in arriving at sound intelligence estimates: lack of intelligence sources near the Shah or in all the opposition groups, little discussion of CIA intelligence estimates within the bureaucracy or the airing of disagreements on those estimates, the inadequate use of publicly available sources, and conflicting meanings drawn from words and phrases used in the intelligence estimates.[60] Finally, doubts were also raised about the failure of the intelligence community to assess more accurately the Soviet military buildup of the 1970s and the strength of the Soviet economy in the 1980s.[61]

In the 1980s and into the early 1990s, questionable intelligence estimates recommended the use of a grain embargo against the Soviet Union after that country's invasion of Afghanistan and failed to predict the bombing of the marine barracks in Lebanon in October 1983 that killed 241 Americans. More recently, failures to anticipate dramatic changes in Eastern Europe and the Soviet Union raised doubts about the CIA's ability. In particular, critics point to the opening of the Berlin Wall in November 1989, the sudden, violent fall of Nicolae Ceausescu in Romania in December 1989, and the initial reforms within the Soviet Union throughout 1989 and 1990. Even the successes during the Persian Gulf War of 1991 did not come without some intelligence failures: U.S. intelligence estimates placed the number of Iraqi forces in the Kuwaiti theater at 540,000, when the number was really closer to 250,000; they estimated the number of mobile Scud launchers at 35, although the number totaled up to 200; and they reported that Iraq had many chemical weapons in the Kuwaiti theater, but none were found.[62]

We may advance several reasons for these intelligence and policy failures. One reason focuses on the quality of intelligence produced by the CIA analysts. As one of President Bush's advisors put it with reference to the changes in Eastern Europe, the CIA is "good at analyzing trends" and "poor at predicting the timing of events in the collapse of Eastern Europe." A former Defense official in the Reagan administration put it more bluntly: "The CIA's analysts...collect a lot of facts and organize them very nicely. But their predictions are wrong."[63]

Another reason focuses on excessive reliance upon technology for intelligence assessments at the expense of human intelligence and analysis. With the increasing use of satellites and electronic interceptions of messages, for example, less reliance has been placed on agents in the field. Even those analysts who are at work are criticized as either too timid in their assessments, more interested in protecting their reputation than in taking risks, or overzealous and too often driven by ideological bias. Further, some intelligence analysts themselves lack the necessary skills. While political analysts are plentiful, sometimes analysts with sociological and anthropological backgrounds are needed to assess more fully the changes occurring in a foreign society.[64] An illustration from the Persian Gulf War makes this point. More than sophisticated technology was needed to judge Saddam Hussein's determination to hold onto Kuwait or to estimate the loss of morale in the Iraqi military as it was subjected to continuous allied bombing in January and February of 1991.

A third reason for the failure of intelligence is competition among the various bureaucracies. The Defense Intelligence Agency (DIA), for example, often gives different intelligence estimates than the CIA. The DIA has tended to be more hawkish on Soviet intentions than the CIA, and the two agencies have also sparred over estimates in particular regions (e.g., the likelihood of Soviet success in Afghanistan) or particular weapons systems (e.g., the capabilities of Soviet air defenses).[65] Thus, intelligence estimates may simply become compromises between or among differing intelligence bureaucracies.

A fourth reason is the structure of leadership within the intelligence community. The director of the CIA is also the head of the intelligence community, which cuts across many different foreign policy bureaucracies. The degree to which the director can be an honest broker among these bureaus has been called into question, whether in distilling intelligence estimates or in assigning areas of responsibility. Indeed, the need for separating these two roles has been recommended as an important necessary reform.[66] Nonetheless, the result of all these problems has been that the intelligence community's "product" has not always been as useful as it might be.

Despite criticisms along these lines, the CIA still has enjoyed acceptance, if not outright support, from the American people, Congress, and the executive branch throughout the greater portion of the post–World War II years. Part of this trust and support is associated with the Cold War environment in which the CIA was born and the considerable amount of threat that existed during its formative years. In fact, intelligence scholar Harry Howe Ransom hypothesizes that the degree of tension between the United States and the Soviet Union is inversely related to the degree of restrictions placed on CIA activities.[67] The greater the tension in the relationship, the fewer the restrictions on the CIA. Part of the acceptance and policy influence of the Central Intelligence Agency, however, hinges on the darker, covert side of intelligence, which we will explore next.

CIA "SPECIAL ACTIVITIES" AND POLICY INFLUENCE

U.S. covert intelligence operations, or "special activities" as they are euphemistically called, have included propaganda campaigns, secret electoral campaign assistance, sabotage, assisting in the overthrow of unfriendly governments, and, apparently, even assassination attempts on foreign officials. These activities are far more numerous than we often think and form an important aspect of foreign policymaking. The sending of clandestine military forces into Iraq to hunt down mobile Scud missile launchers during the Persian Gulf War illustrates one recent type of covert action, while the U.S. funneling of campaign money to the Nicaraguan opposition in its 1990 electoral battle with the Sandinistas (admittingly using an organization to promote democracy, and with congressional compliance) represents another.

Such covert (and not so covert) operations immediately raise questions about their compatibility with democratic values and their accountability. Are they compatible with a democratic society? Can they be justified in a democratic society? How are they controlled? The public has often been divided on the wisdom of such activities and has expressed this uneasiness in public opinion polls. In 1990, for example, 45 percent of the public thought these activities were acceptable, but 40 percent did not.[68] For most administrations in the post–World War II years, however, such ambivalence has apparently not existed. Covert activities have been widely used, and, as we shall see, ultimately stirred a concern about accountability and their role in foreign policymaking.

ORIGINS AND USAGE OF COVERT OPERATIONS

Under the National Security Act of 1947, the CIA not only was authorized to collect intelligence, but was also authorized "to perform such other functions and duties related to intelligence...as the National Security Council may from time to time direct."[69] Through successive directives by the NSC and succeeding presidents, they have continued to hold that imperative. In President Reagan's 1981 executive order, which remains in effect, these covert operations were defined as those "activities conducted in support of national foreign policy objectives which are planned and executed so that the role of the United States Government is not apparent or acknowledged publicly, and functions in support of such activities, but which are not intended to influence United States political process, public opinion, policies, or media, and do not include diplomatic activities or the collection and production of intelligence or related support functions."[70] As this directive suggests, the mandate is broad and open-ended.

As such, as Marchetti and Marks have noted, the appeal of these measures to various presidents has been unmistakable: "Clandestine operations can appear to the President as a panacea, as a way of pulling the chestnuts out of the fire without going through all the effort and aggravation of tortuous diplomatic negotiations. And if the CIA is somehow caught in the act, the deniability of these operations, in theory, saves a President from taking any responsibility—or blame."[71] These activities thus are not—and should not—be traceable to the White House.

The use of such activities has, indeed, been substantial during the post–World War II years, even if the exact number is not readily available. In its final report in 1977, the Senate Select Committee on Intelligence Activities (the Church Committee, named after its chair, Senator Frank Church of Idaho), which investigated the covert activities of the CIA over the postwar period, hints at the broad portrait of the usage of these activities over the years and provided some figures as well:

> . . . covert actions operations have not been an exceptional instrument used only in rare instances. . . . On the contrary, presidents and administrations have made excessive, and at times self-defeating, use of covert action. In addition, covert action has become a routine program with a bureaucratic momentum of its own.[72]

The Church Committee reported that 81 projects were approved by the director of central intelligence between the years 1949 and 1952. In the Eisenhower administration, 104 covert operations were approved; in the Kennedy administration, 163; and in the Johnson administration, 142.[73]

Yet the exact totals go well beyond these numbers, as evidenced by a 1967 CIA memorandum, which noted that only 16 percent of the covert operations received approval from a special committee set up to monitor them. By yet another estimate, several thousand covert actions were undertaken from 1961 on, with only a small percentage (14 percent) receiving review by the National Security Council or its committees.[74] Along with the number of activities, the justifications for undertaking covert operations have greatly expanded, "from containing International (and presumably monolithic) Communism in the early 1950s, to merely serving as an adjunct to American foreign policy in the 1970s."[75]

Covert operations, moreover, were an important instrument of foreign policy for the Reagan administration and remain so for the Bush administration. As former National Security Advisor Robert McFarlane has noted, the United States must have an option between going to war and taking no action when a friendly nation is threatened. In McFarlane's view, there must be something available between "total peace" and "total war" in conducting foreign policy.[76] Covert activity seemed to have fit that middle category for a number of American administrations, including the Bush administration. Since President Bush served as the director of the CIA for a time in the 1970s, he is particularly attuned to the role covert operations can play in providing another foreign policy alternative for the United States.

ACCOUNTABILITY AND COVERT ACTIONS

The revelations in the Church Committee report and in several other investigations have raised the question of political accountability for these covert operations. Because the lines of accountability were not always operating, and because the CIA often carried on special activities without the full approval of the rest of the government, and particularly the White House, the agency's influence on policy was substantial. In effect, the agency could seemingly shape foreign policy.

This discretion was evident from the beginning. In the initial 1947 NSC directive for covert operations (NSC-4), no formal guidelines were established to approve or coordinate these activities. The only requirement was that the director of central intelligence would be certain, "through liaison with State and Defense, that the resulting operations were consistent with American policy." Up to 1955, for instance, there were still no clear procedures for approval of CIA covert operations. At best, the National Security Council required that consultation take place with the Department of State and the Department of Defense, but formal consultation with the president or his representative was not required. In fact, during the period from 1949 to 1952, the director of central intelligence apparently granted approval for covert operations without assistance.[77]

Even when clear NSC directives were issued for committee approval of covert operations (beginning in 1955), the procedures were not without some loopholes. As a CIA memorandum in 1967 reports:

> The procedures to be followed in determining which CA [covert action] operations required approval by the Special Group or by the Department of State and the other arms of the U.S. government were, during the period 1955 to March, 1963, somewhat cloudy, and thus can probably best be described as having been based on value judgments by the DCI [Director of Central Intelligence].[78]

Although new directives were issued in 1963 and 1970, slippage in accountability remained. Not all covert actions were discussed and approved by the new NSC committee, the Forty Committee. Nor were the covert action proposals always coordinated with the Departments of State and Defense.[79]

Coupled with this weakness in executive branch accountability of CIA activities was the lack of any greater accountability by the Congress during the bulk of the post–World War II years. Although in principle the Armed Services and Appropriations committees in the House and the Senate had oversight responsibility (and the CIA argued that it reported fully to the appropriate subcommittees), in practice, the CIA was under only "nominal legislative surveillance" throughout much of the Cold War period.[80] Chairmen of these committees did not want to know of or did not make concerted efforts to monitor CIA activities. Further, Congress, as a whole, seemed reluctant to inquire significantly into intelligence activities.

One analysis has dubbed this inaction on the part of Congress as a result of the "buddy system," a cozy relationship between top CIA officials and the several "congressional barons," usually key committee chairs or ranking minority members in the House and Senate Armed Services and Appropriations committees.[81] Such members as Senators Richard Russell (D-Georgia) and Leverett Saltonstall (R-Massachusetts) and Congressmen Carl Hayden (D-Arizona), Mendel Rivers (D-South Carolina), and Carl Vinson (D-Georgia) did not always want to know about all CIA activities or, if they did, they were able to squelch any attempts to let them get beyond a small group. As a result, CIA covert activities were at best shared with a small congressional constituency whose inclination was not to challenge or disrupt any "necessary" CIA activity.

What such procedures allowed was that the CIA could by itself begin to *shape*, although perhaps not *direct*, American foreign policy. Without adequate accountability or control, the CIA could take actions that might be outside the basic lines of American policy or, at the very least, might create difficulties for the overt foreign policy of the United States. This latter problem arose once covert actions were revealed. In this sense, the foreign policy influence of the intelligence community through the use of its covert side could be quite substantial. The exact significance of the CIA's influence cannot be fully determined, owing once again to the secrecy surrounding its operation.

THE HUGHES-RYAN AMENDMENT

Several key events weakened the congressional acquiescence to CIA covert operations and ultimately produced more congressional oversight by the early 1970s. First, the Bay of Pigs attack against Castro's Cuba in 1961, almost solely a CIA-designed operation, proved to be a fiasco. As a result, President Kennedy became increasingly suspicious of reliance on that organization in policy formation. Second, the Vietnam War produced a large increase in CIA covert operations, which, in turn, stimulated more congressional interest in these kinds of activities. Third, investigations over America's involvement in destabilizing the government of Salvador Allende in Chile raised questions about CIA activity abroad. And finally, the "Watergate atmosphere" of 1972–1974 emboldened the Congress to challenge executive power across a wide spectrum, including intelligence activities.[82]

The first result of this new congressional interest was the Hughes-Ryan Amendment. Sponsored by Senator Harold Hughes (D-Iowa) and Representative Leo Ryan (D-California), this amendment to the 1974 Foreign Assistance Act began to impose some control on the initiation and use of covert activities. Its key passage is worth quoting in full:

> No funds appropriated under the authority of this or any other Act may be expended by or on behalf of the Central Intelligence Agency for operations in foreign countries, other than activities intended solely for obtaining necessary intelligence, unless and until the President finds that each such operation is important to the national security of the United States and reports, in a timely fashion, a description and scope of such operation to the appropriate committees of the Congress.[83]

Thus this amendment required that the president be informed about covert operations (hence eliminating the "plausible denial" argument for the executive) and that the president must certify (or "find") that each operation is "important to the national security of the United States." Further, the amendment directed the president to report, "in a timely fashion," any operation to the "appropriate" committees of the U.S. Congress. Under this provision, eight committees needed to be informed: the Armed Services and Appropriations committees in the House and the Senate, the Senate Foreign Relations Committee, the House Foreign Affairs Committee, and, later, the Senate and House intelligence committees established in 1976 and 1977, respectively.

In addition to these new reporting requirements under the Hughes-Ryan Amendment, two separate investigations by the executive and legislative branches recommended several other changes in the monitoring of intelligence operations. An executive-ordered inquiry into intelligence activities in 1975 (the Rockefeller Commission) and a legislative inquiry by the Senate in 1975 and 1976 (the Church Committee) recommended several substantive and procedural changes in the operation of the Central Intelligence Agency, especially regarding covert operations. New legislative acts were proposed for gaining greater oversight of the CIA through joint or separate intelligence committees in the Congress, through the establishment of an intelligence community charter by Congress, and through more stringent control over covert actions. The investigations also recommended consideration of a more open budgeting process, a limitation on the term of the directorship of the CIA, and the consideration of appointing a director from outside the organization.[84]

Aside from the establishment of intelligence committees in each house, few of these recommendations actually became law; some reforms, however, were incorporated in executive orders issued by Presidents Ford and Carter. President Ford issued an executive order in February 1976 in which the lines of authority over covert operations were spelled out and that expressedly prohibited political assassination as an instrument of American policy. Two years later, in January 1978, President Carter issued another executive order on the reorganization of the intelligence community that also included some recommended reforms.[85] Even though few reforms were translated into statutes, the various reform proposals did have the effect of calling attention to the accountability problem of the intelligence community as a whole, and especially to its covert side. As a result, they did serve to lessen the influence of the intelligence community in foreign policymaking.

Furthermore, Stansfield Turner, CIA director during the Carter administration, proceeded to undertake an organizational reshuffling to increase the powers of the director and to focus more on analytic intelligence than on covert operations. Turner also initiated a reduction in personnel within the CIA's Directorate of Operations, the bureau that handles clandestine operations. Veteran intelligence officers were dismissed from the intelligence service; by one account, over 800 members of the intelligence community were forced out by the end of 1977.[86] Both of these actions were said to have hurt morale within the agency and especially within the clandestine services.

INTELLIGENCE OVERSIGHT ACT OF 1980

Despite these efforts at greater control, the intelligence community and its allies were successful in stopping any further legislative restrictions. Most notably, proposed legislation to establish an intelligence community charter never was enacted. In fact, by 1980, the intelligence community was able to persuade the Congress to repeal the Hughes-Ryan Amendment and its reporting requirements and to pass legislation that was deemed more workable.

This act, the Intelligence Oversight Act of 1980, retained the Hughes-Ryan provision that the president must issue a "finding" for each covert operation, but it modified the reporting requirements of that earlier act. (An intelligence finding is a statement, later refined as a written report, in which a covert operation is defined and in which the president has certified that the operation is "important to the national security of the United States.") Now, the executive branch (either the director of central intelligence or the appropriate agency head) was required to report only to the Select Committee on Intelligence in the Senate and the Permanent Select Committee on Intelligence in the House.[87] Prior notification of all covert operations, however, was now specified in the law and not simply "in a timely fashion," as required under the Hughes-Ryan language. Further, the act also required that the executive branch report to the committees any intelligence failures, illegal intelligence activities, and any measures undertaken to correct such illegal activities.

Some reporting discretion was also afforded to the president by two exemptions included in the statute. First, if the president deems that a covert operation is vital to the national security, the president may limit prior notification to a smaller group (the "Gang of Eight," as they came to be called) listed in the statute: the chair and the ranking minority members of the House and the Senate intelligence committees, the Speaker and minority leader of the House, and the majority and minority leaders of the Senate. Even in these exceptional instances, though, the president must ultimately inform the entire intelligence committees "in a timely fashion." Second, a more oblique and potentially more troubling exemption was also incorporated. The statute specifies that reporting of covert operations was to be followed "to the extent consistent with all applicable authorities and duties, including those conferred by the Constitution upon the executive and legislative branches of the Government." While the meaning of this passage is purposefully vague, it invites the executive branch to claim constitutional prerogatives on what information it will share with the legislative branch. (And, indeed, the Reagan administration apparently invoked this exemption to defend its delay in disclosing covert operations surrounding the Iran-contra affair.)

By this legislation, a balance seemed to have been struck between the requirements of secrecy, as demanded by the intelligence community and the executive branch, and public accountability, as sought by the U.S. Congress and the public. The intelligence community gained the repeal of the Hughes-Ryan legislation, which it disliked, and the Congress was able to gain knowledge of covert actions prior to their occurring, except in rare instances.

The initial application of even these requirements were not without controversy, however. When it was publicly revealed in April 1984 that the CIA was involved in the mining of Nicaraguan harbors, the Senate Intelligence Committee reacted strongly in the belief that it had not been properly informed. (In fact, Senator Daniel Patrick Moynihan, vice-chair of the Senate panel, resigned in protest for a time, although he later withdrew his resignation after CIA Director William Casey apologized for not keeping the committee fully informed.) Subsequent evidence indicated that, in fact, the CIA had informed the House and Senate committees, although the briefing on the Senate side was not as complete as it might have been. As a result of this episode, the CIA pledged to notify the Senate and the committee in advance of "any significant anticipated intelligence activity."[88] On balance, then, this incident demonstrates that the congressional intelligence committees seem determined to preserve accountability on covert operations ordered by the executive branch.

THE IRAN-CONTRA AFFAIR: A CASE OF FAILED ACCOUNTABILITY

Only two years later, however, the revelations surrounding the Iran-contra affair once again raised questions about how well congressional prerogatives regarding covert operations were respected. After Congress had cut off CIA funds to the contras with the Boland Amendment in October 1984 (see Chapter 8) and after the seizure of several American hostages in Lebanon beginning in the early 1980s, including the torture and killing of the CIA station chief in Beirut, members of the Reagan administration initiated covert operations to assist the Nicaraguan contras in their struggle against the Sandinistas and to sell arms to Iran for that nation's help in freeing the American hostages in Lebanon. In turn, and without President Reagan's knowledge (according to his testimony), these two operations were linked when a portion of the Iran arms sales profits was funneled to the contras. These covert actions unfolded from 1984 to 1986 without any congressional accountability or knowledge. Indeed, the House and Senate Intelligence committees were kept in the dark about all of these activities until CIA Director William Casey testified before the committees on November 21, 1986. This testimony occurred nearly three weeks after the arms sales were revealed in a Lebanese newspaper, after it had been admitted by President Reagan, and after extensive reporting by the media. (See Chapter 5 for a fuller discussion of the background to this affair and its broader policy implications.)

A FAILURE TO COMPLY WITH EXISTING STATUTES?

Critics charged that this whole episode was a failure on the part of the executive branch to comply with the requirements of the Boland Amendment and the Intelligence Oversight Act. House and Senate select committees were established to investigate this episode, and their final joint report outlined numerous specific violations of the legislative statutes and agreed-upon congressional-legislative procedures. Three general violations will serve to illustrate the difficulty of congressional oversight of covert operations.[89]

First, contrary to the prohibitions in the Boland Amendment, CIA and NSC staff of the Reagan administration sought a private organization (called "the Enterprise") "to engage in covert activities on behalf of the United States." This organization became involved in both the arms sales to Iran and aiding Nicaraguan contras, used "private and non-appropriated money" to carry on these activities, and received support from CIA personnel around the world. Beyond the specific prohibition of the Boland Amendment, this covert operation violated the Intelligence Oversight Act. No finding was prepared and approved by the president for this "Enterprise" activity, nor was the Congress informed of the existence of this operation. Indeed, when the press reported that this operation was underway in August 1985, the president "assured the public that the law was being followed," and in letters and appearances before Congress, National Security Advisor Robert C. McFarlane testified that "the letter and spirit" of the law was being obeyed with regard to aiding the contras. (In March 1988 McFarlane pleaded guilty to charges that he misled Congress with such testimony.)

Second, the covert arms sales to Iran were carried out in a manner inconsistent with the Intelligence Oversight Act. Intelligence findings were neither properly prepared and approved by the president in all instances, nor were they reported to the Congress "in a timely fashion." The first arms sale to Iran in August-September 1985, in which Israel supplied the military hardware and the United States promised to resupply the Israelis, was completed only through an oral finding. By his testimony, however, President Reagan could not remember exactly when he approved this sale. A retroactive finding was prepared to cover the CIA's involvement in the second arms sale to Iran in November 1985, but this finding was ultimately destroyed by National Security Advisor John Poindexter in February 1986 and never shared with the Congress. Finally, a finding on arms sales to Iran was signed and approved by the president on January 17, 1986, but this finding was never shared with the intelligence committees of the Congress or even the smaller "Gang of Eight," as allowed under the Intelligence Oversight Act. In fact, the Congress did not discover its existence until November 1986.

Third, the transfer of a portion of the profits from the Iran arms sales to the Nicaraguan contras was inconsistent with government policy. It not only violated the Boland Amendment regarding military aid to the contras, but was done largely outside the established channels of government and represented a significant privitization of U.S. covert operations. At the very least, proper executive-legislative procedures involving covert operations were not followed, since these private individuals were not subjected to the same accountability procedures as public servants.

In light of these and other violations, the congressional investigating committees concluded their report with several recommendations. First, however, they noted that the episode "resulted from the failure of individuals to observe the law, not from deficiencies in existing law or in our system of governance. . . . Thus, the principal recommendations. . .are not for new laws but for a renewal of the commitment to constitutional government and sound processes of decision making." Nonetheless, though, the committees report that "some changes in law, particularly relating to oversight of covert operations," may be helpful.

Hence, the majority report of the committees proposed twenty-seven reforms for strengthening such oversight. A first set of recommendations focused on improving the preparation and dissemination of presidential "findings" on covert operations. Findings should be in writing and reported in that form to Congress "prior to the commencement of a covert action except in rare instances and in no event later than 48 hours after a Finding is approved." They should include the names of all U.S. agencies involved in such operations but should restrict National Security Council members from participating in covert operations. Findings also should be limited to a one-year duration (before possible recertification). All National Security Council members should be informed of such findings. And finally, no finding should recommend actions that are presently illegal under existing law. A second set of recommendations called for a series of executive branch changes in monitoring the participation of private individuals used in covert operations, in preserving executive documents of such operations, and in strengthening treaties regarding foreign banks' records of U.S. individuals so that the executive and congressional branches can gain access to them. In addition, the Congress called for improved legal review of covert operations. Finally, a third set of recommendations focused on steps that Congress could take to improve its oversight capacity by reviewing the adequacy of contempt statutes currently on the books, the effectiveness of several laws dealing with arms sales and arms transfers, and congressional procedures for safeguarding classified information.

EXECUTIVE CHANGES IN CONDUCTING AND MONITORING COVERT OPERATIONS

After the Iran-contra affair was revealed publicly, but prior to the final report of the two committees, President Reagan issued a new policy directive for conducting and monitoring covert operations and for notifying Congress of these activities.[90] Several of the changes conform with the final recommendations of the committees, but at least one important one does not.

President Reagan ordered changes regarding those who should carry out covert operations and those who should be informed about them within the government. Members of the National Security Council were barred from conducting covert operations. All executive branch agencies (and private individuals) participating in these operations were ordered to report in the same manner as currently required of the Central Intelligence Agency. An intelligence finding for a covert operation must be in writing and completed before the operation had begun, except when an "extreme emergency" arises. Oral and retroactive findings were no longer to be permitted. All findings must be available to members of the National Security Council, thus ensuring that the secretary of state and the secretary of defense will be informed of such operations, which had not occurred in the Iran-contra case. And finally, all findings must be limited in duration and periodically reviewed.

On the notification of Congress, however, President Reagan's directive did not necessarily represent a tightening of reporting requirements; instead, it opened the possibility of even more delay. In his directive, Reagan pledged that his administration would notify Congress within two working days *after* a covert operation had begun, "in all but the most exceptional circumstances." Thus, a real possibility existed that the reporting of more and more covert operations would be delayed until after they had begun and, in some instances, perhaps very long after they had begun.

The Congress, howver, initiated legislation to tighten the Intelligence Oversight Act and to eliminate this loophole. Under legislation introduced in 1987, the president would have been required to notify the Congress of *any* covert activity within forty-eight hours, much as the Iran-contra investigation had recommended and in sharp contrast to the Reagan directive. While this legislation passed in the Senate in 1988, it failed to pass in the House.

When President Bush took office, and in a gesture of bipartisanship by the Congress to the new president, the Speaker of the House decided not to take up this legislation for consideration by the full House.[91] As a result, the only wide-ranging initiative to result from the Iran-contra investigation failed to become law, and the only real change in the executive-legislative procedures for handling covert operations was President Reagan's 1987 directive. This directive, moreover, remained the policy of the Bush administration.[92]

The Congress did, however, adopt several limited legislative remedies in 1988 and 1989 that dealt in part with covert operations and that grew directly out of the Iran-contra affair. The first legislation dealt with "third parties" transferring American supplies to another country. It specifically required the president to allow Congress thirty days to pass legislation to block such transfers. In the case of the Iran-contra affair, as was noted earlier, Israel had transferred American-made anti-aircraft missiles to Iran. Under this amendment, Congress would have the right to stop such action within thirty days of being notified of it if Congress were inclined to do so. A second remedy strengthened prohibitions on the sales of arms to countries supporting global terrorism. The third required the president to appoint an independent inspector general for the Central Intelligence Agency as one mechanism for closer monitoring of covert actions. And finally, an amendment was added to a foreign aid appropriations bill that prohibits the use of such aid as a lever to gain support for some foreign policy activity (e.g., aiding the contras).[93]

In 1991, however, new legal procedures governing covert operations were passed by the Congress and signed into law by President Bush as part of the intelligence authorization bill for FY 1991. In effect, the law put into statute some of the changes that were originally part of President Reagan's executive order, albeit in a more flexible way. The law, for the first time, provided a legal definition to a covert operation, required that the president approve, in writing, all covert activity by any executive agency, and outlawed all retroactive findings of covert actions. The bill, however, does allow some executive discretion on the use of third parties in carrying out such operations and allows the president to notify Congress "within a few days" of the initiation of such activities. Furthermore, the law continues to affirm the president's prerogative to assert "his constitutional authority to withhold information for more than a few days."[94]

POLICY COORDINATION AMONG COMPETING BUREAUCRACIES

For the sake of convenience and clarity, we have described the role of the various executive bureaucracies in the foreign policy process separately. While each department may have its own impact on policy, the formulation process is also coordinated across departments. In the last section of this chapter, we briefly discuss how this coordination is achieved and how "bureaucratic politics" is played out among the foreign policy departments.

THE NATIONAL SECURITY COORDINATING SYSTEM

Beginning in 1966, and initially as a means of placing the Department of State more fully at the center of the foreign policy process, a series of Interdepartmental Regional Groups (IRGs) was established as a way of coordinating policy recommendations. Each of these IRGs was headed by the appropriate assistant secretary of state.[95] An IRG, for instance, might consist of representatives from Defense, AID, the National Security Council, the Joint Chiefs of Staff, or whatever departments were appropriate for a particular region or issue. The principal aim in seeking widespread representation was to gain policy advice from various bureaucracies throughout the government. While these groups became a source of bureaucratic coordination, they also became a source of bureaucratic competition. Beyond the IRGs, a Senior Interdepartmental Group (SIG), composed of higher-level representatives from the foreign policy bureaucracies and headed by the under secretary of state, was established as a means of coordinating the activities of the IRGs. The SIG, in turn, would be accountable to the NSC or the various departmental secretaries.

These kinds of working groups were the principal means of carrying the policy process across departments and became the model for subsequent administrations. Although succeeding presidents changed the IRGs to interdepartmental or interagency groups (IGs), their use as the principal mechanism for coordinating policy options continued. Even in the very hierarchical arrangements of the national security system during the Kissinger years, the use of IGs was not wholly abandoned, although it was altered. A description of the Reagan and Bush administrations' approaches to the interagency process will give a sense of how these groups provide both coordination and competition among the various bureaucracies.

THE REAGAN ADMINISTRATION AND THE NSC SYSTEM

The Reagan administration initially followed the same design as the other recent presidents, with a system of SIGs and IGs, but with a clear division of responsibility among the secretary of state, secretary of defense, and director of central intelligence for different aspects of policy.[96] Specifically, the Reagan administration established four SIGs, which reflected the four major areas of national security issues. The first SIG dealt primarily with foreign policy issues and was under the general direction of the secretary of state, although formally chaired by the deputy secretary of state. Its other members included the director of central intelligence, the national security advisor, the deputy or under secretary of defense, and the chairman of the Joint Chiefs of Staff. The second SIG dealt with defense policy and was under the general control of the secretary of defense, but it was formally chaired by the deputy secretary of defense. The members were the same as for the foreign policy SIG. The third SIG concentrated on intelligence issues, with the director of the Central Intelligence Agency serving as its chair. The membership, once again, is the same as for the other SIGs. The fourth SIG dealt with international economic policy and was headed by representatives from the Treasury Department. In addition, The Reagan administration established the National Security Planning Group (NSPG), a small select group of National Security Council members, for even closer consultation on policymaking.

Under this arrangement, each SIG created its own IGs for development and review of policy options. The foreign policy SIG was directed to establish IGs corresponding to the regional bureaus in the Department of State and IGs for Politico-Military Affairs and International Economic Affairs. On each IG, there would be representatives of the intelligence community, the National Security Council, the Department of Defense, the Joint Chiefs of Staff, and, of course, the Department of State. The other SIGs also established IGs. The defense IGs were based upon the functional areas within the Department of Defense, the intelligence IGs were formed at the discretion of the director of central intelligence (although one IG for counterintelligence was explicitly called for in the original presidential directive on organization), and the international economic IGs were the responsibilities of the Department of Treasury. All of these IGs would include representatives from other appropriate bureaus and agencies.

By the second term of the Reagan administration, and in light of the Iran-contra investigation, several changes resulted in this arrangement. Only the SIG on intelligence continued to operate by this time, although it was ultimately supplanted by the National Security Planning Group (NSPG) in monitoring covert operations. Instead, the Crisis Preplanning Group and the Strategic Arms Control Group largely assumed the functions of the SIGs on Foreign and Defense Policy, while the international economic SIG was transferred to the Economic Policy Council.[97] Further, as a response to the Tower Commission report on the Iran-contra affair and its conclusion that the Reagan administration had failed to operate the national security system with sufficient accountability, the system was changed once again with the establishment of the Policy Review Group (PRG) in early 1987. This body was chaired by the deputy national security advisor and other sub-cabinet officials from various foreign policy bureaucracies. Along with the NSPG for covert operations monitoring, these groups became the key forums for policy coordination in the last two years of the Reagan administration. By one account, the PRG met over 170 times and coordinated policy on a wide range of activities.[98]

THE BUSH ADMINISTRATION AND THE NSC SYSTEM

The Bush administration sought to streamline the policy coordination system across the various bureaucracies and to give greater control to the national security advisor and his staff in shaping policy.

As a result, a relatively simple three-tier hierarchical system of committees was established, leading to the National Security Council itself. Figure 10.3 portrays the Bush administration's national security committee system and the membership on each one.

The most important committee for policy coordination below the NSC itself is the NSC Principals Committee (NSC/PC).[99] It is the senior interagency group for the consideration of all national security questions and comprises key cabinet-level officials with foreign policy responsibilities. The chair of this committee is the national security advisor, who has responsibility for calling its meetings, setting its agenda, and preparing the appropriate policy papers. While the chair is to work closely with the other members of this committee in carrying out these tasks, the fact that the national security advisor has been appointed chair reflects the Bush administration's view that the national security advisor will be at the center of policy formulation and coordination.

The second ranking committee in this process is the NSC Deputies Committee (NSC/DC). This committee reviews the initial work of the interagency groups or the NSC Policy Coordinating Committees and makes its recommendations on policy as well. It is composed of sub-cabinet level officials from the various foreign policy bureaucracies (see Figure 10.3) and is chaired by the deputy assistant to the president for national security affairs. Once again, the prominent role of the NSC staff is indicative of the Bush administration's desire to have that bureaucracy take the lead in foreign policy formation. The responsibilities of this committee are wide-ranging, indicating its critical importance in the policy process. By presidential directive, it has the responsibility to "ensure that all papers to be discussed by the NSC or the NSC/PC fully analyze the issues, fairly and adequately set out the facts, consider a full range of views and options, and satisfactorily assess the prospects, risks, and implications of each."

The last sets of committees in the policy coordination hierarchy are the NSC Policy Coordinating Committees (NSC/PCC). These committees, comparable to the interagency groups (IGs) used by other administrations, are the ones that initially develop and prepare the policy options across departments for the administration. In one sense, then, the policy coordination process really begins with these committees, since they may be appointed by the National Security Council itself, the NSC Principals Committee, or the NSC Deputies Committee, or, at the direction of the president, by the national security advisor, albeit in consultation with the secretary of state and the secretary of defense.

FIGURE 10.3   National Security Council
Policy Coordination Committees in the Bush Administration

| National Security Council |

NSC Principals Committee (NSC/PC)
Members: Secretary Of State
Secretary Of Defense
National Security Advisor (Chair)
Director of Central Intelligence
Chairman, Joint Chiefs of Staff
White House Chief of Staff

Chair - NSA

NSC Deputies Committee (NSC/DC)
Members: Deputy National Security Advisor (Chair)
Under Secretary of State for Political Affairs
Under Secretary of Defense for Policy
Deputy Director of Central Intelligence
Vice-Chairman, Joint Chiefs of Staff

NSA dep.

NSC Policy Coordinating Committee (NSC/PCC)

Regional PCCs	**Functional PCCs**
Europe	Arms Control
Soviet Union	Defense
Latin America	Intelligence
East Asia	International Economics
Africa	
Near East/South Asia	

Members: Appointed from appropriate foreign policy bureaucracies with an interest in a particular area or issue. Each NSC/PCC is chaired by an assistant secretary, with the secretary of state appointing the regional representatives, the secretary of defense the defense representative, the secretary of treasury the international economics representative, the director of the CIA the intelligence representative, and the national security advisor the arms control representative.

Source: U.S. Army War College, Carlisle Barracks, Pennsylvania, December 1989, and
National Security Council Organization, April 17, 1989, memo from National Security Council.

These committees are both regional and functional in nature (Figure 10.3), a pattern we encountered in the organization of the Department of State in Chapter 9. The regional NSC/PCC covers all regions of the world, while the functional committees focus on particular issues that are current. The number of these committees changes with the issues that arise, but about a dozen committees are likely to be active at any one time. While the membership varies by the type of committee and the chairs come from various departments (the regional ones are headed by an assistant secretary of state or equivalent from the Department of State, while the functional chairs are distributed among the Departments of Defense and Treasury, the CIA, and the NSC), a staff member from the National Security Council serves as the executive secretary on each committee to enhance overall policy coordination. In this way, too, the Bush administration's policy coordination procedures continue to ensure a large role for the NSC. Effectively managed, moreover, these committees serve as a ready mechanism for coordinating policy and managing conflicts among departments and bureaus.

CONCLUDING COMMENTS

The diplomatic, economic, military, and intelligence bureaucracies that we have discussed over the last two chapters all contribute to the shaping of the foreign policy of the United States. The influence of some has increased in recent years, while that of others has declined. The National Security Council (and especially the NSC staff and the national security advisor) and the Department of Defense, for instance, have gained influence in the shaping of policy, as have some of the economic bureaucracies. By contrast, the influence of the Department of State and the intelligence community has probably been reduced over the post–World War II years. The precise contribution of any bureaucracy in an administration, however, is heavily dependent upon how the president chooses to use it and on the individuals within it.

In the next two chapters, we expand our analysis of the foreign policymaking process by examining those participants outside of the formal governmental structure. Political parties and interest groups are the focus of attention in the next chapter. Our aim in that chapter is to assess how America's two major political parties have shaped foreign policy and to determine which interest groups play a role in policymaking on international issues, and under what conditions they do so.

NOTES

1. See Stanley Lieberson, "An Empirical Study of Military-Industrial Linkages," *American Journal of Sociology* 76 (January 1971): 562–584.

2. See, for example, Adam Yarmolinsky, *The Military Establishment: Its Impacts on American Society* (New York: Harper & Row, 1971).

3. See the chapter entitled, "Is There a Military-Industrial Complex Which Prevents Peace?" in Marc Pilisuk, with the assistance of Mehrene Larudee, *International Conflict and Social Policy* (Englewood Cliffs, NJ: Prentice-Hall, Inc., 1972), pp. 108–141.

4. In November 1989, the Congress approved a defense authorization bill for $305 billion for fiscal year 1990, but only appropriated $285 billion. See "Chronology 1989" in William G. Hyland, ed., *America and the World 1989/90* Foreign Affairs 69 (February 1990): 213–214. The defense contract data is from the Department of Defense, *Prime Contract Awards by State, Fiscal Year 1988* (Washington, D.C.: Department of Defense, Washington Headquarters Services, n.d.), p. 3.

5. Directorate for Organizational and Management Planning, Office of the Secretary of Defense, *Organization and Functions Guidebook* (Washington, D.C.: Department of Defense, August 1988), p. 9. This is only a partial listing of the "mission of the OSD." A more complete statement is contained on pp. 9 and 10.

6. See Hoopes, *The Limits of Intervention* (New York: David McKay, 1968), pp. 33–34, for a statement of ISA's role during the Kennedy-Johnson period.

7. *U.S. Government Manual 1989/1990,* July 1, 1989, p. 186.

8. See Henry T. Nash, *American Foreign Policy* (Homewood, IL: The Dorsey Press, 1985), pp. 94 and 114, for the "little State Department" (and a variant) labeling of ISA. By contrast, the Bureau of Politico-Military Affairs in the Department of State has also been labeled the "Little DOD" by Nash because of the military considerations in policy examined by this bureau (p. 114). Further, there tend to be regular personnel exchanges between this bureau and the Pentagon, which facilitates this military analysis. The "Little DOD" was particularly important during the tenure of Secretary Alexander Haig because of the close working relationship between its director, Richard Burt, and Secretary Haig. On the changes in the role of ISA in the policy process, see Geoffrey Piller, "DOD's Office of International Security Affairs: The Brief Ascendancy of an Advisory System," *Political Science Quarterly* 98 (Spring 1983): 59–78.

9. *U.S. Government Manual 1989/1990,* p. 186.

10. See Strobe Talbott, *Deadly Gambits* (New York: Vintage Books, 1985) for a discussion of the key role of Assistant Secretary of Defense Richard Perle in arms control policy.

11. Amos A. Jordan, William J. Taylor, Jr., and Associates, *American National Security: Policy and Process* (Baltimore: The Johns Hopkins University Press, 1981), p. 165. On the responsibilities of the JCS, also see Lawrence J. Korb, *The Fall and Rise of the Pentagon: American Defense Politics in the 1970s* (Westport, CT: Greenwood Press, 1979), p. 112; Korb's *The Joint Chiefs of Staff: The First Twenty-Five Years* (Bloomington: Indiana University Press, 1976), p. 7; and *U.S. Government Manual 1982/1983,* pp. 165–166.

12. Jordan, Taylor, and Associates, *American National Security: Policy and Process,* pp. 165–167; and Korb, *The Fall and Rise of the Pentagon,* pp. 112–137.

13. Jordan, Taylor, and Associates, *American National Security Policy and Process,* p. 165.

14. Korb, *The Fall and Rise of the Pentagon,* p. 115.

15. See the discussion in *The Pentagon Papers, the New York Times Edition* (New York: Bantam Books, 1971), pp. 234–270, on the bombing of North Vietnam and on the acceptance of the domino theory. Although DOD and its advisors did not get all they proposed, its influence in these decisions is still evident.

16. Jordan, Taylor, and Associates, *American National Security: Policy and Process,* p. 166.

17. Ibid.

18. David C. Martin and Michael A. Lerner, "Why the Generals Can't Command," *Newsweek,* February 14, 1983, p. 22.

19. Lawrence J. Korb, "The Joint Chiefs of Staff: Access and Impact in Foreign Policy," *Policy Studies Journal* 3 (Winter 1974): 171.

20. Ibid., pp. 171–173.

21. Martin and Lerner, "Why the Generals Can't Command," p. 22.

22. "Excerpts from Reagan's Testimony on the Iran-Contra Affair," *New York Times,* February 23, 1990, p. A18.

23. This discussion of the Goldwater-Nichols Reorganization Act is taken from *Congressional Quarterly Almanac 1986* (Washington, D.C.: Congressional Quarterly, Inc., 1987), pp. 455–457.

24. Richard Halloran, "Bush Plans to Name Colin Powell to Head Joint Chiefs, Aides Say," *New York Times,* August 10, 1989, pp. 1 and 10.

25. Eleanor Clift and Thomas M. DeFrank, "Bush's General: Maximum Force," *Newsweek,* September 3, 1990, p. 36. For another view on Powell's commitment to the use of force in the Persian Gulf, see Bob Woodward, *The Commanders* (New York: Simon & Schuster, 1991).

26. The reform acts strengthening the secretary's role within the Department of Defense are "Reorganization Plan No. 6 of 1953," 67 STAT. 638–639, and the "Department of Defense Reorganization Act of 1958," P.L. 85-599, 72 STAT. 514–523.

27. See James Schlesinger, "The Role of the Secretary of Defense," in Robert J. Art, Vincent Davis, and Samuel P. Huntington, eds., *Reorganizing America's Defense: Leadership in War and Peace* (Washington, D.C.: Pergamon-Brassey's, 1985), p. 261; and Laurence E. Lynn, Jr., and Richard I. Smith, "Can the Secretary of Defense Make a Difference?" *International Security* 7 (Summer 1982): 45–69. The former discusses the role of the secretary of defense more generally, while the latter looks at his role in the weapons development and acquisition process and the impact of the bureaucracy within the Pentagon in shaping outcomes.

28. Korb, *The Fall and Rise of the Pentagon,* p. 85.

29. On McNamara's evolution in nuclear strategy and strategic thinking generally, see Lawrence Freedman, *The Evolution of Nuclear Strategy* (New York: St. Martin's Press, 1981), pp. 227–249; Michael Mandelbaum, *The Nuclear Question: The United States and Nuclear Weapons, 1946–1976* (Cambridge: Cambridge University Press, 1979), pp. 106–113; and Richard A. Stubbing with Richard A. Mendel, *The Defense Game: An Insider Explores the Astonishing Realities of America's Defense Establishment* (New York: Harper & Row, 1986), pp. 268–269.

30. See, for example, James A. Stegenga, "The Immortality of Nuclear Deterrence," *Arms Control* 4 (May 1983): 65–72.

31. Korb, *The Fall and Rise of the Pentagon,* p. 85.

32. Stubbing with Mendel, *The Defense Game: An Insider Explores the Astonishing Realities of America's Defense Establishment,* p. 265.

33. Korb, *The Fall and Rise of the Pentagon,* pp. 83–94.

34. Ibid., p. 100.

35. Ibid., pp. 107–108.

36. Bernard Weinraub, "Browning of the Pentagon," *New York Times Magazine*, January 29, 1978, p. 44.

37. Brzezinski, *Power and Principle: Memoirs of the National Security Adviser, 1977–1981* (New York: Farrar, Straus, Giroux, 1983), pp. 44–47.

38. Theodore H. White, "Weinberger on the Ramparts," *New York Times Magazine*, February 6, 1983, p. 18; Alice C. Maroni, *The Fiscal Year 1984 Defense Budget Request: Data Summary* (Washington, D.C.: Congressional Research Service, February 1, 1983); and Ellen C. Collier, "Arms Control Negotiations At Home: Legislative-Executive Relations," paper presented at the Annual Meeting of the International Studies Association, March 1984, p. 8.

39. Calculated from Table IX in Alice C. Maroni, "The Fiscal Year 1989 Defense Budget Request Data Summary," Congressional Research Service, No. 88-182F. The data are for the National Defense function category, which included DOD and defense-related programs carried out by other agencies. If only the DOD budget is used, the average increase from 1981 to 1985 is 9.1 percent, while the average decline in 1986–1988 is 2.0 percent.

40. White, "Weinberger on the Ramparts," p. 18.

41. See, for example, Hedrick Smith, *The Power Game: How Washington Works* (New York: Ballantine Books, 1988), pp. 570–576.

42. John M. Broder and Melissa Healy, "Likable Dick Cheney Can Get Mad When He Has To," *Los Angeles Times*, March 16, 1989, p. 20.

43. Andrew Rosenthal, "Cheney Steps to Center of the Lineup," *New York Times*, August 24, 1990, p. A7.

44. *Intelligence: The Acme of Skill* (Washington, D.C.: Central Intelligence Agency, Public Affairs, n.d.), pp. 12–13.

45. Victor Marchetti and John D. Marks, *The CIA and the Cult of Intelligence* (New York: Dell, 1974), p. 95, provides a breakdown of spending in the intelligence community for 1974 totaling $6.2 billion. Charles W. Kegley and Eugene R. Wittkopf report that for fiscal 1980 the budget for the intelligence community was thought to be $10 billion, based on *Congressional Quarterly* reports. See their *American Foreign Policy: Patterns and Process* (New York: St. Martin's Press, 1982), p. 373. The quoted passage is from "Reagan Puts Bombing Blame on Democrats: Carter-Era Intelligence Cuts Cited," *Des Moines Register*, September 27, 1984, p. 13A.

46. "Intelligence Budget Calls For a Record $30 Billion," *Des Moines Sunday Register*, April 8, 1990, p. 2A; and Robin Wright, " '91 Intelligence Budget Still Targets East Bloc," *Los Angeles Times*, April 8, 1990, p. A1.

47. See Executive Order 12333, "United States Intelligence Activities," December 4, 1981. This executive order can be found in *Code of Federal Regulations* (Washington, D.C.: Office of the Federal Register, National Archives and Records Service, 1982), pp. 200–216.

48. Ibid., p. 201.

49. The interagency membership listing is from *Central Intelligence Agency Factbook* (Washington, D.C.: Central Intelligence Agency, Public Affairs, July 1982), p. 12. The reference to the National Security Planning Group draws upon the discussion in the unclassified extract from National Security Decision Directive (NSDD) 286, released on December 12, 1987, by the National Security Council.

50. See the memo from the National Security Council on "National Security Council Organization," dated April 17, 1989.

51. Marchetti and Marks, *The CIA and the Cult of Intelligence*, pp. 291–296.

52. See Chester L. Cooper, "The CIA and Decisionmaking," *Foreign Affairs* 50 (January 1972): 221–236.

53. John H. Esterline and Robert B. Black, *Inside Foreign Policy: The Department of State Political System and Its Subsystems* (Palo Alto, CA: Mayfield Publishing Company, 1975), p. 35.

54. David E. Rosenbaum, "U.S. Sees Threats to Soviet Economy," *New York Times*, April 21, 1990, p. 4.

55. Philip Taubman, "CIA Taking Control of Nicaraguan Policy," *Des Moines Register*, April 20, 1984, p. IA.

56. See Irving Janis, Victims of Groupthink, pp. 14–49, for a discussion of the decision making on the Bay of Pigs invasion and the crucial involvement of the CIA. Also see Marchetti and Marks, *The CIA and the Cult of Intelligence*, p. 294, for how dissatisfied President Kennedy was over CIA action in the Bay of Pigs and how this might have affected his view of intelligence estimates during the Cuban Missile Crisis.

57. Esterline and Black, *Inside Foreign Policy*, p. 35.

58. Harry Howe Ransom, *The Intelligence Establishment* (Cambridge, MA: Harvard University Press, 1970), p. 240.

59. The note is quoted from Stansfield Turner, *Secrecy and Democracy: The CIA in Transition* (Boston: Houghton Mifflin Company, 1985), p. 113.

60. The "Iran Postmortem" report is discussed in Bob Woodward, *Veil: The Secret Wars of the CIA, 1981–1987* (New York: Pocket Books, 1987), pp. 106–108.

61. Robert F. Ellsworth and Kenneth L. Adelman, "Foolish Intelligence," *Foreign Policy* 36 (Fall 1979): 147–159. President Carter is quoted here at p. 148. Michael Wines, "C.I.A. Faulted on Rating Soviet Economy," *New York Times*, July 23, 1990, p. A5.

62. Several sources report some of these intelligence failures. See, for example, John Barry, "Failures of Intelligence?" *Newsweek*, May 14, 1990, pp. 20–21; "NBC Nightly News," June 9, 1990; and Wines, "C.I.A. Faulted on Rating Soviet Economy," p. A5. On the Persian Gulf War failures, see "Intelligence Goofs," *Newsweek*, March 18, 1991, p. 38.

63. Quoted in Barry, "Failures of Intelligence?" p. 20.

64. Turner, *Secrecy and Democracy: The CIA in Transition*, pp. 113–127, especially at p. 125.

65. Barry, "Failures of Intelligence?" pp. 20–21.

66. Turner, *Secrecy and Democracy: The CIA in Transition*, pp. 273–274.

67. See Harry Howe Ransom, "Strategic Intelligence and Intermestic Politics," in Charles W. Kegley and Eugene R. Wittkopf, *Perspectives on American Foreign Policy* (New York: St. Martin's Press, 1983), p. 500.

68. John E. Rielly, ed., *American Public Opinion and U.S. Foreign Policy 1991* (Chicago: Chicago Council on Foreign Relations, 1991), p. 36.

69. P.L. 253 in *United States Statutes At Large*, Volume 61, Part 1, 80th Cong., 1st Sess., p. 498.

70. See Executive Order 12333, "United States Intelligence Activities, p. 215. See Marchetti and Marks, *The CIA and the Cult of Intelligence* and the *Church Committee Report* (note 81) for a discussion of types of covert operations.

71. Marchetti and Marks, *The CIA and the Cult of Intelligence*, pp. 281–282.

72. "Foreign and Military Intelligence," Book 1, Final Report of the Select Committee to Study Governmental Operations with Respect to Intelligence Activities, United States Senate, April 26, 1976, p. 425. (hereafter, the *Church Committee Report*)

73. Ibid., p. 56.

74. Ibid., pp. 56–57.

75. Ibid., p. 57.

76. Bernard Gwertzman, "Top Reagan Aide Supports the Use of Covert Action," *New York Times,* May 14, 1984, pp. 1 and 6.

77. *Church Committee Report,* pp. 49–50.

78. Ibid., pp. 51–52.

79. Ibid., p. 54.

80. Ransom, *The Military Establishment,* p. 162.

81. Gregory F. Treverton, "Intelligence: Welcome to the American Government," in Thomas E. Mann, ed., *A Question of Balance* (Washington, D.C.: The Brookings Institution, 1990), pp. 72–76.

82. Ibid., pp. 74–75.

83. See P.L. 93-559, 88 Stat. 1804. The quoted passage is from section 32.

84. See *Church Committee Report,* note 68, and *Report to the President by the Commission on CIA Activities Within the United States* (Washington, D.C.: U.S. Government Printing Office, June 1975), note 76, for a complete listing of the recommendations. The latter was named the Rockefeller Commission, after its chairman, Vice-President Nelson Rockefeller.

85. On this point, see Harry Howe Ransom, "Strategic Intelligence and Intermestic Politics," p. 313. President Ford's Executive Order 11905 can be found in *Weekly Compilation of Presidential Documents* 12 (February 23, 1976): 234–243.

86. "Controversy Over 'Czar' for Intelligence," *U.S. News and World Report,* February 6, 1978, pp. 50–52.

87. "Intelligence Authorization Act for Fiscal Year 1981," P.L. 96-450, 94 STAT. 1981–1982. This section and the following one draw upon earlier work reported in James M. McCormick and Steven S. Smith, "The Iran Arms Sale and the Intelligence Oversight Act of 1980," *PS* 20 (Winter 1987): 29–37.

88. The passage is quoted in Philip Taubman, "Moynihan To Keep Intelligence Post," *New York Times,* April 27, 1984, p. 7. On the extent to which the intelligence committees were informed, see Philip Taubman, "House Unit Says Report on Mines Arrived Jan. 31," *New York Times,* April 14, 1984, pp. 1, 6, and his "How Congress Was Informed of Mining of Nicaragua Ports," *New York Times,* April 16, 1984, pp. 1, 4.

89. The following examples draw upon the "Executive Summary" in *Report of the Congressional Committees Investigating the Iran-Contra Affair.* Washington, D.C.: U.S. Government Printing Office, 1987, pp. 3–21. The quoted phrases are from this report as well.

90. Unclassified extract from National Security Decision Directive (NSDD) 286, and "Text of Letter on Covert Operations," by President Reagan to Senator David Boren in *New York Times,* August 8, 1987, p. 5. See also James M. McCormick, "Prior Notification of Covert Actions," *Chicago Tribune,* September 8, 1987, p. 11.

91. See Michael Oreskes, "Wright, in Gesture to Bush, Shelves Bill on Covert Acts," *New York Times,* February 1, 1989, p. 8.

92. Personal communication from the National Security Council, August 15, 1990.

93. *Congressional Quarterly Almanac 1988* (Washington, D.C.: Congressional Quarterly, Inc., 1989), pp. 498–499; and *Congressional Quarterly Almanac 1989* (Washington, D.C.: Congressional Quarterly, Inc., 1990), p. 541.

94. Elaine Sciolino, "Conferees Agree to Curb President on Covert Action," *New York Times,* July 27, 1991, pp. 1 and 8, and *Congressional Record,* July 25, 1991,

pp. H5898-H5907. The first quote is from the conference report in the *Congressional Record* at p. H5905 and also quoted in the *New York Times* at p. 8, while the second quote is from the *New York Times* at p. 8.

95. Esterline and Black, *Inside Foreign Policy,* p. 23. On the Kissinger reorganization, see pp. 24–26.

96. The following discussion of SIGs and IGs in the Reagan administration is based upon the statement of the president, "National Security Council Structure," January 12, 1982, reprinted in Robert E. Hunter, *Presidential Control of Foreign Policy: Management or Mishap?* The Washington Papers/91 (New York: Praeger, 1982), pp. 109–115 (also see Hunter's discussion of this system, pp. 96–102, upon which we also relied); and Colin Campbell, *Managing the Presidency: Carter, Reagan, and the Search for Executive Harmony* (Pittsburgh: University of Pittsburgh, 1986), p. 43. In the original directive, only the first three SIGs were established. Only later was the international economic SIG added.

97. Ibid. The reference to the NSPG draws upon the unclassified extract from National Security Decision Directive (NSDD) 286.

98. The discussion of the changes since the Tower Commission report is based upon Paul Schoot Stevens, "The National Security Council: Past and Prologue," *Strategic Review* (Winter 1989): 61.

99. The description of the Bush administration's NSC policy coordination process is based upon material provided by the U.S. Army War College, Carlisle Barracks, Pennsylvania, December 1989, and a memo from the National Security Council on "National Security Council Organization," April 17, 1989.

CHAPTER 11   POLITICAL PARTIES, BIPARTISANSHIP, AND INTEREST GROUPS

''. . . our great parties have too often been far apart and untrusting of each other.

It's been this way since Vietnam. That war cleaves us still. . . . A new breeze is blowing—and the old partisanship must be made new again.'' **PRESIDENT GEORGE BUSH, INAUGURAL ADDRESS, JANUARY 20, 1989**

''. . . ethnic politics, carried as they often have been to excess, have proved harmful to the national interest. . . . Ethnic advocacy represents neither a lack of patriotism nor a desire to place foreign interests ahead of American interests; more often it represents a sincere belief that the two coincide.'' **FORMER SENATOR CHARLES McC. MATHIAS, JR., "ETHNIC GROUPS AND FOREIGN POLICY," *FOREIGN AFFAIRS*, SUMMER 1981**

Beyond the president, the Congress, and the bureaucracies, other participants also influence the American foreign policy process. Two additional key participants are political parties and interest groups. While these groups probably have less direct impact upon policy than the other participants discussed so far, they are increasingly viewed as important to the foreign policy process. By political parties we mean those organized groups who pursue their goals by contesting elections and potentially controlling political offices.[1] These political organizations can influence foreign policy decisions directly by controlling elective offices, but they can also influence the policy content of others who control executive and legislative offices through criticism and debate. By interest groups we mean those portions of the population who are organized and seek political goals that they are unable to provide on their own.[2] These groups seek their political goals through the use of various lobbying techniques, ranging from making campaign contributions to a political candidate to face-to-face discussions with policymakers.

In the first half of this chapter, we examine the contribution of America's two principal political parties to the foreign policy process over the post–World War II decades. We begin our discussion by focusing on the concept of bipartisanship in foreign affairs—a notion often invoked by policymakers to dampen partisan divisions over U.S. foreign policy—and assess its overall success. Next we turn to examine how the Vietnam War and the events surrounding it weakened any bipartisanship that may have existed. Finally, we summarize some recent evidence that challenges the notion that bipartisanship ever existed and, instead, points to the consistency in partisan differences in foreign affairs. In the second half of the chapter, we discuss the several traditional foreign policy interest groups, identify some newer ones that have emerged in the foreign policy arena, and assess the relative impact of these various groups on the decision-making process. To illustrate the increased importance of foreign policy interest groups generally, we focus on two types—economic groups and ethnic groups—that often have been viewed as particularly important in shaping U.S. foreign policy.

POLITICAL PARTIES AND THE BIPARTISAN TRADITION

America's two political parties do not, as a rule, differ in their programmatic or ideological positions on many domestic and foreign issues. Both the Democratic and Republican parties are more often seen as pragmatic parties that adopt policy positions on taxation, bank reform, and health care to attract as many adherents as possible. While this description of the two major parties can be overstated and tends to apply more to party followers than to party leaders, it generally represents an accurate portrait of U.S. political parties, especially when compared to their European counterparts.[3]

This depiction of America's two major parties, moreover, has been applied particularly to the foreign policy arena. Despite the fact that the Republican party has more often controlled the White House and the Democratic party the Congress since World War II, bipartisan has frequently been used to describe the nature of America's approach to foreign affairs. The origins of bipartisanship usually are attributed to the circumstances that the U.S. faced in the late 1940s and early 1950s. Because the international environment was so threatening during that period, a united approach seemed to be required for U.S. national security. In the words of one prominent politician of the time, "partisan politics . . . stopped at the water's edge."[4] In this approach, the U.S. national interest would necessarily supplant any partisan interest in foreign policy, and bipartisan cooperation between Congress and the president would supplant both institutional and partisan differences as well.

The exact meaning of bipartisanship was not always clear, but it seemed to require at least two different, albeit complementary, kinds of cooperation between the legislative and executive branches. One kind focused on achieving "unity in foreign affairs" and referred to the degree to which "policies [are] supported by majorities within each political party" in the Congress. The other kind referred to a set of "practices and procedures designed to bring about the desired unity."[5] Put differently, the Congress and the president would develop procedures in which each would participate in and consult with one another in the formulation of foreign policy, and, in turn, a majority of congressional members from both parties would support the policy developed. These two kinds of cooperation implied that bipartisanship would involve collaboration in both the *process* of foreign policymaking and its *outcome*.

THE COLD WAR YEARS AND BIPARTISANSHIP

The beginning of this bipartisan effort is usually attributed to the foreign policy cooperation that developed between Democratic President Harry Truman and the Republican chair of the Senate Foreign Relations Committee, Senator Arthur Vandenberg of Michigan, in the immediate post–World War II years. After Senator Vandenberg

had altered his isolationist stance and after President Truman committed himself to global involvement for the United States, the two
leaders consciously sought to build a bipartisan foreign policy
against communist expansionism. To a large extent, they were successful in doing so. Indeed, the major foreign policy initiatives of the
late 1940s were accomplished with substantial support across political parties. The passage of the Bretton Woods agreement, the United
Nations Charter, the Greek-Turkish aid program, and the Marshall
Plan, among others, garnered support from both parties and passed
the Congress with over 83 percent support on average.[6]

The acceptance of the Cold War consensus by the major political
parties and the public at large seemingly continued this bipartisan
tradition in foreign policy through the Eisenhower and Kennedy administrations and into the Johnson one as well. Despite some party
divisions over the attacks by Senator Joseph McCarthy upon "communists" within the U.S. government, the "loss" of China, and the
Korean War, the essential foreign policy unity of the two parties remained.[7] Even with the so-called "missile gap" issue of the late 1950s
that was eventually carried into the 1960 presidential campaign, the
parties continued to display markedly similar foreign policy orientations. Both parties in their 1956 party platforms expressed a desire
for a bipartisan foreign policy, and the Republicans expressed this
sentiment again in 1960.[8]

Both Democrats and Republicans came to stand for a similar posture toward world affairs: a strong national defense, an active global
involvement by the United States, and staunch anti-communism. To
be sure, some divisions existed within the two parties. The Republicans had to contend with a wing that still cherished isolationism,
and the Democrats had to contend with a wing that was initially suspicious of the confrontational approach toward the Soviet Union.
Further, the Democrats had to live with popular perceptions that
portrayed them as the party associated with war (but also with prosperity), while the Republicans probably enjoyed the label as the
party associated with peace (but not the one associating them with
recession).[9] Democratic presidents, such as Franklin Delano
Roosevelt with his role in leading the U.S. into World War II and
Harry Truman with the outbreak of the Korean War, often conveyed
the former perception, while Republican presidents, such as Herbert
Hoover in the interwar years and Dwight Eisenhower after the Korean War, conveyed the latter.

Despite these different party factions and popular labels, the
members of the two parties tended to stand for the same general
principles in foreign policy. As political scientist Herbert McClosky

and his associates report from their 1957–1958 survey data on party leaders and followers, the foreign policy differences between the parties were indeed small. In fact, the average difference between Democratic and Republican leaders was smaller for foreign policy than for any of the four domestic policy areas that they examined. A similar result occurred when Democratic and Republican followers were examined.[10]

This bipartisanship was also reflected in the policy "planks" that each party placed into its national platforms during the Cold War years. In a systematic analysis of the platforms of the Democrats and the Republicans from 1944 to 1964, political scientist Gerald Pomper reports that 47 percent of the party pledges on foreign policy were essentially the same in each and only 6 percent were in conflict.[11] Defense policy pledges were also quite similar: 73 percent were the same and only 2 percent were in conflict. Such a level of bipartisanship on foreign policy was second only to civil rights among eight different policy categories analyzed, while the level of bipartisanship on defense policy was tied for third position with labor and agricultural issues. Finally, the percentages of conflicting pledges across the parties were equally low in comparison with the other policy categories.

The important consequence of this bipartisanship tradition is that separate party influence, as such, seemingly did not have a strong effect on the general strategies of American foreign policy. Instead, policy influence was mainly confined to the executive branch, because the president could generally count on congressional and public support across political parties. Recall the high level of presidential success in foreign policy that we discussed in Chapter 7.

THE LIMITS OF BIPARTISANSHIP
THROUGH THE VIETNAM ERA

Although bipartisanship was indeed the preeminent way to describe the roles of the two political parties during the Cold War years and beyond, some analysts recently (and even some at the time) have argued that the degree of partisan unity on foreign affairs was often overstated. I. M. Destler, Anthony Lake, and Leslie Gelb best capture this alternate view in describing the first fifteen years of the Cold War:

> These were said to be the halcyon days of bipartisanship or nonpartisanship, of Democrats and Republicans putting national in-

terests above party interests. But such a description has always been more myth than reality. Conservatives and liberals were at one another's throat constantly. There was never a time when Truman was not besieged. . . . [Adlai E.] Stevenson tried to make foreign policy a key issue in the 1956 [presidential] campaign, and Mr. Kennedy succeeded in doing so in 1960.[12]

Destler et al. do acknowledge, however, that part of the reason for the apparent unity in policy is explained by the fact that politicians would primarily "rally around the President's flag in East-West confrontations." But on "second-order issues," the parties "would squabble" regularly.[13]

Two decades earlier, a prominent foreign policy analyst, Cecil Crabb, reached a similar conclusion in characterizing the magnitude of bipartisanship from the late 1940s to the late 1950s.[14] In reviewing several cases of foreign policy and bipartisanship in that period, Crabb concluded that "there have been relatively few genuinely bipartisan undertakings in American postwar relations." While a bipartisan approach may provide stability and continuity in policy, he noted, it may also weaken the level of executive leadership, reduce the vigor of opposition party debate, and even weaken the party system. Such disadvantages, of course, could ultimately be harmful to the quality of U.S. foreign policy. In short, the characterization of the period as a bipartisan one was not wholly accurate, nor was the attempt to achieve such a policy approach necessarily a wise one.

PARTISAN DIFFERENCES AND FOREIGN POLICY

Indeed a closer examination of several foreign policy issues during those years lends credence to the more limited view of bipartisanship that Destler et al. and Crabb suggest. On foreign aid, military aid, defense expenditures, and trade issues, for example, a rather continuous degree of partisan division has been evident, even at the height of presumed bipartisan cooperation. On foreign economic assistance, for instance, northern Democrats and Republicans in the 1950s supported these programs, while southern Democrats opposed them. In the 1960s through the early 1970s, northern Democrats generally continued their support and southern Democrats their opposition. Republicans, on the other hand, fluctuated from opposition in the early 1960s to support late in that decade and into the 1970s.[15]

On the issue of military assistance, northern Democrats in the Senate generally supported the increase or maintenance of the same levels of funding until the early 1960s. By contrast, southern Democrats fluctuated in their support of military aid during the height of the Cold War, but they became more supportive during the Vietnam period. Republicans increasingly have come to support such assistance over the course of the postwar period, albeit starting with some initial reluctance in the early 1950s. In the House, the voting trends on military assistance have tended to be much more irregular across party lines, but the general direction for the parties is about the same as in the Senate.

For defense expenditures, partisan differences are also detectable. Northern Democrats in the Senate, but less so in the House, were supportive of increasing or at least maintaining defense expenditures in the 1950s, but these Democrats in both houses began to oppose such expenditures in the 1960s and 1970s. Republicans, on the other hand, were more opposed to such expenditures in the 1950s than were Democrats, but they tended to be much more supportive from 1960 onward when compared to the Democrats. The southern Democrats exhibited less variation in their behavior and have generally remained supportive of defense expenditures.

On trade policy, too, some partisan differences in congressional behavior have been evident. Democrats generally were more supportive of a free trading system in the 1950s, while the Republicans were generally more protectionist in their orientation. By the middle of the 1960s, however, these trends had reversed, with Democrats becoming more protectionist and Republicans becoming more free-trade oriented.

The upshot of these analyses suggests that party influence—even at the height of bipartisanship—had an impact on specific details of foreign policy. To the extent that bipartisan foreign policy was achieved, it always had to operate within the confines of party differences. In this sense, partisan politics assisted in shaping U.S. foreign policy behavior to a greater extent than some might wish to acknowledge. Nevertheless, as Hughes and others have reminded us, the position and party of the president still played an important role in these congressional voting results.[16]

THE EFFECTS OF VIETNAM

Although Destler, Gelb, and Lake acknowledge that some bipartisanship (or more accurately, "majorityship") existed from the 1940s to the 1960s, they go on to argue that "Vietnam changed all this."[17] As American involvement in Vietnam deepened in 1965, and as the war began to appear on the news every night, President Johnson had to confront a serious domestic problem—one virtually as difficult as conducting the war itself. The results of the war were profound for domestic harmony and for any great semblance of cooperation across party lines. As they note, "The conceptual basis of American foreign policy was now shaken, and the politics of foreign policy became more complicated."

Zbigniew Brzezinski has aptly summarized the effect of Vietnam on any domestic unity in foreign policy in yet another way:

> Our foreign policy became increasingly the object of contestation, of sharp cleavage, and even of some reversal of traditional political commitments. The Democratic Party, the party of internationalism, became increasingly prone to the appeal of neo-isolationism. And the Republican Party, the party of isolationism, became increasingly prone to the appeal of militant interventionism. And both parties increasingly found their center of gravity shifting to the extreme, thereby further polarizing our public opinion.[18]

These changes in bipartisanship become evident when we examine the support patterns for the Vietnam War within the Congress. President Lyndon Johnson had to rely upon conservative (largely southern) Democrats and Republicans for much of his support on Southeast Asian policy.[19] Opposition began to come from liberals within his party and from a few Republicans. Party and ideological lines began to be drawn; strong support across party lines on a major foreign policy initiative was beginning to erode. As contentious as this issue was, it is significant that the Congress (controlled by a Democratic majority in the House and the Senate) never was successful in defeating Presidents Johnson or Nixon (through 1972) on a major funding bill on the Vietnam War.[20] In this sense, both the essence of party loyalty and bipartisanship remained, although both forces were drawn taut by the Vietnam involvement.

Toward the end of the Vietnam War, bipartisanship began to wear even thinner. With a Republican president in the White House and a Congress controlled by the Democrats, the consequence was a series of foreign policy reforms, as we discussed in Chapter 8. While both parties supported a number of these reforms, Democrats, and particularly liberal Democrats, were generally more favorable to placing limits on the foreign policy powers of the executive than were the Republicans. Moreover, the major foreign policy reforms enacted by the Congress occurred when Republican presidents were in office and the Democrats controlled both the Senate and the House.

When we examine another indicator of foreign policy bipartisanship in the Vietnam period, we also find increasing evidence of foreign policy partisanship, especially when compared to the Cold War years. The party platforms for 1968, 1972, and 1976 showed a marked decrease in bipartisanship.[21] Only 24 percent of the foreign policy pledges for these platforms were the same for Republicans and Democrats, while only 11 percent of the defense policy pledges were bipartisan. (Recall that the bipartisan pledges were about two to three times those figures during the Cold War.) The two parties seemed to be moving in different directions in that the preponderance of pledges on foreign and defense policy was unique to each party. At the same time, the degree of foreign policy conflict on pledges remained low (at about 6 percent) for each policy area. In short, then, while bipartisanship was declining, outright partisan conflict had still not emerged.

By the 1980s, however, the level of partisan division on foreign policy increased even more. Key foreign policy issues like Central America, the Middle East, and national defense policy elicited clashes along party and ideological lines.[22] Congressional voting on covert aid to Nicaraguan rebels, for example, often saw Democrats pitted against Republicans in the Congress. On key defense votes, such as the development of the MX missile, the B-1 bomber, and the Strategic Defense Initiative (SDI), the pattern was much the same.[23] In this way, there has been clear movement away from the bipartisan tradition of the past, especially on crucial defense and foreign policy issues.

BIPARTISANSHIP: DID IT EVER REALLY EXIST?

In contrast to much of our discussion to this point, an alternative view on partisanship and its role in shaping American foreign policy has recently been advanced in the research by McCormick and Wittkopf.[24] In several analyses of congressional foreign policy voting over the last four decades, we have argued that partisan and ideological conflict were more often the norm in foreign policymaking than any bipartisan harmony. Indeed, our analyses over 2,400 congressional foreign policy votes on which the president indicated a position suggest that bipartisanship was as often fantasy as fact.

Figure 11.1 portrays our results for the extent of bipartisan voting in the House and Senate for eight different U.S. administrations between 1947 and 1988. With few exceptions, bipartisan voting has been more infrequent than conventional wisdom suggests. Only during the Eisenhower administration did bipartisan support (defined as the majority of both parties supporting the president) exist across the House and Senate on more than 50 percent of the foreign policy votes. While bipartisan support was greater in the Senate than in the House across these administrations, the level of bipartisanship

FIGURE 11.1 BIPARTISAN FOREIGN POLICY VOTING
IN THE CONGRESS, 1947–1988

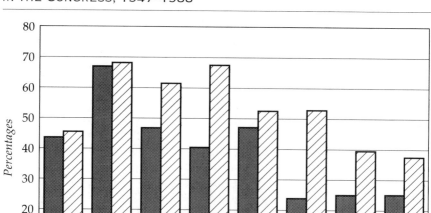

Note: Each bar represents the proportion of foreign policy votes on which a majority of both parties supported the president's position.

Source: James M. McCormick and Eugene R. Wittkopf, "Bipartisanship, Partisanship, and Ideology in Congressional-Executive Foreign Relations, 1947–1988," *The Journal of Politics* 52 (November 1990): 1085. Reprinted by permission of the University of Texas Press, publisher of *The Journal of Politics.*

was especially low in the latter chamber. If the Eisenhower administration were excluded, no more than 50 percent of the votes in any
other administration obtained bipartisan support in the House.
These results hardly support the view that bipartisanship was the
norm for any extended period in the post–World War II years.

By contrast, Figure 11.2 illustrates the substantial degree of partisan divisions in these administrations since World War II. While
the partisan gaps are greater in the House than in the Senate across
these administrations, the divisions between the parties are still
quite substantial. On average, the difference between parties in each
chamber is about 20 percentage points, with only the Eisenhower administration (in both the House and the Senate) and the Johnson administration (in the Senate) obtaining a noticeably smaller gap.

FIGURE 11.2 Partisan Differences in Congressional Voting on Foreign Policy Issues

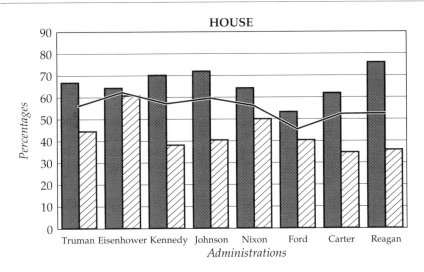

HOUSE

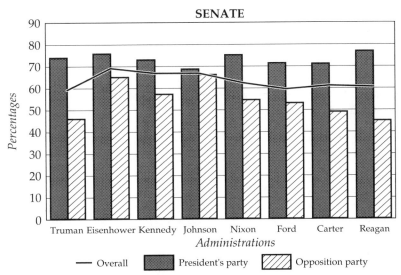

SENATE

—— Overall ▓▓ President's party ▨ Opposition party

Note: Each bar represents for each party the average percentage of support by members of Congress for the president's position on foreign policy votes. The overall line measures the average level of support for the president regardless of party.

Source: James M. McCormick and Eugene R. Wittkopf, "Bipartisanship, Partisanship, and Ideology in Congressional-Executive Foreign Relations, 1947–1988," *The Journal of Politics* 52 (November 1990): 1090. Reprinted by permission of the University of Texas Press, publisher of *The Journal of Politics.*

These partisan gaps have held across different foreign policy issues considered by the Congress as well. Figure 11.3 shows the average congressional support for the president's party and the opposition party averaged across the eight administrations for foreign aid, foreign relations, national security, and trade votes. As the figure makes clear, the partisan differences are pronounced across all of them. In short, these results suggest that congressional voting on foreign policy issues has always been more partisan and less bipartisan than often portrayed.

When the Vietnam War was factored into these analyses, it did not change the overall conclusions. While partisan divisions increased somewhat in the post-Vietnam period, the impact of the war could generally not be separated from the effects of other factors. Only on national security voting did the pre- and post-Vietnam periods show some marked differences. Overall, though, the Vietnam War appeared not to be the singular watershed in postwar bipartisan or congressional-executive relations, as it has sometimes been portrayed.

PARTISAN DIVISIONS TODAY: THE REAGAN AND BUSH YEARS

While debate continues over whether bipartisanship ever existed and over how much it has declined, there is little doubt that today that partisan acrimony on foreign policy issues is quite pronounced. Indeed, the party differences in the foreign policy arena were so substantial during the first term of the Reagan administration that the president felt compelled to undertake at least two important steps in an effort to rebuild bipartisan support.

First, he appointed bipartisan presidential commissions to deal with two particularly divisive foreign policy issues. The first was the Commission on Strategic Forces, more popularly known as the Scowcroft Commission. Its specific task was to "review the strategic modernization program with particular focus on our land-based intercontinental ballistic missile system and basing alternatives for that system."[25] The second was the Bipartisan Commission on Central America, more popularly called the Kissinger Commission. Its task was to review and to recommend policy options for that particular region of the world.[26] The larger task of both commissions, however, was to diffuse the partisan bickering over both of these issues and to build support across party lines.

FIGURE 11.3   PARTISAN SUPPORT IN CONGRESSIONAL VOTING
ON FOUR FOREIGN POLICY ISSUES, 1947–1988

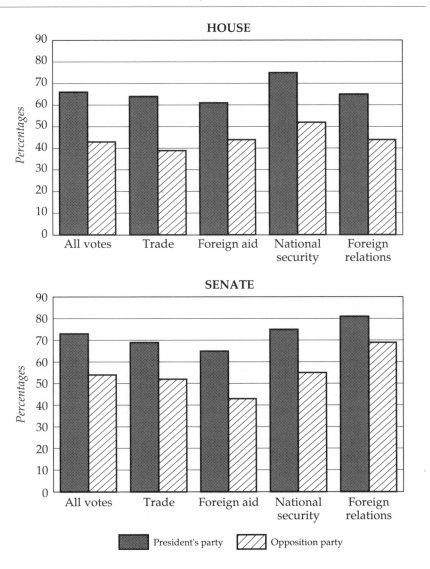

Note: Each bar represents the average percentage of party support on that issue across the
eight administrations.

Source: James M. McCormick and Eugene R. Wittkopf, "At the Water's Edge: The Effects of Party,
Ideology, and Issues on Congressional Foreign Policy Voting, 1947–1988," *American Politics Quarterly*
20 (January 1992): 42.

Second, President Reagan also felt compelled to go directly to the American people and the Congress to appeal for bipartisanship. In April 1984, at the height of partisan criticism of his Middle East and Central American policies, President Reagan delivered a major foreign policy address in which he called for a return to an earlier era of executive-legislative cooperation.

> We must restore bipartisan consensus in support of U.S. foreign policy. We must restore America's honorable tradition of partisan politics stopping at the water's edge, Republicans and Democrats standing united in patriotism and speaking with one voice....Bipartisan consensus-building has become a central responsibility of Congressional leadership as well as of executive leadership.[27]

In addition, President Reagan undertook a series of speeches in 1984 and 1986 in an attempt to rally support for his Central American policy, and particularly for support of the Nicaraguan contras. His efforts hardly fell on receptive ears, however, and there was little evidence of success in restoring the partisan harmony that he sought.

In Reagan's second term, party differences were as sharp as ever, and, arguably, seemed to have accelerated. Fueled by the controversy surrounding the Iran-contra affair and the divisiveness of the congressional override of Reagan's veto of the Anti-Apartheid Act of 1986, Congress and the president and Republicans and Democrats were deeply divided over the conduct of U.S. foreign policy. The Speaker of the House, Jim Wright, attempted, moreover, to intervene directly into efforts to obtain a negotiated settlement with Nicaragua. His actions further divided and accelerated partisan divisions within the Congress and between the Congress and the president.

Indeed, when President Bush took office, partisan discord was at such a low ebb that he felt it necessary to appeal for bipartisanship in foreign policy in his inaugural address. Two key passages summarize his view:

> We need a new engagement...between the Executive and the Congress....There's grown a certain divisiveness....And our great parties have too often been far apart and untrusting of each other.
> It's been this way since Vietnam. That war cleaves us still. ...A new breeze is blowing—and the old bipartisanship must be made new again.[28]

Despite some initial efforts by both Republicans and Democrats and an important initial bipartisan contra aid package early in 1989, President Bush has still faced partisan divisions over his foreign policy actions. Spirited debates have occurred over defense expenditures in the post–Cold War era, the amount of assistance to Eastern Europe, and the response to the Chinese crackdown in Tiananmen Square. In his first year, in fact, President Bush was only able to obtain bipartisan support on issues in which he had indicated his position about 25 percent of the time in the House and 40 percent of the time in the Senate. Such levels are not markedly different from those of other recent presidents (e.g., Carter and Reagan), and do not portend well for the future. Important exceptions to partisan discord for the Bush administration were the bipartisan unity over U.S. intervention in Panama and the seizure of Manuel Noriega in 1989 and the initial bipartisan response to Iraq's seizure of Kuwait in August 1990.

PARTISAN POLITICS AND THE FUTURE

Despite some exceptions, though, the long-term prospect for a restoration of the "old bipartisanship" (to the extent that it ever really existed) does not appear bright; instead, the more likely outcome is that partisan divisions will continue for the foreseeable future. Several reasons make this projection likely. First, continuing domestic divisions support a continuation and intensification of partisan conflict, not a diminution in its level. The Republicans continue as the majority presidential party, having won five of the six presidential elections between 1968 and 1988, and the Democrats continue as the dominant congressional party, having won control of both chambers in seventeen of the twenty-one congressional elections between 1950 and 1990. In contrast to the prospects of bipartisan cooperation provided by ideologically conservative southern Democrats, recent Republican gains in congressional elections in the South and losses in the North have brought partisan differences more fully in line with ideological ones. Partisan and ideological differences have been increased, and the incentives for foreign policy compromise have been diminished.

Second, the proliferation of new issues and the transformation of old ones portend more, not fewer, partisan divisions. The anticommunist, anti-Soviet prism, which for so long had served as the guide to policy in East-West and North-South relations, and which dampened debate to some extent, has been largely undermined. Partisan divisions will more easily surface and grow, not diminish. Trade issues, for example, are likely to assume a larger role in foreign policy and are likely to exacerbate political divisions. As these kinds of economic issues are increasingly viewed as both foreign and domestic policy questions, and as Americans are affected differentially by these policy choices, partisan debate will intensify.

Third, the rise of environmental issues only reinforces this prognosis. Even if scientific agreement can be reached on the dimensions of such ecological challenges as acid rain, nuclear waste disposal, and global warming, common political actions to address these global issues will remain elusive and, hence, ripe for partisan discord. Since virtually any political decision on these issues is likely to affect the public differentially, more, not less, dissension will result.

On balance, then, the influence of partisan politics on the direction of U.S. foreign policy is likely to become more identifiable than it has been in the past. And it is likely to intensify in the future.

INTEREST GROUPS AND THE FOREIGN POLICY PROCESS

Another participant in foreign affairs whose role has increased in importance is that of interest groups. The number of interest groups participating in the American political process is astounding, estimated at over 11,600 firms or groups and an additional 12,500 individuals in one recent assessment.[29] The interest groups concerned either with foreign policy exclusively or with foreign and domestic policy in combination are surely less than that total, but they are still numerous by any count. These foreign policy interest groups range from the oldest and most numerous—the economic interest groups—to the newest and the fewest—foreign lobbying groups. Within and between these two types of organizations, several other categories of foreign policy interest groups can be identified: labor unions, agricultural organizations, religious groups, ethnic groups, veterans' organizations, single-issue interests, academic think-tanks, and ideological groups, among others.

Most of the efforts by these interest groups is directed toward the Congress through the use of professional lobbyists or their own staff personnel. Yet a considerable portion of interest-group activities is also directed toward the foreign policy bureaucracies. The Department of Defense and the Department of State, for example, are important targets for these various pressure groups.

TYPES OF FOREIGN POLICY INTEREST GROUPS

In order to give some sense of the magnitude of these groups (although without pretending to provide an exhaustive list) and some of their foreign policy concerns, let us identify examples of the different types of foreign policy interest groups that are operating today.

BUSINESS GROUPS   Economic interest groups probably comprise the largest number of foreign policy groups. Several umbrella economic organizations lobby for business interests. For example, the National Association of Manufacturers, the U.S. Chamber of Commerce (and its global affiliates), the Committee on Economic Development, and the Business Roundtable would fit into this category.[30] Beyond these umbrella groups, particular manufacturing, industrial, and commodity interests usually engage in separate lobbying activities. The American Petroleum Institute, the American Textile Manufacturers Institute, the American Footwear Manufacturers Association, the National Cotton Council, and the National Coal Association are examples of such lobbying groups. In addition, virtually all major corporations actively lobby for their particular foreign policy interests. The major defense contractors (such as General Dynamics, McDonnell Douglas, United Technologies, and General Electric) lobby the Congress and the Department of Defense in particular. In short, it is probably safe to say that virtually every major corporation in the Fortune 500 list has some kind of representation in Washington, and a large percentage of them are involved in foreign policy lobbying as well. All of these business lobbies generally share similar foreign policy goals: to increase foreign trade, to expand their own exports, and, in a number of instances, to promote a strong national defense policy.

LABOR UNIONS   A second important economic interest group is the American labor movement. This movement actively lobbies the Congress and the executive branch on foreign policy issues. Its main interests are policy decisions that would affect the job security of its workers or increase the amount of foreign imports. The labor movement recently has worked to protect American workers from the importation of cheaper goods and the export of jobs by American multinational firms that seek cheaper labor markets abroad. As might be expected, such policy positions are often directly opposed to those of the business groups on both foreign and domestic policy questions.

The most prominent labor unions that have extensive lobbying efforts are the American Federation of Labor and the Congress of Industrial Organizations (the AFL-CIO) and the United Auto Workers of America (UAW). In addition, over 100 separate affiliate unions within the AFL-CIO umbrella organization also lobby to protect their interests.[31] The United Steelworkers of America actively sought to limit the importation of foreign steel from Japan and Europe in the 1980s as a way of protecting the jobs of American steelworkers, and

that union and others have sought to have legislation passed in recent trade bills that would protect American jobs at home.

Although the labor unions, like the major industrial concerns,
are primarily interested in economic issues, they also have adopted
positions on more general foreign policy questions. Under the long-
time leadership of George Meany, the AFL-CIO was particularly
known for its staunch anti-communist stances and for its effort to assist the global trade union movement that would foster these positions.[32] Lane Kirkland, the successor to Meany as president of the
AFL-CIO, has continued this policy. For instance, he was one of the
first to suggest a reimposition of a grain embargo on the Soviet Union after the shooting down of a Korean airliner by that nation.

Still another and more direct way that the AFL-CIO has become
involved in the foreign policy process has been through the National
Endowment for Democracy (NED) program initiated during the
Reagan administration. As a result of some 1983 legislation, the NED
provided the AFL-CIO with funds to promote democracy in foreign
countries. Such funds were to be used to set up seminars for foreign
labor leaders, bring them to the United States, and assist them in promoting free and democratic institutions within their own countries.[33]

AGRICULTURAL GROUPS   Agricultural interests also attempt to influence the foreign policy process. The principal lobbying groups in
this area are the American Farm Bureau Federation, the National
Farmers Union, and the National Farm Organization.[34] While these
organizations vary in the degree to which they believe that the federal government should intervene into the market economy, they all
support efforts to increase the exports of farm products. Once again,
while these organizations are primarily concerned with promoting
agricultural interests, they also take stands on a variety of other foreign policy issues. At its 1990 national convention, the American
Farm Bureau Federation adopted foreign policy positions on international trade, agricultural exports, immigration, the United Nations,
and the Panama Canal, among other issues.[35]

RELIGIOUS ORGANIZATIONS   Another set of readily identifiable interest groups on foreign policy are religious organizations. The most
prominent among these groups are the National Council of
Churches (various Protestant churches), the American Friends Service Committee (Quakers), and the National Conference of Catholic
Bishops. Major religious groups, including Methodists, Unitarians,
Presbyterians, and Baptists, have also been involved in foreign policy
lobbying.[36] In addition, numerous affiliates of these different religious movements have engaged in lobbying efforts. By one estimate,

there are thirty different religious lobbies in Washington, D.C., alone.[37]

"Peace and justice" and "social concern" committees have been established by these various religious groups as a better means of informing and involving their memberships in both foreign and domestic policy matters. Indirectly, these efforts assist members of the religious faiths in petitioning their representatives if they choose to do so. The American Friends Service Committee (AFSC), for example, has long been involved in group discussions of current international issues, in aiding the various conflicting parties in the Middle East and elsewhere, and in offering suggestions for a resolution of the conflict between the Palestinians and Israelis.[38] Similarly, the May 1983 pastoral letter by the National Conference of Catholic Bishops on the possession and use of nuclear weapons, *The Challenge of Peace*, signaled a major illustration of foreign policy activism by that organization.[39] Various religious groups, largely led by members of the Catholic Church, were also active in opposition to the Reagan administration's policy in El Salvador and Nicaragua.[40]

ETHNIC GROUPS   Ethnic groups are another set of important interests active in the foreign policy arena. The most active American ethnic groups have been those of Jewish, Irish, and East European heritage. More recently, Greeks, Hispanics, and African-Americans have also sought to influence American foreign policy.[41] For these ethnic groups, American policy toward a particular country or region, rather than general foreign policy questions, has mainly been the dominant theme of their participation in foreign affairs. On policy issues related to Israel, Ireland, Cyprus, Central America, South Africa, and Poland, these groups have been most active and have made their voices heard. Ethnic groups, as a whole, have been identified as an especially important source of American foreign policy, and we shall have more to say about their influence below.

VETERANS' GROUPS   Veterans' groups or associations are also active in trying to influence the foreign policy of the United States. Such organizations as the Veterans of Foreign Wars, the American Legion, and the American Veterans of World War II are the best known of these groups.[42] Near the end of the Vietnam War, the Vietnam Veterans Against the War also entered the political arena, seeking at first to end American involvement in that war and, later, to petition for better treatment of the returning Vietnam veteran. Perhaps as an indication of how effective the veterans' groups have been over the years, a separate cabinet department was established in 1988 to serve these interests more directly.

IDEOLOGICAL GROUPS   Ideological groups have long been active in American politics. Although these groups are often identified with questions of domestic politics, some are also active on foreign policy issues. The most prominent ideological groups are the Americans for Democratic Action, the principal liberal interest group in Washington politics, and the Americans for Constitutional Action, the principal conservative interest group in the nation's capital. Both of these groups evaluate members of Congress on foreign and domestic policy from their particular perspectives and issue yearly voting scores for all senators and representatives. These groups also actively work to make known their positions on major foreign policy issues.

Many other ideological groups have also been active on foreign affairs issues from both ends of the political spectrum. Those with a conservative viewpoint include the American Security Council, the John Birch Society, and the National Conservative Political Action Committee (NCPAC), while those with a liberal viewpoint include the Women's International League for Peace and Freedom, the World Peace Through Law Association, the World Federalists, and the World Policy Institute.[43]

THINK TANKS   Another set of organizations that might not be immediately identified as interest groups are the numerous "think tanks" that exist in Washington.[44] These are organizations funded by individuals, corporations, and foundations that focus on analyzing a particular problem or array of problems to offer policy advice. These organizations share their results with the congressional and executive branch through testimony on Capitol Hill, through the publication of scholarly books and articles, and through opinion pieces appearing in several key elite newspapers, such as the *Christian Science Monitor*, the *Los Angeles Times*, the *New York Times*, the *Wall Street Journal*, and the *Washington Post*. In these various ways, they seek to influence policy. The number of think-tank groups is quite large, even if we were to consider only those devoted exclusively to foreign policy issues. Nonetheless, even a brief word or two about the major think tanks will illustrate the range and policy orientations of these organizations.

The best known conservative think tanks in Washington are the Heritage Foundation and the Cato Institute. The Heritage Foundation analyzes both domestic and foreign policy issues from a relatively hardline conservative position. Its views are disseminated through a quarterly magazine entitled *Policy Review* and through a myriad of reports on current topics. The Heritage Foundation gained prominence particularly during the Reagan administration. Several Reagan officials were drawn from its ranks or went there after serving in government. The Cato Institute is much newer than the Heritage Foundation, and it generally favors a libertarian view on policy matters. On foreign policy issues, this view often is translated into policy recommendations that promote a more isolationist or non-interventionist approach on the part of the United States in global affairs.

Somewhat in the middle politically are such institutions as the American Enterprise Institute (AEI) and the Center for Strategic and International Studies (CSIS). As its annual report states, AEI's goal is "preserving and improving the institutions of a free society—open and competitive private enterprise, limited and public-spirited government, strong and well-managed defense and foreign policies, and vital cultural and political values."[45] This think tank began as a strong conservative voice on foreign policy issues. While AEI has retained that characteristic on most foreign policy matters, it has also begun to broaden its political perspective in recent years. CSIS began as an institute affiliated with Georgetown University and, while generally a conservative institute, it has occasionally moved toward more moderation in its outlook. Since 1987, it has operated independently and now has begun to attract some distinguished names to its staff, including Zbigniew Brzezinski and Henry Kissinger. Like AEI and most other think tanks, CSIS publishes a foreign policy journal, *The Washington Quarterly,* holds periodic seminars, and publishes various foreign policy materials.

The best known liberal-leaning think tank is the Brookings Institution. Brookings has several divisions, with one devoted exclusively to foreign policy studies. Its policy recommendations are usually moderate and liberal in orientation, and it sometimes has been referred to as the "Democratic government in exile," since it has often been staffed by officials from Democratic administrations. Its seminars, conferences, and publications—including a wide array of foreign policy books annually—are highly regarded among those of all political stripes. Along with the other think tanks, its policy recommendations are often relied upon for policy innovations on Capitol Hill and in the executive branch.

SINGLE-ISSUE GROUPS   The single-issue interest group represents somewhat of a residual category for different kinds of groups that have sought to influence foreign policy because of their deeply held views on a particular policy question. These groups range widely, from the United Nations Association of the United States, which seeks to enhance support for the UN, to the Union of Concerned Scientists and the Arms Control Association, which back efforts to achieve arms limitations, to the Friends of the Earth or Greenpeace, which support efforts to preserve the global environment.[46] Moreover, these kinds of groups probably dwarf in size any other category we might identify, since they can form, lobby, and disband rather quickly.

Perhaps the leading illustration of a single-issue foreign policy group in the postwar period was the anti–Vietnam War movement of the 1960s and early 1970s. This group (really a coalition of groups such as the National Mobilization to End the War, the Moratorium movement, the War Resisters League, and even the radical wing of the Students for a Democratic Society, the Weathermen) was highly successful in rallying support among the American public and, eventually, altering the course of American policy in Southeast Asia. At the height of the détente period in the early 1970s, other single issue groups arose. Supporters and opponents of détente with the Soviet Union vigorously lobbied for their point of view with the Congress and the executive.

In the 1970s and early 1980s, the most prominent single-issue foreign policy groups were those supporting and opposing the development of more nuclear weapons. In the late 1970s, the Committee on the Present Danger, composed primarily of conservative ex-government officials, was most active in opposition to the ratification of the SALT II treaty signed by President Jimmy Carter. The nuclear freeze movement—a broadly based coalition of individuals from various walks of life that arose in opposition to the nuclear arms buildup by the Reagan administration—called for the enactment of a mutual and verifiable freeze on the production and development of all nuclear weapons.[47]

In the mid-1980s, the largest set of single-issue groups arose around the question of American policy in Central America. A decade-long debate developed over whether to provide or withhold aid to the Nicaraguan contras in their fight against the Sandinista government. One study identified about 100 interest groups that were involved in lobbying the Congress and the president on that issue. Table 11.1 portrays a few of these different groups to show the diversity of organizations that participated in this debate.[48] Some were formed exclusively to address Central America; others had a larger policy agenda but were still very involved in this issue.

FOREIGN LOBBIES   The newest recognized lobby groups on foreign policy have been foreign lobbies. In the main, these are often Ameri-

---

TABLE 11.1 INTEREST GROUP ACTIVITY OVER
THE CONTRA AID ISSUE IN THE 1980S

Some Contra Aid Supporters	*Contra Aid Opponents*
Citizens for Reagan	Religious groups (Catholics,
American Defense Lobby	Lutherans, Baptists, Unitarians)
Fund for a Conservative Majority	ACLU
Concerned Women of America	Common Cause
U.S. Defense Committee	SANE
The Conservative Caucus	OXFAM America
Eagle Forum	National Network in Solidarity with
Council for Inter-American Security	the Nicaraguan People
National Endowment for the	Pledge of Resistance
Preservation of Liberty	Quest for Peace
Students for America	Coalition for a New Foreign and
The Freedom Federation	Military Policy

Source: Cynthia J. Arnson and Philip Brenner, "The Limits of Lobbying: Interest Groups, Congress, and Aid to the Contras," paper presented at a conference on Public Opinion and Policy Toward Central America, Princeton University, May 4–5, 1990.

---

can citizens who have been hired to explain the policy of another nation and to try to persuade the Congress to give more favorable treatment to that nation. Recent prominent examples are the lobbying efforts by South Africa, El Salvador, Saudi Arabia, and other Third World nations. Saudi Arabia, for instance, was particularly active in its lobbying efforts on the AWACS aircraft sale in 1981 and enlisted the support of several large American corporations to back its position.[49]

Perhaps the best known and the most often maligned foreign lobby today is the Japanese lobby. Japan has hired numerous former members of Congress—e.g., James Jones (D-Oklahoma) and Michael Barnes (D-Maryland)—and former administrative officials—e.g., Eliott Richardson, former attorney general during the Nixon administration, and Stuart Eizenstat, former domestic policy aide to President Carter—to serve as its lobbyists and to attempt to influence Congress and the executive branch on U.S.-Japanese relations, especially trade policy. In addition, it has also hired some of the best-known public relations firms in Washington to get its message out. Both of these tactics have made its lobbying effort formidable, and often successful.

But Japanese lobbying has also done more than this. It has provided research money for several Washington think tanks, such as the Brookings Institution, the AEI, and the Center for Strategic and International Studies, to support various studies, conferences, and academic chairs. While any direct Japanese benefit from such think-tank support is obviously not specified with the support, it does at least raise the question of whether independent analysis can be undertaken with such arrangements. A similar problem, albeit less directly so, occurs over its funding of a Japanese studies program at various universities. By one estimate, "Japan funds about three-quarters of university research about Japan." All of these efforts allow Japan access in Washington, and they make its lobbying effort formidable, although "the Japan lobby rarely wins battles on its own."[50]

These kinds of activities by Japan and many other foreign countries reflect the "internationalization" of the lobbying efforts that have taken place today, and reflect how lobbying, and even foreign lobbying, has become yet another part of the American foreign policy process.

THE IMPACT OF INTEREST GROUPS

How successful are these interest groups in affecting foreign policy? Unlike the president, the Congress, or the foreign affairs bureaucracies, which have direct control over policy, interest groups have at best only an indirect effect. By definition, interest groups do not control policy; rather, they seek to influence it. Most analysts suggest that, on the whole, the foreign policy interest groups do not do very well at that task. Several reasons are given for this view.[51] First of all, American foreign policy tends to be made more in the executive branch than in the congressional branch, as we noted in Chapter 7. Access by interest groups to the executive branch is more difficult than access to the Congress, with its varied committee and subcommittee structures. While interest groups do lobby the foreign affairs bureaucracies, this process has not proved very successful and may actually end up serving the bureaucracies' interests more than the lobbyists'.[52] Second, important foreign policy decisions are often made under crisis conditions—short decision time, high threat, and surprise in the executive branch. Under such conditions, foreign policymaking is likely to be even more elitist than normal—more confined to a few members of the executive branch and more restricted in the amount of congressional participation. In such situations, avenues of influence for interest groups are further limited. Third—and perhaps most pivotal—with the magnitude of interest groups operating, it is likely that "countervailing" groups will arise to balance the impact of any interest group and, therefore, allow the policymakers more freedom of action.[53] Competing interest groups on contra aid, as illustrated in Table 11.1, or competing interest groups on trade policy (e.g., labor unions versus business lobbies) give the member of Congress or the executive branch official some latitude in making his or her own decision on a foreign policy question.

Despite such difficulties, interest groups still do affect policy on some key issues. The principal areas appear to be on budget issues related to defense and foreign economic policy in general and on issues involving American long-range policy toward the international system.[54] While the president often takes the lead on such policy questions, congressional approval of actions in these areas is almost always required. Since the Congress allows more avenues of access by interest groups, such groups are likely to be more successful on these issues.

Two kinds of interest groups appear especially influential on these kinds of issues and especially in the Congress. One is ethnic groups, the other can be loosely identified as the "military-industrial complex."[55] The impact of the former set of groups is based upon the interest that many Americans have in the U.S. policy toward the country of their origin or toward a country with which they identify, e.g., Israel.[56] The impact of the latter set of groups is based upon the extensive interest and involvement by numerous corporations in the economic and defense issues that so often arise in the Congress. Let us examine both of these types of interest groups in a little more detail.

THE MILITARY-INDUSTRIAL COMPLEX

The most often-mentioned interest group in affecting American foreign policy is, in reality, a coalition of different organizations, the "military-industrial complex (MIC)." The name comes from the presumed symbiotic relationship between the major industrial firms in the United States and the American defense establishment. These industries become dependent upon the Defense Department for military defense contracts and often apply pressure for a policy of strong military preparedness or even global military involvement as a means of continuing their economic well-being. In addition, the military-industrial concept has also been used to describe the informal ties that have developed among the top corporate sectors of American society and the political-military sectors of the American government.[57]

The principal assumption underlying the military-industrial complex argument is that there is a unified structural elite within American society that dominates all important national and foreign policy decisions. This elite is held together by a set of interlocking structural relationships and by psychological and social constraints among the occupants of the key institutions.[58] In other words, the elites share similar educational and social backgrounds and frequently interact with one another to promote their common interests. The result, as C. Wright Mills stated as long ago as 1958, is that:

> There is no longer, on the one hand, an economy, and, on the other, a political order, containing a military establishment unimportant to politics and to money-making. There is a political economy numerously linked with military order and decision.[59]

A few years later, President Dwight Eisenhower, in his 1961 farewell address to the nation, warned of the danger of this elite's dominating the policy process. Ironically, it was President Eisenhower, a decorated World War II general, who coined the "military-industrial complex" phrase:

> Our military organization today bears little relation to that known of any of my predecessors in peacetime—or, indeed, by the fighting men of World War II or Korea....But we can no longer risk emergency improvisation of national defense. We have been compelled to create a permanent armament industry of vast proportions. Added to this, three and a half million men and women are directly engaged in the defense establishment. We annually spend on military security alone more than the net income of all United States corporations.
> Now this conjunction of an immense military establishment and a large arms industry is new in the American experience. The total influence—economic, political, even spiritual—is felt in every city, every state house, every office of the Federal Government. We recognize the imperative need for this development. Yet we must not fail to comprehend its grave implications. Our toils, resources, and livelihood are all involved; so is the very structure of our society.
> In the councils of Government, we must guard against the acquisition of unwarranted influence, whether sought or unsought, by the military-industrial complex. The potential for the disastrous rise of misplaced power exists and will persist.[60]

Critics contend that this single elite's domination of policymaking would produce a foreign policy supporting its own interests. Such a policy would emphasize high military spending, interventionism abroad, and the protection of private property.[61] By pursuing such a strategy, the private interests of the military-industrial complex would be safeguarded, especially in a world of ideological tension between the United States and the Soviet Union. The challenge for the MIC, however, is whether its influence will wane with the change in global politics that we have witnessed since the beginning of the 1990s.

Support for the MIC   Various pieces of evidence exist, however, to support the dominance of the military-industrial complex within American policymaking: the kind of personnel in governmental offices, the interactions between the political and economic sectors, and the policy outcomes in awarding defense contracts and in making foreign policy decisions.

The first piece of evidence is the personnel who occupy the political and economic institutions. Gabriel Kolko reports that 60 percent of 234 officials in mainly the foreign affairs bureaucracies (Department of Defense, Department of State, the Central Intelligence Agency, etc.) came from important business, investment, and law firms during the years of his inquiry (1944 to 1960). Furthermore, a relatively small number of these individuals (84) held over 63 percent of the positions. In his view, then, a few key individuals dominated the foreign policy bureaucracies and circulated in and out of the government during the 1940s and 1950s.[62]

Thomas Dye provided other evidence to make a similar point. His research has documented the extensive business involvement on the part of several key foreign policy officials in the postwar years.[63] Various secretaries of defense, for example, have had extensive ties to large American corporations. Charles E. Wilson (1953–1957) was the president and a member of the board of directors for General Motors; Thomas Gates (1960–1961) was chairman of the board and chief executive officer of Morgan Guaranty Trust and also served on the boards of directors of General Electric, Bethlehem Steel, Scott Paper Company, and Insurance Company of America, among others; Robert S. McNamara (1961–1967) was president and a member of the board of directors of the Ford Motor Company; and Caspar Weinberger (1981–1987) was a vice-president and a corporate director for the Bechtel Corporation, a California-based engineering and construction firm with worldwide involvement, and served on the boards of directors of such companies as Pepsico and Quaker Oats.

The same pattern has held true for secretaries of state in the postwar years. John Foster Dulles (1953–1959) was a partner of Sullivan and Cromwell, a prominent Wall Street law firm, and was on the boards of directors for the Bank of New York, Fifth Avenue Bank, the American Cotton Oil Company, and the United Railroad of St.

Louis, among others; Dean Rusk (1961–1968) was a former president of the Rockefeller Foundation; and William P. Rogers (1969–1973) was a senior partner in Royal, Koegal, Rogers, and Wall, another prominent Wall Street law firm. Alexander Haig (1981–1982) not only served as military attaché to Henry Kissinger and as supreme allied commander of NATO, but he also served as an executive with United Technologies, a leading defense contractor. His successor at State, George Schultz (1982–1989), also had considerable involvement with the business community. Just prior to his appointment, Shultz was a high-ranking official with the Bechtel Corporation and also had served on the boards of directors for the Borg-Warner Corporation, General Motors, and Stein, Roe, and Farnham, a Chicago-based investment advisory firm.

In the Bush administration, the patterns are largely similar, with several foreign policy members of the cabinet drawn from wealth and privilege and with important business ties. First of all, George Bush himself came from an old-line patrician family in Connecticut and gained his own considerable wealth through the development of an oil firm in West Texas. The Secretary of State, James Baker, came from a background of the law and wealth. (Baker's father owned the Texas Commerce bank, a leading bank in that state.) The national security advisor, Brent Scowcroft, was educated at West Point and Columbia University, worked for Kissinger and Associates, a private global consulting firm, and served as director of a Washington, D.C., bank prior to his appointment. The secretary of the treasury, Nicholas Brady, was a former head of Dillon, Read & Co., an important global investment banking firm, and served on the boards of directors for the Purolator Company, NCR, and Georgia International. The Secretary of Commerce, Robert Mosbacher, owns his own energy company and served as a director of a Texas bank and a life insurance company. The only two key foreign policy advisors without this kind of background are Secretary of Defense Richard Cheney, a former Member of Congress, and the chairman of the Joint Chiefs of Staff, General of the Army Colin Powell.

The assumption undergirding such an analysis of government officials' backgrounds is that their previous experience in corporate America will greatly influence their assessment of foreign policy questions. The interests of important economic groups will be taken into account in any foreign policy calculations that are later made. If the assumption does not always go quite that far, at the very least this common background will allow ready access by the lobbying efforts of the various business groups.

A third type of evidence for the dominance of the MIC is provided by former Senator William Proxmire. His evidence focuses on the personnel interchange between the Department of Defense and the major military contractors. In 1970, Proxmire entered into the *Congressional Record* evidence of the number of former high-ranking military officers who were working for prime defense contractors in 1959 and 1969. In 1959, for instance, the total number of ex-military personnel (with the rank of colonel or navy captain and above) employed by the top 100 companies was 721. By 1969, the number had increased to 2,072 former military personnel in the top 100 defense contractors. While Senator Proxmire rejected calling such interchange a conspiracy, he did assert "that there is a continuing community of interest between the military, on the one hand, and these industries on the other."[64]

According to some recent evidence, these ties hardly ceased in the 1970s and 1980s, despite legislation restricting the so-called "revolving door" between the DOD and defense contractors. In a 1986 survey of former DOD personnel, the General Accounting Office reported that 73 percent had defense contractor responsibilities while at DOD and 26 percent had similar responsibilities for defense contractors for whom they subsequently worked. Further, about 82 percent of the former DOD personnel had continued to have "work-related" communications with DOD officials after they had left their positions. While legislation now restricts some former DOD officials from being employed by certain defense contractors for two years after leaving government service and now requires governmental reporting on such hirings, recent studies indicate that these reporting requirements have not been very effective and that, because of several loopholes in the law, "the legislation limited few DOD personnel from obtaining post-DOD employment with defense contractors."[65]

This symbiotic relationship between the DOD and defense contractors is given even more credence in light of the various criminal charges that have been brought against lobbyists for defense contractors and in light of the large number of revelations about cost overruns and overcharging by defense contractors themselves. Several lobbyists have been charged and convicted of bribing DOD procurement officers to obtain lucrative contracts, for example, and major defense contractors (e.g., General Electric and the Electric Boat division of General Dynamics) have been accused of dramatic cost overruns. Still others have been accused of charging exorbitant prices for commonplace supplies to the military. By one analysis, "the military paid $511 for light bulbs that cost ninety cents, $640 for toilet seats that cost $12, $7,600 for coffeemakers, and $900 for a plastic cap to place under the leg of a navigator's stool" in an airplane.[66]

A final piece of evidence that is often used to demonstrate the influence of the military-industrial complex within American society is the pattern of awarding defense contracts and their constancy over time. The prime military contractors often turn out to be among the largest industrial corporations, and they are often the same ones year in and year out. For instance, in an analysis of the largest defense contractors for fiscal year 1988, we found that 24 of the top 50 and 35 of the top 100 defense contractors were also ranked among the 100 largest corporations in America, based on the Fortune 500 list[67] (see Table 11.2). Further, political scientist James Kurth has pointed out even more concentration and continuity in defense contracting: the defense contractors have largely remained the same over the last three decades, mainly the aircraft industries, and more recently the electronics industries; they have maintained their same ties with particular military branches (e.g., Boeing and Rockwell International with the Air Force and Grumman primarily with the Navy); and they have maintained the same "product specialties," particular kinds of weapons systems for each manufacturer. Such continuity provides further evidence on how and why certain defense systems are purchased rather than others and why some manufacturers are advantaged over others.

While these pieces of evidence suggest the opportunity for the military-industrial complex to shape policy, they do not, in and of themselves, demonstrate its success in always doing so. Several case analyses of American foreign policy decisions attempt to do just that. In their analysis of policy decisions ranging from the Marshall Plan of 1948 to the decision not to intervene in Indochina in 1954, to the decision to cut back the bombing in Vietnam in 1968, Berkowitz, Bock, and Fuccillo contend that "it would be difficult to point to a single decision that directly contravenes the interests of the business elite within the presidential court."[68] While they quickly add that the business elite may not have been successful on every decision, "when major issues are at stake, or when its interests are clearly and incontrovertibly involved, . . . the business elite proceeds with absolute unity of purpose and action."[69] Moreover, they contend that the business elite view of foreign policymaking provides the best explanation for America's actions abroad.

QUESTIONS ABOUT THE INFLUENCE OF THE **MIC**   Others raise doubts about the success of the military-industrial complex to shape

TABLE 11.2   TOP 100 U.S. DEFENSE CONTRACTORS
AND THEIR CORPORATE SALES RANKS FOR FY 1988

Defense Contract Rank	Company	Corporate Sales Rank
1.	McDonnell Douglas Corp.	25
2.	General Dynamics Corp.	41
3.	General Electric Corp.	5
4.	Tenneco, Inc.	24
5.	Raytheon Co.	53
6.	Martin Marietta Corp.	77
7.	General Motors Corp.	1
8.	Lockheed Corp.	33
9.	United Technologies Corp.	16
10.	The Boeing Corp.	19
11.	Grumman Corp.	*
12.	Litton Industries, Inc.	96
13.	Westinghouse Electric Corp.	27
14.	Rockwell International Corp.	28
15.	Unisys Corp.	38
16.	Honeywell Inc.	60
17.	Textron Inc.	61
18.	TRW Inc.	62
19.	Texas Instruments, Inc.	68
20.	IBM	4
21.	The LTV Corp.	56
22.	FMC Corp.	*
23.	Ford Motor Corp.	2
24.	The Singer Co.	*
25.	ITT Corp.	*
26.	Allied-Signal Inc.	29
27.	CRS Sirrine Metcalf & Eddy JV	*
28.	Gencorp, Inc.	*
29.	Avondale Industries, Inc.	*
30.	AT&T Co.	*
31.	CFM International, Inc.	*
32.	Northrop Corp.	75
33.	Hercules, Inc.	*
34.	Harsco Corp.	*
35.	Loral Corp.	*
36.	Teledyne, Inc.	*
37.	Bell Boeing JV	*
38.	GTE Corp.	*
39.	Dyncorp Inc.	*
40.	MIT	*
41.	Gibbons Green Van Amerongen	*
42.	Morton Thiokol Inc.	*

TABLE 11.2 TOP 100 U.S. DEFENSE CONTRACTORS
AND THEIR CORPORATE SALES RANKS FOR FY 1988 (CONTINUED)

Defense Contract Rank	Company	Corporate Sales Rank
43.	Royal Dutch Petroleum Co.	*
44.	Motorola Inc.	52
45.	Harris Corp.	*
46.	Computer Sciences Corp.	*
47.	The Aerospace Corp.	*
48.	The Mitre Corp.	*
49.	Pan Am Corp.	*
50.	Johns Hopkins University	*
51.	Science Applications Int'l Corp.	*
52.	Olin Corp.	*
53.	Penn Central Corp.	*
54.	Chevron Corp.	11
55.	Control Data Corp.	*
56.	Atlantic Richfield Corp.	17
57.	Mobil Corp.	6
58.	Philips Gloeilampenfabrieken	*
59.	Exxon Corp.	3
60.	E Systems, Inc.	*
61.	Forstmann Little & Co.	*
62.	Oshkosh Truck Corp.	*
63.	Emerson Electric Corp.	66
64.	Black River Constructors	*
65.	Zenith Electronics Corp.	*
66.	Contel Corp.	*
67.	Sequa Corp.	*
68.	Eaton Corp.	*
69.	Coastal Corp.	54
70.	Chrysler Corp.	7
71.	MIP Instandsetzunsbetric	*
72.	Bahrain National Oil	*
73.	General Electric Co., P.L.C.	*
74.	Westmark Systems, Inc.	*
75.	AMOCO Corp.	12
76.	Eastman Kodak Corp.	18
77.	Draper Charles Stark Lab Inc.	*
78.	Sundstrand Corp.	*
79.	Kaman Corp.	*
80.	Emhart Corporation	*
81.	Digital Equipment Corp.	30
82.	Morrison Knudsen Corp.	*
83.	Rolls-Royce Corp.	*
84.	Arvin Industries, Inc.	*

TABLE 11.2 TOP 100 U.S. DEFENSE CONTRACTORS AND THEIR CORPORATE SALES RANKS FOR FY 1988 (CONTINUED)

Defense Contract Rank	Company	Corporate Sales Rank
85.	United Industrial Corp.	*
86.	ITT & Varo Joint Venture	*
87.	CSX Corporation	*
88.	Daimler-Benz No. America	*
89.	Motor Oils Hellas Corinth Ref.	*
90.	Hewlett-Packard Co.	39
91.	Honeywell Bull AG	*
92.	Tiger International Inc.	*
93.	Day & Zimmermann Inc.	*
94.	Phelps, Inc.	*
95.	Royal Ordnance Ammunition PLC	*
96.	Braintree Maritime Corporation	*
97.	EG & G Inc.	*
98.	Texaco, Inc.	*
99.	Bundesamt Fuer Wehrtechnik	*
100.	Figgie International Inc.	*

*Indicates companies that were not listed in the top 100 companies in corporate sales.

Source: Defense contract ranks were taken from *100 Companies Receiving the Largest Dollar Volume of Prime Contract Awards Fiscal Year 1988* (Washington, D.C.: Department of Defense, Directorate for Information Operations and Reports, n.d.); the corporate sales ranks for 1988 were taken from "The 500 Largest U.S. Industrial Corporations," *Fortune*, April 24, 1989, pp. 354 and 356.

and influence foreign policy. They point out that the military-industrial complex is far from the conspiratorial arrangement sometimes implied in discussions of it. Instead, the military-industrial complex is a convergence of defense-oriented organizations that are constantly pursuing their interests. It has not been as successful as commonly viewed: defense spending has hardly been as dramatic as sometimes implied, and its negative effect on the American economy may be less than is often assumed. Further, the MIC has met public resistance and interest group opposition, especially in the post-Vietnam period, and it is likely to meet even more resistance with the presumed end of the Cold War. Several pieces of evidence seem to bear out this somewhat more benign view of the MIC.

First, until the dramatic expenditures during the Reagan administration, defense spending, measured either as a percentage of the gross national product or as a percentage of the national budget, had actually declined over time. With the former measure, defense spending dropped below the 6 percent level, and with the latter measure, defense spending fell to about 25 percent. Viewed in this way, the clout of the military-industrial complex on defense spending has hardly been as pronounced as some imply.

Second, have American industries really been as dependent on defense spending for their prosperity as some imply? In the aggregate, as reported in a classic study by sociologist Stanley Lieberson, few of the 100 largest industrial corporations in 1968 depended on military contracts for the bulk of their sales; in fact, 78 of the top 100 had less than 10 percent of their sales from military contracts, and only 5 corporations had more than 50 percent of their sales by military contracts.[70] In addition, Lieberson demonstrated that corporate income over time has been less dependent on military spending of the federal government than on non-military spending. Finally, he shows that defense spending cutbacks would only seriously harm certain sectors of the economy (aircraft, ordinance, research and development, electronics, and nonferrous metals) rather than the economy as a whole. In short, while Lieberson does not deny the existence of the military-industrial complex, his evidence suggests that its pervasiveness is less than others might contend.

Third, to what extent has the MIC been responsible for military spending? Political scientist Bruce Russett, long a student of American defense expenditures, cast some doubt on its pervasiveness. He argues that the explanation for high defense budgets cannot be attributed to the military-industrial complex only. Most assuredly, the military-industrial complex contributes to continued defense spending, but other factors in combination (such as domestic bureaucratic politics, technological momentum, and international actions) better explain the overall defense levels. Russett is quick to acknowledge, however, that domestic factors tend to have somewhat greater weight in this explanation than do international factors alone.[71]

Russett's work also has examined the reliance of the American economy on defense spending and its effect on the rest of the economy. His results, once again, raise some doubts about the power of the MIC. The profits in defense industries, he finds, are not systematically higher than in non-defense industries, and the economy as a whole does not suffer dramatically with defense cutbacks. Instead, as with others, Russett sees the impact of defense spending tied to particular industries, and specifically to the aircraft industry.[72] Further, he argues that military spending did not come at the expense of health and educational spending over the years 1941-1979. Only in the early part of the Reagan administration did military spending come directly from major cuts in health and education.[73]

A more recent study by Alex Mintz largely confirms Russett's earlier analysis and extends it to near the end of the Reagan administration. Only for the Reagan administration does Mintz find that defense expenditures hurt other domestic spending, and that effect was almost exclusively on the funding for education. On average, for example, education expenditures fell 4.6 percent from 1981 to 1987 as various kinds of military expenditures (military personnel, procurement of new weapons, operations and maintenance, and research and development) increased.[74] In essence, then, neither the dependence of the American economy on high defense spending, nor its substantial negative effects across the entire American economy are easily demonstrable. And to the extent that these effects have been demonstrable, they have been so only in the context of the Reagan administration.

The debate about the relative influence of the military-industrial complex in policymaking is likely to increase. With the reunification of Germany and the collapse of the Soviet empire, the rationale for defense expenditures is seriously challenged. The real test of these interest groups' influence is really yet to come. Can this array of interest groups continue to affect policy and achieve its goals in an environment of a seeming decline in defense needs and in an environment of severe budget deficits? If it can, then perhaps the argument about the relative impact of the MIC will become clear. If it cannot, those who took a more differentiated view of its power may be more accurate.

What should not be lost in such a discussion of the military-industrial complex is the continuing size and impact of these sets of interests. No matter what one's judgment is about the degree of control of the MIC, it does appear fair to conclude that the military-industrial sector seems to occupy a potentially important position in the shaping of foreign policy decisions, especially when compared to other interest groups. Moreover, the success of many high-tech weapons in the 1991 Persian Gulf War (e.g., bombs sent down air shafts into Iraqi storage facilities, the success of the Patriot defense system against incoming Scud missiles in Israel and Saudi Arabia, and the accuracy of the cruise missiles in attacking Baghdad) may well have provided a resurgence in political clout for the military-industrial complex on Capitol Hill.

ETHNIC GROUPS

The second major type of interest group that has enjoyed some success in influencing American foreign policy has been ethnic groups. The leading ethnic lobbies today are probably the Jewish and Greek communities, two relative newcomers to the American political process. The Jewish lobby has been able to obtain a remarkable level of economic and military assistance for Israel over the postwar years and has been able to assist in steering American policy toward supporting that state since 1948. Only in the past decade or so has this strong support for Israel begun to wane a bit. In a more limited way, the Greek lobby has also enjoyed some success, especially in the middle 1970s.[75] It was able to garner sufficient congressional support to impose an American arms embargo on Turkey during the middle 1970s, despite active opposition by the executive branch.

By contrast, the influence of the older ethnic lobbies—those Americans of Irish and Eastern European heritage—has generally declined over the past forty years. The Irish lobby enjoyed its greatest success prior to World War II, while the East Europeans seemed most influential in the early Cold War years.[76] A possible exception is the Polish community. With the development of the Polish trade union Solidarity, the 1981 imposition of martial law in Poland, and the eventual movement of that country to democracy, this ethnic segment of American society has once again exercised some political influence in seeking to obtain American development aid.

Newer American ethnic groups are increasingly joining the foreign policy arena and are likely to exercise some influence over the next decade or two. Hispanics and American blacks have begun to exert some policy influence and are likely to be more active in the future. TransAfrica, an organization to promote the interests of African-Americans in foreign policy, especially with respect to Africa and the Caribbean, was only formed in 1977, but it has already had a noticeable effect on American foreign policy.[77] This group lobbied to keep economic sanctions on Rhodesia in the late 1970s in an effort to complete the country's movement toward majority rule and bring about the creation of the nation of Zimbabwe. Its influence has probably been most pronounced in the effort to pressure the Reagan administration to move away from its policy of constructive engagement toward South Africa and to impose economic sanctions until the policy of apartheid was replaced. In conjunction with the "Free South Africa Movement," TransAfrica was crucial in the Reagan administration's executive order applying some economic sanctions in 1985 and in passing the Anti-Apartheid Act of 1986, which imposed even greater sanctions.

With the increasingly large percentage of Hispanics in the South and Southwest, this ethnic group seemingly would begin to make known its concerns about American policy toward Central America, South America, and the Caribbean. So far, though, the evidence is quite mixed about overall Hispanic influence. The most powerful Cuban-American lobby, the Cuban-American National Foundation (CANF) has had a noticeable impact on policy toward Cuba and toward Central America generally. In various congressional votes over aid to the Nicaraguan contras, for example, one would be hard pressed to find a member of Congress with a sizeable Cuban-American constituency failing to support this action. Further, members from such districts also would most likely be receptive to stringent actions against Castro's Cuba. Mexican-Americans, by contrast, have neither had the same interest nor the same effect on policy toward Mexico or toward Central America generally. On many issues regarding Central America, for instance, their attitudes are not much different than those of the rest of the American public.[78]

Why have some of these ethnic groups been so successful? How can only some 6 million Jewish Americans, 3 million Greek Americans, 22 million Hispanic Americans, or 30 million African Americans exercise any influence in a nation of over 250 million citizens? While we suggested some of the possible reasons earlier, a brief examination of perhaps the most successful ethnic lobby, the Jewish lobby, is particularly instructive in understanding how this influence can occur.

THE JEWISH LOBBY: A CASE EXAMPLE   First of all, the Jewish lobby appears to be very well organized and directs its energies primarily toward foreign policy issues related to a single state, Israel. By one estimate, for instance, over seventy-five organizations exist that support Israel, and most are Jewish. Furthermore, these groups have two umbrella organizations to coordinate and guide their activities, the Conference of Presidents of Major American Jewish Organizations and the American-Israel Public Affairs Committee (AIPAC). According to this same analyst, this comprehensive organizational structure greatly assists the overall Jewish effort: "The multitiered structural pyramid that links individual Jews in local communities across the country to centralized national foreign policy leadership groups in Washington and New York is the primary organizational factor that can explain the ability of the pro-Israel movement to mobilize rapidly and in a coordinated fashion on a national scale when important foreign policy issues arise."[79]

Second, AIPAC has particularly good access to Capitol Hill, although less access to the executive branch. Through its frequent contacts with members of Congress, and particularly congressional staff, it has been able to garner remarkable levels of support for some pro-Israeli legislation. For instance, the Jackson Amendment to the

Trade Act of 1974 had some seventy-six co-sponsors in the Senate. This legislation disallowed most-favored-nation status to any state that failed to have a free emigration policy and was clearly directed at the Soviet Union and its policy on Jewish emigration. A few years later, an identical number of senators co-authored a letter to President Ford urging him to stand behind Israel in any search for peace in the Middle East.[80] More generally, one study demonstrated a remarkably high level of pro-Israeli voting (about 84 percent support) in the Senate in the early 1970s, with strong support existing across party lines.[81]

A third reason for the success of the Jewish lobby is tied to the degree of sympathy for Israel among the American public. Such latent support allows Jewish interest groups to obtain considerable overt support within the Congress. The American public is often sympathetic toward Israel for moral and ethical reasons. It represents a people who have suffered greatly in their history and who are believed to deserve a homeland of their own. But support is also tied to political reasons. Israel represents a democratic and Western-oriented state in a region of the world that does not seem to have many such examples.[82]

Equally important, perhaps, is the support for Israel that can be generated for domestic electoral considerations. The Jewish community is quite a small percentage of the nation's population (less than 3 percent), but it is concentrated in some key states, especially along the East Coast and in California, Illinois, and Ohio.[83] As a consequence, its support can be pivotal in the success of any potential congressional or presidential candidate. Furthermore, because the Jewish population has traditionally been quite active politically, there is even more incentive for potential presidents, senators, and representatives to be sympathetic to its view on the question of Israel.

Finally, the pro-Arab lobby, the counterpart of the pro-Israeli lobby, is not as well organized or as active as the Jewish lobby. While the National Association of Arab Americans (NAAA) has increased its visibility and its activism since the Arab oil embargo of 1973–1974, it remains much less potent than the supporters of Israel.[84] The American-Arab Anti-Discrimination Committee, a more recent Arab lobby, has faced similar difficulties. As its leader, former Senator James Abourezk, indicated, his committee faces a formidable task of money and organization: "To have influence in Congress you have to have money for candidates or control a lot of votes. We're trying to build a grass-roots network; it's difficult for us to raise money."[85] Furthermore, these Arab lobbies have to contend with the impression they are more anti-Israel than pro-Arab. It is a charge they deny, but one that continues to remain. In addition, the Arab lobby is often divided. After all, it represents a variety of different Arab states with different political traditions in each and with considerable rivalries with one another. For these reasons, the pro-Arab lobbies do not yet serve as a good counterweight to the influence of the Jewish lobby.

Although the Jewish lobby is arguably the most successful ethnic organization, its overall influence still remains hotly debated. To some observers, it remains far from omnipotent over American policy toward Israel or the Middle East in general. Moreover, some of its recent difficulties illustrate the limits of its influence. Prior to the late 1970s and the Camp David Accords on the Middle East, the Jewish lobby had generally been able to forestall the providing of military supplies to the Arab states and had been able to gain large military assistance for Israel from the American Congress. By 1978, however, success in these areas began to wane a bit, as the United States sought to pursue a more evenhanded policy in the post–Camp David period. The Jewish lobby was unable to stop the supplying of U.S. fighter aircraft to Saudi Arabia and Egypt, despite strong lobbying efforts. In addition, the sale of AWACS and other technologically advanced aircraft equipment to Saudi Arabia in October 1981 also was approved by the Congress. The proposed sale of arms to Saudi Arabia in light of the crisis over the seizure of Kuwait by Iraq, at one time estimated at $20 billion, will be yet another test of this lobby's strength.

Others also discount its overall success with the Congress and the executive branch. Some suggest that its perceived influence within the Congress is overstated and fails to account for the political and strategic reasons for supporting Israel, with or without the Jewish lobby. Others, too, point to the lobby's lack of success within the Department of State and the willingness of recent administrations to criticize the Israeli government, despite the possibility of domestic opposition from the Jewish lobby.[86] Still others cite the internal discord within the American Jewish community, especially after the massacres at the Palestinian camps of Shabra and Shatilla outside Beirut in September 1982, the intransigence of recent Israeli governments over several peace proposals, and the repressive response of the Israeli government to the *intifada*, the Palestinian uprisings in Israeli-occupied territories on the West Bank and the Gaza Strip. Such actions caused fissures within the Jewish community and undoubtedly weakened the overall impact of this group in American policy.[87]

Finally, one former Carter administration aide observed that the president can still challenge the Jewish lobby successfully: "The president can take a position that Israel opposes if the American people as a whole are behind him. . . . Then the Jewish community will support him also. That happened with Ike [President Eisenhower] and the Sinai and it is still true."[88] Another lobbyist for Arab clients characterized the notion that the Jewish lobby cannot be defeated on stopping arms sales to Arab states as "hogwash." If the members of the administration "want to win, they will win."[89]

Despite such views, the Jewish lobby shows how an ethnic group can affect foreign affairs and, more generally, how a well organized and committed interest group can enter the foreign policy arena. Increasingly, interest groups, like political parties, are exercising an independent effect on U.S. foreign policymaking.

CONCLUDING COMMENTS

Political parties and interest groups are playing a more important role in foreign policymaking today. Despite the American tradition of bipartisanship in foreign affairs, partisan differences have always been a characteristic of policymaking. In recent decades, moreover, partisan (and ideological) differences on foreign policy questions have actually intensified and are likely to remain part of the American political landscape, especially as the U.S. confronts the dramatic changes of the 1990s. Interest groups, too, have become more pervasive in the foreign policy process. Both a greater number and a wider array of interest groups have begun to participate in foreign affairs activities. While economic and ethnic groups remain particularly effective, foreign interests are increasingly seeking to influence policy as well.

In the next chapter, we complete our analysis of the policymaking process by examining the role of American public opinion. Because the public is at such distance from where foreign policy decisions are made, considerable skepticism and questions often accompany such a discussion. Does the public really hold any consistent views on foreign policy? Can the public effectively convey its view to public officials? Do those officials listen? It is to these and other questions that we must now turn to get a full picture of how U.S. foreign policy is made.

NOTES

1. On the various definitions of political parties, see Frank J. Sorauf, *Party Politics in America* (Boston: Little, Brown & Co., 1984), pp. 6–28.

2. L. Harmon Ziegler and G. Wayne Peak, *Interest Groups in American Society*, 2nd ed. (Englewood Cliffs, NJ: Prentice-Hall, Inc., 1972), p. 3.

3. Herbert McClosky, Paul J. Hoffmann, and Rosemary O'Hara, "Issue Conflict and Consensus among Party Leaders and Followers," *American Political Science Review* 14 (June 1960): 408–427.

4. The quote is taken from a speech by Senator Arthur H. Vandenberg to the Cleveland Foreign Affairs Forum. See John Felton, "The Man Who Showed Politicians the Water's Edge," *Congressional Quarterly Weekly Report*, February 18, 1989, p. 336.

5. Cecil V. Crabb, Jr., *Bipartisan Foreign Policy* (Evanston, IL: Row, Peterson and Company, 1957), p. 5.

6. Robert Dahl, *Congress and Foreign Policy* (New York: Harcourt, Brace and Company, 1950), p. 229.

7. See the Republican party platform of 1952, which strongly attacks the Democrats, reprinted in Donald Bruce Johnson and Kirk H. Porter, *National Party Platforms, 1840–1972* (Urbana: University of Illinois Press, 1973), pp. 497–500.

8. See the 1956 party platforms in ibid., pp. 524, 556; and the 1960 Republican platform, p. 606.

9. These trends have shifted lately, with the Democrats more associated with peace and the Republicans with prosperity. Public opinion data on these questions of war and peace and prosperity and recession from 1951 to 1984 were recently summarized in George Gallup, "GOP Edges Democrats in Poll on Prosperity Helm," *Des Moines Sunday Register*, April 29, 1984, p. 4A.

10. See McClosky, Hoffmann, and O'Hara, "Issue Conflict and Consensus among the Party Leaders and Followers," Table I, p. 410. At the same time, they argue against the view that the two parties "hold the same views" on foreign policy (p. 417). Some differences are detectable.

11. Gerald Pomper, *Elections in America: Control and Influence in Democratic Politics* (New York: Dodd, Mead & Co., 1965), p. 194.

12. I. M. Destler, Leslie H. Gelb, and Anthony Lake, *Our Own Worst Enemy: The Unmaking of American Foreign Policy* (New York: Simon and Schuster, 1984), p. 17.

13. Ibid., pp. 60–61.

14. Crabb, *Bipartisan Foreign Policy*, p. 256.

15. This discussion and the following on military assistance, defense, and trade policy is drawn from the data and discussion in Barry Hughes, *The Domestic Context of American Foreign Policy* (San Francisco: W. H. Freeman and Company, 1975), pp. 130–144. On foreign aid voting, also see Barbara Hinckley, *Stability and Change in Congress*, 3rd ed. (New York: Harper & Row, 1953), p. 272.

16. Ibid. Also see Aage R. Clausen, *How Congressmen Decide: A Policy Focus* (New York: St. Martin's Press, 1973), pp. 192–212.

17. Destler, Gelb, and Lake, *Our Own Worst Enemy*, p. 61.

18. Zbigniew Brzezinski, "The Three Requirements for a Bipartisan Foreign Policy," in *The Washington Quarterly White Paper* (Washington, D.C.: Center for Strategic and International Studies, Georgetown University), pp. 14–15.

19. Leslie H. Gelb with Richard K. Betts, *The Irony of Vietnam: The System Worked* (Washington, D.C.: The Brookings Institution, 1979), p. 216.

20. "Congress Took 94 Roll-Call Votes on War 1966–1972," *Congress and the Nation, 1969–1972*, Volume III (Washington, D.C.: Congressional Quarterly, Inc., 1973), p. 944.

21. These figures were computed for these years by the author from the data provided in Pomper, *Elections in America*, and Gerald M. Pomper with Susan S.

Lederman, *Elections in America: Control and Influence in Democratic Politics*, 2nd ed. (New York: Longman, 1980), p. 169. The former volume covered 1944–1964 party platforms, while the latter covered the 1944–1976 ones.

22. One recent explanation has suggested that personal ideology more than any other factor (including party) may explain congressional voting in the post-Vietnam period. See, for example, Robert A. Bernstein and William W. Anthony, "The ABM Issue in the Senate, 1968–1970: The Importance of Ideology," *The American Political Science Review* 65 (September 1974): 1198–1206; Wayne Moyer, "House Voting on Defense: An Ideological Explanation," in Bruce M. Russett and Alfred Stepan, eds., *Military Force and American Society* (New York: Harper & Row, 1973), pp. 106–141; and James M. McCormick and Michael Black, "Ideology and Senate Voting on the Panama Canal Treaties," *Legislative Studies Quarterly* 8 (February 1983): 4563.

23. See, for example, "House Votes to Aid El Salvador, Denies Nicaragua's Rebels," *Des Moines Register,* May 25, 1984, pp. IA 20A, and "House Curb's MX, Votes $284 Billion To Military," *Des Moines Register,* June 1, 1984, pp. IA, 12A. For a systematic analysis of partisan differences in congressional voting on the MX, B-1, and SDI in the 1970s and 1980s, see James M. Lindsay, "Parochialism, Policy, and Constituency Constraints: Congressional Voting on Strategic Weapons Systems," *American Journal of Political Science* 34 (November 1990): 936–960.

24. The following sections draw upon these pieces of research by James M. McCormick and Eugene R. Wittkopf: "Bush and Bipartisanship: The Past as Prologue?" *Washington Quarterly* 13 (Winter 1990): 5–16; "Bipartisanship, Partisanship, and Ideology in Congressional-Executive Foreign Policy Relations, 1947–1988," *Journal of Politics* 52 (November 1990): 1077–1100; and "At the Water's Edge: The Effects of Party, Ideology and Issues on Congressional Foreign Policy Voting, 1947–1988," *American Politics Quarterly* 20 (January 1992): 26–53.

25. Statement by the president, "President's Commission on Strategic Forces," *Weekly Compilation of Presidential Documents* 19 (January 10, 1983): 3.

26. See "Summary of Kissinger Commission Report," *Congressional Quarterly Weekly Report,* January 14, 1984, pp. 64–66.

27. "Excerpts from President Reagan's Speech on Foreign Policy and Congress," *New York Times,* April 7, 1984, p. 5.

28. These passages are taken from the inaugural address by President Bush, January 20, 1989.

29. Arthur C. Close, Gregory L. Bologna, and Curtis W. McCormick, eds., *Washington Representatives 1990* (Washington, D.C.: Columbia Books, Inc., 1990), p. 3.

30. Norman J. Ornstein and Shirley Elder, *Interest Groups, Lobbying, and Policymaking* (Washington, D.C.: Congressional Quarterly Press, 1978), pp. 35–39. The discussion in this paragraph also draws upon the list of organizations in Thomas L. Brewer, *American Foreign Policy: A Contemporary Introduction* (Englewood Cliffs, NJ: Prentice-Hall, Inc., 1980), p. 85, and upon Hughes, *The Domestic Context of American Foreign Policy,* pp. 157–171, for the foreign policy goals of business, labor, and farm groups.

31. Ornstein and Elder, *Interest Groups, Lobbying, and Policymaking,* p. 24.

32. For an overview of the foreign policy of the labor movement, and especially the AFL-CIO, see Carl Gershman, *The Foreign Policy of American Labor, The Washington Papers,* vol. 3, no. 29 (Beverly Hills, CA: Sage Publications, 1975).

33. "Program to Promote Democracy Passed...After Deleting Funds for Two Parties," *Congressional Quarterly Almanac 1983* (Washington, D.C.: Congressional Quarterly, Inc., 1984), pp. 148–149.

34. Hughes, *The Domestic Context of American Foreign Policy,* pp. 168–171.

35. See *Farm Bureau Policies for 1990,* Resolutions on National Issues Adopted at the 64th Annual Meeting of the American Farm Bureau Federation (Orlando, FL, January 1990).

36. *The Washington Lobby,* 4th ed. (Washington, D.C.: Congressional Quarterly, Inc., 1982), pp. 150–151, includes a list of the religious groups active over U.S. policy toward El Salvador.

37. Close et al., *Washington Representatives 1990,* p. 6.

38. See, for instance, any of the myriad publications from the American Friends Service Committee. A notable book on the Middle East conflict is *Search for Peace in the Middle East,* rev. ed. (Greenwich, CT: Fawcett Publications, Inc., 1970).

39. See *The Challenge of Peace: God's Promise and Our Response* (Washington, D.C.: United States Catholic Conference, May 3, 1983).

40. *The Washington Lobby,* pp. 152–153.

41. For an excellent overview of the key American ethnic groups and their role in foreign policy, see Charles McC. Mathias, Jr., "Ethnic Groups and Foreign Policy," *Foreign Affairs* 59 (Summer 1981): 975–998. Also see Abdul Aziz Said, *Ethnicity and U.S. Foreign Policy,* rev. ed. (New York: Praeger, 1981).

42. Hughes, *The Domestic Context of American Foreign Policy,* pp. 171–174.

43. For one recent discussion of the development of the conservative movement and its foreign policy goals, see Richard A. Viguerie, *The New Right: We're Ready to Lead* (Falls Church, VA: The Viguerie Company, 1981). For a listing of other liberal and conservative interest groups as well as other types, see Brewer, *American Foreign Policy,* pp. 85–86.

44. This section draws upon the following sources: Close et al., *Washington Representatives 1990,* pp. 480, 513, 517, 518, and 520; the *1988–1989 Annual Report of the American Enterprise Institute for Public Policy Research* (Washington, D.C.: American Enterprise Institute, 1989); and Howard J. Wiarda, *Foreign Policy Without Illusion* (Glenview, IL: Scott, Foresman/Little, Brown Higher Education, 1990), pp. 162–168.

45. *1988–1989 Annual Report of the American Enterprise Institute for Public Policy Research,* p. 1.

46. For a compilation of different categories of foreign policy interest groups (partly upon which we draw in our discussion), see Brewer, *American Foreign Policy: A Contemporary Introduction,* pp. 85–86.

47. Indeed, the freeze movement was very broadly based in terms of the kinds of groups and individuals that participated in it. See Fox Butterfield, "Anatomy of the Nuclear Protest," *New York Times Magazine,* July 11, 1982, pp. 14–17ff, for a discussion of the nature of this movement. For more recent assessments of the nuclear freeze, see Pam Solo, *From Protest to Policy: The Origins and Future of the Freeze Movement* (Cambridge, MA: Ballinger Publishing, 1988), and Douglas C. Waller, *Congress and the Nuclear Freeze: An Inside Look at the Politics of a Mass Movement* (Amherst, MA: University of Massachusetts Press, 1987).

48. See Cynthia J. Arnson and Philip Brenner, "The Limits of Lobbying: Interest Groups, Congress and Aid to the Contras," paper presented for presentation at a conference on Public Opinion and Policy Toward Central America, Princeton University, May 4–5, 1990.

49. "How U.S. Firms Lobbied for AWACS on Saudi Orders," *Des Moines Sunday Register,* March 14, 1982, p. 1C.

50. The section on the Japanese lobby is based on John B. Judis, "The Japanese Megaphone," *The New Republic,* January 22, 1990, pp. 20–25. The quoted

passages are at p. 22 and p. 24. For a more comprehensive and critical treatment of the lobbying efforts of Japan, see Pat Choate, *Agents of Influence* (New York: Alfred A. Knopf Inc., 1990).

51. The most succinct argument for this limited influence of interest groups is in Hughes, *The Domestic Context of American Foreign Policy*, pp. 198–202, from which part of this argument is drawn. Also see, however, Bernard Cohen, *The Public's Impact on Foreign Policy* (Boston: Little, Brown & Co., 1973), and Robert H. Trice, "Domestic Interest Groups and the Arab-Israeli Conflict: A Behavioral Analysis," in Abdul Aziz Said, *Ethnicity and U.S. Foreign Policy*, pp. 128–129, on the problem of gaining access to the Congress and the executive on some types of issues.

52. See Cohen, *The Public's Impact on Foreign Policy*, pp. 100–103, and his discussion of how interest groups can be used by the executive branch.

53. Brewer, *American Foreign Policy: A Contemporary Introduction*, p. 89.

54. On these points, see Hughes, *The Domestic Context of American Foreign Policy*, pp. 200–201, especially Table 7.1.

55. Cohen, *The Public's Impact on Foreign Policy*, p. 96, asserts that economic and ethnic groups appear most prominently, although his analysis is based primarily on interviews with the executive branch.

56. For some reasons for the strength of ethnic influence, see Mathias, "Ethnic Groups and Foreign Policy," pp. 980–981, 996.

57. See C. Wright Mills, *The Power Elite* (New York: Oxford University Press, 1956), and Gabriel Kolko, *The Roots of American Foreign Policy* (Boston: Beacon Press, 1969).

58. For a good summary presentation of this argument, see Marc Pilisuk with the assistance of Mehrene Larudee, *International Conflict and Social Policy* (Englewood Cliffs, NJ: Prentice-Hall, Inc., 1972), pp. 108–141.

59. C. Wright Mills, "The Structure of Power in American Society," in Richard Gillam, ed., *Power in Postwar America* (Boston: Little, Brown & Co., 1971), p. 55.

60. Dwight D. Eisenhower, "The Military-Industrial Complex," in Richard Gillam, ed., *Power in Postwar America*, p. 158. Emphasis added.

61. See, for example, Pilisuk with Larudee, *International Conflict and Social Policy*, 108–132, especially p. 129.

62. Kolko, *The Roots of American Foreign Policy*, pp. 17–23.

63. The following data on the key foreign policy officials are from Thomas R. Dye, *Who's Running America? Institutional Leadership in the United States* (Englewood Cliffs, NJ: Prentice-Hall, Inc., 1976), pp. 56–58; and *Who's Running America? The Bush Era* (Englewood Cliffs, NJ: Prentice-Hall, Inc., 1990), pp. 89–105. The dates of service for some individuals have been corrected from what Dye reports. For a complete description of the background of Reagan administration appointees, see the national security section of Ronald Brownstein and Nina Easton, *Reagan's Ruling Class* (Washington, D.C.: The Presidential Accountability Group, 1982).

64. William Proxmire, "The Community of Interests in Our Defense Contract Spending," in Richard Gillam, ed., *Power in Postwar America*, p. 163.

65. The sources for this paragraph are the following General Accounting Office Reports: "DOD Revolving Door: Relationships Between Work at DOD and Post-DOD Employment," July 1986; "DOD Revolving Door: Processes Have Improved but Post-DOD Employment Reporting Still Low," September 1989; and "DOD Revolving Door: Few Are Restricted From Post-DOD Employment and

Reporting Has Some Gaps," February 1990. The quoted passage is from the last cited report at p. 2.

66. Michael Parenti, *Democracy for the Few*. 5th ed. (New York: St. Martin's Press, 1988), p. 88.

67. These statistics were calculated from the list of the top 100 defense contractors for fiscal year 1988 and from "The 500 Largest U.S. Industrial Corporations," *Fortune* (April 24, 1989), pp. 354 and 356. For the information on the continuity and concentration in defense contracting, see James R. Kurth, "The Military-Industrial Complex Revisited," in Joseph Kruzel, ed., *1989–1990 American Defense Annual* (Lexington, MA: Lexington Books, 1989), pp. 195–215, especially pp. 196–199. The "product specialties" notion is his at p. 198.

68. Morton Berkowitz, P. G. Bock, and Vincent J. Fuccillo, *The Politics of American Foreign Policy* (Englewood Cliffs, NJ: Prentice-Hall, Inc., 1977), p. 289.

69. Ibid.

70. Stanley Lieberson, "An Empirical Study of Military-Industrial Linkages," *American Journal of Sociology* 76 (January 1971), especially pp. 568–572, 575–581.

71. Bruce Russett, *The Prisoners of Insecurity* (San Francisco: W. H. Freeman and Company, 1983), pp. 77–96.

72. Ibid.

73. Bruce Russett, "Defense Expenditures and National Well-being," *The American Political Science Review* 76 (December 1982): 767–777.

74. Alex Mintz, "Guns versus Butter: A Disaggregated Analysis," *The American Political Science Review* 83 (December 1989): 1290.

75. For a study that judges the Greek lobby second behind the Jewish lobby in influence, see Mathias, "Ethnic Groups and Foreign Policy," p. 990. Also see Morton Kondracke, "The Greek Lobby," *The New Republic*, April 29, 1978, pp. 14–16. For two studies that raise doubts about the importance of the Greek lobby over the Turkish arms embargo issue, see Clifford Hackett, "Ethnic Politics in Congress: The Turkish Embargo Experience"; and Sallie M. Hicks and Theodore A. Couloumbis, "The 'Greek Lobby': Illusion or Reality?" in Abdul Aziz Said, ed., *Ethnicity and U.S. Foreign Policy*, pp. 33–96.

76. Mathias, "Ethnic Groups and Foreign Policy," pp. 982–987.

77. Robert W. Walters, "African-American Influence on U.S. Foreign Policy toward South Africa," in Mohammed E. Ahrari, ed., *Ethnic Groups and U.S. Foreign Policy* (New York: Greenwood Press, 1987), pp. 65–82.

78. See Damian J. Fernandez, "From Little Havana to Washington, D.C.: Cuban-Americans and U.S. Foreign Policy," and Rodolfo O. de la Garza, "U.S. Foreign Policy and the Mexican-American Political Agenda," in Mohammed E. Ahrari, ed., *Ethnic Groups and U.S. Foreign Policy* (New York: Greenwood Press, 1987), pp. 115–134 and 101–114, respectively.

79. Robert H. Trice, "Domestic Interest Groups and the Arab-Israeli Conflict: A Behavioral Analysis," p. 126. The earlier points are at pp. 121 and 122.

80. *The Middle East: U.S. Policy, Israel, Oil and the Arabs*, 3rd ed. (Washington, D.C.: Congressional Quarterly, Inc., 1977), p. 96.

81. Robert H. Trice, "Congress and the Arab-Israeli Conflict: Support for Israel in the U.S. Senate, 1970–1973," *Political Science Quarterly* 92 (Fall 1977): 443–463.

82. Some of these reasons are discussed and indirectly tested in ibid.

83. Ibid., p. 457.

84. *The Middle East: U.S. Policy, Israel, Oil and the Arabs*, pp. 102–108.

85. Christopher Madison, "Arab-American Lobby Fights Rearguard Battle to Influence U.S. Mideast Policy," *National Journal,* August 31, 1985, p. 1936.

86. For some discussion of the relative influence of the Jewish lobby, see ibid., pp. 96–101.

87. For a discussion of some of the dilemmas that the Jewish community faces in its advocacy of American policy in the Middle East, see Stephen S. Rosenfeld, "Dateline Washington: Anti-Semitism and U.S. Foreign Policy," *Foreign Policy* 47 (Summer 1982): 172–183.

88. Quoted in Charlotte Saikowski, "America's Israeli Aid Budget Grows," *Christian Science Monitor,* November 30, 1983, p. 5. The reference is to President Eisenhower's decision to stand firm against Israel after it invaded the Sinai Peninsula during the Suez crisis of 1956 and to demand its immediate withdrawal, despite a pending election.

89. Madison, "Arab-American Lobby Fights Rearguard Battle to Influence U.S. Mideast Policy," p. 1937.

CHAPTER 12 PUBLIC OPINION: MOODISH OR STABLE?

"...the characteristic response [of the public] to questions of foreign policy is often one of indifference. A foreign policy crisis, short of the immediate threat of war, may transform indifference to vague apprehension, to fatalism, to anger; but the reaction is still a mood, a superficial and fluctuating response." GABRIEL ALMOND, *THE AMERICAN PEOPLE AND FOREIGN POLICY*, 1960

"...the [public opinion] data... conclusively refute the notion that Americans' foreign policy preferences are volatile or fluctuate wildly. Collective opinion tends to be stable; it sometimes changes abruptly, but usually only by small amounts; and it rarely fluctuates....we feel justified in speaking of a 'rational' public." ROBERT Y. SHAPIRO AND BENJAMIN I. PAGE, "FOREIGN POLICY AND THE RATIONAL PUBLIC," *JOURNAL OF CONFLICT RESOLUTION*, JUNE 1988

The final participant in the American foreign policy process that we shall discuss is the public at large. The attitudes and beliefs of the American public can and do affect the shape of U.S. foreign policy. While their impact is less continuous and direct on foreign policy issues than particular interest groups or political parties may be, they do influence the foreign policy process over time. The views of the public are not usually transmitted directly to the executive or legislative branches on each and every individual issue, as we saw with interest group activity; rather, their views are conveyed largely through periodic polling results and through direct contacts with their elected officials. Many members of Congress, for example, hold "town meetings" in their constituencies or conduct surveys of their district or state to get the pulse of the public on a variety of matters. Executive branch officials often travel widely throughout the country to get a sense of the public's concern on foreign and domestic issues. In this way, public opinion is directly conveyed to elected officials, and it begins to serve in part as a guide on what those public officials are likely to undertake in the foreign policy arena. Finally, elections at both the congressional and presidential levels are other ways for the public to convey its sentiments on foreign as well as domestic issues.

In this chapter, we first examine two differing perspectives about public opinion and foreign policy. One view of foreign policy opinion essentially argues that the public is largely uninterested, ill-informed, and subject to considerable leadership from the top on foreign policy matters. In the strongest form of this position, public opinion is less a shaper of U.S. foreign policy and more likely to be shaped by it. As a consequence, this view argues that public opinion plays little or no role in shaping American foreign policy. A second, and more recent, view suggests a somewhat larger, albeit still limited, role for public opinion in foreign policy. While the public may not be fully informed on foreign policy and lacks sustained interest in such matters, its views are more structured and consistent over time than many have previously contended. As such, the public can affect foreign policymaking, especially over time. Finally, we evaluate how much impact public opinion has on policymaking through its effect on presidential and congressional elections and on policy actions.

FOREIGN POLICY OPINION: UNINFORMED AND MOODISH

Except for very rare occurrences, the role of public opinion is usually characterized as highly limited in its impact on the foreign policy process. In this view, only during wars or international crises is the public sufficiently concerned about foreign policy to affect it directly. The principal reason for this limited impact is the public's lack of interest in and knowledge about foreign policy. Even when specific foreign policy views of the public are expressed, they often prove susceptible to short-term shifts—produced, for example, by presidential leadership, question wording in public opinion polls, or rapidly changing international events. In this context, public opinion serves as a relatively weak restraint on policymakers.

PUBLIC INTEREST AND KNOWLEDGE OF FOREIGN AFFAIRS

Low public understanding of and concern about foreign policy issues has existed throughout the post–World War II years. In a 1947 study in Cincinnati, Ohio, for instance, only 30 percent of the public were able to explain in a simple way what the United Nations did. In an analysis two years later, the public was equally uninformed. By this assessment, only 25 percent of the public were judged to possess reasonably developed opinions, 45 percent had only limited knowledge of world affairs, and 30 percent were classified as uninformed.[1]

Public opinion data from later decades were not much different. According to studies by Free and Cantril, only 26 percent of the American population were well informed on foreign policy issues during the 1960s, another 35 percent were moderately informed on foreign affairs, and 39 percent were simply uninformed. Somewhat indicative of this low level of knowledge was the public's information on the North Atlantic Treaty Organization (NATO), the center of America's containment efforts. According to this analysis, 28 percent of the public had never heard of NATO, only 58 percent knew that the U.S. belonged to that organization, and only 38 percent indicated that the Soviet Union did not belong to NATO.[2]

Through the 1970s and the 1980s, the level of interest in and knowledge of foreign affairs did not change appreciably—even in the context of a more educated electorate—although the latest 1990 survey suggests perhaps a bit more interest. The public has continued to demonstrate a low level of interest in and knowledge of global affairs. In public opinion surveys of the American people on foreign policy issues in 1974, 1978, 1982, 1986, and 1990, local community news received the highest level of interest (between 55 and 61 percent over the years), while news about other countries was much lower (about 31 percent on average).[3] News about America's relations

FIGURE 12.1   PERCENT OF THE AMERICAN PUBLIC VERY INTERESTED
IN VARIOUS TYPES OF NEWS, 1974–1990

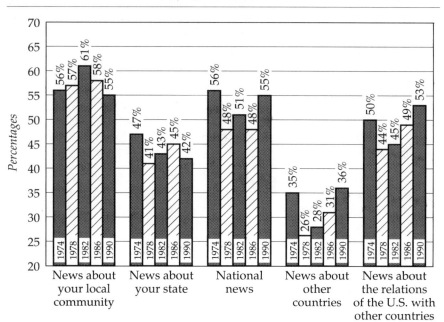

Source: John E. Rielly, ed., *American Public Opinion and U.S. Foreign Policy 1987* (Chicago:
The Chicago Council on Foreign Relations, 1987), p. 8, and John E. Rielly, ed., *American Public Opinion
and U.S. Foreign Policy 1991* (Chicago: The Chicago Council on Foreign Relations, 1991), p. 9.

with other countries, however, was a bit higher, ranging from 44 to
53 percent across the surveys. News about U.S. relations with other
countries now stimulates more interest than news simply about
other countries and, at least for the 1990 data, now rivals the interest
in local community affairs. Part of this recent interest is no doubt a
function of the dramatic events and political changes in Europe and
the Persian Gulf. Figure 12.1 shows a comparison of interest in different types of news over the five survey years.

What is important to note, though, is that on no occasion did the
interest in the news about other countries surpass interest about national or community affairs. What was even more revealing in these
surveys was the general lack of interest in specific issues; few Americans could discuss major foreign policy problems in detail.

With interest in foreign affairs relatively low, it is hardly surprising to find that knowledge on foreign affairs is equally limited. In

fact, these surveys concluded that only about 21 to 23 percent of the American public are fully informed on foreign policy matters and constitute what has been called the "attentive public." The results for 1990 are a little higher, with 29 percent of the public surveyed characterized as "high attentives," although the criteria for attentiveness were less demanding in this survey than in earlier ones.[4]

This paucity of knowledge among the public at large is particularly telling when one major foreign policy event of the 1980s is examined in detail: U.S. policy toward the Sandinista regime in Nicaragua. This issue was arguably the most dominant and divisive policy question on the foreign policy agenda of the Reagan administration, and it engaged the Congress and the executive branch in the most extensive and bitter foreign policy debate since Vietnam. Moreover, the struggle to fund or not to fund the Nicaraguan contras in their battle against the Sandinista regime became the perennial question for the Reagan administration from 1982 through 1988 and even continued into the first year of the Bush administration. Yet, for most of this time period, a majority of the public did not know with certainty which side the United States was backing: the contra rebels or the Sandinista government.

Based upon a series of public opinion surveys by ABC/*Washington Post* and CBS/*New York Times* from 1983 through 1987 (-Table 12.1), it was not until a March 1986 poll that a majority of the public correctly noted that the U.S. government was supporting the contras. Even at that late date in American involvement with the contras, a third of the public still had "no opinion" when asked which side the United States was backing in Nicaragua. Indeed, throughout 1983, 1984, and 1985, "no opinion" was generally the most popular response when asked this same kind of question.[5]

FOREIGN POLICY AS AN IMPORTANT ISSUE

Despite the low level of knowledge and interest concerning international affairs generally, the public has often viewed foreign policy as an important issue facing the country. During large portions of the last four decades, foreign policy issues have been identified as the most important issue facing the nation. In fact, only more recently has foreign policy been replaced by economic concerns as the principal issue identified by the American people.

During the height of the Cold War and throughout America's involvement in Vietnam, for instance, national security issues usually were cited by 40 to 60 percent of the public as the most important problem.[6] In the early-to-middle 1980s, foreign policy issues (such as

TABLE 12.1 LEVEL OF PUBLIC KNOWLEDGE REGARDING WHICH SIDE THE U.S. GOVERNMENT SUPPORTED IN NICARAGUA, 1983–1987

ABC/WP: Do you happen to know which side the U.S. is backing in Nicaragua, the rebels or the government?

	7/83	8/83[a]	11/83	1/84[b]	5/84[c]	3/85	6/85	3/6/86[d]	3/20/86	5/87	8/87
Rebels	29%	22%	26%	25%	26%	37%	46%	50%	59%	52%	54%
Government	24	45	24	27	33	23	20	14	13	21	20
Neither	1	*	*	1	1	1	1	2	1	1	1
No opinion	47	32	50	47	40	39	34	33	27	26	24
N	1,505	1,505	1,505	1,524	1,511	1,506	1,506	543	1,148	1,509	1,205

[a] Which side do you think the United States government is backing. . . ?

[b] . . .the U.S. is backing (in the fighting between the Sandinista government in Nicaragua and the rebels seeking to overthrow the government), the rebels or the government?

[c] How about in Nicaragua: is the United States government backing the government there, or the rebels trying to overthrow the government?

[d] Is the United States backing the government there (in Nicaragua), or the rebels trying to overthrow the government?

* Less than 0.5 percent.

CBS/NYT: Which side does the U.S. government support in Nicaragua—the current government, the people fighting against the government, or haven't you been following this closely enough to say?

	6/83	4/84	5/85	4/86
Government	7%	8%	6%	4%
People fighting / Opponents of government	13	19	26	38
Not following / Neither (voluntary)	9	62	59	47
No opinion	71	11	10	11
N	1,365	1,367	1,509	1,601

Note: *ABC/WP* refers to polls conducted by the American Broadcasting Company and the *Washington Post*, and *CBS/NYT* refers to polls conducted by the Columbia Broadcasting Company and the *New York Times*.

Source: Richard Sobel, "Public Opinion about United States Intervention in El Salvador and Nicaragua," *Public Opinion Quarterly* 53 (Spring 1989), p. 120. © 1989 by the American Association for Public Opinion Research. Published by the University of Chicago Press.

FIGURE 12.2   THE RELATIVE IMPORTANCE TO THE AMERICAN PUBLIC
OF FOREIGN AND DOMESTIC ISSUES: 1982, 1986, AND 1990

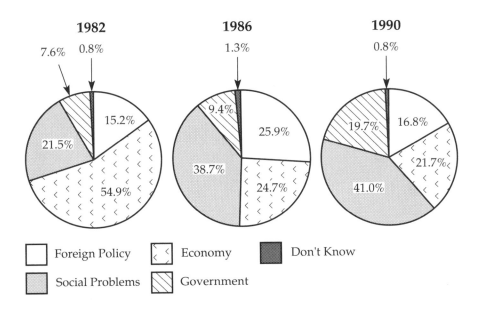

Source: Taken from a portion of Table I-2 in John E. Rielly, ed., *American Public Opinion and U.S. Foreign Policy 1991* (Chicago: The Chicago Council on Foreign Relations, 1991), p. 10.

fear of war or international tensions) were occasionally listed as "the most important problem facing this country today" in the periodic polls taken by the Gallup organization.

In the immediate post-Vietnam years (1973 through 1980) and in much of the 1980s and early 1990s, however, domestic issues, and particularly domestic economic issues, have often outstripped any foreign policy issue as the most important concern of the public.[7] By one estimate, economic concerns from about 1975 through 1985 often captured "over 60 percent of the public. The level of [economic] concern rarely dropped below an absolute majority and typically fell below the 50 percent mark only when energy concern periodically peaked at 10 percent or higher."[8]

Figure 12.2, which portrays the relative importance of foreign and domestic policy issues among the American public from the three most recent Chicago Council on Foreign Relations surveys discussed earlier, shows most strikingly the importance of economic and social issues to the American public. Note that these two issue areas generally outdistanced all other problems, except for foreign policy issues in 1986. In that year, foreign policy problems were slightly ahead of economic problems (25.9 percent and 24.7 percent of the total, respectively), while social issues were most pronounced, with 38.7 percent of the total.

Still, if foreign policy has captured a portion of the public's attention in the decade of the 1980s as expressed in the "most important question" in periodic surveys, why has the public not been more informed and more influential in shaping policy? Part of the explanation is tied up with the two earlier factors we discussed: the low level of sustained interest in foreign policy and the low level of knowledge of foreign policy. Because the public concern has largely been episodic and tied to particular international events, and because the public's knowledge of foreign policy questions has remained relatively low, its ability to influence policy has remained relatively weak.

PRESIDENTIAL LEADERSHIP

Another important reason why the public has not been more influential is related to the American public's susceptibility to presidential leadership. According to evidence provided by political scientist John Mueller, the president has often been the most admired person in the country.[9] As a consequence, because the public is not well informed on foreign policy issues, a tendency has developed to defer to his judgment on such matters. Several recent examples illustrate this phenomenon.

When President Lyndon Johnson changed war policies during the Vietnam conflict, the public generally was willing to shift to support that policy—even if it were a reversal of their earlier-expressed position. Prior to the bombing of oil depots around Hanoi and Haiphong, a majority of the public opposed such bombing. After the bombing policy was begun by the Johnson administration, however, 85 percent supported this new policy. A similar shift dictated by a presidential initiative occurred later in that war. Before President Johnson initiated a bombing halt in 1968, 51 percent of the public supported the continuation of bombing. After President Johnson announced his decision for a partial bombing halt, a majority (64 percent) of the public favored this new policy option.[10] In both instances, then, the American public was very susceptible to presidential leadership.

A similar example occurred during President Nixon's handling of the war in Southeast Asia. Just prior to the American invasion of Cambodia, a Harris Poll asked whether the public supported the commitment of the American forces to that country. Only 7 percent favored such a policy. Yet, after President Nixon went on national television to explain his decision to send American troops into Cambodia, another Harris Poll indicated that 50 percent of the American public supported such a policy.[11] In other words, in a matter of three weeks, public opinion turned around rather dramatically, with only the president's speech as the important intervening event.

In the post-Vietnam and post-Watergate periods, such ready acceptance of presidential leadership might seem more difficult to obtain, but, in fact, it has continued. Prior to the seizure of American hostages in Iran in November 1979, President Jimmy Carter's approval rating was only 32 percent. By the end of December, his approval rating had jumped up to 61 percent. Furthermore, President Carter initially got high marks from the public over his handling of the Iranian situation, with 82 percent of the American people applauding his actions.[12] While this "rallying around the president" can be short-lived, as President Carter was to find out, it nevertheless allows the executive considerable latitude to take foreign policy initiative without suffering any immediate domestic repercussions.

President Reagan also was able to exercise presidential leadership to influence public opinion on foreign policy issues. Although he met resistance over placing American forces in Lebanon in 1982, over his policy in Central America, and over the nuclear freeze issue, he was able to increase support for his policy positions among the American public even in the context of some dramatic international events. After the terrorist bombing of the Marine headquarters in Beirut, Lebanon, and the loss of 241 Americans, the level of the public's approval of U.S. troops in that country increased from 36 percent in late September 1983, to 48 percent by late October 1983. Similarly, President Reagan's decision to send U.S. troops to Grenada won quick approval from the American public, with 55 percent supporting this action and 31 percent opposing it. Coupled with both of these levels of support for the president was an increase in overall approval of his handling of the presidency.[13]

Despite consistent overall disapproval of the Reagan administration's policy toward Nicaragua, President Reagan's efforts on behalf of that policy had some noticeable effect on public opinion. After he gave a speech to a joint session of Congress in April 1983, for instance, the public's support for his handling of Nicaraguan policy rose from 21 percent to 44 percent.[14] Similarly, when he engaged in a series of speeches to the public and Congress from March to June

1986, we find some increase in public approval for his "handling the situation in Nicaragua." In early March 1986, the approval rating was only 37 percent, but by April it rose to 47 percent and remained at about that level (45 percent) through June 1986.[15]

Finally, President George Bush has also been able to use his foreign policy actions to gain support for his handling of foreign policy. In the first two years of President Bush's term, he generally enjoyed strong support for his foreign policy actions, but his decisions to intervene into Panama in December 1989 to topple and seize Manuel Noriega and to respond with military forces to Iraqi President Saddam Hussein's intervention into Kuwait in August 1990 won him even greater approval. After the U.S. assault on Panama, President Bush's approval rating went up to 80 percent in January 1990, and after his decision on August 8, 1990, to send American forces to support Saudi Arabia against Saddam Hussein, his approval rating shot up again, reading 77 percent in mid-August 1990.[16] As the Persian Gulf involvement extended over time, though, Bush's support began to suffer, a phenomenon common among extended involvements abroad by American presidents, although the decline was partially attributable to the U.S. budget crisis at home. Nonetheless, the initial foreign policy actions in Central America and in the Middle East illicited a common "rally-round-the-flag" phenomenon by the American public and aided in the public acceptance of President Bush's actions in both of these areas.

After the Congress gave its approval to use force in the Gulf against the Iraqis and as the air war, and then the ground war, began, President Bush's popularity shot up once again. Indeed, his popularity reached almost 90 percent by the time of the cease-fire in March 1991.[17] Dramatic and decisive foreign policy actions have often tended to rally support for the president. The question that inevitably accompanies this rise is how long it will be sustained. The general answer is that as other events capture the public's attention, such support begins to erode.

In short, then, the potency of the presidency as a shaper of foreign policy opinion continues, and it serves as an important restraint on the effectiveness of overall public sentiment in directing foreign policymaking. Yet, it is not all-encompassing, as we shall show toward the end of this chapter in the discussion of policy toward the Nicaraguan contras by the Reagan administration.

GAUGING PUBLIC OPINION

Other difficulties also seemingly diminish the effectiveness of public opinion. Because the public's views are not always well developed or firmly held, question wording, and even the terms used in public opinion polls, can alter the public's view from survey to survey. As Rosenberg, Verba, and Converse hypothesize, the concepts used to describe American involvement in Vietnam could influence the level of public support or opposition to that war. If negative terms were used (such as "defeat" or "communist takeover"), the public would likely be more defensive and hawkish in its response. If other negative terms were used ("the increase in killings" or "the continued costs of the war"), the public might respond in a more dovish or conciliatory manner.[18]

A recent study of question wording of the various public opinion polls regarding aid to the Nicaraguan contras confirmed just such effects. When the public was asked about funding these opposition forces and specific references were made to "President Reagan," "the contras," or the "Marxist government" in Nicaragua, the level of support for contra aid was generally higher among the American public than when such references were left out. By contrast, when references to the amount of money involved in supporting the contras was mentioned, or when the question format was more "balanced" in treating the competing parties involved in the conflict, the level of public support was lower than in polls without such characteristics. While the overall effect of question wording on support or opposition to contra aid was relatively modest, it did have a discernible effect.[19]

Similarly, the number of options presented to a respondent can also be important in affecting the result. One analysis of public attitudes on the SALT II Treaty in the 1970s illustrated how different question wordings produced different policy implications. Two sets of polls (a Harris Poll and an NBC-AP Poll) asked only the questions of support or opposition to the SALT II Treaty; another set of polls (Roper) provided information on the treaty and provided more options. The latter found only about 40 percent support for SALT, while the former found that between 67 and 77 percent approved.[20] The explanation for such disparity in the results was tied to the kind of options and information provided to the respondents. While question wording is always a possible source of error in gauging public opinion, it is a particularly crucial one when the public's views are not well developed or deeply held.

Public opinion polls asking which side the United States was supporting in Nicaragua illustrate the same problems of how knowledge levels and question options can shape the results. As we noted earlier, the public generally was not able to identify correctly which side the U.S. was backing in Nicaragua until early 1986. Those polls, however, generally used only two options in seeking to discern which side the U.S. was backing ("the rebels" or "the government"). Polls conducted by CBS/*New York Times*, however, used *three* options for ascertaining which side the U.S. was backing ("the current government," "the people fighting the government," or "haven't you been following this closely enough to say?"). In these polls, the last option obtained the highest percentage of responses at the same time as the polls with only two options showed the American public more knowledgeable. Thus, in an environment of limited foreign policy knowledge and of a variety of options, one may get different responses to the question. Such results, once again, raise questions about how much credence officials should give to competing results, and thus erode the impact of public opinion.[21]

PUBLIC OPINION AND FLUCTUATING MOODS

Gabriel Almond, an early pioneer in the analysis of public attitudes on foreign policy, has aptly summarized the characterization of the American public that we have sketched so far. The American public view is essentially a "mood" toward foreign affairs that lacks "intellectual structure and factual content." This mood is largely "superficial and fluctuating," "permissive," and subject to elite leadership influence "if they [the policymakers] demonstrate unity and resolution."[22]

With these fluctuating and permissive moods, the role of public opinion as a shaper of foreign policy is surely diminished. While the public can exercise some impact during periods of crises or war, in general it is more apt to follow the direction of the leadership. Similarly, while the fluctuations in moods may not be as great as they once were, as Almond later acknowledged, public opinion is still largely unstable and unstructured. As such, and as Almond put it, public opinion "cannot be viewed as standing in the way of foreign policy decisions by American governmental leaders."[23]

FOREIGN POLICY OPINION: STRUCTURED AND STABLE

Recent research on public opinion reaches a less pessimistic conclusion about public opinion and its role in the foreign policy process. In this view, even in the context of a relatively uninformed mass public, and one that is susceptible to elite or presidential leadership, foreign policy attitudes of the American public are not as irrelevant to policymaking as others might suggest. At least two interrelated reasons are offered to support this view: (1) the public's attitudes are more structured and stable than has often been assumed; (2) the public mood is more identifiable and less shiftable and potentially more constraining on policymakers' actions than sometimes suggested.

THE STRUCTURE OF FOREIGN POLICY OPINIONS

How is it possible that opinions can be structured and stable if, as we demonstrated earlier, knowledge and interest in foreign affairs is so relatively low among the American public? Political scientists Jon Hurwitz and Mark Peffley have begun to untangle this apparent anomaly. They have argued that individuals utilize information shortcuts to make political judgments and to relate preferences toward specific foreign policy issues from general attitudes. Thus, paradoxically, ordinary citizens can hold coherent attitude structures even though they lack detailed knowledge about foreign policy. As Hurwitz and Peffley write:

> Individuals organize information because such organization helps to simplify the world. Thus, a paucity of information does not *impede* structure and consistency; on the contrary, it *motivates* the development and employment of structure. Thus, we see individuals as attempting to cope with an extraordinarily confusing world (with limited resources to pay information costs) by structuring views about specific foreign policies according to their more general and abstract beliefs.[24]

Research by political scientists Eugene Wittkopf, Benjamin Page, and Robert Shapiro has begun to demonstrate more fully the accuracy of this position. In an extensive analysis of public opinion surveys from the 1930s to the 1980s, Shapiro and Page have demonstrated that public opinion has changed relatively slowly over time. "When it has changed, it has done so by responding in rational ways to international and domestic events. . . ." In their view, public opinion does not tend to be "volatile or fluctuate wildly." Instead, they conclude that "collective opinion tends to be rather stable; it sometimes changes abruptly, but usually by only small amounts; and it rarely fluctuates."[25] In short, the public is markedly "rational" and stable in its foreign policy beliefs.

Eugene Wittkopf has more fully discerned the structure and stability in foreign policy opinion through his extensive analysis of the four Chicago Council on Foreign Relations surveys.[26] His analysis revealed that the American people have been divided not only over *whether* the U.S. should be involved in foreign affairs but also over *how* they should be involved. At the same time, the public has been remarkably consistent in what they have believed about foreign affairs over the years.

In his analyses, the American public is divided along two continua: a continuum of *cooperative internationalism* and a continuum of *militant internationalism*. Where Americans fall on those continua are based upon three underlying attitudes: attitudes toward the use of American force abroad, attitudes about communism, and attitudes about U.S.-Soviet relations.[27] The intersection of those two continua produce four distinct belief systems that best describe the structure of American foreign policy opinion today. Figure 12.3 visually displays the structure of the belief systems across the four quadrants.

The four segments of the public holding these belief systems have been labeled as *internationalists, isolationists, accommodationists,* and *hardliners*.[28] Internationalists are those individuals who support both cooperative and militant approaches to global affairs and are largely reflective of American attitudes prior to the Vietnam War. Both the unilateral use of American force and cooperative efforts through the United Nations would be acceptable to this segment of the public. In the Persian Gulf War, for example, internationalists likely supported both the UN efforts to resolve the conflict over Kuwait and the use of American and coalition forces to expel Iraq from Kuwait. Isolationists are those individuals who tend to reject both cooperative internationalism and militant internationalism and would favor a reduced role for the United States in global affairs. In the Gulf War, they would probably not have supported the use of force toward Iraq or even believed that a vital interest was at stake over the seizure of Kuwait. Accomodationists are those individuals who favor cooperative internationalism but oppose militant internationalism. They would likely have supported the use of economic sanctions against Iraq over Kuwait, but they would not have supported the use of force. By contrast, hardliners are those individuals who favor militant internationalism and oppose cooperative internationalism. In the Gulf War example, hardliners would likely have wanted to use force earlier against Iraq than the other segments of the public that we have discussed so far.

By Wittkopf's assessment, these segments are almost evenly divided among the public. As such, the restraints upon American policymakers come from a variety of directions. Internationalists, for example, constitute about 29 percent of the public, isolationists about 22 percent, accommodationists 26 percent, and hardliners 23 percent.[29] These percentages, moreover, have remained remarkably stable from the initial survey in 1974 to the most recently analyzed one (1986), as Figure 12.3 shows.

FIGURE 12.3   THE DISTRIBUTION OF THE MASS PUBLIC
AMONG THE FOUR TYPES OF FOREIGN POLICY BELIEFS, 1974–1986

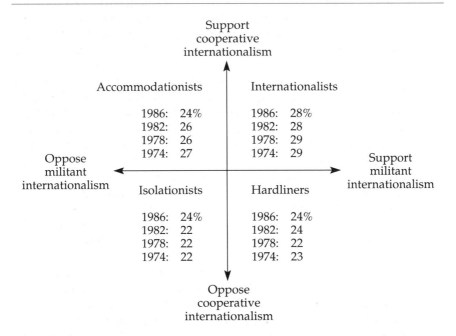

Source: Eugene R. Wittkopf, *Faces of Internationalism: Public Opinion and American Foreign Policy*,
p. 26. Copyright © 1990, Duke University Press. Reprinted by permission of the publisher.

These underlying belief systems among the public are important
for understanding the role of public opinion and foreign policy for
several reasons. First, they are highly predictive of what policy these
segments of the public will support. An overwhelming majority of
both internationalists and hardliners, for example, are strongly supportive of coming to the aid of Japan if it were invaded, but only a
minority of accommodationists and isolationists are. Similarly, internationalists and hardliners are strongly supportive of matching Soviet capabilities, but accommodationists and isolationists are not.
Indeed, these two coalitions are evident across a wide array of issues
that have been examined.[30]

Second, the different foreign policy belief systems are closely
tied to a number of other socio-political characteristics of the American public. As such, these foreign policy divisions are deeply in-
grained within the American political landscape. In particular, the
political ideology of an individual and his or her level of education
are good predictors of where an individual falls among these belief

systems.[31] Political "liberals," for instance, tend to be accommodationists, political "conservatives" tend to be hardliners, and political "moderates" tend to be internationalists. College-educated individuals tend to be both internationalists and accommodationists, those with a high school education tend to be both internationalists and hardliners, and those with less than a high school education tend to be hardliners.

The patterns of these belief systems are less clear-cut by region and party, however. During the four surveys, the East was found to be, by and large, accommodationist; the Midwest and the West fluctuated among the accommodationist, internationalist, and hardline categories; and the South varied between the hardline and internationalist camp. Most interestingly, though, these belief systems are not closely tied to partisanship. While there was some tendency for those possessing hardline or internationalist belief systems to be Republicans and those possessing accommodationist and internationalist belief systems to be Democrats, the differences among these belief systems were sufficiently blurred across the parties to make accurate predictions quite difficult.

Third, because these divisions exist within the public and have been consistent over time, the leadership is now more constrained than some might argue. Foreign policy decision makers must now gauge which groups will support or oppose particular foreign policy actions and must calculate the acceptable limits of their foreign policy actions. In any earlier era, if previous research findings were accurate portrayals of the public, the president, for example, did not have to make such calculations; instead, he could rather routinely count on public support. With these persistent divisions, though, that possibility is less assured. In this sense, this kind of structure and consistency in belief, far from freeing the foreign policy leaders to pursue their own course, may actually constrain the actions of various administrations.

AN ALTERNATIVE VIEW OF THE PUBLIC MOOD

If we can take this initial conclusion one step further, we can begin to suggest a somewhat larger role for the public mood in the policy process. Two political scientists, Bernard Cohen and V. O. Key, writing shortly after Almond's initial work on the public mood and foreign policy, suggest as much with their concepts of "climate of opinion" and the "context of public opinion."

Bernard Cohen introduced the concept of "climate of opinion" to summarize the public's view on foreign policy actions. This notion refers to the foreign policy decision-making environment, which, "by creating in the policymaker an impression of a public attitude or attitudes, or by becoming part of the environment and culture milieu that help to shape his own thinking, may consciously affect his official behavior."[32] A few years later, V. O. Key expanded upon this notion by introducing what he called the "context of public opinion." This notion suggests how the public's overall views can affect governmental action, including the foreign policy arena. His description of this concept and how it operates is worth quoting:

> That context is not a rigid matrix that fixes a precise form for government action. Nor is it unchangeable. It consists of opinion irregularly distributed among the people and of varying intensity, of attitudes of differing convertibility into votes, and of sentiments not always readily capable of appraisal. Yet, that context, as it is perceived by those responsible for action, conditions many of the acts of those who must make what we may call "opinion-related decisions." The opinion context may affect the substance of action, the form of action, or the manner of action.[33]

These alternate views of the public mood suggest that the foreign policy opinions of the American people form a part of the political milieu—even in the foreign policy realm. In this way, foreign policy opinion might be thought of as setting the broad outlines of "acceptable" policy without necessarily dictating the day-to-day policy choices of decision makers. Thus, gauging the public mood, and acting within the constraints of that mood, becomes an important task for the successful policymakers. A brief survey of the recent public moods or climates of opinions, gleaned from several sources, will illustrate their relationship to, and impact on, American foreign policy. Keep in mind, however, that policymakers will also try to alter or adjust that public mood to their liking, much as Almond and others have suggested.

THE COLD WAR MOOD   During the height of the Cold War period, for instance, the public expressed strong support for an active American role in global affairs. The level of support for global involvement was also quite predictive of public commitments to the Marshall Plan, NATO, and a willingness to stop communism through military action. In fact, after examining a number of public opinion polls from the late 1940s through the early 1960s, political scientist William Caspary concluded that the American public demonstrated a *"strong and stable* 'permissive mood' toward international involvements."[34] Further, another analyst saw the Cold War period as one in which "policymakers became imprisoned by popular anticommunism even though, in most cases, the policymakers were too sophisticated really to share the popular perspective."[35] Thus the values of the postwar consensus (see Chapters 2 and 3) were firmly embedded in the public and policymakers alike and largely shaped the policy choices.

THE "VIETNAM SYNDROME"   The "searing effects" of the Vietnam War on the beliefs of the American public toward international affairs have been widely analyzed.[36] In the immediate post-Vietnam period, for instance, there was a decided turn inward on several important dimensions of foreign and military involvement. In late 1974, roughly one third of the American public favored a cutback in the defense budget, and over 50 percent believed that "we should build up our own defenses and let the world take care of itself."[37] In addition, there was considerable public aversion to sending U.S. troops to support friendly nations that were attacked or even to sending military and economic aid to such states. Only in the case of an attack upon Canada did a majority of the public (77 percent) support American military involvement. Attacks upon Western Europe or Israel gained support from only 39 percent of the public in the case of the former region and only 27 percent in the case of the latter state. Support for using military and economic aid to help friendly countries that were attacked was equally low. Only 37 percent of the public supported the American government's using these tactics. Finally, the American public also favored a cutback in military aid and opposed CIA political operations, presumably because each of these areas further involved the United States abroad.

While the public mood tended to reject an active military and political involvement in international affairs in the immediate post-Vietnam period, this view should not imply an abandonment of an "active role" for the U. S. in world affairs. In fact, 66 percent of the public still supported a continued global role for the United States. This global role was to take a different form than that prescribed by the Cold War consensus. When asked to rank the importance of a variety of different goals for the United States, the public placed greatest importance on such aims as keeping the peace and promoting and defending America's security. Next, however, the public indicated that the United States should concentrate on a large number of domestic and global *economic* problems—such as securing adequate energy supplies, protecting American jobs, and solving global food, inflation, and energy problems. Most importantly, perhaps, the traditional goals of the Cold War period, such as containing communism, defending allies, and helping spread democracy and capitalism abroad, were ranked relatively low by the public. In the words of one analyst at that time: "The cold war sense of urgent threat is gone from Americans' political consciousness."[38]

In essence, then, the public sought a *more limited political role, but a larger economic one.* Moreover, the public wanted the United States to emphasize *cooperation* with other nations in solving common problems. Finally, the public seemed to back away from acceptance of some of the crusading goals summarized under the Cold War consensus.

This mood, moreover, seemed to have a dampening effect on the actions of both the Ford and Carter administrations. The ability to use force and to intervene globally was sharply reduced. The Ford administration, for example, was unable to win any public (or congressional) support for last-minute aid to South Vietnam and Cambodia prior to their collapse in 1975. Nor was President Ford able to muster support for vigorous action on behalf of the National Front for the Liberation of Angola in its struggle with the Soviet-backed Popular Movement for the Liberation of Angola. An exception, however, was the popular response to the swift military action ordered by President Ford over the seizure of the American merchant vessel, the *Mayaguez,* by Cambodia in May 1975.

In the context of this foreign policy mood, the appeal of a Jimmy Carter presidential candidacy is quite understandable. With Carter's call for an emphasis upon global issues, downplaying of the East-West dispute, and call for universal human rights, his candidacy was well within the limits of the public mood in the middle 1970s. In essence, the popular mood, summarized under the heading of the "Vietnam syndrome," was in place among the American public and was generally respected by the political leadership.

THE "SELF-INTEREST" MOOD[39] The public mood changed somewhat, however, by the late 1970s, especially as the relationship between the United States and the Soviet Union began to deteriorate during the second and third years of the Carter administration. Moreover, there was an increased perception of threat from the Soviet Union among the American public. By one analysis, concern with the power of the Soviet Union had replaced Vietnam as the "central preoccupation of American foreign policy."[40] As a result, the public mood began to move away, albeit slowly, from the limits of the "Vietnam syndrome."

In this context, the public was now more willing to increase defense expenditures, support American military actions abroad, and tolerate CIA activities in other nations.[41] Thirty-two percent of the public now said that the U.S. spent too little on defense (as compared to 13 percent in 1974) and only 16 percent said that the U.S. spent too much (as compared to 32 percent in 1974). A majority of the public now supported sending troops if Panama closed access to the Canal or if the Soviets invaded Western Europe. Furthermore, a plurality (48 percent of the public) favored the use of American troops if West Berlin were attacked, and 42 percent favored a U.S. response to a Soviet invasion of Japan. The public was now also more supportive of allowing the CIA to work inside other countries to support American interests. In 1978, 59 percent of the public supported such actions, compared to only 43 percent in 1974. While this interventionist sentiment still had its limits, it had increased from the 1974 period.[42]

At the same time, there was a certain amount of ambivalence about any rekindling of past crusading efforts on the part of the United States. Although some Cold War goals (such as protecting allies and containing communism) had increased in importance as foreign policy preferences from the 1974 levels, domestic and foreign economic concerns (such as "keeping up the value of the dollar," "securing adequate supplies of energy," and "protecting the jobs of American workers") remained most important for the American public.[43]

This ambivalence was especially demonstrated in the mixed reaction to the Soviet Union. Although 56 percent of the public believed that the United States was "falling behind the Soviet Union in power and influence," the public remained committed to greater cooperation in joint energy efforts, joint scholarly exchanges, and the pursuit of arms limitation.[44] In short, sentiment for maintaining détente seemed still in place, especially among the attentive public.[45]

In sum, then, the public mood was for a more "self-interested" and nationalistic foreign policy than in 1974, but one that continued to maintain elements of economic and political cooperation with other nations. Furthermore, the public continued to be "wary of direct involvement that characterized United States policy in the 1960s," but they still remained determined to defend important commitments in the world.[46] In this context, the success of the Reagan candidacy is explainable, especially as President Jimmy Carter was increasingly perceived as incapable of dealing effectively with foreign policy matters.

The Public Mood in the 1980s The public mood in the 1980s changed little from that of the late 1970s. Yet the Reagan administration adopted some policies at variance with the public mood. In this situation, it is important to evaluate the ultimate effect of the public mood.

The foreign policy goals, as expressed by the public in two national polls conducted in late 1982 and late 1986, remained essentially the same as in 1978.[47] Global and domestic economic concerns continued to have the highest priority, while containing communism and defending allies retained their somewhat lower ranking. At the same time, the public expressed a slight increase in the level of interventionism than they did in the late 1970s. For instance, the public supported sending U.S. troops to Western Europe and Japan if they were attacked. No other country or region received over 45 percent approval for such action, but a third of the public favored using U.S. troops "if the Arabs cut off oil shipments to the U.S. or if Arab forces invade Israel."[48] The public thus seemed to be selective in choosing between vital and secondary interests that were necessary to protect. There was, for example, substantial opposition to sending American troops into El Salvador if the leftists were succeeding or into Taiwan if China invaded.[49]

On the question of the Soviet Union in 1982 and 1986, the public remained ambivalent, much as they had in 1978. While the Soviet Union ranked the lowest or second lowest of any nation (after Iran) when the public was asked to rank states on a "thermometer scale," the public remained committed to seeking better ties with the U.S.S.R.: 77 percent in 1982 and 82 percent in 1986 favored arms control agreements, 64 percent in 1982 favored undertaking joint energy projects with the Soviets, and 70 percent in 1982 and 76 percent in 1986 favored the resumption of cultural and educational exchanges.[50]

Such a public mood generally clashed with the priorities of the Reagan administration, especially during its first term.[51] While President Reagan brought back some of the rhetoric and policies of the Cold War consensus, the public mood opposed several of these foreign policy priorities. The Reagan administration wanted to increase defense spending and engage in a defense buildup; the public was now content to keep the budget as is and to seek arms control agreements instead. The Reagan administration wanted to engage in a more confrontational policy toward the Soviet Union; the public wanted to seek more cooperative exchanges with that nation. The Reagan administration wanted to increase military assistance; the public continued to oppose such aid by a wide margin.

Such disagreements between the public mood and public policy undoubtedly put some strain on what the Reagan administration could do in its foreign policy. In this sense, it contributed to a political climate that ultimately facilitated accommodation with the Soviet Union, and it served as a restraint on the extent of the policy course pursued toward Nicaragua.

THE PUBLIC MOOD IN THE 1990S   With the dramatic events of 1989 and 1990—the emergence of democracy in Eastern Europe, the fall of the Berlin Wall, the unification of Germany, and the Iraqi invasion of Kuwait—will the public mood change dramatically in the 1990s and beyond? Indeed, several political analysts have already begun to suggest just such a change. Some have called for reducing the U.S. role in the world, and others have called for substituting new rationales to replace the anti-communist one that had guided policy for the 1945–1990 period.[52]

A recent national survey of American public opinion in the post–Cold War and post–Persian Gulf War years gives some hint of where we may be heading and suggests some fundamental change in public sentiment toward international affairs. Public opinion analyst John E. Rielly summarizes the new mood in this way:

> The mood of the American public and its leaders has shifted. The Cold War and the U.S.-Soviet competition are passing from center stage, and a new age of global economic competition has emerged. Americans enter this new era with increased confidence about their military preeminence, but with a growing sense of economic vulnerability.[53]

While about two thirds of the public remained committed to an active role for the U.S. in global affairs, the public is more concerned about domestic economic and social problems than foreign policy ones. Drug abuse and the budget deficit are two leading issues on the public's mind.[54] To the extent that foreign policy concerns are identified as providing important goals for the U.S., those associated with foreign economic activities receive the highest priority from the public. Three key goals are particularly attractive to the public: "protecting the jobs of American workers," "protecting the interest of American business abroad," and "securing adequate supplies of energy."[55] In this same vein, the public recognizes that the U.S. failure to solve its economic problems has contributed to its decline as a global power, but it also identifies Japan and Europe as sources of some of these economic problems. Indeed, 71 percent of the public believe that Japan is unfair in its trade practices, and 40 percent believe that Europe is unfair.[56] While this emphasis upon domestic and foreign economic issues is not wholly a break from the earlier surveys for the 1970s and 1980s, the intensity may well be.

What was perhaps better evidence of the public's changed view was its opinion toward foreign policy issues of the recent past. First, the public's view of the Soviet Union has changed markedly. The public now sees that nation "as one of the three leading countries where America has a vital interest."[57] It also saw the Soviet Union as more friendly and viewed it more favorably than in the past. Indeed, the Soviet Union was now tied for fourth (with Italy) out of twenty-two countries evaluated in the "feeling thermometer" ranking—surpassed only by Canada, Great Britain, and Germany. Soviet leader Mikhail Gorbachev also was favorably received by the public, ranking only behind Pope John Paul II and British Prime Minister Margaret Thatcher in late 1990.[58] Even as they express these views, the substantial majority of the American public still has some doubts about whether the Cold War is fully over. Nonetheless, the overall summary of these results stand in contrast to the 1986 survey by the Chicago Council on Foreign Relations, in which U.S.-Soviet relations ranked at the top as a foreign policy problem and in which the Soviet Union was ranked near the bottom in the favorability index.[59]

Second, some traditional defense attitudes have changed as well. The public is less concerned about arms control issues and nuclear war. It prefers a smaller American troop commitment to NATO, although a majority of the public still support that organization. Almost a third of the public now favors cuts in the defense budget. And the public remains cautious and selective of where it would support the use of U.S. military force abroad.[60]

Third, albeit understandable given the timing of the survey, the key foreign policy problems were different from those of the past. Middle East issues ranked as the most important foreign policy problems facing the American public. Interestingly, too, foreign aid, trade, and oil issues were mentioned as the next most salient issues.[61] Not unexpectedly, one new adversary and one familiar one from the 1980s—Iraq and Iran, respectively—now ranked at the bottom on the feeling thermometer by the public.

The overall portrait of the public mood suggests a continued, but limited, role for the U.S. in foreign affairs. As the success of the Persian Gulf War fades in the public's mind, the global foreign economic issues will likely remain and continue to dominate the foreign policy agenda in the 1990s.

THE IMPACT OF PUBLIC OPINION ON FOREIGN POLICY

One of the most difficult analytic tasks is to assess the overall effect of public opinion on foreign policy. Even if public opinion can be characterized as structured and stable, as we have suggested, a fundamental question remains: How much real difference does public opinion make in the foreign policy process? Are congressional and presidential elections mechanisms of popular control on foreign policy issues? Is the Congress or the president really constrained in its policy choices by what the public thinks? Some recent analyses provide partial answers to these questions, but the questions remain subjects of debate.

FOREIGN POLICY OPINION AND PRESIDENTIAL ELECTIONS

One way for public opinion to register an impact on foreign policy is through the electoral process, and especially through presidential elections every four years. In this way, the electorate can use their votes to punish political candidates with unpopular foreign policy views and reward those with whom they agree. Yet numerous analyses have raised doubts as to whether presidential elections are really referenda on foreign policy.

First, for example, presidential elections are rarely fought on foreign policy issues. Instead, domestic issues, and especially domestic economic issues, have dominated American presidential campaigns in the post–World War II years. By most assessments, only in the 1952 and 1972 presidential elections was foreign policy a central campaign issue between the candidates. Both of these elections, however, occurred in very special circumstances, with the U.S. involved in two highly unpopular wars, Korea and Vietnam.

Second, even when foreign policy might be an issue in a presidential election, the stances of the candidates are not sufficiently different from each other for the public to distinguish between them. In the 1968 presidential campaign, for example, the Vietnam War was an issue, but the two candidates, Richard Nixon and Hubert Humphrey, were not perceived to differ markedly in their positions on the war.[62] As a result, foreign policy did not turn out to be decisive in deciding how the public voted in that campaign.

Third, even if foreign policy was viewed as salient by the public, its overall effect on an election outcome is viewed as quite small. In a classic analysis on this point, Warren Miller reports that the decline in support for the Republican candidate from the 1956 to the 1960 election based upon his foreign policy stance was miniscule—one half of one percent. Instead of the Republicans having a 2.5 percent vote advantage because of their foreign policy position in 1956, the advantage fell to 2.0 in the 1960 election.[63] Two decades later, in the 1980 contest between Jimmy Carter and Ronald Reagan, a similar small effect was reported. Despite the popular impression that the impact of the Iran hostage situation would severely hurt Carter's re-election prospects, a careful analysis of voting behavior in that election found otherwise. Ronald Reagan's issue position on foreign and domestic matters produced only about a 1 percent difference in the vote outcome. Instead, the voters' decisions were more fully related to the overall dissatisfaction with President Carter's performance in office and with doubts "about his competence as a political leader."[64]

Left unanswered by these and similar analyses, however, is whether even these small differences between the candidates in the aggregate did not affect the outcome in particular states, and hence the electoral votes of one presidential candidate over another. Especially in a close national election, such as the 1960 election between Kennedy and Nixon, in which less than one percentage point separated the candidates, foreign policy opinion may have mattered. Put more precisely, in close state votes during such presidential elections, a swing of even a few percentage points could dramatically affect the national electoral vote count. To date, however, detailed studies of presidential elections are not available to answer such questions.

Also left unanswered by these analyses is whether the activities in the foreign policy arena by incumbents contributes to creating an image of competence that can also affect the outcome of elections. While specific foreign policy opinion may not be a central factor in voting decisions, presidential actions can convey a general impression of effectiveness in the global arena. On the face of it, this description seems to fit what happened in 1980, when President Carter's inability to manage foreign affairs probably hurt him at the polling booth with the public. In this, albeit indirect, way, foreign policy mattered.

Finally, one recent study has begun to reconceptualize the relationship between foreign policy opinion and recent presidential elections. This approach suggests that when candidate differences are large and foreign policy issues are salient, the public's views do affect the election outcomes. Not only did these conditions exist in 1952 and 1972, as is often noted, but they also were prevalent in the 1964, 1980, and 1984 presidential elections.[65] In such circumstances, public opinion on foreign policy matters probably made a difference in the election outcomes. Voters could see differences between the candidates, and these differences influenced voting decisions.

FOREIGN POLICY OPINION AND CONGRESSIONAL ELECTIONS

To even a greater degree than presidential elections, congressional elections are rarely depicted as referenda on foreign policy questions. Elections for the House of Representatives, in particular, are hardly ever fought on foreign policy questions. Foreign policy questions in U.S. Senate races are only occasionally salient. In both instances, the foreign policy positions of candidates are likely to be marginal to their campaigns.

Still, foreign policy may play a role in these elections in some negative and positive ways. On the one hand, if an incumbent is perceived as too involved in foreign affairs or as spending too much time on foreign policy matters, he or she could be subject to electoral punishment by the public for neglecting the "folks back home." On the other hand, congressional candidates are often sure to be on the "right" side of particular issues related to foreign affairs to foreclose electoral punishment. Candidates from districts or states with substantial military spending are unlikely to oppose such activities; candidates with large Jewish constituencies are likely to be very supportive of Israel; and candidates from south Florida districts, for example, were likely to support the Nicaraguan contras consistently during the 1980s. In this sense, foreign policy opinion matters to congressional candidates, although in a slightly different way than we normally think of it.

FOREIGN POLICY OPINION AND POLICY CHOICES

If it is difficult to argue that elections are referenda on foreign policy opinion, it is perhaps even more difficult to sustain the view that foreign policy opinion matters for particular policy choices. Only in rare instances, when the public has been mobilized by the president with a nationwide television address or by some interest groups over an upcoming vote in the Congress, does the opinion of the public matter on an immediate foreign policy decision facing the country. In this sense, the effect of public opinion on individual policy decision is sporadic and exceptional.

Over the last two decades, though, we have witnessed examples of just these kinds of sporadic events, although the public's success level in controlling the outcomes has been mixed. In the late 1970s, public opinion, as expressed in various polls, was strongly opposed to the treaties calling for the transference of the Panama Canal back to the country of Panama by the year 2000. As a result, President Carter had a very difficult time gaining Senate approval. Despite his initial opposition to any changes in the treaties, he had to accept several understandings and amendments to make them more acceptable at home. Further, President Carter was forced to lobby hard for their passage with members of the U.S. Senate. Only then was he able to squeak out the two-thirds majority needed to win in the Sen-

ate, 68 to 32. While public opinion did not ultimately stop these treaties, it affected the nature of the debate and their final shape.

President Reagan had a similar experience over the issue of aid
to the Nicaraguan contras, as we have alluded to earlier in this chapter. He went on nationwide television several times to appeal for
public support for his position. In this case, though, he was not always successful in obtaining increased support for the contras. Indeed, in the aggregate, public opinion remained opposed, and
Congress generally gave him much less than he wanted. In this particular case, then, public opinion, more than in the Panama Canal
debate, ultimately contributed to a change in policy course by the
Reagan administration, and later by the Bush administration.

The latter case is especially instructive in another sense. The
public's consistent opposition to aid to the Nicaraguan contras made
it much more difficult for the Reagan administration to pursue the
more assertive course that it favored. The Congress often reflected
that public discontent, and military and economic funding for the
contras throughout the 1980s was a constant political problem. Further, if the public had been more supportive of the Reagan administration's policy in Nicaragua, according to a former high-ranking
official, the administration would have sought more money for the
contras and would have been more assertive in the American role in
the area as well.[66] Such a statement does not imply that the public
opinion in any real sense directed each and every U.S. foreign policy
action toward Nicaragua, but it did serve a more important role than
it is sometimes afforded.

More generally, though, public opinion (or the public mood)
serves as a guide to policy direction, as opposed to each individual
decision. Political scientists Benjamin Page and Robert Shapiro examined directional changes in public opinion and public policy over
five decades from 1935 to 1979, and they sought to answer this central question. When public opinion moved in one direction on an issue, did public policy follow that direction? What they report is
directly relevant to our discussion. They report that policy changes
generally *did* follow the direction of opinion in both the domestic and
foreign affairs arenas in the period of their analysis. For the foreign
policy arena, in particular, they report that policy and opinion were
congruent in 62 percent of the foreign policy cases examined. Further, policy really did seem to follow opinion, rather than the other
way around. As they conclude, "It is reasonable in most of these
cases to infer that opinion change was a *cause* of policy change, or at
least a proximate or intervening factor leading to government action,
if not the ultimate cause."[67] Nonetheless, they also indicate that their
analysis could not and did not answer how much opinion was

affected by the efforts of politicians and interest groups. While normatively optimistic about the effect of public opinion on policy formation, they caution that all the intervening linkages between opinion and policy are yet to be fully explored.

CONCLUDING COMMENTS

The foreign policy opinions of the American people play a part in the foreign policymaking process in the United States. What remains open to debate, however, is the magnitude of the impact of those opinions. One view sees those opinions as "moodish," relatively shiftable, and subject to leadership from the top; another view sees them as structured, relatively stable, and setting some limits on executive (or even congressional) action.

This debate over the public's impact on foreign policy extends to other questions as well. Differing views exist on the overall impact of public opinion on specific foreign policy decisions and general policies adopted by the government. Even the impact of foreign policy opinion on presidential and congressional elections remains unclear. In short, then, while the precise impact of public opinion on foreign policy may still be debated, the fact remains that political leaders, or prospective ones, cannot (and do not) wholly ignore the public's views—even on seemingly distant foreign policy issues.

NOTES

1. These data are from Gabriel A. Almond, *The American People and Foreign Policy* (New York: Praeger, 1960), p. 82.

2. These data are from Lloyd A. Free and Hadley Cantril, *The Political Beliefs of Americans: A Study of Public Opinion* (New York: Simon & Schuster, 1968), pp. 60–61.

3. See John E. Rielly, ed., *American Public Opinion and U.S. Foreign Policy 1987* (Chicago: The Chicago Council on Foreign Relations, 1987), p. 8; and John E. Rielly, ed., *American Public Opinion and U.S. Foreign Policy 1991* (Chicago: The Chicago Council of Foreign Relations, 1991), p. 9.

4. Rielly, *American Public Opinion and U.S. Foreign Policy 1987*, p. 9; and John E. Rielly, ed., *American Public Opinion and U.S. Foreign Policy 1983*, p. 9. The results for 1990 can be found at p. 9 in Rielly, *American Public Opinion and U.S. Foreign Policy 1991*.

5. Richard Sobel, "Public Opinion about United States Intervention in El Salvador and Nicaragua," *Public Opinion Quarterly* 53 (Spring 1989): 120; and William M. LeoGrande, "Did the Public Matter? The Impact of Opinion on Congressional Support for Ronald Reagan's Nicaragua Policy," paper presented at the

conference on Public Opinion and Policy Toward Central America, Woodrow Wilson School of Public and International Affairs, Princeton University, May 4–5, 1990, Table 7.

6. On this point, see John E. Rielly, "American Opinion: Continuity, Not Reaganism," *Foreign Policy* 50 (Spring 1983): 88; and Bruce Russett and Donald R. Deluca," 'Don't Tread on Me': Public Opinion and Foreign Policy in the Eighties," *Political Science Quarterly* 96 (Fall 1981): 393–395.

7. Gallup Polls citation and John E. Rielly, ed., *American Public Opinion and U.S. Foreign Policy 1975, 1979, 1983, 1987* (Chicago: The Chicago Council on Foreign Relations).

8. Tom W. Smith, "The Polls: America's Most Important Problems, Part I: National and International," *Public Opinion Quarterly* 49 (Summer 1985): 264–274.

9. John E. Mueller, *War, Presidents, and Public Opinion* (New York: John Wiley & Sons, Inc., 1973, chap. 8.

10. Ibid., pp. 70–74.

11. Milton J. Rosenberg, Sidney Verba, and Philip E. Converse, *Vietnam and the Silent Majority* (New York: Harper & Row, 1970), pp. 26–28.

12. See "Opinion Roundup," *Public Opinion* (February/March 1980), pp. 27 and 29.

13. These *New York Times*/CBS News Poll results are reported in David Shribman, "Poll Shows Support for Presence of U.S. Troops in Lebanon and Grenada," *New York Times*, October 29, 1983, p. 9.

14. LeoGrande, "Did the Public Matter? The Impact of Opinion on Congressional Support for Ronald Reagan's Nicaragua Policy," p. 8.

15. These changes are shown in poll data on the assessments of Reagan's "handling the situation in Nicaragua" as reported by Sobel in his "Public Opinion about United States Intervention in El Salvador and Nicaragua," p. 127.

16. These data are taken from Michael Oreskes, "Support for Bush Declines in Poll," *New York Times*, July 11, 1990, p. A8; and Andrew H. Malcolm, "Opponents to U.S. Move Have Poverty in Common," *New York Times*, September 8, 1990, p. 6.

17. On the patterns in President Bush's popularity, see Robin Toner, "Did Someone Say 'Domestic Policy'?" *New York Times*, March 3, 1991, pp. 1E and 2E. A CNN (Cable News Network) poll and a *Newsweek* poll placed President Bush's popularity at about 90 percent at the immediate end of the Persian Gulf War. See Ann McDaniel and Evan Thomas with Howard Fineman, "The Rewards of Leadership," *Newsweek*, March 11, 1991, p. 30.

18. Rosenberg, Verba, and Converse, *Vietnam and the Silent Majority*, pp. 24–25. They do not actually use poll data to make this point about question wording; instead, they rely upon these hypothetical examples to demonstrate the underlying argument.

19. Brad Lockerbie and Stephen A. Borrelli, "Question Wording and Public Support for Contra Aid, 1983–1986," *Public Opinion Quarterly* 54 (Summer 1990): 195–208.

20. David W. Moore, "The Public is Uncertain," *Foreign Policy* 35 (Summer 1979): 68–70.

21. See LeoGrande, "Did the Public Matter? The Impact of Opinion on Congressional Support for Ronald Reagan's Nicaragua Policy," note 34, where it raises this concern. Also see Sobel, "Public Opinion about United States Intervention in El Salvador and Nicaragua," p. 120, where he reproduces these poll results.

22. Gabriel A. Almond, *The American People and Foreign Policy* (New York: Frederick A. Praeger, 1960), pp. 53, 69, and 88. The original edition of this book was published in 1950 by Harcourt, Brace and Company, Inc.

23. Ibid, p. xxii, from the new introduction to the 1960 edition.

24. Jon Hurwitz and Mark Peffley, "How Are Foreign Policy Attitudes Structured? A Hierarchical Model: *American Political Science Review* 81 (December 1987): 1114. Emphasis in original.

25. Robert Y. Shapiro and Benjamin I. Page, "Foreign Policy and the Rational Public," *Journal of Conflict Resolution* 32 (June 1988): 211 and 243.

26. Eugene R. Wittkopf, *Faces of Internationalism: Public Opinion and American Foreign Policy* (Durham, NC: Duke University Press, 1990), pp. 25-33.

27. Ibid., p. 25.

28. Ibid., pp. 25-30. The application of Wittkopf's typology to the Persian Gulf War was aided by a personal communication with him.

29. Ibid., p. 26. The numbers are rough averages within each quadrant for the four surveys.

30. Ibid., pp. 27-32, especially the table at p. 28 and the discussion at p. 30.

31. Ibid., pp. 44-49.

32. Bernard Cohen, *The Political Process and Foreign Policy: The Making of the Japanese Peace Settlement* (Princeton, NJ: Princeton University Press, 1957), p. 29.

33. V. O. Key, Jr., *Public Opinion and American Democracy* (New York: Alfred A. Knopf Inc., 1961), p. 423.

34. William R. Caspary, "The 'Mood Theory': A Study of Public Opinion and Foreign Policy," *The American Political Science Review* 54 (June 1970): 546. Emphasis in original.

35. Bruce Russett, "The Americans' Retreat from World Power," *Political Science Quarterly* 90 (Spring 1975): 9.

36. The phrase is from ibid., p. 8. For other judgments of the Vietnam War and its impact on the foreign policy beliefs of the American public and its leaders, see for instance, Eugene R. Wittkopf and Michael A. Maggiotto, "Elites and Masses: A Comparative Analysis of Attitudes Toward America's World Role," *The Journal of Politics* 45 (May 1983): 303-334; and Ole R. Holsti and James N. Rosenau, "Vietnam, Consensus, and the Belief Systems of American Leaders," *World Politics* 32 (October 1979): 1-56.

37. John E. Rielly, ed., *American Public Opinion and U.S. Foreign Policy 1975* (Chicago: The Chicago Council on Foreign Relations, 1975), p. 12. The rest of the data in this section are from this report. The national sample survey was conducted in December 1974, by Harris and Associates for the Chicago Council on Foreign Relations.

38. Russett, "The Americans' Retreat from World Power," p. 8.

39. The title is from John E. Rielly, "The American Mood: A Policy of Self-Interest," *Foreign Policy* 34 (Spring 1979): 74-86.

40. John E. Rielly, ed., *American Public Opinion and U.S. Foreign Policy 1979* (Chicago: The Chicago Council on Foreign Relations, 1979), p. 4.

41. The data cited here are from ibid.

42. A Harris survey in early 1980 showed majority public support for use of U.S. troops if the Soviets attacked the Persian Gulf area, Iran, or Pakistan. See "Use of U.S. Troops to Defend Invaded Countries Endorsed," *Houston Post*, February 26, 1980, p. 3C.

43. Rielly, *American Public Opinion and U.S. Foreign Policy 1979*, p. 12.

44. Ibid., p. 15.

45. Ibid., p. 12.

46. Ibid., p. 7. Also Rielly, "The American Mood: A Foreign Policy of Self-Interest."

47. Rielly, *American Public Opinion and U.S. Foreign Policy 1983*, p. 4.

48. Ibid., p. 6, and Rielly, *American Public Opinion and U.S. Foreign Policy 1987*, p. 32.

49. Rielly, *American Public Opinion and U.S. Foreign Policy 1983*, pp. 6 and 31; and Rielly, *American Public Opinion and U.S. Foreign Policy 1987*, p. 32.

50. These results are taken from Rielly, *American Public Opinion and U.S. Foreign Policy 1983*, p. 32; and Rielly, *American Public Opinion and U.S. Foreign Policy 1987*, p. 31.

51. See the tables in Rielly, *American Public Opinion and U.S. Foreign Policy 1983*, p. 35; and Rielly, *American Public Opinion and U.S. Foreign Policy 1987*, p. 35, which compare the public's views with those of the Reagan administration. Also, see p. 29 of the latter report for a discussion of public attitudes on military expenditures.

52. See, for example, Charles William Maynes, "America Without the Cold War," *Foreign Policy* 78 (Spring 1990): 3–25; and Norman J. Ornstein and Mark Schmitt, "Dateline Campaign '92: Post–Cold War Politics," *Foreign Policy* 79 (Summer 1990): 169–186.

53. John E. Rielly, "Public Opinion: The Pulse of the '90s," *Foreign Policy* 82 (Spring 1991): 79.

54. Ibid., p. 83.

55. Rielly, *American Public Opinion and U.S. Foreign Policy 1991*, p. 15.

56. See Figure IV-4 in ibid., p. 28.

57. Rielly, "Public Opinion: The Pulse of the '90s," p. 80.

58. See Figures III-4 and III-5 in Rielly, *American Public Opinion and U.S. Foreign Policy 1991*, p. 21, and the discussion on pp. 19–21.

59. Ibid., p. 6, for comparison with earlier assessments of the Soviet Union in 1986 and before. For doubts about the Cold War really being over, see ibid., Figure VI-1, p. 37.

60. Rielly, "Public Opinion: The Pulse of the '90s," pp. 83, 86, and 89.

61. Rielly, *American Public Opinion and U.S. Foreign Policy 1991*, p. 13. The reference to Iran and Iraq is from Figure III-4 at p. 21.

62. See John H. Aldrich, John L. Sullivan, and Eugene Borgida, "Foreign Affairs and Issue Voting: Do Presidential Candidates 'Waltz Before a Blind Audience'?" *American Political Science Review* 83 (March 1989): 136.

63. Warren E. Miller, "Voting and Foreign Policy," in James N. Rosenau, ed., *Domestic Sources of Foreign Policy* (New York: The Free Press, 1967), p. 226. Also, see LeoGrande, "Did the Public Matter? The Impact of Opinion on Congressional Support for Ronald Reagan's Nicaragua Policy," p. 6; and John Spanier and Eric M. Uslaner, *American Foreign Policy Making and the Democratic Dilemmas* (Pacific Grove, CA: Brooks/Cole Publishing Company, 1989), p. 216.

64. Gregory B. Markus, "Political Attitudes During an Election Year: A Report on the 1980 NES Panel Study," *American Political Science Review* 76 (September 1982): 558. This point is also discussed in Spanier and Uslaner, *American Foreign Policy Making and the Democratic Dilemmas*, p. 216, from which we draw.

65. See the chart in Aldrich, Sullivan, and Borgida, "Foreign Affairs and Issue Voting: Do Presidential Candidates 'Waltz Before a Blind Audience'?" p. 136.

66. This assessment was based upon remarks made by former Assistant Secretary of State Eliot Abrams at a conference on "Public Opinion and Policy To-

ward Central America: The Case of Aid to the Nicaraguan Contras" at Princeton University, May 1990.

67. Benjamin I. Page and Robert Y. Shapiro, "Effects of Public Opinion on Policy," *American Political Science Review* 77 (March 1983): 186. Emphasis in original. The discussion in this paragraph is drawn from the article.

PART III CONCLUSION

The last chapter examines both the need and prospects for a new consensus in U.S. foreign policymaking. As we entered a new decade and a new era in global politics, the need for such a consensus appeared to be greater than ever before. If U.S. policy is to be both coherent and consistent in the post–Cold War environment, the most compelling task for the policymakers and the public must be to develop a set of beliefs to guide future action. The constant shifts in policy emphasis from one administration to the next—a process so prevalent over the last three decades—no longer serve American interests. At the same time, the task of achieving such a consensus is formidable and, at present, only alternate outlines of what that consensus might be are evident.

CHAPTER 13 AMERICAN FOREIGN POLICY IN THE POST–COLD WAR ERA

"The post–Cold War world will certainly be different in some important ways: Power will be distributed differently; ideological rivalry will be less prominent; nuclear and biological weapons, and the missiles to deliver them, will be more widely dispersed." OWEN HARRIES, "DEFINING THE NEW WORLD ORDER," *HARPER'S*, MAY 1991

"The United States is likely to remain the only country with a leading position in both economic and military power, yet it will have to cope with unprecedented problems of interdependence that no great power can solve by itself. . . . Many of the new issues in international politics— ecology, drugs, AIDS, terrorism—involve a diffusion of power away from states to private actors and require organizing states for cooperative responses." JOSEPH S. NYE, "AMERICAN STRATEGY AFTER BIPOLARITY," *INTERNATIONAL AFFAIRS,* 1990

In Part I of this book, we suggested how the formulation of American foreign policy was marked by a considerable degree of value consensus prior to the Vietnam War and by a substantial number of value shifts from one administration to the next after that war. In Part II, a central message was how the various political institutions—the executive, the Congress, and the bureaucracies, for example—have become increasingly competitive in the shaping of American foreign policy in the post-Vietnam period. Indeed, the impetus for foreign policy change has gained even more momentum since the collapse of the Berlin Wall, the unraveling of communism in Eastern Europe in 1989 and 1990, and the dramatic changes in the Soviet Union after the August 1991 coup attempt. But a crucial problem remains for American foreign policy: can a coherent foreign policy be developed without the emergence of a new foreign policy value consensus to replace the one first challenged by the Vietnam War and now eroded further still by the end of the Cold War? Can American policy long endure the constant shifts and changes in approach that have marked the last two decades? Put more generally, should and will the U.S. remain active in global politics? And, if so, what should be the shape of that role and its rationale?

In this last chapter, we conclude our analysis by discussing the underlying value conflicts and their implications for American foreign policy in the decades ahead. First we highlight more fully the extent of underlying value conflict among the leaders of American foreign policy in recent years. Then we turn to evaluating the problems of and prospects for developing a new foreign policy consensus within the United States for the 1990s and beyond. Finally, we provide a brief sketch of the three alternate approaches that may well shape the future role of the U.S. in the post–Cold War world.

A NATION DIVIDED

An abundance of evidence exists at both the mass and elite levels on the degree of value conflict over the direction of foreign policy in the current age. As we have noted, the United States has witnessed discernible shifts in its foreign policy approach with the coming of each new administration over the past two decades. From the rejection of the values of the Cold War consensus, to the power politics of the Kissinger period, to the moralism of the Carter years, to the revival of containment of the Reagan years, and now the realism of the Bush administration, the American approach to foreign policy has gone through substantial modification almost every four years. Although two leading scholars on American foreign policy contend that a considerable stability in goals and objectives have remained over the postwar years (including the recent administrations), this view fails to account adequately for the changes in emphasis from one administration to the next.[1] Similarly, this view fails to capture the pervasive divisions in value orientation among the leadership (the foreign policy elites) and the American people.

VALUE DIFFERENCES WITHIN ELITES

Over a decade ago, political scientists Ole Holsti and James Rosenau first suggested three different foreign policy belief systems now prevalent among the American leadership over how the U.S. should approach foreign policy problems in the post-Vietnam period.[2] Despite the end of the Cold War, these differing orientations probably remain in place today, and, in some respects, they have actually become more sharply defined, as evidenced in more recent research.

Holsti and Rosenau first summarized the content of these distinct foreign policy orientations with three very descriptive labels: one belief system was labeled the Cold War internationalists, another, the post–Cold War internationalists, and a third, the isolationists (or semi-isolationists).[3] The first segment of elite opinion, the Cold War internationalists, basically continue to adhere to the values of the Cold War consensus and adopt policy prescriptions from that perspective. The principal global issues are defined along the East-West divisions, and the Soviet Union continues to be the dominant reference point for all foreign policymaking. Moreover, the international system is still viewed as predominantly conflictual, and policy has to be made from that perspective. For this group, "the overarching reality of the global system remains the confrontation between an expansionist Soviet Union and its allies, on the one hand, and the noncommunist nations on the other."[4] President Reagan's values and beliefs reflected this approach to foreign policy (see Chapter 5).

A second segment, the post–Cold War internationalists, has moved beyond the East-West divisions to also include the North-South divisions (i.e., divisions between rich and poor countries) in their view of the world. While the Soviet Union is not removed as a policymaking consideration for this group, it no longer dominates the process (in contrast to the Cold War internationalists). Instead, "global issue" questions—world poverty, regional hostilities, global justice—not just superpower politics, inform policy considerations for the post–Cold War internationalists. In other words, the "multidimensional" nature of the present global system is not susceptible to the narrow response embodied in the Cold War consensus.[5] This perspective is largely a reaction to the earlier Cold War view and probably constitutes the largest segment of the American leadership as a whole. The values and beliefs of President Jimmy Carter serve as a good illustration of this second segment of America's leadership (see Chapter 4).

A third segment of leadership opinion, the isolationists, perceives the greatest challenges from the unresolved problems within the United States and wants to reduce involvements abroad to only those concerned with clearly shared interests. To this grouping, then, the Soviet Union or North-South issues are of considerably less importance than to the first two segments; instead, domestic issues such as inflation, unemployment, crime, and environmental damage—and the impact of foreign affairs on such issues—should dominate the policymaking agenda. Spokespersons for this view have included Senators George McGovern, J. William Fulbright, and Mike Mansfield. Moreover, even the original author of the containment policy, George Kennan, has increasingly adopted this perspective.[6]

While adherents to these three belief systems were fundamentally divided by their attitudes toward the Vietnam War, Holsti and Rosenau also found that basic political ideology (liberal versus conservative) was predictive of the different foreign policy orientations as well.[7] Liberals tended to adopt more post–Cold War internationalist and isolationist positions, while conservatives tended to be Cold War internationalists. Similarly, occupations tended to divide the adherents among the different foreign policy belief systems. Media people, the religious community, and educators were often post–Cold War internationalists; military officers were mainly Cold War internationalists; and labor leaders were more likely to be isolationists. Finally, and most interestingly, age, or generational differences, did not prove to be significant in distinguishing among the people who were placed in the three categories.

In sum, Holsti and Rosenau demonstrated that the three foreign policy belief systems deeply divided the American leadership and that those divisions extended "across a spectrum of issues, ranging from the most fundamental purposes of American foreign policy to the appropriate strategies and tactics that might be used in the pursuit of external goals." Further, these divisions at the elite level were assumed to have serious foreign policy consequences. While American policymakers may still be able to take globalist foreign policy actions, they "are more likely to engender vigorous political controversy than unquestioning support from various sectors of American leadership."[8]

Other post-Vietnam analyses of elite beliefs by Wittkopf and by Wittkopf and Maggiotto have largely confirmed and more fully specified the foreign policy divisions that Holsti and Rosenau initially suggested.[9] By sophisticated statistical analyses of the leadership sample gathered by the Chicago Council on Foreign Relations in 1974, 1978, 1982, and 1986, Wittkopf in particular found that elite beliefs, like public beliefs (Chapter 12), can generally be divided into four major categories—accommodationists, internationalists, isolationists, and hardliners—based upon the respondents' attitudes toward militant and cooperative internationalism. Only for the 1982 results does this fourfold categorization not hold. In the main, though, these four divisions are markedly stable and consistent over the three other survey years.[10] In this sense, consistency and coherence exist in elite opinion, as it does in their foreign policy differences.

The foreign policy divisions found by Wittkopf and by Wittkopf and Maggiotto largely correspond to those of Holsti and Rosenau, although the former is less reliant than the latter on policy toward the Soviet Union to capture the differences in belief systems. The hardliners are analogous to the Cold War internationalists, the accommodationists and internationalists correspond to the post–Cold War internationalists, and the isolationists are the same. Indeed, in a recent re-analysis of their survey data for 1976, 1980, and 1984 using the Wittkopf schema, Holsti and Rosenau report that their data correspond to that fourfold categorization very well.[11]

This lack of consensus within elites (and even among the mass public, as we indicated in Chapter 12) is further complicated in yet another way: the failure of both elites and masses to share these policy orientations to the same degree. That is, despite the fact that attitudes of elites and masses are similarly structured into comparable belief systems, some of the different belief systems are not held in the same proportion by the foreign policy elites and the public. For instance, the American leadership tends to be much more *internationalist* (in both the militant and cooperative varieties) than is the mass public. By contrast, the mass public tends to favor more *hardline* (a more militant internationalism) and *isolationist* policies than do the elites.[12] The implication of such disparities between elites and masses is that effective foreign policymaking is further hampered.

These elite/mass issue differences are more directly portrayed in some data from the latest comprehensive foreign policy opinion survey published by the Chicago Council on Foreign Relations. Table 13.1

TABLE 13.1   DIFFERENCES BETWEEN THE LEADERS AND THE
PUBLIC, 1990

	Percentage in Agreement		Gap (Leaders minus Public)
	Public	Leaders	
Involvement Abroad			
Best to take an active part in world affairs	69%	98%	+29%
U.S.–Soviet Relations			
Goal of containing communism very important	58%	10%	−48%
Cold War not really over	66%	25%	−41%
Goal of matching Soviet military power very important	58%	20%	−38%
U.S. military stronger than Soviet	34%	71%	+37%
Favor economic aid to Soviets to modernize their economy	40%	71%	+31%
Military Spending and Alliances			
Cut back defense spending	33%	77%	+44%
Favor decreasing commitment to NATO	31%	62%	+31%
Use of Military Force			
Favor using U.S. troops if Iraq invaded Saudi Arabia	58%	90%	+32%
Favor using U.S. troops if Soviet Union invaded Japan	45%	76%	+31%
Favor using U.S. troops if Mexico were threatened by revolution	54%	20%	−34%
Favor Economic Aid			
Favor economic aid to other countries in general	50%	91%	+41%
Favor cutting back economic aid to other countries	64%	21%	−43%
Favor increasing economic aid to Eastern Europe	27%	75%	+48%
Other			
Goal of protecting American business abroad very important	65%	27%	−38%
Favor 25-cent-per-gallon tax on gasoline to reduce oil dependency	11%	62%	+51%

Note: Percentages are of those holding an opinion.

Source: John E. Reilly, ed., *American Public Opinion and U.S. Foreign Policy 1991* (Chicago: Chicago Council on Foreign Relations, 1991), Figure VI-1, p. 37.

compares some responses to several foreign policy questions of a general public survey and a leadership survey (composed of knowledgeable Americans from government, business, communications, education, and foreign policy institutes). Both surveys were conducted in October and November 1990.

Sharp policy differences are evident in attitudes toward the world and toward specific policies. The public, for instance, is less committed to an active world role and is more skeptical of changed U.S.-Soviet relations than are those in the leadership sample. The leaders (or elites) are more willing to cut defense spending or the commitment to NATO more significantly than is the public as a whole. The public, on the other hand, is generally less willing to use force than the leaders (although the defense of Mexico is an exception), while it is more skeptical of foreign aid than is the leadership. Finally, and the results are not fully revealed in Table 13.1, the public is much more supportive of efforts to protect the economic interests of Americans than are the leaders. The public is much more supportive of efforts to protect American business abroad and the jobs of American workers at home, and it also reveals a greater sensitivity to the impact of foreign policy on food prices, unemployment, and gasoline prices than does this sample of American elites. In short, even as the shape of public opinion has changed, as we noted in Chapter 12, the gap between elites and masses on several foreign policy questions has remained. Indeed, according to the most recent assessment, the magnitude of the differences between elites and masses has actually widened in the early 1990s.[13]

In sum, then, major analyses of post-Vietnam opinion portray the same picture of America's leadership: a foreign policy elite divided over how the United States ought to act in the world. Further, the divisions between the elite and the masses on a number of important foreign policy questions remain as well. Whether the formal end of the Cold War will enable consensus to reemerge remains a question, but, given the significant divisions over the past three decades, the challenge remains a formidable one.

A NEW FOREIGN POLICY CONSENSUS

Indeed, the shifts in policy from one president to another and the cleavages that have developed both among and between American leaders and the public seems to point to the need to develop a new foreign policy consensus that will engender widespread support among the American people and will lend coherence and direction to U.S. policy.

THE CALL FOR A NEW CONSENSUS

This call for a new foreign policy consensus is hardly new; in reality, it has been frequent, beginning in the 1970s and continuing to the present. Sprinkled throughout the writings of foreign policy scholars and practitioners are numerous such appeals. Beginning in the 1970s, Lincoln Bloomfield, Philip Windsor, and Thomas Hughes called for new approaches to replace the Cold War consensus in guiding American foreign policy.[14] By 1974, when Charles Maynes called for a foreign policy directed more toward promoting the interests of ordinary citizens, a lively exchange ensued among experts of varying philosophical persuasions on the whole consensus question.[15]

In the middle 1970s, calls for consensus continued. Two prominent examples will illustrate this point. Prior to his becoming national security advisor in the Carter administration, Zbigniew Brzezinski argued that the Vietnam experience had shattered the WASP foreign policy elite and that Henry Kissinger's global design failed to replace the lost elite. Thus, he contended, there was a "need for national leadership that was capable of defining politically and morally compelling directions to which the public might then positively respond."[16] A little later, political scientist Stanley Hoffmann published a lengthy volume on this very topic.[17] Beginning with an extensive critique of what he called the "containment cycle" (1946 to 1968) and the "Kissinger cycle" (1969 to 1976) of U.S. policy, Hoffmann proceeded to suggest why a new approach was needed and why the time was right. Further, he actually set forth the value and policy requirements of this new approach.

In the 1980s, the debate continued unabated. Thomas Hughes lamented that foreign policy consensus had not emerged and that the U.S. was experiencing a foreign policy "crack-up."[18] As American leaders and the public became increasingly divided into what Hughes called those concerned with the "security culture" and those concerned with the "equity culture," foreign policy had faltered badly. Thus, a new foreign policy coalition was still needed to replace the working coalition of the Cold War years. In his Senate confirmation hearings, secretary of state appointee Alexander Haig stated the need in bold terms: "Our task is to reestablish an effective foreign policy consensus."[19] He then proceeded to argue that such a consensus must be based upon presidential leadership, supported by congressional bipartisanship, and implemented by a professional bureaucracy.

Later, political scientist John Sigler, eminent historian Arthur Schlesinger, Jr., and political observer Dick Clark continued the discussion of the consensus issue. Sigler concluded that a new consensus might emerge combining elements of idealism and realism.[20] Schlesinger yearned for a foreign policy that was more fully reflective of the empirical or practical strain in American character, in contrast to the ideological policy pursued by the Reagan administration.[21] Finally, Dick Clark, a former U.S. senator, took a different tack by proposing a series of policy positions that generally reflected a consensus among leading students of American foreign policy. Such common policy positions could presumably be the basis for a new consensus.[22]

In the early 1990s, and with the demise of communism in Eastern Europe and the changes within the Soviet Union itself, calls for a new consensus, or at least new approaches, are once again rampant.[23] Yet, such a consensus has not emerged and remains the most formidable challenge for American foreign policy. But is there any real prospect that it come about in the near future?

At least three lingering and important questions remain over forming a new consensus: (1) Should it really be developed? Will a new consensus really be necessary or functional for American policy in the 1990s and beyond? (2) Can it be developed? That is, in the context of a divided leadership and a divided public, how is a new consensus going to be formed? (3) Most importantly, perhaps, what values should constitute this new consensus?

Some analysts doubt that a foreign policy consensus can be constructed in the near future and believe that any short-term consensus that might emerge may be detrimental to sound foreign policy. One view, for example, is that the foreign policy interests of the United States today are too diverse to be summarized under a single rubric as anti-communism did during the height of the Cold War. Furthermore, domestic interests are now often perceived to be closely linked to foreign policy (e.g., trade policy and domestic employment), so that foreign policy action might only reinforce existing domestic policy divisions. Thus, the likelihood of widespread public unity remains in doubt. In such circumstances, the United States "may simply have to learn to conduct foreign policy for a very long time without a single unifying theme on which to base a broad national consensus."[24] Instead, foreign policy will have to be made piecemeal—on a case-by-case basis—and in the same manner as domestic policy, by building coalitions as issues come along.

Another approach—less demanding than an overarching consensus, but more than a case-by-case approach to policy—would be to identify and obtain agreement on dealing with key issues or key nations of the world.[25] For instance, a consensus might be built on the need to pursue arms control in today's nuclear world, regardless of occurrence in other issue-areas. Similarly, it might be possible to gain some consensus among the American public and its leadership on how to conduct future relations with the Soviet Union as the traditional ideological gulf narrows. In short, this immediate approach to consensus building would be less demanding and, in this sense, more achievable.

If a consensus were to emerge, however, dangers exist with it. If a premature consensus develops—i.e., one that is not firmly embedded in the elites and the public at large—it might simply be a set of simple moral slogans that would not reflect the complexity of policy needed for today's world.[26] For instance, both the Carter and Reagan administrations might have been accused of employing such a strategy—with the resultant consequence that neither's effort sufficed as a satisfactory consensus for the public as a whole. A consistent complaint about the Bush administration, too, is that it tends to make its foreign policy decisions based upon their popularity at home, and perhaps not always in the long-term interests of the United States.

At the same time, a premature consensus could easily turn out to be an excellent counterpoint for those opposed to a particular approach. Once again, the efforts of recent administrations come to mind as illustrations of this argument. The Bush administration, for instance, moved quickly in confronting Iraq's Saddam Hussein with military action, even as the American public and the Congress were becoming increasingly skeptical over the wisdom of such a policy. President Bush undoubtedly assumed that the public concern over Iraqi aggression against Kuwait and the need to maintain the steady flow of oil from the Middle East would produce a policy consensus quickly, despite the prospect of a war looming on the horizon.

Instead, a premature consensus could actually serve as a rallying point for the opposition. This danger is especially likely in the context of a divided public, as the Iraqi case initially suggested. In this sense, allowing more time for a consensus to develop through normal political dialogue and bargaining among various segments of the American public is likely to yield greater benefits. In the short run, the result of this bargaining process would be a more episodic policy as one elite group, and then another, attempts to mold policy. In the long run, however, a consensus might emerge with wider public support through such a procedure.

A related and more critical danger for any consensus has been aptly summarized by Gelb and Betts.[27] First of all, they are quite skeptical of any new consensus or doctrine because of its impact on policymaking. "Doctrine and consensus," they note, "are the midwives to necessity and the enemy of dissent and choice." Because the military containment belief system had been so firmly interwoven into the American policy process in the 1950s and 1960s, America's Vietnam policy became almost a certainty. Thus, once beliefs become so dominant in the policy process, movement away from them becomes extraordinarily difficult.

Nonetheless, Gelb and Betts acknowledge that some doctrinal consensus is necessary in foreign policymaking ("It lends coherence and direction to policy; it puts particular challenges in perspective; it enables the bureaucracy to handle routine problems without constant and enervating debates; it translates values into objectives. . . ."), but they call for one "with escape hatches."[28] A more pragmatic consensus that will be adaptive to changing circumstances is the key in their view. Given America's past, however, that task may be more difficult than it sounds. Somewhat ironically, they note, while Americans often pride themselves on pragmatism in domestic affairs, they have been much more prone to adopt ideological postures in foreign affairs. In their view, a new consensus must avoid this tendency.

DEVELOPING A NEW CONSENSUS

Can a workable foreign policy consensus emerge that takes into account these possible dangers? The answer, of course, is still very much open to question, but we would nonetheless agree with one proponent of a new consensus: "There is no sensible alternative but to try."[29] At a minimum, the following requirements would seem to be necessary.

Political leadership will undoubtedly be the first requisite. This leadership, however, must not be one that yearns for some past glory; instead, it must accept the changed global reality—a world divided into many diverse sections—and be willing to shape foreign policy in such an environment. The second requisite is that the leadership must be willing to educate the public continuously on foreign policy. A third, and crucial, requisite for this new consensus is that the public itself evaluate its beliefs and values on what the United

States should stand for in the world, the extent to which domestic values should shape American policy, and the degree to which various political, economic, and military instruments are acceptable for implementing foreign policy.

None of these requisites will be easy to obtain. Political leaders often opt for domestically attractive foreign policy stances, and they find educating the public on international issues difficult. Similarly, the public has too often shown little interest in or knowledge about foreign affairs; traditional beliefs remain appealing. A coherent foreign policy, however, requires that such an effort be made by the leadership and the public. The leadership task is especially difficult today because the elite-mass value divisions are ideologically based and because these divisions are *within* generations rather than across them. Thus, simple appeals to only one segment of the American public will not suffice; instead, the leadership must be much more creative in identifying values and policies that will appeal across groups. Furthermore, with pressing international political problems—whether it be the potential spread of nuclear weapons, the continuing global debt crisis, or the effects of global warming—American political leadership probably does not have the luxury of waiting until dramatic international events help to forge a new value consensus (as the events of the late 1940s and early 1950s assisted in forging the Cold War consensus).[30]

ALTERNATE APPROACHES TO BUILDING A CONSENSUS

What, then, might be some of these overarching values that the political leadership could use to mold any new consensus? Several alternate approaches have been advanced recently and largely conform to the different segments among the public elites and masses at the present time. For simplicity's sake, let us list them under three headings: (1) a reduced American involvement, (2) an emphasis on democratic values, and (3) the development of a new world order. While we cannot do full justice to any of them in this short space, we can give some sense of the range of options that have been suggested.

A NEW UNILATERALISM   The first alternative might be labeled "a return to unilateralism" or even "isolationism" as the guiding theme for American foreign policy. In the immediate aftermath of the Vietnam War, for example, several calls arose for neo-isolationism as the most promising path for American foreign policy. Public opinion surveys at the time conveyed just such sentiments, with both the foreign policy leadership and the public at large concerned about America's overextension in world affairs.

With the end of the Cold War, at least two variants of this theme have arisen once again. One variant was offered by a former government official, Earl C. Ravenal, and it portrays the view of those who yearn for a reduced role for the United States in world affairs.[31] This approach, Ravenal argues, will be less the result of a conscious policy decision on the part of the U.S., and more the result of changed international circumstances.

In particular, Ravenal believes that "both of the superpowers will increasingly have to take the international system as they find it," and mutual disengagement will be the result. Because the emerging international system will be more fragmented and regionalized, the United States should move toward greater "strategic independence" by seeking "to quarantine regional violence and compartmentalize regional instability." The best approach to achieve this outcome will not be "by active intervention" but by encouraging "regional balances of power, whether bipolar or multipolar."[32]

In this new international system, the national security strategy of the United States would involve protecting only limited key values: "the lives and domestic property of citizens, the integrity of national territory, and the autonomy of political processes."[33] Promoting and protecting values beyond these will lose their relevance. Efforts to reshape the international system, for example, or to expand human rights globally would no longer be core U.S. values. As a consequence, defense plans could be scaled back, American commitments through extended deterrence would be substantially weakened, and U.S. actions would assume a more limited role in shaping global politics. On balance, the U.S. will be able to do nothing less because, in Ravenal's view, the nation must "adjust to a world beyond order and control."[34]

A second variant of this approach also suggests a reduced, albeit more focused, role for the United States in world affairs. The goal in pursuing this unilateral variant would be for the U.S. to pursue more singlemindedly its global economic interests. In particular, economic nationalism would be adopted to replace anti-communism as the unifying force in American foreign policy and would be used as the means to restore America's competitiveness and global standing.[35] In effect, the U.S. would adopt a more protectionist trade policy and take more selective and vigorous economic actions worldwide. The political/miltary emphasis in U.S. foreign policy would necessarily take a backseat in any such strategy. The most recent survey of American public opinion by the Chicago Council on Foreign Relations seems to imply some support for this position. Note, as we discussed in Chapter 12 and earlier in this chapter, how important foreign economic issues are to the American public at the current time.[36]

THE DEMOCRATIC IMPERATIVE   A second alternative, first suggested a decade ago by George Quester, might involve a return to America's traditional emphasis upon its domestic values in dealing with the world.[37] That is, the United States should place greater reliance upon the principles of political democracy (e.g., "free contested elections with a free press") as the basis of our policy toward other nations. According to Quester's original formulation, the consensus that really was lost by the Vietnam War was a sense of confidence in our own values and our sense of worth to the rest of the world. As a result, Americans applied a double standard in approaching the international system. While we were willing to apply the standards of political democracy in conducting foreign relations with Western Europe and Canada, for instance, we were unwilling to apply those same standards in dealing with states of the developing world. Regimes that engage in political repression and that are not committed to democratic principles have become increasingly tolerable to the United States. Economic progress in these countries has replaced progress toward democracy as the key goal in these (mainly Third World) nations.

This movement away from the "democratic ideal" has had serious consequences for the United States. To many Americans, the United States no longer served as a model to the world. Instead, other states, without democratic values, have assumed that position. Further, as these nations have moved away from traditional American beliefs, the "altruistic impulses" within the U.S.—its social and economic concern for other nations—have declined. In fact, an isolationist sentiment has gained some credibility. To arrest such trends, a return to democratic values as a basis of policy remains crucial in Quester's view.

This democratic impulse has surely gained renewed currency with the demise of communism in Eastern Europe and the Soviet Union, and, hence, the demise of anti-communism as the raison d'être of American foreign policy. As one prominent member of the House put it, "You might actually organize American foreign policy behind a rigorous and internally consistent policy of supporting democracy—a vision of supporting the good guys in the world, a Wilsonian foreign policy."[38] Such a policy would have another attraction. By perfecting democratic institutions at home and then seeking to promote them abroad, "democracy promotion would forge a sense of community that would make both the internal and international purpose of the United States not just a 'government policy' but a source of national identity."[39]

A NEW WORLD ORDER   A third proposal would consciously focus upon building a new world order—a rather dramatic break from the essentially bipolar arrangement of the past to a multipolar world in the future. Indeed, the Bush administration has called for just such an order with the changes in Europe and new dangers in the Middle East (see Chapter 6). Although the details of this new world order have not been spelled out very well, it would presumably involve sustained global involvement for the U.S., combined with more concerted cooperation among the major political and economic powers, as the principal mechanisms for ensuring global stability and peace.

Stanley Hoffmann outlined something akin to this idea over a decade ago, and his insights are worth considering in contemplating the details of this new world order.[40] In his view, this kind of foreign policy would emphasize world order values as the dominant theme for American foreign policy, and it would be based upon three strategic guidelines for implementing such a foreign policy. The first premise would be an emphasis upon building on the world order that presently exists—whether through international institutions (e.g., the United Nations), through formal ties (e.g., a new nuclear arms agreement between the superpowers), or through informal beliefs and standards (e.g., the increasing recognition of global interdependence). More generally, this premise would call for some erosion of ideology (as has now occurred) as the basis of foreign policy and the strengthening of global rules and norms. Second, the United States would have to adopt a much more pluralist approach to the world by showing greater willingness to adapt to changed global conditions and by demonstrating a strong commitment to negotiating differences between states. Third, according to Hoffmann, national security policy would also need to be turned "into an aspect of world order policy." In other words, the emphasis would not be on maximizing the national interest, but on seeking global accommodation. Hoffmann recognizes that this guideline will be particularly difficult to implement because of underlying conflict in the world, as illustrated by the conflict between the United States and the Soviet Union since the late 1940s or as illustrated by the continuing conflicts today (e.g., the Arab-Israeli dispute). Thus, while the balance of power must necessarily be maintained, its pursuance should not blind American policy into seeking it as an end in itself. Instead, efforts at cooperative exchanges in line with the requisites of building world order must always be continued—even within a conflictual environment.

Hoffmann also outlines the methods or the "operational code" for putting these general guidelines into effect. They consist of a policy that remains consistent, employs bargaining, and recognizes the ultimate "politics" of foreign policy. First, in pursuing a world order policy, the United States should follow a consistent course in which international concerns must prevail over domestic concerns. In other words, domestic political considerations should not be allowed to sidetrack efforts to build world order. Second, negotiations must be sought with all states, no matter the degree of commonality with them. Further, in bargaining situations, we must not be put off by new coalitions that might emerge—even if some of our presumed partners join that new coalition. Third, we must understand, even while searching for global order, that foreign policy is ultimately a political process among *states.* Thus we need to foster an order among these states that shows "an awareness of their perspectives, an understanding of their interests, a concern for their future course."[41]

A more recent proponent of this approach has been political scientist Joseph Nye. He has argued that the United States needs to remain actively involved, but that it will need to seek global assistance of other states because of the "unprecedented problems of interdependence." The problems of global ecology, drug trafficking, AIDS, and international terrorism demand global solutions. Such problems transcend national boundaries, and "no great power, not even the United States, can deal with these issues alone. As the largest country, America will have to take a lead in organizing international cooperation."[42]

On a political level, this new world order is already in evidence in a variety of ways: the peaceful unification of Germany; the suspension of all allied rights by Britain, France, the U.S., and the U.S.S.R. in German affairs; the official ending of the Cold War at the November 1990 Conference on Security and Cooperation in Europe; the remarkable degree of U.S.-Soviet cooperation over Iraq's invasion of Kuwait; the unprecedented use of the United Nations in the Persian Gulf crisis; and upheavals within the Soviet Union itself. On an economic level, such an order seems to be evolving, but important differences remain. Consider, for example, the unprecedented economic assistance offered by the U.S. to the Soviet Union to meet its food needs during the winter of 1990-91, the movement toward a North American free trade area, and the proposed completion of the single market within the European Community by 1992. But, on the other hand, also consider the continuing economic friction between the U.S., Japan, and the European Community; the agonizing efforts to liberalize international trade through the GATT (the General Agreements on Tariffs and Trade) during the early 1990s; and largely unresolved trade problems between the developed and developing states since the 1970s.

CONCLUDING COMMENTS

Which approach (or combination of these approaches) will emerge as the basis of a new foreign policy consensus in the years ahead? A return to domestic values? A movement toward greater unilateralism? The development of a new world order? We obviously cannot say with any certainty, because the public and elite debate continues. Nevertheless, these three contrasting approaches continue to highlight the fact that one important part of the value debate has largely been resolved, while another remains largely unresolved. These and other approaches generally agree upon the need for continued American *involvement*, albeit in sharply different forms, but the degree of domestic *moralism* in that policy is still sharply debated. In this sense, one key value that was closely associated with America's past has been changed dramatically, but the other continues to be a center of controversy.

While we believe that the consensus debate—which has been going on for two decades—needs to be brought to some resolution soon, its continuance does not have to be wholly debilitating for the American public. Writing at the end of the Vietnam War, political analyst Richard Holbrooke captured the painful, yet hopeful, situation the United States faced at that time, and his comments remain equally applicable to the 1990s:

> We have been going through a relentless and grueling reexamination of ourselves, a period of self-revelation and public exposure that might have caused a revolution in a country less strong than ours. . . . What is vitally important is that we learn from our mistakes and our past, but not give up our dreams and values as a nation.[43]

NOTES

1. See Charles W. Kegley and Eugene R. Wittkopf, *American Foreign Policy: Pattern and Process*, 4th ed. (New York: St. Martin's Press, 1991) for an argument along these lines.
2. Ole R. Holsti and James N. Rosenau, "A Leadership Divided: The Foreign Policy Beliefs of American Leaders, 1976–1980," in Charles W. Kegley, Jr.,

and Eugene R. Wittkopf, eds., *Perspectives on American Foreign Policy* (New York: St. Martin's Press, 1983), pp. 196–212. Lengthy discussion of the policy implications of each of these belief systems can be found in this article. The inferences about these competing leadership belief systems are based upon analysis of a 1976 survey of 2,282 individuals and "included military officers, business executives, Foreign Service officers, media leaders, clergy, labor leaders, public officials, and lawyers, among others" (p. 208). An earlier article by Holsti, "The Three-Headed Eagle: The United States and System Change," *International Studies Quarterly* 23 (September 1979): 339–359, also discusses these three belief systems and was used as a reference here.

   3. Holsti and Rosenau, in their book on the subject, *American Leadership in World Affairs* (Boston: Allen and Unwin, 1984), now label this third grouping as "Semi-Isolationists," although the description of the group remains the same as before. For the purposes of our analysis, we shall retain the earlier label.

   4. Holsti and Rosenau, "A Leadership Divided: The Foreign Policy Beliefs of American Leaders, 1976–1980," p. 199.

   5. Ibid., pp. 200–204.

   6. The issues and the spokespersons are from Holsti and Rosenau, *American Leadership in World Affairs*, pp. 122–123, 125–126.

   7. Holsti and Rosenau, "A Leadership Divided," pp. 208, 210.

   8. Ole R. Holsti and James N. Rosenau, "America's Foreign Policy Agenda: The Post-Vietnam Beliefs of American Leaders," in Charles W. Kegley, Jr., and Patrick J. McGowan, eds., *Challenges to America: United States Foreign Policy in the 1980's* (Beverly Hills, CA: Sage Publications, 1979), pp. 263, 267. Holsti and Rosenau also conducted a leadership survey in 1980 similar to their 1976 one. The results of their analysis were remarkably similar to those for 1976: "Deep cleavages on many fundamental issues persisted, and they tended to reflect differences on the Vietnam War, ideology, and occupation, rather than such other attributes as sex, generation, or military service." See Holsti and Rosenau, "A Leadership Divided: The Foreign Policy Beliefs of American Leaders, 1976–1980," p. 210.

   9. See Eugene R. Wittkopf, "Elites and Masses: Constancy and Change in Public Attitudes Toward America's World Role," a paper delivered at the annual meeting of the Southern Political Science Association, Birmingham, Alabama, November 1983; Eugene R. Wittkopf and Michael A. Maggiotto, "Elites and Masses: A Comparative Analysis of Attitudes Toward America's World Role," *The Journal of Politics* 45 (May 1983): 303–334; and Eugene R. Wittkopf, *Faces of Internationalism: Public Opinion and American Foreign Policy* (Durham, NC: Duke University Press, 1990), pp. 107–133.

   10. Ibid.

   11. Ole R. Holsti and James N. Rosenau, "The Structure of Foreign Policy Attitudes Among American Leaders," *Journal of Politics* 52 (February 1990): 94–125.

   12. See Wittkopf and Maggiotto, "Elites and Masses: A Comparative Analysis of Attitudes Toward America's World Role," especially pp. 312–323, and Wittkopf, "Elites and Masses: Constancy and Change in Public Attitudes Toward America's Role" for these arguments; also Wittkopf, *Faces of Internationalism: Public Opinion and American Foreign Policy.*

   13. The table and the discussion is from John E. Rielly, ed., *American Public Opinion and U.S. Foreign Policy 1991* (Chicago: The Chicago Council on Foreign Relations, 1991), pp. 37–38.

14. Lincoln P. Bloomfield, ''Foreign Policy for Disillusioned Liberals,'' *Foreign Policy* 9 (Winter 1972/73): 55–68; Thomas L. Hughes, "The Flight from Foreign Policy," *Foreign Policy* 10 (Spring 1973): 141–156; and Philip Windsor, "America's Moral Confusion: Separating the Should from the Good," *Foreign Policy* 13 (Winter 1973/74): 139–153. A survey of *Foreign Affairs*, the other leading journal on foreign policy, produced a number of commentaries on this breakdown of the old consensus and a need for another set of unifying values purposes. Interested readers should see, for example, John V. Lindsay, "For a New Policy Balance," *Foreign Affairs* 50 (October 1971): 1–14; Kingman Brewster, Jr., "Reflections on Our National Purpose," *Foreign Affairs* 50 (April 1972): 399–415; Zbigniew Brzezinski, "U.S. Foreign Policy: The Search for Focus," *Foreign Affairs* 51 (July 1973): 708–727; and Max Lerner, "America Agonistes," *Foreign Affairs* 52 (January 1974): 287–300.

15. Charles W. Maynes, "Who Pays for Foreign Policy?"*Foreign Policy* 15 (Summer 1974): 152–168. See the exchange among Earl C. Ravenal, Charles W. Maynes, Jr., Richard A. Falk, Hans J. Morgenthau, Daniel P. Moynihan, Bruce M. Russett, and Arthur Schlesinger, Jr., in "Who Pays for Foreign Policy? A Debate on Consensus," *Foreign Policy* 18 (Spring 1975): 80–122.

16. Zbigniew Brzezinski, "America in a Hostile World," *Foreign Policy* 23 (Summer 1976): 89.

17. Stanley Hoffmann, *Primacy or World Order* (New York: McGraw-Hill, 1978).

18. Thomas L. Hughes, "The Crack-Up: The Price of Collective Irresponsibility," *Foreign Policy* 40 (Fall 1980): 33–60. Actually Hughes argues that the two "cultures" have always existed in the postwar period, even during the time of presumed consensus before Vietnam. At that time, however, there had been a "workable dissensus" (p. 52). This point raises the larger issue of the extent to which the Cold War consensus was a true consensus. Admittedly, the systematic empirical evidence for the present dissensus among the leadership and the public is more readily available than that for the consensus of the immediate postwar years. Some systematic research, however, is available to evaluate the generally held assumptions. See Eugene R. Wittkopf and James M. McCormick, "The Cold War Consensus: Did It Exist?" *Polity* 22 (Summer 1990): 627–653.

19. Alexander Haig, "Opening Statement at Confirmation Hearings" (Washington, D.C.: Bureau of Public Affairs, Department of State, January 9, 1981), p. 3.

20. John H. Sigler, "Descent from Olympus: The Search for a New Consensus, *International Journal* 38 (Winter 1982/83): 18–38.

21. Arthur Schlesinger, Jr., "Foreign Policy and the American Character," *Foreign Affairs* 62 (Fall 1983): 1–16.

22. Dick Clark, *A Foreign Policy for the United States in the 1980's and 1990's* (New York: Aspen Institute for Humanistic Studies, 1983).

23. See, for example, Andrew Rosenthal, "Farewell, Red Menace," *New York Times*, September 1, 1991, pp. 1 and 14.

24. James Chace, "Is a Foreign Policy Consensus Possible?" *Foreign Affairs* 57 (Fall 1978): 16.

25. I am indebted to Professor Ole Holsti of Duke University for suggesting this point about consensus on issues.

26. Chace, "Is a Foreign Policy Consensus Possible?" p. 15. Actually Chace quotes from Hoffmann's *Primacy and Order* to make this point.

27. Leslie H. Gelb with Richard K. Betts, *The Irony of Vietnam: The System Worked* (Washington, D.C.: The Brookings Institution, 1979), pp. 365–369.

28. Ibid., pp. 365 and 366.

29. Hughes, "The Crack-Up: The Price of Collective Irresponsibility," p. 59.

30. For the classic statement of the impact of international events on domestic images, see Karl W. Deutsch, "External Influences on the Internal Behavior of States, in R. Barry Farrell, ed., *Approaches to Comparative and International Politics* (Evanston, IL: Northwestern University Press, 1966), pp. 5–26.

31. Earl C. Ravenal, "The Case for Adjustment," *Foreign Policy* 81 (Winter 1990/91): 3–19.

32. Ibid., pp. 3, 4, 6, and 8.

33. Ibid.; p. 15 is the source of the quotation. The discussion of changed defense needs follows at pp. 16–17.

34. Ibid., p. 19. An even more recent statement of a unilateralist approach can be found in Alan Tonelson, "What is the National Interest?" *The Atlantic Monthly* (July 1991): 35ff.

35. Norman J. Ornstein and Mark Schmitt, "Dateline Campaign '92: Post–Cold War Politics," *Foreign Policy* 79 (Summer 1990): 176–182.

36. See Rielly, *American Public Opinion and U.S. Foreign Policy 1991* (Chicago: The Chicago Council on Foreign Relations, 1991), and his "Public Opinion: The Pulse of the '90s," *Foreign Policy* 82 (Spring 1991): 79–96.

37. This section relies upon Quester, "Consensus Lost," *Foreign Policy* 40 (Fall 1980): 18–32. The quoted phrases are at pp. 22, 29, and 31. A more complete analysis of his views is presented in George Quester, *American Foreign Policy: The Lost Consensus* (New York: Praeger, 1982).

38. The comment is by Congressman Les Aspin (D-Wisconsin), quoted in Ornstein and Schmitt, "Dateline Campaign '92: Post–Cold War Politics," p. 184.

39. Ibid., p. 185.

40. This discussion is drawn from Hoffmann, *Primacy or World Order*, pp. 241–266.

41. Ibid., p. 265.

42. Joseph S. Nye, Jr., "American Strategy after Bipolarity," *International Affairs* 66 (July 1990): 513–521. The quotations are from pp. 520–521.

43. Richard Holbrooke, "A Sense of Drift, A Time for Calm," in Steven C. Spiegel, ed. *At Issue: Politics in the Global Arena* (New York: St. Martin's Press, 1977), p. 12.

A SELECTED BIBLIOGRAPHY

Acheson, Dean. *Present at the Creation*. New York: W. W. Norton & Company, 1969.

Adler, David Gray. "The Constitution and Presidential Warmaking: The Enduring Debate," *Political Science Quarterly* 103 (Spring 1988): 1–36.

Aldrich, John H., Sullivan, John L., and Borgida, Eugene. "Foreign Affairs and Issue Voting: Do Presidential Candidates 'Waltz Before a Blind Audience'?" *American Political Science Review* 83 (March 1989): 123–141.

Allison, Graham. *Essence of Decision: Explaining the Cuban Missile Crisis*. Boston: Little, Brown & Co., 1971.

Almond, Gabriel A. *The American People and Foreign Policy*. New York: Praeger, 1960.

Almond, Gabriel, and Verba, Sidney. *The Civic Culture*. Boston: Little, Brown & Co., 1963.

Alperovitz, Gar. *Atomic Diplomacy: Hiroshima and Potsdam*. New York: Random House, 1965.

Ambrose, Stephen E. *Rise to Globalism: American Foreign Policy 1938–1976*. New York: Penguin Books, 1976.

Aron, Raymond. "Ideology in Search of a Policy." In *America and the World 1981*, William P. Bundy, ed. New York: Pergamon Press, 1982.

Bailey, Thomas A. *A Diplomatic History of the American People*. New York: F. S. Crofts & Co., 1942.

———. *The Man on the Street: The Impact of American Public Opinion on Foreign Policy*. New York: Macmillan, Inc., 1948.

Bay, Christian. *The Structure of Freedom*. New York: Atheneum Publishers, 1965.

Bennet, Douglas J., Jr. "Congress in Foreign Policy: Who Needs It?" *Foreign Affairs* 57 (Fall 1978): 40–50.

Beres, Louis René. *People, States, and World Order*. Itasca, IL: F. E. Peacock Publishers, Inc., 1981.

Berkowitz, Morton, Bock, P. G., and Fuccillo, Vincent. *The Politics of American Foreign Policy*. Englewood Cliffs, NJ: Prentice-Hall, Inc., 1977.

Bernstein, Robert A., and Anthony, William W. "The ABM Issue in the Senate, 1968–1970: The Importance of Ideology." *American Political Science Review* 68 (September 1974): 1198–1206.

Berry, Nicholas O., ed. *U.S. Foreign Policy Documents, 1933–1945: From Withdrawal to World Leadership*. Brunswick, OH: King's Court Communications, Inc., 1978.

Betts, Richard K. "Misadventure Revisited." In *A Reader in American Foreign Policy*, James M. McCormick, ed. Itasca, IL: F. E. Peacock Publishers, Inc., 1986.

Blechman, Barry M., and Kaplan, Stephen S. *Force Without War.* Washington, D.C.: The Brookings Institution, 1978.

Bliss, Howard, and Johnson, M. Glen. *Beyond the Water's Edge: America's Foreign Policies.* Philadelphia: J. B. Lippincott Co., 1975.

———. *Consensus at the Crossroads: Dialogues in American Foreign Policy.* New York: Dodd, Mead & Co., Inc., 1972.

Bloomfield, Lincoln P. "Foreign Policy for Disillusioned Liberals?" *Foreign Policy* 9 (Winter 1972/73): 55–68.

———. "From Ideology to Program to Policy." *Journal of Policy Analysis and Management* 2 (Fall 1982): 1–12.

———. *In Search of American Foreign Policy.* New York: Oxford University Press, 1974.

Boorstin, Daniel J. *America and the Image of Europe: Reflections on American Thought.* New York: Meridian Books, 1960.

Brewer, Thomas L. *American Foreign Policy: A Contemporary Introduction.* Englewood Cliffs, NJ: Prentice-Hall, Inc., 1980.

Brewster, Kingman, Jr. "Reflection on our National Purpose." *Foreign Affairs* 50 (April 1972): 339–415.

Brown, Seyom. *The Faces of Power: Constancy and Change in United States Foreign Policy from Truman to Reagan.* New York: Columbia University Press, 1983.

Browne, Majorie Ann. *Executive Agreements and the Congress.* Issue Brief Number IB75035. Washington, D.C.: The Library of Congress, 1981.

Brownstein, Ronald, and Easton, Nina. *Reagan's Ruling Class.* Washington, D.C.: The Presidential Accountability Group, 1982.

Brzezinski, Zbigniew. "America in a Hostile World." *Foreign Policy* 23 (Summer 1976): 65–96.

———. "How the Cold War Was Played." *Foreign Affairs* 51 (October 1972): 181–204.

———. *Power and Principle: Memoirs of the National Security Adviser, 1977–1981.* New York: Farrar, Straus, Giroux, 1983.

———. "U.S. Foreign Policy: The Search for Focus." *Foreign Affairs* 51 (July 1973): 708–727.

Buckley, William F., Jr. "Human Rights and Foreign Policy." *Foreign Affairs* 58 (Spring 1980): 775–796.

Bull, Hedley. "A View From Abroad: Consistency Under Pressure." In *America and the World 1978,* William P. Bundy, ed. New York: Pergamon Press, 1979.

Bundy, William P. "A Portentous Year." In *America and the World 1983,* William P. Bundy, ed. New York: Pergamon Press, 1984.

Campbell, Colin. *Managing the Presidency: Carter, Reagan, and the Search for Executive Harmony.* Pittsburgh: University of Pittsburgh, 1986.

Campbell, John Franklin. "The Disorganization of State." In *Problems of American Foreign Policy,* 2nd ed., Martin B. Hickman, ed. Beverly Hills, CA: Glencoe Press, 1975.

Carter, Jimmy. *Keeping Faith.* New York: Bantam Books, 1982.

Caspary, William R. "The 'Mood Theory': A Study of Public Opinion and Foreign Policy." *The American Political Science Review* 54 (June 1970): 536–547.

Chace, James. "Is a Foreign Policy Consensus Possible?" *Foreign Affairs* 57 (Fall 1978):1–16.

The Challenge of Peace: God's Promise and Our Response. Washington, D.C.: The United States Catholic Conference, May 3, 1983.

Choate, Pat. *Agents of Influence.* New York: Alfred A. Knopf Inc., 1990.

Christopher, Warren. "Ceasefire Between the Branches: A Compact in Foreign Affairs." *Foreign Affairs* 60 (Summer 1982): 989–1005.

Clarke, Duncan L. "Why State Can't Lead." *Foreign Policy* 66 (Spring 1987): 128–142.

Clausen, Aage R. *How Congressmen Decide: A Policy Focus.* New York: St. Martin's Press, 1973.

Clausewitz, Carl von. *On War,* edited and translated by Michael Howard and Peter Paret. Princeton, NJ: Princeton University Press, 1976.

Cohen, Bernard. *The Political Process and Foreign Policy: The Making of the Japanese Settlement.* Princeton, NJ: Princeton University Press, 1957.

———. *The Public's Impact on Foreign Policy.* Boston: Little, Brown & Co., 1973.

Cohen, Stephen D. *The Making of United States Economic Policy,* 3rd ed. New York: Praeger, 1988.

Coles, Harry L. *The War of 1812.* Chicago: The University of Chicago Press, 1965.

Collier, Ellen C. "Foreign Policy by Reporting Requirement." *The Washington Quarterly* 11 (Winter 1988): 75–84.

Congress and the Nation 1945–1964. Washington, D.C.: Congressional Quarterly, Inc., 1965.

Congressional Quarterly's Guide to Congress, 3rd ed. Washington, D.C.: Congressional Quarterly, Inc., 1982.

Cooke, Jacob E., ed. *The Federalist.* Middletown, CT: Wesleyan University Press, 1961.

Cooper, Chester L. "The CIA and Decisionmaking." *Foreign Affairs* 50 (January 1972): 221–236.

Corwin, Edward S. *The President: Office and Powers 1787–1957.* New York: New York University Press, 1957.

Crabb, Cecil V., Jr. *Bipartisan Foreign Policy.* Evanston, IL: Row, Peterson and Company, 1957.

———. *The Elephants and the Grass: A Study of Nonalignment.* New York: Frederick A. Praeger, Inc., 1965.

———. *Policymakers and Critics: Conflicting Theories of American Foreign Policy.* New York: Frederick A. Praeger, Inc., 1976.

———, and Holt, Pat M. *Invitation to Struggle: Congress, the President, and Foreign Policy.* Washington, D.C.: Congressional Quarterly Press, 1980.

Dahl, Robert A. *Congress and Foreign Policy.* New York: Harcourt, Brace and Company, 1950.

———. *Modern Political Analysis,* 2nd ed. Englewood Cliffs, NJ: Prentice-Hall, Inc., 1970.

Dallek, Robert. *The American Style of Foreign Policy.* New York: Alfred A. Knopf Inc., 1983.

De la Garza, Rodolfo O. "U.S. Foreign Policy and the Mexican-American Political Agenda." In *Ethnic Groups and U.S. Foreign Policy,* Mohammed E. Ahrari, ed. New York: Greenwood Press, 1987.

Destler, I. M. "Dateline Washington: Congress as Boss?" *Foreign Policy* 42 (Spring 1981): 167–180.

———. "National Security Advice to U.S. Presidents: Some Lessons from Thirty Years." *World Politics* 24 (January 1977): 143–176.

———. "National Security Management: What Presidents Have Wrought." *Political Science Quarterly* 95 (Winter 1980/81): 573–588.

———. *Presidents, Bureaucrats, and Foreign Policy.* Princeton, NJ: Princeton University Press, 1974.

————, Gelb, Leslie H., and Lake, Anthony. *Our Own Worst Enemy: The Unmaking of American Foreign Policy*. New York: Simon and Schuster, 1984.

Deutsch, Karl W. "External Influence on the Internal Behavior of States." In *Approaches to Comparative and International Politics*, R. Barry Farrell, ed. Evanston, IL: Northwestern University Press, 1966.

Devine, Donald J. *The Political Culture of the United States*. Boston: Little, Brown & Co., 1972.

Donovan, John C. *The Cold Warriors: A Policy-Making Elite*. Lexington, MA: D. C. Heath and Company, 1974.

Drew, Elizabeth. "A Reporter At Large: Brzezinski." *The New Yorker* (May 1, 1978): 90–130.

Dye, Thomas R. *Who's Running America? Institutional Leadership in the United States*. Englewood Cliffs, NJ: Prentice-Hall, Inc., 1976.

————. *Who's Running America? The Bush Era*. Englewood Cliffs, NJ: Prentice-Hall, Inc., 1990.

Easton, David. *The Political System*. New York: Alfred A. Knopf Inc., 1953.

Eisenhower, Dwight D. "The Military-Industrial Complex." In *Power in Postwar America*, Richard Gillam, ed. Boston: Little, Brown & Co., 1971.

Esterline, John H., and Black, Robert B. *Inside Foreign Policy: The Department of State Political System and Its Subsystem*. Palo Alto, CA: Mayfield Publishing Company, 1975.

Etzold, Thomas H. "The Far East in American Strategy, 1948–1951." In *Aspects of Sino-American Relations Since 1784*, Thomas H. Etzold, ed. New York: New Viewpoints, 1978.

Executive Legislative Consultation on Foreign Policy: Strengthening Foreign Policy Information Sources for Congress. Washington, D.C.: U.S. Government Printing Office, February, 1982.

Falk, Richard A. "What's Wrong with Henry Kissinger's Foreign Policy?" *Alternatives* 1 (March 1975): 79–100.

Fenno, Richard F., Jr. *Congressmen in Committees*. Boston: Little, Brown & Co., 1973.

Ferguson, Yale H., and Mansbach, Richard W. *The Elusive Quest: Theory and International Politics*. Columbia, SC: University of South Carolina Press, 1988.

Fernandez, Damian J. "From Little Havana to Washington, D.C.: Cuban-Americans and U.S. Foreign Policy." In *Ethnic Groups and U.S. Foreign Policy*, Mohammed E. Ahrari, ed. New York: Greenwood Press, 1987.

Ferrell, Robert H. *American Diplomacy: A History*. New York: W. W. Norton & Company, 1975.

————. *American Diplomacy: The Twentieth Century*. New York: W. W. Norton & Company, 1988.

Fisher, Louis. *The President and Congress: Power and Policy*. New York: Free Press, 1972.

Fleisher, Richard. "Economic Benefit, Ideology, and Senate Voting on the B-1 Bomber." *American Politics Quarterly* 13 (April 1985): 200–211.

————, and Bond, Jon R. "Are There Two Presidencies? Yes, But Only for Republicans." *The Journal of Politics* 50 (August 1988): 747–767.

Fleming, D. F. *The Cold War and Its Origins, 1917–1960*. New York: Doubleday & Co., Inc., 1961.

Franck, Thomas M., and Weisband, Edward. *Foreign Policy by Congress*. New York: Oxford University Press, 1979.

Free, Lloyd A., and Cantril, Hadley. *The Political Beliefs of Americans: A Study of Public Opinion*. New York: Simon & Schuster, 1968.

Freedman, Lawrence. *The Evolution of Nuclear Strategy.* New York: St. Martin's Press, 1981.

Fulbright, J. William. *The Arrogance of Power.* New York: Vintage Books, 1966.

Furlong, William L. "Negotiations and Ratification of the Panama Canal Treaties." In *Congress, the Presidency, and American Foreign Policy,* John Spanier and Joseph Nogee, eds. New York: Pergamon Press, 1981.

Gaddis, John Lewis. "Containment: A Reassessment." *Foreign Affairs* 55 (July 1977): 873–887.

———. *The Soviet Union and the United States: An Interpretative History.* New York: John Wiley & Sons, Inc., 1978.

———. *Strategies of Containment.* New York: Oxford University Press, 1982.

———. *The United States and the Origins of the Cold War 1941–1947.* New York and London: Columbia University Press, 1972.

———. "Was the Truman Doctrine a Real Turning Point?" *Foreign Affairs* 52 (January 1974): 386–402.

Garnham, David. "Foreign Service Elitism and U.S. Foreign Affairs." *Public Administration Review* 35 (January/February 1975): 44–51.

———. "State Department Rigidity: Testing a Psychological Hypothesis." *International Studies Quarterly* 18 (March 1974): 31–39.

Gelb, Leslie H., with Betts, Richard K. *The Irony of Vietnam: The System Worked.* Washington, D.C.: The Brookings Institution, 1979.

Gershman, Carl. *The Foreign Policy of American Labor.* The Washington Papers, 3, no. 29. Beverly Hills, CA: Sage Publications, 1975.

Grosser, Alfred. *French Foreign Policy under DeGaulle.* Boston: Little, Brown & Co., 1965.

Gulick, Edward V. *Europe's Classical Balance of Power.* Ithaca, NY: Cornell University Press, 1955.

Hackett, Clifford. "Ethnic Politics in Congress: The Turkish Embargo Experience." In *Ethnicity and U.S. Foreign Policy,* Abdul Aziz Said, ed. New York: Praeger, 1981.

Haig, Alexander. *Opening Statement at Confirmation Hearings.* Washington, D.C.: Bureau of Public Affairs, Department of State, January 9, 1981.

———. *A Strategic Approach to American Foreign Policy.* Washington, D.C.: Bureau of Public Affairs, Department of State, August 11, 1981.

Halperin, Morton H., with the assistance of Priscilla Clapp and Arnold Kanter. *Bureaucratic Politics and Foreign Policy.* Washington, D.C.: The Brookings Institution, 1974.

Hamilton, Lee H., and Van Dusen, Michael H. "Making the Separation of Powers Work." *Foreign Affairs* 57 (Fall 1978): 17–39.

Hansen, Roger D., Fishlow, Albert, Paarlberg, Robert, and Lewis, John P. *U.S. Foreign Policy and the Third World Agenda 1982.* New York: Praeger, 1982.

Hart, Albert Bushnell. *The Monroe Doctrine: An Interpretation.* Boston: Little, Brown & Co., 1916.

Henkin, Louis. *Foreign Affairs and the Constitution.* Mineola, NY: The Foundation Press, Inc., 1972.

———. "Foreign Affairs and the Constitution." *Foreign Affairs* 66 (Winter 1987/88): 284–310.

Herring, George C. *America's Longest War: The United States and Vietnam 1950–1975,* 2nd ed. New York: Alfred A. Knopf Inc., 1986.

Hicks, Sallie M., and Couloumbis, Theodore A. "The 'Greek Lobby': Illusion or Reality?" In *Ethnicity and U.S. Foreign Policy,* Abdul Aziz Said, ed. New York: Praeger, 1981.

Hilsman, Roger. *To Move a Nation.* Garden City, NY: Doubleday Publishing, 1964.

Hinckley, Barbara. *Stability and Change in Congress,* 3rd ed. New York: Harper & Row, 1983.

Hoffmann, Stanley. "Carter's Soviet Problem." *The New Republic* 79 (July 29, 1978): 20–23.

———. *Gulliver's Troubles, or the Setting of American Foreign Policy.* New York: McGraw-Hill, 1968.

———. *Primacy or World Order.* New York: McGraw-Hill, 1978.

———. "Requiem." *Foreign Policy* 42 (Spring 1981): 3–26.

———. "A View From At Home: The Perils of Incoherence." In *America and the World 1978,* William P. Bundy, ed. New York: Pergamon Press, 1979.

Holbrooke, Richard. "A Sense of Drift, a Time for Calm." In *At Issue: Politics in the Global Arena,* Steven C. Spiegel, ed. New York: St. Martin's Press, 1977.

Holloway, David. "Gorbachev's New Thinking." In *America and the World 1988/89,* William P. Bundy, ed. New York: Council on Foreign Relations, 1989.

Holsti, Ole R. "The Belief System and National Images: A Case Study." *The Journal of Conflict Resolution* 6 (September 1962): 244–252.

———. "The Three-Headed Eagle: The United States and System Change." *International Studies Quarterly* 23 (September 1979): 339–359.

———, and Rosenau, James N. *American Leadership in World Affairs.* Boston: Allen & Unwin, 1984.

———. "America's Foreign Policy Agenda: The Post-Vietnam Beliefs of American Leaders." In *Challenges to America: United States Foreign Policy in the 1980s,* Charles W. Kegley, Jr., and Patrick J. McGowan, eds. Beverly Hills, CA: Sage Publications, 1979.

———. "Does Where You Stand Depend on When You Were Born? The Impact of Generation on Post-Vietnam Foreign Policy Beliefs." *Public Opinion Quarterly* 44 (Spring 1980): 1–22.

———. "A Leadership Divided: The Foreign Policy Beliefs of American Leaders, 1976–1980." In *Perspectives on American Foreign Policy,* Charles W. Kegley, Jr., and Eugene R. Wittkopf, eds. New York: St. Martin's Press, 1983.

———. "The Structure of Foreign Policy Attitudes among Leaders," *Journal of Politics* 52 (February 1990): 94–125.

———. "Vietnam, Consensus, and the Belief Systems of American Leaders." *World Politics* 32 (October 1979): 1–56.

———, Brody, Richard A., and North, Robert C. "The Management of International Crisis: Affect and Action in American-Soviet Relations." In *Theory and Research on the Cause of War,* Dean G. Pruitt and Richard C. Snyder, eds. Englewood Cliffs, NJ: Prentice-Hall, Inc., 1969.

Hoopes, Townsend. *The Limits of Intervention.* New York: David McKay, 1968.

Hopkins, Raymond F., and Puchala, Donald J. *Global Food Interdependence: Challenge to American Foreign Policy.* New York: Columbia University Press, 1980.

Hormat, Robert D. "The World Economy Under Stress." In *America and the World 1985,* William G. Hyland, ed. New York: Pergamon Press, 1986.

Hsiao, Gene T., ed. *Sino-American Détente and Its Policy Implications.* New York: Praeger Publishers, Inc., 1974.

Hughes, Barry B. *The Domestic Context of American Foreign Policy.* San Francisco: Freeman, 1978.

Hughes, Thomas L. "The Crack-Up: The Price of Collective Irresponsibility." *Foreign Policy* 40 (Fall 1980): 33–60.

———. "The Flight from Foreign Policy." *Foreign Policy* 10 (Spring 1973): 141–156.

Hunt, Michael H. *Ideology and U.S. Foreign Policy.* New Haven, CT: Yale University Press, 1987.

Hunter, Robert E. *Presidential Control of Foreign Policy: Management or Mishap?* The Washington Papers/91. New York: Praeger, 1982.

Hurwitz, Jon, and Peffley, Mark. "How Are Foreign Policy Attitudes Structured? A Hierarchical Model." *American Political Science Review* 81 (December 1987): 1099–1120.

Hyland, William G. "U.S.-Soviet Relations: The Long Road Back." In *America and the World 1981,* William P. Bundy, ed. New York: Pergamon Press, 1982.

Janis, Irving. *Victims of Groupthink.* Boston: Houghton Mifflin Company, 1972.

Jensen, Lloyd. *Explaining Foreign Policy.* Englewood Cliffs, NJ: Prentice-Hall, Inc., 1982.

Jentleson, Bruce W. "American Diplomacy: Around the World and Along Pennsylvania Avenue. In *A Question of Balance,* Thomas E. Mann, ed. Washington, D.C.: The Brookings Institution, 1990.

Jervis, Robert. "The Impact of the Korean War on the Cold War." *The Journal of Conflict Resolution* 24 (December 1980): 563–592.

Joffe, Josef. "The Foreign Policy of the German Federal Republic." In *Foreign Policy in World Politics,* 5th ed., Roy C. Macridis, ed. Englewood Cliffs, NJ: Prentice-Hall, Inc., 1976.

Johnson, Loch, and McCormick, James M. "Foreign Policy by Executive Fiat." *Foreign Policy* 28 (Fall 1977): 117–138.

———. "The Making of International Agreements: A Reappraisal of Congressional Involvement." *The Journal of Politics* 40 (May 1978): 468–478.

Jordan, Amos A., Taylor, William J., Jr., and associates. *American National Security: Policy and Process.* Baltimore: The Johns Hopkins University Press, 1981.

Kahler, Miles. "The United States and Western Europe: The Diplomatic Consequences of Mr. Reagan." In *Eagle Defiant: United States Foreign Policy in the 1980s,* Kenneth A. Oye, Robert J. Lieber, and Donald Rothchild, eds. Boston: Little, Brown & Co., 1983.

Kaiser, Fred. "Congressional Control of Executive Actions in the Aftermath of the *Chadha* Decision." *Administrative Law Review* 36 (Summer 1984): 239–274.

———. "Oversight of Foreign Policy: The U.S. House Committee on International Relations." *Legislative Studies Quarterly* 2 (August 1977): 233–254.

———. "Structural and Policy Change: The House Committee on International Relations." *Policy Studies Journal* 5 (Summer 1977): 443–451.

Kaiser, Karl. "Germany's Unification." In *America and the World 1990/1991,* William P. Bundy, ed. New York: Council on Foreign Relations, Inc., 1991.

Karnow, Stanley. *Vietnam: A History.* New York: The Viking Press, 1983.

Katzmann, Robert A. "War Powers: Toward a New Accommodation." In *A Question of Balance,* Thomas E. Mann, ed. Washington, D.C.: The Brookings Institution, 1990.

Kavass, Igor I., and Michael, Mark A. *United States Treaties and Other International Agreements, Cumulative Index 1776–1949.* Buffalo, NY: William S. Hein and Company, Inc., 1975.

Kegley, Charles W. "The Bush Administration and the Future of American Foreign Policy: Pragmatism or Procastination?" *Presidential Studies Quarterly* 19 (Fall 1989): 717–731.

———, and Wittkopf, Eugene R. *American Foreign Policy: Pattern and Process*, 4th ed. New York: St. Martin's Press, 1991.

———. "Beyond Consensus: The Domestic Context of American Foreign Policy." *International Journal* 38 (Winter 1982/83): 77–106.

Kellerman, Barbara, and Barilleaux, Ryan J. *The President as World Leader.* New York: St. Martin's Press, 1991.

Kennan, George. *American Diplomacy 1900–1950.* New York: Mentor Books, 1951.

———. "Containment Then and Now." *Foreign Affairs* 65 (Spring 1987): 885–890.

———. "Is Détente Worth Saving?" *Saturday Review* (March 6, 1976): 12–17.

———. *Memoirs 1925–1950.* Boston: Little, Brown & Co., 1967.

———. "The Sources of Soviet Conduct." *Foreign Affairs* 65 (Spring 1987): 852–868.

Kennedy, Robert F. *Thirteen Days.* New York: Signet Books, 1969.

Kihl, Young W. *Politics and Policies in Divided Korea: Regimes in Contest.* Boulder, CO: Westview Press, 1984.

Kirkpatrick, Jeane J. "Dictatorships and Double Standards." *Commentary* 68 (November 1979): 34–45.

Kissinger, Henry A. *American Foreign Policy,* 3rd ed. New York: W. W. Norton & Company, 1977.

———. "Domestic Structure and Foreign Policy." In *International Politics and Foreign Policy,* rev. ed., James N. Rosenau, ed. New York: Free Press, 1969.

———. *A World Restored: Metternich, Castlereagh, and Problems of Peace 1812–1822.* Boston: Houghton Mifflin Company, 1957.

Knight, Andrew. "Ronald Reagan's Watershed Year?" In *America and the World 1982,* William P. Bundy, ed. New York: Pergamon Press, 1983.

Kolko, Gabriel. *The Roots of American Foreign Policy.* Boston: Beacon Press, 1969.

Kolodziej, Edward A. *French International Policy under DeGaulle and Pompidou.* Ithaca, NY: Cornell University Press, 1974.

———. "Revolt and Revisionism in the Gaullist Global Vision: An Analysis of French Strategic Policy." *Journal of Politics* 33 (May 1971): 448–477.

Kondracke, Morton. "The Greek Lobby." *The New Republic* (April 29, 1978): 14–16.

Korb, Lawrence J. *The Fall and Rise of the Pentagon: American Defense Policies in the 1970s.* Westport, CT: Greenwood Press, 1979.

———. "The Joint Chiefs of Staff: Access and Impact in Foreign Policy." *Policy Studies Journal* 3 (Winter 1974): 170–173.

———. *The Joint Chiefs of Staff: The First Twenty-Five Years.* Bloomington, IN: Indiana University Press, 1976.

Korbel, Josef. *Détente in Europe: Real or Imaginary?* Princeton, NJ: Princeton University Press, 1972.

Krasner, Stephen D. "The Tokyo Round: Particularistic Interests and Prospects for Stability in the Global Trading System." *International Studies Quarterly* 23 (December 1979): 491–531.

Kurth, James R. "The Military-Industrial Complex Revisited." In *1989–1990 American Defense Annual,* Joseph Kruzel, ed. Lexington, MA: Lexington Books, 1989.

Ladd, Everett C., Jr. "Traditional Values Regnant." *Public Opinion* 1 (March/April 1978): 45–49.

LaFeber, Walter. *America, Russia, and the Cold War 1945–1975.* New York: John Wiley & Sons, Inc., 1976.

———. *The American Age: United States Foreign Policy at Home and Abroad since 1750.* New York: W. W. Norton & Company, 1989.

———. *Inevitable Revolutions: The United States in Central America.* New York: W. W. Norton & Company, 1984.

Lasswell, Harold D. *Politics: Who Gets What, When, and How.* New York: Whittlesey, 1936.

Lawson, Ruth C. *International Regional Organizations: Constitutional Foundations.* New York: Praeger, 1962.

Legg, Keith R. "Congress as Trojan Horse? The Turkish Embargo Problem, 1974–1978." In *Congress, the Presidency, and American Foreign Policy,* John Spanier and Joseph Nogee, eds. New York: Pergamon Press, 1981.

Legum, Colin. "The African Crisis." In *America and the World 1978,* William P. Bundy, ed. New York: Pergamon Press, 1979.

LeLoup, Lance T., and Shull, Steven A. "Congress Versus the Executive: The 'Two Presidencies' Reconsidered." *Social Science Quarterly* 59 (March 1979): 704–719.

Lerche, Charles O., Jr., and Said, Abdul A. *Concepts of International Politics,* 3rd ed. Englewood Cliffs, NJ: Prentice-Hall, Inc., 1979.

Lerner, Max. "America Agonistes." *Foreign Affairs* 52 (January 1974): 287–300.

Levgold, Robert. "The Revolution in Soviet Foreign Policy." In *America and the World 1988/89,* William P. Bundy, ed. New York: Council on Foreign Relations, 1989.

Lieberson, Stanley. "An Empirical Study of Military-Industrial Linkages." *American Journal of Sociology* 76 (January 1971): 562–584.

Lindsay, James M. "Congress and Defense Policy: 1961 to 1986." *Armed Forces and Society* 13 (Spring 1987): 371–401.

———. "Parochialism, Policy, and Constituency Constraints: Congressional Voting and Strategic Weapons Systems." *American Journal of Political Science* 34 (November 1990): 936–960.

Lindsay, John V. "For a New Policy Balance." *Foreign Affairs* 50 (October 1971): 1–14.

Lipset, Seymour Martin. *The First New Nation.* Garden City, NY: Anchor Books, 1967.

Locke, John. *The Second Treatise of Government.* Oxford: Basil Blackwell, 1966.

Lockerbie, Brad, and Borrelli, Stephen A. "Question Wording and Public Support for Contra Aid, 1983–1986." *Public Opinion Quarterly* 54 (Summer 1990): 195–208.

Lomperis, Timothy J. *The War Everyone Lost—and Won.* Washington, D.C.: CQ Press, 1984.

Lynn, Laurence E., Jr., and Smith, Richard I. "Can the Secretary of Defense Make a Difference?" *International Security* 7 (Summer 1982): 45–69.

Maggiotto, Michael, and Wittkopf, Eugene R. "American Public Attitudes Toward Foreign Policy." *International Studies Quarterly* 25 (December 1981): 601–632.

Maier, Charles S., ed. *The Origins of the Cold War and Contemporary Europe.* New York: New Viewpoints, 1978.

Marantz, Paul. "Prelude to Détente: Doctrinal Change under Khrushchev." *International Studies Quarterly* 19 (December 1975): 501–528.

Marchetti, Victor, and Marks, John D. *The CIA and the Cult of Intelligence*. New York: Dell, 1974.

Mark, Eduard. "The Questions of Containment: A Reply to John Lewis Gaddis." *Foreign Affairs* 56 (January 1978): 430–441.

Markus, Gregory B. "Political Attitudes During an Election Year: A Report on the 1980 NES Panel Study." *American Political Science Review* 76 (September 1982): 538–560.

Mathias, Charles McC., Jr. "Ethnic Groups and Foreign Policy." *Foreign Affairs* 59 (Summer 1981): 975–998.

May, Ernest R. *"Lessons" of the Past: The Use and Misuse of History in American Foreign Policy*. New York: Oxford University Press, 1973.

Mayne, Richard. *The Recovery of Europe 1945–1973*. Garden City, NY: Anchor Books, 1973.

Maynes, Charles W. "America without the Cold War." *Foreign Policy* 78 (Spring 1990): 3–25.

———. "Who Pays for Foreign Policy?" *Foreign Policy* 15 (Summer 1974): 152–168.

McClosky, Herbert, Hoffmann, Paul J., and O'Hara, Rosemary. "Issue Conflict and Consensus among Party Leaders and Followers. *The American Political Science Review* 14 (June 1960): 408–427.

McCormick, James M. "The Changing Role of the House Foreign Affairs Committee in the 1970s and 1980s." *Congress & the Presidency* 12 (Spring 1985): 1–20.

———. "Congressional Voting on the Nuclear Freeze Resolutions." *American Politics Quarterly* 13 (January 1985): 122–136.

———. "The NIEO and the Distribution of American Assistance." *The Western Political Quarterly* 37 (March 1984): 100–119.

———, ed. *A Reader in American Foreign Policy*. Itasca, IL: F. E. Peacock Publishers, Inc., 1986.

———, and Black, Michael. "Ideology and Voting on the Panama Canal Treaties." *Legislative Studies Quarterly* 8 (February 1983): 45–63.

———, and Mitchell, Neil. "Human Rights and Foreign Assistance: An Update." *Social Science Quarterly* 70 (December 1989): 969–979.

———, and Smith, Steven S. "The Iran Arms Sale and the Intelligence Oversight Act of 1980." *PS* 20 (Winter 1987): 29–37.

———, and Wittkopf, Eugene R. "At the Water's Edge: The Effects of Party, Ideology and Issues on Congressional Foreign Policy Voting, 1947–1988." *American Politics Quarterly* 20 (January 1992): 26–53.

———. "Bipartisanship, Partisanship, and Ideology in Congressional-Executive Foreign Policy Relations, 1947–1988." *Journal of Politics* 52 (November 1990): 1077–1100.

Mee, Charles L., Jr. *Meeting at Potsdam*. New York: M. Evan & Co., Inc., 1975.

Mendelbaum, Michael. *The Nuclear Question: The United States and Nuclear Weapons 1946–1976*. Cambridge: Cambridge University Press, 1979.

The Middle East: U.S. Policy, Israel, Oil, and the Arabs, 3rd ed. Washington, D.C.: Congressional Quarterly, Inc., 1977.

Miller, Hunter, ed. *Treaties and Other International Acts of the United States of America*, Volume 2. Washington, D.C.: U.S. Government Printing Office, 1931.

Mills, C. Wright. *The Power Elite*. New York: Oxford University Press, 1956.

———. "The Structure of Power in American Society." In *Power in Postwar America*, Richard Gillam, ed. Boston: Little, Brown & Co., 1971.

Molineu, Harold. "Human Rights: Administrative Impact of a Symbolic Policy." In *The Analysis of Policy Impact*, John G. Grumm and Stephen L. Wasby, eds. Lexington, MA: Lexington Books, D. C. Heath and Company, 1981.

Moore, David W. "The Public Is Uncertain." *Foreign Policy* 35 (Summer 1979): 68–73.

Morgenthau, Hans J. *Politics among Nations: The Struggle for Power and Peace.* New York: Alfred A. Knopf Inc., 1973.

Moyer, Wayne. "House Voting in Defense: An Ideological Explanation." In *Military Force and American Society*, Bruce M. Russett and Alfred Stepan, eds. New York: Harper & Row, 1973.

———, and Josling, Timothy E. *Agricultural Policy Reform: Politics and Process in the EC and the USA.* New York: Harvester Wheatsheaf, 1990.

Mueller, John E. *War, Presidents and Public Opinion.* New York: John Wiley & Sons, Inc., 1973.

Nash, Henry T. *American Foreign Policy: Changing Perspectives on National Security.* Homewood, IL: The Dorsey Press, 1978.

Nelson, Michael, ed. *Congressional Quarterly's Guide to the Presidency.* Washington, D.C.: Congressional Quarterly, Inc., 1989.

Newhouse, John. "Profiles (James Baker)." *The New Yorker* (May 7, 1990): 50–82.

Nivola, Pietro S. "Trade Policy: Refereeing the Playing Field. In *A Question of Balance*, Thomas E. Mann, ed. Washington, D.C.: The Brookings Institution, 1990.

Nixon, Richard M. "Asia after Viet Nam." *Foreign Affairs* 46 (October 1967): 111–125.

———. *U.S. Policy for the 1970s: A New Strategy for Peace: A Report to the Congress.* Washington, D.C.: U.S. Government Printing Office, February 12, 1970.

North, Robert C. *The Foreign Relations of China*, 2nd ed. Encino and Belmont, CA: Dickenson Publishing Company, Inc., 1974.

Nye, Russel B. *This Almost Chosen People.* East Lansing, MI: Michigan State University Press, 1966.

Ogley, Roderick, ed. *The Theory and Practice of Neutrality in the Twentieth Century.* New York: Barnes and Noble, Inc., 1970.

Oldfield, Duane M., and Wildavsky, Aaron. "Reconsidering the Two Presidencies." *Society* 26 (July/August 1989): 54–59.

Organski, A. F. K. *World Politics.* New York: Alfred A. Knopf Inc., 1968.

Origins and Development of Congress. Washington, D.C.: Congressional Quarterly, Inc., 1976.

Ornstein, Norman J., and Elder, Shirley. *Interest Groups, Lobbying, and Policymaking.* Washington, D.C.: Congressional Quarterly, Inc., 1978.

———, and Rohde, David W. "Shifting Forces, Changing Rules, and Political Outcomes: The Impact of Congressional Change on Four House Committees." In *New Perspectives on the House of Representatives*, Robert L. Peabody and Nelson W. Polsby, eds. Chicago: Rand McNally, 1967.

———, and Schmitt, Mark. "Dateline Campaign '92: Post–Cold War Politics." *Foreign Policy* 79 (Summer 1990): 169–186.

Osgood, Robert E. *Ideals and Self-Interest in America's Foreign Relations.* Chicago: The University of Chicago Press, 1953.

———. "The Revitalization of Containment." In *America and the World 1981*, William Bundy, ed. New York: Pergamon Press, 1982.

Page, Benjamin I., and Shapiro, Robert Y. "Effects of Public Opinion on Policy," *American Political Science Review* 77 (March 1983): 175–190.

Park, Richard L. "India's Foreign Policy." In *Foreign Policy in World Politics*, 5th ed., Roy C Macridis, ed. Englewood Cliff, NJ: Prentice-Hall, Inc., 1976.

Pastor, Robert. *Congress and the Politics of U.S. Foreign Economic Policy 1929–1976.* Berkeley, CA: University of California Press, 1980.

Payne, James L. *The American Threat.* College Station, TX: Lytton Publishing Company, 1981.

The Pentagon Papers, New York Times Edition. New York: Bantam Books, 1971.

Percy, Charles H. "The Partisan Gap." *Foreign Policy* 45 (Winter 1981/82): 3–15.

Perkins, Dexter. *The American Approach to Foreign Policy.* Cambridge, MA: Harvard University Press, 1962.

———. The Evolution of American Foreign Policy, 2nd ed. New York: Oxford University Press, 1966.

———. *Hands-Off: A History of the Monroe Doctrine.* Boston: Little, Brown & Co., 1941.

Pierre, Andrew J. *The Global Politics of Arms Sales.* Princeton, NJ: Princeton University Press, 1982.

Pilisuk, Marc, with the assistance of Larudee, Mehrene. *International Conflict and Social Policy.* Englewood Cliffs, NJ: Prentice-Hall, Inc., 1972.

Pomper, Gerald. *Elections in America: Control and Influence in Democratic Politics.* New York: Dodd, Mead & Co., Inc., 1968.

———, with Lederman, Susan S. *Elections in America: Control and Influence in Democratic Politics*, 2nd ed. New York: Longman, 1980.

Pringle, Robert. "Creeping Irrelevance at Foggy Bottom." *Foreign Policy* 29 (Winter 1977/78): 128–139.

Proxmire, William. "The Community of Interests in Our Defense Contract Spending." In *Power in Postwar America*, Richard Gillam, ed. Boston: Little, Brown & Co., 1971.

Quester, George. *American Foreign Policy: The Lost Consensus.* New York: Praeger, 1982.

Ransom, Harry Howe. *The Intelligence Establishment.* Cambridge, MA: Harvard University Press, 1970.

Ravenal, Earl C. "The Case for Adjustment." *Foreign Policy* 81 (Winter 1990/91): 3–19.

———, et al. "Who Pays for Foreign Policy? A Debate on Consensus." *Foreign Policy* 18 (Spring 1975): 80–122.

Ray, James Lee. *Global Politics*, 2nd ed. Boston: Houghton Mifflin Company, 1983.

Report of the Congressional Committees Investigating the Iran-Contra Affair. Washington, D.C.: U.S. Government Printing Office, November 1987.

Report of the President's Special Review Board (Tower Commission Report). Washington, D.C.: U.S. Government Printing Office, February 26, 1987.

Report to the President by the Commission on CIA Activities within the United States. Washington, D.C.: U.S. Government Printing Office, June 1975.

Rielly, John E. "Public Opinion: The Pulse of the '90s." *Foreign Policy* 82 (Spring 1991): 79–96.

———. "America's State of Mind." *Foreign Policy* 66 (Spring 1987): 39–56.

———. "American Opinion: Continuity, Not Reaganism." *Foreign Policy* 50 (Spring 1983): 86–104.

———. "The American Mood: A Foreign Policy of Self-Interest." *Foreign Policy* 34 (Spring 1979): 74–86.

———, ed. *American Public Opinion and U.S. Foreign Policy 1975*. Chicago: Chicago Council on Foreign Relations, 1975.

———, ed. *American Public Opinion and U.S. Foreign Policy 1979*. Chicago: Chicago Council on Foreign Relations, 1979.

———, ed. *American Public Opinion and U.S. Foreign Policy 1983*. Chicago: Chicago Council on Foreign Relations, 1983.

———, ed. *American Public Opinion and U.S. Foreign Policy 1987*. Chicago: Chicago Council on Foreign Relations, 1987.

———, ed. *American Public Opinion and U.S. Foreign Policy 1991*. Chicago: Chicago Council on Foreign Relations, 1991.

Ripley, Randall. *Congress: Process and Policy*, 2nd ed. New York: W. W. Norton and Company, 1978.

Rizopoulous, Nicholas, ed. *Sea-Changes: American Foreign Policy in a World Transformed*. New York: Council on Foreign Relations Press, 1990.

Robinson, James A. *Congress and Foreign Policy-Making*, rev. ed. Homewood, IL: The Dorsey Press, 1967.

Rockman, Bert A. "America's Departments of State: Irregular and Regular Syndromes of Policymaking." *American Political Science Review* 75 (December 1981): 911–927.

Rokeach, Milton. *Beliefs, Attitudes, and Values*. San Francisco: Jossey-Bass, Inc., 1953.

Rosenberg, Milton J., Verba, Sidney, and Converse, Philip E. *Vietnam and the Silent Majority*. New York: Harper & Row, 1970.

Rosenfeld, Stephen S. "Dateline Washington: Anti-Semitism and U.S. Foreign Policy." *Foreign Policy* 47 (Summer 1982): 172–183.

Russett, Bruce. "The Americans' Retreat from World Power." *Political Science Quarterly* 90 (Spring 1975): 1–22.

———. "Defense Expenditures and National Well-being." *American Political Science Review* 76 (December 1982): 767–777.

———. *The Prisoners of Insecurity*. San Francisco: W. H. Freeman and Company, 1983.

———, and Deluca, Donald R. " 'Don't Tread on Me': Public Opinion and Foreign Policy in the Eighties." *Political Science Quarterly* 96 (Fall 1981): 381–399.

———, and Hanson, Elizabeth C. *Interest and Ideology: The Foreign Policy Beliefs of American Businessmen*. San Francisco: W. H. Freeman and Company, 1975.

Said, Abdul Aziz. *Ethnicity and U.S. Foreign Policy*, rev. ed. New York: Praeger, 1981.

Salisbury, Harrison E. *War Between China and Russia*. New York: W. W. Norton & Company, 1969.

Schlesinger, Arthur, Jr. "Congress and the Making of American Foreign Policy." *Foreign Affairs* 51 (October 1972): 78–113.

———. "Foreign Policy and the American Character." *Foreign Affairs* 62 (Fall 1983): 1–16.

———. "Human Rights and the American Tradition." *Foreign Affairs* 57 (Winter 1978/79): 503–526.

———. *The Imperial Presidency*. Boston: Houghton Mifflin Company, 1973.

Schlesinger, James. "The Role of the Secretary of Defense." In *Reorganizing America's Defense: Leadership in War and Peace*, Robert J. Art, Vincent Davis, and Samuel P. Huntington, eds. Washington, D.C.: Pergamon-Brassey's, 1985.

Schoultz, Lars. "Politics, Economics, and U.S. Participation in Multilateral Development Banks." *International Organization* 36 (Summer 1982): 537–574.

Scott, Andrew M. "The Department of State: Formal Organization and Informal Culture." *International Studies Quarterly* 13 (March 1969): 1–18.

———. "The Problem of the State Department." In *Problems of American Foreign Policy,* 2nd ed. Martin B. Hickman, ed. Beverly Hills, CA: Glencoe Press, 1975.

Scudder, Evarts Seelye. *The Monroe Doctrine and World Peace.* Port Washington, NY: Kennikat Press, 1972.

Search for Peace in the Middle East, rev. ed. Greenwich, CT: Fawcett Publications, Inc., 1970.

Sewell, John W. *The United States and World Development Agenda 1980.* New York: Praeger, 1980.

———, and Mathieson, John A. "North-South Relations." In *Setting National Priorities, Agenda for the 1980s,* Joseph A. Pechman, ed. Washington, D.C.: The Brookings Institution, 1980.

Shapiro, Robert Y., and Page, Benjamin I. "Foreign Policy and the Rational Public." *Journal of Conflict Resolution* 32 (June 1988): 211–247.

Sigelman, Lee. "A Reassessment of the Two Presidencies Thesis." *Journal of Politics* 41 (November 1979): 1195–1205.

Sigler, John H. "Descent from Olympus: The Search for a New Consensus." *International Journal* 38 (Winter 1982/83): 18–38.

Sigmund, Paul E. "Latin America: Change or Continuity?" In *America and the World 1981,* William P. Bundy, ed. New York: Pergamon Press, 1982.

Smith, Hedrick. *The Power Game: How Washington Works.* New York: Ballantine Books, 1988.

Smith, Jean Edward. *The Constitution and American Foreign Policy.* St. Paul: West Publishing Company, 1989.

Smith, Tom W. "The Polls: America's Most Important Problems, Part I: National and International." *Public Opinion Quarterly* 49 (Summer 1985): 264–274.

Sobel, Richard. "Public Opinion about United States Intervention in El Salvador and Nicaragua." *Public Opinion Quarterly* 53 (Spring 1989): 114–128.

Solo, Pam. *From Protest to Policy: The Origins and Future of the Freeze Movement.* Cambridge, MA: Ballinger Publishing, 1988.

Spanier, John. *American Foreign Policy Since World War II,* 9th ed. New York: Holt, Rinehart and Winston, 1982.

———. *The Truman-MacArthur Controversy and the Korean War.* New York: W. W. Norton & Company, 1965.

———, and Uslaner, Eric M. *American Foreign Policy Making and the Democratic Dilemmas,* 5th ed. New York: Holt, Rinehart and Winston, 1989.

Spero, Joan Edelman. *The Politics of International Economic Relations,* 2nd ed. New York: St. Martin's Press, 1981.

Steinbrunner, John D. "Nuclear Decapitation." *Foreign Policy* 45 (Winter 1981/82): 16–28.

Stillman, Edmund, and Pfaff, William. *Power and Impotence: The Failure of America's Foreign Policy.* New York: Vintage Books, 1966.

Stoessinger, John G. *Crusaders and Pragmatists,* 2nd ed. New York: W. W. Norton & Company, 1985.

———. *Henry Kissinger: The Anguish of Power.* New York: W. W. Norton & Company, 1976.

_____. *Nations in Darkness: China, Russia, and America*, 3rd ed. New York: Random House, 1978.

_____. *Why Nations Go to War*, 5th ed. New York: St. Martin's Press, 1990.

Story, Dale. "Trade Politics in the Third World: A Case Study of the Mexican GATT Decision." *International Organization* 36 (Autumn 1982): 767–794.

Stubbing, Richard A., with Mendel, Richard A. *The Defense Game: An Insider Explores the Astonishing Realities of America's Defense Establishment.* New York: Harper & Row, 1986.

Talbott, Strobe. "Buildup and Breakdown." In *America and the World 1983*, William P. Bundy, ed. New York: Pergamon Press, 1984.

_____. *Deadly Gambits: The Reagan Administration and the Stalemate in Nuclear Arms Control.* New York: Vintage Books, 1985.

Terhune, Kenneth W. "From National Character to National Behavior: A Reformulation." *Journal of Conflict Resolution* 14 (June 1970): 203–264.

Tower, John G. "Congress Versus the President: The Formulation and Implementation of American Foreign Policy." *Foreign Affairs* 60 (Winter 1981/82): 229–246.

Treverton, Gregory F. "Intelligence: Welcome to the American Government." In *A Question of Balance*, Thomas E. Mann, ed. Washington, D.C.: The Brookings Institution, 1990.

Trice, Robert H. "Congress and the Arab-Israeli Conflict: Support for Israel in the U.S. Senate, 1970–1973." *Political Science Quarterly* 92 (Fall 1977): 443–463.

_____. "Domestic Interest Groups and the Arab-Israeli Conflict: A Behavioral Analysis." In *Ethnicity and U.S. Foreign Policy*, rev. ed., Abdul Aziz Said, ed. New York: Praeger, 1981.

Truman, Harry S. *Year of Decision.* New York: Doubleday & Co., Inc., 1955.

Tucker, Robert. "America in Decline: The Foreign Policy of 'Maturity.' " In *America and the World 1979*, William P. Bundy, ed. New York: Pergamon Press, 1980.

_____, and Hendrickson, David C. "Thomas Jefferson and American Foreign Policy," *Foreign Affairs* 69 (Spring 1990): 135–156.

Turner, Stansfield. *Secrecy and Democracy: The CIA in Transition.* Boston: Houghton Mifflin Company, 1985.

Varg, Paul A. *Foreign Policies of the Founding Fathers.* East Lansing, MI: Michigan State University Press, 1963.

Viguerie, Richard A. *The New Right: We're Ready to Lead.* Falls Church, VA: The Viguerie Company, 1981.

Waller, Douglas C. *Congress and the Nuclear Freeze: An Inside Look at the Politics of a Mass Movement.* Amherst, MA: University of Massachusetts Press, 1987.

Walters, Robert W. "African-American Influence on U.S. Foreign Policy toward South Africa." In Mohammed E. Ahrari, ed., *Ethnic Groups and U.S. Foreign Policy.* New York: Greenwood Press, 1987.

The Washington Lobby, 4th ed. Washington, D.C.: Congressional Quarterly, Inc., 1982.

Weeks, Joseph. *The Fifteen Weeks.* Chicago: Harcourt, Brace and World, Inc., 1955.

Westphal, Albert C. V. *The House Committee on Foreign Affairs.* New York: Columbia University Press, 1942.

Whalen, Charles W., Jr. *The House and Foreign Policy: The Irony of Congressional Reform.* Chapel Hill, NC: The University of North Carolina Press, 1982.

Whiting, Allen S. *China Crosses the Yalu.* Stanford, CA: Stanford University Press, 1960.

Wiarda, Howard J. *Foreign Policy Without illusion.* Glenview, IL: Scott, Foresman/Little, Brown Higher Education, 1990.

Wildavsky, Aaron. "The Two Presidencies." *Trans-action* 3 (December 1966): 7–14.

Willetts, Peter. *The Non-Aligned Movement: The Origins of a Third World Alliance.* London: Frances Pinter, Ltd., 1979.

Willrich, Mason, and Rhinelander, John B., eds. *SALT: The Moscow Agreements and Beyond.* New York: Free Press, 1974.

Windsor, Philip. "America's Moral Confusions: Separating the Should from the Good." *Foreign Policy* 13 (Winter 1973/74): 139–153.

Winham, Gilbert. "Developing Theories of Foreign Policy Making: A Case Study of Foreign Aid." *Journal of Politics* 32 (February 1970): 41–70.

Wiseman, Henry, and Taylor, Alastair M. *From Rhodesia to Zimbabwe: The Politics of Transition.* New York: Pergamon Press, 1981.

Wittkopf, Eugene R. "Elites and Masses: Constancy and Change in Public Attitudes Toward America's World Role," a paper delivered at the Annual Meeting of the Southern Political Science Association, Birmingham, Alabama, November 3–5, 1983.

———. *Faces of Internationalism: Public Opinion and American Foreign Policy.* (Durham, NC: Duke University Press, 1990).

———. "Public Attitudes Toward American Foreign Policy in the Post-Vietnam Decade," a paper delivered at the Annual Meeting of the International Studies Association, March 27–31, 1984.

———, and Maggiotto, Michael A. "Elites and Masses. A Comparative Analysis of Attitudes Toward America's World Role." *Journal of Politics* 45 (May 1983): 303–334.

———, and McCormick, James M. "The Cold War Consensus: Did It Exist?" *Polity* 22 (Summer 1990): 627–653.

Woodward, Bob. *Veil: The Secret Wars of the CIA, 1981–1987.* New York: Pocket Books, 1987.

Wormuth, Francis D. "Presidential Wars: The Convenience of 'Precedent.' " In *Problems of American Foreign Policy,* 2nd ed., Martin B. Hickman, ed. Beverly Hills, CA: Glencoe Press, 1975.

Yankelovich, Daniel. "Farewell to 'President Knows Best.' " In *America and the World 1978,* William P. Bundy, ed. New York: Pergamon Press, 1979.

Yarmolinsky, Adam. *The Military Establishment: Its Impact on American Society.* New York: Harper & Row, 1971.

Yergin, Daniel. *Shattered Peace: The Origins of the Cold War and the National Security State.* Boston: Houghton Mifflin Company, 1977.

Zagoria, Donald S. *The Sino-Soviet Conflict 1956–1961.* Princeton, NJ: Princeton University Press, 1962.

Ziegler, L. Harmon, and Peak, G. Wayne. *Interest Groups in American Society,* 2nd ed. Englewood Cliffs, NJ: Prentice-Hall, Inc., 1972.

NAME INDEX

Acheson, Dean, 69, 104, 266, 366
Adams, John, 272
Adenauer, Konrad, 96
Allen, Richard V., 172, 176
Allende, Salvador, 417
Allison, Graham, 355
Aquino, Benigno Jr., 202–203
Aquino, Corazon, 202–203, 316, 318, 321
Arafat, Yasir, 204
Aristotle, 6
Aspin, Les, 338

Baker, James A., 213, 218, 225, 230, 254, 266, 366, 369, 376
Ball, George, 137
Barnes, Michael, 337
Begin, Menachem, 155–156
Bevin, Ernest, 50
Bingham, Jonathan, 329
Bishop, Maurice, 183
Blechman, Barry M., 81–82
Bloomfield, Lincoln P., 78–79, 83, 145
Boland, Edward, 327
Bradley, Omar, 68
Brady, Nicholas, 218
Brandt, Willy, 98, 187
Brezhnev, Leonid, 125, 152, 220
Bricker, John, 308
Brooke, Edward W., 326
Brown, Harold, 150, 403
Brzezinski, Zbigniew, 87–89, 91, 140, 150, 161, 365, 373, 403
Buckley, William, 136
Bukovsky, Vladimir, 148
Bundy, McGeorge, 365, 372
Bush, George, 192, 202, 206, 213–217, 219–221, 224–225, 239–242, 245–246, 250–254, 256, 265, 274, 286, 290, 292–293, 300, 316, 320, 340, 366–367, 376–377, 384–385
Byrnes, James, 47, 50

Carlucci, Frank, 405
Carter, Jimmy, 2, 8, 117–118, 138–141, 143–145, 147–162, 170–171, 177, 180, 199, 216, 266, 282–283, 291–292, 300, 315, 318, 321, 365, 367, 373
Case, Clifford, 310
Casey, William, 199–200, 218, 420, 421
Castro, Fidel, 22, 81, 91, 102
Ceausescu, Nicolae, 230, 411
Chamberlain, Neville, 82
Chamorro, Violetta, 24
Cheney, Richard, 218, 405
Chiang Kai-shek, 56
Christopher, Warren, 284
Church, Frank, 325, 414
Churchill, Winston, 44, 48–49
Clark, Dick, 312
Clark, William, 365, 374, 404
Clausen, Aage, 292, 294
Clausewitz, Karl von, 26
Cleveland, Grover, 19
Conyers, John, 285
Cooper, John Sherman, 325
Corwin, Edward S., 270–272
Cutler, Robert, 372
Cyr, Arthur, 353

Dahl, Robert, 6
de Gaulle, Charles, 95–98
Destler, I.M., 339
Diem, Ngo Dinh, 105, 107
Douglas, William, 282
Drew, Elizabeth, 140
Dulles, John Foster, 105, 366, 371

Eagleburger, Lawrence, 218, 225
Easton, David, 6
Eisenhower, Dwight, 57, 81–82,
    89–90, 105, 220, 292–294, 297,
    309, 366, 371–372
Ervin, Sam, 311

Falk, Richard, 135
Fascell, Dante, 290
Fenno, Richard, 289
Findley, Paul, 318
Ford, Gerald, 8, 103, 132, 138, 148,
    170, 216, 266, 291–292, 300,
    315–316, 320, 373, 398
Forrestal, James V., 47
Franck, Thomas, 339
Fulbright, J. William, 80, 289, 334

Gates, Robert, 218
Gejdenson, Sam, 337
Gemayel, Amin, 186
Genet, Edmond, 271
Glaspie, April, 249
Glenn, John, 311–312
Goldwater, Barry, 283
Gorbachev, Mikhail, 189–192, 196,
    231, 234–238, 240–243, 250–251
Gromyko, Andrei, 148, 180, 235
Guzman, Jacobo Arbenz, 22, 80

Haig, Alexander, 171–173, 179, 181,
    187–189, 266, 319, 365, 374, 404
Halperin, Morton, 355
Hamilton, Alexander, 268–269
Hamilton, Lee, 337
Harriman, Averell, 47
Havel, Vaclav, 227, 229
Hayden, Carl, 416
Hayes, Peter, 229, 233
Henkin, Louis, 268, 282
Herring, George C., 132
Hills, Carla Anderson, 219, 353
Hitler, Adolf, 82
Holmes, Oliver Wendell, 280–281
Honecker, Erich, 229
Hughes, Harold, 417
Humphrey, David, 271
Hussein, King of Jordan, 204
Hussein, Saddam, 247, 249, 253–254,
    274, 412
Hyland, William, 216–217

Jackson, Henry, 328
Jackson, Robert, 269
Jaruzelski, Wojciech, 228
Jefferson, Thomas, 5, 9, 11, 272–273
Jervis, Robert, 69
Johnson, Lyndon, 22, 81–82, 92,
    107–108, 274, 292–293, 365, 372

Kaiser, Fred, 335
Kaplan, Stephen S., 81–82
Kavass, Igor I., 15
Kennan, George F., 39, 49, 51–52
Kennedy, John F., 77, 81–82, 90, 102,
    106–107, 292–293, 365, 367
Khomeini, Ayatollah, 197–198
Khrushchev, Nikita, 89–90, 94
Kiesinger, Kurt, 98
Kimmett, Robert, 218
Kirkpatrick, Jeane, 146
Kissinger, Henry, 2, 8, 25–26, 62, 118,
    121–122, 124–126, 128, 130–133,
    135–140, 142, 144, 148, 150, 155,
    170, 178, 216, 218, 365, 373–374
Kohl, Helmut, 231–232

Laird, Melvin, 402–404
Lasswell, Harold, 6
Leahy, William, 47
Lincoln, Abraham, 273
Locke, John, 10, 267
Lugar, Richard, 334

MacArthur, Douglas, 67–68
McCarthy, Joseph, 64, 369
McCormick, James M., 85, 87
McFarlane, Robert, 200, 202, 374–375,
    404, 415, 421
McGovern, George, 136
McKinley, William, 28, 274
McNamara, Robert, 398, 401–404
Mansfield, Mike, 325
Mao Zedong, 56, 67, 93–94, 136
Marchetti, Victor, 414
Marcos, Ferdinand, 202–203, 334
Marks, John D., 414
Marshall, George C., 39, 57, 366
Marshall, John, 272
Mazowiecki, Tadeusz, 226, 228
Michael, Mark A., 15
Miller, Hunter, 19
Minh, Ho Chi, 104
Modrow, Hans, 231–232

Monroe, James, 13, 17, 272
Morgan, Thomas Doc, 289, 311
Mossadegh, Mohammed, 80
Moynihan, Daniel Patrick, 420
Murville, Couve de, 97

Napolean, 27
Nasser, Gamal Abdel, 56, 100
Nehru, Jawaharlal, 80, 98, 100
Nelson, Gaylord, 329
Nitze, Paul, 61
Nixon, Richard M., 2–3, 8, 26, 91,
    108, 117, 120–121, 124–126, 128,
    130, 132–133, 135–138, 158, 162,
    170, 216, 274, 278, 291–292, 300,
    313, 318, 324, 365
Nkrumah, 100
Noriega, Manuel Antonio, 24,
    223–224, 265, 316, 318
North, Oliver, 199–200, 202, 379
Nunn, Sam, 307, 339

Oldfield, Duane, 294
Olney, Richard, 19
O'Neill, Thomas P. Jr., 290
Organski, A.F.K., 7
Ortega, Daniel, 24

Pell, Claiborne, 335
Percy, Charles, 289, 334
Perkins, Dexter, 26
Perry, Jack, 367
Poindexter, John, 199, 202, 365, 379
Polk, James K., 17, 273
Powell, Colin, 405

al-Qadhafi, Muammar, 197

Ransom, Harry Howe, 412
Reagan, Ronald, 162–163, 169, 171,
    174, 176, 179–180, 183, 187–189,
    191–193, 195–198, 200–204, 214,
    215, 216, 219, 221–223, 247, 274,
    292, 300, 315, 317, 319–321, 325,
    326, 327, 330, 365, 374–375
Rockman, Bert, 377, 379
Rogers, William, 365
Rokeach, Milton, 7
Roosevelt, Franklin, 29, 40, 42, 44–45,
    47, 104, 277, 279
Roosevelt, Theodore, 21, 24, 274
Rostow, Walt W., 365, 372

Rumsfeld, Donald, 403
Rusk, Dean, 365
Russell, Richard, 416
Russett, Bruce, 99
Ryan, Leo, 417

Sadat, Anwar, 144–145, 154–155
Sakharov, Andrei, 148
Saltonstall, Leverett, 416
Savimbi, Jonas, 196
Schlesinger, Arthur Jr., 270, 344
Schlesinger, James, 403
Schmitt, Eric, 243
Schultz, George, 365
Scott, Andrew, 364
Scowcroft, Brent, 218, 376–377
Shevardnadze, Eduard, 234–236, 250
Shultz, George, 189, 204, 362,
    374–375
Sigelman, Lee, 293
Smith, Hedrick, 376
Smith, William French, 200
Solarz, Stephen, 337
Somoza, Anastasio, 197
Sorenson, Theodore, 216
Spanier, John, 25, 27
Sparkman, John, 334
Sprudzs, Adolf, 15
Stalin, Joseph, 44, 48–49
Starr, Harvey, 99
Stettinius, Edward, 47
Stevenson, Adlai, 329
Stimson, Henry, 47
Stone, Richard, 22
Sukarno, Ahmed, 100
Sutherland, George, 265, 281

Taft, William Howard, 274
Tikhonov, Nikolai, 235
Tito, Marshall, 80, 100
Tower, John, 200, 218, 341
Truman, Harry S., 45, 47–48, 51, 58,
    67–68, 81–82, 92, 103–105, 277,
    286, 288, 292, 297, 366, 371
Turner, Stansfield, 418

Vance, Cyrus, 22, 145, 150, 365
Vandenberg, Arthur, 288
Vanik, Charles, 328
Vinson, Carl, 416

Walesa, Lech, 226–228

Washington, George, 12–14, 17,
    271–272, 356
Weber, Max, 6
Webster, William, 218
Weinberger, Caspar, 172, 175, 184,
    375, 404
Weisband, Edward, 339
Whalen, Charles, 341
Wildavsky, Aaron, 291, 294
Wilson, Woodrow, 5, 29–30, 32, 45,
    47, 246

Winham, Gilbert, 58
Wittkopf, Eugene R., 84–85, 87
Wright, James C. Jr., 290

Yeltsin, Boris, 236, 238
Yergin, Daniel, 43
Yeutter, Clayton, 385

Zablocki, Clement J., 289, 310, 319
Zhivkov, Todor, 230

SUBJECT INDEX

Achille Lauro, 320
Aeroflot, 179
African Development Fund, 330
Agency for International
    Development (AID), 61, 298, 356,
    358–359, 385
Agreement on Ending the War and
    Restoring the Peace (in Vietnam),
    108
Agricultural Trade Development and
    Assistance Act, 384
Agricultural Trade and Development
    Mission Program, 385
Airborne Warning and Control
    Systems (AWACS), 185, 316–317,
    341
Alliance for Germany, 229
Allies, 28, 47, 49
American Revolution, 10
Anti-Apartheid Act (1986), 333
Anti-Ballistic Missile Treaty (1972), 91,
    126–127, 175, 339–340
ANZUS Treaty, 52, 55
Apollo-Soyuz flight (1975), 126
Arab League, 249–251
Arms Control and Disarmament
    Agency (ACDA), 298, 356, 358
Articles of Confederation, 267, 356
Asian Development Bank, 330
Austrian State Treaty, 89
Authorization for Use of Military
    Force Against Iraq Resolution, 323
Axis Power, 49

Baker Plan (1985), 383
Basic Principles of Relations between
    the U.S. and the Union of Soviet
    Socialist Republics, 126
Bay of Pigs invasion, 22, 81, 91, 274
Berlin Wall, 90, 229, 231–233

Boland Amendment of 1984, 198,
    327–328, 420
Boston University, 219
Brady Plan (1989), 383–384
Brezhnev Doctrine, 220
Bricker Amendment, 308
Bureau of Inter-American Affairs,
    367–368
Bush administration, 8, 205, 292, 318,
    323, 327, 330, 337, 368
    Central Europe after Cold War,
        238–247
    CIA intelligence activity and,
        411–412
    covert intelligence operations and,
        415–418
    Eastern Europe and, 225–238
    new world order, 245–247
    NSC system and, 427–430
    Panama and, 24
    Persian Gulf War and, 247–254
    values underlying foreign policy,
        215–218
Byrd Amendment, 145

C. Turner Joy, 107
Camp David Accords, 156–160,
    184–185
Carter administration, 2–3, 112, 128,
    174, 178, 184, 317, 330, 356, 368,
    398
    Camp David meetings, 156–160,
        184–185
    CIA intelligence activity and,
        410–411
    human rights and, 142–149
    idealism as basis for foreign policy,
        138–163
    Joint Chiefs of Staff (JCS) under,
        399–400

secretary of defense's role, 403
Carter Doctrine, 161
Case-Zablocki Act, 309–312, 331
CENTO (Central Treaty
    Organization), 52, 55
Central Intelligence Agency (CIA), 65,
    81, 143, 198–200, 218, 222–223,
    264, 296–298, 360, 366, 406–430
  Boland Amendment of 1984 and,
    198, 327–328, 420
  Casey, William, 199–200, 218
  Church Committee hearings,
    414–415
  covert operations, 413–425
  Hughes-Ryan Amendment, 417–419
  Intelligence Oversight Act of 1980,
    419–420
  policymaking influences, 409–412
Central Treaty Organization
    (CENTO), 52, 55
China,
  Chiang Kai-shek, 56
  Chinese People's Volunteers, 68
  Mao Zedong, 56, 67, 93–94, 136
Chinese People's Volunteers, 68
Christmas bombing (1972), 132
Church Committee hearings, 414–415
CIA. See Central Intelligence Agency
Civil War, 273
Clark Amendment to the Arms
    Export Control Act, 196, 326
Clark Field, 202
Clayton-Bulwer Treaty, 17
Coast Guard Academy, 219
Cold War, 1–3, 8, 39, 61, 64–65, 70,
    118, 163, 169, 171–172, 205, 219,
    226, 231, 240–241, 244–247, 250,
    255, 274, 299, 339
  accommodation with Soviet Union
    under Reagan, 188–195
  Airborne Warning and Control
    Systems (AWACS), 185, 316–317,
    341
  "Basic Principles of Relations
    between the U.S. and the
    USSR," 126
  Bay of Pigs invasion, 22, 81, 91, 274
  Bush administration and, 2–3
  Carter's idealism and, 141–142
  Central Intelligence Agency, 65, 81,
    143, 198–200, 218, 222–223, 264,
    296–298, 360, 366

  consensus regarding, 77–98
  Conventional Arms Forces in
    Europe (CFE), 241, 358
  Cuban Missile Crisis, 22, 78, 91,
    101–103, 355
  Declaration of the Belgrade
    Conference of Heads of State
    and Government of Nonaligned
    Countries, 100
  domestic containment policies,
    61–66
  Ford administration, 159, 216, 218,
    317, 330
  Foreign Relations Authorization Act
    (1979), 310
  General Agreements on Tariffs and
    Trade (GATT), 153, 241, 385
  Glasnost, 190, 234–235
  Helsinki Accords, 131, 145
  House Foreign Affairs Committee,
    181
  House Intelligence Committee, 327
  House Un-American Activities
    Committee, 64
  intelligence agencies and, 406–430
    see also Intelligence agencies
  Interim Agreement on Offensive
    Strategic Arms, 126
  Kissinger and, 2, 8, 25–26, 62, 118,
    121–122, 124–126, 216, 128, 130,
    131, 132, 133, 135, 136, 137–140,
    142, 144, 148, 150, 155, 170, 178,
    218, 365, 373–374
  Korean War's effects, 64, 66–70, 78
  Litvinov Agreement, 281–282
  Moscow Summit (1972), 126–127,
    137
  Moscow Summit (1988), 193
  Moscow Summit (1991), 91, 235,
    241
  Mutual Security Act of 1951, 59
  National Security Act of 1947 and,
    296, 370, 413
  nonaligned movement and, 98–101
  NSC-68 and, 61–64
  Olympics 1980 Moscow, 161
  Olympics 1984 Los Angeles, 181
  patterns of interaction, 86–92
  postwar origins of, 46–55
  public attitudes, 83–85
  Reagan administration, 2–3, 8, 24,
    104, 112, 162–163, 169, 170–204,

215, 219, 221–223, 247, 317, 325,
327, 330, 337, 339–340, 355, 368,
383
Reagan Doctrine, 195–198, 200, 203,
205
SALT (Strategic Arms Reduction
Treaty) talks, 127, 132, 152, 161,
180, 242, 258
Senate Foreign Relations
Committee, 80, 189
Strategic Arms Limitation Talks
(SALT I), 91, 126, 137, 150, 242
Strategic Arms Reduction
Agreement (START), 191–192,
220, 236, 241–242, 358
Strategic Arms Reduction Treaty
(1991), 243
Strategic Defense Initiative (Star
Wars), 175–176, 192–193, 221,
339–340, 374
Truman Doctrine, 49–51
Vietnam War effects, 103–112
Committee on Foreign Affairs, 267
Commodity Credit Corporation
(CCC), 385
Communist Party, 189
Concert of Europe, 10
Conference on Security and
Cooperation in Europe (CSCE),
244–245
Congress, 13, 17, 19, 21, 27, 48, 51,
58–59, 109, 111, 120, 125, 146–147,
157, 174, 200–201, 205
Congress of People's Deputies,
234–235, 237
Congressional Research Service
(CRS), 299, 335
Constitution (U.S.), 62, 266–268, 272,
278–279, 281, 287, 307, 309
Containment, NSC-68, 61–64
Containment policies, 52–66
domestic, 61–66
Conventional Arms Forces in Europe
(CFE), 241, 358
Conyers v. *Reagan* (1985), 283
Covenant on the Prevention and
Punishment of the Crime of
Genocide, 146
Covert intelligence operations, 413–425
Church Committee hearings,
414–415
Hughes-Ryan Amendment and,
417–419

Intelligence Oversight Act of 1980,
419–420
Iran-contra affair, 195, 200, 202,
290, 307, 420–425
policy after Iran-contra affair,
423–425
see also Intelligence agencies
Crockett v. *Reagan* (1984), 283, 285
Cuban Missile Crisis, 22, 78, 91,
101–103, 355
CIA intelligence activity and, 410

Declaration of the Belgrade
Conference of Heads of State and
Government of Nonaligned
Countries, 100
Declaration of Independence, 6
Declaration of the United Nations, 15
Defense Intelligence Agency (DIA),
406
hawkishness of, 412
Department of Commerce, 380
Department of Defense (DOD),
394–406
Joint Chiefs of Staff (JCS), 397–400
Pentagon structure, 394–397
secretary of defense's role, 400–406
Department of Energy,
intelligence agencies and, 406
see also Intelligence agencies
Department of State,
intelligence agencies and, 406
see also Intelligence agencies
Department of the Treasury, 382, 384
intelligence agencies and, 406
Depression the, 20
Destroyer-for-Bases (1940), 277
Development Coordination
Committee, 359
Dien Bien Phu battle of, 105
Drug Enforcement Agency, 360

Eastern Europe, CIA intelligence
activity and, 411
Economic Support Fund, 328
Edwards v. *Carter* (1978), 282–283
Egypt, Camp David talks, 156–157,
160, 184–185
Egyptian-Israeli Peace Treaty, 316
Eisenhower administration, Joint
Chiefs of Staff (JCS) under,
397–398
Eisenhower Doctrine, 295

European Common Market, 95–96
European Economic Community, 186, 359
European Recovery Program, 58
Executive Agreements Review Act (1975), 311
Export Enhancement Program, 385

Farabundo Marti National Liberation Front (FMLN), 22
FBI, 65
Final Act of the Conference on Security and Cooperation, 130
First Russian Insurance Company, 282
Fletcher School of Law and Diplomacy, 363
Food for Peace Program, 359
Ford administration, 159, 216, 218, 317, 330
Foreign Agriculture Service (FAS), 384–385
Foreign Assistance Act, 332
Foreign policy,
 Bush administration and, 225–247
 Carter's idealistic approach, 138–163
 containment policies, 52–66
 Department of Defense (DOD) and, 394–406
 global involvement, 70
 idealism as basis for, 118–119
 intelligence agencies and, 406–430
 isolationism in, 11–24
 Kissinger's influences, 121–138
 Korean War's effects, 64, 66–70, 78
 moralism in, 25–33
 NATO and, 52, 55, 59, 69, 95–96, 159, 174, 186, 221, 233, 240, 275, 288, 291
 Nixon's doctrines, 119–133
 nonaligned movement and, 98–101
 Reagan administration and, 173–202
 realism as basis for, 118–138
 Truman Doctrine, 49–51, 61, 291
 values and beliefs underlying, 6–11
 Wilson's Fourteen Points, 30–32
Foreign Relations Authorization Act (1979), 310
Foreign trade,
 Agricultural Trade Development and Assistance Act, 384

Agricultural Trade and Development Mission Program, 385
Asian Development Bank, 330
Economic Support Fund, 328
European Economic Community, 186, 359
Food for Peace Program, 359
Foreign Agriculture Service (FAS), 384–385
Foreign Assistance Act, 332
General Agreements on Tariffs and Trade (GATT), 153, 241, 385
International Affairs and Commodity Programs, 384
International Agreements Consultation Resolution, 312
International Monetary Fund, 241, 244
International Trade Commission, 381
Jackson-Vanik Amendment to the Trade Act of 1974, 133, 220, 241, 328, 342
Office of International Cooperation and Development, 385
Office of Technology Assessment, 299
Office of the U.S. Trade Representative (USTR), 380–382
Omnibus Trade and Competitiveness Act (1988), 330–331, 381
Organization for Economic Cooperation and Development (OECD), 153
Trade Act (1974), 343
Trade Act (1988), 343
Trade and Development Program, 359
Formosa Resolution, 294
Fouchet Plan, 96
Fourteen Points, 30–32

Gadsden Treaty, 16
GATT. *See* General Agreements on Tariffs and Trade (GATT)
Gaza Strip, 156
General Accounting Office (GAO), 299
General Agreements on Tariffs and Trade (GATT), 153, 241, 385
Geneva Conference, 154

Genocide, Covenant on the
    Prevention and Punishment of
    the Crime of Genocide, 146
Glasnost, 190, 234–235
Goldwater et al. v. *Carter*, 283–285
Gorbachev Plan, 236
Gulf of Tonkin Resolution, 107, 295,
    313

Harvard University, 39, 363
Hawk anti-aircraft missiles, 199–200
Helsinki Accords (1975), 131, 145
Helsinki Monitoring Group, 148
House Foreign Affairs Committee, 181
House Intelligence Committee, 327
House Un-American Activities
    Committee, 64
How Congressmen Decide (Clausen),
    292
Hughes-Ryan Amendment, 417–419
Human rights, Carter administration
    policies, 142–149

Immigration, National Origins Act
    (1924), 309
Immigration and Naturalization Service
    v. *Chadha* (1983), 286–287, 343
In Search of American Foreign Policy
    (Bloomfield), 78–79
Indochina, Sukarno, 100
INS v. *Chadha* (1983), 284, 286
Intelligence, Central Intelligence
    Agency (CIA), 65, 81, 143,
    198–200
Intelligence agencies, 406–430
    Boland Amendment of 1984 and,
        198, 327–328, 420
    Central Intelligence Agency (CIA),
        406–430
    covert operations, 413–425
    Defense Intelligence Agency (DIA),
        406
    Hughes-Ryan Amendment, 417–419
    Intelligence Oversight Act of 1980,
        419–420
    Interdepartmental Regional Groups
        (IRGs), 425–430
    Iran-contra affair, 195, 200, 202,
        290, 307, 420–425
    National Security Act (1947), 296,
        370, 413

National Security Agency (NSA),
    406–408
National Security Council (NSC),
    61, 102, 145, 199, 203, 218–219,
    264, 296, 369–373, 375, 377, 379,
    386
    policymaking influences, 409–412
    Russian KGB, 238
    Senior Interdepartmental Group
        (SIG), 426–430
    see also Central Intelligence Agency
        (CIA); National Security
        Agency (NSA)
Intelligence Oversight Act of 1980,
    200, 419–420
Inter-American Development Bank,
    177, 330, 383
Interdepartmental Regional Groups
    (IRGs), 425–430
Interim Agreement on Offensive
    Strategic Arms, 126
Intermediate Nuclear Forces Talks
    (INF), 180, 191–192, 194, 205, 358
Intermediate Nuclear Forces Treaty
    (1987), 159, 358
Internal Revenue Service, 359
International Affairs and Commodity
    Programs, 384
International Agreements
    Consultation Resolution, 312
International Atomic Energy Agency
    (IAEA), 330
International Civil Aviation
    Organization, 359
International Convention on the
    Elimination of All Forms of Racial
    Discrimination, 146
International Covenant on Civil and
    Political Rights (1966), 146
International Covenant on Economic,
    Social, and Cultural Rights
    (1966), 146
International Development
    Cooperation Agency, 356, 358–359
International Human Rights Bill, 146
International Monetary Fund, 241, 244
International Security Assistance and
    Arms Export Control Act (1976),
    330
International Security and
    Development Cooperation Act
    (1981), 326

International Trade Commission, 381
Iran, CIA intelligence activity and, 410
Iran-contra affair, 195, 200, 202, 290, 307, 420–425
Iraq, CIA intelligence activity and, 412
IRGs (Interdepartmental Regional Groups), 425–430
Iron Curtain, 58, 172
Isolationism,
  challenges to following World War II, 41–54
  nineteenth century, 15–20
  twentieth century, 20–24
  in U.S. foreign policy, 11–24
Israel,
  Camp David talks, 156–157, 160, 184–185
  Six-Day War (1967), 247, 409
  Yom Kippur War (1973), 133

Jackson State University, 108
Jackson-Vanik Amendment to the Trade Act of 1974, 133, 220, 241, 328, 342
Jay Treaty, 271–272
Johns Hopkins University, 363
Johnson administration, 64, 107, 137
  Vietnam involvement, 107–109
Joint Chiefs of Staff (JCS), 68, 397–400
  secretary of defense and, 400–406

Kellogg-Briand Pact, 20
Kennedy administration, 61, 137
  CIA intelligence activity and, 410–411
  Cuban Missile Crisis, 22, 78, 91, 101, 103, 355, 410
  Vietnam involvement, 106–108
Kent State University, 108
KGB, 238
Khyber Pass, 161
Korean War, 26, 56, 59, 64, 66–70, 78, 88, 104, 286
Kremlin, 62–63

Lancaster House, 157
Latin America, Organization of American States (OAS), 22, 224
League of Nations, 20, 30, 32, 43

Legislative Reform Act (1970), 299
Lend-Lease Act, 28, 44
Leninism, 169
Limited Test Ban Treaty (1963), 91
Litvinov Agreement, 281–282
London Summit (1991), 235, 244
Louisiana Purchase, 16, 272
Lowry v. *Reagan* (1987), 283, 286
Lublin Committee, 44
Lusitania, 28

McCarthy, Joseph, 64
Maddox, 107
Maine, 28
Malta Summit (1989), 240
Marshall Plan, 57–59, 291
Marxism, 169
Middle East,
  Arab League, 249–251
  Arafat, Yasir, 204
  Camp David Accords, 156–157, 160, 184–185
  Carter administration, 140–142, 146–147, 149–154, 157–163, 174, 178, 184, 317
  CIA intelligence activity and, 410–413
  Egyptian-Israeli Peace Treaty, 316
  Farabundo Marti National Liberation Front (FMLN), 22
  Gaza Strip, 156
  Hussein, King of Jordan, 204
  Sadat, Anwar, 154–155
  Six-Day War, 247, 409
Migratory Bird Act, 280
Military (U.S.),
  Department of Defense and, 394–306
  Joint Chiefs of Staff, 68, 397–400
  Pentagon and, 339, 394–400
  Persian Gulf War and, 214, 217, 222, 251–252, 254, 322
  World War I and, 20–21, 27, 30, 42, 70, 246
  World War II and, 27–29, 33, 40–43, 66, 70, 78, 103–104, 112, 226, 278, 281, 296, 299
  see also Department of Defense (DOD)
Missouri v. *Holland* (1920), 280–281
Molotov Soviet Foreign Minister, 48

Monroe Doctrine, 12–14, 19–22, 24, 29, 272
Moralism, in U.S. foreign policy, 25–33
Moscow State University, 192
Moscow Summit (1972), 126–127, 137
Moscow Summit (1988), 193
Moscow Summit (1991), 91, 235, 241
Multinational Force in Lebanon Resolution (1983), 319
Multinational Force and Observers (MFO), 315
Multinational Forces (MNF), 185–186, 198
Mutual Defense Assistance Act of 1949, 59
Mutual Security Act of 1951, 59

National Commitments Resolution, 309
National Front for the Liberation of Angola, 326
National Military Establishment, 296
National Opinion Research Center, 84
National Origins Act (1924), 20
National security,
   coordinating system, 425–428
   domestic containment policies, 61–66
   intelligence agencies and, 402–430
   IRGs (Interdepartmental Regional Groups), 425–430
   National Security Council (NSC), 61, 102, 145, 199, 203, 218–219, 264, 296, 369–373, 375, 377, 379, 386, 426–430
   see also Intelligence agencies; specific agencies by name
National Security Act (1947), 296, 370, 413
National Security Agency (NSA), 406–408
National Security Council (NSC), 61, 102, 145, 199, 203, 218–219, 264, 296, 369–373, 375, 377, 379, 386
   Bush administration and, 427–430
   covert intelligence operations and, 415–418
   NSC-68, 61–64
National Security Directive 1 (NSD-1), 376
National Security Planning Group (NSPG), 426–427

National Union for the Total Independence of Angola (UNITA), 196–197
National Union for the Total Liberation of Angola, 326
NATO. *See* North Atlantic Treaty Organization
Nelson-Bingham Amendment to the 1974 Foreign Assistance Act, 329
Neutrality Treaty, 154
New Deal, 40
"New world order," 3, 245–247
New York Times v. *United States* (Pentagon Papers case), 287
Nicaragua,
   CIA intelligence activity and, 410
   Iran-contra affair, 195, 200, 202, 290, 307, 420–425
Nixon administration, 2, 108, 118–119, 219, 398
   foreign policies, 120–138
   realism as basis for foreign policy, 118–138
   secretary of defense and, 402–404
   Vietnam involvement, 108–109
Nonaligned movement, 98–101
North Atlantic Treaty Organization (NATO), 52, 55, 59, 69, 95–96, 159, 174, 186, 221, 233, 240, 275, 288, 291
NSC-68, 61–64
Nuclear Non-Proliferation Act, 330, 342–343
Nuclear Non-Proliferation Treaty (1968), 91

Offensive Arms Pact of SALT I, 278
Office of the Assistant Secretary for International Affairs, 383
Office of Budget and Management, 386
Office of International Cooperation and Development, 385
Office of Technology Assessment, 299
Office of the U.S. Trade Representative (USTR), 380–382
Olympics 1980 Moscow, 161
Olympics 1984 Los Angeles, 181
Omnibus Trade and Competitiveness Act (1988), 330–331, 381
OPEC, 249
Operation Brightstar, 184

Operation Desert Shield, 251, 339
Operation Rolling Thunder, 107
Operation Staunch, 198
Oregon Territory, 17
Oregon Treaty, 16
Organization of American States
   (OAS), 22, 224
Organization for Economic
   Cooperation and Development
   (OECD), 153
Overseas Private Investment
   Corporation, 359

Palestine Liberation Organization
   (PLO), 185, 203–204, 317
Palestine National Council, 204
Pan Am flight 103 (Lockerbie), 197
Panama Canal, 153–154
Panama Canal Treaty, 154–155, 284,
   294
Paris Peace Conference, 30
Party of Democratic Socialism, 230
Pearl Harbor, 29
Pentagon, 339
   Joint Chiefs of Staff (JCS) and,
      397–400
   structure of, 394–397
Pentagon Papers (*New York Times* v.
   United States), 287
Perestroika, 190, 234–235, 238, 242
Pershing II missiles, 193
Persian Gulf Debate (1991), 307
Persian Gulf War, 214, 217, 222,
   251–252, 254, 322
   CIA intelligence activity and, 412
   debate over, 307
Philippines, 316, 318, 321
   Reagan administration and, 202–205
Plaza Pact (1985), 383
PLO, 185, 202, 203–204, 317
Point Four Program, 57–59
Policy Review Group (PRG), 427
Popular Movement for the Liberation
   of Angola, 326
Potsdam Agreement, 277
Potsdam Conference, 48
Presidency. *See* specific
   administrations by name
Presidential Directive, 13, 152
Princeton University, 363
Pueblo incident, CIA intelligence
   activity and, 410

Radio Marti, 358
Reagan administration, 2–3, 8, 104,
   112, 215, 219, 221–223, 247, 317,
   325, 327, 330
   accommodation with Soviet Union,
      188–195
   covert operations policy following
      Iran-contra affair, 423–425
   Joint Chiefs of Staff (JCS) under,
      399–400
   Panama and, 24
   policy approach of, 173–186
   values underlying, 170–173
Reagan Doctrine, 195–198, 200, 203,
   205
Realism, in foreign policy, 118–138
Riga Axioms, 43, 49
Rockefeller Commission, 418
Romania, CIA intelligence activity
   and, 411
Roosevelt administration, 24
Roosevelt Corollary to the Monroe
   Doctrine, 21
Royal Navy, 27
Rush-Bagot Agreement (1817), 277

SALT I, 127, 132, 180, 242
SALT II, 152, 161, 180, 242
Sandinistas, 223
   CIA intelligence activity and, 410
SDI (Star Wars program). *See*
   Strategic Defense Initiative
The Second Treatise of Government
   (Locke), 267
Secretary of defense, role of, 400–406
Senate, 201
Senate Foreign Relations Committee,
   80, 189
Senate Select Committee on
   Intelligence Activities. *See* Church
   Committee hearings
Senior Interdepartmental Group
   (SIG), 426–430
Shah of Iran, CIA intelligence activity
   and, 410
Shanghai Communique, 128–130
Shuttle diplomacy, 131
Six-Day War, CIA and, 247, 409
Smoot-Hawley Tariff of 1930, 20
"Solidarity" movement, 226, 228
Southeast Asia Collective Defense
   Treaty, 295

Southeast Asia Treaty Organization
    (SEATO), 52, 55
Soviet Union,
    NSC-68 and, 61–64
    see also Cold War
Spanish-American War, 27–28, 70
"Special activities." *See* Intelligence
    agencies, covert operations
Star Wars program. *See* Strategic
    Defense Initiative
State Committee for the State of
    Emergency, 236, 238
Statement of Principles of the
    Conference on Security and
    Cooperation in Europe, 145
Stealth aircraft, 174
Stevenson Amendment, 328–329, 342
Stinger anti-aircraft missile, 342
Strategic Arms Limitation Talks
    (SALT I), 91, 126, 137, 150, 242
Strategic Arms Reduction Agreement
    (START), 191–192, 220, 236,
    241–242, 358
Strategic Arms Reduction Talks, 180,
    258
Strategic Arms Reduction Treaty
    (1991), 243
Strategic Defense Initiative (SDI, Star
    Wars), 175–176, 192–193, 221,
    339–340, 374
Supreme Court decisions,
    Conyers v. *Reagan* (1985), 283
    Crockett v. *Reagan* (1984), 283, 285
    Edwards v. *Carter* (1978), 282–283
    Goldwater et al. v. *Carter*, 283–285
    Immigration and Naturalization Service
        v. *Chadha* (1983), 286–287, 343
    INS v. *Chadha* (1983), 284, 286
    Missouri v. *Holland* (1920), 280–281
    New York Times v. *United States*, 287
    United States v. *Belmont* (1937),
        281–282
    United States v. *Curtiss-Wright Export*
        Corporation (1936), 265, 279–280
    United States v. *Nixon* (1974), 287
    United States v. *Pink* (1942), 282
Sussex, 28

Terrorism, Christmas bombing (1972),
    132
Texas A&M University, 219
Trade Act (1974), 343

Trade Act (1988), 343
Trade and Development Program, 359
Treaties and Other International Acts of
    the United States of America
    (Miller), 19
Treaty of Amity and Commerce, 16
Treaty on the Final Provisions
    Regarding Germany (1990), 233
Treaty of Nerchinsk (1659), 93
Treaty of Peace and Friendship, 17–18
Treaty Powers Resolution, 312
Tripartite Treaty of Alliance, 49
Truman administration, 64, 68
Truman Doctrine, 49–51, 61, 291
Twentieth Party Congress, 89

U.S. Department of Agriculture
    (USDA), 384
U.S. Information Agency, 356
U.S. Naval Academy, 151
U.S. Rapid Deployment Force, 161,
    174, 184
U.S. v. *Belmont* (1937), 281–282
U.S. v. *Curtiss-Wright Export*
    Corporation (1936), 265, 279–280
U.S. v. *Nixon* (1974), 287
U.S. v. *Pink* (1942), 282
U.S.S. Elmer Montgomery, 318
U.S.S. Samuel B. Roberts, 318
U.S.S. Stark, 247
U.S.S. Vincennes, 318
United Nations, 45, 47, 56, 91, 102,
    146, 192, 223, 246, 288, 291, 359
United Nations General Assembly,
    245
United Nations Security Council, 45,
    50, 67, 250–253, 323
United Nations Treaty, 309
United States,
    Department of Defense (DOD),
        394–406
    intelligence agencies, 406–430
    see also Department of Defense
        (DOD); Foreign policy (U.S.)
United States Information Agency
    (USIA), 358
United States Treaties Cumulative
    Indexes, 15
Universal Declaration of Human
    Rights (1948), 146
University of Michigan, 401

University of Notre Dame, 117, 139, 142

Vandenberg Resolution, 288
Versailles peace treaty, 32
Vietnam Veterans Memorial, 77
Vietnam War, 2, 26, 52, 64, 78, 101, 103–112, 131, 274, 324
Gulf of Tonkin Resolution, 107, 295, 313
military involvement, 107–109
origins of, 104–107
Voice of America (VOA), 358

Wake Forest University, 151
War of 1812, 27, 29, 77
War Powers Resolution, 274–275, 283, 285–286, 290, 313, 315–316, 318–324, 331, 343
Warsaw Pact, 94, 97, 220, 233, 245
Washington Summit (1990), 241
Washington's Farewell Address, 12–13

Watergate, 143, 263, 266, 288, 300, 308
Western Alliance, 97
Westminster College, 48
White House, 199, 238, 294, 366, 368, 379
Wilson administration, 20
Wilsonianism (moralism), 30
Wilson's Fourteen Points, 30, 32
World Bank, 241, 244, 330, 383–384
World War I, 20–21, 27, 30, 42, 70, 246
League of Nations, 20, 30, 32, 43
World War II, 27–29, 33, 40–43, 66, 70, 78, 103–104, 112, 226, 278, 281, 296, 299

Yale University, 363
Yalta Agreement, 277
Yalta Axioms, 43, 49
Yalta Conference, 44, 231–232
Yom Kippur War (1973), 133

Zimmermann telegram, 28

THE BOOK'S MANUFACTURE

American Foreign Policy and Process was typeset by Point West, Inc., Carol Stream, Illinois. The typefaces are Palatino and Copperplate. Printing and binding were done by Arcata Graphics/Kingsport, Kingsport, Tennessee. Cover and interior design was by Lesiak/ Crampton Design, Inc., Chicago, Illinois.